THE LIFE AND TIMES OF THE
SHAH

THE PUBLISHER GRATEFULLY ACKNOWLEDGES THE
GENEROUS SUPPORT OF THE HUMANITIES ENDOWMENT FUND
OF THE UNIVERSITY OF CALIFORNIA PRESS FOUNDATION.

THE LIFE AND TIMES OF THE
SHAH

GHOLAM REZA AFKHAMI

UNIVERSITY OF CALIFORNIA PRESS

BERKELEY   LOS ANGELES   LONDON

University of California Press, one of the most distinguished
university presses in the United States, enriches lives around
the world by advancing scholarship in the humanities, social
sciences, and natural sciences. Its activities are supported by
the UC Press Foundation and by philanthropic contributions
from individuals and institutions. For more information, visit
www.ucpress.edu

University of California Press
Berkeley and Los Angeles, California

University of California Press, Ltd.
London, England

Library of Congress Cataloging-in-Publication Data

Afkhami, Gholam R.
   The life and times of the Shah / Gholam Reza Afkhami.
      p.   cm.
   Includes bibliographical references and index.
   ISBN: 978-0-520-25328-5 (cloth : alk. paper)
   1. Mohammed Reza Pahlavi, Shah of Iran, 1919–1980.
2. Iran—History—Mohammed Reza Pahlavi, 1941–1979.
I. Title.
DS318.A653   2009
955.05'3092—dc22   2008015848
[B]

Manufact ured in the United States of America
17   16   15   14   13   12   11   10   09
10   9   8   7   6   5   4   3   2   1
This book is printed on Natures Book, which contains 30%
postconsumer waste and meets the minimum requirements
of ANSI/NISO Z39.48-1992 (R 1997) (Permanence of Paper).

They knew me as they were,
Not as I am

Rumi

CONTENTS

The Iranian revolution of 1979 was a watershed in world history, although the events that followed did not flow in the direction many observers had expected. Most scholarly and political "experts" assumed that revolutions propelled history forward and so took the Iranian revolution as an instance of progressive change. None of them was inclined to examine the revolution's leadership, ideology, organization, strategy, or tactics. If the revolution seemed to be run by the devout in and around the mosques, this was assumed to be a needed catalyst. Over the preceding years, these experts argued, a hasty modernization policy had created a two-tiered society—a veneer of modernity superimposed on a vast body of tradition. They said that the Ayatollah Khomeini's appeal was to the vast traditional majority, but that he was not after power; rather, being a saintly figure, he could be expected to yield power to the forces of democracy once tyranny was overthrown. No one suspected that a seemingly popular revolution might usher in a theocracy.

But that is exactly what it did. Khomeini forced a formulation of legitimacy at odds with both tradition and modernity—a political and ideational dispensation in which God's word became the people's word, and he, the religious jurist, the arbiter of the word. He substituted faith for freedom and thereby sublimated warfare to jihad, soldiers to martyrs, and death to salvation. He redefined in Islamist terms human felicity, social progress, economic development, individual freedom, and popular sovereignty. In his person, power spoke to truth.

The new dispensation, however, hit hard at the human and material foundations of development that had been built in Iran over the previous fifty years. In the 1920s, Iran had been one of the world's least-developed nations. By the mid-1970s it had become a showcase of development among the Third World countries, boasting one of the highest rates of economic growth and a superior record of social services. It had developed the critical mass of educated people needed for takeoff in science and technology. It was also making steady progress in fields ranging from women's rights and environmental protection to intercultural and cross-cultural communication to literacy and lifelong education, among others. As a result of these and other changes, the country was a "braingainer" in 1975, attracting educated workers to its growing economy, a situation then unprecedented in the Third World. The new Islamic regime disparaged and discredited every accomplishment of the Iranian society during the half-century of Pahlavi rule, dispersed the critical masses that had developed over the years, denounced the culture of development, and turned the brain gain into brain drain. War with Iraq—which Iran's diplomacy and military power under the shah had kept at bay—quickly followed and devastated the country. Whereas during the fifteen years before the revolution Iranians' per capita income had increased twelvefold, from $195 annually in 1963 to approximately $2,400 in 1978, it plunged thereafter and was still less than $2,400 in 2004, twenty-five years after the revolution.

Clearly, Iran would be very different today had the revolution not occurred. So would the rest of the Middle East. There would almost certainly have been no Iran-Iraq war; an untold number of Iranians, Iraqis, and others might not have died, become maimed, or suffered displacement and exile; and an untold amount of wealth, property, and infrastructure might not have been destroyed. It is possible that Islamism would have been contained, that clashes of civilizations would not have been conceived or carried out. The United States would not have been involved in wars in the Persian Gulf or found itself diminished as a beacon of hope for millions of people across the world. It is even possible that globalization might have taken a slightly kinder turn.

All this, of course, is mere speculation. What has been and what might have been, however, can alert us to our past mistakes, present options, and future possibilities.

Studying the life and times of the shah dispassionately helps us gain some understanding of how systems rise and fall, but only if we remember that while hindsight is 20/20 at predicting the past, it does not necessarily explain it. For most who have felt compelled to explain the Iranian revolution, the urge to fashion reality to suit their interpretation has been especially strong. The shah seemed extremely powerful, but his power was not as easily explicable as that of the other Third World leaders. To show how a Saddam Hussein or Hafiz al-Asad captured and maintained power is not difficult. They could and did kill people or order people killed. The shah was the opposite. Every person who knew him intimately—wife, relative, friend, military and civilian official, foreign statesman—attests to the essential mildness of his character, his aversion to violence, his hatred of bloodshed, his proclivity to turn from adversity rather than to face it. One could hardly imagine a popular revolution toppling a Saddam Hussein or Hafiz al-Asad. They would kill it before it blossomed. The shah would not kill. How, then, did a man of such mild traits achieve the power he commanded in a volatile country such as Iran? Conversely, how and why did the power that seemed so mightily present in his person implode, as it were, so easily and unexpectedly? Why would the shah, so experienced in the affairs of state, prove so fragile?

This book addresses these questions by placing the shah in context, that is, in interaction with the political, economic, social, and cultural dynamics of the country and the world in which he lived and worked. The narrative tries to make it possible for the reader to see the shah's world through the shah's eyes. It lets the shah speak his thoughts and express his judgments about what he did, why he did it, and how he felt about it. It lets his friends, enemies, officials, and other interlocutors, Iranian and non-Iranian, tell their experiences with him and express themselves about him. By placing the shah in interaction with his environment, the narrative encourages the reader to draw his or her conclusions about the shah's character, personality, and performance and to judge him, if judge one must, not in the stratosphere of ideals, but in the crucible of life.

As I studied the shah and his environment, the events of his life, his friends and foes, and his visions of Iran's future, I became increasingly convinced of the utility of the concept of irony, first employed by Reinhold Niebuhr in *The Irony of American History,* for understanding the history of the shah. Niebuhr defined irony as "apparently fortuitous incongruities in life which are shown upon closer examination to be not merely fortuitous." Irony, wrote James Billington in his seminal work on Russia's cultural history, "differs from pathos in that man bears some responsibility for the incongruities; it differs from comedy in that there are hidden relations in the incongruities; and it differs from tragedy in that there is no inexorable web of fate woven in the incongruities."[1] Irony at once binds and unbinds comedy, tragedy, and pathos, the last suggesting touches of melodrama. The shah's life hovers on tragedy in that his personality, seemingly inexorably, moves to certain decisions that contain the germ of his undoing. On the other hand, disaster was never inherent in what he did unless things got out of hand. And things did not seem to be getting out of hand until they actually did. This introduces another concept as a possible explanatory tool: chaos. Chaos is the probability that any disturbance may over time produce results disproportionate to the disturbance or perhaps qualitatively different from it. Irony and chaos are woven into individual and collective human experience; they were a part of the processes that catapulted Iran from a development showcase to a state of revolution—to almost everyone's surprise. To know irony helps one accept fortune's slings and arrows with patience and equanimity. To know chaos helps one doubt one's certainties. The wisdom that knowing irony and chaos leads to is *qist,* an old Eastern concept meaning balance.

Irony, chaos, and balance, I hope, inform the narrative of this history.

This narrative is composed in five parts: Father and Son; Hard Times; Securing the Realm; Revolution and Irony; and Exile. It begins with Mohammad Reza's childhood experiences, which shaped his personality and character—above all his father's influence, but also that of his Iranian nanny, his French governess, and his schooling at Le Rosey. Part 2 is devoted to the shah's first decade on the throne—his practical education in the craft of kingship as he faced the challenges of the occupation, the separatist movement in Azerbaijan, oil nationalization, and the coup d'état. Part 3 begins with the Consortium Agreement and follows the shah through the successful years in which Iran became a showcase of development and a principal regional power. It brings together the shah's notion of justice and vision of the future with the political positions he adopted and the policies he pursued in domestic and international arenas. Part 4 discusses the shah and the revolution—why he and his regime proved vulnerable and why and how the revolutionaries won. And part 5, the shah in exile, recounts how he faced illness, rejection, and the final place of rest his friend Anwar Sadat afforded him in Egypt.

The information on which this narrative is based comes mainly from primary sources, although academic publications as well as nonacademic books, articles, and press reports also have been consulted. The documents in the Public Records Office in London and the U.S. Foreign Relations Archives in College Park, Maryland, have been used in the discussions of Anglo-Iranian and U.S.-Iranian relations. Material gathered from three Moscow archives—the Russian State Archive of Social and Political History (the former archive of the Communist Party of the Soviet Union), the Russian State Archive of Modern History, and the Archive of Russian Foreign Policy—have been consulted on Soviet-Iran interactions, especially the evolution of the Tudeh Party. An effort has been made to use, as much as possible, Iranian primary sources such as the "Documents from the U.S. Espionage Den" and *Tarikh-e muʿaser-e iran* (Iranian Contemporary History).[2] Also, my personal acquaintance with the academy, the government, and the royal court in Iran, and with the Iranian grassroots in my position as secretary general of Iran's National Committee for World Literacy Program from 1975 to 1979, has helped give shape to the context in which this story is told.

The narrative reflects the work and vision of many individuals who were directly involved with the decisions that shaped Iran during the reign of the shah. Most of these individuals worked for the regime; some of them worked against it. I am fortunate to have known many of them personally and to have benefited from their experience. It is these relationships that make this book different from the mainstream academic accounts of how things were in Iran before the Islamic revolution, how decisions were made, and what motivated the decision makers. It is impossible to name, let alone thank, here every person on whose kind support I have drawn in preparing this volume, but my chief guides in this endeavor must be acknowledged.

I am grateful to the Pahlavi royal family, especially Queen Farah Pahlavi and Princess Ashraf Pahlavi, for the information they offered through interviews and archival material. Queen Farah granted me a number of interviews over several years in which she answered my queries openly, kindly, and patiently. I am also grateful to her for the photographs of the shah, family, and friends that appear in this volume.

My debt to Princess Ashraf is especially profound, not only because she was a unique source of information about the shah's childhood and youth, but also because her endowment in 1982 to the Foundation for Iranian Studies (FIS) made possible the establishment of two major sources of information for students of Iranian studies: *Iran Nameh,* the foundation's journal of Iranian studies, and the foundation's Oral History Program and Archives, without which this narrative would not have its special character. Oral history interviews with individuals close to the shah—friends and members of his household—have been invaluable in bringing to light the shah's personal traits. Interviews with individuals in the public and private sectors who were directly involved in decision making at various periods of the shah's reign have provided unique insights into the shah's personality, style, and thinking. Interviews with members of Iranian student organizations in Europe and the United States have opened a fresh view into the organizational as well as the ideological and emotional milieu of the students' anti-shah activities. The oral history of American envoys associated with the United States civil and military missions in Iran, conducted for FIS in collaboration with Columbia University's oral history program, has been instrumental in deconstructing myths and stereotypes about the shah's relations with the United States government. I must also thank the princess, and especially her bureau chief, Gholamreza Golsorkhi, for placing at my disposal a set of taped interviews the shah gave in exile in Cairo in March 1980 to his editors for background information on the final draft, in his words "the definitive text," of his *Answer to History*.

I am indebted to Ardeshir Zahedi, Iran's former minister of foreign affairs, ambassador to the United Kingdom, and twice ambassador to the United States, as well as the shah's sometime son-in-law and always friend and confidant, for speaking with me on several occasions, responding with patience and equanimity to my often probing questions. As General Fazlollah Zahedi's son, he had a pivotal part in the events known as the CIA coup d'état of 1953. Much of the account of this event in this narrative is based on a critical comparison of his account with that of the CIA.

The late Professor Yahya Adl, surgeon, statesman, and the most distinguished of the shah's old-time personal friends, honored me with several hours of taped interviews in which he discussed in detail the shah's personality, attitudes, commitments, and perceptions of himself and others, as discerned over the nearly forty years he was in almost daily contact with the shah.

In conjunction with the oral history program, which I directed, I conducted several focused interviews, nine of which were published between 1994 and 2003 as a Foundation for Iranian Studies Series in Iran's Development, 1941–1978. The project helped me better understand the interaction of the shah and the officials who worked with him. Indeed, by talking to me for the series, each interviewee contributed also on some subject discussed in this book: Abdorreza Ansari, a former minister of the interior and managing director of the Khuzistan Water and Power Authority, and his deputies in KWPA, Hassan Shahmirzadi and Ahmad Ahmadi, on the intricacies of taking over from foreign developers the management of one of Iran's early major development projects; Akbar Etemad, the first president of Iran's Atomic Energy Organization, on Iran's nuclear politics; Parviz Mina, director of the International Bureau and member of the board of the National Iranian Oil Company (NIOC), on the post-Consortium oil policies; Manuchehr Gudarzi, minister and secretary general of the State Organization for Administration and Employment, Khodadad Farmanfarmaian, managing director of the Plan and Budget Organization, and Abdolmajid Majidi, minister of state for Plan and Budget, on the politics of development planning; Taqi Mosaddeqi and Mohsen Shirazi, managing director and director of the National Iranian Gas Company, respectively, on the structure and functions of Iran's gas industry; the late Baqer Mostofi, managing director, National Iranian Petrochemical Company, on the development of petrochemicals and the role they played in the shah's thinking; Alinaghi Alikhani, minister of economy, on the thinking behind the economic policies that made Iran a showcase of both development and development contradictions; Mehrangiz Dowlatshahi, president and founder of Women's New Path Society, on the role women played in generating the consciousness that led to women's enfranchisement; and Mahnaz Afkhami, minister for women's affairs and secretary general, Women's Organization of Iran, on how women achieved rights and powers in Iran beyond those achieved in most other Muslim-majority societies.

Over the past ten years, I have had the good fortune of being a part of a weekly gathering (*dowreh* in Persian) with five other permanent members and occasional guests at the Foundation for Iranian Studies, each with exceptional knowledge and experience of government and society in Iran before and after the revolution. I have already mentioned three members of this gathering—Gudarzi, Shahmirzadi, and Ahmadi—in connection with the series. The other two—Farrokh Najmabadi, a high-ranking official at NIOC and a minister of industry and mines in Amir Abbas Hoveyda's cabinet in the 1970s, and Reza Qotbi, managing director of the National Iranian Radio and Television (NIRT)—have been invaluable in helping me better understand the operations of Iran's government. I have learned from them in such subtle ways that by now I can no longer state which of my ideas I have not received through them. This narrative is replete with references to them, especially to Reza Qotbi, whose ability to contextualize his practical knowledge of the shah, the royal court, and the bureaucracy in Iran's history and political culture is simply remarkable.

Others also have helped with their special knowledge of Iranian affairs: Hassanali Mehran, a former president of Iran's central bank, on the structure and operations of the banking system and its role in the evolution of development policy; Kambiz Atabai, the shah's adjutant and master of the horse, on the shah's personal habits, the military's moods and expectations, the court atmosphere in the last months of the shah, and especially the life and times of the royal family in exile; and Ahmad Ghoreishi, an old friend and colleague, whose conversation for as long as I remember has alerted me to the critical in a mass of seemingly important issues. Ghoreishi led me to Mahmud Khayami, who kindly explained to me the role of the private sector, especially modern enterprises such as the Iran National Corporation, which he and his brother had established and turned into a showcase auto industry, and their interactions with the government in Iran's development. Habib Ladjevardi further enlightened me on the practical aspects of government-business relations in Iran. I must also acknowledge my debt to Ladjevardi for the Harvard Oral History of Iran Program, which he edited and on which I have drawn profusely. In this respect, the oral history of the left, including the interviews published by Hamid Ahmadi in Germany and Hamid Shokat in Germany and the United States, also has been indispensable to me for tracing the evolution of the Iranian left's mindset from the Leninisms of the 1930s and 1940s to the Romanticisms of the 1960s and 1970s.

My thanks go to Negar Esfandiary, who helped me with research at the Public Record Office in the United Kingdom, and to several colleagues who read parts of the early manuscript, made comments on both content and form, and otherwise helped me find my way: Cyrus Ghani, especially on chapters on Reza Shah and Mohammad Reza Shah's early years; Hormoz Hekmat, Shahla Haeri, Ali Gheisari, Farah Ebrahimi, and Azar Nafisi on several parts of the book, ranging from the early years to exile; and especially Vali Nasr, who not only advised on several aspects of the manuscript, but also guided me to the University of California Press, Berkeley.

For editing, thanks are due to Phil Costopoulos of the *Journal of Democracy* for putting me in touch with Lucy Ament, who as an accomplished editor with no experience with Iran read the manuscript and showed me where I fell short or exceeded the mark for the intelligent nonexpert, non-Iranian reader. I am especially indebted to Bahram Nowzad, a former editor-in-chief of *Finance and Development* at the International Monetary Fund, who made a valiant effort to read the manuscript in the inordinately short time I could give him, and made suggestions that significantly improved its structure and form.

I received invaluable assistance and support from the editors at the University of California Press. Niels Hooper, history editor of the Press, gave me much needed advice on the appropriate length and intellectual balance of the book, and showed much courage in taking up a narrative that runs counter to mainstream scholarship on Pahlavi Iran. I thank him for his steadfast support. Editorial assistant Rachel Lockman was most helpful keeping me informed and on schedule. And I am profoundly impressed by the competence, precision, and remarkable professionalism with which Suzanne Knott, the book's principal editor, and especially Ellen F. Smith, the copy editor, approached and edited this work. The responsibility for the book's shortcomings, of course, remains solely with me.

Finally, I would not have written this book were it not for the encouragement of my wife, Mahnaz Afkhami. She insisted that I take on the challenge and helped me deal with the vagaries of my disposition as well as the demands of this work, despite her own enormous efforts in founding and running an international organization to promote women's human rights across the world. In this, as in so many other things over nearly half a century, she has been my spouse, partner, friend, guide, and support.

NOTES ON TRANSLITERATION
AND TRANSLATIONS

I have used a simplified system of Persian transliteration to reflect Persian pronunciation as closely as possible: for example, Hossein rather than Hussein; Reza rather than Rida; Mosaddeq-us-Saltaneh rather than Musaddiq al-Saltaneh. For consonants I have used *q* for *qaf*, *gh* for *ghayn*, *kh* for *khe* as in Khomeini, and *zh* for *zhe* as in Hazhir. When authors' names are used in the text, I have followed each author's preference as the name appeared on the volume in question. I have omitted diacritical marks, except for *ayn* and *hamza,* especially when Arabic terms are used.

Unless otherwise noted, all translations from written or oral Persian or French to English are the author's.

PART I

FATHER AND SON

1

The Father

On a soft October evening in 1919 a young theology student walked slowly along a narrow alley in a recently built part of Tehran, not far from the city gate that opened on the road to the town of Qazvin. He was headed to a house his father, also a cleric, visited often, sometimes taking the young man along. The young cleric remembered his father and the master of the house sitting on the stone platforms in the narrow street at each side of the entrance to the house chatting about various subjects. The elder cleric was a *hujjat al-Islam,* learned in shii jurisprudence, and a religious leader in this part of the town. As a member of the ulama, the body of mullahs trained in Islamic law and doctrine, he had the right and the duty to advise on practically all aspects of believers' lives and therefore wielded considerable social and political power. Tonight, however, the *hujjat al-Islam* was ill, unable to preside over the ceremony that would launch his friend's expected child into the world armed with his blessing. He had sent his son instead.

The man the young cleric was visiting, Reza Khan, was a Cossack, a member of a military establishment organized and run by Russian officers. The Cossack Brigade had been established in 1878, the year Reza was born. When Nassereddin Shah, the Qajar king, passed through Russia that year on his second visit to Europe, Tsar Alexander II entertained him with a parade of his personal Cossack guards at Champ de Mars in St. Petersburg. The shah fell in love with these mounted soldiers and forthwith asked the tsar to lend him a few officers to establish and train a similar outfit in Tehran as his own personal guard. The Russian, foreseeing the merits of the proposition for his country's interests in Iran, obliged, and the two royals put their signatures to an agreement drawn up for the occasion. Russian military officers, commanded by Colonel Alexey Ivanovitch Dumantovitch, arrived in Tehran in July 1879 and a Cossack Brigade was born.[1]

Reza Khan was one of the thousands of ordinary Iranians who joined this force over the years. He had been born in Alasht, a village in Savadkuh in the heart of the Alborz Mountains in Mazandaran, a province by the Caspian Sea. Many of the men in his family had military careers, and some had held middle-rank positions in the Cossack units protecting the Qajar shahs. His father, Abbasali, died of unknown causes when Reza was only a few months old. His mother, Nushafarin, who was of Georgian origin, died not long after, leaving Reza in her brother's care in Tehran. The uncle, Abolqasem Beig, was a warrant officer with the Cossacks. His ability to provide for the young boy was limited, though he tried to be a good father. Reza received no formal education and passed his time in the streets playing marbles with stray boys. Being taller and stronger than most, he was respected by some and considered a bully by others.

To take Reza off the streets, Abolqasem Beig enlisted him in the Cossack Brigade in 1891 when the boy was fourteen. Still too young to be a soldier, Reza was given odd jobs cleaning the canteen or working as an orderly for junior officers. A year later, he was allowed to join an artillery unit, where he became proficient in the use of machine guns, particularly the type called Maxim. His mastery of this sixty-rounder helped him become an officer and gained him the sobriquet "Reza Maxim." In the meantime, Reza learned the ways of the military and the culture of soldiering. Part of being a soldier in those days was to build a reputation for toughness. Reza became known as a rough soldier, strong-willed, hard drinking, and daring. Russian Cossacks had always fostered a certain rash adventurousness and now encouraged the same in the Iranian Cossacks. Reza built a reputation for himself as a kind of *luti,* a man somewhere between a lout and a knight, rough in manners yet ready to risk his life to help a friend, rescue a woman in distress, or save a man in need of saving. In time, he worked at learning how to read and write whenever he got a chance, though no one knows exactly who taught him the skill or how literate he actually became.

In 1903, at the age of twenty-five, Reza married a young orphaned girl named Tajemah, who lived in his uncle's house. The marriage, however, soon ended in sorrow. Tajemah died as she gave birth to a baby girl, leaving Reza with a baby whose needs he could neither comprehend nor fulfill. This time another uncle, Kazem Aqa, a mid-ranking Cossack officer, and his wife came to the rescue, taking Reza and the baby into their home. (The aunt and uncle became the baby's sur-rogate parents, and she remained in their care until she was grown.) For the next five years Reza worked and fought under Kazem Aqa's command and protection.

These were the fateful years in which ideas of individual freedom, limited and responsible government, and popular sovereignty, which had been germinating for some time in the minds of a small number of Iranians, came to a head in the Constitutional Revolution of 1906. Widespread protests forced Mozaffareddin Shah to accept a constitution known as the Basic Law, which established a National Consultative Assembly (the Majlis) and included a Supplement defining the duties, obligations, and limits of the government and enumerating the rights of Iranian citizens.

The movement that led to the adoption of the Constitution had begun rather innocently within the tradition of the common folk seeking redress. The people were unhappy with the conductor of the only existing train in Iran that took them on pilgrimage to the shrine of Shahzadeh Abd ul-Azim, a few miles to the south of Tehran—the man was dictatorial and charged high prices. The people were also unhappy with Joseph Naus, the Belgian customs director recently appointed head of the treasury, for his strict observance of customs rules matched by a callous disregard of local lore. They were unhappy with the governor of Tehran for his tyrannical rule, particularly his proclivity to punish corporally anyone disobeying his edicts, including the clerics. What the simple folk wanted was "ʿadalat," justice according to the traditional rules of equity. What they asked for was an "ʿadalatkhaneh," a house of justice, where their complaints could be considered and redressed. These demands, however, would be overtaken by ideas grounded in histories and cultures alien to the experience of a majority of those who participated in the movement known as the Constitutional Revolution.[2]

The Constitutional Revolution is commonly dated from the late autumn of 1905 when Tehran's governor, Ala-ud-Daula, supported by the chancellor, Ain-ud-Daula, accused the sugar merchants of hoarding and ordered them to release their sugar to the public. The merchants refused. The governor went to the warehouses and ordered his men to open up the stores and distribute the sugar among the people. He also ordered two merchants flogged in public. After several like incidents, a group of ulama left Tehran in protest to take shelter *(bast)* first in the holy city of Qom and subsequently in the shrine of Shah ʿAbd al-ʿAzim, where they were joined by some two thousand religious students, mullahs, merchants, and ordinary people.[3] The *bast* lasted twenty-five days and, according to Edward Browne, was financed by disgruntled merchants and a former chancellor's supporters.[4] The shah dispatched his uncle to negotiate, but Chancellor Ain-ud-Daula ordered his troops to surround the Friday Mosque, where many had taken shelter, prevent food from reaching the refugees, and arrest anyone suspected of working against the government. On 20 July 1906 a small number of merchants, tradesmen, and ordinary people took refuge in the British legation in Tehran, according to the British against the wishes of the legation, though provisions had been assembled in anticipation of the event. Gradually the number of refugees rose, reaching by some accounts twelve thousand and by others twenty thousand.[5]

The ideas of democracy, constitutionalism, a legislature, and elections came mostly from those who had taken shelter in the legation. From there they spread to other parts of the town and eventually to most of the country, taking on a life of their own, though not many citizens understood them in their historical context. The framework remained local until writing a constitution became the issue. In the meantime, popular pressure forced Governor Ala-ud-Daula to resign and the shah to dismiss Chancellor Ain-ud-Daula and to replace him with Moshir-us-Saltaneh, a man on better terms with the revolutionaries. On 5 August 1906, the shah issued a *farman* (decree) for the establishment of "an assembly [Majlis] of the representatives of the princes, the ulama, the Qajars, the nobles, the landowners, the merchants, the guilds—in the capital to consult on the important business of the government . . ." and charged the chancellor to implement his decree.[6] The chancellor invited the leaders of the groups mentioned in the shah's *farman* to meet and asked them to choose from among themselves those who would prepare the code for electing a Majlis. The leaders chose five men—all grandees of the realm who would play important parts in the political events of the future, as they had in the past. They prepared the code in less than a month, according to which, of the 120 members of the proposed Majlis, 60 were to be elected from Tehran and 60 from the provinces, and had it signed by the shah. The Tehran elections were finished in October, and before the end of the month the shah, who was ill and had to be carried into the hall in a pushchair, opened the Majlis with an emotional message. This first Majlis, representing the estates general of Iran, wrote a Basic Law (Qanun-e Asasi), which the shah signed on 30 December 1906. This document and its Supplement, signed by Mozaffareddin Shah's successor on 4 October 1907, became Iran's Constitution.

The Basic Law set the number of deputies from Tehran and provinces at 136 (the number could be ultimately increased to 200), elected for two years and eligible to be reelected as long as the "electors were satisfied." The Basic Law of 30 December 1906 also stipulated (articles 43–48) a Senate, to be composed of sixty members. Thirty were to be appointed by the shah and thirty elected by the people; in each category, half were to be from Tehran and half from the provinces. The two houses had equal power except in budgetary matters, in which the Majlis had the final say. In fact, however, no Senate was convened until 1949. The Basic Law and the Supplement further stipulated a governmental structure based on the principle of separation of powers, which meant that no deputy could serve as a government executive and Majlis deputy simultaneously.

When the constitutional decree was issued and the First Majlis convened, no one seemed to have a clear idea of the character, functions, and powers of this new assembly. The *farman* seemed to suggest that the proposed Majlis was to help the king's ministers in the discharge of their duties. A corrective to the original *farman* referred to the Majlis as the Islamic Consultative Assembly. Slowly ideas began to evolve within the Majlis that gave it a truly legislative role — not only watching over the government and holding it answerable for its deeds, but also making laws. The 1907 Supplement to the Basic Law was a document borrowed mainly from the Belgian and French constitutions, introducing a bill of rights and specifying the powers and responsibilities of the shah as well as those of the executive and judicial branches. Although it pronounced the shah exempted from responsibility, it gave him substantial powers as the head of state, commander-in-chief of the armed forces, head of the executive branch, with power to appoint and dismiss the ministers, and a partner in legislation, among others. At the same time, faced with the combined forces of the court and the clergy, the constitutionalists agreed to the inclusion of an article whereby a body of five *mujtahid*s (those learned in Islamic law) was empowered to pass judgment on the admissibility of laws based on their agreement with the *shari'a* (Islamic law). Thus, the Constitution was at best a dream and a promise. Reza's future — and that of the son who would be born in 1919 — would unfold largely against the incongruities between the ideals contained in the dream and the society that was to host them.

Mozaffareddin Shah died unexpectedly not long after agreeing to the new Constitution, which was soon rescinded by his son and successor, Mohammad Ali. War then broke out between the constitutionalists and the new shah, who sought support from Russia. In 1907, Russia and England, longtime rivals in the "Great Game" of influence in the Middle East and Central Asia, took advantage of the unrest and divided Iran into "zones of influence," Russia in the north (including Tehran) and England in the southeast, with the central region left nominally to the Iranian government as a buffer. In the midst of this Reza saw himself as a soldier fighting for the king, or more likely for whomever Kazem Aqa fought for. Kazem Aqa, however, was killed in 1908 in a battle near Tabriz. Although Reza was by now indispensable for his prowess with the artillery, he nevertheless insisted on and received permission to take his uncle's body to the holy city of Qom for burial.[7] The conflict ended in 1909 with the defeat of the government forces. Mohammad Ali Shah was forced to abdicate in favor of his underage son, Ahmad, under a regency of constitutionalists. Now, Reza fought for the new shah, on the side of the constitutionalists against the enemies of the Constitution—the deposed shah and his allies, who wished to reinstate him as king. In due course, Mohammad Ali Shah's forces were once again defeated, his claim to the crown coming to naught. In early 1914, Ahmad Shah came of age and was formally crowned. Two months later, the Austrian crown prince was assassinated, and World War I was launched.

The world war was, paradoxically, a godsend to Iranian nationalists. Many of them believed that it saved Iran from the disintegration that had threatened the country since the Russo-British Agreement of 1907 and even before.[8] Neither the Russians nor the British had ever been shy when expressing what they expected from Iran. In 1904, Russia's foreign minister, Count V. N. Lamsdorf, sent a memo to A. N. Shteyer, his minister in Iran, explaining to him Russia's aims: "We have tried gradually to subject Persia to our dominant influence, without violating the external symbols of its independence or its internal regime. In other words, our task is to make Persia politically obedient and useful, i.e., a sufficiently powerful instrument in our hands. Economically—to keep for ourselves a wide Persian market using Russian work and capital freely therein."[9]

By 1914, Russian influence in the Iranian north had become fully entrenched. Two months before the outbreak of the war, George Buchanan, the British ambassador in St. Petersburg, complained to the tsar that "Northern Persia was now to all intents and purposes a Russian province."[10] The tsar, according to Buchanan, offered to divide the neutral zone also, but fortunately for the Iranians the war broke out and nothing came of the offer.

Throughout the turmoil of the years before and during World War I, Reza mostly fought in western Iran—in Hamadan, Kermanshah, Kurdistan, and Luristan. He began as a captain, finished as a colonel. A good part of this period he served under Abdolhossein Mirza Farmanfarma, a major prince of the realm. Reza observed the ways of politics and the culture that framed the practice of ruling. He developed a close relationship with the prince, but had little taste for his politics. These were the years that built his military stature among his colleagues. His regiment, first the Hamadan, and later the Kermanshah, was recognized as the most valorous, used wherever the situation hardened and the circumstance demanded. He fought for the government, not necessarily the side he preferred and not always winning. But he was brave and increasingly respected by his colleagues. As he matured, he began to think about the plight of the country—the squalor, the inhumanity, the corruption, the weakness, the helplessness. He hated the cruelty of his command, talked to his officers about his feelings, and found them sympathetic to his complaints and receptive to his ideas. These were the years he built both camaraderie and leadership; many of the officers who would serve him later—some with brutality, many with distinction—became his devoted followers during this time. He became more self-confident, mastered the details of military command, tried to learn about Iran and the world, and questioned the legitimacy of civilian politics. The higher he climbed in rank, the more he resented the Russian presence and control. But he understood hierarchy and submitted to the order of things.

The year 1917 was a particularly difficult time. The fighting in Iran had taken its toll, and by this time the country was in the throes of famine. Revolution in Russia deposed the tsar, confusing the line of command within the Iranian Cossack forces. Russia's new government under Alexandr Kerensky sent a Colonel Clergé to Iran to take command, but Clergé was accused of having communist leanings, which brought him into conflict with his second in command, a Colonel Starosselsky. Starosselsky managed to mobilize several Iranian officers, including Reza Khan, to oppose Clergé and demand his resignation. Reza brought his forces to the Russian commander's headquarters, entered his office after Starosselsky informed Clergé of the Iranian officers' demand, and extracted his resignation by force. Clergé left Iran in 1918, and Reza Khan, enjoying Starosselsky's patronage, was promoted to the rank of brigadier general. This event changed his position qualitatively, extending his moral authority beyond his regiment.[11] Reza still had no influence among the statesmen who ran the country, most of whom did not yet know him, but in the military he had become a force. Soon he would challenge Starosselsky and become known to others, particularly the British, as a personality to watch.

In 1916, Reza Khan married again, a girl named Nimtaj (later known as Taj-ul-Moluk, a title meaning "crown of kings"). He had to work hard for the marriage because the father of the bride—an officer named Ayromlu—thought Reza was rough, poor, and unlikely to have much of a future. Reza persisted and had several of his friends intervene, until, finally, he received the father's blessing. Reza's friends and the bride's family staged a major effort for the wedding and got several notables to attend. Many of those present would be given important offices of the state when the groom's fortunes changed. In a year's time Nimtaj gave birth to a daughter they named Shams. By this time Reza was a brigadier, well known in the Cossack division, commander of the Hamadan Regiment, stationed mostly near Qazvin. His family lived in the house he had rented in Tehran near Darvazeh-ye Qazvin, the gate opening to the road to Qazvin.

It was to this house that the young cleric made his way on 26 October 1919, for what would be the birth of twins, Mohammad Reza first, followed by his sister Ashraf. Reza had asked Sheykh Abdolhossein Malayeri to be present to recite from the Koran near the baby's ear at the birth. But Sheykh Abdolhossein was ill and sent his nineteen-year-old son, Abolqasem, in his place. Abolqasem recited from the appointed verse while Reza Khan held his two newly born babies in his arms. After the prayer, he put Ashraf down, held forth his son, and, turning his face skyward, prayed in a solemn voice: "O God, I place my son in your care. Keep him in the shelter of your protection."[12]

About two months before Reza Khan's first son was born, Prime Minister Hassan Vosuq (Vosuq ud-Daula) had put his signature to a treaty that in effect placed all of Iran under British tutelage in military, financial, developmental, administrative, and foreign affairs. The Anglo-Persian Treaty, known to history as the 1919 Agreement, was the brainchild of Lord Curzon, an extraordinary man soon to become British foreign secretary — an avid reader and prolific writer, knowledgeable in many fields, arrogant, and authoritarian. His project was to preserve India for England at all costs (the Great Game again), his strategy to establish a *cordon sanitaire* to separate the subcontinent from putative predators — Russia always; other nations, Germany in particular, now and again as the opportunity arose. Iran was critical because it was independent, a rarity in that part of the world, and at the center of the protective belt. To achieve his goal, Curzon, who was at that time serving in the British War Cabinet with responsibility for the Near East, maneuvered into office an agreeable Iranian cabinet headed by Vosuq and appointed as British minister in Iran Sir Percy Cox, a man whom Curzon, while he was viceroy of India (1899–1905), had been grooming for such a part.

When Curzon became foreign secretary in October, he was able to carry out his policy in Iran almost at will. The 1919 Agreement, extremely unpopular among Iranians, needed to be ratified by the Majlis, which had not been convened since the Third Majlis had expired in 1916. Curzon, however, was adamant, and Cox, a former military officer who had spent much of his career in the Persian Gulf dealing with the Arab sheiks, relentlessly pushed for its adoption. The fight for the agreement became a sordid affair. Vosuq and two members of his cabinet, Nosrat ud-Daula Firuz and Sarem ud-Daula, were accused of receiving bribes from the British, as was the young king, Ahmad Shah. All this produced intense bitterness against both the British and the Iranian ruling class.[13]

A year and a half into the struggle to get the agreement ratified, Percy Cox was reassigned to the British mandate in Iraq (to deal with outright rebellion there) and was replaced in Iran by Herman Cameron Norman, a diplomat by métier who was intellectually quite different from Cox. The British government's decision to retrench and collect its forces at the end of the war, for both strategic and budgetary reasons, forced Norman to think about other ways and means of achieving stability in Iran. This brought him into conflict with Curzon, who would not accept rescinding the agreement as an option. He pressured Norman, as he had pressured Cox, to keep Vosuq and his cabinet in power until the agreement was ratified, disparaging Norman's arguments that the policy was failing and that ratification had become well-nigh impossible.

In the meantime, the British cabinet, forced to reappraise British military deployment in the Middle East, especially in light of the revolution occurring in Iraq, decided to recall its troops from northern Iran by early 1921.[14] This put Curzon in a difficult position, and he increased the pressure on Norman and their Iranian allies to get the agreement approved. Conditions on the ground, however, took their own turn. The Soviets defeated the White Russian resistance to the Bolshevik Revolution in the Caucasus and pushed south into Iran, inciting various red-tinged movements along their route. The most defiant of these movements, the Jangali in the Caspian province of Gilan, led by Mirza Kuchek, presented a serious challenge to the Iranians and the British both. The Vosuq government commissioned Reza Khan to deal with the Jangalis, a successful campaign that further enhanced Reza's reputation and brought him, possibly for the first time, to the attention of the British advisory team that had come to Iran as part of the 1919 Agreement. Brigadier General William E. R. Dickson, whose charge in Iran was to reorganize the Cossacks, the gendarmerie, and provincial units into an integrated army, was impressed by Reza's military prowess. Dickson's mission, however, did not go well. Neither the Cossacks nor the gendarmes would acquiesce to unification under British command or to the new rules that stipulated Iranian officers would not be promoted above the rank of major. The humiliation was too much for Colonel Fazlollah Aghevli, a respected Iranian gendarmerie officer assigned to the Dickson mission, whose suicide reflected the bitterness that pervaded the country.[15]

Reza Khan was also unhappy, despite his initial success against the Jangalis. He had requested reinforcements and the salaries that had not been paid over several months, but he had received neither. He was disgusted with the parade of cabinets in and out of office, containing the same individuals who succeeded one another without making any noticeable difference in the country's domestic or international affairs. "If only God would help us rid this country of these foreign masters that leech-like suck our blood," he complained to then lieutenant Mohammad Ali Saffari, later to serve as police chief and governor-general in several provinces.[16] His complaints came to naught; what he received instead was a medal and a brigadier's baldric.[17]

In 1920, despite some fourteen years of constitutional experience, conditions in Iran were not palpably better than in 1900; in some cases they had deteriorated. The nation's military was controlled by foreign officers. The clergy, at the height of its power, influenced every aspect of national life. Socioeconomic conditions had worsened. Government coffers were empty, and the salaries of civil and military employees constantly in arrears. Roads were unsafe, and travel in much of the country was impossible without privately organized armed escort. Cities had turned into the bailiwicks of thugs, *lutis,* and *pahlavans,* who controlled their territories with iron hands, exacted booty, and meted out their version of justice.[18] Around the country, Kurds in the northwest, Lurs in the west, Bakhtiaris and Qashqais in the center and south, Baluchis in the southeast, and Turkmans in the northeast ruled their own territories, at best ignoring the government in Tehran, at worst openly opposing it. More important, the Jangali movement in Gilan, the Simitqu rebellion in Kurdistan, and the flirtation of Khaz'al, the Sheykh of Mohammareh, with independence in Khuzistan threatened the territorial integrity of the country. Adding to the chaos was Curzon's single-minded commitment to the 1919 Agreement and the pressure he continued to exert on the shah and government for ratification. Public displeasure finally forced Vosuq to resign on 24 June 1920. Norman spoke with Ahmad Shah and found him more concerned about the monthly allowance he received from the British than the fate of his country. To Norman's protestation that the money was tied to the duration and success of the Vosuq cabinet, the shah retorted that the money was promised him as long as he supported pro-British governments.[19] Six months later Norman would reiterate to Curzon his own disappointment in the shah: "If the Shah had shown more interest in affairs of state and less in increasing his private fortune and remitting it abroad he might have become popular, but as it is his indifference to everything save his own interest has disgusted all classes of his subjects, and if he left the country it is unlikely that he would ever be able to return."[20]

Into this muddle stepped General Sir Edmund Ironside, taking command of the British forces in Iran on 4 November 1920. Ironside's interest was mainly to guarantee the safe redeployment of British forces out of Iran, and his success depended on grooming a support system that could protect his rear units to provide him safe passage. He needed a strong Cossack force under a command that was pro-British and that would assure authority and discipline, which he thought could not be had if the force was commanded by British officers. He found in Norman a like-minded soul. The two together became a hand of fate, able to set in motion a train of events, perhaps inadvertently, very much at variance with Curzon's wishes because no one in Iran imagined they might pursue a policy not explicitly directed from London. Reza Khan became the Iranian force in this game.

The new prime minister, Moshir-ud-Daula, had exacted from the Bolshevik government in Moscow a note that the Russians would not militarily assist any Iranian insurgents. He had then ordered Colonel Starosselsky, still in command of the Cossacks, to face the rebellious contingents in the north, which he quickly moved to do. Reza Khan was given command of infantry in the campaign. Starosselsky, however, failed to follow the rebels as they were retreating; instead he remained in Rasht to reinforce his troops. This hiatus gave the Bolshevik forces time to reorganize and to attack from both land and sea—and gave Ironside, who wanted to get rid of Russian officers in Iran, the opening to order his troops to attack Starosselsky by air, although he later claimed they had mistaken those forces for the Bolsheviks. Starosselsky and his Cossacks were defeated, with great casualties—two thousand men killed in battle, drowned in the marshes near the Caspian, or otherwise lost. The fiasco angered Iranian officers and, after much haggling between the British, the government, and the shah, led to Starosselsky's resignation. Meanwhile, Reza asked Tehran for uniforms, food, and back wages for what was left of his troops, but received none. He brought his men to Qazvin, where the British units were ensconced under General Ironside's command and there met Ironside for the first time.

It was a fateful meeting in a series of events that came together by a blend of chance, personality, and political will. Ironside entered the room where the Iranian officers were gathered and spoke to them about the importance of pushing the Bolsheviks out of Iran and cooperation between British and Iranian troops. He asked a senior Iranian officer to order the troops to hand in their weapons until the British military instructors engaged to train Iranian troops arrived. For a few moments a heavy silence fell on the room. Then, a tall, dark, strong-faced Cossack officer bearing a battle scar between the eyebrows, a medlar-wood cane in his hand, stepped forward and addressed the interpreter:

"Who are you and who is this man you have brought with you to this meeting?"

"My name is Kazem Khan Sayyah. I am a captain in the gendarmerie. This man is General Ironside, commander-in-chief of the British forces in Iran."

"Well, then, will you kindly translate the following for the general. The officers of the Cossack Division obey the orders of His Majesty the Shah of Iran. The Cossack Division is His Majesty's special guard. If the general wishes to make a request of us, he should first take it up with His Majesty or His Majesty's government, and if the government approves, then it is the government that has the authority to talk to us, not a commander of alien forces.

"Now, on the question of surrendering our weapons: We remained noncommittal when the Russian officers were disarmed because we knew they had been dismissed by the order of our king and by the act of our government. They were traitors. It was our heartfelt desire to be rid of them. That is why, when you disarmed them, we said nothing. But such would not be the case with the Iranians. We hand our weapons to no one. To take our weapons you shall have to pass over our dead bodies."

Ironside was impressed. He smiled, protesting that Kazem Khan had not translated correctly what he had meant to say. He did not mean to suggest that the Cossacks were to be disarmed; rather, they might temporarily leave their arms with the British military if they came into the city of Qazvin. "The Bolshevik threat in Gilan remains, and we should work together to defeat it," he said as he shook hands with the Iranian officers, asking their names. He learned the officer who had spoken the brave words was named Reza.[21]

There is much that is not known, perhaps will never be known, of the details of the coup d'état of 1921. The murkiness has given wing to imagining all sorts of tales about what happened. The British have offered the gamut of possibilities over the years, from claiming total hands-off to claiming they masterminded the whole event, depending on what served their interests at various times. Iranians have almost unanimously attributed the coup to British machinations — some because they could not imagine anything of political importance happening in Iran without England's involvement, others because of ideology or personal interest. England being everywhere in Iran, it must indeed have been difficult for the Iranian ruling aristocracy to think it possible for two relative unknowns to launch a coup unless directed by the British government. Still, history is ironic and events sometimes fall in the purview of chaos. It was probably impossible for the British not to be involved; and yet it is possible that no necessary connection existed between their involvement and the end achieved. As noted, Ironside and Norman, apparently quite independently of the government in London, set a train of events in motion that could go several ways. Reza Khan and Seyyed Ziaeddin Tabatabai, being who they were and facing whom they faced, took it in their own direction, but only part of the way. Tabatabai, a politician of lower social status, had no chance of competing with the entrenched aristocracy once the latter overcame their stupor and the shock of events. Reza, on the other hand, commanded the military, which was matchless in power, and which could overcome, as did the master of arms in *Le bourgeois gentilhomme,* by demonstrative reason.

In most of the accounts of the coup Ironside is depicted as a hero, in some Iranian accounts a hero of Herculean stature. But all we know about what Ironside did is by deduction based on his assumed qualities. He writes little directly about his role in the coup. To his immediate superior, General Haldane, he reported the Cossacks had gone to Tehran by the shah's order to arrest other unruly Cossacks who were looting the city. Privately, he was pleased that many people thought he "engineered the coup d'état," which, he wrote in his diary, he supposed he had, "strictly speaking."[22] That is about it. He left for Baghdad the day the Cossacks left Qazvin for Tehran.

Reza Khan and Seyyed Ziaeddin Tabatabai, Ironside and Norman came together fortuitously in one place at one time to produce a dramatic set of events that would change Iran's history. But Reza was the mover. There would have been no coup without him, and every idea of a coup led to him. Several more Englishmen were involved in the process, however: Colonel Smyth, who recommended Reza to Ironside; A. W. Smart, the counselor at the legation who dissuaded the gendarmes from challenging Reza's Cossacks; Colonels Huddleston and Haig, who made a show of dissuading Reza Khan from proceeding to Tehran; and others who only tangentially affected the events. But it was the Iranian military that could make the coup, and there was only Reza who had the will to do it. To his friends he pretended to be only a soldier innocent of politics. In fact, he showed a high political acumen. Most of the time he was at the right place taking the right step. Not being the ranking officer among the Cossacks, for example, he realized he must have the support of his Iranian superiors. He spoke with those he knew and asked the most senior among them, Sardar A'zam, to talk to the others on his behalf. The old man did and received their approval for Reza to be appointed commander of the Cossack Division.[23] This endorsement greatly increased Reza's authority among the other officers.

Seyyed Zia and Reza Khan agreed on the need to revamp the government but differed on focus and intensity. Seyyed Zia had a more comprehensive idea of what was to be done. The 1919 Agreement was no longer tenable, but much could be done with British help to reform the existing political system, rationalize the administration, and improve the social and economic conditions. The titled aristocracy, particularly those who had governed in the past, however, would have to be discarded, surgically, in one swoop, as soon as possible. Reza agreed tacitly with most of this, but his focus was mainly the military. Much of this discourse may have been at the time beyond his intellectual compass, and he was smart enough to know his limitations. Honesty, military prowess, and nationalism were his assets, and they were indispensable virtues. The rest, his supporters thought, would follow. He impressed Ironside, who had come to believe that Iran needed a strong, honest leader, and that such a leader would satisfy his objectives—get his forces out of Iran safely, see a government installed that could stand on its feet, and keep the shah on the throne. He asked and received Reza Khan's agreement to these points. He wrote in his diaries: "Reza promised glibly enough and I shook hands with him. I have told Smyth to let him go gradually."[24]

Seyyed Zia meant something to Norman but not much to Ironside. Norman, on the other hand, did not know Reza Khan and was not sure what to make of Ironside's confidence in him. Based on what the general told him, Norman suspected Reza might be dangerous to the status quo in Iran, including the future of the throne, which London wished resolutely to preserve. Not having many choices, however, he decided to fall in line with Ironside—to let the Cossacks go, as the latter confided to his diary on 17 February, the day before he left Iran. The phrase "to let him go" suggests that the Cossacks had been held back on a political and military leash. Now they were free to move, and once they moved there was not much that could stop them.

In the early dawn of 22 February 1921, the Hamadan Brigade, commanded by Brigadier Reza Khan, entered Tehran from the west and took over critical points. There was not much resistance—none by the Cossacks in Tehran or the gendarmes and very little by the police. On the 23rd, Reza announced martial law, the declaration signifying his character as much as the requirements of control. "I command," began the statement. Citizens of Tehran were ordered to abide by each and every article of the declaration on pain of severe punishment. The articles that followed were not unusual for martial law, but the tone was patriotic, harsh, and serious. Kazem Khan, who had translated for Ironside in Qazvin and whose rank Reza Khan now identified as colonel, was appointed commandant of Tehran and forthwith arrested approximately seventy members of the aristocracy, including several members of the shah's immediate family. Seyyed Zia was appointed prime minister on 25 February, with the war portfolio going to his friend and ally Mas'ud Khan Keyhan. But it would not last long. Reza Khan was confirmed as commander of the Cossacks and was given the title Sardar Sepah (commander of the army) by the shah. Soon the war portfolio passed to Reza, who in fact had decided military policy from the beginning of the coup. In the meantime, Ahmad Shah found Reza amiable and in his own way loyal. Seyyed Zia, on the other hand, struck the shah and his allies as politically and ideologically suspect. Reza cultivated the shah's good will; Seyyed Zia befriended the crown prince, the shah's brother Mohammad Hassan Mirza. Within three months, the shah asked Seyyed Zia to resign; knowing he had no support from Reza Khan, Seyyed Zia acquiesced. The old crowd returned from dungeons to lofty government positions, if not to power. Qavam-us-Saltaneh, Moshir-ud-Daula, and Mostowfi-ul-Mamalek—great names from an era already past—succeeded each other as prime minister, but they merely followed Sardar Sepah's wishes until they handed him the mantle on 26 October 1923.

The old aristocracy had quietly acquiesced to Reza Khan's becoming minister of war, hoping his new position in the cabinet would put him in civilian clothes and thus separate him from the armed forces. They were disappointed. Reza Khan refused to surrender his uniform. The army was his home, his power, and his freedom. He would attend the cabinet when he pleased, sometimes refusing invitations from the prime minister or the crown prince purely to impress them with his independence and his power. He remained deferential to the shah, but not to the point of changing his word once he had uttered it. On 15 June 1923, a new cabinet under Moshir-ud-Daula was presented to the shah, who had come to town specifically for the occasion. Reza Khan, given the war portfolio for the eighth time in a row in a span of two and a half years, declined to attend on the ground that he was ill. The shah sent word he had something important to discuss and wished to meet with him in the afternoon even if he was sick. Reza refused. The shah sent word again, this time almost begging Reza Khan to go to him, "only for five minutes," said the messenger, but the general would not go.[25]

Reza Kahn had amassed too much power to be trifled with, and he knew how to use it politically. By 1922, the military under his command had changed into a more efficient fighting force, wielding considerable political influence. Whenever Sardar Sepah threatened to resign, the military threatened to rebel, forcing everyone to yield, including the current British representative in Iran, Sir Percy Lorraine, who had willy-nilly concluded that a stable and centralized Iranian government, regardless of who was in charge, would be more in Britain's interest than a weak government that would inevitably succumb to Soviet pressure. Lorraine had also concluded that the only man in Iran honest and capable enough to achieve the kind of stability both Iran and England required was Reza Khan.

Reza Khan was named prime minister on 26 October 1923. By this time his relationship to shah, aristocracy, and state had fundamentally changed. His authority now extended to every decision made, and his power became the arbiter of every action taken. The shah chose to travel to Europe on the day he appointed Reza Khan, leaving the affairs of the royal court mostly to the crown prince. He found the idea of Reza Khan becoming the arbiter of the realm repugnant, more so now that the aristocracy, the men who had run the state over the past twenty years, began to split into those for and those against the new rising power. The political horizon, however, became increasingly murky as those against, facing superior power, chose *taqiyeh,* the politics of stealth.

To a majority in the Qajar aristocracy Reza Khan's power implied a catastrophe. In Iran's neighborhood, the Ottoman caliphate had yielded to a new, republican Turkey and with it a host of ideas that would inevitably affect Iran's politics: republicanism, nationalism, populism, statism, secularism, and revolution, concepts still in the making in 1923 but containing enough substance and form to strike fear in the heart of the traditional believer. Though such ideas did not resonate with the masses, they were attractive to the intellectuals. For the first time in many centuries in Iran, religion and national identity began to diverge, creating a rift between the traditional masses and the emerging nationalistic elite. Patriotism, of course, had always existed among Iranians, but was expressed mostly in ethnic and religious terms. Nationalism, a modern concept grasped and variously defined by only a small contingent of society, rejected both ethnicity and religion. Many among the nationalists saw Islam as the main reason for Iran's backwardness. Iran, therefore, had to be purged, if not of Islam's core values, at least of its Arabisms. The pre-Islamic empire became the image toward which the new nation was to aspire.

Turkey, invariably, excited the imagination, but it was Europe that provided the axis around which tradition and modernity clashed. A group of modernists argued that the only salvation for Iranians was for them in effect to become Europeans. "Iran," declared Seyyed Hassan Taqizadeh, "must become Europeanized in form, substance, body and soul. That is the only way."[26] By contrast, Ahmad Kasravi, the historian, a former cleric turned civilian intellectual, questioned the virtue claimed for the European vision. Does it lead to the good life? he asked. If not, how do we get the best we can from it without losing our soul? But how, too, to redeem the soul when religion, shiism in Iran, was soiled with so much superstition? Between them, Kasravi and Taqizadeh represented the strains of Iranian nationalism as it developed in relation to the West: admiring European law as the backbone of Europe's advancement yet defining nationalism in opposition to European cultural and political domination; vaguely realizing economic and technological development as the cause of Europe's superior power yet falling back on tradition as the only weapon of survival against the European challenge.

Such ideas were in the air, touching those in positions of power, each taking a portion according to his intellectual curiosity or political interest. Reza Khan, as prime minister, was caught in this web, recognizing the importance of the debate without absorbing all its intricacies. He was impressed with Mustafa Kamal Pasha in Turkey, what he had achieved and what he was about to achieve. Republicanism, nationalism, secularism—all resonated in his mind. Other forces were also at play. He had experienced the Constitutional Revolution of 1906 as a soldier with little political or intellectual involvement. Not much had happened in the constitutional era that he could think of as beneficial to the people. Same men, same ideas, same interests, same pettiness; no wonder the country was where it was.

What struck him most forcefully in all of this was the need for a strong state. Nothing could be done if the government did not establish control over the country, he told his adjutant, Lieutenant Morteza Yazdanpanah. He had effected some improvement in the army because he had power. State, however, was a different matter. To build a strong state you needed first and foremost intelligent, educated, and forward-looking men. These men hailed from social backgrounds different from his. They were likely aristocratic, better educated, ideologically sophisticated, but not comparably strong or committed. Almost all of them were old enough to have experienced the Constitutional Revolution, though by the time Reza Khan came to power many had lost their fervor for constitutionalism. They fell into two broad categories: those who held important posts in the Qajar government and those, generally younger, who had chosen or who had been forced to leave the country during Mohammad Ali Shah's reign.

Reza Khan was better acquainted with the first category, as he served with them in the cabinet and called on them for political advice. Mostowfi-ul-Mamalek, Moshir-ud-Daula, Mohammad Mosaddeq, Yahya Dowlatabadi, Mokhber-us-Saltaneh Hedayat, Zoka-ul-Malk Foroughi, and their friends fell in this group. Most of them were social democrats. They wanted a separation of church and state, universal education, some kind of land reform[27]—ideals they now realized they could not implement without power.

Reza Khan's eye was on the second category, younger intellectuals who now resided in Europe and who communicated with their compatriots in Iran through their writings in such publications as *Kaveh, Iranshahr,* or *Nameh Farangestan.* They were influenced by what had happened in Iran since the revolution and also what was happening around them in Europe. Fifteen years past, at the time of the Constitution, the debate was clear: secularism or Islam. The new generation found that debate simplistic. If Iran were to become modern, it had to change, and the change had to be fundamental. The right legal framework was necessary, but not sufficient. Iranians had to acquire new ways of looking at the world. They had to be reeducated. Whether one thought religion was good or bad, it was a fact of life. Religion cleansed of superstition led logically to a separation of church and state. But this had to be addressed, that is, Iran needed its Luther and Calvin. By the same token, it might be good for Iranians to become like Europeans, but that would not be perfect. The better way was to be eclectic, remain true to yourself by recreating in your image what you borrowed from the West. Where lay the golden mean?

There was much debate among the new intellectuals, and many opinions, but invariably everything converged on the state. In part this reflected the way Europe was going. The war had torn Europe asunder, and now the continent was rapidly diverging from the ideas of individual freedom and political democracy that Wilson and the League of Nations had so optimistically enunciated. In Russia, sovietism was beginning to take on the structural characteristics of Stalinism. In western and central Europe a specter of the power state tinged with racial overtones was rising, already becoming a reality in Italy. Fascism seemed to bring together within the nation-state security, discipline, development, and pride. Erstwhile democrats like Taqizadeh now spoke of the "enlightened despotism" of Peter the Great in Russia, the Mikado in Japan, and Mohammad Ali in Egypt as the preferred way for Iran; Mussolini was presented as a kind of philosopher king, a dictator possessing ideals and knowledge, an enlightened leader with an iron fist.[28] Constitutionalism now took a backseat to nationalism, and nationalism increasingly took on a German rather than an Anglo-Saxon tint.

The young Iranians studying in Europe returned to Iran in the first years of the 1920s. They entered various professions, mostly in the government, and they remained interested in politics and in Iran's future. Several joined in establishing a political association named Iran Javan, or the Young Iran Society, whose members played important roles in the development of Iran during the next two decades. One of them, Ali Akbar Siassi, wrote the following in his memoirs:

> Not long after we established the Iran Javan, Prime Minister Sardar Sepah summoned Iran Javan's representatives. The society accepted Sardar Sepah's invitation. Well, in truth, it could not do otherwise. Esma'il Mer'at, Mosharraf Naficy, Mohsen Ra'is, and I went to his residence, then facing the military schools on Sepah [Army] Street. We were told to wait for him in the garden. After a short time, we saw him approach from a distance, tall, awesome with his cape hanging down on his shoulders. He sat on a bench and pointed to us to sit on the bench near him. "You are all young energetic men educated in Europe. What is it that you are saying? What do you really want? What's the meaning of this society, Iran Javan, you have established?" he asked.
>
> "The society," I replied, "consists of a group of patriotic young men. We abhor Iran's backwardness and the chasm that separates us from Europe. We wish to fill this chasm; we wish to see Iran great and progressive. That is the foundation of our beliefs on which we have based our charter."
>
> "What beliefs?" he said. I handed him the society's printed charter. He read it slowly and deliberately. Then he fixed his piercing gaze on us and said in a kind and approving voice: "What you have written is laudable, very good. I see you are patriots, you want progress, and you entertain grand and sweet hopes for your country. It wouldn't hurt if you propagated your ideas, opened the people's eyes and ears, and acquainted them with these subjects. You will speak and I will act.... I assure you—no, not assure only—I promise you that I will fulfill all these wishes, and will implement your ideas, which are also my ideas, from the beginning to the end. Leave this copy of the charter with me. You will hear of it in a few years."[29]

Iran Javan's charter proposed to repeal the capitulatory system, which provided special judicial procedures for certain foreign nationals; build railroads; establish an independent customs; liberate women; send students, both boys and girls, to Europe; reform the judiciary; expand knowledge and primary education; establish secondary schools; stress technical and industrial education; build libraries and museums; and adopt the good aspects of European civilization.[30] Siassi's account is important for the nexus it provides between the man and the idea. Reza Khan, disaffected with the failure of the state, wished to put Iran on the path to progress, but except in the army's case where he had some precise ideas, he did not know how. None of the proposals in the charter was new, but they had never been presented to him cohesively as a program. He was intelligent enough to catch the relevance of their cohesiveness to policy and the relevance of power to their intellectual development and practical implementation. As prime minister and king he would adopt the charter as the main component of his program, call on the young men who had drafted it and on others like them to define and elaborate it, provide them with political support, and give them authority to implement it. It was the beginning of a symbiosis of power and idea—power inevitably defining the contours of the idea.

First, however, it was necessary to consolidate power. In the wake of the coup d'état a wave of republicanism spread across the country, particularly among the intellectuals. Many of them even expected the coup to culminate in a republic until it became clear that Reza Khan had become friendly with the shah. The Qajar king, however, continued to lose legitimacy, partly for sheer incompetence, partly for corruption, and partly for lacking any ardor for his office or his country. As time passed, Reza Khan appeared to assume that legitimacy and increasingly to be seen as the man to head a republic.

Then, a little over a month after Sardar Sepah was appointed prime minister, the Ottoman caliphate was dissolved, and the parliament elected Mustafa Kamal Pasha as the first president of the Turkish Republic. The event hit Iran with cataclysmic force. When the Fifth Majlis convened on 11 February 1924, changing the regime became the major issue. A majority of the deputies seemed to be for a republic, among them many of the Qajar grandees—including Prince Abdolhossein Mirza Farmanfarma—who signed a declaration in Reza Khan's residence pledging their support for a republic and exhorting others to join them.[31] The aristocratic support, however, was disingenuous, again more in the spirit of *taqiyeh,* political dissimulation, than belief and commitment. As Mokhber-us-Saltaneh Hedayat, a signatory to the declaration, wrote in his memoirs: "Perhaps one could vote for his [Reza Khan's] kingship. But this country and republic don't go together. There will be an upheaval every so many years. Such discourse does not sit happily on one's heart."[32] Direct opposition centered on religious leaders, led by Hassan Modarres, a frail but politically astute cleric; they thwarted the movement by obstructing legislation in the Majlis and by mobilizing the people in the street. Turkey had become un-Islamic, profane and lost in the eye of the Lord, claimed the clerics. Once the issue was raised in the street and cast in those terms, the republicans found it difficult to compete. Reza Khan soon realized he was losing support and, rather than continuing the fight for republicanism, met with the religious leaders in the holy city of Qom and renounced the idea of a republic. The movement fizzled out, but at the same time Reza Khan's stature suddenly shrank, and he was clearly rebuffed by his opponents for the first time since the coup. Unless he took the right measures he most likely would be pushed out of the political scene.

By design or chance, Reza Khan resigned on 7 April 1924, citing as his reason "domestic and foreign conspiracies" against him, and announced he would take up residence in a neighboring country. This was a risk that could have backfired. The shah sent a telegram to the Majlis expressing his satisfaction with the turn of events and nominating as prime minister Hassan Mostowfi (Mostowfi-ul-Mamalek), who had held the post many times in the past. Reza Khan's supporters, especially the commanders of the armed forces, however, began a coordinated campaign to force the Majlis to reinstall him. Ali Dashti, a renowned writer and politician, lamented the departure of "the father of the Iranian people" in his newspaper *Shafaq-e sorkh* (The Red Dawn) and predicted a dire future if he did not return. Military commanders across the country threatened to march on Tehran. On the 8th, a delegation of Majlis deputies, clerics, guilds, and merchants went to Rud-e Hen, a small village to the north of Tehran where Sardar Sepah was staying, to ask him to return as prime minister, in defiance of the shah's telegram. Now armed with a popular mandate, he agreed and returned to Tehran that same day.

During the next year, Reza Khan weathered several challenges posed by the clerics and tribal leaders. In the most important he forced Khaz'al, the Sheykh of Mohammareh, to yield to him unconditionally without a single battle, which raised his political stature among Iranians and impressed the British. It also diminished his opponents, particularly Modarres, who had openly plotted with the Sheykh to oust him and to have the Qajar shah return to Iran from his stay in Europe. As Reza Khan's stature rose, ideas of regime change slowly transmuted to dynasty change. In fact, the shah had been urged to return to Iran or at least to devolve authority to the crown prince, but he refused until it was too late. Not until the fall of 1925 did he talk of return. The suggestion led to a flurry of telegrams from the provinces denouncing the idea. On 28 October, delegations representing various social and economic groups gathered in the military school and at the prime minister's home to demand a constituent assembly to be convened to depose the Qajar dynasty. On 31 October 1925 the Fifth Majlis voted to abolish the dynasty and to convene a constituent assembly to decide the future government of Iran. The assembly convened on 6 December. In the course of five sessions it voted to change Articles 36, 37, 38, and 40 of the Supplementary Basic Law, conferring the Iranian kingship on Reza Pahlavi.[33]

2

Father and Son

Mohammad Reza was his father's love—the light of his eye, as the Persian saying goes. His birth eclipsed all else in the household, including his twin sister, Ashraf. "He loved him beyond measure," she recalled many years later. "He had daughters before and prayed for a son. When God answered his prayer and gave him one, he was beside himself with joy."[1]

Mohammad Reza was two years old in 1921 when the coup d'état occurred. Three months later the family moved to a larger house, which Reza Khan had built on land he had bought. The boy was too young to understand the meaning of the subtle changes in his surroundings—the gradual picking up of traffic in the outer house; the increasing deference showed his father and him; the freedom allowed him in his demeanor and behavior. His father was about the only man he saw, except for the orderlies who served the family and a few others, mostly in uniforms like his father's, whom he might pass by when he was taken to his father. He lived among women—mother, sisters Shams and Ashraf, and a baby brother born in 1922 named Alireza. "Henpecked" complained the father. "Mamal Jan," a term of endearment only Reza Khan was allowed to use when he referred to his son, needed a more masculine environment, he told his wife. But the boy was still too young and fragile to be plucked from his mother's arms and placed in the company of men. So, the father was content for now to have lunch with his son at his side whenever his time permitted.[2] But if the idea was for the boy to rough it around men, it did not quite work. Mohammad Reza, still a baby, had a strong hold on his father. "I was never afraid of him," he reminisced about his father many years later in exile. "I respected him immensely. We had our time together—father and son—just like, I presume, other fathers and sons. He used to go on his knees, make like a horse, and I would ride on his back, pretending to whip and spur him on. Well, if someone knocked on the door, we would each regain our appropriate place, and suddenly life assumed its formality."[3] He called his father *pedar*—father—and when the father became king, he kept on calling him *pedar* when alone, Your Majesty at other times.

■

Reza Khan did not practice religion; religious superstition, however, was a staple of belief in Iran, and Reza Khan's sons and daughters were not immune to it. As in most other families of the same socioeconomic station, maids and nannies recounted stories, legends, and fairy tales tinged with religious and epic lore. From them, Mohammad Reza, Ashraf, and their older sister, Shams, learned the folk culture: Amir Arsalan of Rum; Rostam, the hero of the *Shahnameh* (The Book of Kings); Ali, the First Imam and commander of the faithful, wielding the Zu'lfaqar, the double-bladed sword; and Hussein, Lord of the Martyrs and the central figure in the pageant of Karbala. In these tales, time was supple, history nimble, nationalism and shiism blended. In them, Rostam, the protector of the kings in mythic, pre-Zoroastrian times, raised his sword in support of Ali against the enemies of Islam. In later years, Princess Ashraf talked of a nanny who told them stories of goblins and *div*s and fire-breathing dragons until she and her siblings trembled with fear. The tragedy of Karbala, where Hussein, his family, and friends were slaughtered defending their beliefs and rights, never failed to bring tears to the children's eyes.[4] These stories left an indelible mark on young Mohammad Reza, who was a sensitive, impressionable child and, as Ashraf would recall, painfully shy. He became intimately attached to the shii saints, seeing them as his personal angels protecting him from social and natural peril.

Mohammad Reza's urge to religion may have resulted also from the slender physique he and his siblings had inherited from their mother and his susceptibility to illness. He contracted almost all the diseases that children were likely to get in a traditional society and came close to dying from typhoid, which he contracted soon after he was pronounced crown prince. A local doctor, Amir A'lam, was brought in to give whatever care was available, but, recalled Ashraf, "really all we could do was wait and pray. My father was always extremely conscientious about his work, but he would leave his office every few hours to sit at my brother's bedside."[5]

Amir A'lam worked hard to treat Mohammad Reza, but the boy believed he was cured through Imam Ali's intercession.[6] He later wrote about a vision he had during one of the critical nights of this illness. "I dreamed that the Lord of the Faithful, Ali, his sword Zu'lfaqar on his knees, was sitting next to my bed holding in his hands a glass. He ordered me to drink of the glass. I obeyed. The next day my fever was gone. I was only seven years old, but I knew that there was a connection between the dream and my recovery."[7]

In the same book he recounts two more events in support of his belief that some higher power protected him from harm. Imamzadeh Davud, one of the many hundreds of shrines across Iran, is at the foot of the Alborz Mountains, not far from Tehran. Most Tehranis, particularly the older generation, have visited it more than once in their life. To reach it, one had to travel on foot or on mount through narrow passes winding up and down the edge of the mountain. Before Reza Khan was crowned king, his family, like many others, went on pilgrimage to the shrine every year.

> In one of the trips I was sitting on a horse in front of a relative of ours who was an army officer. Suddenly the horse fell and both of us hit the ground. My head hit a stone, and I passed out. When I came to, everyone was amazed nothing had happened to me. I was perfectly safe. I had to tell them that as I was falling off the horse, I was caught in the air by Imam Ali's exalted son Abbas. My father was not present when the accident occurred. Later I told him what had happened to me, but he did not take my account seriously. Knowing him, I did not force the matter, but I never doubted, not for a moment, that I was saved by Abu'l Fadl al-Abbas.

And again, one day as he walked with his tutor in the royal summer gardens in Saʿdabad, north of Tehran:

> Suddenly I saw a man with a divine visage, a halo about his head, not unlike the faces Western painters make of Virgin Mary, and I knew I was in the presence of the Lord of the Time, the Twelfth Imam. The visage appeared only for a moment. I asked my tutor, anxiously, "Did you see Him?" He answered, amazed at my question, "See whom? There is no one here!" But I was so certain of the truth of my experience that my tutor's doubt affected me not at all.[8]

He believed in these experiences, and because he did, he would repeat them throughout his life in Iran and abroad, even when it clearly hurt his credibility. He inserted them in *Answer to History,* his last book written in exile, retelling them with undisputed sincerity to his interviewers for that book in the privacy of his room in Cairo a few months before his death:

> For me religious beliefs are the heart and soul of the spiritual life of all communities. Without this, all societies, however materially advanced, go astray. True faith is the best guarantee of moral health and spiritual strength. It represents for all men a superior protection against life's vicissitudes; and for every nation it constitutes the most powerful spiritual guardian.[9]

Mohammad Reza was softer than his father but not averse to discipline. Indeed, he appreciated order, a quality that appealed to his father. Court Minister Abdol-hossein Teymurtash instructed him in how to carry himself during Reza Shah's coronation, and Mohammad Reza, then six years old, followed his instructions flawlessly. He did not know yet what being crown prince entailed, but he was familiar with the term. For some time, his personal servant, Hashem, had begun to address him endearingly as "vali'ahd junam," or "my dear crown prince,"[10] a title soon emulated by the neighborhood shopkeepers. Once he was formally designated crown prince, he lived in a separate house in the Golestan complex, formerly the residence of the Qajar kings.

Despite the new pomp and ceremony, the crown prince was at ease when circumstances allowed everyone to behave normally.[11] Majid A'lam, the son of Amir A'lam and a lifelong friend, remembers the first time he met Mohammad Reza. A'lam was no older than six, attending a garden party organized to raise funds for the Red Lion and Sun Society, Iran's version of the Red Cross. There were several spectacles for children, one of which was rams fighting. Little A'lam was fascinated watching two rams locking horns. Next to him he noticed a boy, younger than he, in a military uniform, his hand in the hand of a soldier, also watching the spectacle. Then, he remembers, his uncle came over, patted him on the head, and said to him "Come meet Sardar Sepah's son, Mohammad Reza Khan." The boys then watched the battling rams together.

A short time later Reza Khan was crowned king, and Mohammad Reza was designated crown prince. One day a call came from the court summoning the young A'lam to play with the crown prince. He was told he should be very polite and ceremonious. "Remember to bow. Call him 'Your Highness,' never 'Mohammad Reza.'" He went to the court, and did as he had been told. "Don't you remember the day we met at the garden party?" asked the crown prince. "Then you treated me as an equal. Now you bow and call me highness."

"That is what I have been instructed to do," said A'lam.

"Ah, that is just the protocol here," the prince said. "Between us, we don't need it. We are friends, and I do hope that from now on we will act as friends toward each other."[12]

Of the few who played with him, Hossein Fardust and Mehrpur Teymurtash were the closest, the first a son of a noncommissioned officer and the second a son of the minister of court, the most powerful man in Iran after Reza Shah. Fardust was there because Mohammad Reza had developed a liking for him and also because Reza Shah thought that the crown prince should have contact with all levels of society.[13] Reza Shah, however, did not particularly like Fardust and wondered why his son was so fond of him. He ordered that each Thursday Fardust be taken to the public bath, then to his father, where he would stay until Saturday—the first day of the week. Fardust was rather morose; Princess Ashraf thought he was not happy at court. "Sometimes he would disappear, and we did not know where he had gone. My brother then would be unhappy and send for him. He liked him very much."[14] The crown prince made a point of treating Fardust as an equal. When the time came for him to go to Switzerland, he insisted Fardust also accompany him and made sure both of them had the same brands of suitcases and clothes.[15]

There were no girls except Ashraf, who, because of her tomboyish character and natural closeness to her brother, often forced herself on the boys. Ashraf was not treated well by her mother or her older sister, Shams, who was the favorite of both the shah and the queen. Mohammad Reza liked Ashraf and used his influence as crown prince to guard her against the inequities that pervaded her small world. His support made a big difference to his sister. "He was my savior in those years, keen on giving me a fighting chance," Ashraf later said. She felt very much alone when the crown prince left for Switzerland.[16]

The crown prince received his elementary education at a specially designed military school established in the court premises, where he and twenty other students who had been carefully selected from among the sons of military and civilian officers studied under the best available teachers. Military training was a part of the curriculum, and the students, only six or seven years old the first year, attended class in military uniform. Reza Shah had sent word that he wanted his son to be treated exactly like the other students, a message that helped somewhat level the field. But here was the crown prince, beloved of the king as everybody well knew, and no amount of admonishment could change that fact. He was treated with deference, but he was a disciplined student, energetic, sometimes noisy, but never rowdy. He was good at sports. He liked wrestling, which was a national sport. He was fast and ran well. He climbed trees, which were plentiful in Saʿdabad in Shemiran, where the family spent the summer. He learned to ride horses, though he did not perfect this sport until he was in his teens. He became good at soccer, and at polo on bicycles, which was a novelty in Iran. In the games he played with his friends, he was always the police inspector catching thieves, though he confessed later his system, like Iran's, was far from perfect.[17] In short, he was very active, even though he continued to suffer a number of illnesses, including a very difficult spell of malaria at the age of eight, the effects of which remained with him throughout his life.

The young prince was a democrat by temperament. In 1960, when he was forty years of age and twenty years into kingship, he observed that his character was fundamentally different from his father's and that this was as it ought to be because each character suited the historical conditions to which it belonged.[18] There was also a part to his character — a propensity to question and to doubt — that was learned, reflected in him mostly as tension between his father's influence, which was the standard against which all other influences were to be measured, and that of Madame Arfaʿ, the governess who occupied a special place in his early education.

Madame Arfaʿ was a Frenchwoman who had married an Iranian named Arfaʿ in Paris and come with him to Iran. Reza Shah commissioned her to teach the crown prince and his other children French, "the finer things in life," as he put it. Madame Arfaʿ was elegant, sophisticated, chauvinistic about France, and, like most French patriots of the time, anti-German. She imbued the children with "things French" that remained with them the rest of their lives — above all that Paris was a city apart from all other cities, beautiful, rich, shining with human creativity, the birthplace of the best in modern culture and civilization, not only in the arts, literature, and science, but also in statecraft. Shams and Ashraf were tantalized by Madame Arfaʿ's account of the marvels of Paris;[19] young Mohammad Reza learned from her about the virtues of democracy springing from the ideas of the French Revolution. She talked to him about Montesquieu, Voltaire, and Rousseau, but also about Napoleon and Peter and Catherine of Russia, about what great kings and leaders might do for their country. Madame Arfaʿ also planted in the young boy's mind, ever so subtly, that his father was right to look back to Iran's past grandeur as a model for Iran's future glory, but also that there was more to culture and civilization than power and brute force. To become truly civilized, Iranians needed to change culturally; they needed a French revolution of sorts led by a shah steeped in things modern.

Madame Arfaʿ might have become too much of a "feminine" influence, because soon Reza Shah, who had made a point of having lunch with his son daily after he became nine years old, decided the crown prince needed more "manly" company and placed him under strict military discipline. No matter. Later, Switzerland would nourish the seeds the French governess had planted. He would "forever remain indebted to this lady," who died in France in 1959.[20]

■

Switzerland was chosen carefully. It was a Western country par excellence, but not politically suspect. These were difficult years. Communism under Stalin was challenging Europe, which in turn was becoming increasingly fascist. Major

European countries were heading for conflict, and Iran was sure to experience its impact. Iran's interest in maintaining balanced relations with all factions made neutral Switzerland the ideal Western country for the schooling of Iran's heir to the throne as well as his brother Alireza. The crown prince was allowed to choose two friends to accompany him, and he chose his old companions Hossein Fardust and Mehrpur Teymurtash. Ali Asghar Khan Mo'addab Naficy was chosen as the prince's guardian and adviser.[21] Mr. Mostashar, his Persian language teacher, was also sent along to see to his education in Persian language and literature.

On 5 September 1931, the crown prince left for Enzeli (later renamed Bandar Pahlavi) on the Caspian, accompanied by Court Minister Teymurtash and his guardian, Naficy. Reza Shah set out for Gilan on the same day, ostensibly to review the projects in the Caspian provinces, but in reality to be in Enzeli to see his son off as he embarked for Europe. On the 7th, the crown prince boarded a Soviet naval vessel for Baku. He remained on the deck as the ship moved out, looking at the coastline where his father stood until the land faded in the horizon. He would later say to Ashraf that he was of two minds as he stood on the deck: leaving his father for the first time filled him with a sadness tinged with distress; being on his own for the first time and on his way to Europe, on the other hand, excited him. All the things Madam Arfa' had told them about Europe passed through his head. Of course, Lausanne was no Paris and Switzerland no France, but they were as close as he could think possible, and the expectation made him boil inside with excitement.[22]

From Baku the young men and their chaperones were transferred to a train that crossed Poland and Germany to Geneva. They stayed two weeks at the Iranian consulate in Geneva before moving to Lausanne to attend school. In Lausanne, Mohammad Reza and his brother stayed with a family named Mercier, while the other boys were boarded at the school. The crown prince loved his life among the Merciers, the man and his wife, three sons and two daughters. "They were such a kind family," he later wrote. They probably were too accommodating, because after a year he was moved to Le Rosey, at the time an all-male school located between Geneva and Lausanne. "I was transferred to Le Rosey on my guardian's advice and my father's order because my father wished a more disciplined environment for me which could be provided at a boarding school. The school I had attended had 150 students and was coeducational. Le Rosey had a student body one and a half times larger, and it did not accept girls."[23] Although there is no evidence that the crown prince was misbehaving, clearly Mo'addab Naficy had decided he should be in a stricter environment, away from girls, and totally focused on schoolwork.

Le Rosey had all the trappings of a rich boy's school. At the same time, it was a serious school that challenged its pupils intellectually, requiring them to strive for good academic results, making them compete. It valued discipline and had a code of conduct based upon a set of moral principles about how to behave honorably. It also provided an opportunity for its pupils to form privileged relationships on an international scale that would be very useful in their future endeavors.[24]

The crown prince found Le Rosey challenging, although he received good grades. "In Tehran, I always received excellent grades, but I was never sure I had received them because I deserved them. In Switzerland, where social position did not affect grades, I also received excellent grades." He excelled in math (except for plane geometry) and natural sciences, liked history and geography, and loved French literature, in which he "made very good progress." He was proud he could write to his father about the honors and prizes he received for getting good grades in nearly all his courses. He also proved good at sports, the other side of the Le Rosey curriculum. To his own surprise, his health improved greatly during this time; he began to grow taller at a faster rate and his muscles "found strength," he later wrote. He won medals in throwing discus and spear and in various track competitions. He was elected captain of the school's soccer and tennis teams.[25]

Naficy was a strict guardian, too strict for the young prince's taste, even though he should have been used to it, for his father, for all his indulgence of his son, was a strict disciplinarian. Naficy made him stay at school when his classmates went to town. "I was not allowed to go with them. On Christmas and New Year's Eve my friends went happily and freely dancing, celebrating the New Year, but I had to remain in my room, alone and unhappy. The only means of amusement at my disposal were a radio and a record player, no competition for what my friends had for having a good time. I do not believe this method was right, and when I have a son, I will never bring him up in this manner," he wrote just before his own son was born in 1960. His course load at Le Rosey was heavy. In addition, he had to study Persian grammar and literature, which Mr. Mostashar, probably under Naficy's prodding, insisted was just as important, if not more so, than his regular subjects at school. "To this day I do not know whether Mr. Naficy was so strict because of my father's directives or because of his personal dedication to my education and proper upbringing. In any case, I was like a prisoner. I could not leave the school except in very special circumstances and then only in the company of my guardian."[26]

He was ordered to write a letter to his father reporting on his and his brother's progress every week at an appointed time so that the shah would receive it on Tuesdays before noon. This became a matter of grave importance for the royal court, especially for Shokuh-ul-Mulk, the shah's special bureau chief charged with receiving this letter and delivering it personally to the shah. On Tuesdays, the shah would anxiously wait for his son's letter, refusing any other before he read this one. The post office looked for it and made sure it arrived at court on time. The crown prince had been warned by Mo'addab Naficy, who made a point of having him write the letter, taking it from him, and personally mailing it, that any dereliction in this duty had severe consequences for others, thus appealing to the young man's sense of equity and compassion. At court, the civil and military officers who were scheduled to meet the shah on Tuesdays always first inquired about the status of the letter. The audience with the shah would be less than happy, or safe, if the letter had not arrived. Fortunately, most of the time the system worked; Shokuh entered the room first with the prince's letter only, retired discreetly to the antechamber to give the shah room to read it privately, and reentered after a time with the rest of the day's correspondence to meet the shah's smiling face.

The letter was also an occasion for those who met the shah on that day to compliment him on his accomplishments and service to the country and on the alacrity with which the crown prince studied and prepared for returning to help his father. The shah had a set reply: "Yes, I have served my country, but my greatest service to Iran is my choice of the crown prince. It cannot be known now, but it will be when he begins his work. Then the people shall know who he is."[27]

At the beginning, his disciplined nature, enhanced by his native shyness and Naficy's admonishments about his position and obligations as the crown prince of Iran, made Mohammad Reza rather timid in his relations with his schoolmates. He did not know how to behave among boys who did not care who he was, did not treat him as others had done in Iran, and even made fun of Iran and of him as Iran's crown prince and future king. Their behavior annoyed him greatly, but he always kept his temper in the face of their remarks. His inaction irritated his friends, who scolded him, asking why he did not respond to rudeness. "Fight them. Hit them the next time they insult you," said the friends. "Is it appropriate for me to engage in fistfights?" he asked. "Of course it is," they said. "It is your right, your duty." He challenged the next boy who made a derogatory remark to a fistfight, and all insults stopped. After the spar he was treated with respect, though he never felt himself truly "one of the boys."[28]

To the Austrian prince Paul Metternich, his classmate and the source for this anecdote, Mohammad Reza had a sense of his person and position that separated him from the others. He was neither a wimp nor a bully. His private and public personae differed. In private he was friendly, affable, not without a sense of humor. In public he was stiff, distant, and seemingly haughty. He maintained a space clearly marked private, inviolable. The urge for privacy was partly a result of his innate shyness. The insistence on inviolability came from his understanding of his office as crown prince and future king. For as long as he could remember, his father had made the point, directly and by example, that he was not like other boys, including his brothers. He would be king, and this placed him apart. He craved the moments he was free, but there were not many individuals with whom he could cast off the burden of his position.

Le Rosey was instrumental in another way. Here he saw democracy at work, albeit a democracy of the aristocrats. Still, right, law, individual participation, community decision making (if rudimentary and incomplete given the character of the school) pointed to a different possibility of social and political organization. He did not dare write about this to his father, but he thought about it, mulled it over in his mind, and discussed it with his friends. Nothing in Switzerland or at school was as glamorous as Madame Arfa's Paris, not even the system of government, but here was the real thing, people acting so differently from the way people he had known acted toward each other, him, or the shah in Iran. He would be a different king—not that his father was not a great king and worth emulating, but he was not like him, and Iran in his time would not be like it was now.

Strangely, he felt he needed religion. For the first time he began to pray daily—the ritual five times each day, seventeen *ruk'a* as the *shari'a* required. He would pray to God to help him find the straight path. And when he became king, he would help peasants to have enough capital to build their own homes and to buy the wherewithal for farming.[29] Both Mostashar and Naficy talked to him about Iran's past, the grandeur of the court and the glory of the empire. The Persian school texts he studied contained a piece on the Sasanian Khosro Anushiravan, the only Iranian king titled "The Just," and the story of the chain at the palace gate connected to a bell that supplicants could ring by pulling on the bell, thus informing the *shahanshah* (king of kings) they sought justice. The text in the book used the tale of a donkey that rubbed its back against the chain to relieve the discomfort produced by a prick. This showed, the text suggested, the extent of the shah's attention to the plight of his subjects. Such a chain was no longer practical, of course, but Mohammad Reza would instead establish a bureau to receive on his behalf petitions from anyone and about any grievance, private or public.

It is the measure of Reza Shah the man that despite his overriding attachment to his son he nonetheless determined to send him to school in a faraway land so that he would learn things about progress and modernity that he himself never had the opportunity to learn. On the other hand, the traditional Middle

Easterner in him would not allow the same opportunity to his daughters. When the girls were sent to Switzerland to visit their brother, Ashraf wrote their father for permission to enroll in school "to become educated as befitted her station." The shah's response was terse: "Stop this nonsense. Return immediately."[30] She returned, to be ordered at scarcely older than sixteen to marry a man the king had chosen for her and whom she disliked immensely.

On 11 May 1936, five years after he had left, the crown prince returned to Iran. The royal family received the crown prince at the port from which he had left, now called Bandar Pahlavi. The shah appeared at the wharf a good while before the ship was to drop anchor, standing alone, watching, calmly it seemed, as the boat approached from a distance. No one spoke to him. He asked no questions. Finally, the boat attached to the jetty. The crown prince disembarked and walked straight toward his father. The father, hardly knowing his son, who now appeared to him more like a man, shook hands with him, and they briefly embraced. Then the two entered the limousine and drove away.[31] Mother and sisters looked from a distance at the scene with no chance to approach the young man. Emotions had to be contained until later when the shah released him to them.

"I felt at the time that Bandar Pahlavi had profoundly changed and was in no way comparable to the time when I left it for Europe. It seemed an Iranian village had been transformed to a European city," wrote Mohammad Reza Shah about his first impression of his surroundings as he entered Iran.[32] He learned from his father that changes had also occurred in other provinces and cities. Indeed, much had been accomplished or begun since his father had become king in 1925, including the projects Ali Akbar Siassi and his friends in the Young Iran Society had presented to him when he was prime minister. The capitulatory system had been annulled; the judiciary had been modernized and taken largely out of clerical jurisdiction; bureaucracy had been reformed; women had been unveiled; new industries had been launched; a trans-Iranian railway was being constructed; roads had become safe; and some cities had begun to modernize. In addition, education had been substantially secularized; new schools had been built and teachers trained; girls had been encouraged to enroll in schools; technical education had been given priority; students had been sent to Europe for higher education; and a modern university had been established in Tehran.

These were some of the achievements. But other events, some not so savory, had also occurred that, though the crown prince could not foresee at the time, would haunt him when he was king. On 24 December 1932, his father had dismissed the powerful court minister Teymurtash and had him tried for taking bribes. Teymurtash was found guilty and on the appeal condemned to five years' imprisonment and payment of fines. He died in prison on 1 October 1933. The unexpected death led to persistent rumors of foul play, although no evidence was adduced. Reza Shah is said to have been involved, but he is also reported to have been unhappy at the plight of his friend and ally, and he unloaded his rancor on two editors of Tehran dailies who had welcomed Teymurtash's dismissal: "Yesterday they were praising and flattering him, and today they are abusing him without knowing why he had been dismissed, and that shows baseness."[33]

On 2 December 1935, Prime Minister Mohammad Ali Foroughi, another pillar of Reza Shah's rule, was dismissed because he had interceded on behalf of Mohammad Vali Asadi, his son-in-law's father, who had served as trustee of the Shrine of the Eighth Imam in Mashhad during a clergy-instigated uprising in the city against the introduction of Western clothing. Reza Shah had ordered an investigation and received extensive reports from both the central and provincial authorities that must have convinced him beyond doubt of Asadi's involvement in the riots, and this in turn led him to dismiss Foroughi, whom, according to most accounts, he trusted and consulted more often than any other of his collaborators.[34] Asadi was tried before a military tribunal, convicted, and executed. Foroughi fell out of favor but, as we shall see, would be called upon to manage the transition of the crown to Reza Shah's son after the shah's resignation in 1941.

And on 10 February 1937, a few months after the crown prince's return from Switzerland, Minister of Finance Ali Akbar Davar committed suicide in his home. Davar, arguably Reza Shah's most effective minister, is credited with several critical reforms, including the modernization of Iran's government bureaucracy, judiciary, and finances. His death produced many rumors but no satisfactory explanation.

These incidents and others gave ammunition to Reza Shah's enemies and marred his reputation. But none would reflect as critically on the son when he became king as the renegotiation of the D'Arcy oil concession in 1933.

William Knox D'Arcy, a British-Australian businessman, had received in 1901 a sixty-year concession from Mozaffareddin Shah to explore and exploit oil in Iran, except in the provinces in the north bordering on Russia. There a Russian concern had secured a concession about the same time as D'Arcy but had determined early on there was no appreciable oil and stopped activity. In the south, however, oil was discovered in large quantity in May 1908, and to extract and market it D'Arcy had formed the Anglo-Persian Oil Company in 1909. In 1913, Winston Churchill, then First Lord of the Admiralty, prevailed on the British government to replace coal with oil as fuel for British warships. In

1914, at the dawn of World War I, again under Churchill's prodding, the British government bought 52.5 percent of the Anglo-Persian Oil Company's stock to ensure control over an adequate, inexpensive, and secure source of oil for the royal navy. This purchase made the British government Iran's main interlocutor in controversies over oil.

Reza Shah, like most Iranians, considered the D'Arcy concession unfair, extracted when Iran had been at its lowest level of power and prestige while Britain had been at its highest. In 1907, Britain had colluded with Russia to divide Iran into zones of influence, despite Iran's protests. The British had established special relations with the Bakhtiari and Qashqai tribes in Isfahan and Fars, respectively, and with Khaz'al, the Sheykh of Mohammareh, in the Khuzistan area, the center of Iran's oil fields. The 1919 Agreement, though it was never ratified, had threatened to put Iran formally under British control. Throughout its existence, the Anglo-Persian Oil Company had paid Iran a pittance compared to what it made as profit and paid the British government in taxes. By 1920, a year before the coup d'état, the Iranian position had so deteriorated that in the negotiations toward a settlement of disputes with the company Iran was represented by Sir Sidney Armitage-Smith, a British treasury official sent to Tehran by the British government. The agreement that had been reached, however, was not ratified by the Majlis, as the law required, allowing Reza Shah to consider it immaterial. He had ordered the government to look into the original D'Arcy agreement soon after his coronation, but the formal negotiations that had finally begun in 1929 yielded no results and ended in August 1931. In the meantime, Iran's oil revenues had fallen by 76 percent from 1930 to 1931, a decline far exceeding the 36 percent fall in company profits. Informal discussions that ensued also had failed, which increasingly frustrated the shah and his government. On 27 November 1932, Reza Shah, presiding over the council of ministers, had called for the text of the D'Arcy agreement and records of the discussions and in a fit of anger had ordered them thrown in the stove that heated the room. He had then instructed the minister of finance, Seyyed Hassan Taqizadeh, to inform the Anglo-Persian Oil Company that the D'Arcy concession was cancelled.[35]

The British government objected to the cancellation on the ground that the agreement stipulated arbitration in case of dispute and threatened to take the case to the Permanent Court of International Justice. Iran argued that it was a sovereign state, that only the Iranian courts had jurisdiction in the case, and that the British had no right to interfere in Iran's internal affairs. On 15 December 1932, the British took the case to the League of Nations. After some discussion, the League asked its president, Eduard Benes of Czechoslovakia, to mediate between the Iranian government and the Anglo-Persian Oil Company and begin discussions toward reaching an agreement on a new concession. On 4 April, Sir John Cadman and Sir William Frazer of the Anglo-Persian Oil Company arrived in Tehran to begin negotiation. Soon, however, negotiations reached a deadlock and Cadman, ostensibly to say good-bye, requested an audience with the shah. Reza Shah managed to prevail on Cadman to continue discussions, and an agreement in principle was reached on 21 April. Taqizadeh signed it on 29 April, and the Ninth Majlis ratified the new concession, subsequently called the 1933 Agreement, on 28 May. Cadman later said, "The Shah, and only the Shah, made the agreement possible."[36]

The agreement, which, as we will see, would be criticized during the oil nationalization struggles of the 1950s, was celebrated at the time as a success. It significantly reduced the area under concession, increased Iran's revenues, reduced the company's intrusion in local affairs, and made the company's accounts more transparent. It also obligated the company to give priority in employment and promotion to technically eligible Iranians and to train Iranians for taking over technical responsibilities. Indeed, most Iranians who took over the operations and management of the National Iranian Oil Company when it was formed during the nationalization movement had been trained in England pursuant to Article 16 of the 1933 Agreement. But the agreement also increased the life span of the concession. The original D'Arcy agreement was for sixty years, terminating in 1961; in 1933 more than half of its life had passed. The new concession, also for sixty years, thus extended it from 1961 to 1993. The issue of the extension was raised toward the end of the negotiations and Reza Shah, according to Taqizadeh, like the Iranian participants in the negotiations, was surprised. He objected but finally acquiesced because he was in the midst of several development projects, including the construction of a trans-Iranian railway, and could not afford to lose the oil revenues.[37]

But these were matters for the future. First, Reza Shah told his returning son, he must become a soldier: one could never become a good king if one was not a good soldier, the father kept telling him. "My father wished for me to have my higher education at the Officer Cadet College and at the same time learn how to become a king under his tutelage. His wish was not unwelcome to me, for I had always liked the intricacies of military training, and, of course, it was necessary for me to be close to him if I were to become acquainted with his responsibilities. This is why I thought he made a very wise decision."[38]

The Iranian military organization, as it was then, had been modeled after the French. The Officer Cadet College was patterned after Saint-Cyr, the famous French school, following a two-year curriculum in purely military subjects. The crown prince entered the college on 3 October 1936 and graduated not long before his nineteenth birthday as an infantry second lieutenant on 22 September 1938. The shah's instructions about the crown prince were direct and precise: He was to be treated, tested, graded, and evaluated exactly like his classmates. However, this was easier said than done. The prince ate lunch and dinner at home and slept in the palace when his class was not out on maneuvers in the field. When he was not on some official visit with his father, he presented himself at the appointed hour in the morning and participated in the classes and exercises with his classmates. He was a sharp cadet and asked many questions, keeping his teachers on their toes.[39] He was also acclaimed as a superior athlete. His first experience at the military school was to test the mettle of the soccer team, of which he became captain. He was impressed with Fathollah Minbashian, a cadet he met at the school, initially because Minbashian stopped his penalty kick. Minbashian, for his part, found the crown prince a good player with a solid physique, "except that his left kick was not as good." On the other hand, he ran very well: "He did the hundred meter dash in almost eleven seconds on the chronometer," observed Minbashian.[40] He was a team player and aware of his instructors' predicament, but he was also the crown prince, and that was a fact people ignored only at their peril.

After his son's graduation Reza Shah made him the inspector of the Imperial Armed Forces, a job the young man was made to take very seriously. He also included his son in his own royal activities, sometimes even in making decisions about important matters of state. The son went to his father a half hour before others arrived for lunch, and often he was summoned to his father's presence in the afternoons as well. He also accompanied the shah on his inspection trips across the country and was often invited to comment on policies, though, as he later wrote, "The government officials were so frightened of him and so careful to be polite and deferential that there remained no room for having a 'discussion' in the true sense of the term. I was also usually brief when I uttered my opinion, so I did not engage in discussions either. Nevertheless, although I was only nineteen years old, I sometimes expressed myself clearly and forcefully. Surprisingly, he usually listened to what I said with patience and equanimity and very rarely rejected what I proposed."[41]

Indeed the shah did listen to his son, though it took some time before the son learned to speak his mind without crossing the threshold. Mohsen Sadr (Sadr-ul-Ashraf) remembered that once when he was minister of justice during Reza Shah's reign, in order to help free from jail a man named Farahi, who had made derogatory remarks about the shah, Sadr advised Farahi's wife to write a letter to the shah, but to make sure the letter reached the shah through the crown prince. The woman wrote the letter and waited at the royal court's gate for the crown prince to appear. She handed the letter to the crown prince one afternoon when he was riding out of the palace on horseback. Soon, Sadr received a call from the shah ordering him to let the man out, which he immediately did. Shortly after, the shah asked him again if the man were let out.[42]

In 1936, when Ali Mansur (Mansur-ul-Molk), then minister of roads, was accused of taking bribes, the shah, who had received the reports of bribery in the ministry, became very angry and ordered Mansur to be tried and punished. Minister of Justice Sadr argued with the shah on the points of law, stating that Mansur could not be convicted or punished unless the charges against him were proven in the court. If the charges were not proven, he could not be lawfully pronounced guilty even if he in fact had committed the crime. The crown prince, who was present at the meeting, took Sadr's side, saying that Sadr was "the very embodiment of the law," a wise and well-intentioned servant of the shah and the state. Reza Shah then "yielded to Sadr's reasoning."[43] Interestingly, Mansur went on to become Reza Shah's last prime minister before the Allies invaded Iran in 1941.

Despite the love he bore his father, Reza Shah seemed an awesome figure to the son, whose description of his father, repeated on numerous occasions and in several of his books, testifies to the mix of feelings he had for him:

> Our love for him was full of admiration though we held him in respectful awe. Broad-shouldered and tall, he had prominent and rugged features, but it was his piercing eyes that arrested anybody who met him. Those eyes could make a strong man shrivel up inside. Eventually I was able to say to him what needed saying without fear of contradiction or censure. But that took a long time. He was a powerful and formidable man and the good heart that beat beneath his rough cavalryman's exterior was not easily reached. Yet even his enemies realized that he was one of those men sent by Providence through the centuries to keep a nation from slipping into oblivion.[44]

"They talked together all the time," recalled Princess Ashraf, "always, from the earliest time I remember, but even more often after the crown prince returned from Switzerland."[45]

In September 1936, two days before he began his military training, the crown prince attended his sisters' betrothal ceremonies, which turned out to be something of a preview for his own marriage. The shah had decided the time had come for his daughters to marry. He went through the eligible candidates with some care and finally settled on two: Ali Qavam, son of Qavam-ul-Mulk, an important chieftain and political personality in Fars province, and Fereydun Jam, an officer cadet, son of then prime minister Mahmud Jam. Qavam was chosen for Shams, Jam for Ashraf. The two girls saw their future husbands for the first time when the grooms-to-be were playing tennis with the crown prince. Ashraf, who had been terrified of getting married at seventeen, now found Jam handsome and elegant. To her chagrin so did Shams, who asked their father to let her marry Jam. Ashraf objected. The father was reluctant at first but finally acceded to Shams, reasoning that as the elder sister she had prior claim. The decision was hateful to Ashraf, who could not stand Qavam. She went to her brother asking him to intervene, at least to ask their father to exempt her from marrying at all. "You know you can't change our father's mind. He believes you have reached the age girls ought to be married. It would be a waste of time to try to change his mind. You must do as he says."[46] Her mother also was no help. She advised Ashraf not to cry; rather, accept the inevitable. Qavam was a good man, she said, educated in England, from a very good family; many girls would love to marry him. Ashraf knew there was no escape from this fate but remained committed not to go gently into the marriage: if she was forced to marry, she would do so on her terms, and the marriage was dissolved shortly after the end of her father's rule.

Mohammad Reza's marriage to Princess Fawzieh of Egypt would also occur largely independently of his will. But he had accepted it as his fate to marry for the good of the state, which in his case meant marrying the woman his father chose as the future queen. For his part, Reza Shah was not a man to take such a step lightly. Like most conquerors coming to greatness from lowly origins, he wished to marry his son to a great and established line. Once he confided to two of his close courtiers he wished he could have as a bride for the crown prince Princess Ingrid of Sweden, later queen of Denmark, who was at the time accompanying her parents on a visit to Iran.[47] There was talk of selecting an appropriate girl from among the elite Iranian families, including, improbably for legal reasons, a daughter of the last Qajar king. In the end, however, he focused on Princess Fawzieh of Egypt.

Rumor had it that when Reza Shah was visiting Turkey, Ataturk had told him that a marriage between the Iranian and Egyptian courts would be propitious for the two countries and for strengthening the Iranian dynasty. It is not clear why the Turkish leader, who had recently supplanted a traditional Islamic government with a modern republic, should be interested in such an arrangement. What is known is that on one of his trips to Baghdad sometime in early 1937, Turkish Foreign Minister Rushdi Aras told Muzaffar A'lam, Iran's ambassador to Iraq, that the Turkish government, particularly Ataturk, thought such a marriage would be in the interest of all countries in the region, especially Iran and Egypt. Later, Qasem Ghani, who was present throughout most of the process of betrothal (and later, divorce), heard from Egyptian Crown Prince Muhammad Ali that Aras had insistently recommended this marriage to him in 1938. Aras spoke admiringly of the Iranian crown prince's personal traits, his solid education in Switzerland, which he claimed he knew of firsthand because he had visited the crown prince at Le Rosey on several occasions, and his superb upbringing under his father's loving but disciplined supervision.[48]

Fawzieh's Egyptian nationality posed a constitutional problem for the future of the dynasty. Article 37 of the Supplementary Basic Law stipulated that the shah of Iran had to be born of Iranian parents who were themselves of Iranian origin. To overcome the constitutional hurdle, the Eleventh Majlis passed a law on 5 November 1938 interpreting the term "Iranian origin" in the article to include also a mother who, because of high national interest, is declared to be Iranian by a royal decree pursuant to a proposal by the government and a corresponding act of the Majlis, provided such measures are taken before the woman marries the shah. On 29 November the Majlis passed a law based on this interpretation, making Fawzieh an Iranian woman of Iranian origin.[49] On 15 March 1939, the crown prince and Fawzieh were married in the Abedin Palace in Cairo.[50] Reza Shah did not attend the wedding.

3

The Man

Mohammad Reza acquired many of his father's habits, though, as we have seen, temperamentally he was his father's opposite. Where Reza Shah was naturally aggressive, Mohammad Reza was shy and reserved even when at the apogee of power. He had been sent to military school at the age of six to learn to be tough. But, except for self-discipline, which he learned primarily from his father, not much else of military toughness stuck with him. Rumor had it that Reza Shah had once said he wished his son was more like his sister Ashraf, bold and assertive. Princess Ashraf finds the rumor ludicrous: "Anyone who says such nonsense has no idea how my father loved and upheld the honor of my brother. He would never say anything to anyone that might diminish his heir."[1]

As crown prince, Mohammad Reza had been taught to be Spartan in his personal life; he remained so as king. His father slept on the floor in an unadorned room. The son also lived in relative simplicity, though the difference in the circumstances of their respective birth and childhood made his surroundings more opulent. The father dressed invariably in a plain soldier's uniform — no adornment, no medal, no pomp. The son was in full regalia when in military uniform. But this was reserved for formal occasions. Normally he wore civilian clothes, which his valet selected for the day.[2] He was not interested in his physical surroundings, and indeed during the times he was unmarried, his household looked shabby as the furniture became old, tablecloths odd colored, dishes haphazard. He was punctual, disciplined, and given to daily routines he followed almost religiously, even when he was on vacation.[3] Like his father, he also paced energetically in his office as he received government officials and discussed state affairs.[4]

His eating habits were also like his father's. Reza Shah ate simple food in small portions.[5] The son too was not a big eater: "Very little at each course, and never between courses."[6] He rarely drank alcoholic beverages. The cook decided the menu, which could not be too varied because the shah had to follow a special diet for his rather delicate digestion. Grilled fish, chicken, or meat constituted the household routine. "Cutlet and roasted chicken" was his favorite, according to Amir Pourshoja, his personal servant. "If you saw the remains of the chicken he ate you'd think the bones had been washed with Fab [dish soap]."[7] More elaborate Persian dishes were reserved for parties. He was fond of kalleh pacheh, a traditional Iranian dish of mutton's head and foot specially boiled, prepared famously well in the Queen Mother's house, though he could eat very little of it "because his stomach could not take it."[8]

Mohammad Reza liked women but only once did he fall passionately in love. His first wife, the Egyptian princess Fawzieh, was chosen for him. She was beautiful, and he grew to like her, but his affection was not reciprocated. Fawzieh remained cold and distant. In the beginning he had no choice but to be attentive to her because his father demanded it, especially after the birth of their daughter, Shahnaz, for whom the old shah had great affection. They had no other children, however, and after Reza Shah was forced to abdicate and left Iran in 1941, he felt less constrained. Still, he was discreet, seldom embarrassing his queen.

When Fawzieh left for Egypt in June 1945, Mohammad Reza did his best to get her to return, writing letters and sending several envoys to plead with her and with her brother, King Faruq.[9] Eventually, however, in 1948 they resolved to divorce, and as time passed, he became freer with women. "They brought women for him, but he never fell in love with any one. Girls at the time assumed he liked them, but that was wishful thinking," said Princess Ashraf.[10] His relationship with women, however, appears to have been mostly innocent and drab. His friends, including Majid A'lam and Yahya Adl, who were members of his inner circle, attended royal parties with their wives and attested that nothing really exciting ever happened.[11]

With Soraya Esfandiari Bakhtiari, who became his second wife, he truly fell in love, allowing her to dominate him in family matters. Soraya liked neither the shah's mother nor his older sister Shams (though Shams had discovered her) nor his daughter, Shahnaz, forcing the shah to visit his child surreptitiously. Mohammad Reza and Soraya were married on 12 February 1951. Contrary to court gossip, Soraya got along with Princess Ashraf best, according to Majid A'lam, because Ashraf loved her brother and felt obligated to do whatever necessary to make him happy.[12] Princess Ashraf confirms the shah's love: "His Majesty loved her, and they would never have separated if she could have given him an heir."[13] According to the shah's son-in-law, Ardeshir Zahedi, doctors in New

York suggested an operation that was not difficult or dangerous and assured Soraya and the shah that she would subsequently be able to become pregnant. But she refused, much to Zahedi's surprise, because later, after their divorce, she submitted to a complicated facial operation to prepare for a part in a movie.[14] If the refusal did not diminish the shah's affection, it did lead to divorce. The imperative of having an heir to the throne trumped both the shah's love and the public censure that might follow a second divorce.[15]

The shah insisted that the divorce be announced formally, giving the queen the best possible send-off. The rest was choreographed. The shah formally posed the issue of an heir to the throne and the need for assuring the continuation of the dynasty. A group of elders debated the issue on 16 February and 1 March 1958 and concluded that an heir was essential to the country's future security and well-being. The shah then sent an envoy to inform the queen and to ask for her decision. The queen graciously declared her readiness to forego her own interest in order to uphold the nation's well-being. The shah then declared to the nation that Queen Soraya had always had the welfare of the country at heart and had performed her duties as queen with utmost diligence, impeccable decorum, and absolute devotion to the people, and that it was with great sorrow that he, the shah, following the counsel he had received, and putting aside his personal feelings in the face of the nation's high interests, had decided on separation.[16]

The issue of an heir to the throne being critical, everyone close to the court now scrambled to find a suitable queen for the shah. As Princess Ashraf observed, suddenly every young girl became a candidate, every father thinking his daughter the most eligible. Some of those close to the shah also began to think of non-Iranian options, including an approach to an Italian princess that came to nothing.[17] Others continued to look around for appropriate native candidates. In the fall of 1959, the shah met Farah Diba, a young girl from a solid Iranian family who was studying architecture in Paris. They were betrothed in November and married on December 21.

Farah was born in Tehran on 14 October 1938. Her father, Sohrab Diba, was one of four sons of Mehdi Diba, a *seyyed,* that is, a descendant of the Prophet, from a distinguished Azerbaijani family, and a diplomat. Sohrab, an army officer who had gone to school in St. Petersburg and, after the Bolshevik Revolution, in France, died when Farah was still a child, leaving her with fond memories of a father idealized in a daughter's dreams. Her mother, Farideh Qotbi, was from the Caspian state of Gilan, a descendant of Qotb-ud-Din Mohammad Gilani, a Sufi master revered not only in Iran but also abroad. After Sohrab's death the family lived with Farideh's brother, Mohammad Ali Qotbi, and his wife, Louise. The Qotbis had a son, Reza, who was six months older than Farah. The two grew up together, and Reza, as Farah wrote in her memoir, became the brother she never had.[18]

Farah was enrolled in an Italian school in Tehran when she was six years old and then at École Jeanne d'Arc, a French institution established and run by Catholic nuns intent on bringing the "spirituality of St. Joseph and vocational commitment of the sisters of the church" to the education of young girls. The school was one of the more successful educational establishments in Tehran, where many of the upper-class French-educated families enrolled their daughters. Farah proved a superior student, excelling at both scholarship and sports. Sister Claire, Farah's teacher and mentor, described her as "brilliant, gifted, and conscientious" with "a good, precise mind," and active, energetic, and lively, exuding "joie de vivre." She continued at Jeanne d'Arc until the tenth grade, when she transferred to Lycée Razi to prepare to go to France for higher education. By the time she enrolled in École Spéciale d'Architecture in Paris in 1957, she had thought of living in that city more times than she could remember. Paris was a great center of the arts, and she would be only the second woman architect in Iran. "What other sector would offer me so many opportunities to express myself while helping to contribute to my country's growth?" she wrote in her memoir.[19]

The shah met Farah through his daughter Shahnaz and her husband, Ardeshir Zahedi. Like many upper-class Iranian families, Farah's family was old, rooted, and respected but not rich. She was forever looking for scholarships, which had eluded her in her previous applications to the government. In 1958, Zahedi was in charge of financial aid to students in foreign universities, and Farah asked her uncle, who knew Zahedi, to arrange an appointment for her with him. The uncle not only insisted on Zahedi's meeting his niece, but, according to Zahedi, also asked him to consider her as a possible candidate to marry the shah. Zahedi was reluctant at first because, he said, "in such cases the go-between always loses. If the marriage is a success, he is forgotten; if a failure, he is blamed."[20] Nonetheless, he agreed to ask his wife, Shahnaz, to take a look at Farah as he interviewed her. Shahnaz did and apparently was impressed. A day or two later Farah was asked to meet with the Zahedis at their home.

At the Zahedis', Farah suddenly sensed a commotion and was told the shah had arrived unexpectedly. She felt her heart pounding with excitement, even though she half-expected his arrival. She had met the shah briefly two months before during his visit with Iranian students in Paris. The chief adviser to the students, Jahngir Tafazzoli, had introduced her as a diligent and superior student. The shah had asked her one or two questions, to which she was satisfied she had given appropriate answers. She wrote her mother that she had been ladylike, not like the girls who had rushed the king. And one of her friends had told her the shah liked her because he had looked at her as he left the room.[21] All this was done and said with innocent girlish excitement suggesting she was mindful of the possibility, finding it thrilling, no matter how improbable.

The shah talked to her with quiet warmth when they met again at the Zahedis'. Farah responded with calm and dignity, despite the tension of the occasion. The shah was impressed, although he would go on interviewing other candidates. But after he met with Farah once more at the Zahedis' house, on Zahedi's suggestion, he talked to his mother about his interest in Farah. "I must marry for my country; I would like to marry someone this time that my daughter and mother also like," he told his son-in-law.[22] The shah and Farah continued to meet, he driving her in his sport cars and once in a Morane-Saulnier four-seater jet with Shahnaz along. A rumor began that the shah proposed to Farah during this flight. In fact, the jet developed a problem with the landing gears, forcing the shah to call on Farah to help with the manual controls. Excited with the company and the flight, she did as instructed, unaware of the danger. Only after they landed and she saw the fire engines waiting and the worried look on the faces of the people on the ground did she realize something had gone wrong.

The hours she had spent with the shah, the driving and the flying, the excitement of being near this man she considered so exceptional left Farah with excruciating expectation. "He had a real gift for putting me at my ease with a word or a smile, and so I could just enjoy the pleasure of being there beside him."[23] The shah was warm, kind, and attentive, but he said nothing about marriage. Zahedi found it appropriate to remind him he should let Farah return to Paris if he was not serious.[24] The shah then asked Farah to spend an afternoon with him to talk and to swim. It was not easy for her to be alone in a swimming suit with the most powerful man of the realm. But she surprised him with her calm, saying she adapted easily to circumstances. "It was a disturbing and delightful afternoon," she wrote enigmatically.[25]

Several days, "maybe it was two or three weeks," she reminisced, passed without any news from the shah. She decided to ask Zahedi if she should go back to her school in Paris. She was told to wait. "I felt upset, but what were my feelings compared to his responsibilities?" Wisely, she decided to strike a stoic pose. Finally, an invitation came from Princess Shahnaz. Farah described the scene at the Zahedis:

> There were a lot of us there with the king that evening, maybe twenty. I was happy and relieved to see him again. The conversation was light and the king smiled, showing nothing of the care and tensions that must invariably have been on his

mind. As we were in the drawing room, I suddenly noticed that the guests were leaving one by one. The king and I were there alone on a sofa. Then he told me very calmly something of his two former marriages: the first to Princess Fawzia of Egypt, who had given him his daughter Shahnaz, the young princess, and the second to Soraya Esfandiari Bakhtiari, who he had vainly hoped would give him a son. Then he stopped talking, took my hand, and gazing into my eyes, said to me, "Will you consent to be my wife?"

She said yes immediately; there was nothing for her to ponder: "I loved him and was ready to follow him."[26]

Farah was twenty-one years old when she married and became queen, almost the same age as the king's other brides at the time of marriage. The shah, however, had moved on in age and experience. Fawzieh was the same age as he when they married, Soraya ten years younger, and Farah half his age. He was more experienced now and commanded greater authority, no less than his father, he had been heard to boast. He told Farah that in being a queen she would have responsibilities that were unique to her position and that separated her from other women.[27] He did not want a hands-off queen, as Fawzieh and Soraya had been, but one engaged in social work and also dedicated to her duties as wife and, he hoped, mother.

Farah turned out to be different from Fawzieh and Soraya for reasons other than the shah's serious though affectionately worded sermon. She was smarter, more energetic, more active, and considerably more interested in the affairs of the nation. More important, she bore the shah a male heir in less than a year, which made her position secure and the shah's relation with her unique. The birth of Reza Cyrus on 31 October 1960 was a source of pride for the shah, a link to his father by reaffirming the dynastic chain. His father had held him up when he was born and prayed to the Almighty to protect him. He paid homage at the tomb of his father to mark the continuity of his dynasty and in 1961 conferred the pre-Islamic title *shahbanu* on his queen. In time he and Farah would have three more children, Farahnaz, Alireza, and Leila.

The shah was good at sports, and serious about them. At tennis he practiced regularly with George Aftandelian, Iran's champion player, and he kept up playing until eventually it became difficult for him to continue because of his eyesight.[28] He had learned skiing at Le Rosey and, back in Tehran, never missed a chance to ski on the rare days snow filled the rather primitive ski slopes of the hills near the city. In the 1940s, he was a role model to the few men and women who skied, seeing him carry his skis on his shoulder walking up the Elahiyeh hills by Pahlavi Boulevard.[29] In later years, he frequented the much more advanced ski slopes constructed in Shemshak and Gajereh on the slopes of the Alborz, and in the Alps near his winter cottage in St. Moritz. He was also an accomplished horseman, the kind who liked his horses sprightly, quick to the touch, requiring no encouragement to move. He disliked spurs, never used them, and never wore them unless as part of the uniform in ceremonial military functions.[30] When he went to the stables at the royal hunting grounds in Farahabad, he often took with him sugar and carrots for the horses and always noted how they had been groomed, asked questions, and commented on their appearance and poise.

He liked speed and courted danger beyond the boundaries of propriety for a king. His queens, though with him at different periods of his life, were equally afraid to be in the car when he drove and told him so. Others, also afraid, dared not speak, though General Karim Ayadi, his personal physician, once was so frightened that he lost control and, according to Queen Farah, who was also in the car, shouted at the shah to slow down, to which outburst the shah quietly but sternly remarked: "If you don't keep quiet, I will be distracted and may have an accident and consequently will not be able to guarantee your safety or promise you a long life." The queen, though sympathizing with Ayadi, could not help laughing, and Ayadi, fearing both time present and time future, fell silent.[31]

It was the same when he piloted a plane or a helicopter. He followed the rules but also took risks. He had several accidents, one potentially fatal. His small propeller-driven airplane's engine stopped in flight, forcing him to land in a mountainous area near Kuhrang in Isfahan. The plane hit the top of the hill, lost its wheels, and overturned when it hit the ground, leaving him and the general who accompanied him strapped to their seats upside down. He found his posture comical and began to laugh, to his companion's consternation. Later, he explained that he and the general were unharmed because he was protected by the Almighty.[32] This escape made him even more confident and prone to taking risks, particularly in later years, when he flew the Falcon or the Mystère, his favorite jet planes, from Tehran to the Caspian and back. He established records for himself and then tried to better them, flying between mountain ridges to save the time that would be needed to gain the required elevation over the mountain. This, of course, frightened the queen and others who happened to be in the plane.[33]

In the 1940s and 1950s, the shah had dinner twice a week at Princess Shams's, twice a week at Princess Ashraf's, and Fridays at his own home, where his friends and guests came for lunch as well. Soraya cut some of the dinners off, but they resumed after she and the shah separated. Early in these years, when the shah and his friends were young, playing at sports was the preferred pastime. In later years, playing at cards became the vogue. Rumor had it that exorbitant sums of money changed hands in both sports and cards. This was not true. The shah played for money, but the amount was small. Volleyball, for example, was played for small bets, the shah making it known he did not countenance any favors. He insisted that everyone do his best, and he himself was often on the losing side, even though he was probably the best player, at least until Mohammad Khatami joined the circle. Khatami, later the commander of the air force and husband of the shah's youngest sister, Fatemeh, was of professional caliber and adept at sports, and everyone, including the shah, accepted his superiority and compensated for it by balancing the teams. After a while, because of the rumors, betting in sports stopped. The same happened with cards. The shah played poker when he attended Princess Ashraf's dinners, but the pots were not big. Indeed, the shah and the rest of the royal family did not have the money in the 1940s and 1950s to gamble big.[34] Still, the shah stopped playing poker; his game now became bridge and subsequently belote (a game similar to but less complicated than bridge). This routine, like most other things in the shah's personal life, continued almost unchanged in the later years when he married Farah. When Princess Shams moved out of town in the late 1960s, her dinners became less frequent. Her friends also were cut off from the shah's presence. On the other hand, Queen Farah's friends, younger and more energetic, became a new and important part of the court crowd. The shah, the queen, and their friends now attended Princess Ashraf's dinners regularly and those of other family members only occasionally.

Dinners, as social occasions meant to help the shah and the queen relax, were attended by friends of the royal family, often also the prime minister, the minister of court, one or two cabinet ministers and their wives, one or two businessmen and their wives, and one or two individuals from the arts world. There was a roster of the eligible to be invited. In the 1970s, Reza Golsorkhi was the master of the roster at Princess Ashraf's, and for any dinner he cleared the list for that evening with the princess. Neither the shah nor the queen saw the list for prior approval.

To be invited to an event where the shah and the queen were present was honor to some and business to others. Some would rather have been passed over, but these were few. Many in a position to be invited, particularly those with business interests, were sensitive and competitive. They would seek ways of being seen at the court by those who could affect their interests and complain if left out. A reputation of friendship with the court was worth a lot, carrying a presumption of favor and therefore power. The rest depended on the presumption-bearer's guile and chutzpah. "There were those who would go to great lengths to ensure they were on the list," Golsorkhi explained. "When I became responsible for sending invitations, I found myself faced with a problem. Princess Ashraf had a personal friend-maid, Iran Khanum, she had grown up with and liked very much. Iran Khanum wielded a lot of influence about the palace. Those who knew how close she was to the princess had cultivated her friendship and called her directly to ask if they could come to the dinner, and she would tell them they could. I had to work for some time to establish the rule that henceforth the invitations would go solely through my office."[35]

The shah's circle of friends was small and over the years remained relatively unchanged. He insisted on keeping his personal friendships separate from his official work, a compartmentalization that was near absolute: friends knew and observed the rule. This, of course, did not mean that those who were with him lacked political clout or did not use it. In the first years of his reign, being his friend did not make much difference because he himself did not carry much political weight. In later years, when he was the near-absolute ruler, being close to him was enough to convey influence and power.

Some of his friends, such as Hossein Fardust and Majid A'lam, went back to his childhood. Fardust was a special case, becoming in later years his eyes and ears and therefore no longer in the same category as his other friends. A'lam was with him when they were both children, but they separated when the crown prince left for Le Rosey and he for Paris. A'lam's father, Amir A'lam, the old shah's physician, had asked Reza Shah to allow his son to go to a school where he could prepare to become a doctor to the crown prince, as he was to the shah. Reza Shah agreed. The son, however, chose to attend the École Polytechnique in Paris instead and became an engineer, a professor at Tehran University, and a successful contractor.[36] Other friends joined the shah after he returned from Switzerland, several after he became king.

Yahya Adl was a scion of a well-established Azerbaijani family friendly with the Qajars.[37] Adl had studied in Paris, become a general surgeon, and taught for some time at the Sorbonne; he was reputed to be one of the best surgeons in Iran. He was several years the shah's senior and perhaps for that reason the shah treated him with deference. Unlike the others, Adl freely criticized the shah's policies, so much so that the shah, exasperated, had once protested he would go happy to his grave if Yahya said one good thing about something he had done for the country.[38] Adl did not seem eager to be at the court. Sometimes he did not show up, which made the shah both angry and unhappy. The shah insisted that he be present on Fridays. He enjoyed having Adl as his partner in bridge or belote, even though Adl would sometimes quit playing to go watch his daughter in equestrian competitions, even when he was the shah's partner. Others wondered how he could do what they dared not, and some of them sometimes tried to get the shah to feel insulted, but the shah always shrugged it off.[39]

Because of their professional positions, both A'lam and Adl were on very good terms with the members of the National Front, a group that in the 1950s became anathema to the shah. A'lam was named chair of metallurgy at the University of Tehran when Mehdi Bazargan, who was a collaborator with Mohammad Mosaddeq and the National Front (and a quarter of a century later Khomeini's first prime minister), was dean at the College of Technology. A'lam's friendship with Kazem Hasibi and engineer Ahmad Zirakzadeh, Mosaddeq's close allies, resulted from their common background as graduates of the École Polytechnique. Adl operated at the Najmieh Hospital, an endowment of the Mosaddeq family, where Mosaddeq's son Gholamhossein was the managing physician. The two were close friends. The shah did not mind. Occasionally he asked A'lam how his friends in the Iran Party, to which several of Mosaddeq's allies belonged, reacted to a certain policy. But this was rare and out of the ordinary. Usually he did not engage his friends in political discussions.

Many of the shah's friends came to him through his relatives, especially his sisters, though usually it took time for friendships to gel. Felix Aqayan was introduced to the shah through Princess Ashraf and her friend Minu Dowlatshahi. Minu, who had been Ashraf's sister-in-law, was a member of the princess's inner circle and was always present at the dinners she gave for her brother. After she divorced her first husband and married Felix, she continued to frequent the dinners but without her new husband. It took some time before Aqayan was admitted and accepted as friend, but once in, he remained to the end, even after he and Minu were divorced.

Amir-Hushang Davallu, the most notorious of the shah's friends, was a member of the Qajar princedom, a born courtier, clever and corrupt, a well-informed conversationalist, tasteful in dress and décor, a sycophant par excellence, and an opium addict. He was also, in Adl's parlance, a superior "pimp,"[40] but did his job so deftly that Queen Farah, though aware of his activities for her husband, nonetheless enjoyed his company and invited his presence at court. Unlike many of the shah's friends, Davallu used his position at court to promote his personal interests. The shah's position was that, all else being equal, Davallu should not be denied his share because he happened to be his friend. He had the same attitude regarding General Karim Ayadi, his physician-friend. Ayadi was of the Baha'i faith and devoted to the shah. Originally a good doctor, over the years he failed to keep up with evolving medical knowledge. The shah did not think highly of his medical skills, but relied on him for ordinary medical advice and especially for his loyalty. He was not amusing, lacked a sense of humor, was a mediocre partner at bridge, belote, or any kind of sport. In latter years he was, among others, the head of Edareh-ye tadarokat-e artesh (ETKA, the Military Procurement Department), which provided for the everyday consumption needs of the imperial armed forces. It was a lucrative post, but unlike Davallu, Ayadi was not interested in personal gain; rather, whatever he could skim from his command he used to prop up the organizations belonging to his faith. Since Baha'is were anathema to the shii clerics, Ayadi's closeness to the royal court created political problems for the shah, but he nonetheless kept him as an assistant and confidant.

Queen Farah brought with her to court several of her close friends. They were young, innocent of the ways of the court, and mostly university types the queen believed the shah enjoyed.[41] Some of them had been critical of the regime before they found their way into the court as a result of their friendship with the queen.[42] They were often referred to as *bacheh-ha,* "the kids." The shah's friends looked at them more as their wards than as competitors. As one of the queen's friends said, there was more competition within the two groups than between them.[43] The shah, for his part, was very correct toward the people around him, including "the kids." He knew, almost reflexively, that his attention to any particular person might work against that person because of the envy it might elicit in the others. On the other hand, if he showed irritation, the object of his ire would be demolished by the others. He took care to be balanced. He rarely showed his true emotions, although those close to him had learned to interpret his mood by his look and his gestures.

As a rule the shah did not talk politics with "the kids." Fereydun Javadi, the queen's childhood friend, was very surprised when one evening in the royal resort in Noshahr, a city by the Caspian, in one of the after-dinner walks, the shah asked them what they thought about abolishing capital punishment. The question, out of character, appeared particularly strange to Javadi because of the terrorist activities of several anti-shah groups at the time. To Javadi, the shah was a man ahead of his time. "He had visions of the future that oozed out of his general statements without his ever speaking about particular policies." Over time, "the kids" developed a kind of affection for him, an empathy that toward the end bordered on reverence. He seemed to them to believe in the sentences he uttered—"never mixing words to protect against intellectual overcommitment," observed Javadi. "He abhorred hypocrisy. I believe deeply that he never said a word in which he did not totally believe. The man was complete sincerity. That's why he was somewhat naïve."[44]

Farah and the shah loved each other, but the love was more companionate than passionate. The shah being a man in an oriental patriarchy had more leeway; the queen was bound by custom and tradition to make sure her actions did not violate the honor of the family and in her case the nation. Both the shah and the queen worked hard, but the shah's work was emotionally and intellectually draining, and the hours were difficult to control, though he was personally disciplined and made sure his discipline infused the environment of his work. His one venue to sanity, as he said to his friend and court minister Amir Asadollah Alam, was the company of other women. These women were brought for him mostly from Europe; Madame Claude of Paris was the supplier of choice. And there were several intermediaries—pimps like Davallu, according to Yahya Adl—who took their duty very seriously, striving to excel, seeking to outdo the competition. The shah met with these women periodically, the tempo picking up when the queen was away. The encounters did not always conclude in sexual intercourse. Often a conversation, a dance, or a drink sufficed. But these occasions were soothing, and the shah enjoyed them. He called them *gardesh,* outings.[45]

Farah knew about her husband's adventures and was generally good-natured about them, but not always. At times she would grumble or cry, and on rare occasions even threaten to harm herself. The worst crisis of this sort occurred in the summer of 1973. A girl named Gilda, with whom the shah had an outing, began blabbering everywhere that the monarch was madly in love with her. The claim led to a widespread rumor that the shah had secretly married the girl as a second wife. Tehran was abuzz with gossip. This was more than the queen could take, and she was very angry with the shah. He ordered Court Minister Alam to warn the girl to keep quiet or she would end up in jail. The gossip, however, did not stop. Farideh Diba, the queen's mother, confronted Alam with the report of the shah's marriage. Alam denied the gossip as an absolute lie. "Even if true," he told Mrs. Diba, "you should not repeat such words. What profit could there be in making a fuss about it?" Mrs. Diba was unrelenting: "Fortunately, my daughter has not become addicted to luxury," she told Alam, intimating a possible divorce. Alam repeated the statement to the shah. "Really," was the shah's sarcastic response. But he was obviously worried. "Find a way out of this," he said to Alam, both a command and a supplication.[46]

The shah's closest friends—those who were privy to his *gardesh*—sometimes witnessed these scenes but did not interfere, and if they did, being male chauvinists, pronounced the queen unreasonable. The man, after all, needed respite from an otherwise suicidal schedule, they argued. But these moments disturbed the shah to no end. He would have given anything to defuse the tension with the queen except, of course, his venue to relaxation. One of the things he gave his wife to keep her pacified was a free hand in the fields of her interest. In due time, Farah became a power unto herself.

Despite his keen intelligence, the shah was never known as an intellectual. Indeed, he disparaged intellectuals, mostly in jest, making it difficult for the people around him to decipher his meaning. Early in life, he showed great interest in literary and philosophical matters, though he was shy about it and self-effacing. At Le Rosey he had apparently become somewhat familiar with French and English writers, as one might in high school. He had even read some Shakespeare in French translation—*Romeo and Juliet,* for example. But he must have found it impolitic to appear adept at such things to his father, who might have seen it as a sissy's avocation. To appear good with horses and football and cars most likely was the right bet for impressing Reza Shah. After Reza Shah's exile, of course, his situation changed but he remained shy on such matters. He was outspoken on politics but not on subjects that assumed an academic background. He was, however, anxious to learn.

When still crown prince he had heard of Allameh Mohammad Qazvini's reputation as a great scholar. He had wished for some time to meet with the learned man, and when he became king, he kept asking his ministers of court to invite Qazvini to the palace. Qazvini, a modest and self-effacing man, had refused, stating that he was only an ordinary scholar and the shah's time was more precious than to be spent with him. "His Majesty has been gracious; that is no excuse for me to overstep my limits." The ministers appealed to Qazvini's friend, Qasem Ghani, who finally prevailed on the old man to meet with the young shah.[47]

The shah knew that several other scholars held regular discussion meetings with Qazvini. He told Court Minister Hossein Ala that he wished to spend one afternoon each week with Qazvini's group. "This is spiritual nourishment for me," he said and forthwith gave Ala the names of the individuals he wished to be present, which Ala wrote down exactly, as was the court's custom.[48] The first meeting was held at the Sa'dabad Summer Palace north of Tehran at the foot of the Alborz Mountains. According to Ghani, the shah entered the room, shook hands with everyone, and sat rather diffidently at the head of the table. A few moments passed in silence. Then the shah said: "I am aware that you gentlemen get together regularly to discuss literary and scientific subjects. I am not knowledgeable enough to be a member of your group or a participant in your discussions. But I wish very much to listen and to learn. That is why I have asked that you periodically hold one of your meetings in my house and think of my house as your own. I will sit and listen. What I wish most is that there be no protocol, that we treat each other as friends." In time, the shah, who was mostly quiet during the first sessions, would be the first to speak, beginning the debate with a question, usually put to Qazvini, who then either opened the discussion or referred the subject to another participant. The meetings continued for several years, discussions ranging over many topics, including philosophy, history, and poetry. Once, when a Hafiz *ghazal* (sonnet) was quoted to him, the shah was particularly moved, commenting that although he was not well versed in Persian poetry, he felt, indeed experienced, the loftiness of its accomplishments. Afterward, Qazvini told Ghani that the shah's love was now ingrained in his heart because he believed any man not moved by good poetry was dead as a stone. "But today," he said, "I saw how this young man was affected by poetry and found him all soul."[49]

In the 1960s and 1970s the shah still enjoyed having around him individuals who dabbled in intellectualism, though he rarely participated in the interaction. Asadollah Alam, who had a penchant for smattering his prose with verse, also had several "intellectual" friends who supplied him with ideas in vogue among the literati. Quoting verse was the way of tradition and of giving assurance that one's connection to Persian culture was firm and unpolluted. But this was not to some of the moderns' liking. They believed that Persian culture had substituted poetry for reason and that the practice was a symptom if not a cause of the ineffectual thinking that had kept Iranians backward; serious people should not take shelter behind the emotional façade it provided in lieu of rational argument.

The shah agreed and extended the thought to cover the intellectuals.[50] However, he did not mean by the term *intellectual* the literati who were against him or his regime, or those who made specific arguments showing why his policies were wrong. He was more concerned with those who cooperated with the regime, but were not serious about the possibilities the country had. He himself was serious. He thought that if Iranians put their efforts behind the projects he proposed to catapult the country into the twenty-first century, they would succeed. Some intellectuals in the regime went through the motions but did not quite believe in the effort. To him they were cynics, naysayers who had neither the intellect to come up with an alternative nor the gumption to pull out. He did not see anything constructive in critique that was mainly deconstructive.

He was familiar with some of the debate that was raging about Western cultural hegemony and the threat it posed to Iran's national identity. He followed some of it in the media — for example, a series of conversations on television in the early 1970s in which Seyyed Hossein Nasr and Ehsan Naraqi, an Islamic philosopher and a sociologist, respectively, discussed the religious and the secular in Iranian culture.[51] He used the term *gharbzadeh* (usually translated as "westoxicated") pejoratively, but he was not familiar with the philosophical underpinnings of the term and, as far as those close to him knew, he had not read books by such authors as Al-e Ahmad, who had popularized the term. His familiarity stemmed from the reports he received, which ordinarily categorized such writers as befuddled ideologically and unbalanced psychologically. His own problem with *gharbzadegi* was the tendency to oversubmit to the West and things Western that he sensed in certain individuals around him, in his regime, or even in the opposition, such as the National Front, and that to him meant being weak on nationalism and patriotic pride. His own pride in things Iranian was inordinately high. He even resented foreigners belittling or undervaluing Iranian movements whose mission was to topple his regime. In the same vein, he appreciated and respected Iranian scholars who spent their lives studying, thinking, and writing, liked to be with them, and often boasted to foreigners about the individuals in his regime he considered intellectual. Once he bragged to King Hussein of Jordan that Fereydoun Hoveyda, "our ambassador to the UN," was a novelist and film critic.[52] He thought such individuals engendered respect for Iran because they had, as he might put it, "coté intellectuel." The same complex of feeling was instrumental in his positive attitude to Amir Abbas Hoveyda, Fereydun's brother, who became the longest-serving prime minister in his reign.

Though not himself an intellectual, the shah often impressed intellectuals. Gunnar Myrdal called him extraordinary after he and his wife visited with the shah and Queen Farah. Indeed, the two men were very impressed with each other. Their meeting, scheduled for a private luncheon, lasted several hours after the queen and Mrs. Myrdal left the table. The shah was familiar with Myrdal's works on race problems in the United States and poverty in South Asia. Myrdal later commented that if there ever was a philosopher king, the shah was it.[53]

The shah admired people of Myrdal's intellectual stature, more so if they were also statesmen—especially Léopold Sédar Senghor, the Senegalese poet and politician, one of the few friends with whom he was on first-name basis. He admired Senghor for his literary and philosophical bent and was taken with his discourse on "negritude" and especially his suggestion about "iranité" as an idea that could be developed as shorthand to identify Iran as a "cultural becoming" to bridge the East and the West. The shah might have wished he could put the thought poetically, but he could not. The best he could do was to use economic and technological language, which he did with comprehensiveness, sometimes with a smattering of exaggeration substituting for poetry.

Perhaps this is why he felt more at ease with the technocrats, though he admired them not as much as the literary crowd. The spirit of the time did not invite poetry in the affairs of the state. Amir Abbas Hoveyda would conduct a scholarly conversation on the French Revolution and the personal habits of Saint-Just. He might even recite a line or two of Hugo or Baudelaire, but no one heard him ever come up with a line from an Iranian poet. This was probably the case with most of the Iranian technocracy. It was the case with the shah also. But, as noted, others did. Alam had poems for all occasions and used them in his conversation with the shah, which the shah appreciated. Jamshid Amouzegar, the tough OPEC negotiator, was versed in the Persian poetic tradition—Hafiz and Sa'di and Rumi—as well as modern poetry, but as in most other things, he used his poetry in private. The first time most people heard him recite poetry was in his speech in the Majlis in 1977 as he explained and defended his government's program in preparation for a vote of confidence. It was an amazing performance, causing the deputies to wonder how a man famous for his toughness knew and, more amazingly, actually used verse in such a serious governmental business—and showed how much life had changed since the time kings composed poetry.

The shah's childhood religious beliefs remained with him to the end. He insisted on honoring the Islamic tenets—the *sha'a'ir-e eslami*. His commitment to religion was emotional more than intellectual, though he reasoned religion was the foundation of morality and that without it morality had no compass. Throughout his reign his policy was to strengthen the foundations of religion but to shun empowering the clerics. An Islamic government had no place in his thinking. Indeed, in the first two decades of his reign the idea of an Islamic government was never an issue. But he believed even the more common understanding of the established religion, one that was grounded in the Iranian constitution, thwarted progress. Nevertheless, Islam was an entrenched religion and the ulama had influence over the people and consequently possessed significant political power. This he considered an important factor in the nation's power equation; one ignored it at one's peril. He was therefore adamant about observing what he believed to be the spirit of Islam and shunning, more on the basis of expediency than belief, anything that contradicted the clear Islamic tenets stated in the Koran. Governments believed that one way to deal with the clerical establishment was to buy it with money and to scare it with force. The shah seemed to think that a carrot other than money was also needed. The regime should befriend the clerics when possible. The policy worked as long as it did not transmute to appeasement, a condition that depended largely on the recipient's attitude. His policy was geared to the likes of the Grand Ayatollah Borujerdi, the *marja' mutlaq,* the "supreme source of emulation," during many formative years of his reign. Borujerdi did not favor a politically aggressive Islam, because his reading of recent history, particularly the history of the Constitutional Revolution, had taught him that political Islam led to damaging and unintended consequences.

What the shah wanted of Islam, on the other hand, was its moral teaching, which he, or someone like him, would interpret. Islam for him had two interconnected dimensions. It was a faith in God and God's saints, who were benevolent and protective. And it was a set of primordial tenets that morally and ethically compelled the individual and the government to be kind and helpful to others because they were God's creation and equal in His eyes. Human beings had needs and rights that changed with time. Unless the ulama understood the importance of moving with time, society did not need them because they would only hinder progress. A majority of ulama understood what he was after, and they disapproved of it. Their opposition annoyed him, but it neither scared nor worried him. As far as he was concerned, the clerics were outmoded, already in history's dustbin, unbeknownst to themselves and to some people. One therefore neither antagonized nor gave them leeway unnecessarily.

PART II

HARD TIMES

4

Ascending the Throne

In 1939, as war broke out in Europe, Russia was Iran's main worry. Communism, a mystery to most Iranians, was generally disliked because it was "Godless," clearly to be shunned and condemned. Its creed ran counter to Iranians' sense of authenticity. They were vexed by the thought of communized property, and they abhorred the idea of sharing their wives and daughters, a false notion that was widely spread across the country by the clerics. They believed communism was a Russian tool of dominion and control. The Molotov-Ribbentrop Pact confused them, but it did little to swing their opinion in favor of the Allies. Rather, it turned them against the war altogether because they believed war would end in Russian supremacy in Iran. The Allies' determination to destroy Germany they thought was a mistake, "almost wicked," because, regardless of who won the war, Europe would be weakened and Iran would be left to the mercy of the Russians.[1]

Reza Shah, who worried more than most others, made his ministers give him their assessment of how war would proceed and ordered several of them to hand him their best judgment in writing. To everyone's surprise, the essays led him to choose as the next prime minister Ahmad Matin Daftary, then minister of justice.[2] Matin Daftary was young, from a family with strong ties to the Qajars, and pro-German. On 26 October 1939, the shah had opened the Twelfth Majlis stating he was saddened by the war, which would harm Iran economically and financially, and prayed for peace to be restored soon for the sake of Iran and the world.[3] After the opening ceremonies, Prime Minister Mahmud Jam and his cabinet met with the shah in the Majlis Hall of Mirrors to seek permission to resign, as the law required. Jam expected to be asked to form the new cabinet, but, to his surprise, the shah looked at the ministers standing in line and after a moment or two of reflection said Matin Daftary would manage the government; looking at Jam he said, "You come to the Ministry of Court and work with me."[4]

The war caught Iran in a bad time. An inflationary spiral had taken hold while salaries had remained fixed. Oil revenues had gone down, retarding industrial growth. For the past several years Germany had been Iran's most important supplier of goods and technology for her industrialization programs—although not for the army. The shah had deliberately bought the weapons he needed for his armed forces from companies in small industrial states, Skoda and Brno in Czechoslovakia and Bofors in Sweden, to minimize foreign domination. Contrary to subsequent British and Russian propaganda, he disliked Hitler and abhorred Mussolini. He believed Mussolini had ambitions in the East and would probably prevail on Hitler to help him invade the countries of the Middle East, including Iran.[5] He also believed that regardless of their expertise or employment, the German nationals so useful to Iran's economy were obliged to follow Nazi directives. Consequently, many of them might indeed be engaged in espionage or propaganda. Just before the war the German embassy requested an entry visa for a German professor, purportedly to study Sasanian irrigation methods because, he argued, ancient Iran excelled in irrigation techniques. The request was forwarded to the shah's special bureau for his permission. The shah rejected it, jokingly asking since when had Iran achieved such renown in irrigation. This man, the shah observed, was a military cadet. His coming to Iran was not advisable.[6]

Sir Reader Bullard, recently appointed British minister to the legation in Tehran, wrote in his report that the shah's government tended to doubt German claims. "It may in fact be said that relations [between Iran and Britain] have remained friendly, and it is certain that the Shah's sympathies, were he to express them, would be found to be more in favor of the Allies than of Germany. The latter's alliance with Russia indeed makes this inevitable." Bullard characterized the shah's attitude as one of "frantic neutrality."[7] The shah had in fact done his utmost to prove Iran's neutrality by word and deed. The press had been ordered to reproduce only news items from the international news agency reports and strictly to refrain from any comment on the war. Diplomatic receptions were duplicated so that the belligerent countries would be invited on separate occasions, while the neutrals were divided between the two camps.

England, however, had cut off Iran's trade with her best customers and despite Iran's pleas had not offered alternative export or import markets of any consequence, making everyone anxious about the future. Shortly after the opening of the Majlis in October 1939, Iran lodged a complaint with England for intercepting a cargo of military and industrial goods from Czechoslovakia. The shah took the matter up with Bullard: "The arms had been ordered from Czechoslovakia not only before the war but even before the seizure of that country by Germany.

These are things I want for the economic development and for the strengthening of the means of defense whereby Iran could the more easily preserve her neutrality: I don't believe England would object either to the one or the other."[8] He also wanted Hurricane airplanes, weapons, and other industrial goods from England. Would Britain replace at least a part of what he needed? Bullard was sympathetic: "Since in recent years Germany not only supplied Iran with industrial material finished goods of all types, but also took by far the greater proportion of her exports, the problem of finding new markets is obviously one of great urgency, and if a solution cannot be found it seems likely that the Iranian Government will direct a greater share of their resentment towards the [British] Government whom they hold responsible for their plight."[9]

In fact, the Molotov-Ribbentrop Pact had made Iran's position vulnerable. Germany had been a counterweight to the Soviet Union. The Soviets had pressured Iran to expel the Germans, accusing them of anti-Soviet activity. Although that pressure had subsided after the signing of the pact in August, the counterweight had also substantially weakened. Iran now considered the Soviets a serious threat to its territorial integrity, especially after Russia's incursions into Poland and Finland, and sought ways and means of protecting herself. The government again approached the British for weapons but was rebuffed, the British stating that they had their own shortages and were in no position to help.

At the same time, Iran's finances deteriorated, in part because of a fall in oil revenues. In 1939, the Iranian official currency, the rial, fell on the open market from 140 to 175 per pound sterling, and the budget continued to show a large deficit. The shah accused the Anglo-Iranian Oil Company (AIOC) of deliberately restricting production, thereby cheating the Iranian government of the royalties that were its due. Lord John Cadman, the AIOC chairman, was sent to Iran in June 1939, but his interventions with the shah did not have a long-term effect. In February 1940, the shah signed a credit agreement with the British for £5 million to buy weapons and industrial goods. At about the same time, he told the company "[that] England should take more Iranian oil and that he had decided that the money he received in the form of oil royalties would be spent in the United Kingdom for the large quantities of material which Iran needed." Surely it was advantageous for both Britain and Iran if more oil was taken from Iran, said the shah—"England must want the Iranian oil, the whole world must want the Iranian oil," and he was tired of the excuses made since 1937 for the results that had so deeply disappointed him. Cadman, the shah insisted, "must understand that the production of oil from Iran must not be less than in 1937."[10] The company informed the British government that it was up to the government to convince the shah that the company was not able to satisfy his demands.

In June 1940, the shah cancelled the credit agreement with the British, arguing that Britain had not honored the terms of the agreement. The terse language of the cancellation and its subsequent publication in the Iranian press vexed the British.[11] Bullard attributed the cancellation to an increase in German influence and called it "a dangerous symptom." Nevertheless, he wrote British Foreign Secretary Lord Halifax, in the matter of credits, "it would have paid us handsomely to be more accommodating, especially as to cement and locomotives."[12] Halifax agreed on both counts but, complaining about the mode and language of cancellation, instructed Bullard to inform the Iranian government that it had made "the worst impression on His Majesty's Government."[13]

The Iranian government now asked the AIOC to be paid in gold convertible to dollars, with the shah threatening to denounce the Anglo-Iranian oil concession before the Majlis on 7 July. The British, fearing drastic action by the shah, began to think more seriously about accommodating him. Cadman was again to be dispatched to Tehran to speak to the shah.[14] Bullard was instructed that England did not wish to become involved in disputes with additional countries and that Iranian oil was of "great strategical importance [because] oil from other alternative sources will have to be bought largely in dollars." However, Bullard was told, "there are limits to patience of His Majesty's Government." England wished to maintain friendly relations with Iran, but Bullard might threaten the Iranian government at his own discretion: "if Iranian Government do not share desire of His Majesty's Government for friendly relations they should reflect carefully upon the obvious fact that His Majesty's Government could and probably would exercise complete control over all exports of oil from Iran."[15]

Bullard did not deliver the threat. The British concluded that they could not risk losing the oil from the world's largest refinery in Iran's southern port of Abadan and must pay something toward what the shah demanded although they considered it blackmail. They seriously believed that the shah might cancel the concession, an alternative they would wish to avoid at all price. They proposed to pay the "blackmail" in the form of an interest-free loan of about "4½ million pounds to which His Majesty's Government would be asked to contribute." In addition, the shah would likely demand that the funds be convertible to dollars, which the Treasury found "very disturbing." The idea of giving in to the shah was hateful to the British. "To give way to the Shah," wrote Chancellor of the Exchequer Sir Kingsley Wood to Lord Halifax, "would create a feeling throughout the East that we are in so perilous a situation that we are ready to submit to any bullying or blackmail, even by a small and poorly armed state such as Iran. I think the damage to our prestige in the United States of America and elsewhere would also be very great." He wondered whether Halifax would want to take up the matter with the War Cabinet for a thorough debate.[16] Halifax, commiserating with Wood, wrote him that England did not have many choices: oil from other sources would have to be paid for in dollars, England could not incur unnecessary military risks in the Middle East, and, he said, "we have to take account of the possible reactions of the Soviet Union if by mischance a serious quarrel with Iran developed."[17]

In the event, the Iranian government did not accept an offer of a loan. The shah had said previously that under no circumstance would he accept oil payments smaller than £3½ million per year, equal to the amount paid in the peak year of 1937. Now he demanded to be given the gold premium as well, which according to the company's calculations gave him an extra £1½ million for the period 1938 to 1941. The shah, of course, knew that the British were in a quandary and that their deteriorating position in the Far East had made them more dependent on the Abadan oil. The British had come to the same conclusion. There was no sense in talking to Reza Shah anymore; Cadman likened him to a brick wall. On 21 August 1940 the dispute was resolved on the following terms: (1) The AIOC undertook to pay the sum of £1½ million on 31 August 1940 and to make up the sums due on account of royalty tonnage, dividend participation, taxation, and gold premium to £4 million in total in respect of each of the years 1940 and 1941. (2) The difference in respect of the years 1940 and 1941 would be paid no later than 31 August of the following year. And (3) in regard to the period after the expiration of the year 1941, differences between the parties in respect to the government claims would be examined at that time with due consideration to the conditions of the time with a view to reaching arrangements agreeable to both parties. These proposals, the two sides agreed, would not affect the terms of the concession.[18]

Even as these negotiations proceeded, Reza Shah remained afraid of Russia. England was in no position to help if Iran was attacked, and it failed to deliver the weapons it had promised to supply Iran before the war. Germany was the only country that could potentially help because, many Iranians believed, it was likely to win the war and if so would behave toward Iran differently than England or Russia had done in the past. However, Germany was also far away, and as long as the war continued Iran would have to guard its independence and territorial integrity mostly on its own. The shah therefore tried not to give offense to the Russians. The British tended to interpret Iran's deference to Russia in the framework of the 1921 Agreement, giving its Article 6, which allowed the

Soviets to bring troops into Iran under certain circumstances, more credence than the Iranians did.[19] The shah would under no circumstance acquiesce to Russian intrusion into Iranian territory, though he knew he did not have the wherewithal to fight off the Russians if they should intrude. The Germans buttered up the shah; the British fought with him. At the time, the only major power the shah was able to pressure was England, because of England's dependence on the Anglo-Iranian Oil Company. This left the British with a bad taste, a sense that England must wait until the right time to balance the score. Lacy Baggallay of the Foreign Office expressed the sentiment in a note to A. P. Waterfield of the Treasury: "However disagreeable it may be to have to give way to the Iranian demands, the price is on the whole a cheap one when one considers the benefits which we secure from retaining our hold *till happier times* on this vital supply of oil."[20] England would now wait for happier times.

Reza Shah was the rare Iranian who was not particularly pleased with the Germans, even though he had approached them for help when an officer in the Cossacks. But that had been before Hitler and Nazism. After Hitler grasped power and particularly after the Molotov-Ribbentrop Pact was made, the shah became increasingly wary. The pact and its aftermath—the fate of Poland, the Baltic States, and Finland—convinced him he could not count on Hitler. On the other hand, the events in Europe, the rise of Hitlerism, the absorption of Czechoslovakia, the Munich Pact, and the swift move into Poland, warned him to beware of antagonizing Germany. The Wehrmacht's spectacular drive westward in the summer of 1940, the fall one after another of Norway, Denmark, the Netherlands, Belgium, and France, dazzled him as it did others. Nevertheless, to reassure the British, he appointed Ali Mansur, reputed to favor the British, as prime minister in June 1940 on the eve of those German victories. The move, however, made little difference because the shah still personally ran the show. Under Mansur, his problems with the British grew despite his own wish to avoid getting into trouble with them. In December Anthony Eden replaced Lord Halifax as foreign secretary, a move that would ultimately alter Anglo-Iranian relations, Eden being a sterner man than Halifax.

The shah insisted on receiving the royalties as agreed, and the British paid them after much haggling at each instance. The more the shah stood on his rights, the more acerbic became the British propaganda against him. In 1939, both Anne Lambton and Bullard had characterized Reza Shah as much admired, particularly by the youth, for his accomplishments. Now, Bullard called him despicable and detested. Leo Amery, secretary of state for India, wrote Eden a private note suggesting that Reza Shah was universally detested and questioning the legitimacy of his rule. "Don't forget that the legitimate Shah, younger brother of the late Shah, Prince [Mohammad] Hassan Kajar, is in this country and could if necessary be flown out any moment."[21]

Eden followed up on Amery's suggestion, put it up for discussion in a ministerial meeting, but finally concluded that a Qajar prince would not find much support among the Iranians. "I can recall no example in Persian history of a 'hark back' to an earlier dynasty," he wrote back to Amery.[22] To Harold Nicholson, who had also taken up the Qajar mantle, he wrote that he "doubted whether any Qajar prince would rally much local support" and that he didn't like "saddling ourselves with a candidate who might collapse at the first opposition. . . . The present Pahlevi Valiahd [crown prince; i.e., Mohammad Reza] has, as you say, some advantages and if Reza Shah should go in some way that did not take the whole family with him this young man might be a possibility. But I think we should keep our hands free till we see how things are likely to shape."[23]

The question of replacing a Pahlavi with a Qajar, however, would recur several times during the 1940s and early 1950s, though the then pretender, Hassan's son Hamid, had taken the name Drummond, enlisted in the merchant marine, and become a British subject, much to Nicholson's amazement. "How it came about that the King of Kings was so careless about his dynastic progeny as to allow his Valiahd to become a member of the British Merchant Navy and to speak no language except English passes my comprehension," observed Nicholson to Eden as he nonetheless recommended Mohammad Hassan for the throne.[24]

Hitler's invasion of Russia on 22 June 1941 drastically changed Iran's strategic position in the war. Everyone, including the shah, expected a quick German victory. The purpose of the attack, said Churchill, was to cut off Britain's lines of economic and military sustenance and to defeat her before the United States entered the war. England, he said, would fight to the end. Reza Shah thought Hitler's next target might be Iran; Hitler would get control of the oil in the Caucasus as well as the two countries of Iran and Iraq, and would use Iran and Afghanistan as a bridge to India. The shah ordered Mohammad Sa'ed, his ambassador in Moscow, to declare Iran's absolute neutrality. He was unusually gracious to Andre Smirnov, the Soviet Union's new ambassador to Iran. He talked to him longer than usual and made a point of telling him that it had always been his ardent wish to have good, constructive, and cordial relations with the Soviet Union. He wished, he said, to move beyond any misunderstanding that might have existed between the two countries in the past. When Smirnov said Russia had certain strategic needs Iran might satisfy, indirectly suggesting that Iran might become a conduit for weapons Russia needed, the shah answered he would do whatever he could as long as it did not violate Iran's neutrality.[25]

Iran was now facing Russia and England without the counterbalance of Germany. Reza Shah put himself on the Allies' side, expecting to help them as much as he could within the bounds of neutrality. This, however, was not enough for the Allies, though they never said so explicitly. In July, Eden explained Britain's policy toward Iran as (1) the maintenance of fully independent Iran; (2) the promotion of Iranian prosperity; and (3) the maintenance of Iran's freedom from the undue influence of any foreign power. England would even continue its commercial relations with Iran, including the export of aircraft material, provided, however, Iran expelled the Germans. "There can be no doubt that these persons will be employed whenever it may seem fit to the German Government for the creation of disorder either in Iran itself or in the neighboring countries," he cabled Bullard. "His Majesty's Government take a grave view of this situation and you should urge upon the Iranian Government the vital importance . . . of a drastic reduction of the number of Germans who are permitted to remain in the country. For your own information, we should wish to see four fifths of the Germans leave in a month. We assume you can check fairly accurately numbers who leave."[26]

The shah had already ordered his government to expel as many Germans as would be possible without appearing completely to have fallen under the Allies' thumb; this had, naturally, drawn angry reactions from the Germans. Being hit by both camps, he did not know exactly how to respond. The press on both sides predicted an inevitable clash between Iran and the Allies. On 10 July Prime Minister Mansur sought a clarification from Bullard, who promised him that no pressure would be brought on Iran to abandon neutrality. "A neutral Iran was strategically to the Allies' advantage," he explained.[27] The British were buying themselves time to resolve two questions: was it wise for the future of India to have the Russians ensconced in Iranian territory; and would it be possible to have a free hand in Iran with Reza Shah at the helm? Soon after Hitler's attack on Russia, Eden had been forced to defend past government policies against a charge of appeasing the shah, brought specifically by the government of India. It was a misreading of the government's intentions, he said. "There has never been any question of appeasement in the policy adopted towards Iran but it has been essential, before embarking on any action that might result in hostilities, to make sure that the necessary forces would be available to deal with any enemy reactions. . . . Once the necessary force had been made available H.M.G. will have no hesitation in exerting all necessary pressure." The government, Eden wrote, did not believe sanctions, as advised by the government of India, were useful. More important, he observed: "There is the very important question of the use of the Trans-Iranian Railway for supplies to Russia, which would be imperative should Vladivostok route become unavailable and vulnerable in any case. This might be secured by show of force but might necessitate extensive military operation in conjunction with Russian occupation of Northern Iran, which Government of India deprecate. This would seem to constitute an argument for making every endeavor to get what we want by friendly means in the first instance."[28]

By the end of July 1941, the British had decided that they probably would invade Iran. The question was from where and how. Amery wrote to Eden how delighted he was that all military preparations were being made "in readiness to support an ultimatum to Iran by the Middle of August" and once more reminded Eden, "we have a possible Pretender here in the legitimate Shah, Prince Hassan."[29] Troops in India had already received orders to move to Iraq. Iraq was to be handled carefully, even rewarded at Iran's expense, to gain its full cooperation as the springboard for invasion. Reza Shah was now treated to a barrage of demands to expel German nationals from Iran. The Iranian government kept assuring England and Russia that she would under no circumstances permit the remaining Germans to interfere in Iran's affairs, but to no avail. On 4 August, the German News Agency reported that sixty German technicians in Iran had left for Turkey and the rest would leave when their visas ended. Nonetheless, the press in England and Russia now began to forecast an early invasion. On 13 August Russia informed England it was prepared to move into Iran but wanted to coordinate with Britain. On the 16th Bullard and Smirnov handed the Iranian acting foreign minister, Javad Ameri, another ultimatum demanding the expulsion of all remaining Germans. Ameri replied that there remained only 470 Germans in Iran, all technicians working in technical and industrial fields. "This number of Germans," he declared, "could in no way threaten the security of the Allies."[30]

On the 20th, the shah attended the graduation ceremonies at the Officer Cadet College. He told the cadets they might not have their customary one-month leave this year, but once they knew the reason, they would burst with pride. "I do not need to impress on you the critical position in which we find ourselves today nor the importance of your sense of sacrifice for the nation. It is enough for me to say that the army and the officers should be fully attentive to the crisis that today faces our country."[31] On the day before this speech, Eden sent British military and civilian leaders a top-secret cable in which he said that the terms of the Iranian reply were "unacceptable and designed in collaboration with Germans to play for time and that military action should begin as soon as the Russians are able to cooperate." The invasion was to take place on or after the 22nd. The Allies needed Iran's railway, but, Eden wrote, "For publicity purposes our reasons for action contemplated will initially be confined to the need to eliminate German influence in Persia. If subsequently military operations develop on a considerable scale our action could be justified on the grounds that we are keeping open a line of communication with Russia."[32] On the 22nd, Reza Shah ordered all German nationals not absolutely needed for technical reasons expelled. On the 25th, England and Russia invaded Iran.

The last days of Reza Shah on the throne were traumatic for him and for his son. Reza Shah had discussed the war with his government, military command, and several Majlis deputies and had determined there was a potential danger for Iran, but not an immediate threat. His policy was to accommodate the Allies while maintaining Iran's neutrality. But he had misread the Russians and particularly the British. His basic problem was himself. Being who he was, whatever he did or could possibly do would not have satisfied the requirements of the Allies.

The Russians had been the first to bring up formally the question of invasion. On 23 July, Soviet Ambassador Ivan Maisky asked to meet Eden and told him his government was prepared to take part with the British in military preparations against Iran. The two countries would first concentrate troops, then present demands, and if the demands were refused they would take action. The demands, Maisky said, should be as follows: "first eviction of the Germans, as [Britain] had suggested; secondly, right of free transit for Russian troops and war material across Trans-Iranian Railway." The second demand, Eden noted, might be difficult to harmonize with "our insistence to Iran that Germans should be evicted based on the need for Iran to observe scrupulous neutrality. It might be a little difficult in the same breath to tell Iranian government that they must give Soviet Union and perhaps ourselves facilities which were difficult to reconcile with neutrality." Maisky brought up the analogy of Sweden's remaining nominally neutral but giving Germany important transit facilities. Eden agreed Sweden was a good precedent and promised to talk about it with his colleagues.[33]

However, neither Eden nor Churchill wished to have Russian troops entrenched in Iran. The government of India had strenuously objected to the idea, even when the Soviet-German pact was still operative. Eden deliberately refrained from instructing Bullard to bring the matter directly to Reza Shah's attention. Bullard, for his part, had become disaffected with the shah. Over the year and a half he had spent in Iran, he had seen the shah rarely and had found him aloof. Based on the opinions he had heard the crown prince offer on the war, he had concluded that both the shah and his heir considered the Germans invincible and partly for that reason had pro-German sympathies. The shah's insistence on more royalties had miffed Bullard. The image he had developed and conveyed of the shah was one of a morose, corrupt tyrant, whom his people detested. Later on, after the shah had left for exile, Bullard called Iranians "a base people" for showing sympathy for their exiled king.[34] Bullard and the Foreign Office doubted that the shah would resign but thought that one way or another he must go. The Qajar alternative did not seem viable to them, except as a puppet run by a local officer. The crown prince was a possibility, but they thought it would be difficult to put up with any Pahlavi after they settled with the shah. In early August Bullard suggested that British financial aid to Iran be designed and offered so as to divide the shah and the government, but on further reflection Eden concluded that this was not practical.[35]

Prime Minister Ali Mansur and Javad Ameri, the acting minister of foreign affairs, were Iran's interlocutors with Bullard and Smirnov, the British and Russian representatives. According to Mansur, Iran followed the principles of neutrality to the letter. The Germans in Iran posed no threat to the Allies. Moreover, the Germans were not the only foreigners in Iran; there were many other nationalities, including Indian, Iraqi, and British. The British indeed had complete information about the Germans, including their number, names, and reasons for being in Iran, and given the Iranian government's vigilance it was impossible for them not to know that they posed no threat to them. Soon, the Iranian government realized that there might be other reasons for the Allies' pressures for which the focus on the Germans was camouflage. The shah ordered Mansur and Ameri to ask the envoys about this. They did, but, according to Mansur, the answer was always the same: the Allies were satisfied with Iran's policy of neutrality; it was the Germans in Iran that were the problem. Mansur directed the Iranian minister in London to put the same question to Foreign Secretary Eden. The answer was the same as Mansur had heard from Bullard.

The shah was baffled and insisted on a rational answer. Sometime toward mid-August, Mansur asked the shah if Iran should ask all the Germans to leave despite the economic and financial losses Iran would incur. The shah was reluctant at first, but soon he relented. Mansur and Ameri approached the German minister, Ervin Etel, and put the question to him. In time Etel agreed to put to his government the Iranians' predicament and reasoning. After several communications he informed Mansur that the German government had acquiesced to Iran's intention to expel all German nationals and hoped to continue to have friendly relations with Iran. "This issue was resolved according to Iran's wishes," added the German envoy, "but this is not the end of it. The British and the Russians have other plans, which will not be satisfied by this move."[36]

The shah, however, was happy with the results and ordered Mansur to inform the British and Russian envoys that now that the Iranian government had Germany's agreement to have all the German nationals expelled, there remained no cause for argument. Mansur in turn directed Ameri and Hamid Sayyah, the political director at the ministry, to inform Bullard and Smirnov. Sayyah reported back to Mansur in writing:

11 August 1941

Prime Minister Mansur,
Your Excellency,

As directed, I went to the Soviet embassy in Zargandeh at the appointed time to present to Ambassador Smirnov the Imperial government's reply to the embassy's 6 August note. Due to Mr. Smirnov's illness, I was received by Mr. Nikolayev, the embassy's political counselor. As directed, I told him since the embassy had given the Imperial government a written note, the Imperial government shall per force present a written answer based on the rules of neutrality. However, I have been charged by the Imperial government formally to present to you an oral statement that in order to eliminate any misunderstanding the government of Iran has decided to expel from Iran all Germans in its employ within two weeks. Mr. Nikolayev asked: "Are you certain the Germans will leave during this period?" I answered I was certain.

Signed Hamid Sayyah.[37]

The German embassy in Tehran asked the government to direct the police department to expedite the issuing of exit visas for the German nationals and to ask the Turkish embassy to do the same with transit visas. All this, however, was of no avail. Mansur writes: "At 4 A.M. on 25 August 1941, without prior notification, the Soviet and British ambassadors arrived at my home delivering notes stating their respective countries' concerns about matters that had been previously answered with respect and assurance. In their notes, they referred to a possibility of eventual military action, when they had already begun military attacks on defenseless Iranian border cities from air and land."[38] Mansur objected to the unprecedented Allied behavior, attacking without prior notice a neutral country that had already done what they had demanded. He asked them to stop their operations so that Iran could learn what it was that they really were after. The envoys declined, saying only that they would report Mansur's statements to their respective governments.

At 4:30 A.M. Mansur called Ameri, and the two of them went to Saʻdabad, the royal summer residence, to report to the shah. The shah was stunned. "Why?" he asked. "Did they give any reasons?" He ordered Ameri to bring to him the two envoys. It took Ameri some time to rouse the ambassadors, who had gone to bed after their call on Mansur; but, finally, the three of them met with the shah. "Ask them why have they done this," the shah ordered Ameri. Ameri translated the shah's query to Bullard, who, knowing some Russian, repeated it to Smirnov. After a short discussion in Russian, the two envoys repeated what they had previously told Mansur: All they knew was that their governments had directed them to convey the notes. The shah was furious. "I have my responsibilities. I need to know why your forces have invaded my country. You haven't declared war on us. Invading another country requires a declaration of war, a rationale, but we were on good terms, why then?"

Same answer: We don't know.

"You don't know that I also have my duty to perform, I must know if we are at war? This cannot be. Why did you not tell us if there was something you wanted?"

Ameri, translating, insisted that Bullard answer. "The country's sovereign asks you a question. You must give him some answer."

Bullard talked with Smirnov and finally said that in their opinion it was the question of the Germans in Iran. "I will expel all the Germans," said the shah. "What then?" The envoys conferred with each other again and then asked for time to consult with their governments and come back with an answer.[39]

That same day in Moscow Molotov told Iranian Ambassador Saʻed that the Allies had attacked Iran because Iran had taken no steps to expel the German agents. He referred to Article 6 of the 1921 Agreement as the basis for the Soviet action and stated that the Soviets would withdraw as soon as the German threat was foiled.[40]

In the afternoon, Mansur informed the Majlis about what had happened, and the shah sent a telegram to President Franklin Roosevelt asking him to mediate for peace. The Iranians had great respect for the Americans, in part because of the positive attitude of the U.S. envoy, Louis Goethe Dreyfus, and the popular charity work of Mrs. Dreyfus in the southern slums of Tehran.[41] Dreyfus, however, was not on good terms with the British or the Russians and would soon have a difficult relationship with the U.S. military in the Persian Gulf.

Mansur believed that the British and the Russians conspired to alienate Dreyfus from the war affairs and soon had him transferred out of Iran.[42] Roosevelt, who knew of the British and Soviet plan, made only a noncommittal response, assuring the shah that Iran's national independence and territorial integrity would be respected. Four years later this assurance would come almost to naught. As George Lenczowski subsequently observed, had the United States made its stand clear on several issues, "it could have prevented many unwelcome events."[43]

Reza Shah ordered a general mobilization. The First and Second Divisions moved out and took defensive positions in the outskirts of the capital. The commander-in-chief's war headquarters was established in the Officers Club under the shah's chief of staff, General Azizollah Zarghami. Reservists were called to service. But it was clear that against combined Russian and British power resistance was useless. On 26 October the war council proposed a unilateral armistice, and the shah approved. That evening the shah summoned the cabinet to his residence at Sa'dabad and declared he intended to resign: "We have done whatever possible to prevent this nefarious war from breaking out on our land. But against all international rules and moral principles, our two neighbors invaded our country. There can be no other reason for this dastardly act but their wish to destroy our system and our progress, which we have achieved with so much labor and human struggle. The bottom line is that they consider me their enemy because I have protected this land. I do not wish to be the cause of enmity toward and misfortune for my country and my people. I have therefore decided to resign." He then looked at Mansur and told him to prepare the proper statement to be announced to the Majlis.[44]

The cabinet demurred unanimously. The shah's decision to resign, the ministers said, ran counter to all that he had done to build the country. His resignation would harm Iran's national interest and even jeopardize the country's independence. The shah asked them to debate the matter among themselves and said he would meet with them to hear their "considered opinion." The cabinet met immediately at the palace, discussed the issue, and again arrived at the same conclusion. The shah and the crown prince now joined the ministers. Mansur stated the cabinet's counsel: the shah's resignation at this time was not in the nation's interest. The cabinet, however, had decided to ask the shah's permission to resign. Mansur and his team had followed a neutral policy, but the circumstances had clearly changed. His Majesty should appoint a new cabinet that was better positioned to negotiate with the invading governments. Also, a council of elder statesmen should be called together to deliberate on the present situation and offer counsel on policy. The shah listened and at the end said he would inform the cabinet of his decision soon.[45]

The next morning, the 27th, the shah informed Mansur he had decided for the time being not to resign. In the afternoon, he called the cabinet to discuss the future government. He proposed Minister of Justice Majid Ahy for prime minister, but Ahy begged to be excused on the ground that the times required a more experienced statesman and promptly suggested Mohammad Ali Forughi, who had been prime minister several times in the 1920s and 1930s but had then fallen out of favor. The shah was reluctant. Forughi was ill and old and had been away from the affairs of state for so many years that he was probably unfamiliar with the needs of the day, the shah complained. "Better get Vosuq-ud-Daula," the shah suggested, perhaps because of Hassan Vosuq's previous close connection with the British. But Vosuq, they told him, was out of the country. The ministers promised they would help as best they could to make Forughi's stewardship a success. The country needed his experience, prestige, and gravitas. The shah sent Nasrollah Entezam, his chief of protocol, to bring Forughi to the court. "You don't look as old as I had been told you are," he said to the old gentleman when he was ushered to his presence. Forughi knew the gravity of the situation and accepted the shah's offer without question. "The nation has groomed us for a day such as this and it is incumbent on us to serve," he explained to his brother and sons.[46] That same afternoon the prime minister designate had his first cabinet meeting with the existing ministers in the presence of the shah. The cabinet decided anew to declare a unilateral cease-fire and to negotiate the terms with the British and Soviet envoys.[47]

On the day Forughi was appointed prime minister, Mohammad Sa'ed, Iran's ambassador to the Soviet Union, was told by the British ambassador there and the Soviet foreign commissar that Reza Shah would have to leave and that his heir was not whom the Allies had in mind for the Iranian throne. One of the younger princes might be chosen, to be governed by a viceroy selected by the Allies from among Iranian statesmen acceptable to them. Sa'ed argued that neither the law nor the people would accept a future king other than the crown prince and that it was to the Allies' advantage to have the crown prince as king. Sa'ed informed Forughi and beseeched him to ensure the crown prince's ascent to the throne.[48]

By 30 October, military discipline had dissolved. On that day an attempted coup d'état in the air force was foiled, but the few junior officers involved managed to escape in two small airplanes. The High Council of War decided to release all the conscripts and so ordered the garrisons. Across the country soldiers poured onto the roads on foot in all directions, heading for their villages. The shah was stunned. He summoned the officers who had signed the decree and accused them of treason. He promised he would personally execute the two commanders he had decided were the main culprits—acting War Minister Major General Ahmad Nakhjavan and G2 Chief Brigadier Ali Riazi—and was dissuaded only by his son's mediation.[49] That day, he called his son-in-law Lieutenant Fereydun Jam and ordered him to take the shah's family to Isfahan. Only the crown prince remained in Tehran.

The young prince, soon to become shah, had come face-to-face with a hard and unexpected reality. He had learned a lot during the past few days about men, fear, selfishness, and loyalty. His father was strict in his treatment of others, but not always unkind. Nevertheless, everyone he knew feared the shah, which naturally conditioned his feeling toward the stern man also. Courtiers had told him that his father had only two loves: his crown prince and Iran. He believed it, but the knowledge did not put him at ease. There was something in the coarseness of the father's character that annoyed him, though he scarcely dared to admit it to himself. He remained deeply loyal to his father and worried about what might happen to him. He would not leave his father under circumstances such as he had experienced in the past several days.

His father had told him over the years that it was folly to trust exceptional men not to develop ambitions beyond their station. He himself, the father had said on several occasions, was the very proof. The advice remained with Mohammad Reza, and many years later, after he had lost the crown, he reiterated it as an argument why he could not have had a Bismarck or a Richelieu as chancellor. But at this time, at only twenty-two years of age, the idea weighed on him as unhappy consciousness. Yet such mistrust went against his instincts, both because he had learned otherwise at Le Rosey and because he did not possess the inner roughness to trust no one. He was markedly democratic and lenient in his relation to others. The shah had taken him everywhere on his trips and given him responsibilities of various kinds, especially with the military. He almost always had chosen to intercede on the side of clemency and fairness. The father, like most others, thought him decent but soft. He had told the son once he hoped he could put everything in order before his death and leave him with an orderly, easily governed country. The young man had interpreted the statement as rather less than complimentary and resented it at the time. "Does he think I am not up to the job?" he had wondered. Now, however, he thought it would have been the most valuable thing he could have received from his father. Later, after his own time had reached the end, he would remember that, sitting at the cabinet meeting next to his father, he had wondered how such a catastrophe could have occurred when his father had had such seemingly airtight control over every man in his administration. How could the military let soldiers go without his knowledge? He had interceded with his father one last time to save the two generals, perhaps because he himself might have unknowingly confused them with his observations. They always talked to him, and as the inspector of the armed forces he said things about the army's morale and combat readiness, but the generals took their orders from the shah and they never mentioned a conversation with him when reprimanded by his father. If his father, so sternly in charge, had failed at the most critical moment of his reign, would he be able to cope? He had thrown words at the ministers, scolded them for not foreseeing the events, inadvertently called them names suggesting they were cowards, but he was not sure he had meant it. Would he be able to control himself in the future, unprotected by his father?

Now they brought him the rumor about the Allies wanting to install his half-brother Abdorreza as king—clearly a reverberation of what Sa'ed had been told in Moscow and transmitted to Forughi. His old friend from Le Rosey, Ernest Perron, mad with anxiety, begged him to have his father take whatever measures necessary to avert this "catastrophe." But such things were no longer in his father's hands. Forughi was the man of the hour, more so as the shah became increasingly convinced that it was impossible for him to continue as king. "I am the target," he had told his ministers, and Forughi had thought the same before he accepted the office. President Roosevelt's noncommittal reply to the shah's appeal for help offered no immediate aid, but it gave some assurance about the future of the country, buoying the new prime minister and encouraging him to move as quickly as possible to take hold of the events.

The invasion had frightened the people everywhere. The dissolution of military discipline had left the country and the people defenseless. Still, it was a testimony to the worth of those of Reza Shah's generals who maintained the peace by their sheer presence. Ahmad Amir-Ahmadi, Iran's first and until then only lieutenant general, appointed military governor of Tehran after the invasion, kept the city quiet by simply walking on Sepah Street "twisting his moustaches," as General Karim Varahram fondly remembered almost a half century later.[50] These were the men who had helped Reza Shah in his ascent to power; now, he counted on them to help his son in a far more difficult and dangerous situation, though he had called them traitors and personally beaten some of them. For the moment, however, the problem was political, the ball was in Forughi's court, and the future of the young prince depended on how the old gentleman played it. As it turned out, Foroughi proved more than equal to the task.

Reza Shah resigned on 16 September 1941. The text of his resignation was prepared by Foroughi. He signed it without comment despite Foroughi's plea for him to look at it carefully and make corrections where he thought necessary. What he signed reads thus:

> I have spent all my power and energy in the service of the country. I am no longer able to continue in the same vein. I feel the time has come for a younger and more energetic power to take charge of the affairs of the nation, which require constant attention, and to work for the happiness and welfare of the people. Therefore, I resign, bequeathing the crown to my heir and crown prince. From today, 25th of Shahrivar of the year 1320 [16 September 1941], it shall be incumbent on all the people, military and civilian alike, to acclaim my crown prince and legal heir as the shah and to give him the same in upholding the interests of the state as they gave me.[51]

The shah then left for Isfahan in a solitary car, accompanied only by the driver. His son-in-law, Lieutenant Fereydun Jam, who had taken the shah's family to Isfahan, drove to greet him several kilometers outside the city. Jam was ill, and at the appointed spot, he got out of the car and lay down by the side of the road, waiting for the shah's car to arrive. He must have dozed off. He was awakened by the tip of a walking stick. He saw Reza Shah standing above him alone asking him what he was doing lying down by the road. The two got in the shah's "ancient, dilapidated" car and drove into the town to the house where the family had been ensconced.[52] As the shah walked toward the building his daughter Ashraf, sitting at the window of the house looking down into the courtyard, spotted "a very old man" walking with two companions.

> As they drew closer, I was stunned to realize that this old man in civilian clothes was my father. In less than a month he seemed to have aged twenty years. . . . In my whole life I never had seen Reza Shah in anything but a military uniform, and I had never known him to be anything other than a proud and vigorous man. His work had been the activating force of his life, and now he was suddenly a man without purpose, sent to join the realm of old men whose usefulness had ended. At my brother's wedding he had expressed the wish to have ten more years to finish the programs he had started, but he was not to have that wish.

The princess thought her father might have suffered some kind of stroke following his abdication.[53]

On the morning of 16 September 1941, after Reza Shah signed the resignation letter Prime Minister Forughi had drafted for him and set out for Isfahan, Forughi and Foreign Minister Ali Soheili drove to Zargandeh, the Tehran suburb where the Soviet embassy was located, to inform Smirnov and Bullard of the shah's resignation. From there the two attended a special session at the Majlis to announce Reza Shah's resignation in favor of the crown prince, whom Forughi referred to as "the new king." The Majlis, whose members had been elected by Reza Shah's grace, was not kind to the departing shah, but the deputies went along with the prime minister, sensing the urgency of the matter. The next day, the 17th, at 4:30 P.M., Mohammad Reza Pahlavi took the oath of office in the Majlis:

> I, in the sight of the Almighty God, swear on the Holy Koran, and on all that is respected before God, that I shall dedicate my life to the preservation of Iran's independence and territorial integrity, and of the rights of the people. I swear to preserve and protect Iran's constitutional system and its Basic Law and to reign accordingly. I swear to promote the Ja'fari Twelver Shi'a religion, to take all my actions conscious of God's keen surveillance, to have no other intent but the grandeur and happiness of the Iranian state, and to ask the Almighty to grant me success in serving the Iranian nation. In all this, I seek the support of the luminous spirits of Islam's *uliya'* [tutelaries].[54]

The new shah was received warmly by the deputies. After taking the oath, he spoke about the rule of law, constitutionalism, separation of powers, and the importance of close cooperation between the government and the Majlis "in these dark days of foreign occupation."[55] He said he would bequeath all that he inherited from his father to the state. On his way back from the Majlis to the palace, the people jamming the streets gave him a jubilant welcome—more ecstatic than the Allies had expected or liked. "The people ensured His Majesty's kingship [*saltanat*] today," commented Forughi, who accompanied the new shah to and from the Majlis.[56] Others claimed the people almost carried the shah and his carriage on their hands. Sir Reader Bullard, the British envoy, noticed the jubilation but was noncommittal in his report to Eden: "The young shah received a fairly spontaneous welcome on his first public appearance, possibly rather [due] to relief at the disappearance of his father than to public affection for himself." The young man, Bullard reported, was thought to have pro-German sympathies and to have maintained close relations with the German legation, "but this may have been politic." But "he [was] not credited with much strength of character," which, "if true, [might] suit present circumstances." The report reveals the extent of suspicion the British bore against the Pahlavis. Bullard cautions that the new shah should not be dismissed as "inevitably a bad sovereign" out of hand because, in any case, "no alternative presented itself, nor could any have been without considerable delay and a welter of intrigue." This, however, was not a matter of grave concern: "The present shah, if unsuitable, [could] be got rid of later." In the meantime, "it should be possible to prevent him from doing much harm."[57]

Forughi told the young shah he should beware of the Allies. Once the option of a Qajar prince had proved unworkable to them, the idea of a republic was said to have popped up, presumably with Forughi as its head.[58] But this option also was impractical. Forughi would not stand for it, nor would other civilian or military officers. The young shah knew the British and the Russians did not want him on the Iranian throne and that given a chance they would support an alternative. But he also knew they did not have many practical choices since the two powers disagreed on which alternative they wanted and for what reasons. The British wished a docile government they could rule as in the beginning of the century; the Soviets believed getting rid of the shah was the first step to a Soviet Republic of Iran, and this made the idea of a republic repugnant to the British. In the midst of such intrigue, the new shah moved cautiously. He sent several messages to Bullard assuring him of his "whole-hearted cooperation." But he also asked Bullard and Smirnov whether it was their desire to administer the country jointly or if they would allow an Iranian government to govern. If the latter, then he asked "how any government can have authority when the capital is surrounded by foreign troops."[59] He sent a telegram to King George to inform him that he had ascended the throne as the constitution demanded. He wrote that he hoped his sincere wishes for the welfare of his people and the desire to fulfill the weighty task he had assumed would yield the results he prayed for. He would like to think that the British king would accord him his friendship as he, for his part, would be happy to renew the best relationship possible between the two monarchs and their two countries. He offered his best wishes for the well-being of the royal family together with his "inaltérable amitié" (enduring friendship). King George's response was formal, but assured him that he could count on the king's "friendship and support."[60]

The advent of the new shah coincided with a new political dispensation. On 19 September he issued a general decree pardoning a mix of political and other prisoners, including the two officers his father had accused of treason for releasing the soldiers in time of war. Two days later, on 21 September, Major General Ahmad Nakhjavan, whose stars and medals the former shah had forcefully torn from his uniform, was appointed minister of war in Foroughi's first cabinet, with his rank and medals restored. On that same day, Justice Minister Majid Ahy read to the Majlis the text of Reza Shah's letter bequeathing his real and movable estate to his son, and the new shah's declaration that he transferred to the state everything he had received from his father.[61] "Munificent gifts," wrote Bullard to Eden.[62]

The day the new shah took the oath of office the Allied forces entered Tehran. Fear engulfed the citizenry. The well-to-do, wishing to escape the Russians, moved south and west however they could. The poor stayed, unsure of what the future held. Foroughi tried to calm the nation, sometimes sounding ludicrously simple: "They come and go, having nothing to do with us." Such statements did not assuage the fear. Already food had become a problem, as had law and order. The disbanded Iranian soldiers had taken with them an assortment of weapons that were now spread across the country. Orders were given to the military to collect these weapons, with a deadline for their return, but everyone knew the task was difficult and orders from the government, once unquestioningly obeyed by the officer corps, no longer commanded such respect. Overnight, the military, which had avoided politics after Reza Shah's ascent to the throne in 1925, had the potential to be a major political player. The bonds that had tied it to the crown still existed, but were unmistakably weakened, if not in loyalty then in discipline.

The changes in the army had parallels in civilian politics, which now took new shape and meaning. Silence, the normal state for some years, became voice, articulated unhindered. On 29 September a group of men gathered in the home of a Qajar prince, Soleyman Mirza Eskandari, to found the Tudeh Party of Iran (the "party of the masses"). Soleyman Mirza, a gentleman of the old order and a former member of Hizb-e ejtema'iyun-e 'amiun, a party with social-democratic leftist leanings, had served in several cabinet positions in the past, including under Reza Khan. He gave the party prestige, but he was not the mover. That distinction fell to his relatives Iraj and Abbas Eskandari, the more active and ideological members of the family, and other frankly communist stalwarts, such as Reza Rusta, Abdolsamad Kambakhsh, Ardashes Ovanessian, and Reza Radmanesh. But the party at its inception was not meant to be revolutionary, despite the wishes of several of its original members. An official communist party could not come into existence without the Soviet embassy's permission and directives. The Soviet government, however, was concerned primarily with the German military advances. It had no wish to antagonize the British, its main ally at the time, or the Americans. Motherland was taking precedence over Marxism-Leninism for the moment, a shift reflected in Stalin's imaginative reintroduction of Russia's traditional heroes, such as Alexander Nevski, the patron saint who defeated the Swedes in the thirteenth century, or Mikhail Ilarionovich Kutuzov, the field marshal who defeated Napoleon.

Thus the need of the moment was to assuage the Allies' fears and suspicions. The directives from Moscow must have surprised at least some of the Tudeh members. The party was to be legal, formally and practically committed to Iran's constitutional monarchy. It was to be ideologically free of Marxism-Leninism; nothing in it should suggest revolutionary inclinations. It was to be totally supportive of the Allies — to fight against the supporters of Germany, Italy, and Japan in Iran and to support unconditionally the international positions of Russia, England, and the United States. The Soviet Union, of course, had primacy; however, the party should under no circumstances take measures that might offend Russia's allies. The party should seek to attract "national personalities," that is, individuals who did not have communist sympathies but were politically and socially respected. And the party activities should not harm the Allies' economic interests, for example, causing labor strikes that closed factories.[63] Things would change as the German threat receded, but at this time there was nothing in the Tudeh Party's program that the young shah could not agree with. Indeed, a year later, when he would meet with several of the party members elected to the Majlis, he would scold them for not paying sufficient attention to the plight of women in their manifesto. "Perhaps you would do so in the future drafts," he said.[64]

In the months to come other notables who had been kept out of politics during Reza Shah's rule would reappear on the political scene. In particular, Ahmad Qavam would return from Europe, Seyyed Ziaeddin Tabatabai from Palestine, and Mohammad Mosaddeq from his estate in Ahmad Abad. More than mere contenders in the political fray, each of these three would present a serious challenge to the crown. The shah would gradually learn how to deal with them, and the experience would shape his attitude to his office, his government, his people, and his country.

◼

The shah's first concern, however, was his father, whom he regarded as a British prisoner on Mauritius. The ex-shah had gone from Isfahan to the Persian Gulf and sailed with several of his children into the Indian Ocean on the *Bandra,* a

British postal vessel, thinking he was free to choose his final destination. Instead, he was deposited on Mauritius, a small tropical island east of Madagascar in the southern waters of the Indian Ocean, whose weather he found heinous. He told the British governor of the island of his objections to living in Mauritius on both climatic and social grounds. It did not matter that he was allowed freedom of movement on the island; the whole island was a prison. He wished to be allowed to go to a neutral country that was friendly to Britain. If German influence in South America rendered those countries unsuitable he would just as soon go to the United States. What he really demanded was a statement about British intentions.[65]

In Iran, the shah pushed Bullard on the subject, along the lines his father had used with the governor of Mauritius. He asked whether his father would be allowed to go to Argentina. Bullard had not much to say to alleviate the shah's concerns. He passed on to him a copy of a letter from the British viceroy in India, saying the British government feared that in South America some members of the imperial family might become instruments of German propaganda.[66]

Bullard, in fact, was concerned that the ex-shah had become popular in Iran. "It is typical of this base people that the ex-shah is becoming popular again as the alleged victim of British cruelty. The myth is being created that we got rid of the shah because he defended the independence of Persia and wanted to modernize the country, whereas we wish to enslave it and make it 'return to camels.' Pro-German propaganda probably has a hand in this, but it has arisen partly because it flatters the Persian to compare the ex-shah with Napoleon and makes him feel less ignoble to believe that the ruler whose slave he was for so long was a great man."[67]

Bullard's telegram resonated in London. The notes exchanged among the functionaries called Persians "an illogical race." Nevertheless, the "Pahlevi legend" was dangerous, merited "serious consideration," and should not be allowed to develop. It was out of the question for the ex-shah to go to a neutral country, where he could not be thoroughly controlled. Canada or South Africa might be considered. This, however, would be too kind. "We are under no obligation, moral or contractual, expressed or implied, in this matter." The shah might say he put his trust in the British or he resigned to facilitate the Allies' cause. "But if the prisoner at the bar pleads guilty, that does not put the judge under any obligation to let him off hard labor, even though he may thereby have saved the Crown the trouble of a prolonged case." Eden signed off on these comments on 28 October. For the time being, the ex-shah was to remain in Mauritius,[68] though, finally, he would be allowed to settle in Johannesburg, South Africa.

The shah followed his father's sad journey through exile attentively, protesting his treatment to the British whenever he had a chance. He sent him letters, which often were delayed in reaching the old man. He awaited his father's letters in return, which also did not come regularly. He recorded a message of love and respect and commissioned his Le Rosey friend Ernest Perron to take it to him in Johannesburg and to bring back a recording of his voice in return. Perron did so. Reza Shah's language is formal and literate. He is thrilled hearing his son's voice, "transformed to invisible waves, but deciphered so clearly by my heart that I was able to treasure it in its most protected corners." Despite the distance that separated them, he saw his son always in his mind's eye, no barrier ever able to bar his view.

> My dear son, since the time I resigned in your favor and left my country, my only pleasure has been to witness your sincere service to your country. I have always known that your youth and your love of the country are vast reservoirs of power on which you will draw to stand firm against the difficulties you face and that, despite all the troubles, you will emerge from this ordeal with honor. Not a moment passes without my thinking of you and yet the only thing that keeps me happy and satisfied is the thought that you are spending your time in the service of Iran. You must remain always aware of what goes on in the country. You must not succumb to advice that is self-serving and false. You must remain firm and constant. You must never be afraid of the events that come your way. Now that you have taken on your shoulders this heavy burden in such dark days, you must know that the price to be paid for the slightest mistake on your part may be our twenty years of service and our family's name. You must never yield to anxiety or despair; rather, you must remain calm and so strongly rooted in your place that no power may hope to move the constancy of your will.[69]

The message touched the son deeply, committing him emotionally and intellectually to the father's words.

Reza Shah died of a heart attack in Johannesburg on 26 July 1944. His embalmed body was placed in temporary interment in Rifaʻi Mosque in Cairo awaiting the completion of a mausoleum near Tehran specially designed to receive it. The mausoleum was finished in early 1950. In April of that year, the shah sent a mission headed by his brothers Alireza, Gholamreza, and Abdorreza, each a son of one of his father's wives, as well as several high-ranking civilian and military officers, including the former prime minister Sadr-ul-Ashraf and the war minister General Morteza Yazdanpanah, representing the government and the military, respectively, to Egypt to accompany the body of the king back to Iran. "One of my most important wishes has been to bring my father back to Iran in full religious and regal dignity," the shah told Sadr. "You must take the body to Medina for the circumambulation in the shrine of the Prophet and then to Qom, the shrine of Maʿsumah, where one of the major *maraji' taqlid* [sources of emulation] shall lead the prayers, before my father reaches his eternal resting place." He ordered Sadr, Court Minister Hossein Ala, and Army Chief of Staff General Haji Ali Razmara to prepare the details of the program of returning his father's body and to bring it for him to see.[70]

The committee was faced with two hurdles at the outset. First, relations between the Egyptian and Iranian royal houses had not been good since the divorce of Fawzieh in 1948. It took several communications and significant diplomatic work by Iran's ambassador in Cairo, Ali Dashti, an important statesman and literary figure, to have the Egyptians agree to give the late shah an appropriate send-off. Qom also proved problematic. The Pahlavi foes among the clerics spoke against taking the remains to the shrine because, they said, Reza Shah had been anti-religion. Sadr met with Grand Ayatollah Borujerdi in Qom, who said he could not control political activists in false religious garb. "You see," mused Borujerdi, "certain clerics may make unwarranted comments that may present the government with a dilemma: to punish them will have unhappy consequences; not to punish them will also lead to the same results." Therefore he advised against bringing the remains to Qom. Sadr reported Borujerdi's words approvingly to the shah, who nevertheless persisted in his decision.

The king's coffin reached Iran at Ahvaz, where it was received by the minister of court and several cabinet ministers and Majlis deputies, and mourned by the people. Sadr was moved by the sincerity of the emotions ordinary men and women of the street showed. "Everywhere people wept. . . . In Arak, there were so many that the train could not move. We disembarked to thank the mourners. One man insisted and was allowed to read the poem he had composed for the occasion. Everyone began to weep anew." The stop in Qom passed agreeably, and the next morning the train arrived in Tehran. The shah went into the train to visit his father's remains for the last time. He fell on the coffin, kissed it, and wept in a spontaneous act of devotion Sadr found "exceedingly touching."[71]

5

Azerbaijan

The Allied invasion of Iran on 25 August 1941 made the preservation of Iran's independence and territorial integrity the government's most urgent task. Reza Shah's letter to President Roosevelt had not produced an immediate effect; but the response it had elicited at least placed on record the United States' assurances about the Allies' commitment to Iran's independence. In late July and early August, Reza Shah's envoy in the United States, Mohammad Shayesteh, had made several visits to the Department of State and Secretary of State Cordell Hull to appeal for American help. The visits had prompted the secretary to talk with the Soviet and British envoys in Washington as early as 21 August 1941, several days before the actual invasion, about the importance of assuring Iran that the Allies were in Iran solely because of the war.[1] The American show of interest, though minimal, nonetheless provided some leverage for Prime Minister Foroughi and Foreign Minister Ali Soheili to negotiate with the British and the Russians a treaty of alliance, known as the Tripartite Treaty, that became a legal and political linchpin of Iran's struggle to maintain its political integrity at the end of the war. The treaty, ratified by the Thirteenth Majlis on 26 January 1942 and signed on 29 January by Foreign Minister Soheili for Iran and ambassadors Bullard and Smirnov for the United Kingdom and the Soviet Union, respectively, obligated Britain and the Soviet Union to respect the political independence and territorial integrity of Iran; to withdraw their forces from Iran no later than six months after all hostilities between the Allies and Germany and its associates were suspended by the conclusion of an armistice; to safeguard Iran's economy and the Iranian people against the privations and difficulties arising as a result of the war; to defend Iran against aggression by Germany or any other hostile power; and to maintain in Iranian territory land, sea, and air forces as necessary with the understanding that these forces did not constitute a military occupation and that care would be taken that these forces "disturb as little as possible the administration and security of forces of Iran, the economic life of the country, the normal movement of the population, and the application of Iranian laws and regulations."[2]

For its part, Iran undertook to cooperate with the Allied forces for the defense of its territory (but was not required to fight against any foreign power); to secure for the Allies unrestricted access to and control of "all means of communication through Iran"; to help provide labor and material for maintaining and improving the means of communication; to establish "measures of censorship control as the Allied Powers may require"; and not to adopt in its foreign relations attitudes or positions contrary to the treaty.[3]

The Tripartite Treaty placed Iran on the side of the Allies, but the relationship remained strained. Many Iranians considered the treaty necessary but also an imposition. The ambivalence caused constant tension between the Majlis and the cabinets. Forughi resigned on 7 March 1942 because the Majlis deputies did not give him the support he needed. His successors Soheili and Ahmad Qavam each lasted about five months before Soheili was reinstalled on 14 February 1943. Part of the problem was that the Allies forced the Iranian government to spy on Iranians and incarcerate those the Allies suspected of pro-German sympathy. In August, the British and the Soviets arrested and exiled a host of Iran's civilian and military leaders, which increased the tension. Also, under the occupation the economy progressively deteriorated, especially after American troops arrived in December 1942. The Iranian government asked the United States to join the Tripartite Treaty, but the Americans procrastinated, prompting both Iranians and the Soviets, each for its own reasons, to complain that the Americans were in Iran without a treaty. What the new shah and his prime minister, Soheili, sought was that the United States guarantee Iran's independence, not only against the Axis powers, but also against the Soviets and the British. Failing to get the U.S. assurance, on 25 July 1943 the Soheili government lodged a request with the Allies to join the United Nations declaration of 1 January 1942. The Allies demanded that Iran declare war on one of the Axis powers before they would consider the request. On 9 September 1943 the shah issued a decree, which the Majlis ratified the same day, declaring war on Germany. The decree opened the way for Iran's adherence to the United Nations and also facilitated the Tripartite Declaration signed by Roosevelt, Churchill, and Stalin on 1 December 1943, the last day of their meeting at the Tehran Conference, where the chief topic was the opening of a second front in the war in Europe.[4]

The Tripartite Declaration complemented the Tripartite Treaty. The Allied powers recognized Iran's contribution to the war effort, especially by facilitating "the transportation of supplies to the Soviet Union" (considered so vital that because of it Iran was dubbed "the bridge of victory"). They acknowledged that the war had "special economic difficulties for Iran" and agreed to "make available to the Government of Iran such economic assistance as may be possible." They agreed that economic problems Iran might face at the close of hostilities "should receive full consideration." And they were "at one with the government of Iran in their desire for the maintenance of the independence, sovereignty, and territorial integrity of Iran."[5]

The declaration and the treaty were meant to help Iran, at the conclusion of the war, to make demands on behalf of its national interests on strategic, legal, and moral grounds. But, as we shall see, such grounds for appeal were conditioned by the exigencies of the emerging Cold War, Soviet expansionism, and British intransigence.

At the beginning of World War II, two oil concessions existed in Iran — the Anglo-Iranian in the southwest and the Kavir-i Khurian, a minor company owned jointly by Russians and Iranians, which covered a very limited area near the town of Semnan in the northeast.[6] In August 1944, the Soviet government informed Iran's ambassador in Moscow that the Soviets were interested in opening negotiations on the Khurian concession. Iran responded that any delegation from the Soviet Union would be warmly received.[7] In early September 1944, however, the Iranian cabinet decided that it would not engage in negotiations on any foreign concession until the end of the war.[8] Two weeks later, in the second half of September, Soviet Deputy People's Commissar for Foreign Affairs Sergei I. Kaftaradze arrived in Iran with a large retinue of diplomatic and technical experts.

Kaftaradze's arrival produced a frenzy of rumors in Tehran but no panic. It was assumed that Russia had concessionary rights to Khurian and therefore any discussion about Semnan oil would be technical only. Soon, however, it was learned that Kaftaradze was after a new concession that would cover the five provinces of Iran bordering on the Soviet Union, among them Azerbaijan. On 16 October, Prime Minister Mohammad Saʻed announced the decision to reject all concessionary offers, including Kaftaradze's. The Soviets then began an attack on Saʻed, accusing him of "neglect for not punishing the 'harmful actions of certain evil-intentioned elements' who had sabotaged the regular flow of Allied supplies to the Soviet Union through Iran and for not opposing the 'intensification of subversive work of pro-fascist elements.'"[9] In hopes of mollifying the Soviets, the shah received Kaftaradze and Soviet Ambassador Mikhail Maximov, along with several members of the embassy and their team, for dinner on 23 October. The gesture was not effective. The next day, Kaftaradze stated in a press conference in Tehran: "I must make this crystal clear that Mr. Saʿed's decision has been received with extreme distaste in the Soviet Union,"[10] and that "the disloyal and unfriendly position taken up by Premier Saʿed toward the Soviet Union excluded the possibility of further collaboration with him."[11] Three days later, members of the Tudeh Party, escorted by several trucks of armed soldiers from the Soviet occupying forces, demonstrated in Tehran against Saʿed and in favor of the Soviet demand for oil concession.[12]

Kaftaradze's attack prompted Saʿed to state in a hastily assembled press conference that his government had only postponed negotiations about foreign concessions till the end of the war and that the decision was in no way directed against the Soviet Union. At the same time, Mohammad Mosaddeq, now an influential Majlis deputy, also responded to Kaftaradze's threats, suggesting Iran would not concede the oil in its northern territories to the Soviet Union, but it would sell all the northern oil not used domestically to the Soviet Union at the average international price "if our northern neighbor needed oil." "I believe," said Mosaddeq, "such a proposition would pass this Majlis."[13] Ambassador Leland B. Morris of the United States observed that his government recognized Iran's sovereign right to refuse the granting of oil concessions. *Izvestia* wrote back that it was the American influence that stood behind Iran's refusal: "As is known, apart from the Soviet and British troops that are on Iranian territory in conformity with the treaty of alliance, there are also American forces in Iran. But these forces stay there entirely without a treaty with the Iranian government."[14]

The Soviet attack forced Saʿed to resign despite his efforts at appeasement, and Saham-us-Soltan Mortezaqoli Bayat was named as his successor. A few days into Bayat's premiership, on 2 December, Mosaddeq introduced a bill, suggested to him by a deputy he would not name and cosigned by many deputies, making it a punishable crime for "any prime minister, minister, or their deputies" to enter into negotiation or sign agreements on any oil concession with any "neighboring or nonneighboring government" or oil company without a prior mandate from the Majlis. The bill was approved on the spot.[15] The next day, on the 3rd, a deputy from Khurasan, Gholam Hossein Rahimian, offered a bill to repeal the 1933 Agreement, and asked Mosaddeq to support it. Mosaddeq refused to go so far, arguing that "treaties result from agreement between two parties, and therefore unless both parties agree, they cannot be rescinded. . . . The Majlis may not repeal a law it has made based on respect for international agreements and treaties for transient reasons and in the absence of a legally sound process."[16]

Mosaddeq's position brought forth the wrath of the Tudeh Party, which accused him of keeping the field safe for Anglo-Iranian Oil.

Early on, the young shah developed a shrewd though as yet unsophisticated sense of the Soviet view of international politics as a set of strategies designed to win the world, on the one hand by using force and on the other by championing history's presumed promise of Marxist liberation. In Iran, the Tudeh Party was a formidable weapon in the Soviet arsenal because it did not have to identify with the Soviet state. For the rank and file, commitment to the Soviet Union was camouflaged in ideology—uncritical, unquestioned, yet intellectually promising and emotionally rewarding. For most ordinary members Russia became history's path and Stalin, history's agent. Resistance to the Nazi war machine made Russia a major world power, and the Soviet Union's anti-fascist alliances led many intellectuals to see it as a force for freedom, democracy, and peace. Armed with a comprehensive ideology and supported by the resources of the Communist International, the party seemed able to pose pertinent social, economic, and political questions about domestic and international issues and to answer them plausibly in a way that seemed different from, more significant than, and superior to those of other Iranian parties. The Tudeh Party impressed Iranian youth as both community and ideology. It provided a social milieu where young men and women interacted much more freely than the larger society allowed. It offered a rather simplistic Marxism-Leninism as a panacea, the intellectual vehicle that led to the right questions and the political vehicle that provided the right solutions. Most party leaders too were uninformed.[17] The panacea was accepted on faith; indeed, at the time there was not much literature on Marxism in Persian available for ordinary members to read.

The rank and file joined the party to seek social and economic justice. Not so the leaders, as revealed by the accusations they hurled at each other after the party's demise. Anvar Khamei, a Tudeh leader in the 1940s, likens the party to *Grand Hotel,* the novel by Vicki Baum that was made into a Greta Garbo movie in 1932. Strangers interact within the various rooms in the hotel to create a plot that none foresaw or intended.[18] According to Fereydun Keshavarz, an early Tudeh leader, Abdolsamad Kambakhsh, who served as a party secretary in the 1940s, received his orders directly from Jaʿfar Baqirov, the first secretary of the Communist Party and president of the Soviet Republic of Azerbaijan, as did Ali Amirkhizi, Ardashes Ovanessian, Nureddin Kianuri, and many other Tudeh leaders. Kambakhsh "had been forced on the party by Aliev, the Soviet chargé in

Tehran," states Keshavarz. Kambakhsh and his brother-in-law, Kianuri, forced assassination, sabotage, and premature revolt on the Tudeh Party in the early 1940s when the party was still legal and had eight deputies in the Majlis.[19]

The public, however, did not know about these atrocities in the early 1940s, including the murders, which the party invariably attributed to the government, the shah, or a member of the royal family. So the party grew and became a shaper of Iran's intellectual climate. And the shah continued to share in the essential values of fairness in social and economic conditions of that climate.

By the time of the first Tudeh Party congress, in Tehran in August 1944, some three years after the party had been established, the tide of the war had changed. The defense of Stalingrad had given the Soviet Union and the Red Army unprecedented prestige. The Soviets had pushed back the German army and were about to move into Eastern Europe. The Allies had landed on the European continent, freed France and parts of Belgium, Holland, and Norway, and begun to enter German territory. The Allied army in southern Europe was moving north, and the British had landed in Greece to preempt the Soviets. Germany's defeat in the war was no longer a matter of conjecture. The question now was who would get what once the war was over. The East-West competition for supremacy had begun.

The situation in Iran reflected the situation in Europe. Germany had lost all influence. The Soviet influence was rising. In general, the Russians and the Tudeh attracted a greater share of intellectuals, politically mobilized youth, and lower classes, while England, and to a lesser extent the United States, attracted former pro-German middle and upper classes. As Soviet power and prestige increased, so did Soviet arrogance. Soviet politics changed from satisfying Western allies to dominating the areas the Red Army occupied, as in the Iranian north, where the Tudeh became the undisputed master under Soviet protection and tutelage. Tellingly, however, power did not produce popularity. The party's close association with the Soviet army repelled the people. At the same time, in the south, where the British held sway, the left was more popular and the British bore the brunt of popular rejection. Still, Soviet power was seen by many as inherently different from that of the West, threatening not only established social and economic relations but also the fundamentals of moral and ethical systems.

By the time the war was coming to an end, the Tudeh Party had become powerful enough to affect the longevity if not the composition of the cabinets, as in the case of Mohammad Sa'ed's late in 1944. The Iranian army was not allowed to enter the Soviet zone, where the party held sway. Consequently, the center lost control of the northern provinces, causing the mood in the Majlis and the royal court to turn sullen and tense, which, in turn, made the lives of governing cabinets short and unhappy. Serious unrest began in the north in late August 1945. In Tabriz and other Azerbaijan cities, members of the Firqeh demokrat (loosely translated as the Democratic Party, Brotherhood, or Group) rose against the central government, spreading havoc, burning, and looting. Jafar Pishevari, soon to be self-proclaimed head of the Republic of Azerbaijan, announced in Tabriz that henceforth Turkish would be the province's first language and Azerbaijan would be a self-governing entity. The government sent a contingent of gendarmes to deal with simultaneous revolts set off by the Tudeh Party in Shahi and Sari, cities in Mazandaran Province by the Caspian, but the gendarmes were stopped at Firuzkuh Pass by Soviet forces. This was a prelude to Soviet military intervention in support of the Firqeh demokrat and the left in Azerbaijan and Kurdestan and in other cities and villages across the north. On 13 September, the Azerbaijan branch of the Tudeh Party declared it had formally joined the Firqeh demokrat. On 27 September, the Majlis voted for Mohsen Sadr as prime minister and denounced the situation in Azerbaijan, the chaos in Khurasan, the arsons in Qazvin, the killings in Zanjan, and the government of the rabble in Mazandaran.[20] But it was too little too late, for Soviet Ambassador Maximov utterly refused to communicate with Sadr. Exasperated, Sadr asked Majid Ahy, Iran's ambassador to Moscow, to contact Foreign Minister Vyacheslav Molotov to complain about Maximov's behavior. Molotov procrastinated for several days before he sent a message to Ahy instructing him to advise Sadr to take his business up with Maximov when the latter returned to Tehran. Maximov, however, still refused to meet with Sadr.[21] On 21 October, Sadr resigned because, he explained to the shah, he had failed to gain the confidence of the Majlis or its cooperation. The Majlis then voted again for Ebrahim Hakimi, who had served as prime minister in May but had been forced by the Majlis to resign after only a month in office.

A few days after the new cabinet was presented to the Majlis, the gendarmerie in Azerbaijan reported movements of trucks distributing arms to several groups of men, who then attacked the gendarmerie stations in cities around Tabriz.[22] By November, the Soviet support of the insurgents in Azerbaijan had become increasingly open. Army and gendarmerie units ordered to move to support the contingents in Kurdistan and Azerbaijan were stopped by Soviet forces. On 20 November, Iran's interior ministry informed Iran's foreign ministry that unless some accommodations with the Soviets were reached, it would be difficult to foretell what might happen in the north.[23] Foreign Minister Abolqasem

Najm then sent a note to Maximov asking him to order Soviet armed forces to desist from interfering in internal Iranian affairs in Azerbaijan and Kurdistan.[24] He also formally asked the United States and Britain to intervene to protect Iranian rights. On the 24th the United States delivered a note to the Soviet Union proposing U.S., Soviet, and British withdrawal from Iran by 1 January 1946. The British agreed and sent a note to the Soviets reminding them of the 1942 Tripartite Treaty and the 1943 Tripartite Declaration guaranteeing Iran's national independence and territorial integrity. The Soviet response to the American note was that nothing untoward was happening in the north; the people were simply demanding "their national ideals." The Soviet government, the note said, "opposed the dispatch of new Iranian troops to northern districts of Iran" and more Iranian troops in the north would increase disorder and bloodshed, which "would compel the Soviet Government to introduce into Iran further forces of its own for the purpose of preserving order and insuring the security of the Soviet garrison." Ominously, the note invoked Article 6 of the 1921 Treaty, giving the Soviet Union "the right of introduction of Soviet troops into the territory of Iran."[25] The United States then asked the Soviets and the British to leave Iranian territory before the agreed-upon date of the Tripartite Declaration, 1 March 1946.

On 12 December 1945, Tabriz was occupied by the military contingents of the Firqeh demokrat, and a National Assembly of Azerbaijan was inaugurated, electing Seyyed Mahmud Shabestari speaker and Jafar Pishevari prime minister. The next day the governor of Azerbaijan, Saham-us-Soltan Bayat, now helpless, returned to Tehran, and General Ali Akbar Derakhshani unconditionally surrendered the Azerbaijan 3rd Infantry Division, which he commanded, to Pishevari. The new government sent the general and his officers back to Tehran by plane, bus, and rail. Mosaddeq addressed the Majlis on 19 December, the day General Derakhshani arrived in Tehran, saying: "Do not fight in Azerbaijan; attend to its grievance and it becomes obedient to the center."[26] Iran clearly needed its George Kennan.

British Foreign Secretary Ernest Bevin and U.S. Secretary of State James Byrnes arrived in Moscow for a conference of foreign ministers on 15 December—three days after Azerbaijan had declared itself an autonomous republic. Bevin, supported by his area expert, the former ambassador Sir Reader Bullard, suggested several schemes, including one for the creation of local governments in Iran to accommodate both Soviet and British interests. The Russians initially seemed interested in this reformulation of the 1907 division of Iran into zones of influence but subsequently demurred, possibly because they had come to believe they could have the whole of the country.[27] Soviet intransigence and the seemingly relaxed attitude of the United States disquieted Bevin. According to the London correspondent of the *New York Times,* he came back from the Moscow conference far less happy than Byrnes: "It is felt here that Americans are inclined to overlook the vital importance of Iran and the whole Middle East to the British Empire. What may have seemed to be a relatively minor question to Mr. Byrnes was a major one to Mr. Bevin."[28]

On 9 January 1946, Hassan Taqizadeh, Iran's ambassador to the United Kingdom and representative to the United Nations, sent a note to Prime Minister Hakimi and Foreign Minister Najm warning that, based on what he was hearing, unless something urgent was done, not much would remain of Iran's independence. Other countries, former enemies of the Allies, were receiving many advantages. "Why is it," he asked, "Iran, a nation so instrumental in the Allied victory, should now find its independence endangered?"[29] On 16 January, he submitted Iran's case against the Soviet Union to the Security Council. Four days later, Hakimi and his cabinet resigned under pressure from the Majlis, led by Mosaddeq; Hakimi was succeeded by Ahmad Qavam. On the 29th, Taqizadeh again brought Iran's complaint about the Soviet activities in Iran to the Security Council's attention and demanded the Council's intervention. Soviet Deputy Foreign Commissar Andrei Vishinski argued that Iran's demand was made by a government no longer in power and therefore had no material foundation. If the present government of Iran agreed to negotiate the matter directly with the Soviet Union, he said, the Security Council no longer possessed jurisdiction on the matter. The Council recommended that the two parties try to reach agreement on Azerbaijan through direct negotiation—clearly a blow to Iran.

The shah had taken an active role in the selection of Qavam as prime minister. He conferred with his military commanders and civilian counselors and decided that of the two contenders for premiership, Qavam and Motamen-ul-Mulk Pirnia, a former Majlis president, Qavam was the more suitable candidate for the job ahead.[30] The competition was tight, forcing the current Majlis president, Seyyed Mohammad Sadeq Tabatabai, a friend of the shah, to cast the deciding vote for Qavam, who at the time was ill in bed. It took some time before Qavam was able to form a cabinet, but, in the meantime, he and the shah actively sought an invitation from Stalin for Qavam to go to Moscow to negotiate the Azerbaijan crisis. By the time Qavam presented his ministers to the Majlis, the invitation had been received.[31] He set out for Moscow on 18 February 1946, accompanied by Javad Ameri, Reza Zadeh Shafaq, and Abolhassan Amidi Nuri, among others.

When his plane arrived in Moscow, Foreign Minister Molotov was not at the airport to receive him. Qavam remained inside the plane for half an hour until the foreign minister arrived. When he finally exited the plane, Molotov asked him to say a few words at the microphone for the benefit of the press. Qavam resisted at first but then acquiesced, visibly unenthusiastic about the whole affair. His interpreter added a few words thanking Molotov for the reception, thanks that Qavam had intentionally or unintentionally failed to express.[32]

In his two weeks in Moscow, Qavam had three serious encounters with the Russian leaders. The first was with Stalin, who harassed him no end, accusing Iran of stabbing Russia in the back at every opportunity and saying that it had become very difficult for him to trust Iranians. The encounter left Qavam desolate, almost ready to pack up and return to Iran. His meeting with Molotov, who invited Qavam and his colleagues to an afternoon reception, was just as difficult. Following his boss, Molotov also gave Qavam a dressing-down on Iranian treachery, accusing him of duplicity and suggesting that his days as prime minister were numbered, since Seyyed Ziaeddin Tabatabai, the arch-reactionary controlling the Majlis, had already planned his government's downfall. Molotov then brought up the question of oil, accusing Iran of treating the Soviet Union unfavorably compared to England. Iran, he said, would be wise to show even-handedness by negotiating an oil agreement with the Soviet Union, which, unlike the British, was prepared to negotiate a participatory arrangement on discovery, extraction, and marketing. On Azerbaijan, said the Russian, Iran should respect the wishes of the people, who demanded the political rights that were legitimately theirs. The Soviets, he said, would take their armed forces out of Iran, but only if they were assured of Iran's goodwill.

Qavam directed Reza Zadeh Shafaq to prepare a response explaining why he could not accept any of the propositions Molotov had made. "If that was to be our answer, why did we come here at all?" asked Amidi Nuri. "Don't you see," retorted Qavam, "they want me to give them the oil. If I comply with their demand, Mosaddeq will surely take me to court for breaking the law. I will be tried and forced to spend the few years that remain to me in jail. No, thank you."[33] Amidi Nuri explained this was not the case, that nobody could charge him with a breach of the law, because what the Majlis had forbidden was negotiations about concessions, not about participatory arrangements. At this, Qavam became interested and asked for further explication. Amidi Nuri referred the matter to Javad Ameri, a law professor, a former minister of justice, and a parliamentarian who had voted for the law. Ameri did not remember the exact letter of the law but said that if it was as Amidi Nuri said it was, then Amidi Nuri would be in the right, because concession is not the same as participation or cooperation in developing oil resources. Qavam asked to see the law, which was found among the documents the delegation had brought along and read to him. Ameri now stated that the prime minister would not be in breach of the law if he agreed to negotiate a mixed organization or a joint stock company for discovery, extraction, and exploitation of oil, provided Iran owned a majority of the shares. Qavam ordered Shafaq to rewrite the part on the oil according to the proposed formula but to insist that there could be no compromise on Azerbaijan or the Soviet military withdrawal.[34]

On 2 March 1946 the British withdrew their forces from Iran, as their commander had informed the shah they would on 23 February. But there was no sign of evacuation of the Soviet troops in Azerbaijan. The Soviets announced they would move their forces out of Khurasan, Shahrud, and Semnan as of 2 March but not from Azerbaijan or other locations. The Soviet troops did, indeed, leave Tabriz, Azerbaijan's provincial capital, but they did not move toward the Soviet borders; rather, they pushed in three columns in the directions of Tehran, Iraq, and Turkey, followed by hundreds of tanks moving south from Russia in support. The British and the Americans protested, as did Qavam personally to Molotov and Stalin, to no avail. By this time more than ten days had passed since the delegation had arrived in Moscow, and Qavam, snubbed and frustrated, ordered a plane to be readied to take him back to Iran. Suddenly he received an invitation from Stalin to a reception that turned out to be both exquisitely sumptuous and surprisingly friendly. Qavam's memorandum had obviously pleased Stalin, who personally introduced Ivan Sadchikov to him and declared triumphantly that he would send Sadchikov to Tehran to begin negotiations. The Soviet negotiating points, however, were not easy for the Iranians to accept:

1. Soviet troops would continue to stay in some parts of Iran for an indefinite period.
2. The Iranian government would recognize the internal autonomy of Azerbaijan. If the Iranian government acquiesced in this request, the Soviet government offered to take steps to arrange that:
   a. The prime minister of Azerbaijan, in relation to the central government, would bear the designation of governor general.
   b. Azerbaijan would have no Ministry of War or Ministry of Foreign Affairs.
   c. Thirty percent of the Azerbaijan revenue would be paid to Iranian central government.
   d. All correspondence with the central government would be in Persian.
3. The Soviet government would abandon its demand for an oil concession. Instead it proposed that an Iranian-Russian joint stock company be set up with 51 percent of the shares owned by the Soviets and 49 percent by Iran.[35]

Qavam left Moscow on 10 March, refusing to accept formally the Soviet demands but signing a joint communiqué stating negotiations would resume when Sadchikov, the new Soviet plenipotentiary, arrived in Tehran.[36]

■

On 20 March 1946, the eve of Noruz, the Iranian New Year, the new ambassador to the United Nations, Hossein Ala, delivered a note to the Security Council protesting the Soviet Union's refusal to evacuate Iran, which he called an egregious violation of international law and the Tripartite Treaty, and its blatant interference in Iran's internal affairs through its agents, officials, and armed forces.[37] On the 21st, the shah explained Iran's plight in his traditional Noruz radio message to Iranians, exhorting them to patience and a demonstrative commitment to religious and moral principles as well as social and national traditions. The speech expressed a sense of desperation, an exhortation to national resistance, and a yearning for international support. This Iran received through President Harry S Truman's message to Stalin urging him to pull out of Iran and implying that unless he did so the United States would take serious measures. Truman believed that the Iranian problem had implications that went beyond the region, affecting the world balance of power. Russian control of Iran's oil would seriously damage the economies of the West, he wrote in his memoir, and Stalin could not have failed to understand that Iran was strategically important to the United States and England.[38] But until the note was delivered, it was not at all clear that Stalin had been impressed with American resolve.

On 25 March Stalin announced that his government had reached an agreement with the government of Iran, providing for the evacuation of Soviet troops within six weeks after 24 March "if no unforeseen circumstances occur."[39] On the 26th, the Soviet envoy to the United Nations, Andre Gromyko, demanded that the Iranian appeal be withdrawn from the Security Council. Qavam, pressured by the Soviets and encouraged by the apparent progress in the negotiations, ordered Ala to take back Iran's complaint. Ala, supported by the shah, declined on the ground that Qavam must have made the request under duress.[40] Faced with the Soviet claim that it would withdraw its troops, however, the U.S. delegation proposed and the Council agreed on 4 April to accept the Soviet statement and "to defer further proceedings on Iranian appeal until May 6th, at which date the Soviet government and the Iranian government are requested to report to the Council whether the withdrawal of all Soviet troops from the whole of Iran has been completed and at which time the Council shall consider what, if any, further proceedings on the Iranian appeal are required."[41]

On the day the Council decided to defer the Iranian case, Qavam and Sadchikov signed an agreement comprising the following: The Red Army would, as previously announced, evacuate Iran within six weeks after 24 March 1946; peaceful arrangements would be made between the central government and the people of Azerbaijan "for the carrying out of improvements in accordance with existing laws and in benevolent spirit toward the people of Azerbaijan"; and a joint-stock Irano-Soviet oil company would be established and ratified by the Fifteenth Majlis within seven months after 24 March, in which, according to the letters exchanged between Qavam and Sadchikov, the Soviet government would own 51 percent and the Iranian government 49 percent of the stock. The agreement was to hold for twenty-five years, after which Iran and Russia would each own 50 percent of the stock for another twenty-five years. The Soviets seemed to have won, but their victory was to prove politically and economically ephemeral. Qavam, for his part, also claimed victory, though the agreement he signed proved unpopular and exposed him to the caprices of adverse political and economic interests, both domestic and international.

During the first months of Qavam's premiership the Tudeh and the Firqeh demokrat in Azerbaijan became increasingly powerful and vocal, prompting people in both Tehran and the provinces to ask the government to take appropriate countermeasures. In the Zanjan region in the northwest, the war raging between the Firqeh demokrat and the local population led by the Zolfaqaris and the Afshars intensified after the Pishevari group took over Azerbaijan. In the south, particularly in Khuzistan, the Tudeh staged mammoth strikes and demonstrations, showing its mobilizing powers. The apparent alliance between Qavam, the Soviets, and the Tudeh with the signing of the agreement added to the anxieties of the provincial elite, particularly the landowners and tribal khans, or chiefs. The military worried — as subsequently proved to be correct — less about the Firqeh demokrat's martial prowess than about the Tudeh's growing political clout. The shah became increasingly aware of the country's changing mood. So did Qavam, though he remained steadfast in courting the Soviets. On 22 May, Hossein Ala, Iran's ambassador to both the United States and the United Nations, reminded the Security Council that not all Soviet troops had yet left the country. The Council decided to retain Iran's complaint on its agenda until Soviet evacuation was completed. Subsequently, Sadchikov wrote Qavam that the Red Army had indeed left Iran, prompting Qavam to remove Ala from his position at the United Nations.[42]

On 11 June Qavam dispatched his deputy, Mozaffar Firuz, at the head of a delegation to Tabriz to negotiate the terms of the relationship proposed by Jafar Pishevari, the self-proclaimed prime minister of the newly established autonomous republic of Azerbaijan. For many people the fact that the negotiations were to take place in Tabriz rather than Tehran signified obsequious deference to the communists. Firuz signed an agreement on 13 June conceding to Pishevari every controversial stipulation, including his demands on land distribution, governorship, the military, taxes, and elections.[43] On 15 June, Qavam, adhering to the agreement, appointed Salamollah Javid, Pishevari's minister of the interior, as governor-general of Azerbaijan. Two days later, Abbas Eskandari, one of the founding members of the Tudeh, was named governor of Tehran.

Stalin thought it imperative for the new Fifteenth Majlis to be convened as soon as possible to ratify the oil treaty. He instructed Sadchikov to pressure Qavam to expedite the parliamentary elections. Qavam promised to do so but procrastinated to prepare for the contest ahead. His purpose was to launch a political organization to compete with the Tudeh, an idea that received the shah's support. On 29 June he told the nation he was forming the Demokrat Party of Iran because the country needed a unifying political party. The announcement, made on the day the Tudeh and Iran parties, the latter a group of academics and other professionals with social democratic leanings, joined in a coalition, surprised the Tudeh, but its import did not immediately register. The new party attracted many notables who had joined the Tudeh or cooperated with it as fellow travelers but had no strong ideological convictions, diminishing the Tudeh's political influence across the board.[44] The Tudeh leaders, however, were reluctant to criticize Qavam, partly because he was the best prime minister for their cause they could expect, but mainly because the Soviets believed he would deliver the oil. Ehsan Tabari, the party's theoretician, advised his colleagues not to be deceived by the reactionary elements whose project was to distance them from the prime minister. "Qavam-us-Saltaneh has proved himself in action and strived to save the Iranian nation from [foreign and domestic] political interference. As long as he continues on this path, we who seek freedom will support him," he told the Tudeh stalwarts.[45]

On 20 July 1946, Qavam was formally elected leader of the Demokrat Party. On the 24th the shah, reacting to Qavam's power and expectation, conferred on him the title of *hazrat-e ashraf*, "his noblest excellency," a strange move considering that his father had abolished all titles several years back. The royal edict set Qavam apart from the rest of the political elite, giving him a distinctly superior place in the Iranian political hierarchy. On 3 August Qavam reshuffled his cabinet and, to mollify the Soviets somewhat, appointed three Tudeh Party members as ministers for the health, commerce, and education portfolios, a controversial move that led to much haggling and strife, particularly in the case of education. The Tudeh had had representatives in the Majlis before, but this was the first time it had members in the cabinet. To have Iran's foremost province in communist hands and additionally three communists in the cabinet was a veritable political coup.

Soviet control of Azerbaijan (and potentially Kurdistan) together with the Tudeh infiltration of the government could not but put the British and the Americans on guard. Bevin had been quite willing to reach an arrangement with Stalin to divide Iran into zones of influence on the model he had proposed in the Moscow Conference, but the Tudeh becoming one with the central government of Iran was more than he could tolerate. Events in the south now also began to take an ominous turn. Suddenly there were reports that Sheykh Khaz'al of Mohammareh, a British protégé living in exile in Iraq, had amassed an army of Arab warriors and raided several towns in Khuzistan — an obvious British countermeasure to Russian political advances in the north. Concurrently, the British ordered a contingent of their military from India to Basra, in accordance, the Iraqi government explained, with the Anglo-Iraqi treaty of 1930. Several Arabs in Khuzistan complained about their treatment by the Iranians. The Iraqi Independence Party then claimed Khuzistan as a part of "the Arab country."[46] Tribal leaders in Fars and other southern provinces began to voice opposition to Qavam's compliance with communist demands and the rising Tudeh power and influence.

American resistance to Soviet policy in Iran also hardened after the arrival in April of a new ambassador, George V. Allen. Allen had been deputy director of the Office of Near Eastern and African Affairs in the Department of State. He was knowledgeable about the Middle East, younger than his predecessor, Wallace Murray, and more energetic. He and the shah hit it off, and he became a regular guest at court on Fridays, when the shah entertained for lunch and dinner, and a partner in volleyball and tennis games. He agreed with the shah's worries about the Soviets. For Iran, he said, there was no middle way between Soviet totalitarianism and Western democracy, no easy neutrality; Allen counseled aggressive resistance now that the Soviet Union was engaged in Eastern Europe and in need of Iranian oil. The United States would not go to war with the Soviets to save Iran, he told the shah,[47] but the Soviets did not know this. They had just taken their troops out of Iran, and they probably thought that reinvading the country would be extremely risky. Allen gave the same advice to Qavam.[48]

The shah also warned Qavam along the lines Allen suggested. Qavam objected, defending his policy as the only reasonable alternative Iran could follow for the moment that would allow it to remain territorially intact and politically independent. The central government would accommodate the Azerbaijan regime as long as the province remained a part of Iran and would keep Stalin happy by promising him oil. Qavam would certainly control the upcoming Majlis and thus the conditions under which the debate about oil would be conducted. The Tudeh, he believed, could be managed. When the shah expressed his dissatisfaction, Qavam gave him an ultimatum: either make all the decisions or leave all the decisions to me. The shah retreated on the political front but not on the military. He grasped the intent of Allen's conversation better than Qavam; he also had a more realistic understanding of Stalinism than did his prime minister. Qavam, he thought, was wrong and simplistic in believing appeasement would help him maintain both his power and the nation's territorial integrity.[49] There were forces in the country that seriously objected to the inclusion of the Tudeh ministers in the cabinet, and these forces needed to be mollified. Already the government and the military were becoming increasingly—and opposingly—engaged with the tribes in regions ranging from Kurdistan and Khuzistan to Isfahan and Fars.

Clashes between Qavam and the military were inevitable. Qavam was aristocratic, domineering, and anti-Pahlavi; the top brass was pro-Pahlavi, mostly middle class, and unused to taking orders from civilians. To appease the Russians, Qavam had fired the anti-Soviet chief of staff General Hassam Arfa' and appointed in his place General Farajollah Aqevli. At the same time, General Haji Ali Razmara, a former chief of staff and Arfa' rival, was called back from retirement and appointed inspector general of Azerbaijan and Kurdistan, the provinces run by separatist movements. Razmara was a brilliant military tactician, who had been made a general under Reza Shah—a rare occurrence—and extremely ambitious. He was appointed chief of staff on 4 July and with the shah's approval immediately set out to study the strategic and tactical requirements of a possible military excursion in Azerbaijan and Kurdistan.

Soon after he included the Tudeh in his cabinet, Qavam issued a declaration forbidding members of the military to meddle in politics. Given the social disorder and political chaos across the country, the order proved hollow. In early September 1946, Qavam dispatched Mozaffar Firuz, his propaganda chief and political troubleshooter, to calm brewing tribal unrest in the Bakhtiari and Qashqai regions. Firuz, among other decisions, ordered the arrest of Colonel Abdolhossein Hejazi, commander of the Fars Division. Both the minister of war and the army chief of staff resigned in protest. Qavam was forced to appear personally in the war ministry and formally apologize for the incident. The event drew a red line beyond which the army would not accept civilian interference. Now, Qavam assigned the pacification of the south to General Fazlollah Zahedi, who was given command of all the southern forces as well as the governorship of Fars, which had fallen under the sway of the leaders in Qashqai. The Qashqai demanded the ouster of the Tudeh ministers and autonomy for Fars province. Zahedi, however, succeeded in reaching a modus vivendi with the Qashqai chiefs, establishing a semblance of peace in the region.

Further difficulties arose because Qavam had promised he would formally recognize the military ranks Pishevari had given the Firqeh officers as equal to their respective ranks in the Iranian armed forces. He had also promised to reinstate the officers who had left the army to join the rebellion. The military high command would stand for neither. Qavam begged the shah to permit it. The shah refused: "I will have my hands severed before I sign this decree," he said.[50] Instead, he asked Qavam to drop the Tudeh ministers and to prepare at last for the Majlis elections. Elections were to be conducted throughout the country, including Azerbaijan, which meant the presence of the central forces in that province, a situation that put the Soviets in a quandary. They, of course, wished to protect their surrogate government in Azerbaijan; on the other hand, they needed a Majlis to pass the oil agreement. They chose the latter.

The army headquarters studied the military capability of the Azerbaijan republic and determined that it was lacking in organization, leadership, weaponry, strategy, and personnel. "There is nothing in the contemporary organization of Azerbaijan except fear and anxiety. The boasts made about it in Tehran are essentially baseless lies designed to produce fear and awe," the study declared. The rebels had seven hundred officers who lacked qualifications and therefore the ability to organize efficiently to wage war. Given time, however, they could become better organized and pose a real threat to the country. The report stated that immigrants from the Soviet Caucasus were pouring into Iran and would soon take over every vital political or social function of the region. New officers were being rapidly trained, six hundred having been sent abroad already for training, particularly in aviation. Weapons were pouring in, including five thousand machine guns, a hundred thousand rifles, and an untold amount of ammunition. Clearly, said the report, this force, now easy to destroy, would soon become a dangerous threat to the country's independence. Just as clearly, the rebellion's purpose was not to establish an autonomous republic in Azerbaijan only; it aimed to take over the whole of the country. Once it was prepared for action, it would not remain stationary. It was, said the report, the duty of the general staff to state categorically that the time for action was now; inaction would be unconscionable as it would subject the nation to horrendous danger and the country's decision makers to history's harshest of judgments.[51]

The shah concurred. He was certain, he said in his decree, that a group of adventurers were determined to take over one of Iran's most fertile and precious regions and, if allowed to do so, they would threaten the nation's independence. He agreed with and approved the report, he said, and, therefore, based on the duty and responsibility his office and his oath placed on him, he ordered immediate action to be taken to save Azerbaijan and the rest of the country's northern region.[52]

By this time, the prime minister also had come on board. In October and November, the shah, Qavam, General Razmara, and Minister of War General Amir Ahmadi met several times to discuss the military and political ramifications of the election and of the putative decision to send troops to Azerbaijan.[53] Qavam dropped the Tudeh ministers on 20 October, replacing them with Ali Shayegan, Hamid Sayyah, and Manuchehr Eqbal; the latter was subsequently to become one of the shah's closest confidants. On 3 December the prime minister declared that elections would begin on the 7th across the country, except in Azerbaijan, where they would begin as soon as the forces of law and order entered the province. On 6 December the shah and General Razmara flew to Zanjan, where the shah heard the report of Colonel Hossein Hashemi, commander of the forces designated to move into Azerbaijan, and ordered the armed forces to attack. The enemy, he said, was preparing for future assaults. It was therefore

> incumbent on us to save this land, our nation's soul, before our foes' evil dreams take the name of action. We must perform our patriotic duty now. We therefore command our armed forces to march forward to Azerbaijan, to break down all resistance, and to raise the lion and sun standard in every corner of this dear land. We shall wash away the dust of grief settled on the brow of our compatriots during the past year; we shall bring to them pride and hope, which they so anxiously await and richly deserve. But it takes courage and the will to sacrifice. Let me tell you that the names of those who today take part in this battle for our land and country shall forever be inscribed in the annals of our proud and honorable history. I will be close by, watching your brave and fearless feats of action.[54]

That same day, the national forces attacked in three columns, from east, west, and center. The western column had the pivotal task of taking a mountainous stronghold in Qaflankuh, dominating the town of Mianeh, defended by a mix of regular and guerrilla rebel forces under the command of the self-proclaimed general Gholam Yahya Daneshian. The rebel defense, however, was not very effective. The Qaflankuh positions yielded on 10 December. Daneshian reported to Pishevari in Tabriz that the battle lasted a whole day, but the *fadaiyan* (as the guerrillas were called because they were supposed to be ready to give their lives for the cause) retreated because "they were frightened of bombs from the planes and artillery rounds from the batteries." Morale was lost and they left their trenches, he wrote. Pishevari ordered the general to shoot on the spot any soldier or guerrilla who ran.[55] But it was too late. By the 12th, Pishevari and a hundred of his men had crossed the border to the Soviet Union at the town of Jolfa. So did Daneshian—after robbing the bank in Mianeh.[56]

When the central forces reached Tabriz, there were no enemies left for them to fight; instead, they received a rousing welcome from the citizens. "It was as if the arrival in Tabriz of the Imperial Armed Forces illuminated the people's lives," wrote then Colonel Ahmad Zangeneh, who entered the city with the troops. "Men, women and children were united in expressing a joy so intense that one could not but think such expression of feeling had happened in Iranian history only rarely." As Fereydun Ebrahimi, the Firqeh demokrat's prosecutor general, was being brought to the city jail, the people chanted slogans demanding his instant execution. Colonel Zangeneh, appointed military governor that day, told Ebrahimi he would let him loose if he wished it. "I would rather stay here in prison," replied the erstwhile prosecutor.[57] Ebrahimi was tried, convicted, and executed, as were several Firqeh military officers formerly of the Tudeh military organization over the next few months.

The return of Azerbaijan boosted the shah's morale as well as his popularity. He made a political pilgrimage to Azerbaijan, starting out by train on 24 May 1947. At every stop, he was received with utmost affection. In Tabriz, the people came out to receive him twelve kilometers out of town, mostly on foot. A like reception was accorded him in the other cities on his itinerary, the last being Tehran three weeks later, on 11 June. "I was a student, and I remember I was rooting for him before the Tehran University," recalled Alinaghi Alikhani, who some twenty years later would be minister of economy. "He was standing in a jeep, alone, without any protection, saluting the people who mobbed his car, barring its movement. A colonel was trying to push the people away to make room for the jeep to move, but to no avail. The shah was at the height of his popularity."[58]

The elections for the Fifteenth Majlis were tumultuous and uneven. Qavam was accused of rigging the election, occasioning a group of powerful men—Mosaddeq, Jamal Emami, Seyyed Mohammad Sadeq Tabatabai, and Seyyed Mehdi Farrokh, among others—who had little in common other than opposing the prime minister, to petition the shah and to seek asylum in the royal court on 10 January 1947. The shah spoke with Qavam on their behalf, but nothing much came of his intervention. The elections in Tehran produced Qavam, whose name was entered as the leader of the Demokrat Party despite his being prime minister, as the man with the most votes, followed by Ali Amini and the rest of Qavam's supporters. His writ, however, was not as absolute in the provinces, where local powers had always had a greater effect on election outcomes. Since the constitution's separation of powers clause forbad the prime minister to be in the Majlis, Qavam resigned his seat as expected, which allowed his supporter Dr. Reza Zadeh Shafaq, number thirteen on the party list of which the first twelve entered the Majlis, to be admitted in his place.[59]

To many people, Qavam was now Iran's only strong man. But this was more form than substance. Qavam's troubles with the military, begun early in his watch, came to a head when he declared martial law on 8 July 1947, as opposition grew to the oil agreement with the Soviet Union. His minister of war, General Amir Ahmadi, resigned after a row in the cabinet over the declaration. The next day another general in his cabinet, Minister of the Interior Aqevli, resigned in support of his military colleague, objecting to the prime minister's orders to close down a whole array of newspapers and to arrest their publishers indiscriminately. These events exacerbated Qavam's already tenuous hold on the military, forcing him to turn to a civilian, Mahmud Jam, the former prime minister and minister of court, for the war portfolio. On 17 August, Mohammad Mas'ud, the editor of the Tehran daily *Mard-e emruz* (Man of Today), in a damning editorial demanded Qavam's execution and announced a reward of one million rials (approximately $10,000), an exorbitant sum, to any person or his progeny who would kill Qavam while he was still in office; Mas'ud promptly went into hiding.[60] The new Majlis declared for Qavam, however, with a two-thirds majority on 30 August, and on 5 October gave him a vote of confidence by a majority of 93 out of a maximum of 120. Nonetheless, the minority deputies launched a devastating attack on the prime minister for his handling of negotiations with the Soviets on the issue of oil. The anti-Soviet rhetoric spread beyond the Majlis, forcing Qavam again to order several Tehran publishers and editors arrested. This did nothing to diminish his growing troubles in the Majlis, where deputies such as Abbas Mas'udi of the *Ettela'at* daily, Abdolqadir Azad, Abdolhossein E'tebar, and Emami Ahari continued to take him to task for entering into an agreement that they claimed was illegal and harmful—"the worst agreement in the past hundred years of Iranian history."[61] The nationalist fervor took hold of some previous Qavam supporters as well. Hossein Makki, Mozaffar Baqai, and Gholam Hossein Rahimian resigned from the Demokrat Party faction in the Majlis. Qavam's director of propaganda, Ebrahim Khajenuri, went on the radio to plead for a national system of control over oil.[62]

In the meantime, Qavam was faced with Stalin's displeasure at the months-long delay in actually inaugurating the Majlis after it had been elected, and subsequently at delays in getting the oil agreement approved. Sadchikov gave Qavam formal notes on 28 August and 15 September, accusing him of procrastinating and returning to "the policy of enmity towards and discrimination against the Soviet Union."[63] On 22 October 1947, Qavam finally presented to the Majlis a detailed report of his trip to Moscow and a copy of the oil agreement he had signed with Sadchikov. That same day, a bill drafted by Dr. Reza Zadeh Shafaq and several other deputies, rejecting the agreement with the Soviets and charging the government to begin negotiations with the Anglo-Iranian Oil Company for better terms, was presented to the Majlis and passed with a majority of 102 of 104 deputies present.

The surprise rejection of the agreement shocked Stalin, straining further his relationship with Qavam. Stalin was also upset by a military assistance agreement reached between Iran and the United States. Early in October, Iran had entered into an agreement with the United States to establish a military mission to advise the Iranian armed forces. The agreement was in fact an extension of missions instituted for the gendarmerie in 1942 and for the army in 1943.[64] The Soviets had sporadically objected to the presence of the American advisers in Iran, but as long as the United States and the Soviet Union were allies in a joint war effort—and even after the war had ended, while the negotiations for oil were being conducted—the objections had never been vigorous or threatening. With the unexpected rejection of the Soviet oil agreement, however, the U.S.-Iran military agreement suddenly became a casus belli, leading to sporadic invocations of Article 6 of the 1921 Treaty, which the Soviets maintained allowed their forces to enter Iranian territory if they felt threatened by the presence of a third party force in Iran. In response, the U.S. Department of State established a new unit called the Division for Greek, Turkish, and Iranian Affairs, thus putting Iran on a par with the countries that were the original objects of the Truman Doctrine, which declared U.S opposition to Soviet expansion.[65]

Seemingly unassailable before the elections, Qavam's position became unsteady and vulnerable once the Majlis began its work. He needed help, and he thought he would get it from U.S. Ambassador George Allen, with whom he had established good relations. Allen's intervention, however, only served to embolden the opponents of Qavam's agreement. Commercial proposals, said Allen in a speech he delivered in September at the Iran-American Cultural Relations Society, were no concern of the United States. But the United States was concerned when commercial proposals were accompanied by threats. America, he said, would not stand by idly in the face of such threats. He encouraged Iranians to stand firm:

> Our determination to follow this policy as regards Iran is as strong as anywhere else in the world. This purpose can be achieved to the extent that the Iranian people show a determination to defend their own sovereignty. Patriotic Iranians, when considering matters affecting their national interest, may therefore rest assured that the American people will support fully their freedom to make their own choice. Iran's resources belong to Iran. Iran can give them away free of charge or refuse to dispose of them at any price if it so desires.[66]

Allen's statement, which was a clear reiteration of the Truman Doctrine enunciated in April, was encouraging for Qavam's opponents not only for its intrinsic value but also for its contrast with the British attitude. Unlike Allen, British Ambassador Sir John Le Rougetel advised accommodation with the Soviets for obvious reasons: the British were anxious about the probable implications that denying oil to the Soviets would have for the British concession in the south. The speech and the U.S. position it represented clearly influenced the events that finally led to the wholesale rejection of the agreement with the Soviets in October. Allen reported to Secretary of State Dean Acheson that the decline of the Tudeh was due largely to the general belief in Iran, Azerbaijan, and the Soviet Union that the United States was not bluffing. After all, wrote Allen, "Iran is no stronger than the UN and the UN, in the last analysis, is no stronger than the US."[67] Qavam, for his part, considered Allen's view, especially on the collapse of the Tudeh, exaggerated, but he accepted the inevitable, and at least one observer has suggested that he lent his support to the bill drafted by his friend Reza Zadeh Shafaq rejecting his agreement.[68]

Whatever the case, that loss in the Majlis diminished Qavam politically, which meant practically all other factions, including the Tudeh, gained. The interpellation his former ally Gholam Hossein Rahimian brought against him on the day his agreement was rejected further hurt him. He still had a majority in the parliament and believed he could rule as effectively as in the past, but he misread his support. Before the rejection of the agreement, he was the solitary

Iranian statesman the Soviets looked to as trustworthy, and this gave him leverage. The Soviets now attacked him ceaselessly, implicitly making his departure a
condition of improved relations with Iran. On 21 November Sadchikov handed
Qavam an exceptionally harsh note accusing Iran of reneging on its commitment
and objecting to Iran's honoring its concession with the British, which he said
was a testimony to Iran's violation of its treaties of friendship with the Soviet
Union. Indeed, the note hinted at a possible rupture of diplomatic relations.
On 2 December Sadchikov delivered another message, this time responding to
Qavam's explanation of why the Majlis had rejected the agreement, warning
Iran of "dire consequences." Qavam tried to rebut the accusations through a
radio broadcast, but his message served instead further to enrage the Majlis. Two
days later his ministers resigned en masse, except for one, Seyyed Jalal Tehrani,
who had joined him as his parliamentary deputy on 19 November, less than two
weeks before. On 10 December, Qavam explained the government's actions to
the Majlis and asked for a vote of confidence. Of the 112 deputies present, only
46 voted for him.[69] Ironically, Princess Ashraf, whom Qavam occasionally consulted, had warned him the night before that he would be wise to resign because
he did not have enough votes. He had dismissed the advice as uninformed.[70] On
the day he was dismissed, he lamented the legislature's irrational interference in
the executive power, warning that the practice would take constitutionalism to
a tragic end,[71] a follow-up to the shah's admonition a year or two before and a
precursor to the outburst Mosaddeq would make on the same subject as prime
minister half a decade later.

   In hindsight, many Iranians came to believe that a politician as astute as
Qavam would have known the agreement would not pass any Majlis.[72] He therefore must have played the game skillfully enough to dupe Stalin and Molotov.
The proposition makes a hero of Qavam, but it is a moot claim at best. There
was no evidence at the time to point to such a game. He no doubt wished to
cut the Tudeh down to size and believed himself able to do so. The Soviets were
a different story. His game with them was to feed them enough to keep them
satisfied and peacefully at bay. He had a deep comprehension neither of Stalin's
plans nor, most likely, of Marxism-Leninism. He knew that Russians had always
wished to gain access to warm waters and that Iran provided the best geography
for them to do so. But the appetite for this went back for at least two centuries,
so he did not believe there was anything acute or new about the threat. Nor did
he have a modern sense of nationalism, that is, a nationalism that had evolved in
Iran during Reza Shah's reign revolving around the idea of a national grandeur
lost. His idea of grandeur was personal and class oriented. Stalin had power and
could probably do what he pleased with Iran but not with him. He was to be

respected and treated according to his station, which had little to do with being prime minister of Iran and everything to do with who he was. That is why he behaved haughtily toward everyone, including the shah. That is perhaps also how he inspired the shah to carry out the unprecedented and probably illegal act of conferring on him a title as haughty as Qavam's own self-image.

Qavam left Iran on 30 December 1947, two days after Ebrahim Hakimi, his successor, presented his new cabinet to the shah.

6

Nationalizing Oil

If Reza Shah was the greatest influence on his son's attitude toward power and governance, Mohammad Mosaddeq was a close second. Reza Shah was father, Mosaddeq father figure. Reza Shah was martial, uneducated, and rough in demeanor, thinking, and politics; Mosaddeq was frail, educated, and aristocratic. Reza Shah had told his son to beware of anyone securing uncontrolled, independent political power, giving his own career as evidence; Mosaddeq inadvertently proved the truth of Reza Shah's advice by almost deposing the son. Both men left legacies of politics and power the shah struggled to match, and residues of thought and feeling he struggled to discard throughout his reign. The relationship between Mosaddeq and the shah, as it developed in the years after World War II, became for Iranians a tragedy of biblical proportion; the rift it produced in the Iranian body politic penetrated beyond political cleavage into individual psyche. It behooves us to know this man well if we are to begin to understand the shah.

Mosaddeq was born to an aristocratic family, in or about 1880, some twenty-five years before the Constitutional Revolution of 1906. His mother was a granddaughter of the early Qajar shah Fath Ali and thus Nassereddin Shah's cousin. His maternal aunt was married to Muzaffareddin Shah, and his maternal uncle, Abdolhossein Mirza Farmanfarma, a major Qajar prince, was, as noted in chapter 1, a politician and a favorite of the British. His father, Mirza Hedayatollah Vazir Daftar, was a renowned official and financial administrator. When Vazir Daftar died in 1892, Nassereddin Shah conferred on the twelve-year-old son Mohammad the father's office, financial auditor of Khurasan, and his title, Mosaddeq-us-Saltaneh, as was the custom of the day.

The young Mosaddeq was not physically strong and was prone to fainting and bleeding—illnesses that remained with him throughout his life. He was sensitive, irritable, and easily made angry, traits that exacerbated his physical condition. He studied with tutors at home, as was the custom of the rich. When he was sixteen or seventeen, his uncle Farmanfarma engaged him to begin to actually manage Khurasan's finances.[1] He was in Iran during the Constitutional Revolution of 1905–6, but there is no record that he participated in it. Certainly, he remained aloof during the years 1907–11, when Mohammad Ali Shah challenged the Constitution. In 1908, when the shah declared the Constitution null and void, had the Majlis bombed and deputies dispersed, and ordered the Majlis replaced by a Grand Governmental Consultative Assembly, Mosaddeq received through his half-brother, Heshmat-Dauleh Vala Tabar, who held high office in the shah's court but was friendly to the constitutionalists, a royal decree appointing him to the new Grand Assembly.[2] He attended the assembly once, had lunch with other deputies, "and deciding that there was no apparent danger in not attending," made no further appearances.[3]

In 1909, Mosaddeq traveled to Paris to study finance, but he was forced to return to Iran because, as he has written, the courses were hard, the climate did not agree with him, and he fell ill, unable to walk or sit for long stretches. After a few months of rest in Tehran, however, he felt well enough to travel back to Europe, this time to Neuchatel in Switzerland, accompanied by his family. At Neuchatel he studied law, received a bachelor's degree (license), and was admitted to the doctoral program, which apparently required only a dissertation. He returned to Iran to prepare his dissertation on the subject of will and testament in Islam, the Persian version of which was finished in three months with the help of two cleric acquaintances learned in *fiqh*. He then returned to Neuchatel, translated the dissertation into French with the help of a French colleague, and had it published in Paris on his way back to Iran in 1914.[4]

On his return to Tehran Mosaddeq was appointed inspector of finance and in 1917 was made vice minister of finance in the cabinet of Vosuq-ud-Daula, a close relative. In 1919 he left on his third trip to Europe but was called back by Prime Minister Moshir-ud-Daula to serve as minister of justice. Returning via India, he passed through Shiraz in the southern province of Fars. His uncle Farmanfarma had for some time been governor of this province in the British zone but had just been forced to resign because of opposition from tribal chieftains and other local notables. Within hours of Mosaddeq's arrival in Shiraz telegrams were sent to Tehran demanding his appointment as governor to replace his uncle—most likely with British encouragement—and the prime minister agreed.[5] Later that year, when Moshir-ud-Daula fell and Fathollah Akbar Sepahdar became prime minister, the British minister, Herman Cameron Norman, wrote Sepahdar that Mosaddeq was anxiety ridden and that the prime minister should assure him of his continued support.[6]

Mosaddeq's term of governorship in Shiraz coincided with the coup d'état of 1921. He soon had a row with the new prime minister, Seyyed Ziaeddin Tabatabai, a plebeian with the temerity to imprison a host of aristocrats. Seyyed Zia, however, did not last and was succeeded by Ahmad Qavam (Qavam-us-Saltaneh), a relative of Mosaddeq, who promptly appointed him minister of finance. Mosaddeq demanded special powers so that he could reform the finance ministry, which the Majlis at first conferred but later denied, causing him to have one of his fainting spells and leading to Qavam-us-Saltaneh's resignation. When Moshir-ud-Daula returned as the next prime minister, he appointed Mosaddeq governor of Azerbaijan, but there he fell ill, both because the Tabriz climate did not agree with him and because the tensions of the Ministry of Finance had adversely affected his disposition.[7] Nonetheless, in June 1923, Moshir-ud-Daula appointed Mosaddeq minister of foreign affairs, which lasted until October, when Reza Khan Sardar Sepah became prime minister. Mosaddeq then ran for the Fifth Majlis and was elected to represent Tehran.

Between 1921 and 1923, Mosaddeq and Reza Khan had been colleagues while Mosaddeq was in the cabinet. Also, as governor of Azerbaijan he had often needed the military's assistance in performing his tasks, which he had received with Reza Khan's blessing. He came to know Reza Khan well and, as far as can be surmised from his statements at the time, respected him as a man who brought law and order to the country. When the Fifth Majlis voted to depose the Qajar dynasty in 1925, however, Mosaddeq voted against the move on the ground that Reza Khan was better suited to the position he held as the commander-in-chief of the armed forces. The new Reza Shah was not pleased but did not move against him, and Mosaddeq was elected to the Sixth Majlis. Indeed, Mosaddeq later claimed, in a speech he delivered in the Fourteenth Majlis in 1943, that Reza Shah had asked him to form a cabinet, but he did not accept because he did not wish to leave the Majlis.[8] After the Sixth Majlis, however, he retired to his estate in Ahmad Abad, away from politics until Reza Shah was exiled in 1941. In the meantime, some of his close relatives worked with the shah, including his nephew and son-in-law Ahmad Matin Daftary, who was prime minister between October 1939 and June 1940.

When Prime Minister Matin Daftary was dismissed and put under arrest on 25 June 1940,[9] Mosaddeq was also put under arrest although he held no political office at the time. He was then exiled to Birjand, a city in the southeast, but allowed to go there in his own car, to take his cook along, and to be chauffeured by his personal driver, a British subject of Indian parentage. In Birjand, his stay was made as pleasant as circumstances allowed, thanks to Amir Shokat-ul-Mulk Alam, the khan of the region and father of Amir Asadollah Alam, Mohammad

Reza Shah's friend, minister, prime minister, and minister of court in later years. Mosaddeq's evident anxiety and its physical effects on him were severe enough to make his relatives and friends seriously worried, and they sought his release from exile.[10] They got their chance when an old friend of the crown prince became ill.

Ernest Perron, Mohammad Reza's Swiss school friend, was suffering from a damaged kidney. While a student at Le Rosey, he had undergone surgery to remove kidney stones that had cut and infected his kidney, causing insufferable pain. The doctors had told him then that he would not survive another operation. In Iran, the stones and the infection returned, and despite the Swiss doctors' warnings, getting the stones out appeared to be the only reasonable course of action. Perron was taken to the Najmieh Hospital, where Professor Yahya Adl did the surgery. The hospital was an endowment of the Mosaddeq family, and Mosaddeq's son, Dr. Gholam Hossein Mosaddeq, practiced there. Gholam Hossein asked Perron to intercede on behalf of his father, whose health was deteriorating, and Perron conveyed the message to the crown prince. The crown prince, in turn, asked his father to let Mosaddeq go.[11] The shah acquiesced, as he usually did when the future king asked him a favor. But he also told him that he vaguely suspected Mosaddeq was plotting against him in some unverifiable collusion with the British and advised his son to beware of the old man. The father's words, vague as they were, remained uneasily with the son for the rest of his life.[12]

Mosaddeq was ordered freed on 12 September 1941, four days before Reza Shah resigned. He returned to his farm in Almadabad but soon was prevailed upon by his supporters to campaign for the Fourteenth Majlis, the first elected under Allied occupation, which was to open in March 1944. The young shah was not happy with how the elections were proceeding because he thought they were unduly influenced by the Allies. He summoned Mosaddeq while the elections were still going on and asked him to become prime minister, cancel the current election, and conduct a clean one. Mosaddeq agreed to accept the offer with two conditions. First, he wanted full-time personal guards, which the shah immediately granted. Second, he said, British approval must be secured before he could accept the proposal. "How about the Russians' approval?" the shah asked in amazement. "They do not matter. It's the British who make the decisions in this country."[13] The shah objected: "My father was not in the habit of asking for British approval before making decisions." Mosaddeq replied that the shah was young and inexperienced but would in time learn. The shah, though disappointed, nevertheless asked both the British and the Russians. Although the Russians did not object to the shah's proposal, the British ambassador, Sir Reader Bullard, did, arguing that a new election would cause unnecessary turmoil.[14] Thus, the shah's project to make Mosaddeq prime minister abruptly ended.

The Fourteenth Majlis also nominated Mosaddeq for prime minister, but the nomination was withdrawn because he made accepting it contingent on conditions the Majlis found unconstitutional. On 14 November 1944, he wrote the shah that he would accept if he could return to the Majlis after his premiership ended.[15] The shah returned Mosaddeq's letter to the Majlis for a decision,[16] and the body found Mosaddeq's demand contrary to Article 32 of the Constitution. During the Fifteenth Majlis (17 July 1947–28 July 1949) Mosaddeq, at that time not a member, campaigned openly for the premiership and came within one vote (53 to 54) of getting it on 21 December 1947.

He ran for the Sixteenth Majlis even while objecting to the government's conduct of the election. On 13 October 1949 he and a group of some two hundred asked for asylum in the royal court, a time-honored practice. Mosaddeq wrote the shah on behalf of himself and his fellow asylum seekers, complaining about the government's interference in the elections. "The people suffering from cruel oppression and injustice have no other refuge but Your Majesty's Blessed Being *[zat-e mobarak-e shahanshahi]*." The way to correct the injustice, he suggested, was to have a government, and particularly an interior minister, that people trusted. He and the other asylum seekers "offer this petition *[arizeh]*, which is a list of their requests, to Your Majesty's presence, and beg permission to remain in asylum in Your Majesty's Court until Your Majesty's orders shall be issued."[17]

The petition, signed by Mosaddeq, was handed to Court Minister Abdolhossein Hazhir to be presented to the shah. The shah answered through Hazhir that he was always ready to hear any complaint forwarded by any citizen of Iran. He had received many telegrams approving of the elections; however, if the gentlemen wished to remain in the court, they were welcome. Moreover, he was ready to receive their representatives. As conveyed by Hazhir, the shah then said that according to the current laws, the loci to lodge a complaint about elections were the government, the election board, and, finally, the Majlis itself. It seemed to him that his power in this respect was constitutionally limited to dissolving the Majlis. At the moment, he did not know what he could do about a Majlis that had not yet convened. At any rate, the shah thought the complaints were mostly resulting from the shortcomings in the election laws.[18] According to Mosaddeq, the twenty representatives of the asylum seekers admitted to the court then announced the establishment of a National Front with Mosaddeq as leader. The Front persevered with its complaints until the electoral votes in Lavasanat, a suburb of Tehran, were annulled, sending Mosaddeq and his friends to the Sixteenth Majlis, which would prove to be one of the most fateful assemblies of the constitutional period.

◼

The Fifteenth Majlis, which opened on 17 July 1947 and finally voted on the proposed agreement with the Soviet Union for an oil consortium in northern Iran on 22 October, had not only rejected that agreement but had also charged the government to review the 1933 Agreement and to begin negotiations with the Anglo-Iranian Oil Company (AIOC) in order to regain Iran's national rights to all its own oil reserves.[19] After Qavam's cabinet fell, a succession of cabinets under Ebrahim Hakimi, Abdolhossein Hazhir, Mohammed Sa'ed, and General Haji Ali Razmara took up the challenge. Under Hazhir a rather elaborate memorandum consisting of some twenty-five items was prepared for discussion with the AIOC. Hazhir, however, did not last in office to carry out negotiations with the AIOC delegation, headed by N. E. Gass, which arrived in Tehran during the subsequent cabinet headed by Mohammad Sa'ed. In February 1949 Sa'ed assigned a committee under Finance Minister Abbasqoli Golshaiyan to begin negotiations with the delegation. The Hazhir memorandum became the initial basis for negotiations, which, for the most part, were held in secret. On 9 June, Golshaiyan reported to the Majlis that he had stood firm against the AIOC position and followed the existing memorandum, which stated, among other things, that the 1933 Agreement had not been faithfully executed by the company and that now, regardless of the past, changing conditions had rendered it inimical to Iranian interests. The company representatives, however, would not negotiate on these grounds and had threatened to break off discussions. Golshaiyan then had presented two main topics: first, the amount of royalties and taxes and, second, the duration of the concession. He had suggested a fifty-fifty sharing of the profits, as in Venezuela, on the first point and a review every fifteen years of whatever duration was mutually agreed upon, on the second.

Subsequent to the Golshaiyan report, the Sa'ed government decided to continue negotiations rather than submit the Iranian claims to arbitration. The result was a revised oil agreement known officially as the Supplemental Oil Agreement and popularly as Gass-Golshaiyan, named after the chief negotiators. The government tried to push the agreement through in the last days of the Fifteenth Majlis but failed in the face of a determined minority that collectively and simultaneously interpellated the government for failing to secure Iranian rights and for obstructing proper legislative process.[20] The Majlis then adjourned before the bill could come to a vote. The fight made several minority representatives famous, especially Hossein Makki, who led the interpellation through to the end of the session. The struggle also created the nucleus for the National Front, which would be formally established during the election to the Sixteenth Majlis. It was during the "protracted election which preceded the convening of the 16th Majlis," said one observer, that "opposition to the Company and its operation, echoed by virtually all significant political groups and parties, assumed overwhelming proportions. Expressions of moderation were seen as treason."[21]

The 4th of February 1949 was a Friday, the day of rest in Iran. It was also the anniversary of the founding of Tehran University, and tradition, as initiated by Reza Shah, demanded that the shah attend the university and hand out that year's diplomas. The shah arrived at the university's College of Law in the afternoon. As he walked toward the building, a man holding a camera approached and suddenly opened fire with a gun. It took a second or two and three bullets through his hat before the shah realized what was happening. The fourth bullet entered his right cheek and exited through the upper lip. By this time he had begun instinctively to spin away. The fifth bullet hit him in the shoulder, and the sixth misfired as the gun jammed. The assailant threw his gun in anger and attempted to escape, but officers and guards surrounded and killed him.[22]

The shah regretted that the man had been killed before he could be questioned. "Perhaps it was in someone's interest that he not be questioned," he wrote many years later in exile. The assailant was alleged to have had connections to both the Tudeh and religious fanatics, and the shah wondered if the event could have been the "first glimmer of what would later come to be known as 'Islamic Marxism.'"[23] The attempted assassination gave rise to a flurry of rumors, including one impugning the army chief of staff, General Razmara. Later, in Geneva in 1956, the shah asked Ali Amini, then Iran's ambassador to Washington, who he thought was behind the assassination attempt. "You know very well who was behind the attempt, Your Majesty—Razmara," Amini answered matter-of-factly. "Come on, it cannot be," was the shah's response, half denying the statement, half suggesting it was absurd, but remaining open to the possibility.[24]

The assailant, Nasser Fakhrarai, was declared to have been a member of the Tudeh Party though he carried a press pass issued to *Parcham-e eslam* (The Flag of Islam), an Islamist newspaper.[25] The government declared martial law, announced that the Tudeh was now illegal, closed its centers, offices, and newspapers, and arrested several members of the non-Tudeh press as well as a good number of the political opposition. The same day as the attempted assassination, the Tudeh had held a rally at the grave of one of its heroes, Dr. Taqi Erani, in which an estimated ten thousand to thirty thousand members and sympathizers participated. The sizable gathering suggested that the party might be able to significantly affect the elections for the Sixteenth Majlis, scheduled for the summer.[26] The attempt on the shah, however, essentially wrecked its prospects.

Fakhrarai's attack proved a boon to the shah in another way. He had been for some time pressuring the government and the Majlis to convoke the Senate, which was stipulated by the Constitution but had never been elected, and to amend Article 48 of the Constitution to give him the power to dissolve the Majlis. Now he was in a position to demand what he could previously only ask. Three weeks after the attempt on his life, on 27 February, the Majlis voted in favor of a constituent assembly to be convened to amend Article 48. On 21 April, the shah opened the assembly, calling on the members "to keep in mind international conditions and to remember that to persist and prosper, countries will have to move in harmony with the requirements of the times, achieve the characteristics of a progressive civilization, and implement the kinds of change that elicit world approbation."[27] The assembly, meeting under the chairmanship of Seyyed Mohammad Sadeq Tabatabai, an old Pahlavi friend and supporter, changed Article 48 to give the shah the power to dissolve the Majlis free of the specific conditions the original article imposed, thus significantly increasing the shah's power vis-à-vis the Majlis.[28] In June he secured an agreement from the Majlis for the election of the First Senate, to be opened simultaneously with the Sixteenth Majlis on 9 February 1950.[29]

As monarch, the shah favored the appropriation of his country's rights to its own oil but worried about the hurdles on the way. His father had undertaken to renegotiate the D'Arcy concession on an impulse and was forced to agree to conditions he had not foreseen. According to Seyyed Hassan Taqizadeh, who as minister of finance had signed the 1933 Agreement, Reza Shah wished to annul all agreements he deemed harmful to Iran's interest and in most cases of annulment he was successful—save in the case of oil. No one had dared tell him at the time that he should enter into this enterprise warily. He had no intention of prolonging the agreement on oil but was forced to do so once the negotiations had begun. Reza Shah, stated Taqizadeh in the Majlis, "did not wish to extend the concession, and in the first instance of its mention by the British, he exclaimed abusively right in front of them: 'Really! Such an action is quite out of the question! Do you expect us who for thirty years have been cursing our predecessors because of this matter to allow ourselves to be cursed for another fifty years by our successors?'"[30] In the end, however, England and the AIOC had proven too strong, partly because Reza Shah was intent on developing Iran, which he could not afford to do without the guarantee of oil money.

The derogatory statements being made about the 1933 Agreement annoyed the shah. The fact that his father had had to yield to the British, against his will, disturbed him further. He sought to educate himself, to have a more solid grasp of the oil situation, an analysis from someone knowledgeable but not associated with the oil company. Sometime in 1948 he asked Hossein Ala, then Iran's ambassador to the United States, to study the oil issue and recommend to him an appropriate plan of action. Ala approached Mohammad Namazi, a successful Iranian businessman in Washington who was also something of an honorary commercial attaché at the embassy. Namazi did not know much about oil, but he promised Ala to study it and in the end came up with a remarkable set of analyses. The 1933 concession, wrote Namazi to Ala, was far better for Iran than had been the case under the D'Arcy agreement—until the outbreak of the war, when it became gradually worse as a result of the unusual rise in the price of oil on the world market (from $6 per ton before the war to $17 per ton in 1947). The terms of the agreement then lowered Iran's share to about 8 percent of the net profit on crude, not counting the profits on refining and marketing. This fact alone, Namazi argued, was sufficient to prove that a revision in the 1933 Agreement was necessary, though there were other reasons as well—such as the company's failure to reduce the number of its foreign employees. At any rate, according to Namazi, the Iranian government had two good weapons in hand: the threat of nationalization and the threat of imposition of a heavy tax in 1963, as was stipulated in the agreement.

In 1942, the government of Venezuela had revised the concession it had formerly granted, and oil companies operating in Venezuela had agreed to a taxation mechanism that raised Venezuela's income to 50 percent of the net profit on the exploitation of crude oil. Iran, Namazi argued, could accept no less. Even if the cabinet agreed to less than a 50 percent share and the Majlis approved the agreement, the agreement would not last; it would have to be revised soon after. Finally, it was politically intolerable for a foreign company to operate on Iranian soil and to hold one-half the shares of oil. The people would not accept it; and, besides, it would provoke the Russian government to demand a similar concession in the north. AIOC, therefore, should separate its exploitation and refining operations in Iran from its operations in other parts of the world and agree to transfer its exploitation operations in Iran to a new company that would be registered in Iran. The new company would allot half its shares to the Iranian government and half to the shareholders of the original company.[31]

Ala and Namazi believed that the British would approach the issue with understanding and goodwill. This optimism proved false. In Iran, the struggle for vindicating Iranian rights intensified, propelling new faces, and new heroes, onto the political scene as the National Front won seats in Tehran and a few other cities, partly because of the support it received from the shah and the chief of national police, General Fazlollah Zahedi. The shah opened the Sixteenth Majlis on 9 February 1950, stating, "the nation's moral purpose is to provide every member of this society with the five basic rights to which everyone is entitled: food, clothing, housing, health, and education. The best way to achieve these rights is to make the Seven-Year Plan work."[32] It was not to be. The Sixteenth Majlis was consumed with oil, which overshadowed every other issue. Prime Minister Sa'ed resigned a few days after the inauguration of the new Majlis without even asking for a vote of confidence. His successor, Ali Mansur, offered the Supplementary Oil Agreement (Gass-Golshaiyan) bill to the Majlis without committing the government to it. "The previous government tabled this bill, and now the Majlis must make a decision," he said in answer to Mosaddeq's inquiry about where he stood on the issue. He suggested a special committee be established to look into the proposed bill. After some hard debate, a Special Oil Committee of eighteen members was formed, to which the National Front members—Mohammad Mosaddeq, Ali Shayegan, Allahyar Saleh, and Hossein Makki—were elected, though they had originally voted against it. Mosaddeq was elected chairman and Makki rapporteur; other posts were filled by non-Front members.[33]

Mansur resigned on 26 June, the day Mosaddeq was made chair of the committee, and was succeeded by General Haji Ali Razmara, the army chief of staff. Razmara's premiership had been rumored for several months, occasioning vociferous opposition from the National Front and the religious groups associated with Ayatollah Seyyed Abolqasem Kashani, including the Fadaiyan Islam and its leader, Navvab Safavi.[34]

Razmara was methodical, disciplinarian, serious, and ambitious. These traits showed in his approach to his work. The first bill he introduced to the Majlis was to establish city and provincial councils, foreseen in the Constitution but never promulgated. The proposal incurred the wrath of Mosaddeq, who accused Razmara of planning to dismember the country.[35] Razmara's politics, in fact, veered leftward, and his views of oil, while generally against nationalization, was more complicated than his opponents labeled them. He wished to reach a modus vivendi with the Soviets and signed several commercial and border treaties with Soviet Ambassador Ivan Sadchikov. He also terminated the contract of several American advisers and disallowed the work of Voice of America in Iran. He sought to implement, though to no avail, the findings of the Government Corrupt Practices Committee, which deemed a large number of high-level officeholders in the administration and the parliament corrupt and therefore unsuitable to public service.[36] But Razmara's tenure and, in the final analysis, his life were literally and figuratively decided on the issue of oil.

The Special Oil Committee asked Razmara to give it his formal opinion on the Gass-Golshaiyan agreement within ten days. The government failed to do so. A number of National Front deputies then interpellated Razmara and several of his ministers, but the government won out. On 4 November, having just signed a commercial agreement with the Soviets, Razmara, accompanied by Finance Minister Gholamhossein Foruhar, met with the committee at Mosaddeq's invitation. Razmara asked the committee to report to the Majlis on the points in the agreement that they considered contrary to Iran's interests so the Majlis could make a comprehensive decision about what the government ought to do. Only then would he be able to negotiate with the AIOC to either improve the present agreement or replace it with another. Mosaddeq said the 1933 Agreement was invalid. Makki talked about nationalizing oil. This may have been the first time the term *nationalization* had been formally used; thereafter, however, nationalization became the National Front's political mantra.

On 25 November the committee unanimously rejected Gass-Golshaiyan. Mosaddeq and the National Front members further suggested the committee submit a proposal for the nationalization of oil with its report. Committee members Nosratollah Kasemi and Hedayatollah Palizi objected on the grounds that such a proposal was beyond the authority the Majlis had conferred on the committee. Such a bill should be offered at the whole session, they argued. Mosaddeq insisted, however, and subsequently the following proposal, signed by five National Front deputies, was read into the report: "In the name of the felicity of the Iranian nation, and in order to promote world peace, the undersigned propose that the oil industry be declared nationalized without exception across the whole territory of the country; that is, the activities related to discovery, extraction, and exploitation be placed in the hand of the Government. Signed, Dr. Mosaddeq, [Abolhasan] Haerizadeh, Allahyar Saleh, Dr. [Ali] Shayegan, Hossein Makki."[37]

The committee's report, submitted to the Majlis on 17 December, signified the end of Gass-Golshaiyan and the dawn of nationalization. The proposal to nationalize the oil industry was formally presented to the Majlis on the same day.

Mosaddeq, who was sick that day, sent a letter that was read by Makki, in which he said, "Even if we extracted ten million tons of oil instead of the thirty million the company will extract in 1950, and even if we spend 2 pounds for every pound that the company spends, still, based on 5 pounds a ton, which is the reported price of the Persian Gulf oil, Iran will have an income of 30 million pounds."[38] Mozaffar Baqai pleaded: "Gentlemen, let us nationalize this oil. What though the oil was to disappear forever; we need no refinery. We will attend to our own customary farming." In the euphoria of the moment, no one seemed conscious of or concerned with the potential problems that lay ahead. Nationalization became the dominant theme, the mantra, in the Majlis and across the country. Baharestan, the area in the middle of Tehran where the Majlis building was situated, became the hub of demonstrations; from there the excitement traveled first to other quarters in Tehran and then gradually to other major cities.

A few days later, on 24 December 1950, amid a large student demonstration before the Majlis in favor of repealing the 1933 Agreement and abrogating martial law in the southern oil regions, Razmara argued before a special Majlis session about the danger a decision to nationalize oil posed to the Iranian people. "If we are talking about nationalization only, this is already attained. Iran is different from Mexico. Here, according to the law, all mines belong to the government and they are 'nationalized.' In Mexico, underground resources were in private hands. But perhaps the people who make such demands believe that we ourselves should extract and sell our oil. Since this is a matter of grave responsibility before history and before the Iranian people, I must declare here that under the present conditions Iran does not possess the industrial capacity to take the oil out and sell it on the world markets. . . . Gentlemen, you cannot yet manage a cement factory with your own personnel. . . . I say this as clearly as I can: To endanger our country's national capital and underground resources is the greatest of treasons."[39]

On 7 March 1951, Mosaddeq said about Razmara's position on oil: "On behalf of the National Front and armed with the support of the Iranian people, I declare that Iranians find the prime minister's statements hateful and do not consider legitimate a government that yields to such slave-like baseness. No other way exists but to nationalize the oil."[40] That same day Razmara was assassinated.

It is not clear what exactly Razmara was after. There is evidence that he had reached some sort of secret understanding with the AIOC on a fifty-fifty sharing of the profits. In August 1950, Arabian-American Oil Company (ARAMCO) had begun negotiations with the Saudi government, on Saudi demand, with a view to a fifty-fifty profit sharing agreement. In September the negotiation was brought to the attention of the AIOC and the British government by George McGhee, then U.S. undersecretary of state for Eastern affairs. McGhee had received reports from the U.S. ambassador in Tehran, Henry Grady, that the Iranian situation was deteriorating and that "continuing delay in getting Iranian approval of the Supplemental Agreement could result in the collapse of Iran or confiscation of AIOC concession." Razmara, Grady reported approvingly, had demanded four points "to sweeten the agreement in order to obtain Majlis ratification: a ten-year Iranianization program, the right of Iran to examine the AIOC books to determine their share of the profits, oil prices in Iran equal to the lowest given to others, and full information as to destination of oil exported." The prime minister had also insisted on funds to be paid Iran up front against the agreement to start up Iran's seven-year development plan. The U.S. companies told McGhee Razmara's demands were eminently reasonable, Charles Harding of Socony-Vacuum thinking it "inconceivable that AIOC could not accept" them. But the British balked. In September, the Foreign Office told McGhee that AIOC could not agree with any of Razmara's points except those related to the cost of production and the destination of Iranian oil.[41]

In November 1950, ARAMCO formally offered fifty-fifty profit sharing to Saudi Arabia. The agreement made it impossible for Razmara to offer the Majlis anything less. The British procrastinated, even though they had warning from the Americans on the impending U.S. agreement with the Saudis at least a month before it was made. Finally, it seems that, although it was never fully verified, they told Razmara through a "note verbal" on 24 February 1951, a few days before his murder, that they too were prepared to offer a fifty-fifty profit sharing contract.[42] There was much talk about the understanding in Tehran and abroad, but no one seems to have actually seen the contract—if there was one. Razmara had asked for a report on the consequences of nationalization from two Iranian officials of the AIOC, who had been commissioned by the Iranian government to prepare the ground for the establishment of a National Iranian Oil Company (NIOC). The report had concluded that because the international oil market was controlled by a powerful and united cartel, it would be difficult for Iran to sell either refined or crude oil. Oil production in Iran most likely would be limited to domestic consumption needs, and consequently Iran's revenues would be drastically reduced. The report was delivered to the Special Oil Committee, where its drafters—Fathollah Naficy and Baqer Mostofi—were scheduled to appear on 7 March 1951, the day Razmara was shot. Razmara had told them he had the fifty-fifty agreement in his pocket but, again, no one ever actually saw it.[43]

Perhaps Razmara was too intimidated by British power to be able to convince them of the extent of the Iranian nation's commitment to nationalization. At the same time the shah did not think Razmara was the right man to solve the oil dilemma—nor did he trust him fully. Razmara was infatuated with Princess Ashraf and had once, perhaps inadvertently, told her he would make her his queen. The princess told her brother, advising him to be careful.[44] Several of the deputies who frequented Razmara's home and were wooed by him concluded that he might have plans that smacked of treason against the shah and reported it to him. Majlis deputy Nasser Zolfaqari believed that a group of imprisoned Tudeh leaders had been allowed to escape as a result of a plot Razmara had concocted against the shah.[45] He brought up the issue in Razmara's home and was told he had to make a choice. He reported the event to the shah, vowing he would not support Razmara. The shah concurred. According to Mosaddeq, a few days before Razmara was assassinated, the shah sent Jamal Emami, an influential deputy, to ask him if he would agree to become prime minister,[46] but Mosaddeq demurred. "Razmara's murderer," Mosaddeq wrote in his memoirs, "whoever he was, saved His Majesty from having to deal with Razmara, because a few days before Razmara's assassination, His Majesty sought to appoint me in his place, which I did not accept. The assassin did the work he had set out to do."[47]

The days after Razmara's assassination were chaotic, wanting in both moral and legal compass. Razmara, like Hazhir, who had been assassinated in November 1949, was killed by a member of the Fadaiyan Islam—a man named Khalil Tahmasebi, who volunteered that he had killed in order to punish treason. The next day, on 8 March, the Special Oil Committee approved the nationalization of the oil industry. On the same day, Ayatollah Kashani declared Razmara's murder a religiously necessary act and called the murderer the savior of the Iranian nation. In a large demonstration in front of the Majlis, National Front members Hossein Makki and Mozaffar Baqai congratulated the Iranian people on the "killing" of Razmara. Navvab Safavi, leader of the Fadaiyan Islam, declared in a statement addressed to "Son of Pahlavi," read at the same demonstration, that unless Tahmasebi was immediately freed, many others would suffer Razmara's fate.[48]

▪

A week after Razmara's assassination, on 15 March 1951, the Majlis passed the Nationalization Bill with no opposition and charged the Special Oil Committee with determining how it was to be administered. The Senate passed the bill on the 20th, also unanimously, and the shah signed it into law on the same day. In his New Year address on 22 March, the shah urged the people to remain calm because a calm atmosphere was needed if the reform was to be implemented wisely. The country, however, was anything but calm. In Abadan and Bandar Maʿshur, the employees of the oil industry went on strike because of 30 percent cuts in their overtime and other benefits. In a clash between the strikers and the police nine Iranians and three Englishmen were killed and a larger number wounded. This triggered a strike throughout the oil industry, with strikes and clashes expanding to other areas, including Tehran and Rasht.[49] On 24 April, the shah summoned the cabinet, now under Hossein Ala, and expressed his concern. On 26 April the munitions depot in Shiraz exploded, destroying, according to one account, one-third of all Iranian weaponry.[50] The next day, the 27th, the British ambassador, Sir Francis Shepherd, issued a statement calling the decision to nationalize Iranian oil hasty and warning the Iranian government of possible severe consequences. On the same day, Ala offered his resignation because, he complained to the shah, he "had not been consulted — not even once — on the nationalization law's implementation protocol."[51] On the 28th, the Majlis endorsed Mosaddeq as the next prime minister, and the shah appointed him to the post the following day.

In fact, Mosaddeq's becoming prime minister was encouraged, if not engineered, by the shah. On 26 April Mosaddeq had presented a nine-point bill to the Special Oil Committee as the framework for the execution of the law of nationalization of the oil industry, and the committee passed it unanimously that same day. The bill had been prepared initially as seven points by Jamal Emami. To this Mosaddeq added two additional points on compensation to and disempowerment of the AIOC and forced the bill hastily through the committee.[52] That Emami and Mosaddeq had been cooperating for some time was clearly indicated by Mosaddeq's expression of gratitude to Emami on 13 March 1951, the day Ala was appointed prime minister. "I consider myself duty-bound to thank Mr. Jamal Emami, whose considerable assistance in the critical hour paved the way for nationalization of the oil industry," Mosaddeq said then in the Majlis.[53]

Jamal Emami was also the shah's confidant. It was he who had taken the shah's offer of premiership to Mosaddeq when Razmara was in office, as stated by Mosaddeq and his son.[54] The shah clearly wanted Mosaddeq to lead the fight for nationalization — partly because he thought no one else would succeed; partly because he thought only Mosaddeq could afford to fail. On the day Ala resigned, Mosaddeq spoke in the Majlis special session, expressing his anxiety about the fate of the nine-point nationalization protocol in the hands of the next prime minister. Suddenly, Jamal Emami looked at him and said: "Why do you not become prime minister and personally implement the nine-point law!" Mosaddeq said, unhesitatingly, "I accept." In a secret ballot, Mosaddeq received seventy-nine of the one hundred votes cast. He then conditioned his acceptance on the passage of the nine-point protocol by the two houses. The Majlis passed the protocol the same day, the Senate on 30 April; the shah signed it into law on May 1.

Why did Mosaddeq so readily agree to become prime minister now whereas in the past he had consistently refused? Mosaddeq's explanation: "I asked some friends the reason for Ala's resignation. One of them said that *Hazarat* [the British], thinking nothing would come from the likes of this prime minister, intended to bring in Seyyed Ziaeddin Tabatabai, who has had an audience with the Shahanshah, and is now waiting for a nod by the Majlis. One of the deputies, who never thought I would accept the job, suggested it, and I immediately accepted. Had Seyyed Zia become prime minister, he would not leave a Majlis for me to pursue the oil issue. With anyone else also, I could not have nationalized the oil."[55] This, however, hardly explains, even accounting for the agitated climate of opinion, how he received 79 percent of the votes in secret ballots when until then the National Front had been a small minority. It is also unlikely that the shah would have promoted Seyyed Zia, because he believed, as he had told the previous British ambassador, Sir John Le Rougetel, that Seyyed was too much tainted by his pro-British reputation to be of any use in solving the oil issue.[56] The only reasonable explanation for Mosaddeq's succession, then, is that the shah must have encouraged it.

To the British, Mosaddeq was anathema, his becoming prime minister a cataclysmic event. "When the events of 1951 come to be recorded in later years in the wider context of Persian history, I think it will be found that the murder of General Razmara marked a turning point," the British chargé George Middleton wrote in his report to Foreign Secretary Anthony Eden. Mosaddeq would last for some time and therefore, Middleton concluded, "The hopes of Persian advancement which her British and American well-wishers fostered in the immediate post-war years must now be postponed if not altogether abandoned. To many observers it appears that Persia will remain a backward, corrupt and inefficient agricultural state from which the most that can be hoped is that it shall not totally disintegrate or disappear behind the Iron Curtain." Mosaddeq's premiership had affected every aspect of Iranian national life: "The position of the Shah, the authority of Parliament, the loyalty of the Army, the financial and economic stability of the state have all in turn been subjected to strains which have taken a toll from which the country may take many years to recover." This, observed Middleton, was the reality. Mosaddeq, however, clutched "at the shadow for the substance . . . unable to distinguish beyond the two."[57]

In March 1951, when Iran passed the law to nationalize oil and to establish a national oil company to operate the oil industry, the Abadan refinery was the largest in the world, with annual production of about twenty-two million tons of various refined products. Over seven million tons of crude oil had been exported in 1950. The AIOC employed more than sixty thousand persons at Abadan and in the oil fields serving Abadan, of whom over two thousand were British. Besides the oil installations, the oil industry establishment provided services called "non-basics," such as power, water, roads, public health, and housing for the refinery and the municipality that grew around the refinery as well as for the smaller communities around the oil fields.

The British government and the Anglo-Iranian Oil Company claimed that Iran's decision to nationalize the oil industry was illegal and threatened to take the case before the United Nations Security Council in New York and the International Court of Justice in The Hague. The Iranian government argued that the 1933 Agreement was made under duress and was therefore illegal and that at any rate it was Iran's sovereign right to nationalize its resources and consequently neither the Court nor the Security Council had jurisdiction over the matter.

AIOC sent a mission to Iran in June 1951 to attempt to settle the dispute by negotiation, but with no success. At the end of June, the newly established National Iranian Oil Company (NIOC) offered the British employees of the former AIOC employment, but they declined as a group. In August, the United States offered its good offices through Averell Harriman, who went to Tehran with a second British mission headed by Richard Stokes, Lord Privy Seal, to mediate the negotiations. Stokes arrived in Tehran on 4 August and stayed until the 23rd, his negotiations seesawing but his progress at the end almost nil. He and Mosaddeq, however, hit it off on a personal level, remaining civil to the end. In their first meeting on the morning of 5 August, Mosaddeq appeared very "amiable" to Stokes, who "was relieved at the personal approach." As the conversation moved to business, Mosaddeq referred to AIOC as "ma femme divorcée," which phrase, according to Stokes, "cropped up throughout negotiations." That evening, Mosaddeq went to Sahebqaraniyeh Palace, Stokes's assigned residence, to resume the discussions. Stokes began on a light note: "I had never heard it essential to starve 'a divorced wife' to death." Mosaddeq "thought this very funny," a sign of British understated humor, which despite his stubbornness on the oil issue he liked and sometimes commented on. The next day, on the 6th, Stokes met with a delegation of Iranians from the Majlis and the Senate that had no negotiating authority but was very warm and pleasant and seemingly eager to reach agreement. He took it as a good omen: "it might set the tone of subsequent meetings," he thought.[58]

The members were certainly quite different in their attitude from Hossein Makki in Abadan, who had neither welcomed Stokes nor seen him off when he stopped there, causing Stokes to complain and ask Mosaddeq to recall him from Abadan. Mosaddeq responded, lamely, that Makki was ill and would probably return to Tehran shortly anyway. In Baghdad on his way to Tehran, Stokes had consulted with Nuri Said, the Iraqi prime minister and a friend of the British. On Said's recommendation, Stokes also met with Seyyed Ziaeddin Tabatabai to receive his input on Mosaddeq and particularly on the shah, with whom he seemed to have less rapport than with Mosaddeq. Seyyed Zia had advised him to be tough, to threaten to leave if negotiations did not move, to force the shah to intervene. He met with the shah several times, the shah always counseling accommodation but supporting his prime minister. All told, the Iranians dined and wined Stokes, but not much more. He was particularly impressed with a big reception Foreign Minister Baqer Kazemi gave for Averell Harriman, which the British delegation attended. "Beautifully done in gardens of Foreign Office Summer Palace," Stokes jotted down. "Still going on at midnight. Papal Nuncio present."[59]

Stokes went to Iran personally bearing goodwill, hoping to reach agreement, but the instructions he had been given by his government left him little room for maneuver. In hindsight, what he offered in an eight-point proposal was not totally unreasonable, given the Consortium Agreement as the end result of the nationalization process. It acknowledged the principle of nationalization but reserved production, refining, and marketing to a management committee and purchasing organization that were only superficially responsible to NIOC. On compensation, it stipulated that the amount paid in any one year would not exceed 25 percent of the NIOC's net earnings. A Purchasing Organization (PO) was to sign a contract for a minimum purchase of twenty-five million tons of crude a year, containing a clause allowing NIOC to sell up to 12.5 percent over and above the twenty-five million tons of crude each year for the first five years and more afterward. Mosaddeq appeared interested but then retreated under pressure, most likely from Ayatollah Kashani, thought Stokes. "The visit [Kashani's to Mosaddeq] certainly took place and Dr. Mosaddeq was certainly as obstinate as a mule, so the threat may well have been made. He [Harriman] and I were both astonished at this change round."[60]

Stokes saw merit in Iran's position, and a year later, when he no longer was with the government, argued that the Iranian case had never been properly stated in England. The British public, he wrote to the *Times,* did not know Iran received far less for its oil than Iraq and Kuwait, or that the "British Treasury took 50 million pounds in tax on Iranian oil whereas Iran received approximately 16 million pounds," or that the Persian Gulf oil is the cheapest in the world to extract, or that "the Persians were within their rights in nationalizing their oil industry, and in doing so they recognized the principle of adequate and fair compensation," or that the negotiations he had conducted in Iran were not broken by Iranians but by him—because, he wrote, he "could get no agreement on staff employment which seemed [to him] practical." Any proposal made now (September 1952), therefore, would have to be "at least as good as that contained" in his eight-point proposal of August the previous year. He did not believe, under the circumstances, that "any proposal emanating from official sources, either American or British," or from the oil company, would receive a sympathetic hearing. "In these circumstances," he concluded, "the best course is to depute the task of preliminary negotiations and adjustment to independent British commercial or industrial interests who could approach the issue informally and impersonally."[61]

U.S. Ambassador Henry Grady had great influence on Mosaddeq and probably misled him by imparting to him his own sentiments as those of his government's. Grady thought Britain was wrong morally and politically. Britain could not stomach the national independence movements in former colonies and "undervalued Mosaddeq to an incredible degree," failing to see the bond that connected him to his people. Mosaddeq, Grady thought, was "a man of great intelligence, wit, and knowledge" who reminded him of Mahatma Gandhi—frail of body with a will of iron. The AIOC made a net profit of £100 million in 1950 but paid a pittance to the Iranian government. The British attitude in the summer and autumn of 1950, he later wrote, was remarkably unclear and hesitant. The United States, he thought, should give the same strategic importance to Iran as it did to Greece or Turkey. He had taken the post in Iran on the condition that the United States would double its military aid and that the Import-Export Bank would make available to Iran a loan of $50 million; the American government, however, did not follow through during Grady's stay in Iran because it was too much influenced by the British. The British, for their part, now wished to dislodge Mosaddeq by applying economic pressure and expected the United States to stand with them. "If [Mosaddeq] causes great harm and in reality serves the interests of the Soviet Union, it is not because he wishes to do so, but because his real struggle is directed against what he regards as British economic aggression," Grady noted, urging that the United States not blindly follow Britain. Rather it should lead, because it had the financial and military power, and "the British only have this power through the USA."[62]

In October 1951, when Prime Minister Mosaddeq went to New York to present Iran's case in the UN Security Council, his opinion of the United States was very much shaped by Grady's vision of the world. He assumed the Americans were viscerally with the underdog and that with a little prodding they would take Iran's side against their partner and ally. He spent some time in New York and Washington in talks with the U.S. government. In New York, George McGhee — who in addition to serving as undersecretary of state for Eastern affairs was a renowned geologist and oilman — was commissioned by the State Department to talk with Mosaddeq. Their first meeting, on 8 October 1951, was arranged by Nasrollah Entezam, Iran's ambassador to the United States. Entezam left after introducing McGhee and his interpreter and adviser, Vernon Walters, which caused McGhee to reason that "either he had been told to, or he was wise enough to know that the Prime Minister would not speak freely in his presence."[63] This continued to be the pattern, McGhee and Walters meeting Mosaddeq alone. Walters was the official translator and much more, according to McGhee. He had accompanied Averell Harriman to Tehran earlier in 1951 and had acquired a sense of Mosaddeq that McGhee found extremely helpful. The meetings went on over several days in New York and Washington, where Mosaddeq also met with Truman and Acheson on the president's invitation.

The McGhee intervention did not disabuse Mosaddeq of his faith in Grady's view. Rather, it strengthened it, since McGhee was critical of the AIOC's insensitivity to Iran's grievances and inclined to humor Mosaddeq. He told the British ambassador, Oliver Franks, "somehow or other we have got to get our relations with these countries [such as Iran] on a basis of equality and do it in such a way that it is recognized by these countries that they are being treated as equals and partners." Franks transmitted the statement to London, adding that it probably represented "the general opinion of the State Department." The response was that McGhee was ill-advised, as were the Americans in general, but the British would need to take the attitude into account as they made future policy.[64] Truman and Acheson's talks with Mosaddeq seemed to reflect McGhee's opinion, with Acheson remarking on Iran's worries about British intervention in Iranian affairs and the U.S. efforts to see to it that Iran and England negotiated free of such concerns while Truman worried aloud about the Soviet Union — a "sitting vulture on a fence waiting to pounce on the oil. It would then be in a position to wage a world war."[65]

These discussions, however, changed nothing between Britain and Iran. Suggestions then were made that the International Bank for Reconstruction and Development (IBRD) might assist in the dispute between its two member states. The U.S. government encouraged the idea. R. L. Garner, vice president of IBRD, met with Mosaddeq in Washington on 10 November 1951, suggesting the bank was prepared to act as a neutral institution, but only upon the invitation of both Iran and the United Kingdom. The bank proposed to set up temporary management for the operation of the oil properties; arrange a contract for the sale of oil to AIOC; and arrange for the provision of necessary funds for the resumption of operations, to be reimbursed from oil revenues.[66] Oil would once again flow, creating an atmosphere in which the two parties might negotiate and reach a permanent settlement, Garner argued. Mosaddeq agreed. Garner then informed the British but received no response before Mosaddeq left Washington on 23 November. Shortly after, in London, Foreign Secretary Anthony Eden also expressed interest in the bank's "attempting to work out a specific proposal" as long as the bank's involvement was for a limited period. He advised and apparently convinced Garner over several discussions that the bank would have to engage "a large number of British oil technicians to run the industry," though he agreed with the bank that perhaps most of the top executives should be confined to individuals not connected to AIOC.[67]

Eden was confident that England had the upper hand and would prevail if the Americans stayed calm.[68] In fact, oil production from fields in Iraq, Kuwait, Saudi Arabia, and the United States had already increased more than enough to compensate for the Iranian loss. In December he instructed Ambassador Shepherd to tell Mosaddeq and the shah to ponder the matter of nationalization carefully because "the world oil industry has already replaced Persian supplies from other sources, and in a short time it may be a matter of difficulty to reopen to Persia her former markets." He told Garner that England would consider it prejudicial to British interests if the bank were to act as agent or trustee for Iran only. Rather, the bank should act as trustee or agent for both parties until the dispute was settled either by the judgment of The Hague Court or by agreement.[69] Garner in turn proposed to Mosaddeq that the oil operations be conducted, as an interim measure, under the management of a neutral top executive group selected by the bank, which would be free to engage and discharge other personnel as it considered necessary and without restriction in the choice of nationalities. Mosaddeq rejected the proposal. It was his view that the bank could intervene only as an agent of the Iranian government.[70]

George Middleton, the British chargé in Tehran, wrote to London that the shah clung to the hope that a settlement might be reached. However, "Mosaddeq's summary rejection of the Bank's principles and his refusal to give the assurances requested for the continuance of U.S. aid must weaken his position with the shah, and help the opposition."[71] "If he [Mosaddeq] persists in these demands" Eden informed Franks in Washington, "there is little hope of his accepting any detailed proposals from the Bank for an interim solution, but we are nevertheless encouraging the Bank to complete a comprehensive scheme but to hold it in reserve for a successor Government to Musaddiq's."[72]

On 9 January 1952 Radio Tehran broadcast the text of a note from Mosaddeq to be handed to the British later in the afternoon. "According to the reports received by the government," read the note, "the definite activities and interference of British government officials in Iran have been recently intensified. My government is not prepared to tolerate any more such undesirable behavior. . . . Unless officials of your government in Iran change their conduct, my government will be obliged to adopt severe decisions to put an end to this undesirable state of affairs."[73] At 2:30 P.M., the note was read to a congregation of foreign press from which British correspondents were excluded. At 5 P.M. it was sent to the British embassy by courier. Loy Henderson, who had replaced Grady as U.S. ambassador, met with Mosaddeq the next day to object to the tone of the note. The British, who returned the note as unacceptable, concluded from this exchange that Mosaddeq had little to go on, that the challenge of the note was intended to deflect the opposition's interpellation scheduled for 22 January, and that they should expect follow-ups, perhaps the closing of the British consulates or possibly breaking off of diplomatic relations. And indeed Mosaddeq ordered all British consulates closed on 12 January 1952.[74]

The Americans became increasingly nervous as the bank negotiations stalled and Anglo-Iranian relations worsened. The Democrats would soon have a presidential election on their hands. China had gone communist under their watch, and the Republicans never ceased scolding them for it. In Iran, the economy was deteriorating; political leaders were at each others' throats; Mosaddeq was clinging to his position; the shah seemed out of the picture; and the Soviets were aggressively active, all of which prompted Acheson to tell Ambassador Franks that he worried the Iranian situation was creating a serious danger for the West and that he had a plan he wished to discuss with the delegation that was to accompany Prime Minister Winston Churchill to Washington in mid-January.[75] Eden responded to Franks that preoccupation with China must not blind the United States to the fact that "for the maintenance of our own economic strength we must prefer no settlement with Persia to a bad one [such as the one suggested by the Americans]; and this even at the risk of increasing Communism in Persia."[76]

On 4 April 1952, the International Bank for Reconstruction and Development released a review of its negotiations on the Iranian oil, announcing that its mission on the Iranian oil problem had returned to Washington and that the negotiations had been recessed but not terminated. The bank, the announcement said, stood ready to assist in working out any practicable suggestions that offered a reasonable prospect of success.

■

Throughout the negotiations with the IBRD, the shah remained on the sidelines. Mosaddeq met with him before leaving for the meeting of the Security Council in October, and Baqer Kazemi, the acting prime minister in Mosaddeq's absence, kept him abreast of Mosaddeq's activities in New York. On his return to Tehran in late November 1951, Mosaddeq went to the court to report on his trip. But beyond what protocol required, the shah was not admitted to the oil negotiations. He did not meet with the bank delegation or with Mosaddeq during the delegation's stay in Tehran. Ambassador Shepherd, who met with the shah on 15 January 1952 before leaving Tehran at the end of his term of service, observed to Eden, "the shah was merely a spectator and was very little if at all active to guide affairs."[77] Indeed, a parallel drama began to play out for the British, involving former prime minister Qavam, as will be discussed in chapter 7. But in this as well as in their opinion of the shah, the British were misguided.

The shah continued his self-education, seeking to learn about the global disposition of oil companies' power by going over the grounds of the oil dispute with experts, politicians, and diplomats. He continued to believe Mosaddeq was the only man able to bring the nationalization issue to a satisfactory end, provided a way was found for him to save face. He protested to the British and the Americans and tried to find openings where none seemed to exist. He believed that because Mosaddeq was the constitutional leader of the government, he was obligated to support him as long as the prime minister enjoyed the confidence of the Majlis. He had discussions on this matter with his advisers, including Ala, who argued that Mosaddeq was slowly undoing the crown's constitutional rights and duties. But the shah still remained supportive of Mosaddeq for several reasons, not least of which was that he had appointed him prime minister and it was his custom to support his officials and to defend them to others as long as they held office. Nonetheless, it began to seem to him that Mosaddeq knew what he did not want but not what he wanted or, more precisely, how he could get what he wanted.[78] Mosaddeq said he wanted "to make sure that no other body or foreign power would be in a position to exercise the influence in Iran that the Anglo-Iranian Company had possessed."[79] His intent, the shah thought, was unimpeachable. The problem was with the assessment of power, control, and responsibility. In early 1952 Mosaddeq did not believe that Iranian oil had already been largely made up for by oil from other countries. If the British did not need Iran's oil, he reasoned, why did Britain not leave Iran alone? Why annoy Iran by pushing the case in The Hague? When pressed about the future, Mosaddeq would say vaguely that "things should be arranged in such a way as to enable the Government of Iran to carry on even without oil revenue if it were to be stopped."[80]

The shah, on the other hand, was keenly aware that the British and American companies together had replaced the Iranian oil and that they controlled the market. He also believed oil was needed to spur Iran's development. Government might carry on without oil, but economic development, to which he was deeply committed, would be severely damaged without it. For him, therefore, "economy without oil" was a faulty and dangerous slogan. Moreover, he did not think of the British or their power the way Mosaddeq did. It was a generational divide. To Mosaddeq, the British had near occult powers. They would have to be kept away or they would control things and make mischief. He could not readmit the British experts, Mosaddeq told Kingsley Martin of the *New Statesman*. "He had been congratulated by many countries because Iran had gained her independence with the departure of the British. If British experts were to come back, this success would not be real."[81] The shah too was habitually on the lookout for British tricks, but he did not think the game with them was zero-sum, all or nothing. They were powerful, treacherous, wily, and intransigent, but they were a fact of life that could be handled. The trouble, as he saw it, was that Mosaddeq had gotten off on the wrong foot, obstinate, bent on closing doors when wisdom demanded the opposite. Mosaddeq won accolades in the Security Council and among the peoples in Iran and the Third World, but none of it led to the resolution of the problem. On the contrary, the oil issue increasingly became a threat to Iran's security both at home and abroad. The Tudeh Party on the left and the radical Islamists on the right were becoming increasingly powerful and difficult to handle, while others, including the National Front, were weakening by comparison. There were popular demonstrations in support of nationalization, and the most impressive of these were organized and led by the Tudeh and the Islamic right around Ayatollah Abolqasem Kashani and in the bazaar. To deal with the situation Mosaddeq needed power, only some of which he could mobilize in the street. To mobilize the state's power, essential to his struggle, he needed authority, the sources of which were the Majlis and the shah.

The Sixteenth Majlis, however, though it had supported Mosaddeq at the beginning, had become restive at the end. Minority deputies attacked Mosaddeq over the growing strength of the Tudeh, or the closing of the opposition papers, or the use of martial law, and sought to destabilize his government in whatever way they could, including seeking political asylum in the Majlis, remaining there until the end of the session on 19 February 1952. The elections for the Seventeenth Majlis, which were carried out by Mosaddeq's interior ministry in January 1952, turned violent in many districts and ended in the election of deputies not to Mosaddeq's liking. Seeing how the results were going, he stopped the elections before they were completed, complaining that in most districts elections had not been clean or free. The fact was that, except in Tehran and several larger cities where the National Front had the votes, in most electoral districts across the country landlords and tribal khans had always elected to the Majlis whomever they pleased. Although Reza Shah had managed to get the more respected of them to act as real representatives of their constituencies and after the war the Allies had wielded much influence, still many of the same continued to get elected. Mosaddeq's "free" elections would yield the same results. The new Majlis Mosaddeq got elected was in fact not substantially different in form or composition. On 17 December 1951, shortly before the new elections, Mosaddeq had announced that this was to be the first election in Iran's constitutional history that was free of domestic or foreign intervention, but on 28 April, a day after the shah opened the Seventeenth Majlis, he condemned the elections he himself had conducted as fraudulent.[82] He got into fights with his ministers for not producing the right results, so that the minister of the interior responsible for the elections, Amir Teymur Kalali, resigned. Kalali was a Khurasan tribal leader who had been invited to join Mosaddeq's government because he had opposed the Gass-Golshaiyan proposal. Mosaddeq's candidate for the presidency of the Majlis, Abdollah Moazzami, lost to Seyyed Hassan Emami, the Imam Jom'eh of Tehran, who was close to the shah.[83] In the Senate Seyyed Hassan Taqizadeh, not Mossadeq's favorite, was reelected president.

■

The shah and Mosaddeq had an extended discussion on 10 March. The next day, the shah told Middleton, the British chargé, that Mosaddeq had put through the nationalization law and it was up to him to bring it to conclusion. The country was now facing bankruptcy and he, the shah, felt that matters could not be allowed to drift. He had therefore asked Mosaddeq exactly what his program was. Mosaddeq had answered that he "only wished to settle the oil question and resign." The shah then launched into several substantive questions about management and price, which he suggested might be agreeable to Mosaddeq. "As regards price," the shah said, "it was a question of showing that a reasonable profit was accruing to Iran from the refinery; the latter was the main asset which distinguished Iran from her neighbors, and the Prime Minister could not justify to the people an arrangement which only included a refining fee of a few cents a barrel." The question of management "might be settled if a phrase such as 'under power of attorney for the Persian Government' could be accepted instead of the phrase 'for account of the Persian Government' to which the Bank had taken exception." The question of admitting British experts, he said, was better left to the Seventeenth Majlis when it came to ratify the draft agreement with the bank. "Mosaddeq would retire before then and leave it to the judgment of the people." The shah then said he wished to appeal to Britain to make some adjustment on the question of prices. He understood that prices could not be out of synch with the market. But "Mosaddeq's position in the matter was largely a political one and he wished to ask whether [England] could not allow a larger profit on refining even if margin on crude had to be correspondingly reduced."[84]

In late May Mosaddeq presented Iran's case before the International Court of Justice in The Hague in familiar terms: Iran had been a pawn in the Great Power game; Britain had dominated Iran's politics; the AIOC was an implement of British policy in Iran; the 1933 Agreement was made without popular mandate and therefore was invalid; the AIOC and the British government profited, and the British admiralty used Iranian oil to develop the British navy at Iran's expense; the British never actually accepted the principle of nationalization and conspired against Iran even after the fact of nationalization, to inflict military and economic pressure on Iran, to cause boycott of Iran by Western oil trusts, and to deny Iran access to AIOC accounts while the company treated its Iranian employees shamefully, like "domestic animals," and kept them out of technical posts.

The British rebuttals were also the same. After some bizarre statements about how Britain had protected Iran against Russia over the past century by, among other things, entering into the 1907 Agreement, they argued more seriously that the 1933 Agreement was passed by the Majlis and that every Iranian government since, except Mosaddeq's, had recognized its validity and claimed the advantages accruing to Iran from it. Iran could not nationalize the oil industry unilaterally when she had bound herself formally under the "1933 Concession Agreement" not to cancel the agreement by legislation but to refer the disputes to arbitration. The talk about compensation without British involvement in the oil industry was nonsense because no compensation could be made unless the oil industry was run efficiently. England had accepted the principle of nationalization, but only as a basis for negotiation. Were it not for the contract to the admiralty, AIOC would actually have had great difficulty in disposing of the large quantity of fuel oil available and consequently Iran would have received far smaller sums in royalty. The economic measures Mosaddeq spoke of were designed not to hurt Iran but to protect the British economy. Large oil companies were not buying Iran's nationalized oil, not because of British pressure, but because they were not interested in buying and selling oil in penny packets. And finally, the AIOC had given Iran proper access to its accounts' audited copies and, contrary to Mosaddeq's allegations, treated its Iranian employees decently, as recorded in the reports of the International Labor Office Mission in 1950.[85]

By the time Mosaddeq returned from The Hague in June, the economy had further deteriorated. The monthly deficit on day-to-day expenditure was 460 million rials, according to the treasurer-general. Internal sources of revenue, including the Bank Melli's lending capacity, had almost dried up. Drawing on gold reserves or issuing new notes required legislative authority, and the latter option would most likely throw the economy into a rapid upward inflationary spiral. The government needed money and looked to the Americans for succor, but now the Americans were looking to a post-Mosaddeq administration. Iran's current needs, both the British and Americans thought, had built up to levels that might be assuaged but not satisfied solely through foreign aid. The conclusion was that a critical stage was fast approaching in the political and financial situation in Iran and a change of government had become a real possibility.[86]

7

Toward the Abyss

On 17 January 1952 Ambassador Shepherd sent Anthony Eden a cable informing him that he had had a long audience with the shah on 15 January, during
which the shah had mostly asked him questions rather than offering opinions,
and when he had offered an opinion, he had defended Mosaddeq. But he had
made two substantive statements worthy of notice. First, the Allies had been
wrong in forcing his father to abdicate and in invading Iran as they had, because
no one knew as he did that his father was not pro-German. And second, the
opposition to Mosaddeq had no cohesion, and of the two major personalities
among his opponents — Qavam and Seyyed Zia Tabatabai — the first "had come
to the conclusion that he would not be able to do anything" and the second "was
certainly out of the running."[1]

In late January Eden received an enigmatic telegram signed "Peter," stating
that the sender had seen "my friend" in Monte Carlo and was much impressed
"by his propositions and reasons for his present procedures and requirements."
He then stated that he had a more complete message and urged Eden to instruct
the British consul in Nice to accept this full message and pass it on to Eden
in cipher. "Am convinced it is imperative this opportunity should not be lost,"
Peter solemnly wrote.[2]

On 30 January, Eden wrote his parliamentary deputy Anthony Nutting that
he had received "a very odd telegram," which he believed must have been from
Kenneth de Courcy. De Courcy had asked Eden several weeks before to see a
"certain Persian" in London. Eden was out of town at the time, and Nutting
had taken the matter up but had not found "the man in question." Eden now
asked Nutting to take up the matter again and decide whether or not the foreign
secretary should be brought into it.[3]

De Courcy then sent a telegram to Nutting, urgently asking him to inform
Eden "personally" that the telegram signed "Peter" was indeed his and that he

was convinced "immediate action as suggested may prove extremely profitable." Nutting did as requested. By this time, of course, everyone involved knew the person in question was Ahmad Qavam. With Shepherd's observations on his mind, Eden was noncommittal, which led de Courcy to complain that Eden's telegram "would appear to confirm our friend's opinion" about British lack of resolution. The "friend" did not trust Eden's representatives in his locality, namely Nice, and refused to make any move without direct guarantees from Eden personally. He would "doubtless consider his fears well founded and convey them widely." "I am astonished," de Courcy complained, "that you refuse even to study his observations and proposals." In these circumstances, he, de Courcy, would "prefer to withdraw altogether." He had no doubt of the seriousness of the friend's proposals and hoped "we shall not finally lose our vast interest."[4]

Back in England, de Courcy forwarded to Nutting his impressions of Qavam, who, he said, might be completely useless but had nonetheless made "a fairly strong impression" on him. Qavam, observed de Courcy, "is a Persian politician and probably wholly unreliable; but as our situation there [in Iran] does not seem to be particularly good I should have thought [Qavam's] proposals were worth investigating."[5] He intended to drop out of this matter now, he said.

Qavam had met with de Courcy in Monte Carlo in the latter's apartment, warned that de Courcy "was unprepared for anything short of most serious proposals." Qavam was serious. He told de Courcy Iran must come to terms with Great Britain if catastrophe was to be averted. He was convinced he could easily take power into his hands, but he could not succeed if Great Britain did not support him and he was not convinced that it would. He would not be satisfied with promises from the British embassy in Tehran. He would accept only the foreign secretary's direct assurances by meeting him personally in Paris; if the foreign secretary was unable to come, then he would accept a meeting with Lord Salisbury, then the leader of the House of Lords and also Lord Privy Seal. Qavam was prepared to take power and to negotiate an oil agreement very favorable to England if England, on her part, supported him "by such economic aid as may be necessary." He might be obliged by the conditions existing in Iran to "appear somewhat anti-British in his first utterances," but the British should understand the reason and abide by a secret agreement with him. He intended to form "a very strong government," but he feared England might betray him "to appease Russia." Did England really mean to be firm, following "a strong British policy," and how did England stand vis-à-vis the United States? Finally, he did not like or trust the shah. How could he be assured that the British would not work with the shah against him?[6]

Qavam was under the impression that de Courcy was a high official at the foreign office, and when he did not receive a response for some time, he concluded that the British did not favor him or his project. But he soon was informed otherwise. Julian Amery, a Conservative MP and a persistent supporter of the Qajars, got wind of de Courcy's contact with Qavam and asked Nutting if he should visit the old man in Monte Carlo. Nutting discouraged him, suggesting that Qavam was not serious or he would have sent the British government a message before leaving Tehran.[7] Amery did not give up, however. He contacted Selwyn Lloyd, the minister of state for foreign affairs, who encouraged him to go ahead because, Lloyd suggested, Qavam's return to power would be "a change for the better." Amery was, however, to make sure Qavam understood that he did not speak for the British government.

Amery met with Qavam in the latter's hotel in Paris around the 20th of March. Qavam was not alone; he had also invited Prince Hamid Qajar, "the Pretender to the throne," as Amery reported. The invitation may have been with Amery's prior knowledge and approval, though Amery does not say so in his report. Amery knew and was fond of Prince Hamid (alias Captain David Drummond) and had in fact sought to have him reinstated on the Iranian throne when Reza Shah resigned, if Hamid's father, Prince Hassan (whom Avery's father, Leopold, supported) proved unacceptable. But the matter had become irrelevant once Mohammad Reza Shah was formally sworn in as king.

As Lloyd had instructed, Amery assured Qavam that the British government "would regard his return to power as a change for the better," and that the American and British views "were very much closer than they had been." The International Bank negotiations, Amery said, had gone a long way "to disillusion the Americans about Dr. Mosaddeq."[8] Qavam said he intended to return to Iran in about two weeks to take over power. He could not be absolutely sure of how he would accomplish this until he studied the situation in Tehran. The oil issue had to be solved, probably within the terms of the nationalization law. But this was not a problem, he believed, given that Herbert Morrison, the foreign secretary in the previous Labor government, "had publicly accepted the principle of nationalization." He then outlined the essential principles of a settlement: the refinery should work to full capacity, which would require the employment of several British technicians at Abadan; the British should have full control of foreign sales of the oil; and the terms of the agreement should be so presented as not to prejudice British oil agreements with other Middle Eastern countries.

Qavam now raised the question of the dynasty. He did not trust the shah, having suffered from his intrigues before. It might be necessary for him to change the regime and restore Prince Hamid, because a republic would not suit the Iranians. "What would be the British reaction to this?" he asked Amery. "We [have] been rather disappointed by the present shah," replied Amery, "and it would be a matter of complete indifference to us whether he stayed or went." At this point Amery asked Prince Hamid to leave the room, and when alone he asked Qavam if he was serious about the regime change. Qavam was serious. "Admittedly," said Qavam, "the old dynasty had ended badly, but Prince Hamid was a much better man than the present shah and his English education and connections might make for better relations with London." Amery was left with the impression that Qavam was "attracted by the idea of putting in a shah who would be dependent upon him, at least in the early stages of his reign, and who might provide a useful link with London."[9]

Amery asked Selwyn Lloyd to show his letter to Anthony Eden, "as I have written to him previously about Qavam."[10] Lloyd apparently did. On 16 April Eden cabled a telegram "of particular secrecy" to the embassy in Tehran, sending a copy of Amery's report and advising that Qavam would return to Iran to take power and that he would get in touch with the embassy soon after his return. On the question of the dynasty, however, Eden demurred:

> While we certainly have not been impressed by the shah's recent performance, we find it hard to believe that we should gain by an attempt to restore the Qajars, which would probably split the country or at least very seriously weaken it. Moreover, we are by no means certain that if it came to a show of force between the shah and Qavam the latter would win, and we should be blamed by the shah even if we had in fact given Qavam no encouragement. . . . I hope that you will have an opportunity to make it clear to Qavam that we could not countenance any attempt on his part to restore the Qajars and that on the contrary we should expect him to do his best to help support the shah. We for our part would do our best to further good relations between the shah and his prime minister.[11]

Events in Iran between January and April 1952 had caused a change of attitude in London and Washington. A new government in Iran began to seem a possibility. At Acheson's suggestion, Paul Nitze of the U.S. Department of State had met with the British in London in February to discuss the Iranian situation. At that time it was agreed that although the economic and financial situation of the country was becoming increasingly serious, Mosaddeq's position had been strengthened during the past two months and that "there was little or no hope of useful intervention by the shah."[12] Mosaddeq, they agreed, would likely continue as prime minister for the foreseeable future. By June the expectations had changed somewhat. The new Majlis was increasingly hostile, though Mosaddeq still controlled a majority and could use it to obstruct action. The opposition remained sharply divided. And the shah was weak and disinclined to take action either through the Senate or on his own. "In these circumstances it may well be necessary to find means of forcing the Shah to take action," A. D. M. Ross wrote on 23 June to Eden in a brief for an upcoming meeting with Acheson. "This might, in our view, entail a joint Anglo-American approach."[13]

In their meeting on 28 June Acheson told Eden that according to the most recent U.S. assessment, August was the most likely month Mosaddeq might fall. Consequently, it was important to have some idea of the form an agreement with a successor government might take. "Mosaddeq would not fall of his own accord," said Eden. "He would have to be pushed and the one person who could do this was the Shah." At some stage, Eden said, it might be necessary for "the British and US representatives in Tehran jointly to impress on the Shah the need for some sort of action of this sort."[14]

On 6 July the Seventeenth Majlis was officially declared ready for work. As protocol demanded, Mosaddeq resigned, but the next day in a special session the Majlis renominated him by fifty-two votes out of the sixty-five seats that had been filled in the interrupted election. This was a great victory, which owed much to the popular support the prime minister enjoyed. The Senate, however, demurred. Only fourteen of sixty senators supported Mosaddeq; the rest were waiting to vote after they heard Mosaddeq's program, the Senate president reported to the shah on the 9th. Mosaddeq now refused to continue because of the Senate's refusal to support his nomination. The shah asked the senators to come to terms with the prime minister. An agreement was quickly reached, and on the 10th the shah signed the *farman,* or order, naming Mosaddeq prime minister. On the 12th, Mosaddeq asked the Majlis to give his government full authority on economic and financial matters for six months. Unless the authority was granted, he would not continue as prime minister. The demand met with much opposition, not only from his opponents, but also from his erstwhile supporters in the National Front. On the 16th he met with the shah and over a long conversation demanded to be given the war portfolio. As long as the armed forces were not under his command, his enemies would use it to undermine his authority, he told the shah. On this the shah stood his ground. It was a tradition he would not violate, he said. Mosaddeq resigned, stating, "The experience accumulated during the past year teaches that to be successful in the work of government requires that this devoted person personally take charge of the war ministry. Since this requirement has not met with Your Majesty's *[zat-e shah-aneh]* approval, it is of course preferable to have the future government formed by an individual who enjoys royal confidence and is able to carry out the royal purpose. Under the circumstances, it is not possible to conclude victoriously the struggles the Iranian nation has embarked upon."[15] Court Minister Hossein Ala informed the Majlis that the shah had accepted the prime minister's resignation and asked the Majlis to nominate a successor. On the 17th the Majlis met in a secret session and with a vote of forty out of forty-two declared for Qavam. The shah then summoned "the Most Noble Excellency Ahmad Qavam" to serve as the prime minister, in this phrase unceremoniously reinvesting him with the title he had taken away a short time back.[16]

Since his return to Tehran in April, Qavam had worked hard to mobilize support in the parliament, but he had succeeded only partially in the Senate and, despite the vote in his favor, minimally in the Majlis. The British had supported him secretly, depending more on his political acumen to win over the deputies than their own willingness or ability to push. Qavam was able to win the vote on 17 July because Mosaddeq had closed all other possibilities. But he misread the political climate, his own popularity, and the support he would get from his old friends—or the British or the shah. In the summer of 1952, Mosaddeq and his supporters—both those genuinely with him and those with him only because it suited their purpose—were in control of the streets. Moreover, he was loved. He symbolized hope, self-respect, and a glimpse of greatness lost over the centuries of stagnation. For many Iranians, recapturing even a sense of that now faded merit was worth the struggle. Qavam, on the other hand, offered defeat, a return to reality, an acceptance of the practical, the sense of worthlessness. Contrary to what he believed, he commanded little. The shah never gave him his support, and therefore the military remained noncommittal. The British, except for de Courcy, Amery, and a few others on the margin, did not put much weight on his chances to succeed. The speech read on his behalf on the radio was like a drum, sound and fury outside, vacant inside. The threat of military courts, imprisonments, and violence fell on deaf ears. The ship captain commanded setting a new course, but the crew would not hearken.

The five days of Qavam's premiership were spent in riots, demonstrations, and violence, uniting the left and the right against him and, at least momentarily, for Mosaddeq. The military was called out to quell the revolt but to no avail. The shah would not countenance bloodshed, and so he ordered his generals not to shoot. Nevertheless many were killed and many more were wounded in the rioting. Qavam asked for special powers and command of the military, but the shah refused to grant them. By 21 July, the strikes and demonstrations had spread across the country. The shah asked Qavam to resign and instructed Court Minister Ala to canvass the Majlis deputies for a new nominee. It was a foregone conclusion: in the Majlis sixty-one deputies out of sixty-four voted for Mosaddeq; in the Senate thirty-three out of forty-one senators voted for him.[17] In the aftermath of these events, the shah descended to the nadir of his prestige and power.

■

On 20 July, the day Qavam's fate was sealed, the International Court at The Hague ruled it had no jurisdiction in the case of the oil dispute between England and Iran. A triumphant Mosaddeq called in George Middleton, the British chargé, and gave him a dressing-down on how things had turned out. "You have failed at the Security Council, you have failed at The Hague, and you have failed to overthrow my government. Your legal position is hopeless, and you are dealing with a united Iranian people firm in their resolve to maintain the nationalization laws. I want to know whether England wishes to settle the oil dispute or prefers to let it drag on indefinitely." The only outstanding issue to be settled was compensation, said Mosaddeq, and he hoped the British were now ready to start discussion. He then authorized Middleton to convey to his government that he would be prepared to seek the agreement of the Majlis and the Senate to a form of arbitration whereby each government would name its arbitrator, "who would in turn agree on a third sur-arbitre." The two governments would abide by the decision of the arbitral board. No mention would be made of the 1933 Agreement.[18] The matter was extremely urgent, said Mosaddeq, asking for an answer by 28 July. Middleton failed to meet this deadline, causing, or giving an excuse to, Mosaddeq to withdraw the offer.

To Eden, Mosaddeq's offer was not much anyway—"vague and unpalatable as might be expected"—but he wanted to coordinate his policy with the State Department before he answered Mosaddeq.[19] The Americans, by contrast, were impressed. Nitze argued that Mosaddeq might not be "a reliable bulwark against communism but there was nothing else; any change would be to the left."[20] Acheson suggested the United States and United Kingdom make a joint offer to the Iranian government. The British ambassador to the United States, Oliver Franks, wrote Eden that the Americans were beginning to think Britain was prepared to offer nothing that Iran could possibly accept and indeed were of a mind now to go it alone.[21] After much unpleasant communication, Churchill and Truman agreed on the following joint proposal within Iran's nine-point nationalization law.

    1. There shall be submitted to the International Court of Justice the question of compensation to be paid in respect of the nationalization of the enterprise of

the Anglo-Iranian Oil Company in Persia, having regard to the legal position of the parties existing immediately prior to nationalization and to all claims and counterclaims of both parties;

2. Suitable representatives shall be appointed to represent the Persian Government and the Anglo-Iranian Oil Company in negotiations for making arrangements for the flow of the Persian oil to world markets;

3. If the Persian Government agrees to the proposals in the foregoing two paragraphs, it is understood that:

    a. Representatives of the AIOC will seek arrangements for the movement of oil already stored in Persia, and as agreements are reached upon price, and as physical conditions of loading permit, appropriate payment will be made for such quantities of oil as can be moved;

    b. Her Majesty's government will relax restrictions on exports to Persia and on Persia's use of sterling; and

    c. The United States Government will make an immediate grant of $10,000,000 to the Persian Government to assist in their budgetary problem.[22]

On 27 August, Loy Henderson and Middleton took the gist of the joint message to Mosaddeq, who rejected it out of hand.[23] That evening Henderson and Middleton met jointly with Court Minister Ala and impressed upon him "the folly of Mosaddeq's course," and "the importance of not allowing it to become known that Mosaddeq had in fact rejected a message from the President of the United States and the Prime Minister of Great Britain."[24] Middleton had met with the shah the day before and "had done [his] best to persuade His Majesty that the offer [they] were about to make was the most generous possible and that Persia could not afford to reject it."[25] Ala now promised to talk to the shah, and as far as Middleton was concerned, it was the shah who prevailed on Mosaddeq to reconsider and to immediately publish his decision rejecting the message. Churchill wrote Truman suggesting it had been a mistake for the envoys to engage Mosaddeq in a lengthy discussion. "They should have presented our very carefully considered message and withdrawn as soon as possible with all diplomatic courtesy." Mosaddeq no doubt "feels very acutely the pressure of a United States–British message from us both." The message should be published immediately as it is. "We have decided to offer what is right and fair. Let the world judge."[26]

The joint message was formally delivered to Mosaddeq on 30 August. That evening the message and the gist of the meetings were reported on the radio. The Majlis and the Senate were called to prepare a reply. For Churchill and Eden, the game had already been won, because the joint message told the region and the world that America and England were together, allies now as they had been during the war, "a most valuable demonstration to the whole Middle East of Anglo-American solidarity," Eden wrote his envoy in the United States.[27]

On 3 September 1952, in a press conference in Washington, Acheson confirmed that the Churchill-Truman Joint Proposal accepted the nationalization of the oil industry in Iran as a fact and the nine-point law implementing the nationalization of the Iran oil industry as the framework for the Anglo-Iranian Oil Company to make arrangements for the flow of Iranian oil to world markets. The statement differed from the previous six proposals made to Iran in that it accepted not only Iran's right to ownership of the oil resources and the paraphernalia of the oil industry, but also — in principle — the two other demands that Iran insisted on: control of the operations and of marketing. The proposal agreed that the National Iranian Oil Company (NIOC) would take control of the administration of the oil industry. An international consortium would be established to provide the national company with the needed expertise and technology. To expedite the flow of oil, the consortium would buy the Iranian oil and market it, while providing the opportunity for NIOC gradually to enter the international market as an independent agent as it became able to do so.[28]

Mosaddeq rejected — informally, he later claimed to Henderson and Middleton — the joint proposal in a statement to the press on 7 September. Since the International Court had declared itself incompetent in the matter of Iranian oil, the only competent court was an Iranian one, he said. He would accept arbitration by the International Court only if the terms of claims for compensation were declared. He complained of Britain's high-handed attitude, which came close to insulting the Iranian nation. His government would never submit to such unfair proposals. He took up the articles one by one and found each wanting in logic, equity, and civility.[29] The next day, he told Middleton Iran would never agree to any compensation terms beyond the value of the company's physical assets on the ground, including the oil in stock at Abadan, at the time of nationalization.

By the end of 1952 xenophobia had reached a new peak, extending beyond things and people English. Iran broke off relations with Great Britain on 22 October 1952. On 23 December, Foreign Minister Hossein Fatemi announced a decree issued by Mosaddeq forbidding the reassignment "of foreign nationals who have been serving in this country whatever their titles before the enactment of this decree." Only those the minister of foreign affairs and the foreign affairs committee of the Majlis decided had helped improve relations between Iran and their respective governments might be allowed to return. Those who had interfered in Iranian affairs would be forbidden to enter Iranian territory. The decree also forbad establishing any consulate in any part of Iran unless proposed by the foreign minister and approved by the Majlis foreign relations committee."[30]

Meanwhile, economic conditions had deteriorated badly, making all factions nervous. Over the next few days Mosaddeq met with Henderson almost daily, haggling over compensation and U.S. financial assistance, either direct or by purchasing Iranian oil.[31] But not much could be accomplished in the United States as the new Eisenhower administration would take office on 20 January 1953 and needed time to get into the stream of negotiations. The British wished to get Eisenhower and his designated secretary of state, John Foster Dulles, on their side. They had been vexed by what appeared to them to be the gullibility of the Democratic Truman administration, which they thought was the main reason the Iranian government had been able to convince the Iranian people that sooner or later England would have to submit to Iran's terms and that America would be instrumental in forcing her to do so. The American attitude, the British contended, had reached the Iranian government and "greatly helped to stiffen the Prime Minister's obduracy." The Republican victory, however, changed the mood in England. The preliminary talks with the coming administration gave them reason to believe the U.S. position was likely to firm up, especially after 28 January, when Henderson wrote Dulles that he and Mosaddeq had very nearly reached a deadlock.[32]

By mid-February, the British and the new U.S. administration had come to a preliminary understanding. On 20 February, Henderson handed Mosaddeq a proposal for specific compensation for nationalization. Iran was to make payments annually for twenty years of a maximum of 25 percent of gross receipts from oil exports; if more was needed, the rest would be paid by annual deliveries of crude oil or oil products as might be necessary. Mosaddeq argued for 25 percent of net receipts (which he said could be arbitrarily put as 80 percent of gross receipts), but he could not accept the inclusion of the phrase "loss of the Company's enterprise in Iran," or "the British coal law as a basis for determining the amount of compensation owed the company." Henderson, surprised, told him it was regrettable that Mosaddeq would now find unacceptable what he himself had insisted upon in the past. In his judgment this was the most the British could concede, and the U.S. government found it fair and equitable. The happiness and prosperity of eighteen million Iranians depended on the decision Mosaddeq would make. Henderson hoped that "Mosaddeq would make his advisers aware of the grave responsibilities which they also had and that should they begin emasculating the proposals, he would inform them that grave harm to Iran might result from their actions."[33]

"The British do not want a settlement," Mosaddeq warned Henderson three days later, for they were completely aware that he could not accept a settlement that hinted at compensation for the company's future profits. Furthermore, Iran would never accept economic bondage for twenty years. Mosaddeq now wanted to know if the terms of reference could be changed to read as follows: "To determine the sums required to provide compensation to the company as a result of the Iranian oil nationalization laws of March and May 1951." Henderson said he did not know, but asked whether that would mean that if the British accepted Mosaddeq's proposal, Mosaddeq would agree to the rest. Mosaddeq refused to make any commitments. Dulles then instructed Henderson to refrain from discussing any change in phraseology at this time.[34]

The summer and fall of 1952 were hellish for the shah, the nadir of his power and prestige. For him, the Qavam fiasco represented more than losing in a political game, in a way even more than losing the crown, for he came face to face with a possibility he had not entertained in the past: Could it be that his countrymen rejected him? After Qavam, attacks on him grew to new heights. He was called all sorts of derogatory names—stooge, lackey, scourge of the nation. He felt increasingly isolated. The prime minister, now armed with plenary powers and the defense portfolio, retired many of his generals, rejected the Churchill-Truman proposal, broke off relations with England, and caused the shah to sign a constitutionally dubious law that effectively closed the Senate by reinterpreting the Constitution to mean a two-year term for the second legislative body. Mosaddeq's reason for closing the Senate was the senators' disapproval of his policies, especially the plenary powers he had demanded and gained right after his return to power. The trigger was the Senate's refusal to agree to the Majlis bills pardoning Prime Minister Razmara's assassin and expropriating Qavam's property. The Senate tried to stand up to Mosaddeq's attack by assembling in the residence of one of the members, announcing itself ready to function to the end of its four-year term and declaring that it considered laws passed without its approval unconstitutional.[35] The shah's signing of the Majlis bill, however, took the wind out of the senators' sails. In the meantime, Mosaddeq was using his plenary powers to introduce significant changes in the country's judiciary, legislature, finances, and administration.

The shah's powerlessness and Mosaddeq's energetic use of his powers alerted several of the prime minister's politically powerful allies to initially warn and subsequently oppose him. Mozaffar Baqai, the leader of the Toilers Party and one of the initiators of the National Front, was one of the first to break with Mosaddeq. Baqai took Mosaddeq to task on the floor of the Majlis on the draconian "social security" (i.e., national security) law that Mosaddeq had used his special plenary authority to promulgate on 21 October 1952. The law gave the police and the martial law administrator in Tehran and the provinces power to arrest anyone who "encouraged" workers and employees of organizations falling under the labor law or, alternatively, any government employees to strike or otherwise disrupt the normal flow of work; furthermore, such individuals were considered guilty unless the evidence provided by the police was disproved. The law was odious, giving unprecedented power to the police and practically annulling the presumption of innocence in a court of law.[36] Baqai begged Mosaddeq to reconsider, to no avail.

In response, in December Baqai introduced a bill that no decision based on the prime minister's plenary powers could lead to the closing or paralysis of the Majlis. Mosaddeq accused Baqai and his other opponents of playing the British hand: "Is it fair to stab the government in the back when Churchill is traveling to the United States and the Iranian government is busy with important negotiations?" he asked in a message broadcast on the radio. He was not about to close the Majlis, Mosaddeq assured the deputies. Two days later, on 6 January 1953, Mosaddeq asked the Majlis to extend his plenary powers for another year. This time several other deputies joined in objecting, including Ayatollah Kashani, Abolhassan Haerizadeh, and Hossein Makki, who was Tehran's first deputy and known as "the patriot soldier." "Extending Mosaddeq's plenary authority is against the constitution, and the deputies should not approve it," wrote Kashani to the Majlis. Haerizadeh, also a founding member of the National Front, called on Mosaddeq to join him in a rest asylum rather than seek power in this tumultuous world. "God save this country from the chameleons governing it," he said. Baqai called the extension "the death of the Constitution" and resigned from the National Front. "I would rather resign from the Majlis than vote for this bill," Makki declared, handing his resignation to the chair. He was returned to the Majlis by a group of bazaar merchants. In the meantime followers of Mosaddeq and Kashani fought each other in the streets of the capital and in the provinces.[37]

In the end the law passed, but it created an unbridgeable rift, casting asunder erstwhile allies. A few days after the vote Mosaddeq and Kashani met in neutral territory to make peace and to urge the people to remain united against the enemy. But events would prove the reconciliation a sham. Mosaddeq proceeded to arrest several military officers, including General Fazlollah Zahedi. He also sought to deprive the shah of the remainder of his constitutional powers through a committee of Majlis deputies formed ostensibly to reconcile the government and the court. The shah was conciliatory, causing Court Minister Ala to complain that his docility bordered on near complicity in letting the crown's constitutional powers and duties slip away. On 20 February 1953, the day he received the joint Churchill-Eisenhower proposal, Mosaddeq sent a message to the shah through his half-brother Heshmat-Dauleh Valatabar, accusing Hossein Ala and the imperial court of instigating antigovernment activities. Mosaddeq and the shah had talked earlier about the shah's travel to Europe by way of Iraq. He had not favored the shah's decision to go abroad, he said, but having consulted with several National Front leaders, he had concluded that the trip was better than his having to report to the people and to resort to a referendum.[38] The shah was stunned. He had gone out of his way to accommodate the prime minister. He had even suggested to Ala and others that the committee's reinterpretation of the crown's authority was probably within the constitutional framework. After all, it was the Majlis that, according to the Constitution, interpreted the Constitution. Besides, Mosaddeq was the legitimate prime minister as long as he enjoyed the confidence of the parliament. The shah therefore said nothing to Mosaddeq. He and his queen both were anxious to leave. He no longer was sure of his standing with the people. He needed time to weigh his situation, to reassess his relationship to the crown and the nation, to rediscover and reappropriate his persona, as it were. He ordered Ala not to divulge his plan and kept the secret himself.[39] The date of departure was set for 28 February. Mosaddeq issued a secret order to the appropriate authorities to prepare for the shah's voyage. It did not turn out as expected; too many people already knew of the intended trip.

On the 28th, Ala summoned Mosaddeq and his ministers to an audience with the shah—Mosaddeq at 1:00 P.M. and the ministers at 2. It was a short trip from Mosaddeq's house to the shah's. He saw nothing unusual on his way to the palace. He met with the shah and Queen Soraya, saying "what needed to be said" (arayezi arz shod).[40] What needed to be said was another complaint about the court in Ala's presence. "I was extremely unhappy to hear the prime minister disparage me to you after I had worked as diligently as I could over the past two years to bring understanding between the imperial court and the government," Ala wrote to the shah. "I was even more disappointed when the prime minister used the crown as a scapegoat, weakening and belittling it, to hide his own failures despite all the assistance and support Your Majesty had given him."[41] It was not a happy meeting for Mosaddeq or the shah.

The shah then met with the ministers and, according to Mosaddeq, reluctantly agreed also to meet with several Majlis deputies who had learned of his trip and come to ask him to reconsider. The shah then dismissed the ministers and deputies and left to say good-bye to his brothers. As Mosaddeq was walking in the courtyard toward the gate, he heard a crowd outside. He asked if there was another way out and was led out through the adjacent palace belonging to the shah's sister Shams. As he was being driven to his own house, he noticed several people running behind his car but being held back by the police. "Later I learned they wanted to do me in before the gate," Mosaddeq mused to his attorney, Colonel Jalil Bozorgmehr. The mob moved toward his house. Mosaddeq, his foreign minister, Hossein Fatemi, and his son Ahmad left the house for the army headquarters, where they picked up Chief of Staff General Mahmud Baharmast and drove to the Majlis. In the Majlis, Mosaddeq complained to a tumultuous meeting that military officers, including Baharmast, obeyed the commander-in-chief, the shah, not him. He would seek shelter in the Majlis.[42]

The shah had a different experience. Seyyed Mohammad Behbehani and Haj Aqa Baha'-ud-Din Nuri, two influential Tehran clerics, came to ask him not to leave. Ayatollah Kashani, president of the Majlis, sent a message to ask him on behalf of the Majlis to stay. "The news of Your Majesty's unexpected departure has bewildered the populace," he wrote the shah. The bazaar closed, demanding that the shah reconsider his decision. Demonstrations spread that same day to other cities and towns in the provinces. The shah had not expected the people at the palace gate to hail him and beg him to stay. The shouts outside were friendly—"Javid Shah!" (Shah forever), "Ham Shah ham Mosaddeq!" (Both the shah and Mosaddeq); the sound exhilarated him. The court issued a declaration that the shah, acceding to the people's will, had decided not to leave Iran. He came out of the Marble Palace and told the crowd in person he would remain, since "my going out of the country for health reasons does not meet with your approval."[43]

This day brought back to the shah a sense of legitimacy, the confidence that he was wanted, that the people supported him. According to Ala, he and the shah were both completely surprised when they were informed that a great crowd had gathered in front of the palace to prevent the shah from leaving the country. "How can anyone attribute this overflow of natural and sincere feeling to any motive but the people's love for their sovereign and their commitment to their country's national independence and territorial integrity?" At any rate, Ala continues, the imperial court had nothing to do with the event. "Indeed, as soon as the news got around, the same sincere demonstrations broke out across the nation." There may have been certain unsavory individuals, as is always the case in such gatherings, among the people who might have used the occasion for their purpose; however, "it was your exalted person who ordered the chief

of staff to take utmost care to protect His Excellency Dr. Mosaddeq's home."
For Ala the case was clear. "Dr. Mosaddeq has not yet learned that the shah is
loved by his people; that the crown has had power in this country since time
immemorial; and that the people have a special respect for the lofty office which
symbolizes our national unity. The best means of any government's success is
forthright sincerity with His Majesty and teamwork with the shah as the head
of the executive power."[44]

In Washington, Eisenhower and Dulles grew increasingly worried about Iran.
Dulles thought the situation was cloudy; the only clear picture was that the shah
seemed to have lost all authority and therefore the chances of Iran falling to the
communists were now greater than before. Eisenhower believed that something
needed to be done to save the country, but was not sure what. The British, for
their part, wanted the United States to stay away from oil. Eden suggested that
if the Americans wished to help keep Iran from falling into communist hands,
they would do better to give it small direct piecemeal assistance rather than
helping it sell its oil or lubricating the plant in Abadan. Otherwise it would be
very hard to mollify British public opinion or to preserve a united front.

On 8 March 1953 Eden and Dulles issued a joint communiqué, an important part of which raised again the question of the joint proposal. Eden said
the British government was determined to stand on the proposals presented to
Prime Minister Mosaddeq on 20 February.

> These proposals were the result of many conversations and careful study of all the
> factors involved. In the opinion of the United States Government these proposals
> are reasonable and fair. If agreed to: a) Iran would retain control of its own oil
> industry and of its own oil policies. b) The problem of compensation would be
> disposed of in such a way that there would be no sacrifice of principles which
> form the very base of international intercourse among free nations, and the pay-
> ment of compensation would be fully compatible with the rehabilitation of Iran's
> economy. c) Iran would have full opportunity to enter into arrangements whereby
> it could sell its oil in substantial quantities at competitive commercial prices in
> world markets. d) There would be placed at Iran's disposal sufficient funds, to be
> repaid in oil, to meet its immediate financial problems pending resumption of the
> flow of revenue from its oil industry.[45]

Mosaddeq had summoned Henderson to meet with him on 9 March to
discuss once again whether or not the British might indicate immediately the

amount of compensation they planned to request from the International Court of Justice. But when they met, he told Henderson there was no sense in continuing the meeting since the United Kingdom had declared it would stand on the proposals that as written were not acceptable to Iran. Given Eden's statement, the talks had for all practical purposes collapsed. He had therefore decided to ask the United States government the following formal questions, which he would send in a note to the ambassador in the afternoon: Would the United States government, in the absence of a compensation agreement and in order to aid Iran in solving its financial difficulty, be willing (1) to purchase over a period of years at prices to be agreed upon substantial quantities of Iranian oil; (2) to encourage private United States companies to buy oil from Iran and to otherwise aid Iran in producing and exporting its oil; and (3) to immediately grant a loan to Iran which would be paid back with oil. He had to ask these questions, Mosaddeq said, because "it was necessary that he and the people of Iran should know the amount of help they could expect from the United States before they decided what course of action they should pursue."[46]

On 20 March, the eve of the Iranian New Year, Mosaddeq delivered a message to the Iranian people outlining his reasons for rejecting the 20 February joint Anglo-American proposal. He said Iranians had no quarrel with the people of England and the rupture of diplomatic relations between the two governments did not necessitate a rupture between the two nations. The oil dispute had not been settled because, first, the British government counted on its lackeys in Iran to restore the former conditions so it would be able to settle the oil question as it pleased; and second, other international oil companies, duped by British propaganda, had come to believe that if the oil dispute was solved based on Iran's proposal, their interests might be jeopardized. Iran, he said, would keep trying to sell oil abroad and there was a good chance that serious purchasers would now come forward. At the same time, the door to negotiations with the British government would be kept open. Mosaddeq thanked God that the government's economic and financial affairs, though under stress, were still in order and that Iran stood on its feet. "I ask my dear compatriots," he said, "are the British proposals concerning compensation, which is the basis for the settlement of the oil problem, acceptable to the Iranian people?" If they were not acceptable, he asked rhetorically, what, then, was his government to be blamed for?[47] He then reiterated the same proposals he had made in the past on compensation and arbitration.

On the next day, the Commonwealth Relations Office sent out directives to U.K. High Commissioners around the world that the United Kingdom stood on its last offer, stressing the claim for the loss of AIOC's enterprise as a basis for compensation. "We regard it as useless to enter into direct negotiation as long as it is clear that Mosaddeq will not agree to a proper basis for compensation."[48]

■

By April, Tehran was buzzing with rumors of a coup. Mosaddeq declared for American ears that "any right-wing coup d'état against his government would only pave the way for certain Communist dictatorship. . . . It was to America's enlightened self-interest to see that Iran received enough economic support to prevent any further decline in living standards." The $44 million the United States had given Iran under its Point IV aid program and in military aid during his premiership was not enough, but he would not beg, he said to Homer Bigart of the *New York Herald Tribune*. Rather, he wanted the United States and Japan to buy the crude and refined oil he was offering them at half price. Reactionary governments in Iran would be short-lived, and no government would ever again dare let the British interfere in Iran's internal affairs.[49] The Russians and the British were undermining his government, he told Henderson in early May, and unless the United States came to his aid, Iran would go communist.[50]

The uncertainty in Iran continued to disturb Eisenhower, but he was not sure how best to approach Churchill in order to deal with it. On 8 May he wrote Churchill a *tour d'horizon* letter in which he complained about the difficulty of reaching a compromise on the oil issue. The British had rejected an offer by U.S. Treasury Secretary George Humphrey to British Chancellor of the Exchequer R. A. Butler for U.S. oil companies to buy out British interest in the "region" and to start anew. Eisenhower found it disturbing that Churchill apparently considered the situation hopeless and preferred "to face the probability of the whole area falling under Russian domination than to look for a new approach." He respected contracts and understood Churchill's conviction that further retreat might set loose repercussions around the world. Nonetheless, he wrote, "I still regard that area as one of potential disaster for the Western world."[51]

The frustration did not materially change the American position, however. Later in May Mosaddeq wrote Eisenhower that he had hoped the president would devote "attention of a more sympathetic character" to the Iranian situation but unfortunately "no change seems thus far to have taken place in the position of the American government." Iran was suffering at the hands of the AIOC and the British government but was grateful for "the aid heretofore granted by the government of the United States." The Iranian nation hoped that "with the help and assistance of the American government the obstacles placed in the way of the sale of Iranian oil can be removed, and that if the American government is not able to effect a removal of such obstacles, it can render effective economic assistance to enable Iran to utilize its other resources."[52] But Eisenhower would not comply. The United States, the president wrote back in July, would not extend special assistance to Iran but would continue to offer technical assistance.[53]

The president's letter added fuel to rumors about a rapprochement between Iran and the Soviet Union. On 10 June Iran and the Soviet Union had signed a new commercial protocol, and on the 11th Ambassador Ivan Sadchikov had returned to Iran and had a long meeting with Mosaddeq,[54] which had started widespread rumors about Iran and Russia entering a new diplomatic phase whereby the Russians, in a bid for Iran's friendship, would return the Soviet-held Iranian gold, settle the frontier disputes, and agree to revise the 1921 Treaty.[55] Some newspapers wrote of the prospect of significantly improved trade relations. The government implicitly encouraged such rumors, hoping that the United States would be enticed to outbid the Soviet Union for Iran's favor. "All foreign powers must respect Iran's independence," wrote the pro-Mosaddeq weekly *Tehran Mosavvar* on 19 June 1953, "and try on the basis of honest rivalry to win the friendship of our country. Only by this means will the Iranian government be able to profit from this rivalry and protect its policy of neutrality." The same message was reported by the anti-government press, though in a more critical tone: "The government does not wish to lose the support of the Americans," wrote *Dad* on 17 June, "and by magnifying the importance of Iran-Soviet trade relations, it hopes to induce the Americans to give greater financial and economic assistance to this country." Later, on 23 June, *Dad* hinted at secret negotiations between Mosaddeq and Sadchikov following their initial meeting: "The premier is awaiting the return to Tehran of Mr. Henderson to take a stand regarding the future of our relations with the Soviet Union in the light of American aid." As if to fan the rumors, on the 29th Molotov told Iranian ambassador Nader Arasteh that the Soviet Union was very much interested in resolving its differences with Iran.[56]

On 9 July the letters exchanged between Mosaddeq and Eisenhower were published in Tehran, and the people learned that the United States would not extend more assistance and would no longer strive to resolve the oil issue.[57]

8

TPAJAX

As 1953 progressed, Mosaddeq's problems grew worse, in a chain of interconnected events. Tension with the military increased when in February he appointed Brigadier Taqi Riahi to replace Major General Mahmud Baharmast as the army chief of staff and arrested a host of retired general officers as well as civilian politicians. In April, Mosaddeq forced the shah to dismiss Hossein Ala, his trusted court minister, and replace him with Abolqasem Amini. About the same time, Mosaddeq's chief of police, Brigadier Mahmud Afshartus, was abducted and murdered. Several military officers were arrested in connection with the crime, and on 2 May the government accused the Majlis deputy Mozaffar Baqai and General Fazlollah Zahedi of complicity in the Afshartus murder and called for their arrest. On 4 May the Majlis president, Ayatollah Kashani, gave Zahedi asylum in the Majlis, rebuffing Mosaddeq. A week later, the shah, again under pressure from Mosaddeq, agreed to place the Pahlavi belongings under government control, in return for which the government would pay a stipend to the Imperial Organization for Social Services, a royal endowment, to cover the royal family's expenses. In June, the Majlis became a hub of tension as pro- and anti-Mosaddeq deputies fought for control.[1] The fall of the monarchy in Egypt late in June shocked the shah and reverberated across the land. Many in the Majlis and outside now worried seriously that the same fate awaited Iran.

The rift between the prime minister and the Majlis widened as economic and political pressure rose in July. On 10 July, Mosaddeq announced that the time had come for him to settle his account with the Majlis by a referendum, a move that was both expected and surprising, for that day the Majlis elected his friend and supporter Abdollah Moazzami as president in preference to Ayatollah Kashani. Moazzami, a man of moderate demeanor and connected with several factions by both family and politics, tried to heal the wounds that separated the prime minister, the Majlis, and the shah, but failed. Seeing that the Majlis was bound for dissolution, on 20 July he helped General Zahedi, still in asylum in the Majlis, to exit safely to a new hiding place. On 21 July, the anniversary of Qavam's fall and Mosaddeq's return to power, a mammoth demonstration, led by the Tudeh, was organized in Tehran and other major cities. This event led Secretary of State Dulles to express concern about the increasing communist influence in Iranian affairs. On the 29th Mosaddeq announced he would ask the people to vote in a referendum on the fate of the Seventeenth Majlis—the voting would be held on 3 August in Tehran, 10 August in the provinces. This was the first time such a method of decision making was to be used in Iran, prompting the minority deputies to bring criminal charges against the prime minister.

On 2 August Moazzami resigned from the Majlis. On the 3rd, the Tehranis voted in different polling stations set up separately in different locations for those voting for or against the dissolution. Those voting against had to brave bands of thugs who threatened them with sticks and knives. Between the 3rd and 10th the country experienced extraordinary tension. On the 4th, the anniversary of the Constitution, the shah reminded the nation that constitutionalism in Iran had been gained by great sacrifice and that it was incumbent on the people to preserve it even at the cost of life and limb. On the 9th, the Tudeh embarked on another mammoth demonstration to show its power. The demonstration scared many in Tehran and in the provinces. On the 10th, in most provinces demonstrations and riots broke out, both for and against the referendum. On the 11th, the shah flew to the Caspian city of Ramsar and from there to his summer retreat at Kalardasht. On the 12th, Mosaddeq ordered "a large number of his opponents arrested," and several general and field-grade officers retired. On the 13th, the shah signed two *farmans* (orders), one dismissing Mosaddeq, the other appointing General Fazlollah Zahedi prime minister, and he ordered Colonel Nematollah Nasiri, commander of the guards, to meet with Zahedi in Tehran and deliver Mosaddeq's *farman* as Zahedi directed. On the 14th, Mosaddeq announced on the radio that given the results of the referendum, the Seventeenth Majlis must be dissolved. He ordered the number of tanks protecting the shah's palace at Saʿdabad, north of Tehran, reduced to four, and the tanks protecting his own house increased to twelve. On the 15th, he formally asked the shah to order the dissolution of the Seventeenth Majlis. The shah did not respond. Late that evening, Nasiri delivered the shah's *farman* to Mosaddeq, for which Nasiri was arrested. Early on the morning of the 16th the government announced that the officers of the Imperial Guard had attempted a coup but had failed.[2]

At 9 A.M. on 16 August the shah, Queen Soraya, his pilot, and the head of his household flew from Ramsar to Baghdad. Before entering the plane, the shah said:

> I have observed over the past few days that Mosaddeq is intent on vitiating the Constitution and the laws. I have sworn to protect the basic law and constitutionalism as long as I am the king. I therefore issued the *farman* to dismiss Mosaddeq. I heard this morning on the radio that they have arrested Colonel Nasiri, who was executing my order, and that they are calling it a coup d'état. They now want to arouse the people and shed the blood of the innocent. To prevent fratricide, bloodshed, and civil disorder, I have decided to leave the country for some time.[3]

All these events occurred in conjunction with a CIA project code-named TPAJAX.

Fazlollah Zahedi had become a brigadier general in 1922 at the age of twenty-seven, the youngest general in modern Iranian history. He had participated in several major battles against tribal chiefs in the north, west, and south and served as army commander and governor in Khuzistan and Fars under Reza Shah. When World War II broke out, he was appointed commander of the Isfahan army, where he was arrested by the British and exiled to Palestine. Toward the end of the war, he was allowed to return to Iran and was commissioned by Prime Minister Qavam to take command of both the administration and the army in Fars to negotiate a cease-fire with the Southern Tribal Federation, a collection of tribes that had taken arms against the central government. After Court Minister Abdolhossein Hazhir was assassinated on 4 November 1949 by a member of the Fadaiyan Islam, the shah appointed Zahedi chief of national police. This was the beginning of his political association with Mosaddeq and the National Front.

The National Front was then hotly contesting the election to the Sixteenth Majlis. The Tehran ballots had been invalidated by the electoral board on charges of fraud. Zahedi promised that in the new election the National Front members "would not be at a disadvantage." The Front candidates won the second Tehran election handily, which made Zahedi one of their favorites. Soon, the First Senate opened, to which Zahedi was appointed senator from Hamedan, his birthplace. After General Razmara was assassinated on 7 March 1951, also by a member of Fadaiyan Islam, Zahedi was appointed minister of the interior (which oversaw levels of government, elections, and police, among other responsibilities) in Hossein Ala's cabinet, which soon yielded to Mosaddeq and a different political order. Zahedi was retained as interior minister in the new cabinet, a position that gave him control over internal security and politics. He was instrumental in helping the National Front member Mozaffar Baqai and others gain access in June 1951 to the residence of Richard Seddon, the AIOC chief in Tehran, where important documents bearing on the company's interactions with the Tudeh Party and interference in Iranian politics were found.[4]

Zahedi and Mosaddeq, however, were not politically or temperamentally on the same wavelength. Mosaddeq was always on the lookout for conspiracy, worrying especially about the military. He suggested that Major General Hassan Baqai (no relation to Mozaffar Baqai) be appointed chief of national police, to which Zahedi, as the minister in charge of the police, acquiesced. Four days after the appointment, on 15 July 1951, Averell Harriman, President Truman's special envoy, arrived in Tehran. The Tudeh Party came out in force to protest the visit, marching on the Majlis, clashing with opponents and the police. The police fired on the Tudeh, and some twenty people, from both sides, were killed and more were wounded. Mosaddeq ordered General Baqai to be dismissed and tried. Zahedi resigned as interior minister, protesting the police were duty-bound to protect the Majlis, and returned to the Senate, where he became an outspoken critic of the government, voting against the plenary powers Mosaddeq demanded in July 1952. Soon after, he was recognized as a leader in the opposition to Mosaddeq and a probable candidate for premiership. His military background gave him influence with members of the armed forces, leverage not available to most other politicians. He attracted colleagues in the Senate as well as in the government, in the Majlis, and among the people, including the National Front members now gradually falling out with Mosaddeq. On 13 October Mosaddeq accused him of working with foreign agents and, since Zahedi had parliamentary immunity and could not be arrested, ordered the arrest of his collaborators. To rid himself of the Senate, which had failed to support him, and of Zahedi, Mosaddeq forced a vote in the Majlis on 23 October to reduce the Senate's term from four years to two. Despite the act's doubtful constitutional validity, it nonetheless took away the general's immunity and made him available for arrest on 2 May 1953 when Mosaddeq charged him in connection with the murder of Afshartus. On 4 May Zahedi took asylum in the Majlis and remained there until 20 July, when Moazzami smuggled him out. He then went into hiding, only to surface as Mosaddeq's replacement.

■

Zahedi's challenge to Mosaddeq thus had a history that preceded TPAJAX, the code name for the CIA attempt to bring down Mosaddeq. Much of this history, however, has been lost or vitiated because of the CIA involvement in the affairs that led to Mosaddeq's fall. The CIA presence distorted the facts, including the role it played in the event. The American urge to promote the fledgling CIA in 1953 and the Iranian proclivity to assign responsibility to others made of the CIA a seemingly omnipotent force with the power to move heaven and earth. This history, fostered by pro-Mosaddeq Iranians and liberal and leftist Westerners, has diminished Mosaddeq, demonized the shah, and turned Iranians into traitors or wimps. In this history Mosaddeq, a hero supported by a nation that uniformly declares "Mosaddeq or death," succumbs to an American armed with a bag of money. Can this be because Iranians are villains, politically emasculated betrayers, or cowards?

The alternative is to make the United States—in this case its stand-in, the CIA—omnipotent. The intellectual trick is to equate intention with results. It was the CIA that overthrew Mosaddeq because that is what the CIA set out to do, and the CIA, like the United States, like England and Russia before the United States, and like God before all of them, was able to do what it pleased. But except perhaps in spy novels, the CIA has never been as omniscient or omnipotent as it has pretended, or been made out, to be.

■

The Central Intelligence Agency was organized in 1947 out of the wartime Office of Strategic Services (OSS), based on recommendations drafted by a group of experts led by Allen Dulles. In June 1948 the National Security Council (NSC) established the Office of Policy Coordination (OPC) to report to NSC, and directed it to engage, through the CIA, in "propaganda; economic warfare; preventive direct action, including sabotage, anti-sabotage, demolition and evacuation measures; subversion of hostile states, including assistance to underground resistance and support of indigenous anti-Communist elements in threatened countries of the free world." These operations were "to be planned and performed so that if ever exposed, the American government could 'plausibly disclaim any responsibility.'" In 1950, the new director of central intelligence, General Walter Bedell Smith, incorporated OPC into the CIA, along with the Office of Special Operations (OSO), an older branch whose members, relatively less well paid and pampered, resented the more cosseted newcomers.

"In the months following the merger of OPC and OSO in 1952," wrote Richard Helms, "it sometimes seemed unlikely that we [the CIA] would ever effect the coordination Bedell Smith assumed would follow his decision to form a unified organization."[5]

In his book on the CIA, Richard Helms, the quintessential company man, does not elaborate on the 1953 operation code-named TPAJAX, the first and one of the most celebrated undertaken by the CIA. "In two months, and at a cost of two hundred thousand dollars," he writes, "the joint [British and American] coup d'état tumbled Mossadegh from office and brought the Shah back from a prudent sojourn in Rome to the Iranian throne." This is the whole of Helms's comment on the CIA's actual operation in Iran. He also notes the warning by the operation's director, Kermit Roosevelt, to Secretary Dulles: "If we [CIA] are ever going to try something like this again, we must be absolutely sure that [the] people and army want what we want. If not, you had better give the job to the Marines."[6] Beyond this, Helms is silent on TPAJAX. His account of the CIA's state of organizational preparedness, however, suggests that in 1953 the agency was not in a position to launch a well-coordinated clandestine operation — certainly not in the short time allotted. This may very well be the reason behind Helms's unusual, and suggestive, silence.[7] In an interview several years before he wrote his book, Helms said: "My impression is that bringing the shah back and putting General Zahedi as prime minister were generally popular in Iran. It is also my impression that the crowds that came into the streets in support of this measure came there wanting to see this outcome. This operation, I know, has been regarded as being far fancier or larger than it in fact was. There was really not an awful lot of money spent."[8]

To the historian Arthur Schlesinger the CIA in the 1950s was a rogue institution. A year after its inception, Schlesinger writes, Congress gave it authority to use funds as it pleased, largely free of the normal rules of budgetary accountability. After Allen Dulles was named director in 1953, he and his brother, the secretary of state, became the tsars of American foreign policy. "A word from one to the other," Schlesinger quotes Howard Hunt, the original chief of political action for the Bay of Pigs, "substituted for weeks of intra- and inter-agency debate." Schlesinger further notes: "Intelligence agencies, sealed off by walls of secrecy from the rest of the community, tend to form societies of their own. Prolonged immersion in the self-contained, self-justifying, ultimately hallucinatory world of clandestinity and deception erodes the reality principle."[9] And "the intrigue is fascinating," wrote David Bruce and Robert Lovett of the Board of Consultants on Foreign Intelligence Activities, created by President Eisenhower in 1956; "considerable self-satisfaction, sometimes with applause, derives from 'successes'—no charge is made for 'failures'—and the whole business is very much simpler than collecting covert intelligence on the USSR through the usual CIA methods."[10] This last reference is to events in Eastern Europe, China, and Korea and the Soviet bomb, among others, all of which escaped the CIA's intelligence operations.

The CIA report of the coup in Iran and Kermit Roosevelt's book *Countercoup,* in which he describes his role as the director of the coup d'état, read more like prophecy made after the fact.[11] Indeed, to Eisenhower, Roosevelt's report "seemed more like a dime novel than historical facts."[12] Ardeshir Zahedi, General Fazlollah Zahedi's son and a central figure in the events leading to the transition of power from Mosaddeq to Zahedi, believes Roosevelt's account was adopted from "Panj ruz-e bohrani," the "Five Critical Days," a series of articles that appeared in the monthly publication *Ettela'at Mahaneh* and that were based on an interview with Ardeshir Zahedi shortly after General Zahedi took power. His American detractors dismiss Ardeshir's critique of the CIA report (not his account in "Five Critical Days," which, being in Persian, most of them have not read, but his statements to the press and on other media in the West after the publication of the report in 2000) as long-winded and self-exculpatory. Zahedi, however, is persuasive on several important points on the discrepancies contained in the CIA account.

TPAJAX may be studied on three levels: formulation, execution, and explication. The CIA's Secret Report is mostly formulation. There was a plan aimed at the overthrow of Mosaddeq. Since General Zahedi was the only contender for Mosaddeq's post, the planners agreed on him as the candidate for the job. Since the shah was the commander-in-chief of the armed forces, the focus of political legitimacy, and the only person under the Constitution authorized to appoint the prime minister, it was logical to identify him as the plan's pivot. Clearly, the United States and the United Kingdom determined jointly to overthrow Mosaddeq's government. The question is what role the CIA played in the actual process that led to the fall of Mosaddeq, how effective the role was, and how it affected subsequent Iranian politics.

The Secret Report begins with the genesis of the plan to topple Mosaddeq and to replace him with a prime minister amenable to negotiation on oil and willing to curtail the Tudeh Party. The idea originated with the British Secret Intelligence Service (SIS) in December 1952 and was communicated to the CIA; however, given the impending transition from Truman's administration to Eisenhower's, the State Department remained noncommittal. The new administration soon approved the idea, however, and directed the CIA to draw up a plan jointly with the SIS, provided the British government agreed to cooperate with the post-Mosaddeq government and the U.S. government supported it with necessary funds. The CIA and SIS began drafting a plan, but soon the SIS left the planning to the CIA—although the final draft was largely a variation on the general structure developed by C. M. Woodhouse at SIS.[13] Another MI6 officer, Anthony Cavendish, claims Mosaddeq "was removed through skillful planning by SIS, with some little help from the CIA, although Kermit (Kim) Roosevelt, in his book *Countercoup* (1979), claimed virtually all the credit."[14] The same complaint is voiced by a high-ranking MI6 officer, Anthony Verrier: "The CIA has been given credit for the Shah's return and Mosaddeq's subsequent downfall. One former member of the CIA, Kermit Roosevelt, has even claimed as much in an idiosyncratic version of these events. The truth is that the CIA took little part in the business, except in the final phase."[15]

According to the secret report, on 4 April 1953 CIA Director Allen Dulles approved a budget of $1 million to be used by CIA's Tehran station "in any way that would bring about the fall of Mossadeq" and authorized Ambassador Loy Henderson and the CIA chief of station to use it "as long as the ambassador and the station concurred." On 16 April, a study entitled "Factors Involved in the Overthrow of Mossadeq" determined that a "Shah–General Zahedi combination, supported by CIA local assets and financial backing, would have a good chance of overthrowing Mossadeq, particularly if this combination should be able to get the largest mobs in the streets and if a sizable portion of the Tehran garrison refused to carry out Mossadeq's orders." The plotters determined that General Zahedi "stood out as the only major personality in undisguised opposition to Mossadeq." They therefore made plans to take three simultaneous routes toward the plan's execution: to assure the shah's compliance, to get Zahedi and the military ready to move, and to launch a propaganda assault. They would approach the shah principally through his twin sister, Princess Ashraf, General Norman Schwarzkopf, Sr., Asadollah Rashidian, Kermit Roosevelt, and Colonel Hassan Akhavi. In April 1953, the Secret Report states, the CIA reestablished covert contact with General Zahedi through Commander Eric Pollard, the U.S. naval attaché. In June, for reasons of efficiency, reliability, and security, it selected Zahedi's son Ardeshir as "the means of contact with General Zahedi." After 21 July, after he left the Majlis, "contact with General Zahedi was made directly." In the course of time, the CIA and SIS, as the report details, found new agents or mobilized the old ones to carry out their mission. These agents included a small number of officers, a majority of them retired or with no command position, and a handful of civilians, of whom the two claimed to have been most effective—Ali Djalili and Faruq Keyvani—were by and large unknown outside of a small group of journalists. The agent with significant contact at all levels, Asadollah Rashidian, turns out to have been a British "asset." But even in the case of Rashidian (and his brother, also an "asset"), Robin Zaehner, then an MI6 agent and later a professor of oriental religions at Oxford, who "controlled" the brothers, decided that they were unable to deliver and reported them to Woodhouse and London as disappointing. Subsequently in a meeting with Woodhouse and Eden, Zaehner emphasized their irrelevance to any serious undertaking.[16] Here, however, we are particularly concerned with the shah and the Zahedis.

The Secret Report depicts the shah as timid and indecisive by nature, doggedly refusing to be drawn into the plot. Stephen Kinzer, a critic of the shah and of American policy, in his recent book based mainly on Roosevelt's *Countercoup* approvingly quotes a British opinion of the shah: "He hates taking decisions and cannot be relied on to stick to them when taken. He has no moral courage and succumbs easily to fear." Then, in passing: "It was not even clear that the Shah had the legal authority to remove [Mosaddeq]" since "in democratic Iran prime ministers could be installed or removed only with the permission of parliament."[17] This, of course, is the crux of the matter. The Constitution, as we have seen, gave the crown and only the crown the power to appoint or dismiss the ministers (Article 46, Supplementary Basic Law) and made him the head of the executive branch (Article 27, paragraph 3) and a partner in legislation (Article 27, paragraph 1). The parliament (the National Consultative Assembly, or Majlis, and the Senate) could cause the dismissal of a minister or a cabinet by refusing to give a vote of confidence; but it could not appoint ministers. However, over the postwar years it had become accepted practice for the shah to ask the Majlis to express its preference before he appointed a prime minister. Soon after Mosaddeq formed his cabinet, many Iranians and non-Iranians advised the shah to use his constitutional prerogative to dismiss him. He answered invariably that he did not think the Constitution gave him the right to dismiss a prime minister as long as he enjoyed the parliament's confidence. He stuck to this position even when he was made an offer the plotters thought he could not refuse. According to the Secret Report, the shah was told the coup would occur regardless of his decision; however, if he did not cooperate the country might collapse, the dynasty might end, and he would be held responsible. He still refused, much to the plotters' consternation. He told Roosevelt he was not an adventurer. He told Schwarzkopf he was the king and he would take the necessary measures when his office gave him the authority to do so. "Should Mossadeq carry through his referendum and dissolve the Majlis then he, himself, would have full powers under the constitution to dismiss Mossadeq and replace him by a prime minister of his own choice." He had told the Iranians the same. He had advised several Majlis deputies to resign if they were asked to, and several of them did. None of this suggests that he acted as told by the plotters.

Princess Ashraf was approached and asked to help. In Donald Wilber's account in the Secret Report, the princess was contacted on the Riviera and went to Iran with a letter for the shah stating that General Schwarzkopf would follow to discuss the plan. In Woodhouse's telling, Ashraf was in Switzerland.[18] Ashraf herself describes what actually happened in *Faces in a Mirror,* a book she wrote in the United States after the death of her brother. She was in Paris and had a telephone call from a friend she calls "Mr. B," who informed her an English and an American representative wished to see her on a matter of utmost importance to Iran and the shah. She met with them on two occasions in Paris near the Bois de Boulogne and was taken on both occasions to an apartment in St. Cloud. The Englishman, presumably the SIS operative Norman Darbyshire, offered to give her a check as compensation for the dangerous mission she was about to undertake. She was insulted and the meeting almost failed. Later, the man apologized, amends were made, and on 25 July she set out for Iran carrying a sealed envelope. She was received at the airport by Khojasteh Hedayat, a friend she had called from Paris, who spirited her out of the airport, bypassing customs, and took her to the Saʿdabad royal compound at the foot of the Alborz Mountains, to her half-brother Gholamreza, whose wife, Homa Aʿlam, was her best friend.[19] Her arrival, however, was immediately discovered and she was ordered to leave by both Mosaddeq and the shah. She never saw the shah but was able to get the letter to him through their youngest brother, Hamidreza; he handed it to Queen Soraya, who gave it to the shah. Under Mosaddeq's pressure, the shah issued a statement the evening Ashraf arrived that his sister's return to Iran was without his permission and that she would fly back to Paris immediately. According to the Iranian press, she left Iran on 27 July, two days after she had arrived.

The Secret Report names several Americans associated with the CIA who, according to the report, were instrumental in the operations; the most active among them were Kermit Roosevelt, Eric Pollard, Roger Goiran, Joseph Goodwin, and George Carroll. Roosevelt, as the man in charge of the operation, was to be in touch with the shah and the Zahedis; Goiran, Goodwin, and Pollard with the Zahedis; and Carroll mostly with the military.

According to the Secret Report, Asadollah Rashidian met with the shah on 2 August to inform him that Roosevelt was in Tehran and wished to meet with him. According to Kinzer, beginning that evening and apparently continuing for a whole week, Roosevelt and the shah met every midnight (a distinctly improbable arrangement given the curfew that was in effect, Mosaddeq's suspicions, and Tehran's political climate), with Roosevelt delivering to the hapless shah a hefty dose of browbeating every evening, but apparently to no avail since, according to Roosevelt, the shah's mood kept turning to "stubborn irresolution."[20] But, according to Kinzer, Roosevelt would not give up; he would keep on explaining the plan: "First, a campaign in mosques, the press, and the streets would undermine Mosaddeq's popularity. Second, royalist military officers would deliver the decree dismissing him. Third, mobs would take control of the streets. Fourth, General Zahedi would emerge triumphantly and accept the shah's nomination as prime minister."[21] Finally, the hero proves compelling, the irresolute shah loses stubbornness and gives in, but not before Roosevelt helps him find a hiding place: "a hunting lodge that the royal family maintained near Ramsar on the Caspian coast."[22] The shah then dutifully — as Kinzer indelicately tells us — informs Roosevelt that if things go wrong, "the Empress and I will take our plane straight to Baghdad."[23]

Kinzer's is the burlesque version of Roosevelt's account, laying bare the incongruities in this unhappy affair. The shah presumably agrees to sign the *farmans* after Roosevelt pretends to him that he has received a cable that evening in which President Eisenhower has asked him to convey to the shah the following message: "I wish Your Imperial Majesty Godspeed. If the Pahlavis and the Roosevelts working together cannot solve this little problem, then there is no hope anywhere. I have complete faith that you would get this done."[24] It was agreed, according to Kinzer, "that a CIA courier would bring the vital *farmans* to the palace early the next morning." The shah, true to form, takes off before signing the decrees, leaving Roosevelt and his aides cursing. Roosevelt, however, will not give up; ever the hero, he is determined "it not be allowed to upset his plan."[25]

What the Secret Report states formally, and Roosevelt and Kinzer restate casually, is fact fictionalized, fable constructed around an event after it has occurred and become known. The story about Eisenhower's cable is absurd. The shah was meticulous about every piece of information he received, not the sort of man to accept the claim of a cable from the president of the United States without asking to see it. Why would the *farmans,* so important to the plan, arrive late? Why would the shah not wait a few minutes for them to arrive, given that they came on the heels of Eisenhower's alleged cable? Why would the shah tell Roosevelt he would fly straight to Baghdad? He was, at that same time, telling everybody, including Schwarzkopf, that he would not dismiss Mosaddeq as long as the latter enjoyed the support of the Majlis. And if Mosaddeq lost that support or if there were no Majlis, he would dismiss and replace him with a prime minister of his choice, which, under the circumstances, could have been no other than Zahedi. According to the Secret Report, "Headquarters urged that the anti-Mossadeq deputies be given every encouragement to keep their posts and to take up political sanctuary in the Majlis. The theme to be built up was that those who had not resigned from the Majlis would constitute the legitimate parliamentary body." The shah, on the other hand, encouraged some of the deputies to resign. The shah never thought Mosaddeq would not heed his decree; rather, he feared another "30 Tir," the events of the summer of 1952, when the people rose up to reinstate Mosaddeq after he had resigned.

The Secret Report states that by late July the station was in direct contact with General Zahedi, who had left his Majlis sanctuary on 21 July (actually 20 July). Roger Goiran and Joseph Goodwin had had several conversations with him and characterized him as indolent. Ardeshir Zahedi (hereafter referred to by his given name to distinguish the father and the son) denies his father ever had contact with any foreigner: "I know because it was impossible for any foreigner to see him during this period without my knowledge." The general disliked the company of foreigners because, except for a little Russian and Turkish, he spoke no foreign language. In the past he had shunned invitations to foreign embassies. Once, after the war when the British had released him, Ambassador Bullard had invited him to the British embassy, but he refused. As minister of the interior in Mosaddeq's cabinet, he had been invited to a reception in Averell Harriman's honor at the U.S. embassy, which he attended. This, according to Ardeshir, was his first and last visit to the embassy.[26]

Ardeshir, however, knew many Americans because he had served as chief Iranian assistant to the director in the Point IV aid offices in Tehran until late in the fall of 1952, when Mosaddeq asked Director William Warne to dismiss him on account of his father's antigovernment activities. Warne did so reluctantly. He thought highly of Ardeshir: "A tall, handsome young man, he is among the very few I have known whom I believe to be without any sense of fear. He was not reckless beyond reason, but he would and did risk his skin fearlessly when he thought it was important and right to do so. 'Right' to him, meant 'in the interests of Iran.'"[27] Warne arranged to maintain contact with Ardeshir unofficially. Through Point IV Ardeshir had become acquainted with several people connected with the U.S. embassy but, according to Ardeshir, this had no connection with TPAJAX, of which he knew nothing.

This is how Ardeshir recounts the story.[28] The Zahedis were close to the Verbas. Captain Verba, a White Russian officer, had taught military tactics to General Zahedi during his Cossack years, and Mrs. Verba, a Swiss woman, had taught French to Ardeshir and his sister Homa when the general was stationed in Isfahan before the British exiled him to Palestine. Once, at a friend's house, Ardeshir encountered Captain Verba accompanied by a Colonel Gagarin, a tall, handsome American officer, originally from Russia, now a military attaché to the U.S. embassy in Tehran. Gagarin liked horses, and Ardeshir invited him to ride with him. Through Gagarin, Ardeshir became acquainted with another American officer, Navy Captain Eric Pollard. The Americans mingled with others at the parties Ardeshir gave in his father's house in Tehran or in their country place north of Tehran.

A few days after 28 February 1953, the day the shah was dissuaded by popular demand from leaving Iran, Ardeshir visited Yusef (Joe) Mazandi, who was the chief Associated Press representative in Tehran and a supporter of his father. There he encountered Eric Pollard as the latter was leaving Mazandi's home. Ardeshir upbraided him over the U.S. attempt to force the shah out of Iran. Pollard protested vehemently, pronouncing himself and other Americans dismayed at the turn of events. This was the first time Ardeshir had talked about Iranian politics with an American.

Because of his active involvement in his father's political activities, Ardeshir too was eventually forced to go into hiding, moving from house to house but frequently meeting with friends and supporters. Once, when early that summer he was hiding in a house belonging to Mehdi Mirashrafi, the editor of *Atesh* ("Fire," an anti-Mosaddeq daily), in the presence of Nosratollah Moinian (later the shah's special bureau chief) and General Abbas Garzan (the former army chief of staff), he called Pollard and told him he wished to discuss the events then happening in Iran. Pollard tried to arrange for Ardeshir to meet with two individuals he considered appropriate but agreed to come himself when the arrangements he had made did not materialize. At their meeting, Ardeshir told Pollard, "We wish for the United States to remain neutral in our domestic quarrels. Ambassador Henderson sits with Mosaddeq-us-Saltaneh whenever Mosaddeq needs him in order to impress on the Majlis that the United States supports him. What right do you have to support one side under these troubled conditions? If you believe in democracy, how do you explain the government's warrant for my father's arrest simply because he is a candidate for prime minister? What sort of support for democracy is this? This is certainly against the principles I was taught the United States believes in."[29]

Pollard advised Ardeshir to talk to Joseph Goodwin, who, Pollard told him, attended to Goiran's affairs in Iran. Goiran "had been in Iran for some time and had been a friend of General Razmara"; Ardeshir knew him and once had been invited to his home when still working at Point IV. The address Pollard gave him, a house in a street near Tajrish, was next to the home of Brigadier Mozaffar Malik, who was at the time commander of the gendarmerie. Ardeshir found the proximity somehow reassuring. He told Goodwin, who, he later learned, was the deputy CIA station chief in the embassy, what he had previously told Pollard but received in reply only some innocuous discourse on U.S. foreign policy: support for democracy and noninterference in the affairs of other countries. This was the end of Ardeshir's contact with the Americans.[30]

The Zahedis were in touch with the royal court, at first mainly through Court Minister Hossein Ala, whom they considered a good and trusted friend, and subsequently through Abolqasem Amini, who succeeded Ala on 25 April 1953 under Mosaddeq's pressure. Ala had several meetings with General Zahedi at Reza Kaynejad's residence in the suburb of Qolhak. Kaynezhad was an old friend, and his house offered a safe place where the general met with other civilian and military leaders. Among them were General Ahmad Vossuq, sometime acting minister of war in Mosaddeq's cabinet, a number of Mosaddeq's former allies — the Ayatollah Kashani, Hossein Makki, Mozaffar Baqai, Abdolqadir Azad, Abolhassan Amidi Nuri, Abolhassan Haerizadeh — and others who had never been associated with Mosaddeq. Most of them were Majlis deputies who had refused to resign. Some had been outspoken, criticizing Mosaddeq. Haerizadeh, an original founder of the National Front, for example, sent a telegram to the UN secretary general on 9 August, calling Mosaddeq a rebel who had risen against the Constitution and whose actions did not in any way bind the Iranian people.[31] Kashani had warned Mosaddeq against the referendum and vowed to fight him if he acted against the shah. Most of them had urged the shah to dismiss Mosaddeq. Each of these individuals in turn had a circle of people that could be called upon when needed.

Friends and supporters of Zahedi — Yarafshar, Shahrokhshahi, Generals Qaranei, Farzanegan, Gilanshah, and several other military and civilian supporters, as well as Sardar Fakher Hekmat, Mehdi Pirasteh, Khosro and Amir Aslan Afshar, aviation chief Reza Afshar, and others — met with Ardeshir in different pre-arranged spots to discuss the political situation. On 10 August, the day the referendum was being held in the provinces, Ardeshir was meeting with several supporters at the Tehran zoo when Parviz Yarafshar, Zahedi's close friend and personal secretary, arrived with the news that the shah had summoned the Zahedis and that Ardeshir's father had started out for the palace. When Ardeshir arrived at Saʿdabad, the shah had already informed the general that in the absence of the Majlis he had decided to dismiss Mosaddeq and appoint him prime minister. "You have taken upon yourself the grave responsibility of protecting your father," said the shah to Ardeshir. "Be very careful, because not everyone you meet will be trustworthy, and if you judge wrongly you will probably be arrested." The shah then told Ardeshir that one of his military adjutants, Colonel Hassan Akhavi, and General Hedayat Gilanshah would be in touch with him and that he should arrange for the time and place they would meet with his father. The encounter assured the Zahedis that the shah had reached the end of his patience and was ready to act.

The shah left for his summer resort in Kalardasht on 11 August. Mosaddeq informed him of the results of the referendum on the 13th and asked him to issue the dissolution *farman*. The shah did not respond. On that day he went from Kalardasht to Ramsar, another resort town by the Caspian, where he signed two decrees—one to dismiss Mosaddeq, one to appoint General Fazlollah Zahedi prime minister. Not sure of the exact date the *farmans* could be delivered, he left the day out of the dateline to be inserted at the general's discretion. He ordered Colonel Nematollah Nasiri, commander of the guards, to take the *farmans* to Zahedi.

Ardeshir had arranged to meet with Nasiri near a gas station. Nasiri arrived dressed in civilian clothes, wearing a light brown sport jacket. Ardeshir took him to his father's hideout. There, it was decided that Nasiri would take the *farman* of dismissal to Mosaddeq Saturday the 15th late in the evening, because the cabinet convened Saturday evenings in Mosaddeq's residence in Kakh Avenue and the meeting sometimes lasted until midnight. It was arranged that General Mohammad Daftary, then commander of the Border Guard, would escort General Zahedi to his new office once the *farman* was delivered to Mosaddeq.

Mosaddeq, however, was persuaded not to accept the shah's *farman*. The evening of the 15th remains murky, partly because none of the participants on either side was in a position to know everything. Certain points, however, seem clear. For the shah, Zahedi, and Nasiri the popular uprising in support of Mosaddeq in July 1952 was the criterion against which they judged, measured, and took their options. Most likely, this was also Mosaddeq's criterion. In the past the shah had never stood against Mosaddeq's wishes, so Mosaddeq had no reason to expect to be dismissed. "He would not dare" was his matter-of-fact reply to his interior minister, Gholamhossein Sadiqi, when the latter had warned him the shah might dismiss him in the absence of the Majlis.[32] His first reaction to the shah's decree was to do what he had done in July of the previous year—accept the *farman* and appeal to the people, who he believed would rise in his support. He asked Bashir Farahmand, his propaganda chief, to come prepared to record his last message to the people. "I took a tape recorder to Dr. Mosaddeq's home and recorded his message to be broadcast in the morning. In the message Mosaddeq admitted he was dismissed and asked the people to take the rein of their fate in their hands." According to Farahmand, at this time Foreign Minister Hossein Fatemi and several others arrived. Mosaddeq informed them he had been dismissed and had recorded a message to the people of Iran to be broadcast early in the morning. Fatemi objected strenuously, arguing that Mosaddeq was the constitutional prime minister and nobody could legally dismiss him. The debate went on for some time, and at the end everyone acceded to Fatemi's position. At dawn, Farahmand was directed to announce on the radio that the government had foiled a coup d'état and arrested its perpetrators.[33] There was no mention of the shah's decree.

The Zahedis had taken off from Hassan Kashanian's house on Pesian Street in Shemiran where they were hiding to meet Brigadier Daftary and the jeeps that would escort them to the prime minister's office. But there were no jeeps, only General Gilanshah, driving northward to inform them things had gone wrong. The Zahedis retreated to Kashanian's house, then moved twice more, ending at the house of Ahmad Faramarzi on Heshmat-Dauleh Street. General Zahedi now directed Ardeshir to have the *farmans* reproduced as soon as possible. Ardeshir had them taken to Sako, a famous photo shop on Ferdowsi Circle, for reproduction.[34]

On Sunday morning the shah, hearing the government's report of the events, decided to leave the country for Baghdad, as, according to Roosevelt, he had said he would. What in fact happened, however, makes that allegation hard to believe. He had spent the previous four evenings with his friends in Kalardasht, a royal resort he frequented during the summers. None of the friends had any knowledge that a momentous event was about to occur or got any inkling of it from the mood or behavior of the shah or the queen.[35] Kalardasht was not suited for quick escape. Its airstrip could not accommodate a plane able to travel the distance between the Caspian and Baghdad. Nothing had been prepared for an eventual trip. When they departed, the royal couple left without money, food, or clothes, as did their two companions—Abolfath Atabai, the shah's old friend and head of household, and the pilot, Major Mohammad Khatami. The four passengers first had to reach Ramsar, where the shah's plane was kept. Iraq happened to be on the way to Europe and was a monarchy that was likely to accommodate the royals even if the Iranian government objected. All this makes it unlikely that the shah had already told Roosevelt he would fly to Baghdad, which would require planning.

On the same Sunday, in Ahmad Faramarzi's house on Heshmat-Dauleh Street, a meeting of Zahedi supporters was called. The news of the shah's departure that morning had left everyone in utter despair. "Suddenly," Ardeshir recalls, "Mr. Hoda, a brave Azerbaijani nationalist, banged his fist on the table and shouted in Azeri: 'By God, death maybe, but retreat never.'" Hoda's outburst raised everyone's spirits. A decision was made to have the *farmans* shown to domestic and foreign reporters. The question was how. "The only reliable place I could think of," wrote Ardeshir, "was Dr. Sa'id Hekmat's office. I went there directly. Hekmat made a telephone call to the Park Hotel, where most foreign news services in Tehran had their headquarters. I was able to speak with the Associated Press bureau chief Joe Mazandi, a man I trusted. I asked him to come for an interview, and he agreed to inform the other press representatives. Yarafshar volunteered to drive the reporters up into the Velenjak hills, where I would be waiting for them. The reporters expected to see the general; I explained he could not risk coming out, but I was here to convey his words." Ardeshir distributed the copies of the *farmans* and described what had happened. The reporters asked him questions about his father's whereabouts, which, of course, he would not reveal. He said the following on behalf of the general:

> Iran is a constitutional monarchy. The Constitution gives the shah the power to appoint and dismiss the prime minister. This is his prerogative, particularly at this time that Dr. Mosaddeq has dissolved the Majlis and the Senate. The shah has used his constitutional power to dismiss Mosaddeq and appoint General Zahedi prime minister. Therefore, General Zahedi has been the prime minister of Iran since the evening of Saturday 24 Mordad 1332 [15 August 1953]. Consequently, Dr. Mosaddeq is no longer prime minister. His refusal to accept the shah's *farman* and his persistence in giving orders against the Constitution and the laws put him outside of the law and make him a rebel. His line of action may be construed a coup d'état against the Constitution and constitutional monarchy.[36]

The news of the conference sped around the world. The Tehran daily *Ettela'at* printed the *farmans* that evening, attributing the news to foreign sources. The United States government also received the news of these events, mainly from the press and through formal embassy dispatches; Roosevelt and his associates had minimal information about the events and, according to the Secret Report, were told by both British and U.S. governments to withdraw. The streets on Sunday, Monday, and Tuesday belonged to the Tudeh and the remnants of the National Front.

On Sunday, 16 August, the Mosaddeq government announced it had neutralized a military coup but made no mention of the shah's decrees. Several military officers and Majlis deputies were arrested and a large group of police officers were forcibly retired. The Imperial Guard was disarmed. General Zahedi was summoned by the military governor and a reward was posted for his arrest. Foreign Minister Fatemi forbad Iran's envoys in foreign countries to receive "the deposed shah." The Tudeh cadres brought down the statues of the shah and his father in Tehran and other cities, changed the names of the streets, and demanded an end to monarchy. In a giant demonstration in front of the Majlis, Fatemi and Ali Shayegan asked for the abolition of the monarchy and the institution of a republic. On Monday, Mosaddeq ordered the shah's name to be removed from the morning prayers in military garrisons across the country, though few observed the order. On Tuesday, the Tudeh papers called for the establishment of a people's democratic republic. Ambassador Henderson, just returned from Europe, met with Mosaddeq and told him the United States was increasingly worried about the Tudeh influence and the future of Iran. That afternoon, Mosaddeq, who must have been just as worried, ordered Brigadier Daftary, whom ironically he had appointed military governor that day, to stop the Tudeh cadres in the streets. In the evening, the police and the military, shouting "Long live the shah," beat the Tudeh demonstrators. Zahedi moved to his last hiding place, a house on Heshmat-Dauleh Avenue belonging to Seif-us-Saltaneh Afshar. On Wednesday, the Tudeh collapsed, leaving the streets totally to the anti-Mosaddeq forces.

This victory of the royal forces was unexpected everywhere, leaving the CIA as surprised as the KGB. When news of "the coup's success" arrived, it "seemed to be a bad joke, in view of the depression that still hung on from the day before," the Secret Report says. Throughout the day, Washington continued to get most of its information from the news agencies, receiving only two cablegrams from the station. Roosevelt later explained that if he had told headquarters what was going on, "London and Washington would have thought they were crazy and told them to stop immediately," the Secret Report states. More likely, Roosevelt had little or nothing to convey. Nevertheless, the CIA took full credit inside the U.S. government.

Roosevelt and Kinzer are most imaginative on the events of Wednesday, 19 August, the day Mosaddeq's government fell. According to Kinzer:

> Once Roosevelt learned that the assault had begun, he decided to fetch General Zahedi from the hideout where he had been closeted for two days. Before leaving he summoned General Guilanshah, who like Zahedi, was at a CIA safe house impatiently awaiting instructions. Roosevelt asked the general to find a tank and bring it to Zahedi's hideout. He scribbled the address on a scrap of paper and drove there himself.
>
> When Roosevelt arrived, Zahedi was sitting in a basement room wearing only underwear. He was thrilled to hear that his moment had finally come. As he was buttoning the tunic of his dress uniform, there was a rumble outside. General Guilanshah had arrived with two tanks and a cheering throng.
>
> In later years, perhaps inevitably given his grandfather's fame as a swashbuckler, a story took hold that Roosevelt had ridden triumphantly atop the lead tank as it crashed through the streets of Tehran toward Mossadegh's house. In fact, Roosevelt realized as soon as he heard the crowd accompanying General Guilanshah that he should not even be seen in Zahedi's presence. As the door to the basement burst open, he jumped into a small cavity behind the furnace.[37]

The American saga does not end here. Martial music was to be played on the radio before Zahedi "spoke to the nation, and one of Roosevelt agents had brought along a likely-looking record from the embassy library. As Zahedi approached, a technician played the first song. To everyone's embarrassment, it turned out to be 'The Star-Spangled Banner.'" Amidst the mayhem, "around the time that Mossadegh's house was being set afire, a car pulled up at the gate of the American embassy. The driver honked wildly, and Roosevelt hurried out to see who it might be. It was Ardeshir Zahedi." Ardeshir, according to Kinzer, had gone to pay his respects to Roosevelt, but Roosevelt, the quintessential gentleman, asked him to tell Henderson the good news personally. They shared a bottle of champagne before Ardeshir took Roosevelt to the Officers Club, where the general now held court, presumably in the company of many others. Roosevelt, who had previously jumped behind the fireplace to escape being seen with Zahedi, then gave a rousing speech à la Marc Antony—"Friends, Persians, countrymen, lend me your ears"—and graciously telling the Iranians that he could merely accept their thanks, allowing the new prime minister and his men to celebrate Roosevelt and his victory. Through all the mayhem, Kinzer writes,

Mosaddeq "sat with remarkable calm in his bedroom." "If it is going to happen, if it is going to be a coup d'état, I think it is better that I stay in this room, and I die in this room," Kinzer has him say to Ali Reza Saheb.[38] But Saheb was never in Mosaddeq's room on that day.

Interior Minister Gholamhossein Sadiqi, a university professor in private life who was now in charge of domestic politics and security, would have been Mosaddeq's most worthy and credible colleague were it not that he agreed to preside over the flawed referendum to close the Seventeenth Majlis. Mosaddeq had initially asked Chief Justice Mohammad Soruri to oversee the charade. Soruri, a sharp lawyer and clever politician, declined and, when pressured, threatened to resign rather than do what the prime minister asked. The task had then fallen to Sadiqi.

At 6:30 on the morning of the 19th, Sadiqi was summoned to Mosaddeq's residence at Kakh Avenue. He arrived at 7, and Mosaddeq told him to instruct all governors to remain at their posts to prepare for an immediate referendum on a royal council. Sadiqi suggested that the decision be debated and approved at the council of ministers, scheduled to meet that afternoon. Mosaddeq insisted the matter was urgent and needed to be acted on that same morning. Sadiqi, ever the loyal subordinate, arrived at the ministry at 8 A.M. and directed the ministry to prepare and send the appropriate telegrams.[39]

At around 9 A.M. an employee informed Sadiqi that he had encountered a group of people at Sepah Square, not far from the ministry, shouting "Long live the shah" as a truck full of police passed by, waving its approval. Sadiqi called Police Chief Brigadier Nasrollah Modabber, who told him he knew nothing of this. A few minutes later Sadiqi received a call from the army chief of staff, Brigadier Taqi Riahi, who told him Mosaddeq had dismissed Modabber and appointed General Mohammad Reza Shahandeh chief of police. Sadiqi directed his staff to issue the proper appointment orders. Soon he was told that demonstrations for the shah and against Mosaddeq were going on in several parts of the city, including in the square in front of the interior ministry and the bazaar. He could see the crowd outside his window. He called Colonel Hosseinali Ashrafi, the military governor:[40] "What is the meaning of this? Why aren't you stopping it?" "I cannot rely on my soldiers," replied the colonel. "The contingents we have deployed to stop the demonstrations have joined the demonstrators."

At 11 A.M. Mosaddeq called Sadiqi. "I have looked into the matter, and I have now decided to appoint Brigadier Mohammad Daftary as police chief and military governor. Daftary is already at the police headquarters," said Mosaddeq. The prime minister's contradictory orders surprised and frightened Sadiqi. Shortly after, a call came from the city hall, reporting that mobs were assailing the building but the soldiers sent to stop them were taking no action. By 1 P.M., the crowds were rushing the Ministry of the Interior as well as the telephone and telegram bureaus. Sadiqi called Mosaddeq and pleaded with him to mobilize all his forces to defend the radio station, which was situated on the Old Shemiran Road. "Taking the radio means trouble in all provinces," he said. Mosaddeq took in the import of what he was told and ordered General Riahi to take action accordingly. By 2 P.M., several tanks sent to protect the radio station had reached the upper Saʿdi Avenue and stopped there to fill up at the gas station, as their commanding officer explained.

At a few minutes past 1 P.M. Sadiqi had called for his car to go to Mosaddeq's home but was told it was not safe to bring the car in front of the ministry. A car was then brought for him from the mayor's office to the adjacent Ministry of Health. At 2:40 Sadiqi was able to take off for his destination. He encountered tanks and soldiers at the entrance to Kakh Avenue, where the prime minister's house was located, and was told by the officers in charge he had to walk the rest of the way. He saw several tanks and military trucks deployed also "on the two sides of Mr. Mosaddeq's residence." He entered Mosaddeq's private chamber a few minutes after 3 o'clock.

The chamber was quiet and seemed somber to Sadiqi, several of his colleagues—among them Fatemi, Ahmad Razavi, Ali Shayegan, Seyfollah Moazzami, and Ahmad Zirakzadeh—sitting on the chairs and on the floor, brooding. "What news?" the prime minister asked. "Not good," answered Sadiqi, "but we should not despair." "What is to be done?" asked Fatemi. "First protect the radio," Sadiqi answered. "The city is not good. The officers and soldiers are siding with the people."

They heard the sound of people shouting and crying coming from the radio in the next room; they rushed out of the prime minister's room the better to hear the radio. Sadiqi realized the station had fallen. "After a few minutes the radio began to play the national anthem, 'Long Live Our Shahanshah,' and kept on playing it, repeatedly, again and again." Now they were told the prime minister had had one of his spells. "We all went back to his room. He was crying in a loud voice, uncontrollably." Then the telephone rang. They put it on the speaker for all to hear. It was General Riahi asking the prime minister to declare a cease-fire on the part of the government.

"Declare what?" Mosaddeq intoned.

"It is the thing to do, Your Excellency," Riahi pleaded in a broken and tearful voice. "General Fuladvand will come to you. Please listen to him as you would to a trusted adviser." Mosaddeq and his colleagues realized that the army headquarters had also fallen. A few minutes later Fatemi informed Mosaddeq he had received a call from his home. His wife, hearing he had been killed, had passed out and was in a coma; he had to go home to attend to her. He left. Later, it was learned that this had been a setup.

Brigadier Fuladvand arrived at 4:40 P.M. He said: "Two sides are aimlessly shooting at each other, and people are uselessly dying. The continuation of the violence endangers everyone's life, including yours. Issue a declaration to stop the resistance."

"Let them come here and kill me," said Mosaddeq. "I will stay here."

"We will declare this house defenseless," suggested engineer Razavi. Mosaddeq approved. Razavi, Zirakzadeh, and Shayegan prepared the following declaration: "His Excellency Dr. Mosaddeq considers himself the legitimate prime minister. Now that the forces of law and order refuse to obey him, he and his house are declared defenseless. Let no one trespass against his home." Four of the people present signed the declaration and handed it to Fuladvand. At around 5 o'clock Razavi took a white sheet from Mosaddeq's bed and gave it to the soldiers at the gate to hoist above the house. Soon, however, he changed his mind. "It is folly to remain here in this house and die," he said. "Let us get out. Maybe we'll find a way to safety."

They moved out of the building into the courtyard, from where they climbed up a ladder over the wall to the next house, then the next, and the next, where they were recognized by the servants and invited to stay. At 5 the next morning, Mosaddeq, Sadiqi, Shayegan, and Engineer Moazzami went to Moazzami's mother's residence. Now the radio announced that Dr. Mosaddeq was to present himself to the military governor within twenty-four hours. According to the announcement, His Imperial Majesty had ordered the government to take care that no harm came to Dr. Mosaddeq. Moazzami proposed to call Ja'far Sharif-Emami, his brother-in-law, and ask him to inform General Zahedi of Mosaddeq's whereabouts and of his readiness to surrender to the government. Sadiqi recommended to Mosaddeq that he take advantage of the hiatus the deadline provided and wait till the evening before communicating with Zahedi. Everyone agreed, because "there was a faint possibility that things might change and we would return to power."

At 5 P.M. the doorbell rang. Three police inspectors asked to enter the house. "What do you gentlemen want? Are you here to arrest us?" Sadiqi asked. The man in front nodded his head but uttered no word. "Which one of us are you here to arrest?"

This time the man spoke: "All of you."

The inspectors had come on foot. One of them left to fetch a vehicle and returned after a few minutes with a small car, into which the four prisoners and the three inspectors somehow crowded themselves. They drove to the national police headquarters, which housed the offices of the military governor, now Brigadier Farhad Dadsetan. At 6:18 P.M. Major General Nader Batmanqlich, the new army chief of staff, freshly out of jail, arrived and escorted the prisoners to the Officers Club, where General Zahedi was staying. They were taken to his room. Sadiqi writes:

> The general, in khaki summer military uniform, short sleeves and open collar, approached Dr. Mosaddeq, saluted, and shook his hand: "I am sorry to see you here like this. Please, you need rest. A room has been readied for you." Then he turned to us: "Gentlemen, please be my guests for a cup of tea, until later." He shook our hands before we departed. General Batmanqlich, Brigadier Fuladvand, and Colonel Zargham escorted Dr. Mosaddeq to the fifth floor, room 8, Shayegan to room 9, Moazzami to room 7, and me to room 10, facing Dr. Mosaddeq's. . . . Our rooms were equipped with telephone. Dr. Mosaddeq wished to call his family. The operator connected him. We had dinner at 8 P.M., and since we were tired, we each went to our assigned rooms at 9:30 P.M.[41]

■

At 2:30 P.M. on the 19th the tanks that Mosaddeq had ordered out to defend the radio station were still in front of the service station at the upper Saʻdi Street, a north-south artery just south of Shahreza Avenue, an east-west artery stretching across the city, getting fuel. They needed to refuel at the station because, according to the Secret Report, as a precautionary measure Mosaddeq had ordered through General Riahi that petrol for armored vehicles be limited to the amount that would be used in one hour. A crowd of people had gathered about the column of tanks, debating what was to be done. They insisted to the tank commander, Captain Manuchehr Khosrodad, that they move on Mosaddeq's residence to dislodge the old man. A debate ensued between the tank commanders, and in the end the decision was made to do as the people demanded. "Well," said Khosrodad, "Mosaddeq always said we must do what the people want. Clearly, it is the people's will to move to Mosaddeq's house. That is what we shall do."[42] The column began to move, carnival-like, with young men climbing up and down the tanks, shouting slogans, running, walking, talking. It turned westward on Shahreza Avenue, reached Ferdowsi Cricle, turned south on Ferdowsi Avenue, and then westward on Shah Avenue, meeting no opposition or resistance. Suddenly, halfway between Ferdowsi and Kakh, where Mosaddeq's home and the royal palaces lay, there was a burst of gunfire coming from behind the roofs on the south side of the street, wounding several people, some mortally. The column stopped. The firing stopped. The commanders thought it might be possible to negotiate with the opposing forces. But there was no one to negotiate with. The column moved again. The firing resumed, felling several people. The tanks fired, taking the rim off the roofs. The enemy fire stopped and the column, encircled by the crowd, began to move again. No more resistance until the column reached the Kakh crossing. There the units deployed to defend Mosaddeq put up a fight. The seamless connection of the tanks and crowd cracked apart, and the tanks went ahead. There was shooting on both sides, but not for long, for soon it was learned that Mosaddeq and his colleagues had left, and his guards ceased to resist. The crowd began to move again, first onto the street and then into Mosaddeq's house. Some, but not all, looted the house, taking out what they needed or could. It became the shame of the day.

According to Kinzer, quoting Richard Cottam—who was on the Operation TPAJAX staff in Washington and who, in turn, took his cue from Roosevelt—"That mob that came into north Tehran and was decisive in the overthrow was a mercenary mob. It had no ideology and that mob was paid with American dollars."[43] Much is written about and made of the role played by Shaʿban Jaʿfari, known as the Brainless, on 19 August. Jaʿfari was a tough in the south of Tehran who owned a *zurkhaneh*, a traditional Iranian sports club. But he was also dedicated to the shah, and ready to fight for him—as he had fought previously for Mosaddeq and nationalization when the shah and Mosaddeq were on the same side. Whatever his potential to give shape and substance to the movements of the crowd in the streets on the 19th, he was denied the opportunity because in fact he was not there. Kinzer, however, following Roosevelt and Cottam, makes him an important mover and shaker on that day, while claiming Jaʿfari's role was later made to appear less pivotal in order to maintain respectability. Jaʿfari has been interviewed in Los Angeles about his life experiences and the results are now out in a book of oral history, which is an anthropological gem. It opens a hitherto hidden vista to the culture of Jaʿfari's milieu, the way "his people" see the world, the way they evaluate themselves and others, the way they interpret *javanmardi*—chivalry. The narrative resides in a culture that though quaint and somewhat alien has clear and distinct rules that are binding on its members. One of the rules is honesty. Jaʿfari's account of the day is surely more trustworthy than Roosevelt's or Kinzer's, at least for its simplicity—he does not know what happened because he was in jail.[44]

Exaggerated claims are also made about the role of the armed forces, most prominently the role General Teymur Bakhtiar, then commander of the Kermanshah Brigade, is said to have played. Teymur Bakhtiar was appointed commander of the Kermanshah Brigade about ten days before the events of 19 August. General Reza Azimi, then commander of the Western Army Group, of which the Kermanshah Brigade was a component, denies Bakhtiar had any part in the events. "Bakhtiar had not yet taken command of the brigade, did not know it, and certainly could not have moved the brigade without permission from his superior," namely, General Azimi himself. "Later it was rumored that Bakhtiar had gone to Tehran at the head of a division. But there was no division in the west for Bakhtiar, then a colonel, to command."[45]

The shah arrived incognito at the Baghdad airport on 16 August and asked permission to land to receive fuel. Permission was granted, and the Beechcraft landed and was guided to a stop by the customs building. At that same time, King Faisal was returning from Amman, and the king's guard and many Iraqi dignitaries were at the airport to receive him. The shah, seeing the guard, told Atabai, half jokingly, "Perhaps they have come for us?" Atabai got out of the plane and there met by chance an adjutant of the crown prince, Malik Abd al-Ilah, who had accompanied the prince to Tehran on several occasions. The officer was surprised.

"What are you doing here, Mr. Atabai?" he asked.

"We are here on pilgrimage. Their Majesties are in the plane, with Major Khatam."

By this time, the shah and the queen had disembarked. The adjutant was shocked and suddenly cried, "Your Majesty!" Atabai asked him to be quiet for the moment and to take them to a private room. The officer led them to a room next to the customs house and politely asked if they needed anything. It was hot, and Soraya was very thirsty. She asked for water. The officer brought her Coca-Cola. "I was so sad," said Atabai later. "Here is a queen, so tender and so well attended until yesterday, and now she must drink Coca-Cola from the bottle in the desert."[46]

In the meantime, the adjutant informed Seyyed Khalil Kenna, the Iraqi acting minister for foreign affairs, that the shah and queen of Iran were at the airport. The minister, astounded, hastened to see the unexpected guests. The shah asked him if they could be put up in a hotel. Kenna said the shah must regard himself a guest of the Iraqi government and indeed a guest of the king, as "the latter would no doubt desire as soon as he knew of Your Majesty's arrival." He was then led to a government guest villa set aside for distinguished visitors, "on which a strong guard was put."[47] Kenna had lunch with the shah and got the impression that the shah was not sure he had been right to leave Iran. The shah met with King Faisal and the crown prince in the afternoon and received the U.S. ambassador in the evening. He told the ambassador that he had been approached some time ago about the possibility of a coup, but he had decided to exercise his rights as a constitutional monarch to dismiss Mosaddeq and appoint Zahedi as prime minister, "using sufficient force only to ensure a smooth change-over. He had made arrangements to that end, and the attempt had been made after a little delay but had failed owing either to a leak or to the interception of his communications with General Zahedi."[48] He did not wish to cause bloodshed, so he had flown out of Iran. He was now wondering whether he should openly oppose Mosaddeq, and if so, how.

The next morning, the shah met with Ayatollah Shahrestani, an Iranian cleric strongly opposed to Mosaddeq, who was living in Iraq. Shahrestani was contacted by Mozaffar A'lam, Iran's newly appointed ambassador in Baghdad, and advised not to "prejudice his high political reputation by seeing the shah," but if he decided to see him anyway, he should tell him to leave Iraq as soon as possible. A'lam had received a directive from Foreign Minister Fatemi on the 16th stating that the shah was deposed and that he was not to be received.[49] He sent a note to the Iraqi foreign ministry saying that as the shah's arrival in Baghdad had something to do with what he called the abortive coup in Tehran, the Iranian embassy hoped the Iraqi government would see that nothing was done to affect adversely the relations between Iraq and Iran. He asked the Iraqi undersecretary for foreign affairs how long the shah would stay and was told it was not an "Arab custom to ask guests where they had come from, where they were going, and when." A'lam saw Kenna and asked him why the Iraqi government had received the shah as its guest. "He was asked in turn whether the Shah was not still the Shah and who, indeed, had signed the Ambassador's credentials?" Kenna then told A'lam that "while the internal affairs of Iran were Iran's affair, the stability of the country was Iraq's interest too, and Iraq could not stand aside in the matter."[50] When he learned of it, the shah considered Mozaffar A'lam's behavior unforgivable.

The shah received Shahrestani warmly and listened patiently to his advice about what he should do to regain his throne. He also received a friend of Shahrestani's, a Dr. Jamali, and several current and former Iraqi officials. Later in the afternoon of the 17th the shah told the American ambassador that he proposed to leave for Rome early the next morning. "The American ambassador informed me," the British ambassador cabled London, "and we agreed to urge the shah to stay on for two or three more days, so as he might receive such advice as you and the American Secretary of State felt able to give. I asked Dr. Jamali to try to pass the same message. The shah was, however, adamant."[51]

That morning the Iraqi court provided Atabai with a car and money to buy a suitcase and a few items of clothing for the shah and the queen. In the evening, the shah and Atabai flew to Karbala to pray at the shrine of Hussein, the Third Shii Imam, Lord of the Martyrs. The queen, feeling ill (or more likely feigning illness), remained behind. At the shrine, the pilgrims, mostly Iranians, greeted the shah so warmly that Atabai said, "I would have been crushed had the governor of Karbala not come to my aid." They were advised to drive back to Baghdad rather than fly in the small plane at night. The trip turned out unexpectedly pleasant. "It was a beautiful evening, full moon, the river gliding calmly, palm branches stirring slowly under the soft breeze. We stopped along the way. The protocol officer accompanying us ordered bread, cheese, and grapes, wonderful grapes. I took some to His Majesty in the car. He ate them with obvious relish. We were all very hungry."[52]

On the morning of the 18th, before leaving for Rome, the shah met once more with the American ambassador, who again tried to persuade him to stay in Baghdad a few more days, but to no avail. The shah was dispirited by the insulting broadcasts he heard on Radio Tehran. The ambassador tried to cheer him up by pointing out that General Zahedi was still at large, that the shah had a great following in the Iranian armed forces, and that the world media would no doubt give him a fair hearing. The shah said he had decided to speak out, stressing the following themes: He had always tried to act as a constitutional monarch, but Mosaddeq had acted unconstitutionally; he had therefore felt obliged to dismiss Mosaddeq and appoint General Zahedi; when he had found his orders were not being obeyed, he had left the country to avoid bloodshed; and he would always be ready to return to Tehran if he were needed. Meanwhile, he prayed to God for his people in the hope that they would be spared from Tudeh domination.[53] He and his group then left for Rome early that morning on a British carrier.

The shah wondered about how he would be received in Rome and whether Ambassador Khajenuri would be at the airport to receive them. "Of course, Sire," Atabai was certain. "You have given him everything he has. For years he has enjoyed Princess Ashraf's patronage. How could he not?"

"You want to bet, Atabai?" Atabai heard the shah say.[54]

The shah was right. No one came from the embassy. Only two Iranians, Hossein Sadiq, an engineer, and Murad Erieh, a businessman, both civilians unaffiliated with the Iranian government, were among those waiting at the airport. The rest were reporters and Italian officials. Sadiq and Erieh offered their services; Erieh, reportedly, also a signed blank check. The shah and the queen were taken to the Hotel Excelsior in an Italian foreign ministry limousine. Atabai and Khatami, left to fend for themselves, were ambushed by the reporters. Atabai, remembering the war and the accusations of theft leveled at Reza Shah when he left Iran, opened the suitcase for the reporters to see and made them take pictures. "Look, gentlemen, no jewelry, just a couple of suits of clothing, nothing more." The shah liked the gesture when he was told and commended Atabai for his ingenuity.[55]

That afternoon Princess Ashraf was driven by a friend from Nice to Rome to visit with her brother—she had to ask for the ride because she could not afford to buy a plane ticket.[56] Later in the evening, the U.S. ambassador in Rome met with the shah, but the Americans had for some time thought all was lost and did not have much to say that might encourage him. The royals remained in the hotel, the queen ill and unhappy, ambivalent about what lay ahead. She had never been satisfied with her life in Iran, had not got along with her in-laws, had never been eager to perform her queenly chores, though she had tried to do them as best she could. Now, amid the turmoil and chaos, a different future had suddenly become possible. She did not know how to think about it. She could not tell her husband how she felt, partly because she knew how dejected he was and partly because she was not sure of her own feeling. They talked about things past and present. They conjectured about the future. "Perhaps we will go to California, get a plot of land, and farm," said the shah at one point. But this was said in passing, with a smile more like a smirk. It was ironic that they found themselves talking about such a future, though the irony was probably lost on the shah. He did not know that in 1917 in Zurich, a few days before embarking for Russia to make revolution, Lenin had uttered just such words to his wife.[57]

The night they spent at the Excelsior was difficult. In the morning Atabai found the shah's room heavy with smoke and ashtrays filled with half-smoked cigarettes. "You should not smoke so much, Sire, particularly when you feel down. It is not good for you," Atabai remarked. The shah said he had not slept, thinking about what was happening in Iran. Atabai ordered breakfast for the couple. The shah told him the queen had $150 with her that he could use to buy some clothes for himself and for Khatami. Meanwhile, he would remain in the hotel and wait for news. Armed with $150, the two companions went out shopping. It wasn't easy; neither of the two spoke Italian, and Khatami had not worn civilian clothes since he had joined the air force. Atabai bought two suits for each, one for the daytime, one for the evening. "We needed appropriate suits if we were called on to escort Their Majesties in the evenings," he reasoned.

When they returned, Atabai saw a mob-like assembly of men and women pushing toward the hotel. "I trembled with fear. 'My God,' I said to Khatami, 'they have assassinated him.' We jumped out of the car, forcing our way in. Inside, the crowd was everywhere. I could not see the shah or the queen. Then, I saw a hand waving at me. It was His Majesty's. I forced myself toward him, shouting thank God you are safe. 'Look,' he said, handing me a telegram. 'Things seem to have changed.' I took the telegram. It was in English. 'Sire, you know I cannot read English. What does it say?'" The telegram, the first the shah had received from Tehran, was from Hesam-ud-Din Dowlatabadi, Tehran's sometime mayor. But the people and the media had come because they had heard an AP report of the Iranian events on the radio.

That night, the evening of 19 August, a Wednesday, the shah, Queen Soraya, and Princess Ashraf dined outside. Atabai received permission to go out on his own. "I wish to get drunk tonight, Sire," he said. And he did. He had been promoted, Soraya told him as he was allowed to leave. "How, Your Majesty?" Atabai asked.

"Well," said the queen, "I have been answering the telephone calls in the hotel room all day, mostly taking messages for you. Until this evening they hardly could pronounce your name. Now, suddenly, you are addressed as 'Excellency.'"[58]

The coming Friday was Id al-Adhha, the Festival of the Sacrifice, a commemoration of the day God sent Abraham a ram to sacrifice instead of his son. The shah, having been asked to return by General Zahedi, wanted to leave for Tehran on Saturday. Atabai counseled that they leave Rome for Baghdad on Thursday and spend Friday in pilgrimage to the Mausoleums of Ali in Najaf and of Hussein in Karbala. Soraya did not like the idea. It was agreed she would remain in Europe with her father for a few days until the situation in Iran stabilized. The pilgrims had to wait until Friday morning for a suitable plane to take them to Baghdad.

"Your Majesty, I would like to warn you I will kill this Sardar Entesar [Mozaffar A'lam] if I see him this time in the Baghdad airport," Atabai said to the shah.

"You will do nothing of the sort," answered the shah. "We shall be calm and polite as befits us."

In the airport they were received by Crown Prince Abd-ul-Ilah and Prime Minister Nuri Said, King Faisal being indisposed. "The son of a bitch has gone way out of line for someone who is not even an ambassador, for he has yet to be formally presented to the king," said Said to Atabai in Turkish, looking at A'lam, who this time was indeed on hand to receive the shah. Atabai took the telegrams A'lam had brought over but refused to let him approach the sovereign.[59]

The shah and his two companions went on their pilgrimage to the holy places in Iraq in two small planes, then drove back to Baghdad. In the morning the shah's air force uniform, which they had ordered to be sent from Tehran, had arrived, but no other news. In the telegram he had sent on the 20th, however, Zahedi had asked the shah to return expeditiously. "The shah-loving people and the brave army are counting the minutes waiting for Your Majesty's arrival," Zahedi's message read.

"In the name of God Almighty, I thank the Iranian people for supporting me and defending the Constitution," the shah answered. He invited the people, the army, and civilian and military government employees to obey "His Excellency Fazlollah Zahedi, whom I have appointed to head the national and legal government according to the Constitution." He would return to Iran and his people without a moment's delay, he said.[60]

The shah returned to Iran on 22 August a different man. "I knew my people loved me," he exclaimed when he heard the events of 19 August. Until then he had been king because he was his father's son; now he had a mandate from his people, he would later say. At Mehrabad, the prime minister, accompanied by the political and military elite, received him in full ceremony and honor. "Everything had clearly changed," said Atabai, who had traveled in the same plane.[61] The shah was displeased at seeing his commander of the guards, Nasiri, wearing a brigadier's crown and star and said so. "Couldn't you have waited until I arrived?" he asked General Zahedi, who had bestowed the honors on Nasiri in anticipation of the shah's commands.

The shah sat with the prime minister that afternoon for three hours discussing the new cabinet, future policies, budget shortfalls, oil, and, inevitably, Mosaddeq. After the meeting, Zahedi told reporters that Mosaddeq would be tried on two general counts: for illegal acts he had performed as prime minister and for treason against the Constitution and the regime. The shah thanked the people and the army and stated that those accused of attacking the Constitution and the regime would be tried in accordance with the letter of the law. In the next few days, he received the new cabinet and bestowed a "Taj" first class, the highest civilian medal, reserved mainly for prime ministers, on Zahedi while also promoting him to the rank of lieutenant general. He told the members of the chamber of commerce that the national uprising proved that class conflict had no dominion in Iran when high national interests were concerned: "On this day, all of Iran's classes—men and women, rich and poor, police and gendarme, soldier and officer—all came together to participate in the national uprising."[62]

PART III

SECURING THE REALM

9

A New Vista

Never again; the shah might have mulled the thought over in his mind as he flew back to Tehran. Never again would he be so poor and vulnerable as he was in Rome. Never again would he be a plaything of another man as he had been of Mosaddeq. Never again would he forget his father's advice: any man worth asking to help in the arduous work of making a nation will seek your place if allowed. He would not allow men to reach so high a station as to covet his or events to get so out of hand as to put him in jeopardy. He would be alert and vigilant. He would pass beyond the mediating elite to connect directly to his people — the men and women who rose to return him to his crown and who would rise again to help him do what he must. And he would do his best to help them achieve a better, more prosperous life. His country would become strong now that he was in charge. His military would be the best fighting force in the Middle East. He would make a new bargain with the Iranians. Iran would begin anew.

These thoughts were dreamlike; they pointed to directions and possibilities rather than to a plan or even a will. Everything had happened so fast that he had not yet had time to move beyond nebulous dreams. Already he and his new prime minister had come to some disagreements about Mosaddeq. After consulting with the shah, General Zahedi had announced Mosaddeq would be tried for legal and constitutional breaches of his authority. His personal preference and advice, however, was for the shah to pardon him and have the whole problem over with. The shah was too hurt to acquiesce. Mosaddeq had committed treason, not against him only, which he was willing to forgive, but against the Constitution and the regime, for which he had to be tried. At any rate, if there were to be a pardon, it would be after the trial, not before, he said.[1] There were other considerations as well. How would he placate those who had stood up to the old man, fought him, put their lives on the line to protect their king and country? He ordered War Minister General Abdollah Hedayat to ask the prime minister what he intended to do and to inform him that the shah wished an early trial. Zahedi was hesitant. He asked Mohammad Sajjadi, an old hand in politics and many-times cabinet minister, Chief Justice Ali Hey'at, a politically astute Azerbaijani lawyer and judge, and his own son, Ardeshir, to meet with the shah and come to an agreement about an optimal course of action. They asked the shah what would happen if Mosaddeq was tried and convicted. "I will use my power to pardon him," the shah replied. The three agreed with the shah and reported their conversation to the prime minister. Zahedi told them he would, of course, obey the king's command. He was not, however, convinced that this was the best course of action they might take. "If he is going to pardon him anyway, why not do it now and spare everyone the tension that will certainly arise out of the trial," he said.[2]

◾

U.S. Ambassador Loy Henderson found the shah stronger and more self-assured when they met on 23 August, a day after the shah returned to Tehran. Was the change due to his learning that his country was more pro-shah than he had previously thought, Henderson wondered. Was it permanent or would it wear off? He conveyed President Eisenhower's oral message, in which the president congratulated the shah for his moral courage and acts that had helped preserve his country's independence and assure its future development. The message moved the shah visibly. He thanked the president and the American people for their friendship. The miracle that had occurred resulted from Iranians' patriotism, the friendship shown by the West, and God's benevolence. Iran would not have been saved if God had not willed it, said the shah.[3] But he was not happy with the new council of ministers. These were the same old political faces the people had seen for years; he had hoped fresh, younger individuals would now come forth. He wondered whether the Americans had anything to do with the composition of the government. Had they suggested Ali Amini, as he had heard? Of course they had not, answered Henderson. The shah had encouraged Zahedi to bring Abolhassan Ebtehaj into his cabinet—he was more reliable than Amini, he told Henderson—but Zahedi seemed reluctant. He was sure the Americans would not try to influence the choice of Iranian ministers and certainly no one, Iranian or foreigner, should be allowed to come between him and the armed forces, he told Henderson. Henderson asked if the shah was dissatisfied with Zahedi's performance so far. The shah replied that he was very satisfied and had the utmost confidence in him. The new cabinet, however, was a fait accompli; he had not been consulted on its composition.[4] Clearly, he wished to send a message that he was in charge, though as yet he had not found the frame or the style that fitted his newly claimed authority.

The shah and Zahedi had already come to an understanding about the need for swift action on money, security, oil, and development — but not on the army. Even before the fall of Mosaddeq, the shah had insisted that the United States help the Iranian government financially, whether Mosaddeq remained in power or not, in order to prevent the country from falling to communism. After he returned from Rome, he told the American envoy that immediate financial aid was essential to the new prime minister's success. Zahedi wrote Eisenhower on 26 August, thanking the U.S. government and people for the assistance they had given Iran, especially through Point IV. However, Iran needed to begin seriously to address urgent economic issues. Iranians were keen to embark on development, but unless they received technical, financial, and economic assistance, their journey would be slow and long. Now, Zahedi wrote, Iran also wished to mend its foreign relations based on mutual respect and the observance of accepted international rules of conduct. Eisenhower's response was fast and friendly. He was happy to hear that the American assistance in the past was appreciated and that Iran now intended to have amicable relations with other nations. He understood the urgency of Iran's need for help. He had already directed Harold Stassen, director of foreign aid, to send an expert to Iran to consult with Ambassador Henderson on Iran's immediate needs.[5]

Eisenhower proved true to his word. On 5 September, the president announced that $45 million had been made available for immediate economic assistance to Iran. The money was in addition to the $23.4 million in regular technical assistance that had just been approved for Point IV. Two days later, the American Point IV director in Tehran, William Warne, wrote a note to Finance Minister Ali Amini, setting out how the aid money was to be handled and used. That same day Amini agreed to the terms, allowing Warne to proceed with handing the first aid installment over to the Iranian government. "The next morning," Warne wrote in his book, "bright and early I called on Dr. Amini in his office. Since we had estimated what the first month's requirement would be I handed him a check drawn on the United States Treasury for $5.4 million. This he took to the Bank Melli, the state bank of Iran. Immediately 508 million rials were deposited to the ministry's account."[6]

It is possible, however, that Warne sent the check to the government through his organization's senior Iranian legal counsel rather than having gone to the office himself.[7] This check became a subject of rumors and innuendos. The shah's opponents suggested it was a pay-off to Zahedi. This, of course, was nonsense because, however it was delivered, the check drawn on the U.S. Treasury was made out to Iran's treasury at the Ministry of Finance and was deposited to the ministry's account in the Bank Melli.

Zahedi and Henderson hit it off well. After a meeting on 27 August, Henderson judged Zahedi physically strong and mentally alert, and quite capable of tackling Iran's chaotic economic and political situation.[8] On the 31st, they had a discussion on Iran's relations with the Soviet Union. The Soviets were unhappy about the turn of events in Iran and had inquired what they should expect from the new Iranian government. Iran wished to have peaceful and friendly relations with the Soviet Union, Zahedi had replied, provided that: (1) the Soviet Union refrained from interfering in Iran's domestic affairs, including giving moral and material support to the Tudeh and other subversive organizations; (2) the Soviet Union treated Iran as an equal and refrained from threatening her; and (3) the relations between the two countries were based on mutual advantage. Mosaddeq and Razmara had tended to be flamboyant in their relations with the Soviet Union, making a big deal of every trivial negotiation, Zahedi said. From now on, Iran would have a balanced relationship with her great neighbor to the north. The relationship would be essentially commercial. Iran would sell the Soviets whatever nonstrategic goods it could offer and buy from the Soviets whatever they could sell at a more favorable price than Iran might get from other countries.[9]

Henderson now became a Zahedi enthusiast, defending him to the shah. It was rumored that the shah and Zahedi did not see eye-to-eye on their respective roles with regard to the military. Henderson brought up the subject with the shah, who told him there would be no problem if the prime minister realized he should leave the army alone. He understood that it was difficult for Zahedi, a military man, to remember he now occupied a civilian office. He would have no problem discussing with him every decision he made on the military, but he would not countenance establishing precedent by allowing the prime minister to openly interfere in military affairs. Neither would he agree that the military was a political organization, as Henderson suggested, though he understood the political implications of military decisions. He would therefore, as a general rule, inform the prime minister of the decisions he would make but did not see himself bound by such a rule. The army chief of staff would get his orders from the shah, never from the prime minister. The prime minister would communicate on military matters through the minister of war, who would also take his orders from the shah.[10]

■

While the shah generally regarded General Zahedi with some affection, respect, and deference, he felt close to Zahedi's son, Ardeshir, whom he treated with a certain informality. There was a positive chemistry between the shah and Ardeshir, which would grow over the years despite Ardeshir's youthful idiosyncrasies and natural sprightliness. Ardeshir allowed himself ample leeway in the shah's presence, and the shah almost always accepted it with equanimity. (The sympathetic relationship began early, well before Ardeshir married the shah's daughter Shahnaz and continued after their divorce.) A month after the shah's return from Rome, in a royal party at the Caspian resort town of Ramsar, where the royals and the Zahedis were present, the general was dancing with Queen Soraya. Ardeshir had told the shah jokingly to watch his father dancing with his wife because women had a way of falling for the old man. Zahedi, embarrassed, had told the son indignantly to assume some grace even if he did not have it. The shah, however, had only laughed, clearly enjoying the young man's antics.[11]

The relationship between the king and his prime minister was, nonetheless, often strained. The general was older and took his responsibilities seriously. Tensions arose because the shah now was determined to be involved in not only political but also administrative decisions. Zahedi was inclined to the position previously taken by Qavam and Mosaddeq, that the shah should keep his distance from the everyday affairs of the state, not only for constitutional reasons but also in order to be protected against political mishaps that were sure to occur and so also from the blame that just as surely would ensue. The shah's experience with Qavam and Mosaddeq, on the other hand, had taught him otherwise: he must be heavily in or he would be pushed out, as he almost had been by Mosaddeq. This was perhaps the central bone of contention between the two. Nevertheless, he valued Zahedi's advice and asked for it also out of respect. He had been viscerally hurt by a letter Court Minister Abolqasem Amini had written to Mosaddeq when the shah was in Rome, in which Amini had referred to the shah as *pesareh,* a pejorative and disrespectful rendering of *boy.*[12] Clearly a new minister of court was to be appointed, and just as clearly choosing him was the shah's prerogative—the more so since Amini had been forced on him by Mosaddeq. The shah, however, deferred to Zahedi. Once a list of candidates, including Seyyed Jalal Tehrani, Dr. Ali Akbar Siassi, and Hossein Ala, had been prepared, the shah insisted on presenting it to Zahedi for advice. Zahedi, perhaps knowing the shah's preference, advised in favor of Ala, who was then appointed minister of court.[13]

Trumping personal disagreements between the shah and his prime minister were the real problems they both had to tackle. England, oil, elections, and perhaps most immediately the ongoing trials of Mosaddeq and his colleagues converged to make for risky and difficult politics in Tehran and some other cities, though things remained quiet in rural towns and villages. On 1 October

Point IV Director Warne, whose mission was engaged mainly in the country-side, reported what he called "cheering news": "Calm returned to Iran in the month of September so that it was possible for the regional directors, holding their regular meeting, to report the stopping of the organized badgering of our people. No more was being heard 'Yankee Go Home.'" Point IV could now settle, continued Warne, "into a comfortable, unstrained situation."[14]

Tehran, however, was far from the semi-idyllic situation Warne described. The 19th of August, the day Mosaddeq's government fell, was almost eerie, in that after so many days of fevered demonstrations in favor of Mosaddeq and against the shah, on that day literally no one rose to defend Mosaddeq. Once the excitement of the event began to wear off, however, a pall of nostalgia descended on the city. Mosaddeq had given Iran a moment in the sun. His standing up to the colonial powers had exhilarated the Iranians. His fall was a plunge into sobriety and the depressing gray of reality. For the students at the university and in the secondary schools it was just too much to bear. Tehran University was almost always in turmoil. There the Tudeh Party, centered at the College of Technology, was the best-organized group and generally in charge of demonstrations. In the secondary schools, where the groupings were diverse, the anti-Tudeh nationalists and Third Force socialists (the latter inclined to some version of Titoism) had the upper hand. The government cracked down hard on the Tudeh across the land and especially in the armed forces, where a large number of members were caught and tried. Several among them were convicted of treason and executed, severing the party's civilian and military lines of command and control and consequently diminishing its ability to fight or act cohesively. The National Front also began to unravel. Those who had stuck with Mosaddeq capitulated or were found and arrested. Most of them were soon released, the harshest punishments being reserved for those who had openly called for regime change, especially Mosaddeq's foreign minister, Hossein Fatemi.

Several of the former National Front leaders who had broken with Mosaddeq, including Hossein Makki, now objected to Mosaddeq's being tried in a military court.[15] According to the law, cabinet ministers were to be tried by the Supreme Court in ordinary times. The situation, however, was determined to be extraordinary, and the military court assembled to try Mosaddeq decided that it had jurisdiction over the case. This decision became a cause célèbre during the trial, Mosaddeq arguing he was prime minister and therefore what he had done during the four days of August he had done as prime minister, which meant the military court lacked legal authority to try him. The legal referent was Article 46 of the Supplementary Basic Law, which made appointment and dismissal of ministers a prerogative of the sovereign. Mosaddeq argued the article was purely ceremonial, and therefore the shah had no right to dismiss or appoint him unless the Majlis gave a vote of no confidence. He further argued that the Majlis could not dismiss him because it had given him plenary powers. If it chose to dismiss him, first it had to take away the powers. But the Majlis could not meet because elections for the new Majlis were not complete and a quorum of the old Majlis could not be reached after the resignation of a large group of deputies. He therefore was prime minister, even though he had asked the shah to issue a decree for the election of the Eighteenth Majlis because the Seventeenth had actually been dissolved by the referendum. Faced with the shah's inaction, he personally had declared the Seventeenth Majlis dissolved on 16 August, the day the shah had left Iran.

The prosecution argued that this was an admission of guilt, insofar as Mosaddeq did not deny the essence of the charges brought against him based on the facts of the case—that the Constitution gave him no right to interpret the law and that on the basis of the measures he had taken during the four days of August, he had clearly risen against the constitutionally established regime, including the monarchy, and therefore, according to Article 317 of the military code, was guilty of treason, a capital crime for which the punishment was death. The shah now interceded, forgiving Mosaddeq for whatever harm he had done him personally and urging leniency on other counts because of the services the old man had rendered Iran in the first year of his premiership. The court, taking into account Mosaddeq's age and service to the country as well as the shah's intercession, sentenced Mosaddeq to three years in prison.[16] The court's decision was confirmed on appeal on 11 May 1954,[17] two months after Mosaddeq's foreign minister, Hossein Fatemi, was apprehended. Fatemi was severely beaten by a mob as he was taken to prison from the police headquarters where he had been arraigned. He was condemned for treason and sentenced to die on the appeal. A flurry of efforts was launched to save him. The shah was caught between his military officers, who wanted the sentence carried out, and the press and the politicians, who wished the sentence commuted to life in prison. He told Ardeshir Zahedi he had given orders to commute but apparently his orders had arrived too late to save Fatemi, who was executed by a firing squad early on the morning of 10 November 1954.[18]

The British were in a quandary. Since their expulsion from Iran in 1952 after the nationalization of AIOC, the United States had become the dominant Western power in Iran and acted as the intermediary for their interests. The

British, therefore, had to look to the United States for political favor. But they did not trust America's motives. Many of the British, especially among the intelligence community, believed the United States was determined to take control of Iranian oil at Britain's expense. According to Anthony Verrier of the British Secret Intelligence Service (SIS), "Washington had decided that a policy of working with Britain to restore the Shah's powers and against Britain to increase America's stake in Middle East oil (they got 40 percent in the consortium that was subsequently formed) was, indeed, a sound combination of diplomacy and commerce." Further, according to Anthony Cavendish, "It was no secret that the American Embassy was anxious to discredit the British in Iran and that two of their diplomats, Anthony Cuomo and Roy Melbourne, actively negotiated with Mossadegh under the guidance of US Ambassador Loy Henderson."[19]

The Foreign Office was not "optimistic about the prospects of being able to work out a 'new deal' for a settlement of the oil dispute" and was worried about the depressing effect substantial U.S. aid to Iran might have on reaching a final agreement with the Zahedi government, which the British thought was probably no less nationalist or anti-British than Mosaddeq's.[20] Eden suggested that the aid the Americans were contemplating for Iran was probably more than needed and that in any case the policy of "the common front" made it desirable that the British know beforehand what the United States intended to propose so that they could therefore claim they had been consulted and were fully in agreement with the United States government.[21] The Americans, however, kept on pressing the British to assume a more agreeable attitude. Secretary of State John Foster Dulles wrote Lord Salisbury, Lord Privy Seal and leader of the House of Lords, on behalf of President Eisenhower that Iran was "the most dangerous gap in the line from Europe to South Asia" and that if the United States and England could "in coordination move quickly and effectively," they could close it. "I am impressed," the president's message read, "by the approach of the shah and Zahedi and I believe that if we can respond with something which involves a new look without abandoning basic principles, there is a good chance for a resumption of the old cordial relationship which used to exist between Iran and your country and mine."[22]

An agreeable attitude on the part of the British meant reining in their demand for immediate reestablishment of full relations. The British, however, were adamant, realizing that without having a chance at direct contact, they most likely would remain out of the loop. Foreign Minister Anthony Eden met with Dulles on 17 October and told him that England preferred to solve the problem of relationship first, because it would greatly facilitate the process of negotiations. The Iranians were "timid of taking the first step," so he would make it easy for them by giving an upbeat statement about the new Iranian regime in the House of Commons soon.[23]

The idea that American companies would now replace the Anglo-Iranian was hard for the British to swallow. "There seems no compelling reason why [Iranian] oil should be handed to America," wrote the influential London oil journal *The Petroleum Times:* "The view of the British Government should be — as no doubt the view of Anglo-Iranian is — that Britain has prior rights in Persia which have not been affected by the events of the past two years."[24]

The Americans, for their part, seriously doubted that the British could ever have a role resembling what they had had in Iran's oil industry in the past. "Broadly speaking, State Department Officials — and most U.S. oil men familiar with the Middle East — believe a direct British return to Iran, even on a limited basis, is virtually ruled out by the aura of fanatical nationalism that has grown up around the oil dispute," wrote W. M. Jablonski in the *Journal of Commerce.* According to this view, it was no longer a matter of commercial advantage for Iranians. Bringing the British back "would be as politically unthinkable, some say, as for the American Government to have proposed in 1776 to recall the British to manage our tea trade," wrote Jablonski. Washington therefore believed "that any realistic plan for reopening of Iran's nationalized oil industry must have a clearly non-British character (though might include some British participation). If so, the dominant role would of necessity have to be American, because American firms are the only other ones with big enough distribution facilities to handle the job."[25]

By November the Americans in Iran were clearly vexed by British intransigence. Zahedi's government, Henderson wrote the State Department, had its share of public criticism, as was customary in Iran, and this would affect its performance in the future. The British, however, were not helping the matter. They had promised to facilitate the work of the new government but instead had taken a wait-and-see attitude. In fact, Henderson complained, they had hardened their position on oil by demanding to reestablish diplomatic relations before substantial progress was made on the oil issue. If ever Zahedi agreed to such a thing, it would be because of the American pressure. In that case, Zahedi would hold the United States morally responsible for seeing that the British did nothing in Iran that weakened the government's position. England should realize that the United States was acting in Iran on behalf of the free world, which included England, and it should assure the United States that at least for a specified period it would not do or let its supporters within Iran do anything that debilitated the Zahedi government.[26]

Henderson also worried that if the shah sensed a rift between the United

States and the United Kingdom, he would intervene more vigorously in the government's work. The shah had said he would wait until the oil issue was resolved before he entered the fray energetically. His interest was primarily in building up the army and launching a development program, both of which required funds. He needed the income from oil, and he was willing to let Zahedi's government do what it could to expedite the negotiations. Henderson argued that the shah's support in the government's oil negotiations, as well as the election of a Majlis that would ratify the agreement, was essential. But this would happen only if the shah was convinced that the United States and the United Kingdom were in substantial agreement on these matters. Hence, Henderson concluded, the British should be made to behave.[27]

The shah and Zahedi disagreed, however, on the dissolution of the Seventeenth Majlis and the election of the Eighteenth. Zahedi believed the deputies that had refused to resign when Mosaddeq declared the Majlis dissolved should be rewarded and those who had resigned punished. The shah had no problem rewarding the steadfast but doubted the wisdom of punishing those who had resigned, especially deputies who had resigned with his own approval and encouragement. The negotiation between the two went on for some time. The British and the Americans urged new elections because a full Majlis would give the future oil agreement a more solid constitutional base. By October, the shah was urging Zahedi to ask for the dissolution of the two houses and the launching of new elections. Zahedi agreed in mid-October but did not make the request until December. The shah finally signed the decree on 19 December 1953, citing Revised Article 48 of the Basic Law.[28]

December was also the month Iran and the United Kingdom agreed to resume diplomatic relations. The British prevailed on the Americans and the Americans on the shah and Zahedi to move forward on the resumption. The announcement made on 5 December caused a protest at Tehran University, led mainly by the Tudeh Party but also supported by the National Front and other factions, prompting martial law forces to intervene. Ordered to contain the demonstrators, the soldiers fired on the crowd on 7 December (16 Azar), leaving three students dead and several wounded. As the demonstrations in Tehran continued and spread to the provinces, tensions between the government and the clerics, particularly Seyyed Abolqasem Kashani, also rose. Kashani took Zahedi to task for planning to reestablish relations with Great Britain. "The noble Iranian people will never submit to this ignominy. The day the government declares the resumption of relations will be a day of mourning. On that day, the people should wear a black ribbon on their jackets," Kashani told the press on 11 December.[29] Kashani's outburst notwithstanding, the elections for the Eighteenth Majlis were held without major incident, and the assembly was opened on 18 March 1954. That same day Sir Roger Stevens, the new British ambassador, who had arrived in Iran on 18 February, met with the shah and assured him of England's commitment to extending and strengthening friendly relations with Iran.[30]

■

Bringing the Iranian oil dispute to a reasonable conclusion was not easy even though all sides now eagerly wished it. Several issues needed to be addressed simultaneously, but above all the nationalization law, which could be neither ignored nor honestly realized. The shah deliberately kept a low profile, leaving much of the leadership in the negotiations to Ali Amini and Abdollah Entezam, the ministers of finance and foreign affairs respectively. What he wanted was a speedy resolution, so he could get on with the business of economy—developing the nation's riches, as he said in his address at the opening of the Eighteenth Majlis. Everyone understood that an agreement would be reached and the British would not occupy the same position as they had previously held. It was also understood that no agreement could conceivably satisfy the people's hopes and aspirations. Thus criticizing the negotiations would be popular and politically rewarding. Facing that criticism was the government's responsibility—Prime Minister Zahedi, the police chief, General Alavi-Moqaddam, the military governor, General Teymur Bakhtiar, and Zahedi's friends in the parliament and the press.

The oil companies had their own problems. They had to find markets without alienating the countries that had increased their oil production to replace the lost Iranian oil. They also needed to accommodate the companies that demanded a share in the upcoming Iranian operations. Intricate discussions among the oil companies operating in the Middle East involved drawing and redrawing supply equations agreeable to the oil-producing countries as well as the companies involved. Equally intricate negotiations between the British and the American majors on one hand and between them and the other companies on the other hand took place to arrive at a settlement everyone could live with. In the end, a consortium was suggested and provisionally established to satisfy both the requirements of the nationalization law and the demands of the oil companies. Representatives of the Consortium—Orville Harden (later replaced by Howard Page) of Standard Oil (N.J.), Harold Snow of AIOC, and J. H. Loudon of Royal Dutch Shell went to Tehran on 11 April 1954 to negotiate with the Iranian team—Ali Amini, Abdollah Entezam, the National Iranian

Oil Company chairman, Mortezaqoli Bayat, and Fathollah Nuri Esfandiari of the foreign ministry. Concurrently, Amini negotiated with Sir Roger Stevens and Harold Snow on the question of compensation, the issue that had undone Mosaddeq.[31]

The nationalization law stipulated that Iran would have ownership of its oil and control of the related operations. The Consortium was a device to allow formal adherence to the law. On behalf of the Iranian government, which maintained formal sovereignty over the oil, the Consortium would manage the operations pertaining to the extraction, refining, transportation, and marketing of the oil in the concessionary area for a period of twenty-five years, and have the option of three five-year renewals at the end of that period. Two operating companies would be established and registered in Holland to undertake the work of the Consortium — the Iranian Oil Exploration and Producing Company and the Iranian Oil Refining Company, which the Iranian government had the right to inspect and audit. In practice, the decisions would later be made by the Iranian Oil Participants, an organization in London composed of representatives from each member of the Consortium, which decided on planning, capitalization, development, and other important projects having to do with Iranian oil, and in which Iran had no representatives.[32] The exploration and refining companies were in fact executors of this central decision-making body. On compensation, the companies joining the Consortium were committed to pay AIOC £200 million over ten years. Iran agreed to pay £25 million over the same period.[33]

The framework for the agreement was signed on 5 August 1954 by Ali Amini on behalf of Iran, by Page and Snow for the oil companies, and by Roger Stevens for Britain, eliciting widespread reaction across the country. The day corresponded to the forty-ninth anniversary of the signing of the Constitution, which was usually celebrated in the Majlis with a message by the monarch. The shah's message on this date focused on the meaning of constitutionalism and the importance of reason replacing emotion in the affairs of the state.[34] President Eisenhower and Prime Minister Churchill congratulated the shah on his statesmanlike leadership of the issue, Churchill noting how eagerly he awaited the successful conclusion of the treaty as it passed the legal stages to become law. The National Front and others associated with Mosaddeq condemned the agreement as undermining the national interest and asked the Majlis to reject it.[35] Ayatollah Kashani called on General Zahedi not to become the most treacherous of Iranian leaders by "accepting this piece of paper." "I am ready to die to preserve the honor and interest of Iran, and I ask all the Iranians who fought to nationalize our national resource to stop fighting each other and instead unite to defend our national sovereignty and honor," Kashani announced.[36] Zahedi told the Majlis, "It is rare for human beings to achieve all their wishes completely; still, as the honored deputies shall come to see, we have solved the problem of oil in the best way possible under the circumstances." Amini, who was to guide the agreement through the Majlis, told the representatives: "We do not claim to have found the ideal solution to the problem of oil, or that the sales agreement we have reached is what our nation wished. . . . [W]e can reach the ideal solution only when we achieve the power, wealth, and technological means that give us the ability to compete with countries that are big and powerful."[37]

No one in Iran was happy with the Consortium Agreement. For the Iranian government, it was, as Amini said, a necessity that had to be faced for the time being until changing conditions presented a new opportunity. During the later sessions of the talks, the shah spent much of the time traveling in various parts of the country; in the month of July he was mostly in Azerbaijan. He followed the negotiations and received periodic reports from Amini, whom he prodded to expedite the process. The end result was probably the best that Iran could have expected under the circumstances, observed Parviz Mina, director of international affairs at the National Iranian Oil Company (NIOC) during the 1970s, but it was far from satisfactory. Certainly it fell short of expectations; Mina qualified it as "imposed." Unlike the offers Iran had received in the Truman-Churchill or the Eisenhower-Churchill proposals, where the National Iranian Oil Company would have had control of the administration of the Iranian oil industry and a consortium of companies would have become purchasers of Iran's oil, the 1954 agreement gave the power to manage the oil almost totally to the Consortium. Thus the Consortium assumed the greater share of Iran's technical capability as well as its extractable and exportable resources.[38] Iran's oil, wrote Fuad Rowhani, was legally nationalized, but, in practice, the Iranian government and the NIOC had very limited authority in the management of the industry. The companies constituting the Consortium, on the other hand, had extensive powers, particularly in determining Iran's revenues from oil, in which the main factors were price per barrel and rate of production. In these areas the Iranian government and the NIOC were powerless, and the Consortium enjoyed absolute freedom.[39]

The agreement Amini took to the Majlis on 21 September 1954 was debated in a special joint committee composed of thirty-six members, half from the Majlis and half from the Senate. The Majlis passed the bill on 21 October, the Senate on the 28th. These were not happy days for the shah. The oil agreement was not something he could be proud of. In addition, on 26 October, his thirty-fifth birthday, the plane carrying Prince Alireza, his only full brother, from Gorgan province to Tehran was lost over the Alborz Mountains. The shah drove to

Firuz Kuh, the region of the mountains where the plane was most likely to have crash-landed, to oversee the search, but there was no sign of wreckage. On 1 November the commander of the gendarmerie informed him that the plane had been found and that its three passengers, including the sick villager for whose sake the prince had ventured to fly after dark, had perished. The incident saddened the shah profoundly; the devastation was visible on his face as General Mohammad Shahbakhti, the eldest among his officers and his father's sometime colleague, offered condolences on behalf of the military. His grief was equally evident as he followed his brother's funeral cortege from the Sepahsalar Mosque in Tehran on 4 November. Prince Alireza was interred near his father; both graves would be desecrated after the 1978 revolution.

On 24 February 1955 a pact of mutual cooperation between Iraq and Turkey was signed in Baghdad — and therefore dubbed the Baghdad Pact. England joined it on 4 April and Pakistan on 23 December. The United States, although it had instigated the pact, did not join but encouraged others to participate. Iraq became the center of the pact because of the close relationship between Iraq's strongman Prime Minister Nuri Said and England. Turkey and Pakistan had already formally taken sides in the Cold War by joining the North Atlantic Treaty Organization (NATO) and the Southeast Asian Treaty Organization (SEATO), respectively. The Baghdad Pact was to join NATO with SEATO in a defensive arc covering the southern flank of the Soviet bloc. If Iran were to join the pact, that would be certain to incite strong Soviet objection. It was therefore a matter of serious concern for the shah and the government.

The idea of the pact was first floated in June 1953 when Secretary of State Dulles made reference to a northern tier in a report to the nation after his trip to the Middle East. He had not visited Iran because at the time Iran was in the grip of its oil crisis and the United States was in the midst of its scheming to overthrow Mosaddeq. Dulles, however, was clearly hinting at a pact that would include Iran as an important link in the chain of countries close to the Soviet Union. Iran, he said in his comments, may be "preoccupied with its oil dispute with Britain. But still the people and the Government do not want this quarrel to expose them to Communist subversion."[40] Mosaddeq, of course, did not wish to be exposed to communist subversion, but he was. There was also the problem of his neutralist foreign policy. The question was whether the policy would continue after Mosaddeq and, if not, what role the shah would play in reformulating it in favor of the West. Both Dulles and Eisenhower believed the shah was the pivot and that he would shift vigorously to the West because it was to his country's advantage. Eisenhower had an especially positive impression of the shah, whom he considered "a man of good intent, concerned for the welfare of his people."[41] After the fall of Mosaddeq, the shah's role in foreign policy altered significantly, but in 1953 and 1954 he still had to contend with Zahedi as prime minister and Entezam as minister of foreign affairs, neither of whom was in favor of an acute change in Iran's foreign relations.

The issue of the Baghdad Pact was first raised with the shah in early 1955 during a visit to the United States. On a visit to Tehran the previous year, Vice President Richard Nixon had extended the invitation to the shah on behalf of the president. The shah and Queen Soraya left Iran on 5 December 1954 and returned on 12 March 1955, one of the longest trips the shah would ever take outside of Iran, a signal he was confident the situation at home was under control. By the end of 1954, in fact, the political climate had calmed down. Mosaddeq's trial was over. The oil dispute was behind him. He had regained control of the armed forces. And he was in a position to redefine his standing with the Western countries that were important to his future, especially the United States and Great Britain. His people "were thankful for the support they received from the United States in one of the most difficult moments of their history," he said to the press in New York, as he disembarked to receive a routine medical examination. He was confident that his trip would help strengthen the relationship between the two countries.[42] He had already decided that the security of Iran would be critically influenced by the seriousness of the United States' commitment and he was not shy about impressing his view on the Americans. In Washington he said as much to Nixon, who was on hand to receive him, and to Eisenhower at lunch and Dulles at dinner, stressing to all three of them the communist threat and Iran's need for financial and military support. Neither Eisenhower nor Dulles needed convincing; both were already engaged in forming the defensive pact that would join NATO and SEATO. Iran, insisted the shah at the Washington Press Club, would do its best to raise its economic and defensive powers and would not countenance falling behind in the march of the world's civilized nations toward progress. He said the same to Iranian students who had come from across the United States to Washington, D.C., to meet him: "Now that we are confident of Iran's future, it is incumbent on you to get the best theoretical and practical education in your fields and return to serve your country." It was important to remain Iranian and patriotic, he told them. "Individual opinion is to be respected, but no one may be allowed to become a slave to a foreign country, for that is called treason." And "Each Iranian must be a soldier defending his country against foreign aggression with courage and a sense of self-sacrifice. If not, he will have committed treason against his nation."[43] The target in these words was the Soviet Union. During the past year, as part of the fallout of the Mosaddeq affair, a Tudeh military organization had been discovered, with a membership far greater than previously suspected. Many of the members had been detained, then charged with high treason, tried, and convicted. Many among them were executed, although more were saved, their sentences commuted by the shah. All this weighed heavily on his mind. In the past, he had not used the term *treason* lightly. Now, he found himself using it as he spoke to the group of students.

Nevertheless, the shah was acutely conscious of the need to accommodate the Soviet Union as well as Iran's other regional neighbors. On 7 December, the day after he and Soraya arrived in New York, Iran's foreign minister, Abdollah Entezam, offered the Majlis the text of the agreement that Iran and the Soviet Union had reached on long-standing and thorny financial and border disputes. On the 8th the Iranian government declared formally that Iran was intent on reaching amicable agreements on several urgent issues, including oil, diplomatic relations with England, border and financial disputes with the Soviet Union, differences over the Helmand River with Afghanistan, and border disputes, especially around the Shatt al-Arab delta near Abadan, with Iraq.[44] Joining a one-sided defensive pact such as the proposed Baghdad Pact did not seem to help Iran's prospects of achieving these aims. The shah therefore was not committed to such a pact when he left Iran for the United States, nor did he believe he was in a position to decide on the subject without the presence of his government. On 15 December, in his conversations with Eisenhower and Dulles, he stated his wish for stronger relations between Iran and the United States but he also stressed the strategic implications of Iran's proximity to the Soviet Union. According to Ardeshir Zahedi, who accompanied the shah as his adjutant, the question of the pact was not raised in these meetings. Eisenhower, though, assured the shah he was happy that he was in the United States and that the Iranian political situation had changed so manifestly for the better.[45]

The shah left Washington, D.C., for California, and from there flew to Palm Beach, Florida, where he met for the first time Joseph and Rose Kennedy, their children Edward and John, then a U.S. senator, and John's wife, Jacqueline. Jacqueline and Soraya became friends and subsequently met in France on several occasions.[46] While in Florida, the shah and Soraya made several leisure trips to the Caribbean. In the Bahamas the question of the upcoming pact between Turkey and Iraq was raised informally in conversation with the shah. Ardeshir sent a telegram to his father in Tehran to inform him of the events. The prime minister was angry and wired back that His Majesty should not have talked about these matters with foreign leaders in the absence of the minister of foreign affairs. Besides, he added, what did Iran gain from the Saʿdabad Pact to make the country rush into another like it?[47] The shah also was not fond of the Saʿdabad Pact, but neither did he appreciate his prime minister's outburst. The conversation about the pact, however, was not pursued. In England, where the shah visited next, the pact was brought up only cursorily, when Churchill informed the shah that England would join in April. In Iraq, the last country he visited on his way home, his hosts, King Faisal and Crown Prince Abd al-Ilah, also mentioned it in passing, though no serious negotiations were undertaken.

Actually, a pact with Iraq and Turkey meant little to the shah. Neither country could help him against his northern neighbor. He sought an American commitment, and he was given to believe that the United States would join the pact since it had initiated the idea. Still, he would rather have a bilateral agreement with the United States than be in a pact whose purpose he believed was deterring the Soviets but not necessarily defending Iran. What if joining the pact would only serve to incite Soviet ire but provide Iran no real defense? In fact, in July 1954 his government had received a threatening note from the Soviets about Iran's rumored intention to join a Turkey-Pakistan agreement designed to bridge NATO and SEATO. Ambassador Anatoli Lavrentiev complained to Foreign Minister Abdollah Entezam that he understood Iran was being pressured by the United States to join this "aggressive" arrangement and warned Iran to mind the commitments it had undertaken when it signed the security treaty of October 1927 with the Soviet Union.[48] Given this treaty, the note Lavrentiev handed Entezam said, the government of the Soviet Union desired to receive from the government of Iran a formal explanation. Entezam denied that Iran intended to join any bloc, but in an official note he protested it was Iran's right to do so if her security so required, and in any case Iran would act openly and honestly.[49]

What was significant for Iran in all this was that the British were no longer a match for the Soviets in the Middle East. In London the shah had told Churchill that friendly relations now established between their two countries would significantly improve the chances for peace in the Persian Gulf and the Middle East.[50] He believed the British position in the oil consortium made it possible for more rational Anglo-Iranian relations to emerge. He would later write that the oil agreement's most important achievement was that it terminated the British monopolistic hold over Iran. "No longer did a giant private corporation or the government behind it dominate a large sector of our economy. The agreement meant that Iran and Britain now dealt with each other on the basis of full equality, and therefore it paved the way for smooth and neighborly relations." That, however, would take statesmanship on both sides, and no one could predict the future.[51] The fact was that the shah did not trust the British to support him and his country against the emerging revolutionary Arab states, headed now by Egypt. And for the first time since the fall of his father, the opinion of the shah carried real weight in his country; it might not yet have reached the finality it would have in future years but it already was nearly determinative. This made him feel responsible and apprehensive. Sometimes he felt he was the only Iranian who thought strategically about the future. His prime minister objected to his negotiating these points on his own, but, perhaps, the time had come, or soon would come, for him to be his own minister of foreign affairs.[52]

Even before the agreement on the oil consortium was signed, the shah had decided that Abolhassan Ebtehaj was the man to manage Iran's development policy. He had tried to get Zahedi to make Ebtehaj head of finance, but the general had not taken the bait. Instead, he had chosen Ali Amini. But no one could doubt Ebtehaj's credentials for heading the new development program. He was the father of the idea. Besides, he was the shah's close friend, a friendship that went back to the early 1940s, when Ebtehaj's first wife, Maryam, was Princess Ashraf's lady-in-waiting and dear friend, one of the reasons Ebtehaj was admitted to the inner circle of the court. His relationship with the princess deteriorated after he divorced Maryam, but he remained a confidant of the shah.

Ebtehaj's interest in planning for economic development went back to Reza Shah's times, when the concept of "economic development" was unknown. Ebtehaj had talked to interested officials then about the need for what he called an "economic map." In the early summer of 1937 Reza Shah ordered Prime Minister Mahmud Jam to follow up on the idea. But no tangible efforts at development happened until 1947, when Qavam's cabinet, with Mohammad Reza Shah's prodding, established a High Planning Commission and a Planning Board and charged them to take measures to prepare a national development plan.[53]

Ebtehaj, who was then president of Bank Melli, Iran's national bank, once again became the prime mover behind development planning in Iran, finding in the shah a kindred soul and supporter who agreed with him that Iran's economic problems could not be solved except by adopting a measured, comprehensive plan infused with foreign capital and expertise. The government chose Morrison Knudsen Construction Company to develop a plan and assigned Ebtehaj as the Iranian liaison. In four months—January to April 1947—the American company prepared two development plans, one with a budget of $500 million and another with a budget of $250 million, as Ebtehaj had instructed. In August, Prime Minister Qavam deployed Ebtehaj to London to talk to the World Bank president, John J. McCloy, about a loan. McCloy would not agree to $250 million but promised an unspecified amount Iran could manage once the Majlis approved a plan. The bill for the plan was based on a report prepared by Mosharraf Naficy, an Ebtehaj ally, and offered to the Majlis by Prime Minister Hakimi on 4 May 1948. After debate in a special committee on plans, it was passed by the Majlis on 15 February 1949, by then in Sa'ed's premiership.[54] The first development plan, with an expected length of seven years, was launched in September 1949 with a budget fixed at 21 billion rials, or about $100 million per year.

The first seven-year plan, however, did not take off as the shah and Ebtehaj had hoped. Cabinets did not last, the plan was not taken seriously, and the oil nationalization stopped the flow of funds. Once oil income was restored in 1954, Ebtehaj informed the shah that he was there "to fight against those who intend to waste the oil income." The shah knew where he wanted him: "We have thought of two positions for you—NIOC and the Plan Organization. Oil will be run by the companies; you will do better at the Plan Organization."[55]

Ebtehaj became development planning's veritable tsar. He reorganized the Plan Organization. He established a technical bureau headed by Safi Asfia, a professor at Tehran University, and an economic bureau headed by Khodadad Farmanfarmaian, an economist he recruited in the United States, both of whom would later become managing directors of the Plan Organization. He invited foreign experts, mostly American but also other nationalities, to help with planning and execution—with little regard for the sensibilities of his government colleagues. During his stewardship the germ of Iran's development culture was sown. He concentrated planning, execution, follow-up, and oversight in the Plan Organization and succeeded so well that this concentration became the norm even after the rationale for it had long expired. He countenanced no deviation and allowed no one to interfere in his work, a bargain he had made with the shah and the prime minister. The shah assured him he wanted him in the Plan Organization because he wanted the oil money to be spent by someone immune to influence. "Does your prime minister think the same way?" inquired Ebtehaj. "He agrees completely, but talk to him as well," said the shah. Zahedi assured Ebtehaj on his "soldier's honor." But it was not easy to build a government within a government. Inevitably, rifts began to appear. Zahedi wanted action; Ebtehaj would not act until he was convinced he knew what it was that he, Ebtehaj, wanted to do. The shah urged him to take at least some action so he could defend him; he would not. He was an exceptional person but, in British Ambassador Sir Roger Stevens's words, "his outstanding qualities of courage, honesty, and efficiency [were] more than offset by his uncertain temper, his indifference to the feelings of his colleagues, and his determination to get as much power into his own hands and control as much public expenditure as possible."[56]

By the end of 1954 Zahedi was in trouble, he and his cabinet tainted by unproved accusations of corruption. Iranian political culture made it difficult for a neutral observer to conclude confidently whether a reputation of corruption corresponded with the truth or not, because the charge of corruption was often indifferently applied. But the reputation hurt nonetheless, and the Zahedi cabinet, a target for some time, was no exception. Moreover, the shah was not averse to a change of government. He had already intimated the possibility of dismissing Zahedi separately to Henderson and Stevens in the spring of 1954, complaining of the cabinet's unpopularity and tainted standing, but had retreated faced with the ambassadors' strong support for the prime minister.[57] By the end of the year, however, Stevens had come to believe that the cabinet would not last. On 16 March 1955 Zahedi, at the end of his patience, charged three of his ministers to prepare a Three-Year Plan, apparently to challenge Ebtehaj. The next day, on the 17th, Ebtehaj had an audience with the shah, who assured him of his continued support. On the 18th, Zahedi wrote the shah asking him to choose between Ebtehaj and him. On the 19th, the shah wrote back to the prime minister that he was not prepared to dispense with Ebtehaj, whose abilities were outstanding, but he hoped the prime minister would reconsider his decision.[58] Zahedi, realizing he had no future, even if he discounted his problems with Ebtehaj, resigned on 6 April 1955.

Before he left on a trip to Khuzistan on 24 March 1955, the shah had met with his prime minister on several occasions to discuss the intimations of corruption in the government, particularly in relation to the aid received from the United States.[59] To the Majlis and the Senate, the shah suggested administrative reform, especially in pay scales, to obviate civil servants' need to seek graft.[60] These activities led to bizarre rumors about the relationship between the shah and the prime minister, much of it proving false. On his way back from his trip in the south the shah is said to have directed Amir Asadollah Alam to advise the prime minister to resign. According to Jahangir Tafazzoli, an Alam protégé, Zahedi replied that he had come on a tank and he would leave on one. According to Reza Kaynezhad, a friend of Zahedi who was present at the meeting, Zahedi told Alam no intermediary was needed; he would personally speak with the shah.[61] Nasser Zolfaqari recalls General Teymur Bakhtiar, then martial law governor in Tehran and commander of the Tehran Second Armored Division, telling him that Zahedi had boasted that nothing could stop him if he decided not to go, but Bakhtiar had responded that he personally would arrest him if the shah so ordered.[62] Ardeshir Zahedi had only heard his father say he preferred to resign because he felt he was no longer supported by the shah.[63] According to Queen Soraya's reminiscences, the shah had said Zahedi had become too arrogant to remain as prime minister. However, when Zahedi told the shah he was tired and wished to resign, the shah said he would be sorry if the prime minister indeed decided to leave, which left Soraya baffled.[64]

Ardeshir's version is most likely the closest to the truth. A few days before the general was dismissed, Ardeshir accompanied the shah on his trip to Khuzistan. On the way back, he and the shah played backgammon most of the way, the shah enjoying Ardeshir's pranks designed to make him miss the critical moves. By then the shah had already begun the process of dismissing the prime minister.[65] The shah returned to Tehran on 4 April; on the 5th, he flew to Mashhad, where he made a pilgrimage to the shrine of Reza, the Eighth Imam, and unveiled his father's statue in the Khurasan military headquarters. On 6 April, General Zahedi offered his resignation. The shah accepted the prime minister's resignation with regret and issued a *farman* commending him for his distinguished service to the nation. He then appointed his court minister, Hossein Ala, as prime minister. Ala, however, was ill and had already arranged to travel abroad to receive medical care. A reluctant warrior, Ala kept Zahedi's senior ministers—Foreign Minister Abdollah Entezam, Finance Minister Ali Amini, and National Defense Minister Lieutenant General Abdollah Hedayat—appointed Amir Asadollah Alam to Interior, and on 10 April introduced the cabinet, with Entezam as acting prime minister in his absence, to the Majlis and left for Europe. With Zahedi gone, a new era began.

10

The White Revolution

The shah believed in Ebtehaj, though he did not quite grasp the political implications of Ebtehaj's position. The shah's mind moved toward a comprehensive
political framework in which economic planning was an important pillar but
subordinated to the requirements of his politics. Ebtehaj, on the other hand,
saw planning as the frame against which politics was to be assessed. For him,
everything else was subordinate to planning. His was a "wedge approach," said
Khodadad Farmanfarmaian, the head of his economic bureau. There was the
plan — and there was the rest. Everything good was in the plan and the organization that harbored it. The rest was laziness, corruption, and ignorance. The
ministries wished to participate, but Ebtehaj argued that they could not until
they earned the right to participate by becoming knowledgeable, efficient, and
honest. The paradox was that they could not become all of that unless they
learned in practice.

Ebtehaj would stifle all nascent urges to decentralization. While he was in
the process of formulating the Second Development Plan (1956–62), a committee from Khuzistan comprising the province's governor, the two senators, and
several Majlis deputies appeared in his office with a large map of the province
and a plan for Khuzistan's development that they wished to present to the
Majlis for approval and for which they asked his support. The plan called for
an allocation of 7 percent of the oil revenue to the development of Khuzistan.
Ebtehaj would have none of it: "My purpose is to have a comprehensive and
coordinated development plan for the whole country," he said.[1] Several years
before, in the summer of 1950, Prime Minister Razmara had proposed an economic program whereby the central government would allocate lump sums of
money to the provinces, allowing the governor and a council of local leaders to
determine for what development projects the funds would be used. Ebtehaj had
strenuously, and apparently successfully, counseled against the idea.[2] What he

said to Khuzistan's governor and representatives followed the same logic, except that now he was the master. The Khuzistani representatives, dejected and disappointed, left his office, and afterward development planning in Iran was imagined, shaped, developed, executed, and supervised at the center.

Ebtehaj also created another dilemma for the shah. Good management could not be had without good managers, and Iran, as far as Ebtehaj was concerned, was singularly devoid of good managers. He therefore looked to the West, especially the United States, for men who could help him to get his organization off the ground. He had important friends, including the World Bank president Eugene Black, who helped him find the right men for some of the ongoing industrial projects he had inherited—dams, roads, port facilities, and the like. Black sent him several able experts who worked with the World Bank and also talked to David Lilienthal, president of Development and Resources Corporation and a former manager of the Tennessee Valley Authority (TVA). Ebtehaj and Lilienthal met in the fall of 1955 when they both were attending the annual meeting of the International Bank for Reconstruction and Development (IBRD) and the International Monetary Fund (IMF) in Istanbul. Lilienthal expressed interest in what Ebtehaj was doing in Iran, and Ebtehaj invited him to go to Iran to study the prospects for the development of Khuzistan. The idea of irrigating Khuzistan had been launched during Qavam's premiership but had had to be abandoned after opposition from the Anglo-Iranian Oil Company had dried up the British government's support and consequently also the funds that were to be made available by Hambros Bank of London. Ebtehaj saw a new opportunity to relaunch the project, and as far as he was concerned Lilienthal was the ideal candidate for it. The idea, however, was not as welcome in Iran. Lilienthal was not known to Iranians, though, according to Ebtehaj, "contrary to his ministers who had not even heard his name, the shah knew him by reputation" and supported Ebtehaj's decision.[3] Lilienthal and his partner Gordon Clapp went to Iran and began one of the most ambitious projects Iran had ever known.

For the shah, developing Khuzistan, which was reputed to have been one of Iran's most fertile provinces in times past, became a priority. He appreciated Lilienthal's attitude, especially his statement to Ebtehaj that the TVA would have never gotten off the ground had he listened to the experts. In Iran also the expert opinion was skeptical about the cost-effectiveness of the project: the earth and water were too salty, the air was too hot and humid, and the cost was overwhelming, warned the critics. Lilienthal thought otherwise. It was the perfect place for the perfect project, he said. All he needed was financial and political support, which Ebtehaj gave him unreservedly. His enthusiasm for Lilienthal and Clapp was almost unbounded. Lilienthal seemed to him to have come to

Iran for a higher purpose. Lillienthal himself would write in his journal that building one more dam was nothing to him. He was doing in Iran something that he hoped would make a difference in the lives of the people,[4] an ambition whose achievement required more than listening to the experts. Here he was on the same wavelength with Ebtehaj—who had once shouted at Burke Knapp, an IBRD expert who warned him of the inflationary pressures his expenditures might produce, that one could not build a country if one kept listening to the economists who would always warn against doing anything[5]—and also with the shah, who had come to believe, perhaps tutored by Ebtehaj, that "the best economists are those who never studied economics."[6]

Over the years Ebtehaj alienated almost everyone in the government. His disagreements with Zahedi were known throughout Tehran. He made life almost as difficult for Zahedi's successor, Hossein Ala, who was his old friend, but this could not go on forever. Ala (who had survived an assassination attempt in November 1955) resigned on 3 April 1957 and was appointed minister of court, replacing Dr. Manuchehr Eqbal, who, in turn, replaced Ala as prime minister. Eqbal was also a friend of Ebtehaj's, though not as close as Ala. "If I were you, I would not accept the position, given the powers of the managing director of the Plan Organization" (that is, himself), Ebtehaj told Eqbal. "However, you have agreed to become prime minister knowingly. I hope it will not affect our friendship."[7] Eqbal promised to support Ebtehaj but declared in the Majlis that he would not suffer a government within a government. To Ebtehaj, who protested his remarks, he said it was a reference to his ministers, one of whom, Ja'far Sharif-Emami, would become Ebtehaj's nemesis. Sharif-Emami was German-educated, connected with the clergy, head of an important Freemason lodge, politically tough, and professionally ambitious. His turf, industries and mines, overlapped with Ebtehaj's. It would not take long for the two to lock horns, though, in the end, it was Ebtehaj's outburst in front of an American envoy that forced the shah to side with the government and against Ebtehaj.

Early in February 1959, Admiral Arthur W. Radford, a former chairman of the U.S. joint chiefs of staff, and George McGhee, a former ambassador and assistant secretary of state, were on a tour of Turkey, Iran, and Pakistan to study U.S. military aid to these countries. In Iran, they visited the Plan Organization, where Ebtehaj gave them a dressing-down on the problems of military policy in Iran. "Iran needs economic development, not military support," he told Radford. According to Khodadad Farmanfarmaian, who was present at the meeting, Ebtehaj lost control, "banging so hard on the table that the table shook, disorienting Radford, who had turned red and did not know what to say."[8] This apparently was the last straw. The shah naturally learned of what had happened.

Farmanfarmaian believed that the Americans reported what had happened to their ambassador and the ambassador informed the court. A few days later, on 11 February 1959, Prime Minister Eqbal introduced a highest-priority bill to the Majlis devolving the powers and responsibilities of the managing director of the Plan Organization to the prime minister.[9]

Ebtehaj heard that the Majlis had passed the bill while he was in a meeting with his directors. His deputy, Khosro Hedayat, entered the room and whispered in his ear. "Please excuse me. The meeting is over," Ebtehaj said, as he rose to his feet, closing the document in front of him on the table. Later that day, he told Farmanfarmaian: "I have submitted my resignation on three different occasions. Why are they throwing me out like a dog?"[10] As he was being driven home, he heard on the radio the report of the "single bill" in the Nineteenth Majlis. "When Eqbal read the text of the bill, the deputies shouted *ahsant, ahsant,* Hear, Hear. Not one rose to support me, not one was sad to see me go."[11]

■

The Nineteenth Majlis ended on 9 July 1960. The shah had for some time promoted a two-party system and now promised free elections. Amir Asadollah Alam, a confidant of the shah and the leader of the opposition Mardom (People's) Party, declared the defeat of the government party, the Melliyun (Nationalists), led by Eqbal, imminent. Alam, taking up the mantle of a "genuine" opposition leader, had for some time been criticizing the government on every occasion, including in an address in the fall of 1958 to the Iranian Students Association of Northern California assembled at the University of California at Berkeley, where he called Eqbal and his government incompetent and misguided.[12] But this was not all. The Kennedy candidacy—this "young energetic man" speaking of a new generation of Americans who would bring democracy to the world—had helped to revitalize the moribund left and the National Front in Iran. The Second National Front was organized on 19 July, the day the shah ordered elections for the Twentieth Majlis. Eqbal now became a target of concerted attack by an array of opponents. His government tried to "control" the elections, but he was challenged politically in the streets and legally in courts. On 3 August old political stalwarts such as Mozaffar Baqai and Hossein Makki brought suit in the court to annul the Tehran elections for fraud. On the same day Ali Amini and Asadollah Alam called the elections the faultiest and most fraudulent ever conducted in Iran. On the 5th, the shah pronounced himself "dissatisfied" with the elections. Eqbal resigned on the 7th, and two days later the shah called on the newly elected Majlis to resign also because "the parties and their representatives no doubt wish[ed] to enjoy the people's utmost confidence and respect,"[13] which, by implication, the just-elected Majlis did not.

The government that succeeded Eqbal's did not fare better. The ideals espoused by the newly elected John F. Kennedy worked to energize opposition to the shah across the political spectrum—from the Tudeh left to the New National Front to the secular and religious right. The parliamentary elections to replace the flawed Twentieth Majlis became an excuse for demonstrations against the new prime minister, Ja'far Sharif-Emami, his government, and the election process itself. On 1 February 1961, several members of the National Front sought asylum in the Senate, demanding free elections. The next day, Tehran University students took to the streets in demonstrations that continued for several days. On 21 February the shah opened the new Twentieth Majlis, enumerating the country's achievements during the Nineteenth Majlis and the great steps that had been taken for the nation's infrastructure and industrial development. The new Majlis, he said, would have much to do because the country was on the move.

Student unrest continued, however. Two days after the opening of the Majlis, students at Tehran University closed down classes and launched a violent demonstration against Prime Minister Sharif-Emami and the newly appointed university chancellor, the former prime minister Manuchehr Eqbal, burning the latter's car. Police then entered the university walls and forced the university council to close the university. The unrest was embarrassing to the shah, though not unexpected. "Iran enjoys political stability," the shah said in an interview with the *Washington Post*. "The feudal system is on its way out. But we must realize that one cannot create all the elements of democracy in one day. But I am creating an environment in which democracy can grow."[14] The unrest abated after the closing of the university but was rekindled once it opened on 3 April. On 2 May primary and secondary school teachers struck, gathering in front of the Majlis to demand higher salaries. The police opened fire, and one of the teachers, Abdolhossein Khanali, was killed by a stray bullet. Sharif-Emami was interpellated in the Majlis and offered his resignation. The shah at first refused but, upon the prime minister's insistence, reluctantly accepted his resignation. The next day, on 5 May, he appointed Ali Amini prime minister.[15]

◼

Ali Amini was not the shah's favorite. He was a Qajar king's grandson, a Qajar prime minister's son-in-law, close to Qavam and Mosaddeq, and too ambitious—the kind of man the shah's father had warned him against. On the other hand, he was clever, friendly, and politic. He knew how to treat royalty, and he ingratiated himself to the shah by being correct and deferential. He was also an American favorite, which made him both an asset and a threat to the shah. He had shown considerable skill in negotiating the Consortium Agreement, which had made him popular with the Americans. Because of that and his other traits, he thought of himself as a candidate for prime minister, an ambition he did not conceal.

Amini had been appointed ambassador to the United States in the latter part of Ala's premiership and served until March 1958. In Washington he established rapport with Secretary of State John Foster Dulles and friendship with John F. Kennedy, then a U.S. senator from Massachusetts. He was recalled to Iran under curious circumstances. According to documents discovered in relation to an alleged coup d'état being planned by the army's chief of G2 (or intelligence bureau), Major General Vali Qaranei, Amini was to become prime minister. With its discovery the coup fell apart. The shah was incensed, not so much at Amini, who was shown not to have been actively involved in the plot, but at Qaranei, whom, as he told the Eqbal cabinet, he had been grooming for higher positions.[16] Amini had, however, suggested that part of the revenues of the oil-producing countries be placed in an international bank to help oil-poor Third World countries under international supervision.[17] This was totally unacceptable to both the shah (though in the 1970s he would suggest a similar arrangement, but under his own supervision) and the Iranian government, providing further reason for Foreign Minister Aliqoli Ardalan to call Amini back. Amini stayed in France for a few months until tempers cooled—and then returned to Iran as a self-proclaimed candidate for prime minister.

Given the political fever over John Kennedy that invaded Tehran, Amini's reputed friendship with the Kennedys bolstered his position. There were talks of Amini, the left, and the National Front joining forces in the election for the Twentieth Majlis, but the coalition did not materialize. Amini reasoned that the shah would not stand for such a coalition and that he would not succeed if the shah opposed him. Instead, he criticized the cabinets of Eqbal and subsequently Sharif-Emami while currying the shah's favor—and suggesting to others that the shah supported his candidacy. Over the years, he had kept in touch with his *dowreh,* a discussion group consisting of his friends and supporters, even while he was in the United States.[18] Now he sought contact with other groups, including American-educated technocrats in government and private business, among them a band of colleagues and friends centered at the Plan Organization who would play important administrative and political roles in future years.[19] His main liaison with this group was his friend and relative Khodadad Farman-farmaian, then head of the Economic Bureau at the Plan Organization.

The shah would later say, on several occasions, that the Americans forced Amini on him. The Kennedy administration probably would have liked Amini to become prime minister, but it is unlikely that anyone had said so to the shah.[20] A reasonable explanation for the shah's feeling might be that he deduced American inclination from a combination of factors, both domestic and international. The deciding factor might have been Sharif-Emami telling the shah that the Americans had been behind the unrest that led to the death of the teacher Abdolhossein Khanali and his own resignation.[21]

John Kennedy was not fond of the shah; on the other hand, he was too busy elsewhere to be overly concerned with him. As his secretary of state, Dean Rusk, put it: "There weren't major crises involving Iran during that period. Remember that President Kennedy's thousand days were days of high crisis. There had been the Berlin crisis of 1961, 1962 and the Cuban Missile Crisis and the basic decisions on Vietnam, so that Iran did not play a major role because it wasn't in that kind of a critical situation. So I don't know; although President Kennedy had an insatiable appetite for information and took a great interest in what was going on, he did not become greatly concerned about what was happening in Iran."[22]

Five months into his presidency Kennedy had met with Nikita Khrushchev in Vienna, an encounter that had not gone well for the American president. Rumor had it that in Vienna Khrushchev had told Kennedy Iran was ripe for a revolution and would soon fall to the socialist camp. The warning, a part of Khrushchev's testing of the president, was said to have greatly upset Kennedy and made him think about Iran and the shah. If so, Rusk must not have noticed. "I was present for those conversations in Vienna. And I was concerned with the brutal way in which Khrushchev threw an ultimatum at President Kennedy on Berlin and seemed to think that he could somehow intimidate this new, young president of the United States. But, quite frankly, I don't recall that Iran played all that much of a role in those discussions." The rumor about Khrushchev's remarks, attributed to Walt Rostow, Kennedy's adviser on national security affairs, also provided a basis for believing that Kennedy had pushed Ali Amini on the shah. To Rusk this was improbable. "I'd be surprised to learn that we had tried to advise or push the shah to name one man rather than another as prime minister. . . . We were pressing for economic and social reforms, and we were encouraging him [the shah] in the White Revolution. But I think there was a limit beyond which our advice could not go. And such things as the actual choice of a prime minister would be simply beyond our reach."[23]

Whatever the reason, Kennedy ordered a special task force, the first ever in his administration, chaired by Philips Talbot, to study the Iranian condition. Talbot had been appointed assistant secretary of state for the Near East and South Asia in 1961 on the recommendation of Dean Rusk and Chester Bowles. His area extended from the eastern Arab countries and Israel to Turkey, Iran, Afghanistan, and the subcontinent through Sri Lanka (then Ceylon). He represented the new, rather nebulous thinking under Kennedy—though personally he had little previous connection to the Kennedys—that the Eisenhower administration had been too closely and uncritically involved with the shah and his regime and that the time had come to take a new look at the relationship. The Kennedys were critical of the shah in the general way U.S. liberals were critical of Third World leaders who did not fall in the neutralist category. Their attitude was reflected more as a mood rather than a doctrine or specific set of policies. The U.S. foreign policy establishment in the National Security Council (NSC), the State and Defense Departments, the CIA, and Congress did not always see eye-to-eye and so did not project a coherent position the target countries could identify with reasonable assurance. Thus the shah had to guess—and make decisions based on his guesswork. There were those Americans who favored the military as the nexus of U.S.-Iranian relations to assure U.S. security imperatives, which involved a whole array of considerations, from control of the Persian Gulf to the safety of the listening posts that monitored the Soviet strategic and tactical military moves. There were others who stressed social and economic development as the primary goal, which meant also a greater propensity to intervene in the shah's domestic politics and policies, including questions of human rights and democracy.[24] These were tendencies, never exclusive, never black-and-white, that, imposed on specific consideration of weapons or aid packages or loans, might cause them to diverge from the shah's demands and expectations. So it was that the shah was not happy with the Kennedy administration, nor the Kennedy administration with the shah.

Several members on the president's Iran task force had a history with Iran and were vociferously anti-shah. Kenneth Hansen, who in 1961 held a senior position at the Treasury Department and was influential with the Kennedys, had worked in Iran with Ebtehaj at the Plan Organization and had developed a very negative view of the shah. "Hansen, even in the waning Eisenhower days, had been stirring up all kinds of trouble," Ambassador Armin Meyer recalled. "In his view, the shah was an S.O.B., and we Americans shouldn't be dealing with him. He considered him a tyrant, an oppressor, and all that sort of thing—nondemocratic. Hansen got an even a better position, as I recall, in the Kennedy administration, and energetically stirred up things about Iran. I think, probably, he as much as anybody was involved in instigating the idea that we've got to take a good look at Iran."[25]

Robert Komer of the NSC, "a blow-torch type fellow"[26] with strong feelings on Iran, was also on the task force. Originally from the CIA, Komer had gone to the NSC during the Eisenhower White House, but his work on Iran began with Kennedy. He was assigned to Iran because he had correctly predicted to McGeorge Bundy, Kennedy's special assistant for national security affairs, what the shah's first communication with Kennedy contained. Averell Harriman had met with the shah in Tehran on 13 March 1961, bringing him a routine message from the president. The shah, in return, had given Harriman a letter to deliver to the new president, which Harriman did on 29 March.[27] The shah had written that he was happy a young energetic man had taken over the U.S. presidency and that he was sure they would get along well. He then had stated the dangers Iran faced from the Soviet Union and its surrogates, headed by Nasser. He needed economic and military help and he hoped Kennedy understood Iran's predicament and would be more forthcoming than his predecessor. "Well," Komer told Bundy, "I would not give him a blood nickel. His problems are internal more than external. He has always seen the Soviets and Nasser as about eight times larger than they really are." Bundy assigned Komer to write the president's reply. "Because you have been so good," said Bundy, according to Komer, "you can write the answer—over Kennedy's signature."[28]

The letter made Komer the Iran point person at the NSC. His bailiwick—"empire" as he put it—gradually grew to include the whole of the Middle East and South Asia and subsequently also Africa. He reported to Bundy, who had brought together "five or six smart substantive people" and divided up the world among them. Iran, however, was Komer's first problem. The way he saw the shah set the tone for many others in the administration:

> One of the very first problems we had was Iran because the shah, who had returned after Mosaddeq, was feeling much more uncertain in his country. There was a certain increase in pressures on him, though the pressures were mostly domestic rather than foreign. He was frustrated. He was complaining. It looked as though we were heading maybe for an overthrow, or an attempted revolution. This raised the question, first off, of whether the shah was an adequate instrument. Whether the shah could run things in Iran. Or whether he was not likely to be picked off by his domestic opposition. The question became one of "Is the shah modernized enough to get along in the mid-twentieth century?" Or didn't he try to emphasize too much the divine right of kings, which we all knew came from World War I and his father who had been a sergeant in the Cossacks.[29]

The task force picked Julius Holmes as the next U.S. ambassador to Tehran. Holmes, a former military man, turned out not to be as docile as the task force had hoped. He was disciplined and, as both Meyer and Komer agreed, a sharp trouper, able and willing to fight for his beliefs — in both Tehran and Washington. He was also an older man and as such proved to be the last U.S. ambassador whose age gave him leverage with the shah. But he ended up in many cases arguing in favor of the shah's position.

President Kennedy went along with the task force recommendations on Iran, without much personal involvement. The recommendations, which came out in May, somewhat softened by State Department input and therefore somewhat different from the NSC position, were meant to strengthen the shah by making him adopt ways that the United States assumed were politically efficient. The task force was inclined to micromanage Iranian politics and administration in both civilian and military fields. This the shah did not accept. Neither did Julius Holmes.

Khodadad Farmanfarmaian had come to work with Ebtehaj in the fall of 1956. He had studied in the United States and left a teaching appointment at Princeton University to return to Iran to head the Economic Bureau, one of the main offices of the Plan Organization. While he was still in the United States, Ebtehaj commissioned him to study the universities that could best help him to find specialists in the fields he needed. Farmanfarmaian suggested Harvard and Princeton and mentioned Edward Mason, head of Harvard's Littauer Center for Public Administration (later the Kennedy School of Government). Ebtehaj signed an agreement with the Ford Foundation and Harvard University to select and deploy to Iran appropriate consultants for the Economic Bureau of the Plan Organization. Mason, a man of great authority according to Farmanfarmaian, became the main liaison in this process. Farmanfarmaian later recalled: "He was a strong personality. He insisted that we must accept his choice."[30] The Americans and the Iranians agreed that government could and should deliberately manipulate the economy in order to speed up the development process, which to them meant mainly the growth of GDP per capita, at the time a generally accepted thesis.[31] Ebtehaj used it to argue for allocating oil income to development. He succeeded in getting a law passed stipulating an allocation for development projects that would gradually move to 80 percent of oil revenues; in practice, however, the allocation rarely reached 60 percent.

The Economic Bureau had analyzed the Second Development Plan and determined that it was more a hodge-podge of projects than a comprehensive, interconnected plan. In 1962 the bureau proposed a third plan, which would be different from the second in important ways: the length of the plan would be reduced from seven years to five; the projects would be transferred to the ministries; and the government budget—current and development—would be determined in the Plan Organization. The first two items were already contained in the decision to put the Plan Organization under the prime minister; the third was, as Farmanfarmaian argued, to give some teeth to the Plan Organization now that the implementation functions had been taken away. The new plan would also present a balanced concept of development, emphasizing grassroots education, development of rural industry as part of industrial development, and the introduction of a project of land reform. It would also insist on a series of criteria that the government was obligated to observe, including the discipline that the concept of a plan entailed, that is, respecting plan priorities against the vagaries of political preferences. According to Abdolmajid Majidi, the Third Development Plan had significant political implications, particularly in light of the structural relations that were developing among the shah, the executive, the legislature, and the people. "Thus some individuals began to think that those working on the plan intended to interfere with the country's political structure, which inevitably put [the planners] in a very difficult situation."[32]

For the shah, the basic problem with the Third Plan was that it was dominated by the American and European consultants generically known as Goruh-e moshaveran-e harvard, or the Harvard Group.[33] The drafting of the plan, begun during Eqbal's government and continued through Amini's, coincided with Kennedy's election and the impact that it had on the political climate in Iran. In the Plan Organization the relationship between the foreign consultants and Harvard was a known fact and the connection between Harvard and the Kennedy administration was taken for granted. The dominant belief was that with Kennedy's election the Harvard group would become stronger and consequently more assertive. Amini was also supported by the Kennedys. "We believe in Dr. Amini's government, and as long as Amini is prime minister we will do whatever is necessary to help him," Attorney General Robert Kennedy told Farmanfarmaian, who met with him in Bonn on behalf of Amini.[34]

The combination of Amini and the Plan Organization appeared to some to be invincible, but things turned out differently. Amini aspired to some independence but would not go against the shah. His message to Robert Kennedy, which Farmanfarmaian delivered, was to reconsider giving the military aid the shah had requested because "the shah seemed very depressed."[35] Amini did not support the Economic Bureau before the shah as strongly as he might have done. When the strategy of the new plan was presented, the shah responded by emphasizing the importance of defending the nation's territorial integrity and national independence. He did not reject Farmanfarmaian's presentation; he simply talked about a different set of priorities. To Majidi the interaction appeared as a dialogue of the deaf, ships passing in the night. Amini, however, was quiet. Though Farmanfarmaian was both friend and relative, he failed to support him either in moving the budget to the Plan Organization or in implementing the plan. Farmanfarmaian resigned his position as head of the bureau in protest. When his colleagues asked Amini to call him back, Amini retorted: "Khodadad has become delirious."[36]

Farmanfarmaian, of course, was not delirious. It was Amini who had become exhausted, and by now it was clear that he would not last. The shah was unhappy with him, even though Amini had publicly stated his support for a powerful army.[37] Amini's pessimistic view of the economy irked the shah. His reputed closeness to the Americans made him generally unliked. His justice minister's imprisoning of Ebtehaj in November 1961 on bogus charges of corrupt practices had made him many enemies among the modernists in the government and intellectuals in the society. Even though Amini's policies had set the framework for a new take-off, for the moment he was right in his pessimism: the economy was not working well. The military was pressuring the shah to dismiss him. The Americans, who had supported him in the past, now appeared lukewarm in their support, as Kennedy became increasingly sensitive to global security issues. And the shah, freshly back from a trip to the United States in April 1962, felt more self-assured about his standing with the U.S. administration. He had impressed Kennedy as a knowledgeable and rational leader and as one who could not be easily or safely replaced. For what the shah had by now determined to do, especially in land reform, Amini was not the right instrument. The shah also did not wish to implement the reform within the framework of the Third Plan, because he believed it would then be said that land reform was an American project.[38]

But this is not to say that the shah had withdrawn his support of Amini. And at least part of the reason Amini tried to accommodate the shah was that without the monarch's support he knew he would not last long, given his enemies across the political spectrum. In late January 1962 Tehran University students, at the instigation of the National Front and encouraged by the bazaar and such conservative elements as the Rashidian brothers and several clerics on the right as well as the Tudeh on the left, went on a strike against the government. The shah ordered the police and the military to do what Amini asked. On Amini's request, he ordered former SAVAK Chief General Teymur Bakhtiar to leave

Iran. He agreed to have whomever the prime minister thought appropriate incarcerated. Stuart Rockwell of the U.S. embassy reported to Washington that the demonstrations had only one objective—to depose Amini and his cabinet—and concluded that the events showed that the shah strongly supported Amini.[39]

Ultimately, however, Amini resigned on 17 July 1962, declaring he was not able to work out the budget in a way that would satisfy the shah's military plans. He faulted not the shah but the United States for cutting off its financial assistance, putting his government at an impasse, a charge the U.S. government rejected, claiming instead that it had extended more than $67 million in aid to Iran during Amini's fourteen-month tenure.[40] The fate of the Third Plan now fell to the shah. The plan had sought to recreate the influence Ebtehaj once exerted on the government by incorporating a binding intellectual discipline. Neither the shah nor the government really bought the idea. The sovereign in fact may have killed two birds with one stone—ridding himself of both the Harvard Group and the Iranian planners by recasting much of the Third Plan in what would be called the White Revolution.

The shah believed that the industrial nations were responsible for at least part of the economic and technological plight of developing countries. He also agreed with the proposition that much of the industrial and economic progress of developed countries was financed essentially through exploitation, that is, by extracting cheap primary resources from the nonindustrial world, using them for the benefit of the developed countries, and leaving very little for the host country either in money or in know-how. But he considered this the natural condition of his time, brought about because when the West had awoken and moved, countries like Iran slept. Consequently, the world had fallen into an inevitable colonialism because of the economic and technological imbalance that had come about between developed and developing countries. Iran now had to pay for the sins of the previous generations of Iranians; that is, it had to set out on the road to economic and technological development, which the shah thought was the only way for a country to achieve a place in the industrialized world. And the only way to do this was to learn the culture of development and its scientific and ideological elements from the West. It was not easy to seek help at the altar of one's exploiter, but that was the price one had to pay if one sought to become a player on a par with those who ran the world, the shah reasoned. The price of development was an ignominious, if temporary, begging for knowledge, money, and protection. This was the essence of his positive nationalism, the only nationalism, he believed, that would lift his people from the permanent ignominy of poverty, backwardness, and exploitation.

The White Revolution, therefore, was neither a leap of faith nor an act of obedience; it represented the shah's idea of nationalism, geared in part to his concept of democracy, which he defined as an interaction of development, rights, and obligations, which in Iran would materialize only through his intervention. There were several existing models of democracy, but they would not work in Iran, he told British Foreign Secretary Sir Alex Douglas Home in March 1961 on the occasion of Queen Elizabeth's visit to Iran. Finding the right kind of democracy for Iran was a challenge, he said, because of the large percentage of illiterates. The Pakistan model of "basic democracies" was not suited to Iran, because Iran had had universal franchise for a long time. Iran had to make the best of the existing system, "gradually training the people to vote for candidates on political grounds rather than as at present on a purely personal basis." Even then, the shah suggested, the people might very well choose the candidates selected for them beforehand. But he believed this could change, because "Iranians were an intelligent people," and as they went through municipal and local elections "they would, as education spread, get the feel of democracy and, with wise guidance from the top, Iran had a good chance of remaining in and being an asset to the free democratic world." All of this, said the shah, required that he be involved in politics "to a considerable extent." Home wondered whether the extent of the shah's involvement meant that the people would blame the monarchy if things went wrong. On the whole, said the shah, the people understood that he was trying "to introduce a fair political system, to give the peasant population a greater share in the land, to industrialize the country and increase its wealth," and a majority of the people therefore recognized that the "monarchy as such" was on their side. The problem was that the students who returned from Western countries were "impatient for political reform and infected others with their ideas. . . . It was difficult to know how to turn their energies into more constructive channels," he said.[41]

The shah clearly had thought about the issue during the past two and a half years, during which he was preparing his book *Ma'muriat baray-e vatanam* (Mission for My Country), the English version of which had just been published. He was proud of his achievement: "As far as I know," he wrote in the introduction to the book, "I am the first Iranian king since the beginning of Iranian kingship 2500 years ago to write a systematic account of his life." He had written the book because he believed it would help to acquaint Iranians with their country's past as well as with the possibilities it had for a bright future. Iranians had slept through much of the past, their knowledge of it was murky, and until recently they had neglected to make plans for their future. "It was time for the king to redress these shortcomings." He would do this by reminding Iranians of their brilliant historical heritage, of the great contribution his father had made to Iran's awakening and renaissance, of his own childhood preparation for the work he was destined to perform, of the crisis of the war, of the year when "a man named Mosaddeq ran the country in his own peculiar manner," of Iran and the West, and of how he had come to formulate his concept of "positive nationalism." He would speak also of his ideas of social development and the role of oil in the nation's economic and technological development as well as political relations.[42]

In the book, the shah explained his understanding of true democracy, which was, as he saw it, democracy as it applied to Iranian conditions. His view was practical: democracy became meaningful to the extent that the people achieved the ability to become partners in the social and economic and finally political affairs of their society. His vision of democracy was triangular: political and administrative democracy; economic democracy; and social democracy. True democracy, therefore, was a coming together of the three in balance and synergy.

As far as he was concerned, the politics of Iranian democracy were constrained by the Constitution and history and gave him both the right and the obligation to perform certain functions, including appointing and dismissing ministers, vetoing certain financial bills, dissolving the parliament, and appointing governors-general, governors, or ambassadors.[43] After 1957, when the country had become politically stable and the economy began to move again, he, for his part, promoted a two-party system—so that elections always resulted in a majority party and a minority party—an idea that had always been dear to his heart. Now, in 1961, there were two major and several minor parties operating. People joined these parties freely, and although all parties saw more or less eye-to-eye on foreign policy, they sometimes engaged in significant debate about economic, social, or cultural preferences and the ways of achieving domestic goals. He was delighted that Iran's political parties had now moved away from personalities and looked more to ideas and platforms. Unfortunately, he wrote, "certain individuals criticize our party system, arguing that the two parties have not grown from among the people but rather have been imposed on them by the shah or the government." These people did not understand the motives for establishing parties in Iran, a country that had just recently embarked on its march toward progress. The shah wrote:

> Despite my father's untiring effort to educate our children and the progress we have achieved during my reign, there are still a large number of illiterates in our country. Concepts of democracy and political parties are still new to us. In a country where tradition still reigns, no thought is more injudicious than that which

holds our political parties may suddenly rise from among or be instituted by the people, grow and reach perfection. I am the king in a constitutional monarchy. I have no reason not to promote political parties, no reason, as dictators do, to support only the party of my own making. Since I symbolize my country's national unity, I can encourage two or more parties to engage in political activity without my having a special relationship with any one of them.

There were certain literate or illiterate individuals who thought a party of ten or a hundred thousand members might exist without the benefit of guidance from effective and intelligent leaders. But there was no precedent for it in any country. "Only a little exploration shows that, in every free country, parties are established by leaders who have a sufficient number of followers." There were also the self-important one who thought he was too special to participate in party politics, the congenital negativist who disparaged anything that was done for the country, and the faint-hearted person who was simply afraid. But, rejoices the shah, "There are many patriotic Iranians who realize the importance of parties for the establishment of democracy and betterment of the country and consider it a national duty to participate in their operations."[44]

The shah then focuses on administrative issues and the need for administrative reorganization. "It is our plan to continually reform the nation's public bureaucratic organizations as the needs change and as we receive new information. But there is also no doubt that, regardless of how scientifically one organizes, one never gets the right results if the managers remain traditional and out of synch with the times." An important dimension of the reform was to give the provinces and cities as much freedom of action as possible. "We have given more authority to local officials and encouraged the city councils to supervise the functions of the schools, hospitals, orphanages and other responsibilities of the city government." For this, and because the government provided palpable service in a wide array of public needs, the government official was now better received by his constituents. The shah was proud of the public official who "teaches the children, helps villagers fight against malaria, digs deep wells, or builds free clinics. . . . The villager naturally feels that a new relationship is now established between the government and the people." This new relationship was essential to building democracy. People ought to know who does what, vote into office meritorious candidates, and be familiar with the issues the candidates will have to tackle when they are in the two houses of parliament. "I do not pretend that making such a democracy is easy. The only point I wish to emphasize is that we Iranians think of the truth that is at the center of a real political democracy so highly that we think whatever we must do to achieve it is worth doing."[45]

In the shah's mind, political democracy could not be had without economic development. Ironically, his example was the United States, a country, he noted, that was producing more goods and services, gross and per capita, than any other. The important point about the American economy, however, was the democratic distribution of the goods and services it was producing. "What is most striking when one visits large factories in the United States is the hundreds and sometimes thousands of cars one sees in the adjacent parking lots. The blue collar and white collar workers in these factories and companies own and drive them. And a great majority of them eat well, dress well, live in newly built houses that are equipped with the most modern means of living, which give them time and space to live with their family in relative leisure." Income disparity, of course, existed, but the volume of production in America was so high that everyone could satisfy his needs and yet save some money. "This feat does not come from pure capitalism; it is a result of a mixture of capitalism and socialism. The government helps [the thousands of private industrial and financial institutions and hundreds of thousands of private farms] by offering loans, technical assistance, and other services, strengthening them to the benefit of the general public. The government also directly manages an array of institutions such as hospitals, power stations, munitions factories, and huge publishing houses. What is important in all this is that all the goods and services so produced are distributed across the country among the people."[46]

In Iran also the government controlled industrial and commercial affairs for the public good, the shah boasted—for example the labor laws, or retail prices in some critical commodities such as meat, bread, or medicine, sometimes setting them at below the retail price in the producer country. In some cases industries were owned and managed by the government, but the idea was for the government to provide opportunities for industrial entrepreneurs, traders, and farmers. "In my opinion," wrote the shah, "the success of economic democracy in Iran depends on the presence of individuals who directly engage in industrial and commercial affairs [in the private sector]." He wanted to preserve individual freedom. In the agricultural domain Iran would never be like China, "where millions of farmers and agricultural laborers live under a command economy where they have no right even to their own private life or family." Thus, two principles would govern Iran's economic system: continually rising economic well-being and leisure for the people; and an economy in which the rights of laborers, farmers, factory managers, engineers, and experts engaged in production were respected and safe. "I cannot endure a society whose people are illiterate and ignorant, have low productivity, and do not move, strive, or seek, while living in a world where every other nation on earth is making a strenuous effort to get ahead."[47]

How could Iran establish economic democracy quickly? The first step was to have a sound plan. "In the contemporary world, no economy will improve at high speed except by adopting basic, comprehensive projects." The worst mistake would be to build big factories without attending to the availability of appropriate manpower, raw material, means of transportation, or markets. All of this suggested the need for a powerful planning organization and also an economic coordinating agency at the highest levels of decision making, both of which had been established in Iran. That is why "I formed the High Economic Council, headed by the prime minister and composed of the cabinet ministers whose responsibilities relate to economic issues, the managing director of the Plan Organization, and the director general of the National Bank."[48] To achieve high efficiency, the council's secretary general had been made a deputy prime minister, and often the council met in the shah's presence.

This, however, was not enough. Economic democracy needed strong guilds and strong labor unions. During World War II, labor unions had mushroomed across the country. Unfortunately, most of them were dominated by the Tudeh Party. But factory owners, short on democratic spirit and long on unsavory attitudes, were worse than the Tudeh, following their earlier counterparts in England and the United States in hiring thugs to scare workers into submission. Nevertheless, "Reason demands that labor unions keep away from political parties and use their energy to protect and promote the economic interests of their members and leave the long-term complex political issues to the political parties. Otherwise, since members may belong to different parties, inevitable political conflict will split and weaken the union."[49]

In 1946 the shah had identified five basic rights for all Iranians: food, clothing, housing, education, and health care. Now, discussing social democracy, he recalled those rights. They had stuck with him because of the conditions he had witnessed in Iran after he returned from his studies in Europe. "Despite the progress achieved as a result of my father's efforts, still I witnessed individuals who had no shelter, who died of hunger, and who were almost naked because they had nothing to wear. These heartrending scenes tortured my soul and marked my heart." This was not the way he had imagined Iran. It was not how any people should have to live. How could leaders not be concerned about this sordid situation? Worse was that some leaders believed this was how the world had been, was, and would continue to be. Once he became king, he had called several Majlis deputies and told them he was not prepared to see some people, including some members of the parliament, increase their wealth and use all the perks available to them while next to them hundreds of thousands of men, women, and children lived in squalor, poverty, and absolute despondency. The next day, a rumor spread that he had been influenced by communism. "If what I said was communism, so be it," he said. "Of course, if some people gain more than the minimum by legitimate means, more power to them. However, no buts or ifs, and probable consequences notwithstanding, I say every individual ought to have enough income to be able to provide for his family and for himself enough of the five essential categories, and if some of them are not able to provide this minimum, then it is the function of the government or charitable organizations, individually or together, to step forward and to provide the five essentials for them."[50]

He was angered by the "rich and haughty," the upper classes, who claimed poverty resulted from laziness. He remembered a little boy in a village without a school who, "like my father," had learned how to read and write without a teacher's guidance and had also learned how to read and write English by himself. The boy, of course, was blessed with genius. His accomplishment showed nonetheless that he, like a majority of Iranians, was a committed and hardworking soul. "If one is to look for indolence and torpor, one had better look among the rich bums."[51]

Democracy, argued the shah, is a synthesis of the three dimensions he had identified. "Democracy is not just a series of actions a government or a people might take; it is most of all a philosophy of life. Mastering this philosophy has never been easy for either individual or society. However, despite its difficulties and complexities, it is the best method [of governance] that humanity has learned.... We Iranians must seek rapid progress toward democracy, but we must also remember that achieving political, economic, and social democracy requires time, rational and intellectual training, and learning to accommodate contradictory demands. This, in turn, demands attention to individual and collective moral values and feelings of loyalty. More importantly, its successful achievement depends on the proclivities of the members of the country to learn to cooperate with and support each other." There were therefore historical conditions that defined the limits individuals and peoples had to respect if they were to make progress in freedom. Going too fast would not take Iran where it wanted to go. But "if we bring together our desire for reform and progress with patience and perseverance, we shall surely meet with success. Our goal is set and the path to its achievement is open; if we are not short in effort, we shall reach our lofty goal."[52]

■

The shah appointed Amir Asadollah Alam prime minister on 19 July 1962. The Amini cabinet was retained for the most part; newcomers reflected friendship more than policy considerations. Major portfolios—war, interior, foreign affairs, agriculture — were left unchanged. Finance reverted to Abdolhossein Behnia, who had been Amini's first finance minister, an intriguing selection because Behnia had left the Amini cabinet in protest against parts of the land reform law. In other portfolios Alam chose friends — Gholam Hossein Jahanshahi for commerce, Parviz Natel Khanlari for education, and Taher Ziai for industry and mines.

Hassan Arsanjani, the continuing minister of agriculture, was also Alam's friend. Alam had been serving as head of the Pahlavi Foundation, an endowment of the crown. When he was told by the shah that he was to be prime minister, he called on Jahanshahi, his deputy at the foundation, and Khanlari, a renowned academician, to meet with him to discuss the future cabinet. Jahanshahi was against retaining Arsanjani:

> He [Arsanjani] was so intent on disparaging the landlords, on belittling them, insulting them. We did not need to make so much noise doing what we were about to do. I told Alam so: "Bring in someone less rowdy, disruptive, and raucous."
>
> Alam said, "That is precisely His Majesty's view. But I believe it is better for us to keep Arsanjani."
>
> I said, "I am amazed why you think so, because His Majesty's view is the right one and we should go along with it."
>
> "The trouble is," said Alam, "if we keep Arsanjani out, the foreigners will likely think we have given up on land reform."
>
> Well, I said, they may think that, but once they see we actually are going ahead with it, they will be disabused.[53]

Arsanjani, of course, was retained and became the most important pillar of land reform.[54]

Alam's tenure as prime minister was tumultuous. The shah's White Revolution, a phrase first used by Amini when the land reform law passed, was based on two acutely controversial foundations: land reform and women's rights. Both ideas were anathema to the clergy, women's rights even more than land reform. In the land reform case, the clerics had a powerful ally in landlords. The alliance against women's rights was not as well-defined though it was broader, with the clergy providing the focus and the bazaar the money.

The first major clash between the government and the clergy involved women. On 7 October 1962 the cabinet decreed a new protocol for elections to local councils, which implied women as well as religious minorities might vote on a par with Muslim men. The decision elicited strong clerical objection. The Ayatollahs Shari'atmadari, Golpayegani, and Haeri, as well as then Hujjat-ul-Islam Ruhollah Khomeini, determined jointly that each would ask the shah to order the government to rescind the decree and to warn the government of serious consequences if it did not. The shah retreated, assuring the clerics that he supported the Islamic tenets, that he would refer their objections to the government, and that, as always, he wished the ayatollahs success in guiding the nation according to Islam's sacred injunctions. The moderate royal response encouraged the ulama to attack the government more strongly, with Khomeini threatening Alam directly: "Deviating from the laws of Islam, the constitution, and the laws made by the Majlis will surely make you personally responsible." At the same time the implementation of land reform was leading to riots in several tribal areas across the country, including Fars, where a provincial director charged with implementing the law was assassinated. While the government stood firm on land reform, it retreated on women. On 29 November Alam informed the clergy that women would not participate in local elections.[55]

The shah was simply more determined on land reform. He presented the program as a revolutionary act, asked for popular and international support, and in most cases received it. Vice President Lyndon Johnson, for example, visiting Iran in late August 1962, called the land reform program superb and the shah commendable for launching it. The United States, said Johnson, would continue with its economic assistance to Iran.[56]

On the domestic front, the shah campaigned across the country to sell the program to the people. Distributing ownership deeds in Arak, a city in central Iran, he called the farmers far more mature than others had given them credit for. "Our farmers immediately realized the importance of the cooperatives and joined in, and this caused all of us to become more convinced of the rightness of our path. It would not be an exaggeration to claim that perhaps the way we have chosen [to implement the land reform program] in Iran is better than those others have chosen." By September, in Maragheh, a city in Azerbaijan, he would call land reform "the most progressive means of bringing to the Iranian farmer welfare, happiness, and an honorable life." A day or two later in Rezaieh he explained the purpose of the land reform as bringing "a different meaning to Iran, her independence, and her territorial integrity. We mean for Iran to march in step, shoulder to shoulder, with the most progressive countries of the world. For this to happen we must mobilize all of our aptitudes and capabilities in an environment of social justice that is inferior to none. I am convinced that our history, our traditions, and the stability God has bestowed on us, make it possible for us to achieve, calmly but speedily, the utmost progress that a country in the twentieth century can attain and take pride in." In Tabriz: "The reason we are successful is that your hearts and mine beat to the same drummer. We feel alike and we think alike, and it is because of this spiritual and emotional bond God has willed that I understand what your heart and mind desire, and it is thus that by God's will together we have always moved ahead of events."[57]

Back in Tehran, on the occasion of his birthday on 26 October, the shah called the White Revolution "a social transformation unprecedented in Iran's three-thousand-year history." This was "a transformation aimed at requiting the just rights of every member of our citizenry and therefore the more robust the paraphernalia of justice, the stronger and deeper will be our reforms." He felt he had connected with his people and the feeling gave him confidence. The law establishing an education corps, a component of the White Revolution, passed at the end of October, charging the ministries of education and war to train the educated military conscripts and deploy them to villages to teach in special schools. This was also a novel idea that would bring him high accolades not only in Iran but from 113 countries participating in UNESCO's twelfth general conference. On a pilgrimage to the Mausoleum of the Eighth Imam in Mashhad he announced that the feudal system in Iran was coming to an end. "He who works in the field shall be no longer a vassal but a free person working freely and receiving his due honorably in an environment where owner and laborer, each possessing rights, work together in peace and friendship." The education corps was to assure that everyone learned his or her rights. It was only then, he said in Shiraz, that "all individuals would become aware of their rights and interests and aware that others also had rights and interests."[58]

■

During the first months of Alam's premiership a small group of ministers had regular weekly meetings with the shah to discuss national issues. The meetings usually took place on Thursday afternoons, the day before the Sabbath, and usually took several hours. This was an informal representation of the council of government meeting with the shah. It was, Jahanshahi recalls, "collegiate in deportment, with participants speaking freely and easily."[59] The Alam cabinet in full, however, convened only once in the presence of the shah, when the shah summoned it on 5 January 1963 to announce that he was about to address the nation to declare his six-point program and his decision to put it to a popular referendum. He wished to discuss the text of his proposed address with the cabinet. The points had been discussed before, the most critical of them, of course, being land reform, which was the first article, and women's political status, which was the fifth. The cabinet was of several minds: there were those who were against land reform and those who were for it, and a third group that was for it but not in the way it was proposed or was to be implemented. A reasoned debate, Alam had thought, was healthy and for this very reason he had asked Arsanjani, his minister in charge of land reform, not to attend. He wanted neither his other ministers cowed nor a fight in the presence of the shah.

Immediately, however, the referendum itself became the issue. The only other referendum ever conducted in Iran was Mosaddeq's, and that had proved disastrous, not only in the way in which it had been managed, but also for constitutional reasons. Some of those present thought the whole project was too hurried, too unstudied. Behnia and Nasrollah Entezam argued for further political preparation and counseled caution. Jahanshahi brought up the constitutionality of the referendum. There was no constitutional foundation for a referendum, and the shah himself had criticized Mosaddeq's action on constitutional grounds. Now the shah offered a new theory. "Mosaddeq was the head of government; I am the head of state. He did not have the right to resort to referendum; I do." The argument did not satisfy some in the audience, but, as Jahanshahi put it, "Here it was, and he was the shah and head of state."[60]

In the text he read for the ministers, the shah stated, partly in support of his decision to put his proposals to a referendum, that the previous Majlises had not been elected honestly and correctly and therefore they did not truly represent the people. That is why he wanted to have the people vote directly on his revolutionary propositions. In the future, he said, elections would be faultless, and then there would be no need for referendums. This was clearly a very bad idea and prompted several ministers to ask the shah to take it out of the speech. "Surely, Sire, you realize that all the previous Majlises were elected during your watch and they are the source of all the laws we live by," said Jahanshahi, supported by Entezam and Behnia. The shah kept on bringing up evidence to support his position, but finally agreed to delete the reference to the Majlis from his speech.[61]

■

On 9 January 1963, the shah opened the National Congress of the Farmers of Iran in the Mohammad Reza Shah Sports Stadium. The congress consisted of some 4,200 representatives of Iranian farmers, drawn from among individual farmers as well as farm unions and cooperatives. The shah explained the changes that had occurred in Iran in the past and the reasons for the changes he was about to propose and ask the people of Iran to ratify. He spoke in the vein he had used in discussing the issues previously with the cabinet. He was offering six reform bills for the people to ratify directly in order to prevent what he called the agents of black reaction and red destruction from vitiating them. The six reform bills, presented as principles of the White Revolution, were:

1. Abrogation of the feudal system *(nezam-e arbab ra'iyati)* by ratifying the land reform law of 19 Dey 1340 (9 January 1962) decreed by the cabinet and its amendments;
2. Ratification of the law of nationalization of forests and pastures;
3. Ratification of the sale of state-owned factories to the private sector as security for land reform;
4. Ratification of profit sharing schemes for employees in industry;
5. Reform of the electoral law to extend suffrage to women; and
6. Ratification of the bill to establish a literacy corps to facilitate implementation of the law of mandatory universal education.

These were bills that had been passed by cabinet decree, most during Amini's tenure, in the absence of a Majlis. In the last months of Eqbal's tenure in 1960, under the shah's prodding, the cabinet had proposed and the Majlis and the Senate had passed a land reform law prepared by the agriculture minister, Jamshid Amouzegar; certain Majlis deputies (most of them landlords) had, according to the shah, used cunning and sophistry to gut his ideas beyond recognition.[62] He had signed that bill on 6 June 1960 because, he said, it was better than nothing, but the referendum would be his revenge. It would turn the tide in favor of his aspirations and against landlord greed, religious obscurantism, and leftist demagoguery. It would become the instrument binding him and his people. From now on, or beginning soon, it would be the shah and the people together, unmediated, unadulterated, and unbreakable. "There shall be no country on earth with laws more progressive than the laws of Iran," he told the farmers, who had just approved unanimously his referendum proposal. "Be the harbinger of this glad tiding to your people: this is just the beginning." The farmers resolved to give him the title of *dadgostar,* disseminator of justice, but he refused the gesture. What he did was for the country, not for titles, he responded, thanking the Congress.[63]

The shah would win the referendum handily and by most accounts fairly. But it would not be a victory without repercussions. The government announced 26 January 1963 as the voting day, both in Tehran and in the provinces. On the 22nd, Khomeini declared the referendum anathema before God, enjoining believers not to participate. He was supported by several other ayatollahs, the bazaar closed, and there ensued a scuffle between police and demonstrators. On the 23rd the government announced it would not allow any interference with the referendum. Farmers entered Tehran, joining the workers in a demonstration for the shah's program. Women came out, demanding the right to participate in the referendum. On the 24th, the shah went to the holy city of Qom, where the day before, a veritable war had erupted between the *tullab,* students of religion, and the forces of law and order; he prayed at the shrine of Ma'sumeh, the Eighth Imam's sister, and distributed land titles to farmers. "We have eliminated free-loading in this country," said the shah, referring to the clerics. "The masks have been lifted. To me, the black reactionaries are worse than the red destroyers. . . . This gentleman [Khomeini], whose ideal is the government of Egypt, which has bought more than a thousand million dollars of weaponry, tells us to dismantle our armed forces. We have made fifteen million people owners of land whereas this gentleman's leader, the Egyptian Abd al-Nasser, has at least fifteen thousand political prisoners but no Majlis or election."[64]

On the 26th, for the first time in Iran, women also voted, though for political and legal reasons separately from the men. This was a big event and a great victory for women, achieved in good part by their own efforts. Despite its inclusion in the list of reforms in the referendum and the support of Princess Ashraf, then honorary head of the recently formed High Council of Women, the cause was not high on the leadership's agenda. The government had declared the referendum would be carried out according to the general election laws, which meant that women would not vote. Women, however, agitated for the right to vote, arguing that this referendum was a special case and that the shah wanted all of the people to make their opinion known. On 7 January 1963, the anniversary of the 1936 decree that ordered the unveiling of women, representatives from several women's associations had converged on the government chancery to object to the government's retreat on granting women the vote in local council elections and to demand the right to participate in the upcoming referendum. Prime Minister Alam, still reeling from the defeat he had been handed by the clerics and knowing the troubles ahead for the referendum, was in no mood to entertain what he considered at the time a woman's whim and cited existing law to explain why he could not give the women what they wanted. He asked Princess Ashraf to see to it that women did not make the situation more difficult than it was by making waves about elections. The princess met with women leaders privately to discuss Alam's predicament. Women agreed not to act in the name of the High Council of Women but asked for and received her blessing to agitate in the name of their respective organizations. The princess then strategically left town to be beyond government reach.[65]

On the 23rd women in schools and government offices stopped work, demanding the right to participate in the referendum.[66] On the evening of the 25th, the night before the referendum, they were told they could vote, though separately from men. In the morning, women in Tehran and the provinces cast their votes in hurriedly contrived ballot boxes. At 11 that morning the interior minister announced on the radio that women's ballots would not be counted to determine election results. This was a blow to women, setting off accusations of a government ruse from within the country and abroad. But women had voted, and the act had established a precedent, even if the vote would not be included in the final count. When the votes were counted, 16,433 women in Tehran and close to 300,000 in provinces had cast their votes in favor of the shah's proposal, as compared with 521,108 and 5,598,711 men, respectively.[67] And passage of the referendum meant passage of suffrage for women, even if their own votes had not been counted. On 27 February, opening the Grand Economic Congress, the shah declared women eligible to vote and to stand for office in all elections. To the women who converged on his office to thank him he said: "Our revolution, which the world acclaims, would not have become complete if you were denied these elementary human rights."[68]

The first day of the Iranian New Year, 21 March 1963, became a portent of the struggle taking shape between the government and the radical clergy. The shah told the people that Iran's future would be founded on social justice, equitable distribution of wealth, just and lawful return from work and capital, and a provision of a minimum income needed for a reasonably comfortable life.[69] Khomeini announced that the people had no New Year because the principles the shah had put to referendum were against Islam and the referendum was a criminal act.[70] The two sides deployed their forces, though the regime clearly was more powerful, for now. Khomeini was not a known commodity outside the clerics and certain groups in the bazaar. Many people in the government did not know him at all. Alinaghi Alikhani, soon to become Alam's minister of economy, had not heard of Khomeini, though he was politically savvy and had worked as an analyst on SAVAK's foreign relations bureaus.[71] On the other hand, almost everyone knew of the Grand Ayatollahs, such as the late Borujerdi, Hakim, Shari'atmadari, Golpayegani, Kashef-ul-Qita', and the like. Although most of these ayatollahs did not favor Khomeini's radical approach, given the clerical culture, most of them felt obliged to support him in public.

On 1 April, on a pilgrimage to the shrine of the Eighth Imam in Mashhad, the shah called the radical clerics obstacles to the nation's progress. "The good Muslim people of Iran must be shown the Koranic injunctions as they really are; they must learn the truth of Islam. They must become wise to the falsehood some individuals have invented for the benefit of their pockets." What he had done was the very embodiment of what the Prophet and the First Imam had meant for true Muslims, he said on the occasion of 'Id Ghadir, the anniversary of the day when, according to the shiis, Mohammad appointed Ali, the First Imam, as his successor. "Two groups of individuals oppose our policy: they belong to black reaction and red treason. We have deprived the red traitors of their destructive paraphernalia. They have lost their bearings and become speechless and dumb-founded. Like three-year-olds they parrot what they have been taught, unable to relate their word to the reality around them."[72] But it was a mistake to take this war lightly. The shah's leftist opponents were still strong and mostly centered in the university.[73]

His immediate problem, however, was Khomeini and the radical clerics. Although, according to the shah, "the black reaction was losing because the people were increasingly educated and ignorance yielded to knowledge, and therefore soon the clerics would no longer have a mount to ride,"[74] clearly, he thought something needed to be done. He directed the SAVAK to come up with suggestions. To this end, SAVAK Chief General Hassan Pakravan held several meetings with his assistants, including his deputy for internal security, Brigadier Mahutian; Baba Amjadi, the director of Third Bureau, which was charged with domestic security; the director of intelligence, Mansur Qadar; and others. According to Qadar, the group was in favor of making light of Khomeini and his behavior. One participant suggested that the most effective way to deal with the Khomeini hurdle was to ignore him in public but to "do him in" and then give him a great funeral, a suggestion that Pakravan rejected out of hand.[75] But before much could be done, or left undone, the controversy came to a head on 3 June, the 'ashura, or anniversary of the martyrdom of Hussein, the Third Imam. In a lecture in Qom's Faizieh School, Khomeini took the shah and regime to task, comparing the shah to Yazid, the Umayyad caliph who ordered Hussein martyred. Yazid's target, he said, was not only Hussein; it was the Prophet's household. The shah's target also was not the *maraji'*, the sources of emulation, but the very foundation of Islam. "These people do not want Islam. Israel does not want the Koran to be here; Israel does not want the Islamic injunctions in here; Israel does not want the educated in here. . . . Israel uses its agents in this country to do away with the barriers on its way . . . the Koran, the ulama. . . . Oh, Mr. Shah, oh Exalted Shah, I advise you to cease and desist. I do not want to see the people celebrate the day you leave this country by the order of your masters, as they celebrated when your father left."[76]

Khomeini's direct assault on the shah could not be ignored. He was arrested on 5 June, but this did not end the trouble. Riots broke out over Khomeini's arrest in Qom, Shiraz, Mashhad, Tehran, and several other cities. They were quelled hard everywhere, resulting in many dead or wounded. Martial law was declared in Tehran for the first time in almost ten years. The figures given by the opposition for the casualties of the 5th and 6th of June are undoubtedly exaggerated, touching on the astronomical. The real figure is far smaller, though not precise. However, it is generally accepted that the government was determined to stop the riot and the marches, particularly those of the marchers wearing martyrs' shrouds moving toward Tehran. The preponderance of opinion holds that Prime Minister Alam was the man of the hour who saved the regime by standing fast, asking the shah to allow him to do what was needed and to hold him responsible in case the center did not hold or things did not work out. According to his minister of national economy, Alinaghi Alikhani, this was exactly how things happened. Alam, said Alikhani, was by nature calm and self-possessed. He took it upon himself to face the crisis, keeping his colleagues in the cabinet mostly in the dark:

> We heard here and there that there was trouble in the bazaar, among the ulama, big landowners, and the tribal khans in certain areas of the country. We also heard that the National Front was against the reforms. But there was no general discussion in the council of ministers unless some specific matter was brought out. I remember once Alam said several religious students in Qom had demonstrated but he had slapped them in the face and that was that. Beyond such remarks, we had no mental preparation about the events. . . . Consequently, I can tell you that on 15 Khordad [5 June] Alam was absolutely prepared. He had been working to prepare for days. But he had told us nothing. He was cool and self-possessed. He believed there was no reason to make others anxious and afraid. . . . On the afternoon of 5 June, the cabinet met, and Alam laughed and joked more than any other day. His behavior showed that he was the kind of man who could master crises.[77]

Not all Alam's friends agreed, however. Gholam Hossein Jahanshahi thought Alam was too devoted to the shah. In Jahanshahi's words, "he was drowned in him. If the shah wanted land reform, that was the best for the country, regardless of Alam's personal interests. It wasn't that he had a firm economic, social, or political opinion of his own. And if he had one, it was no matter; he discarded it if it conflicted with the king's. It was the shah that counted, and it happened that the shah thought and understood well and wanted the best for the country, so that was that, and that needed to be done, nothing more, nothing less."[78]

Jahanshahi was also skeptical about the proposition that Alam took over in the 1963 Khomeini crisis and ordered the troops to settle the matter:

We probably have to distinguish between two periods of Alam's service to the shah: the period of Khomeini assault in 1963 and the period of his tenure as minister of court a decade later. About 1963, everyone believes, and I like most others have heard Alam say on numerous occasions, it was he who ordered shooting down the rioters and stopping the assault, what later came to be known as the prologue to the revolution. I don't buy this on two counts. First, Alam was so loyal to the shah that he would never embark on any action without his approval, certainly not on an act of such mammoth consequences. Second, in such conditions the military would not obey the prime minister without the shah's approval. I think Alam was so totally and profoundly devoted to the shah that he took the burden of killing people upon himself to exonerate the shah of any possible blame."[79]

The generals concur that they took orders only from the commander-in-chief. Alam would not have been able to control the military without the shah's backing. But this was as far as it went. The shah's backing was not different than in the past, for example, in the summer of 1952. He did not want bloodshed. And the generals—Nasiri of the police, Oveisi of the Guard, Pakravan of SAVAK, Amir-Sadeqi of the military police, and Malek of the gendarmerie—talked to each other and to the prime minister, not to the shah.

Khomeini was arrested in Qom on 5 June at 3 A.M. Nasiri, the police chief and Tehran's military governor, called Oveisi at 5 A.M. to ask him to deploy his units, but Oveisi was at his morning prayers. Nasiri told Kambiz Atabai, then Oveisi's adjutant, in an "excited and quivering voice," that demonstrators were burning the city. At about the same time, Atabai recalls, Mrs. Oveisi called, asking to speak with her husband. When told Nasiri had called but her husband was at prayer, she exploded with anger: "Get him off the prayer rug, and tell him to get a move on," the lady shouted at Atabai, whom she treated as a son. The morning prayers being short, by this time the general had finished, and he and his adjutant set out for the national police headquarters, where the command post had been established. Here, Atabai found, things were not as they should have been, the generals uncertain exactly how to proceed. At about 8 A.M., Oveisi learned that one of his officers had been knifed and seriously wounded. "On God's grandeur, I will not stand here and let them do this to my officers," he shouted, his military hat in his hand as was his custom when he became angry. "What is it that I am to do under these circumstances?" Clearly, the shah's call to caution was frustrating the generals. At about 10 A.M., Alam arrived at the headquarters accompanied by his interior minister, Mehdi Pirasteh. "Order must be restored at all costs. Do what you must within the law to quell this treasonous revolt against the country," Alam told the generals in utter calm, which Atabai felt raised the generals' confidence and sense of authority. "As far as I know, my boss, General Oveisi, had no communication with the imperial court afterwards," said Atabai.[80]

Both the police and the military had been on the alert for some time, but in Tehran the anti-demonstration operation remained essentially a police action, led by Tehran Police Chief Colonel Abdollah Vasiq, who in 1979 would be executed by Khomeini for the part he had played in 1963.[81] Although neither General Nasiri nor General Oveisi played a large part, they held their commands, the police and the Guard, respectively. The fact was that in 1963, despite the ferocity of the riots, a majority of the people, including workers and peasants, were with the shah. He had embarked with them on a path that contained much promise.

11

Women and Rights

The "woman question" in Iran was only sporadically touched on in the nineteenth century.[1] Exceptional women sometimes created ripples in the social fabric, but the ripples did not last. A woman named Tahereh Qorrat-ul-ʿAin, a priestess of sorts, appeared uncovered among men while preaching modernity—one of the audacious acts for which she was executed.[2] Nassereddin Shah Qajar's mother, Mahd ʿUliya, influenced politics while her son was young but lost power once he matured. Nassereddin Shah's daughter, Taj-us-Saltaneh, was a rare woman with an eye for truth and a temperament for inquiry. She wrote about life in the women's quarters where the shah's womenfolk were confined, the "natural" deprivations women were heir to, and the "ugly eunuchs" to whose rule they were made to submit.[3] The condition of women in lower stations was less stringent than that in the royal court but not by much. The work that they did in the field and household allowed a certain freedom to move about and to have contact with others, sometimes men, but the culture was the same. Patriarchy dictated the norms by which they lived, and the clerics, managing education, justice, and culture, dictated the content and form the norms took. In towns women worked in the house, in villages in both the house and the field; in both cases they received their identity from their men. Girls were considered sexually mature at the age of nine as computed by lunar calendar, ready to be married off to whomever their father or guardian deemed appropriate. Men could divorce their wives at will; women could not divorce their husbands, except in very exceptional cases. Men had dominion over women's movements, social relations, and work. Iranian patriarchy, informed by shii lore, abstracted women's honor, concretizing it in the thought, judgment, and behavior of their men—fathers, brothers, and husbands. Women's actions expressing even a modicum of individual freedom almost always contradicted the governing social norms, vitiating men's honor, making life routinely hazardous for women. Women were led to defend themselves using the two main weapons available to them: motherhood and sex. Conversely, men saw women symbolically as either mother (and, by extension, wife, daughter, or sister) or whore—either a symbol of their honor or an instrument of sexual satisfaction. For most men there existed no intermediate space.

The Constitutional Revolution of 1906 brought to Iranians a set of new concepts—freedom, social justice, equality, secularism, popular sovereignty, and the like—offering a different scheme of social organization. The clerics tried to temper these concepts by adding an article to the Supplementary Basic Law requiring legislation to conform to the *shari'a,* the framework of Islamic law.[4] This article was never formally honored, but it left a residue of expectation that critically affected women's condition: political decisions were always made with the *shari'a* in mind, generally making women the sacrificial lamb to appease the ulama. Under Reza Shah, the first Pahlavi king, the nation set out to modernize, but the process left family law largely undisturbed. Still, modernization could not completely leave out half of the population. A new language was invented, mostly by women, to accommodate the clerics: women's education or employment was said to be necessary to social and economic progress. Woman remained man's other half, however, and since the man's station in society was a given, woman's was to adjust to it. The family was the central unit; man the master, woman man's complement. The framework assigned a highly valued position to woman, but the value was qualitatively different from the value assigned to man. Man's worth was inherent; woman's instrumental. This dualism was so strongly entrenched in culture that men and women equally considered it self-evident. Not until well into the twentieth century did women come to see the contradiction in the "self-evident."

The theoretical framework for this dualism was supplied by the shii hermeneutics and the ulama's interpretation of gender relations in Islam. As do the other Abrahamic religions, Islam defines man and woman as inherently different. Since man has the claim to priority, wherever Islam eulogizes woman, it does so from the man's viewpoint, measuring woman's worth in relation to man's need. God speaks to men even when He means to be kind to women. The Prophet commends women to the care of men: "Fear God when you deal with women, for he has left them with you in trust."[5] Woman has been created for man and therefore does not possess an identifiable status outside of man. A just man naturally treats women justly, but since woman is created for man's social and emotional sustenance, justice means little outside the patriarchal frame.[6]

This was the backdrop of modernizing social relations in Iran. Not everywhere were things as bad as this account suggests. Motherhood had its filial authority, and man's honor required respect for women. Married women had dominion over their property, which gave the wealthier among them considerable leeway. And throughout Iranian history there existed a tradition of revolt against rigid religiosity, manifested most clearly in Persian gnosis, especially Gnostic poetry, where love, God, and freedom intertwined. But the clerics were powerful, rigid, and bigoted. It was neither easy nor safe to contradict them, particularly in social fields such as gender relations where they were "naturally" supported by the patriarchal order. It therefore took courage for both women and enlightened men to strive for women's rights. And it is unlikely that much progress would have been made without the support of the state. Reza Shah used the historical need for progress to open education to women, but he did not relish the prospects of his wife and daughters appearing unveiled in public. He sent his sons to Europe to study, but he would not countenance the same for his daughter Ashraf, despite her eager supplications to do so. Women therefore continued to have a hard time of it, though in the fifty years of the Pahlavis they made considerable progress against considerable odds.

Reza Shah was not initially keen on "modernization" of women. Some of his more enlightened officials, especially Court Minister Abdolhossein Teymurtash, talked to him about the veil as a symbol of backwardness and about the linkage that joined modernization and unveiling. "If that be true, then I will divorce my two wives before I embark on such decisions," he once told Teymurtash.[7] Unveiling, which was mandated in 1936, proved to be a difficult transition not only for Reza Shah but also for ordinary men and women; for many it was a traumatic experience. The first day the deputies' wives attended a Majlis ceremony unveiled, several among them fainted, unable to endure being seen "bare" by men. Women were loath to be seen uncovered in the streets, partly because they feared being assaulted for appearing unchaste and partly because they themselves found the practice abhorrent.[8] Soon, the government went so far as to order the police to unveil women in the street, on the theory that most women remained covered out of fear of being molested by religious zealots. The move was not popular and became a stigma on Reza Shah's reign. But the effect, unveiling as a signature of freedom and equality, took hold, and many women remained unveiled after Reza Shah's abdication and exile.

After Reza Shah's exile, however, the ulama regained much if not all of the influence they had lost during his reign. They succeeded in stopping the celebrations of 17 Dey (7 January), the anniversary of the unveiling, but unveiled women had become a fact of life. Their focus became damage control, keeping women as covered and politically contained as possible. Only a small group of clerics, the Fadaiyan Islam, or devotees of Islam, proposed to reshape society by force on the model of the Prophet's rule in Medina in the seventh century. Their project, however, failed; although they assassinated several members of the literati and government, they had little effect on society.

Women fared better with the left, though more in ideology than in practice. The Tudeh, the Soviet-oriented party of the left, invariably subordinated women's rights to the requirements of the grander struggle — the political imperatives of the Third International, which men defined and led. Women's issues were rarely raised or debated, giving the shah, as noted in chapter 4, cause to scold the Tudeh leaders for not paying sufficient attention to women's issues in their politics as well as their charter.[9]

Raising concerns about women fell to several moderate groups, led mostly by women teachers and other women belonging to the establishment. In 1943, Safieh Firuz, Hajar Tarbiat, and other like-minded women organized the Women's Party (Hezb-e zanan), many of whose members were later attracted to Prime Minister Qavam's Demokrat Party of Iran, established as a counterbalance to the Tudeh. Qavam's party did not last beyond his tenure as prime minister, but it did provide a training ground for women activists who later formed several women's associations, including the Council of Women (Shoray-e zanan); these groups did mostly charity work but also debated issues of import to women. In the 1940s, the Council of Women, led by Safieh Firuz, was the foremost women's organization. By the 1950s women had formed several professional organizations, ranging from associations of women nurses and midwives to those of women lawyers.

In 1957 fourteen women's organizations joined in a federation called the Organization for Cooperation of Women's Associations, headed by Princess Ashraf. When the princess had agreed to serve as the honorary president of one association, other groups argued that it was unfair for her to be associated with one organization to the exclusion of others. Court Minister Ala reported the complaints to the shah, who agreed, saying the princess should not have accepted the position, unless she was prepared to do the same for all women's organizations. Thus came into being the Organization for Cooperation, which soon evolved to the High Council of Women, with a domestic and an international agenda and Princess Ashraf as its honorary president.[10]

By the mid-1950s several women's associations had begun studying the law as it applied to women, principally for their own edification. It was clear that the family law existing on the books, mainly a translation of the *shari'a* to modern idiom, was fundamentally unfair to women. Much of it was based either on the Koran or alternatively on the *sunna,* the traditions of the Prophet or the imams. In certain cases, such as the right of women to inheritance, the injunctions were stated clearly in the Koran. In others, such as women's position in society, they were largely clerical interpretations codified as religious injunctions. In reality, there never was a "divine" injunction against women's participating in the political process. Prophet Muhammad's wives, especially Khadija and A'isha, were active political supporters of their husband and his religion. A'isha had memorized the Koran and used her knowledge as a weapon in post-Muhammad Muslim politics. Hind, the wife of Mecca Chief Abu Sufyan and the mother of Umayyad caliph Mu'awiya, was a deadly enemy of Muhammad's cousin and son-in-law Ali, the fourth caliph of the sunnis and First Imam of the shiis. The same uncertainty engulfed the issue of the hijab, the Islamic cover. Early Muslim women did not wear the hijab. Muhammad's wives for the most part appeared in public unhindered by the veil. At least one legend suggests that the Koranic verses about the hijab were meant for the Prophet's wives and no others, after Muhammad's companions complained that it behooved the Prophet to tell his wives not to show themselves without proper cover to men who came to visit him and often ended up in informal proximity to his wives. This interpretation agrees with the custom of the Prophet's time, according to which high-society women but not commoners were to be covered when in public. All of this, however, had changed over time. The clerical position on women had become accepted tradition, and as a result every move toward women's rights conflicted with the patriarchal norm. It took courage and tact to tackle women's issues, and governments burdened with other problems preferred to postpone dealing with women, even if they were inclined to help.

In 1956 a group of younger women professionals, mostly teachers, established a more progressive organization called New Path Society (Jam'iat-e rah-e nov), led by Mehrangiz Dowlatshahi, Mehri Ahy, and Parvin Khanlari, among others.[11] All of the original nine members were either a part of or had contact with the Iranian ruling class.[12] They knew they were no match for the clerics or the establishment. They understood the advantages of working within the system and the utility of the support they could mobilize in the government. They were no revolutionaries. What they asked for were simple rights — the right to work, to travel, to have greater control over their children and themselves. They saw their role at home and in public as complementary to that of men. They were the proverbial other half. They also asked for the right to vote, though in the beginning not insistently. Their primary activities still involved charitable work: helping the poor or the marginalized such as women inmates in Tehran's prisons.[13]

The New Path Society was also interested in the relationship between women and the family. The members managed to interest a well-known judge of the high court, Shahab Ferdows, in their work and persuaded him to prepare a prototype bill on women in the family that did not conflict with Islam. "We needed a bill that could be enacted. We knew it would not be enacted if its language conflicted with Islamic tenets," recalled Dowlatshahi.[14] When the New Path Society became an affiliate of the High Council of Women in 1959, it put its family law project on the council's agenda. The government, now under Manuchehr Eqbal, however, was not keen on the matter. But women kept on talking about the issue, educating other women, and lobbying men in decision-making positions. Partly in response to women's lobbying, in September 1959, the shah told the cabinet that the world had changed and that the laws needed to be changed, though along Islamic lines, to eliminate the unjust conditions that confined women. Specifically, he said, the government should give them the right to vote so that they could participate in social and political affairs.[15] That December the shah married Farah Diba, a young, energetic, and conscientious woman who would prove a sturdy support for the cause of women. The fact that for the first time in recent history Iran's queen would be actively engaged in social issues and would say so even before she married the shah encouraged women. It was her ardent hope to be a source of good and a force for progress, "especially of my nation's women," she told the *Ettela'at Daily* on 22 November. She would try to open up for women the opportunity to be active, to work, and to prosper, she said in an interview with the *Times* of London.[16]

The White Revolution significantly improved the political climate for women. On 11 August 1963, the High Council of Women's member organizations announced their readiness, given the passing of the referendum in January of that year, to take part in the upcoming election to the parliament. On the 12th, they organized a great march in Tehran, despite ongoing extremist threats and occasional violence. On the 17th, a meeting of women, farmers, guilds, and local council members and employees resolved that a national congress be convened in Tehran to choose the candidates that would represent them in the Majlis election. On the 27th, a Congress of Free Men and Free Women was convened in Tehran, chose candidates to stand for the Majlis, and pledged to support them in the elections. For the first time in Iran's constitutional history several women were among the candidates.[17] From among them six were elected to the Majlis and two appointed to the Senate. Most of them had been active in the women's movement. Hajar Tarbiat, elected from Tehran, had founded the Women's Center (Kanun-e Banovan) in 1935, the first organization of its kind. Showkat-Malek Jahanbani was a pioneer in girls' education and a founder of several educational institutions. Farrokhru Parsa hailed from an activist family; her mother was the editor of *Jahan-e zanan* (Women's World), one of the first "feminist" magazines in Iran. A medical doctor, Farrokhru chose to teach girls and work for the advancement of women. Nayyereh Ebtehaj-Samii, a graduate of the American Missionary School in Tehran, was a teacher and member of several women's societies. Dowlatshahi, the founder of the New Path Society, had a doctorate in sociology of journalism from Heidelberg University. Nezhat Naficy was the youngest and least experienced but active in women's affairs. At the time she was married to Ahmad Naficy, Tehran's mayor and the organizer of the Congress of Free Men and Free Women, a fact not totally irrelevant to her candidacy. Most of these women went on to play important roles in promoting women's rights in Iran. Parsa became the first woman minister in Iran's history and Dowlatshahi, the first woman ambassador. Tarbiat and Jahanbani were later elected to the Senate. Ebtehaj-Samii served as a deputy until the end of the regime and became an important leader in the Iran Novin Party. Only Naficy, whose husband fell out of favor, did not serve in future years.

Of the two women senators, Mehrangiz Manuchehrian was a doctor of law and founder and president of the Iranian Federation of Women Lawyers. Shams-ul-Moluk Mosahab, armed with a Ph.D. in pedagogy, had long served as teacher and principal of girls' schools and supervised elementary school text production and publication.[18]

Women in the Majlis became an inside lobby for the proposed family law. However, the government, made up of members of the newly formed Iran Novin Party, was not willing to submit the bill to the Majlis. Majlis President Abdollah Riazi suggested an ad hoc committee of women deputies and others to review the proposal to make sure it did not conflict with Islamic tenets and to educate the deputies. Tarbiat and Dowlatshahi became the sponsors on behalf of the six women, five of whom had joined the Iran Novin. (Naficy joined the Mardom Party.) They took the draft to the Ministry of Justice, where the bill had to be approved on behalf of the cabinet. They had it discussed with the ayatollahs in Tehran, Qom, and Mashhad. They took it to Princess Ashraf and the queen, who in turn kept the shah informed. The bill was debated for three years in committee but was not formally introduced in the Majlis, since the majority party remained hesitant. Finally, the party suggested the women convene a seminar to debate the general issues of interest to women and to draw up a set of proposals, based on which a bill might be introduced and passed in the Majlis. The seminar was opened formally by the queen on 15 October 1966 in Tehran's Hall of Culture, with the announced theme of Iran and women. There was no mention of a family law or the party's involvement. The seminar was then transferred to the Iran Novin Party headquarters, which caused a flurry of criticism of the court and the queen for lending themselves to partisan politics. The shah clearly meant to support the seminar, since he had been assured the outcome would contain nothing that conflicted with Islam. The criticism, he must have concluded, was a risk worth taking. The seminar ended with a resolution about the problems women faced with respect to health, education, employment, and family, and it asked the government and the Majlis to introduce and pass appropriate legislation.

A few days later, on 24 October, however, Senator Manuchehrian introduced a bill in the Senate signed by fifteen senators, as the rules required, on the law of the family. Manuchehrian's bill was daring and had a history that went back to her days as a law student at Tehran University in the 1940s.[19] In 1949, she had, with great difficulty, published *A Critique of Iran's Constitutional, Civil, and Criminal Law from the Standpoint of Women's Rights;* most publishers either considered it anti-Islamic or feared clerical or governmental reaction. The *Critique* was republished in the summer of 1963, this time propped up by Manuchehrian's position as a senator and by the promises of the White Revolution. In a prologue to this new edition she wrote, "The horizon for social reform was dark in those days, the only spark of hope radiating from the shah's vision and luminary conscience preparing the ground for eventual equality between men and women."[20] She felt something needed to be done fast, before the excitement of the White Revolution wore off. "With your help," she had told her colleagues in the Senate in February 1964, she would propose legislation that guaranteed "full and complete equality of men and women, including equality in marriage, guardianship of the child, employment and woman's right to employment free of the required husband's approval, and also equality in the right and condition of divorce, inheritance, and all other social, economic and civil matters." These were sweeping propositions, but she was certain that the Senate would pass them, though "this was not something that could be accomplished overnight."[21]

Her bill was reprinted as the "Proposed Law of Family Based on the Principle of the Equality of the Rights of Men and Women Granted by HIM Mohammad Reza Shah to the People of Iran" in May 1964 in several issues of *Ettela'at Banovan* (Ladies' Ettelaat) and was widely discussed in the press. It caused mayhem in the shrine cities of Qom and Mashhad in Iran and Najaf in Iraq. Worried about clerical reaction, Justice Minister Baqer Ameli denied any connection with it. "Iran's civil law will not change," he said. "Someone may have done a study of sorts, but that is a private matter. There is no study going on in the Ministry of Justice, and the government has no intention of even looking at a proposed bill that may in any way come into conflict with Islam." There was no need therefore to discuss the article in *Ettela'at Banovan,* because the whole project was irrelevant, said Ameli.[22] The Iran Novin Party Secretary General Ataollah Khosrovani intimated that Manuchehrian had been expelled from the party "for lacking in moral and party probity." Manuchehrian responded that she had left the party because it no longer represented the principles of the shah's White Revolution. The shah, said Manuchehrian, "has written in his book, *Enqelab-e sefid* [The White Revolution], that today we can have peace only if there is world peace. And world peace depends most of all not on this or that country's military might but on providing individuals and nations their rights."[23] Khosrovani and the party had acted against the philosophy contained in the shah's statements. It was Khosrovani who lacked in moral rectitude, she said.

When the bill was formally introduced on 24 October 1966 in the Senate and accepted by the Senate president as a normal bill to be studied, it made a furor, not so much in the press but in the government and among the clerics, who threatened to excommunicate Manuchehrian. In the Majlis, the majority party asked one of the women deputies, Showkat-Malek Jahanbani, to dissociate their group and the Majlis from Manuchehrian's bill. "We will do nothing that vitiates Islamic tenets," Jahanbani assured her colleagues and the nation. Prime Minister Amir Abbas Hoveyda directed Iran's envoys in Muslim societies to send him copies of family laws in the country they served. He asked two renowned mujtahids (doctors of Islamic law), Mohammad Kazem Assar and Mohammad Sangelaji, to go over the Majlis proposal to make sure it matched Islamic tenets. The law that this bill finally became, the Family Protection Law of 1967, passed on 13 April, was nothing as daring as Manuchehrian's, but it was a breakthrough in Iran's family relations. (Manuchehrian would have abrogated polygamy, the marriage portion, *mut'a* [temporary marriage], and paternal male guardianship of orphaned children, and would have come close to equalizing male and female inheritance. It was an improbable proposition, as she herself had reasoned a year or so back. "Has this woman gone berserk?" the shah had asked Sharif-Emami, according to Dowlatshahi. "How could so many senators sign off on such a bill?" The answer was they had not read it. "Would they then have signed off on my execution unread if put before them?" he had protested.)[24]

The 1967 law referred all civil complaints incumbent on family relations, inclusive of husband, wife, children, father, paternal grandfather, guardian, and the like, to the courts (Articles 1 and 2). Women obtained the right to sue for divorce, and the courts were enjoined to take on the complaint (Articles 8 and 10). Men were deprived of the right to divorce at will and were constrained to receive court permission to divorce a wife. Men were constrained from marrying a second wife without securing permission from the first wife in court and without proving they could act justly and equitably in relation to their two wives (Article 14). The court now could assign children to the care of the mother, but this new possibility was mentioned in passing: according to Article 12, in cases of divorce the court was required to rule on the children's welfare and "if the children were to be put in the mother's care," to determine the condition and cost of their care. To make these articles consonant with the *shari'a,* which regards marriage as a contractual arrangement between a man and a woman, the law made the inclusion of certain provisions in the text of the marriage contract mandatory (Article 17).

These changes were revolutionary in a Muslim society, despite being tamer than those proposed by Manuchehrian. The law had gone as far as it could without provoking unrest. The ulama did not like it but took it in stride because enough had been done with the text to make it as palatable to them as possible. Contrary to Manuchehrian's bill, which would have replaced existing laws, the bill that passed the parliament and was signed by the shah was advertised as a complement to existing law (Civil Law of 1310 [1931] and Marriage Law of 1315 [1936]). The family protection law therefore was hailed by those in the center of the political spectrum but attacked on both ends: the modernists found it inadequate, the Islamists ungodly. "The law that recently passed the unlawful Majlis under the name of 'family protection law' was passed in order to destroy the Muslim family," Khomeini announced from his exile in Najaf. "It is against Islam, and both its legislators and administrators are sinners against the *shari'a.*"[25] Altogether, however, the law passed without much tumult. There were other matters of greater concern, including the perennial Arab-Israeli tension, which erupted in a full-fledged war on 6 June, claiming most of the region's attention, including the shah's. The family protection law passed the parliament with his blessings but not much direct input. For him, it was another step in the path to modernization, which he routinely supported as long as care was taken not to overwhelm the fine and vulnerable balance he had established with the clerics.

Another event also dominated public attention: the formal coronation of the shah occurred on 26 October 1967, his forty-eighth birthday. He had refused to hold the ceremony before because, he said, "Being king over a mostly poor, ill, and insecure people was no honor."[26] The coronation therefore meant more than just a ritual to him. It was also a statement: Iran had broken out of the vicious circle of poverty, ignorance, and backwardness. Now, he told the nation on 19 August, because of the advancements made under the White Revolution, Iran's ancient social structure, which had no longer accommodated the requirements of the modern age, had changed and become, in principle, one of the most advanced of our time. Women, he said, were an important component of this transformation.[27]

The coronation was to reflect women's heightened status. On 23 August, Prime Minister Amir Abbas Hoveyda presented to a newly elected constitutional assembly a bill to amend Articles 38, 41, and 42 of the Supplement to the Constitution to reform the process of royal succession. The amendments fixed the minimum age of the crown prince at twenty for the assumption of the throne and made the queen regent if at the time of succession the crown prince was not of age. This was a revolutionary act that could not have been achieved had the shah not the power to impose it. Conversely, the clerics and the traditional elite would not have countenanced it had they the power to go against the shah's will. Politically ascendant, he now vowed to advance further. A few days before the ceremonies he told the cabinet that once the nation's primary needs were satisfied and a firm infrastructure for the economy was laid, Iran would embark on the road to a high civilization: "We must begin to prepare ourselves for that time."[28] This was the first time he spoke of a "high civilization," a prologue to what in later years he would present as "the great civilization."

On the coronation day, the royal family was driven to the Golestan Palace in central Tehran in two horse-drawn coaches, the shah and the queen in one coach drawn by six black stallions, the crown prince, not quite seven years old, in the other, driven by white horses.[29] The young prince entered the coronation hall first, in formal uniform, followed by the commander of the Imperial Guard. With considerable poise, he walked to his appointed seat to the left of the throne. Then entered the queen, followed by the young girls carrying her train and her ladies-in-waiting, marching to her seat to the right of the throne. And finally the shah in full regalia, preceded and followed by generals and adjutants carrying the crowns, swords, scepters, and other accoutrements of the ceremony, all moving in unison to their assorted places.

Then trumpets sounded and prayers were offered by the Friday Imam of Tehran, followed by formal statements by Prime Minister Hoveyda, Senate President Ja'far Sharif-Emami, and the Majlis President Abdollah Riazi, in that order.[30]

Then the shah stood at attention while the paraphernalia of royal power were brought to him—first the Koran, which he kissed, then the saber, the scepter, and his father's cloak, which he put on, and finally the crown, which he took and with deliberate motions put on his own head. He sat back on the throne and read the following statement: "I thank God who has allowed me to be of use to my country and my people in every way within my power. I ask God to grant me the power to continue to serve as I have done to this day. The sole aim of my life is the honor and glory of my people and my country. I have but one wish: to preserve the independence and the sovereignty of Iran and advance the Iranian people. To this end, if needs be, I am prepared to lay down my life."[31]

The queen now kneeled before him to be crowned. He placed the crown presented to him carefully on her head. The queen then rose and went back to her seat. The shah now completed his sermon:

> At this time that I wear the crown of the world's oldest monarchy, and that for the first time in history a shahbanu of Iran is also crowned, I feel closer than ever to my dear and honorable people and wish and pray that the Almighty God shall more than ever bestow on this country and this nation His protection, bounty, and grace. For myself, I am delighted and proud that today my people and I are joined by an unbreakable bond of mutual loyalty and love, marching hand in hand on a path of progress, happiness, and greatness.
>
> May Almighty God allow me to bequeath to future generations a happy country, a prosperous society, and may my son, the crown prince, also remain under divine protection in carrying out the heavy task that lies ahead of him.[32]

The coronation was a victory for women. They had already found their way to the representative assemblies and soon they would have their first cabinet minister in Farrokhru Parsa. Now another important advancement had been made by the legal mandate giving the queen the right and duty under certain circumstances to take over the role of the shah. This was a near paradigm change in Iran; the idea that a woman would legally take over the king's functions in his absence had the potential of qualitatively improving all women's status and rights.

More concrete work was undertaken by the Women's Organization of Iran (WOI), a transformation of the High Council of Women into a more structured organization. The impetus for the change came piecemeal from several women and men as well as from Princess Ashraf. Princess Ashraf was an avid traveler, visiting many countries in her capacity as Iran's chief representative at the United Nations and as honorary president of Iran's Human Rights Committee. Since she had assumed the presidency of the High Council, she naturally asked about women's movements and organizations in the countries where she traveled. She was especially impressed with the statistics she received on active women in the Soviet satellite and other socialist countries. "In countries such as Poland, she was given numbers in millions," remembered Dowlatshahi. "She would then tell us, why can't we do it in Iran? We ought to get women involved. How can we increase our membership?" By the mid-1960s, a new generation of Iranians, younger and more energetic, was taking over and moving on in economic, social, and cultural fields. The princess, like her brother, was impatient, constantly asking for something to be done. She appointed an informal committee of men and women whom she knew and considered to be progressive to look into ways and means of broadening the base for the women's movement. The committee suggested an organizational apparatus with more mass appeal, capable, potentially, of extending to the provinces and penetrating the grassroots. The scheme was clearly influenced by socialist ideas, proffered by the princess's friends, among them, Fereydoun Hoveyda, a novelist, film critic, and later Iran's envoy to the United Nations; Majid Rahnema, a diplomat, intellectual, and soon to become Iran's first minister of science and higher education; Ehsan Naraqi, a sociology professor at Tehran University; and Javad Ashtiani, a former dean of the medical school at Tehran University, managing director of the Imperial Organization for Social Services, and an appointed senator. Women participants were also of the same genre — Mehrangiz Dowlatshahi, Nayyereh Ebtehaj-Samii, Mehri Ahy, Farrokhru Parsa, and the like.[33] The ideas corresponded to the climate of the time and to the shah's political proclivities.

The basic unit of the new organization was the branch. Women in cities or villages got together in a committee, usually established by the WOI secretary in the province, city, or county. When the number of volunteers reached thirty they petitioned to join WOI. Each branch had committees responsible for fields of interest to women — education, vocational training, environment, legal counseling, childcare, and the like. Branches elected their leadership, the committee chairpersons, who then elected a branch secretary from among themselves. The branch membership elected the branch's representatives to the provincial general assembly, which elected the province's representatives to the annual national assembly in Tehran. The national assembly in Tehran made general policy guidelines; its major responsibility, however, was to elect a central council that represented it between its sessions. The central council had eleven members, from among whom a secretary general was appointed.

In early 1971 Mahnaz Afkhami became the fourth secretary general of the Women's Organization of Iran. She represented the national gravitation to leadership by the young. She had traveled to the United States at an early age, attended high school in Seattle, Washington, and university in San Francisco and Colorado. She had worked throughout her stay in the United States and when still a teenager had once turned to a labor union in San Francisco to seek redress against a management that had taken advantage of her youth and inexperience to cheat her out of her rightful wages. When at the age of twenty-six she returned to Iran to a teaching position in English literature at the National University of Iran, her understanding of women in society was derived mainly from her experience as a student of literature in the United States and her exposure to the social movements of the 1960s.

At the National University she was exposed to the ideas and experiences of young women students who were drawn to the individual freedoms that women in the narratives of English writers seemed to enjoy, but who were also attached to the customs and cultural traditions that tied them to their families and communities. Their discussions on how to manage a workable transition to a more independent life while keeping the best of their culture and connections led her and her students to establish the Association of University Women. The work of the association became a foundation for developing an Iranian approach to women's rights and led her and other members to become involved with the recently established Women's Organization of Iran and its then secretary general Simin Rejali, a colleague and professor of psychology at the National University of Iran. Sometime in 1969 Rejali told Afkhami that Princess Ashraf was interested in providing young educated women with a chance to participate in the Iranian delegation at the United Nations, which she headed, as a way for them to become familiar with international diplomatic work—would she be interested? Afkhami readily agreed. In New York, she had contact with the princess only occasionally, once when she delivered Iran's speech on Palestine, which the princess, to show her support, attended. She was again asked to accompany the princess on the latter's next annual trip to New York, which she did. It was at this time that she was asked if she would agree to serve as secretary general of WOI. She had no experience, she pleaded. Perhaps that was the advantage she brought to the movement, replied the princess, insisting that youth, energy, and new blood were what was needed. Afkhami accepted the offer, although her family and friends almost universally advised against her taking responsibility for a conflict-ridden and controversial organization.

The new secretary general soon realized that though the princess had been instrumental in her getting the job, she was not around to help. "In the first year I saw her maybe three times, each time for about half an hour," she recalled. "I reasoned I had accepted the position and now it was up to me to make of it what I could."[34] She set out to get acquainted with her environment and the women who had helped bring the women's movement to where it was. She traveled to some forty cities and innumerable villages, speaking to women and men of different economic, social, and educational backgrounds. She realized, even more than for her students at the university, that the theories of feminism she had learned in recent Western tracts did not answer the questions and observations she received from Iranian women at the grassroots. Western authors were concerned primarily with individual rights and emphasized sexual politics. But what the grassroots Iranian women told her was different and more urgent.

> They told me all of this is fair and good; it is great if I am aware of my individual rights and of the law the parliament has passed to preserve those rights. But of what use is the awareness or the law if I do not know how I will provide my child with the needed daily bread, or shelter, or clothing? Well, the studies about women done in the Sixties were more about individual rights. Even Woolf, who spoke more of women's independence, was for my interlocutors a character in fantasy land, a woman writer needing space and quiet to write. The problem of bread or shelter an industrial or agricultural female worker posed was of a different nature, grounded in her reality. It was not that one woman said one thing and the other another thing. Invariably, women in factories and farms posed the ability to support one's life financially as the most important issue and knowing a craft that produced the ability as *the* priority.[35]

WOI took what the grassroots said as a springboard for its organizational, procedural, and political planning. How was it possible to empower women to stand on their own economically and socially? "Empowerment," of course, was not yet a term in common usage. The questions posed, however, were relevant to the concept: What did women need in order to be able to earn a living? How could vocational training be made available to women? Who would provide them with the wherewithal for learning to influence their own lives and the lives of their families? How would one encourage the men in the family to help, or at least allow, their women—wives, daughters, sisters—to get out of the house, to attend classes, to associate with others, as the learning process required? What would a woman who wanted and was allowed to attend a learning environment do with her children during the learning period? Who would feed the children, and what? And who provided the children's health care and hygiene?

These and other questions like them were brought back to the councils in provinces and the central council in Tehran, where they were discussed and refined and
gradually became the stuff of thinking about organization and policy. Changing
archaic laws was the necessary condition for assuring women's rights, but not sufficient. Measures had to be taken not only to educate ordinary women but also to
give them the wherewithal to strive and to survive. This could no longer be accomplished by acts and structures of charity. WOI needed to become an organization
that not only attracted women at the grassroots but also connected them to the
loci where public and private decisions were made. Given the shah's proclivities, if
WOI was to have a chance of success, it had to imagine itself as a part of a developmental process mobilizing the resources of the country in support of women.

In the early 1970s two major laws directly affecting women were proposed — a
passport law and a supplement to the Family Protection Law of 1967. The second
was a real advancement, clarifying the opaque corners of the 1967 law and adding
several important new provisions to facilitate implementation. The first, however, was a failure, even though it would have affected only a small proportion of
women. Existing law prohibited a woman's travel without permission from her
husband and conditioned the issuing of passports to women on the husband's
written approval. The provision was clearly against the principle of gender
equality and was widely opposed by women. Manuchehrian and Mosahab in
the Senate objected to the existing law and demanded supplementary legislation
to delete the offending articles. In 1967, Prime Minister Hoveyda announced
that a new passport bill had been prepared and soon would be presented to the
Majlis.[36] The proposed bill stipulated that women would be issued passports
with the permission of either the husband or the district attorney.[37] The new
bill drew women's objection as not much better than the old law. Dowlatshahi
in the Majlis called it "a step backward" and "unbecoming of the government
to bring such a bill to the Majlis."[38] Hoveyda nonetheless offered the bill in the
Majlis, but there it remained dormant.

In the meantime, women were gaining ground in other areas. In June 1969,
for example, five women were made judges, an uncommon achievement for a
Muslim society. In the passport case, however, the government would not budge.
On 29 June 1972, the bill was brought to the whole Senate for a second reading.
Mosahab called it a tyrannical law that was not only a denial of the best aspects
of the shah's White Revolution but also against the UN Declaration of Human
Rights, which Iran had signed. Manuchehrian, taking the floor, said everything

flowed from the shah; women owed this government nothing. Outside this hall, she said, many of her colleagues agreed with her that "sons and daughters should receive equal inheritance." The statement elicited shouts of "blasphemy," led by Senator Allameh Vahidi, an old hand in *shariʿa* law. Manuchehrian went on about other gender inequities. "A wife should share in the family's wealth," she said. She worked at home as a partner of the man and without her labor "the wheels of life did not turn." This government, she said, "not only has not reformed the existing laws in the direction of the Revolution of the Shah and the People but it has also introduced bills that are in many ways against the Universal Declaration of Human Rights. . . . This bill has flaws of a different sort also; this bill contradicts our religious principles, because in Islam a woman—"

Suggesting that a bill under discussion in the Senate might be against Islam was too much for Senate President Sharif-Emami. He cut Manuchehrian short. "Shia Islam is our official religion, and no part of this bill is against Islam. Do not bring religion in," Sharif-Emami protested. Manuchehrian did not give up. She insisted that husbands had no right to forbid their wives to attend the hajj, or pilgrimage to Mecca. And therefore, by extension, this law was in conflict with Islam because it gave the man the right to deny the woman the ability to perform her religious duties at will.[39]

The argument, somewhat spurious, ended Manuchehrian's career in the Senate. She was radical for her time and relied heavily on the shah's ideological, if not political, support. The shah had no problem with women's right to travel but he would not force it against general consensus. The passport question applied to a small group of women mostly in the upper classes. He would not lock horns with the clerics on that issue. On the other hand, many women could neither understand nor justify the government's obstinacy, precisely because the issue had little to do with the masses. WOI's secretary general wrote an open letter to Sharif-Emami to urge a revision of the passport law on the ground that it contradicted human rights and international conventions, including the declarations on the rights of women, but to no avail.[40] Manuchehrian left the Senate in protest. The shah was sorry to see her go, but he also was in a quandary. Sharif-Emami had apologized to Manuchehrian in private, but he would have a hard time controlling the Senate if he also apologized publicly, which Manuchehrian demanded. In the end, it came to choosing one or the other, almost always a losing proposition for women.[41]

The supplement to the family law had a better ending. The importance of the new law was that for the first time in Iran and in the Middle East the guardianship of the child would pass to the mother rather than to paternal grandparents in case of the father's death.[42] In addition, the law identified the conditions for divorce and stated clearly that man and woman had equal rights in asking for divorce (Article 8). It acknowledged that women had "honor" in their own right by giving them the right to prohibit men from engaging in employment or activities that vitiated the wife's or family's honor (Article 18). The law forbad men to have a second wife without express permission from the first wife and then only under specific, dire circumstances. Minimum marriage age for men was raised to twenty and for women to eighteen, though under certain conditions the court might allow the girl to marry sooner, provided she was not less than fifteen years of age. Furthermore, a set of protocols was promulgated that closed many loopholes and facilitated implementation. This last measure was needed to correct one of the major shortcomings of the 1967 law, the ease with which the husband, notaries public, and the courts colluded to bypass the law in favor of men. Still, this was only the beginning. The prevailing culture had taught women that men had the right to divorce them by just uttering the words "I thee divorce." It would take time, organization, and effort to reeducate women as well as men to the law and the new dispensation.

Over the years, the discourse of women, society, and family changed, as did their actual interactions. In Reza Shah's time and in the first decades after the war, the purpose of educating women was primarily to prepare them for motherhood. As the number of women rose and more of them entered the employment market, women argued, and men concurred, that women had the capacity simultaneously to work both inside and outside the home and to be good mothers and wives in the process. Indeed, this was what the shah had insisted on in his explanation of his mission for his country in his 1961 book:

> Contemporary woman has difficult tasks ahead of her: First, she has to be a good spouse for her husband, that is, she has to go beyond a good bed partner and become a partner also in her husband's intellectual and aesthetic life. Her other important task is to see to the children's intellectual, moral, and physical development. She must be the kernel of love and knowledge and the one who teaches the child the ethics of entering the society. Moreover, the Iranian woman must participate in her country's rejuvenation, and she must commit herself to performing her part in charitable and useful work and do it humbly without regard to her social position.[43]

By the end of the 1960s, as the economy picked up and more women took increasingly demanding jobs, it became clear that the dual responsibility of work at home and outside could not be negotiated satisfactorily without a serious rene-gotiation of the respective duties and responsibilities of men and women. For the most part, the ideational transformation occurred imperceptibly and unevenly, the discourse remaining more or less constant and traditional. The explicit change in the language of the women's movement occurred at a special conven-ing of the WOI General Assembly in 1973. The idea was broached in humble and matter-of-fact terms. "The time had come for us to name our problem and to seek its solution," said Afkhami, as WOI secretary general:

> We all know none of us is a superwoman and that no one should expect us to be one. No one can do so many different things at once and do them well. No one should expect us to take upon our shoulders, by ourselves, alone, unassisted, the responsibilities both of the home and the workplace. Women ought not to be forced to choose either to take on the two burdens of work inside and outside the home unassisted or stay at home. We are not half of anything or anyone. Each of us is a complete human being. We demand to be recognized and treated as one.[44]

The delegates agreed, transcending, at least in principle, the established idea of woman as man's complement. The WOI charter was amended to redefine its objective. The prime duty of the organization now became "defending women's individual, family, and social rights in order to achieve their complete equality in the society and before the law." Three supporting duties included promoting women's education, especially in literacy and vocational and professional skills; assuring women's participation in the modernization of the nation, including economic, cultural, and social development, and helping women to coordinate their efforts; and assisting women in performing their individual, social, cul-tural, and economic responsibilities.[45]

By 1975, the shah had also come to adopt the new philosophy. Addressing a special congress of women on the anniversary of unveiling, he said the laws, rules, and procedures that "in some sense may be discriminatory against women must be reviewed and corrected," albeit "in a studied and reasonable manner." Men must be taught to respect women and to cooperate with them in the chores of the home "to lighten the burden of women who labor to better the society as they also do the work of the home." But women also "must not forget that when they marry they take the name of their husbands and therefore must remain profoundly aware of the great responsibility they bear." The mass media, the press, and the textbooks must be attentive that the picture they give of the Iranian woman "must do justice to her state as the woman of the age of the revo-lution, and employ all their means and all their skill to elevate and uphold her status."[46] These were the points WOI had provided, and he faithfully repeated them at the congress.

Since this was also the international year of the woman, the shah addressed women's condition around the world. The principle of the equality of the rights of men and women, he said, had been recognized in the United Nations Charter as it was in the UN Declaration of Human Rights. But a wide gap separated the principles formally avowed and their implementation in reality. This was "not only unacceptable from the standpoints of human justice and moral principles, it is also injurious economically and materially. . . . Let us not forget that problems such as human rights, population, family planning, illiteracy, and poverty, which define the future of humanity, cannot be resolved without women's effective and determinative participation."[47] A few weeks earlier, in December, his sister Ashraf had offered in his name $2 million to UN Secretary General Kurt Waldheim for promoting women's causes and with it a declaration on the need to close the gender gaps he was emphasizing at the women's congress. Waldheim called the declaration a document that defined the "principal objectives of the International Women's Year," and Iran a country well known for its successful efforts toward economic and social development.[48] Such accolades buoyed the shah, moving him to act more enthusiastically on women's rights, which in turn prompted government agencies to respond positively to WOI.

The First World Conference on Women, in Mexico City (19 June – 2 July 1975), aimed at three key objectives: full gender equality and the elimination of gender discrimination; the integration and full participation of women in development; and increased contribution by women in the strengthening of world peace. To achieve these objectives, the conference adopted a World Plan of Action that set certain minimum targets, to be met by 1980, to secure equal access for women to resources such as education, employment opportunities, political participation, health services, housing, nutrition, and family planning. Whereas previously women had been seen as passive recipients of support and assistance, they were now to be viewed as full and equal partners with men, with equal rights to resources and opportunities. And a new consensus held that economic and social development was not possible without the full participation of women.[49]

Iran's role in the conference was consequential. A preliminary plan for the UN World Plan of Action, devised and prepared by Iran, was distributed by the United Nations Economic and Social Council under the title "Working Paper Submitted by Iran with a View to Facilitating Discussion of the Draft Plan of Action." The draft became a major point of departure from which the debates took off. (Indeed, the above-mentioned targets inserted in the Plan of Action were all suggested in Iran's preliminary draft.)[50] Iran also conceptualized, lobbied for, and was designated the site for two important UN research, training, and policy organizations for women: The Institute for Research on Women and Development of the United Nations Economic and Social Commission for Asia and the Pacific (UNESCAP) and the International Research and Training Institute for the Advancement of Women (INSTRAW). The first was established in 1977 in Tehran but because of the revolution was moved to Bangkok (now named UNESCAP's Gender and Development Section). The second was being negotiated when the revolution occurred and was set up in the Dominican Republic. Tehran was also designated as the site for the 1980 Mid-Decade Conference on Women; the conference had to be moved to Copenhagen following the revolution.

The World Plan of Action asked each country to make "a clear commitment by the highest levels of government to take appropriate action to implement this Plan within the framework of national development plans and programs."[51] Iran was one of the first countries to act on the UN recommendations. The first steps toward the development of Iran's National Plan of Action were taken in 1975 after the Iranian delegation returned from Mexico City. WOI sponsored over seven hundred informal gatherings of women throughout the country to publicize the International Women's Year and the goals of the United Nations Decade for Women and to get information from women about their priorities and needs. Toward the end of the year a High Council for Cooperation, consisting of eight cabinet ministers, the head of the National Radio and Television Organization, and the secretary general of Iran's National Committee for World Literacy Program, was formed to plan programs and to discuss legislation relating to women that came under the jurisdiction of the ministries and organizations involved. At the end of December 1975, Afkhami was appointed minister of state for women's affairs—a first in Iran and second in the world—in Hoveyda's cabinet, to provide formal linkage between government programs and women's issues.[52]

In 1976, the government agreed to establish an executive committee composed of the deputy ministers of the ministries participating in the High Council, under the chairmanship of the new minister of women's affairs, to formulate and put together the basic elements of a national plan of action. The government was in the process of drawing up the Sixth National Development Plan,

1978–83, which represented the national effort in every area of interest to women, making women's participation in its deliberations an unprecedented boon. It was arranged for the deliberative committees each to have at least one WOI representative, who, when practicable, would act as deputy chair of the committee. This was a first in Iran, and likely for most other countries, and a beginning for women's structured involvement in national decisions.

The World Plan of Action stated that national plans and strategies "should pay special attention to improving the situation of women in areas where they have been most disadvantaged and especially of those in rural areas."[53] In Iran, the draft National Plan of Action was submitted to all elective rural and town councils as well as the branches and provincial councils of WOI for review and comment. The results were discussed at a conference of governors-general to inform them of objectives of the plan, to receive their comments, and to enlist their support.[54] The comprehensive review process was completed in late February 1978 and was approved by the cabinet of Prime Minister Jamshid Amouzegar on 1 May 1978, not only for its goals but also for the process by which it was to be implemented and evaluated. Accordingly, each government ministry or organization was to establish a "planning and follow-up committee" headed by a deputy minister and include, among others, the director or representative of the Women Employees Organizations of the ministry or, if such organizations did not exist, a senior woman employee, and a WOI representative to serve as a general advocate of women's issues. Similar planning and follow-up committees were established in the provinces under governors-general to determine the status and needs of women in the province, integrate these needs with the programs and projects conducted in the province, monitor and coordinate agencies' plans and programs, and report quarterly on the progress made.

The chairpersons of the planning and follow-up committees were to meet monthly to discuss implementation problems and coordinate ministry efforts. The Women's Organization of Iran was to serve as a secretariat to this group, and the current secretary general of WOI was to chair the chairpersons committee. This group would look into the coordination of the countrywide implementation plans and submit to the council of ministers an annual report on the achievement of the National Plan of Action. WOI as the secretariat to the committee was to provide a broad perspective in the annual review process through its representatives on the planning and follow-up committees as well as regional and local structures. Thus WOI provided channels for vertical as well as horizontal communications. Coordinating government ministries afforded a means for lateral discussion, with ministries and other agencies talking to each other and to WOI. WOI also provided a channel for reaching and hearing women at the grassroots. The underlying philosophy, a decade or two before the thought became popular worldwide, was that women were stakeholders in everything that happened in society and that all issues were women's issues. It was also the first successful example of what decades later was formulated in the concept of "mainstreaming" of women's issues. The idea was concretized in the Amouzegar cabinet by making the office of minister for women's affairs a clearinghouse for measuring gender impact of cabinet decisions. This was in line with the concept underlying the national plan of action and, like so much else, an idea just beginning to be tested. Helvi Sipila, UN deputy secretary general for social affairs, later wrote that the Iranian model was the most successful of the national plan of action models around the world and that if it were taken up by other countries, it would significantly improve women's situation.[55]

The framework for the National Plan of Action was symbolically presented to and approved by a National Congress of Women of Iran convened on 27 February 1978, the anniversary of women's franchise. Approximately ten thousand women (and some men) were present, some of them ex officio, most of them elected or appointed by WOI branches and provincial councils, village and town councils, and academic and other groups that had taken part in discussions about the National Plan of Action. The shah addressed the congress, mindful that nine days before, on 18 February, a riot in Tabriz had run out of control, suggesting a new pattern of violence as yet not quite understood. He recalled the dismal state of Iran in the past, the ignominy of the "capitulation" regime, Iran's weakness and helplessness, and the dignity his father had brought to the concept of "Iranianness" and the opportunities he himself had provided for the Iranian women to claim their rights. The country, he said, had made phenomenal progress during the past fifteen years. More people had become literate; more people sought and received higher education. The campaign against illiteracy had enabled millions of people to read and write. "These are the people who can go to the voting polls and freely express their preferences. These are the people who not only listen to radio and watch television, but also read newspapers and books, and more is added every year to the number and the content of the books they read." He continued:

> I believe such a society can use all the freedoms except the freedom to betray the country and to sell it to foreigners. In the past two years, people have enjoyed a wide variety of freedoms, increasingly and fully. Is this a proper use of this free-

dom for a small number of individuals in the cradle of knowledge, the university, to say that girls should not be allowed in the university's self-service cafeteria? Is it fair to have this shameful apartheid in the university? Iran's policy is against apartheid. We have condemned apartheid on the international arena and fought against it. The apartheid this group, fortunately this very small group, advocates is even more shameful than the apartheid abroad because it discriminates against one's own kind and race.

At the end of his speech, he said: "Well, this greater freedom has rekindled the unholy alliance of the red and the black in Iran and abroad. But we will continue our policy because the pillars that hold this country, propped by the Shah-People Revolution and the Rastakhiz Party of the nation [established by the shah in 1975], are strong and will not be harmed by the last gasps of this moribund unholy alliance." This caravan, he said, shall never come to a stop: "Let the dog bark; the moon shall beam on."[56]

The women gave him a standing ovation that lasted several minutes. He was clearly touched. As he was approaching his helicopter to leave, he turned to WOI Secretary General Afkhami and said, proudly, she thought, "It seems we said what you wanted to say, but with greater intensity and fervor."[57] He had indeed. The line about the barking dog and beaming moon was especially galling to the clerics. He had used "dog" to allude to Khomeini, a strongly pejorative metaphor in both culture and religion. This was war or seemed like one.

A few months after the national congress, Iranian women, like Iranian men, plunged into revolution. The first groups of revolutionaries demanded the segregation of men and women in university cafeterias, as the shah said in his speech, and intimated other limitations of women's space. The demands, however, were never taken seriously. Most people, including the leadership of WOI, assumed that they were concocted by SAVAK to discredit the dissidents. It was simply unbelievable that students at the university would demand gender apartheid, of which the shah had accused them. The shah, on the other hand, wondered why Iranian women did not respond to such reactionary demands. "Where are the liberated women we hear so much about? Perhaps now that the leader has returned they will show some gumption," he mocked Afkhami in a general audience, obviously miffed at women's silence and inaction. His tone, though, was not angry. He seemed genuinely surprised at what was happening across the country. Afkhami, who had just returned from a mission to the

United States, did not take his words seriously, thinking that such things as were then happening could not be real. A month or two later the shah's chagrin became more palpable. He sent a message to her through Prime Minister Amouzegar: "Tell Afkhami the Women's Organization is worth less than nothing *[Sazeman-e zanan pashizi arzesh nadarad]*."⁵⁸ Amouzegar's successor, Ja'far Sharif-Emami, had no room for women in his cabinet. By that time the revolutionaries had practically won — not formally yet, but by having succeeded in transforming the government to an agent that did their bidding. Appeasement became the order of the day. A month or so into Sharif-Emami's stewardship, in Kerman, a city in the southeast, Afkhami saw women in black veils marching in the street shouting anti-regime slogans. "Who are these women?" she asked Malekeh Yasai, WOI's Kerman secretary. "These are our women. We mobilized them. Now, they are marching shouting death to the shah."⁵⁹

12

Mastering Oil

As we have seen in chapter 9, the Consortium settlement in 1954 was a defeat for Iran. The Consortium received all the operational fields and territory previously conceded to AIOC. Iran remained totally dependent on the Consortium for extracting, refining, transporting, and marketing its oil. The National Iranian Oil Company (NIOC) operations were initially limited to managing the small refinery in Kermanshah and the pipeline that carried oil to it from the Naft-e Shah oilfields to the west; distributing oil from the Abadan and Kermanshah refineries for domestic consumption; and administering nonbasic functions in the south. The Consortium Agreement did not allocate to NIOC oil for export. NIOC could opt to take a part of its owner's share of oil and sell it on the international market, but this was not financially attractive, because Iran's share of the money was based on posted prices, which were almost always higher than the actual sale price.

Given the nature of the Consortium Agreement, the shah sought ways and means of developing an oil industry outside the area controlled by the Consortium. Ineluctably, he was drawn to Enrico Mattei, president of the Italian oil company Ente Nazionale Idrocarburi (ENI). Mattei had tried, unsuccessfully, to get a share of the Consortium. He then had approached other oil-producing countries, offering them an alternative to the so-called Majors, the large transnational oil companies.[1] His purpose, he said, was not only to give the Muslim countries, which had been crudely exploited by big oil, a greater share of the profits, but also to make them a partner in exploration and extraction.[2] With such opportunities in mind, Iran studied the options open to it and enacted a new oil law in 1957 to allow NIOC to draw necessary capital and technology to explore, extract, refine, transport, and sell oil from the fields outside the areas assigned to the Consortium. The draft for the bill, prepared by Fathollah Naficy and Fuad Rowhani of NIOC, was designed to attract foreign investment and technology-rich partners along three structural modes: mixed organization, in which shares and management were equally divided between NIOC and its partner; joint structure, an organization with no independent standing, created to act on behalf of the partners to the agreement; and finally, an agreement in which the second party acted as NIOC's agent.[3] In the meantime, Mattei traveled several times to Iran, met with the shah and government leaders, and, once the law was passed, proposed a mixed structure whereby ENI and NIOC each had a 50 percent share and ENI, in addition, would pay taxes and interest on the income it drew for its share. Thus, for the first time in the history of oil, the oil-producing country, Iran, would receive 75 percent and the foreign-owned company only 25 percent.[4]

The deal angered the Majors. The Mattei project not only deprived them of income but also weakened their control. On 3 May 1957, Howard Page, a director of Standard Oil of New Jersey, warned Fuad Rowhani, then the deputy chairman of the NIOC board, against the agreement with Mattei. "Bringing Mattei to Iranian oil is not in Iran's interest. Mattei asked for a share in the Consortium as a price not to get involved with Iran. We had reasons to reject his proposal. He then said he would close Italy to American companies and deprive us of that part of the European market. I feel obliged to warn NIOC that if he acts on his threat, we will reduce the volume of our lift from Iran equal to the volume of oil we now supply to the Italian market." Rowhani reported the threat to the NIOC board and subsequently to the shah. "NIOC should never pay attention to such statements," said the shah.[5] On 1 August 1957, the shah signed the 1957 Oil Bill into law. The agreement with Mattei was signed on 3 August, and the shah, to make a point, received Mattei in audience.[6]

For the shah, moving beyond the Consortium was politically exciting and technically educational. He studied how the oil market operated, how the companies colluded and manipulated, where their strengths and weaknesses lay. He learned to wriggle through and about them, bide his time, never attack without providing himself a path for retreat or a space for maneuver. His caution was deliberate, a must learned from experience. Mosaddeq's travails had taught him that unless you had the technological, economic, and political ability to contend with those who controlled oil on the world market, your efforts would come to naught. He reasoned that oil was the fuel that drove the West, the commodity the West considered absolutely vital to its interests and would go to any length necessary to protect. Mattei's death in a plane crash in 1962 was a warning to him. He never doubted that the crash was deliberately planned and that Mattei's death was the price the Majors had exacted for his audacity to outmaneuver them in Iran.[7]

In later years Iran would become the first Third World country to engage in refining and distributing oil abroad. In 1969, NIOC, the Oil and Natural Gas Commission of India (ONGC), and Amoco, one of Iran's partners in the Iran–Pan American Oil Company (IPAC), would jointly build a refinery in Madras, where Iranian oil from the Darius and Fereydun fields near Kharg Island in the Persian Gulf would be refined and distributed across India, and NIOC and its partners would have a monopoly market with significant future potential. Another refinery, Natref, would be set up in Johannesburg in 1971 jointly with South Africa's National Oil and Gas Company (Sasol) and the French Total, with Iran supplying 75 percent of the refinery's crude. In South Korea, NIOC and the Korean company Sangyang would build a refinery that would begin operation just before the Iranian revolution of 1978, a deal that fell apart when the Islamic Republic sold Iran's shares to the Arabian American Oil Company (ARAMCO). In Senegal, NIOC, Shell, and the Senegalese government would agree to establish service stations under the NIOC logo. In the mid-1970s, Iran would negotiate with several American and Japanese companies to set up refineries on the Persian Gulf shores to jointly export and sell a variety of oil products on the international markets. Iran also would begin discussions with Shell and ENI to participate in refining and distributing oil products in Europe and the United States.[8]

In the 1950s, however, there was not much the shah could do beyond trying to enter the market with the utmost care. He needed money and the money was with the Consortium. Moreover, big oil controlled 90 percent of the world market. Iran therefore could only enter the remaining 10 percent and then take care not to harm her own income by damaging the price the Consortium received. The shah opted for the simplest solution: he would deal where governments controlled the oil — in Eastern Europe, India, Argentina, Finland, and the like. With these countries the exchange could take a number of forms, including barter, which became a way of trading with Eastern Europe.

■

On 9 August 1960, the Consortium informed the Iranian government and NIOC that it had reduced the price of Iranian light crude by 12 cents per barrel and heavy crude by 6 cents per barrel, the second time in a year the oil cartel had brought down the price of oil. Thus, between February 1959 and August 1960, the average price of Iranian crude fell from $2.04 a barrel to $1.78 a barrel. The shah linked the Consortium's action to the steps Iran had taken to deal with independent oil companies:

> A part of the negative propaganda we see in some foreign press and other propaganda organs began when we signed unprecedented agreements favoring Iran with several important foreign oil companies. . . . Is it right for the oil companies to raise or lower the price of oil as they please without informing us, the owners of the oil? In this, as in every case, we always mind our legitimate rights and interests and shall never fail to take the necessary action to safeguard those rights and interests.[9]

On 28 August, he declared in a special press conference that Iran would send a delegation to Iraq for a conference to discuss the issue of oil with other oil-producing countries. He told Fuad Rowhani, who was to head Iran's delegation, that Iran would cooperate with other oil-producing countries to safeguard Iran's rights and interests, but must also "take care that decisions taken are based on adequate study and research as well as on rational and peaceful discussion." This was a warning to Rowhani not to fall in with the radical Arab states, especially Iraq. Rowhani understood: "The shahanshah's emphasis was particularly important for OPEC's subsequent success because it paved the way for controlling certain radical positions that were impractical at the time and would have weakened the foundation for the participating countries' alliance and cooperation."[10]

The idea of a cooperative association of producers was first aired by Juan Pablo Perez Alfonzo, Venezuela's minister of mines and hydrocarbons. The impetus for the policy was not only nationalism but also a downturn in Venezuela's income from oil. Throughout 1950s the price of Venezuelan oil had increased, reaching its zenith in 1957 as a result of the closing of the Suez Canal. It began to fall after the re-opening of the canal and also the entry into the market of oil from smaller producers. The income shortfall put the new government in a bind, further swaying Perez Alfonzo to seek cooperative association with other producers.[11] Perez Alfonzo found an ally in Sheykh Abdullah Tariqi, Saudi Arabia's oil minister, who was looking for ways and means of gaining some control over the operations of ARAMCO in Saudi Arabia. Perez Alfonzo and Tariqi made a gentleman's agreement to cooperate when they met early in 1959 in Cairo at the First Arab Petroleum Congress, which had been held shortly after the Majors cut oil prices for the first time. Not much came out of this initial meeting, but the Majors' second reduction of prices in 1960 helped establish the mood for collective action. Perez Alfonzo and Tariqi, who would be dubbed the "Red Sheykh" by the Majors, became the force that launched the next round of talks.

The Baghdad conference was convened on 10 September 1960, with representatives from Iran, Iraq, Saudi Arabia, Kuwait, and Venezuela, and observers from Qatar and the Arab League. In the meeting the participants agreed with Iraq's formal proposal to establish a permanent organization for systematic consultation among members and with Perez Alfonzo's suggestion to call it the Organization of the Petroleum Exporting Countries (OPEC).[12] If Perez Alfonzo and Tariqi had originated the idea of a producer collective, it was the Iranian delegation, drawing on its nation's experience in exploration and extraction as well as in international relations, that was instrumental in formulating and building consensus on the conference's declarations on goals, instrumentalities, and protocols. The bylaws that were discussed and agreed on in Baghdad that November were based on the preliminary material prepared and presented by the Iranian delegation, consisting of Farrokh Najamabdi and Amir Jahanbaglu and headed by Fathollah Naficy, then NIOC's director of exploration and production.[13] Subsequently, OPEC was formally set up in Geneva by Iran's delegate Fuad Rowhani (who had been named the organization's secretary general in its Caracas conference in 1961), along with several Iranian colleagues.[14]

The shah was not initially supportive of OPEC, though he trusted and respected Rowhani. He made sure Rowhani and other NIOC directors understood that Iran's oil policy would be determined independently of OPEC and that the connection between NIOC and OPEC would be limited to technical and administrative cooperation. In the first meeting of the participating members, Perez Alfonzo and Tariqi had proposed production pro-rationing (i.e., quotas), which the shah and his government thought would negatively affect Iran's interests.[15] According to Rowhani, a majority of the NIOC directorate believed Perez Alfonzo was trying to strengthen Venezuela's position in North America at the expense of Iran by lowering production in the Middle East and therefore making Iranian oil too expensive to compete for the U.S. markets, which were then just opening to foreign oil. Thus it did not suit Iran to follow Perez Alfonzo. Moreover, Iranians believed it was naïve to think that the other producers would not sell Iran short if it suited their interest. Indeed, Saudi Arabia had begun (and Kuwait was about to begin) to produce more oil than did Iran. Iran pushed for higher production but was systematically rebuffed by the Consortium, whose American members' primary interest lay in Saudi Arabia, Iraq, and Kuwait. Surely, observed Rowhani, past experience pointed to the conclusion that the companies as well as producer states would promote their own interests at Iran's expense.[16]

Also, the shah had no wish to align Iran with Iraq — or with Indonesia, when that country joined OPEC in 1962 — against the West, though he favored pressuring the companies to raise prices. His priority was to increase Iran's revenue from oil. The companies had impressed on him that playing the hawk would inevitably damage Iran's relative position in the market, because the Consortium would not then increase Iran's share to the extent he desired—a message the companies took to all heads of state to discourage them from working in unison. Early on, Howard Page threatened Iranians that following the OPEC propositions would raise the price of Middle Eastern oil 24 cents per barrel, making it uncompetitive with the oil from Venezuela, North Africa, or the Soviet Union. His success, however, was only partial. The Iranian press took him to task: "Companies ought to come to terms with the truth that the times have changed and that OPEC is now armed with undeniable facts and figures. Its actions are now based on reason rather than emotion," wrote *Kayhan Daily*.[17] Maurice Bridgeman of British Petroleum warned the NIOC chairman, Abdollah Entezam, about "unhappy events that would harm Iran's interests and the oil industry and damage the mutual confidence that surely ought to prevail."[18] This veiled threat also had only partial effect. The Iranians took it as a scare tactic. The shah remained supportive of OPEC but advised caution. "The companies must acquiesce to OPEC's demands," he said on 16 October 1963 in a joint press conference with the French president, General Charles de Gaulle, who was then on a state visit to Tehran. "They must realize that OPEC is a powerful organization that member states support and consider indispensable to their interests."[19] Still, this was more lip service than firm commitment.

The oil companies had two main control levers: production and price. The shah believed that the international oil regime and the Majors that controlled it kept Iran's production deliberately low and also kept the price of oil at levels lower than the actual value of oil. The price charged in Europe or the United States was significantly higher than that on the basis of which royalties were paid to producer countries. He believed the difference to be fundamentally iniquitous. He also thought it important to base the demand for higher prices on some economically defensible argument rather than only on need or ownership. One option was comparative pricing—oil priced against the cost of comparable sources of energy, such as coal or nuclear fission. Another was to close the gap between the cost of a barrel of oil at the well and prices it yielded as it reached the final consumer. "Why should the consumer countries gain so much at the tail-end of the production-consumption chain by taxing oil that belonged to the producers in the first place?" he asked. It was unconscionable, he said, that Europe exacted rent from oil consumed at unit rates three or more times higher than that which producer countries received. This, he said, was in part because industrial countries like the United States kept production costs in their territories artificially high, causing prices to be higher, whereas they kept the price of oil in producer countries artificially low.

The companies refused to raise either production or prices; they also refused to recognize OPEC as a negotiating interlocutor, using U.S. anti-trust laws as their excuse. OPEC members, however, kept on the pressure and, finally, in 1962, the Majors agreed to negotiate with one country that would also represent the other members. OPEC elected Iran to negotiate on its behalf. Fuad Rowhani, OPEC's secretary general, began a round of preliminary discussions as Iran's representative. Soon, Iran's minister of finance, Abdolhossein Behnia, was engaged also.[20] Negotiations continued throughout 1963 and into 1964, when the Consortium announced it was prepared to raise payments to Iran and consequently also to other OPEC members. The formula Iran proposed was to discount royalty as an expense, but the result, which was a price rise of about 11 cents per barrel, was more than the companies were prepared to pay. Instead, they proposed to pro-rate "expensing" over several years.[21] This meant that Iran's income would rise initially at about 6 cents per barrel, gradually reaching 11 cents. A supplemental agreement needed to be worked out if this formula was to be implemented. After discussing the proposal with the other OPEC members, Iran entered into an agreement with the Consortium, and the others followed suit.

The 1960s were years of growth and development in Iran. Once the hurdles of the early years were crossed, the shah's attention gradually moved to formulating into precise ideas the images his mind had only vaguely held in the past. He began to press the country into new ventures, including gas and petrochemicals. He educated himself on oil and slowly assumed a role beyond that of arbiter. Increasingly, he dealt directly with the Consortium, not only on policy, but gradually also on technical issues of production and price. He sought greater revenues, which he had been told came only with greater production, something the companies promised but refused to deliver. He concluded that the Consortium partners would not sacrifice their interests in Saudi Arabia, Iraq, or Kuwait for Iran. By the late 1960s he had begun to think differently about OPEC. His domestic and international standing by now had changed. The White Revolution was bearing fruit. The economy was moving forward at high but controlled speed. His relations with the United States had qualitatively improved after the presidency passed from Kennedy to Johnson and promised to become even better under Nixon. He had established with the Soviets a modus vivendi in politics and a mutually beneficial arrangement in trade and economic cooperation. His relations with the Arab states were improving, especially after Egypt's defeat by Israel in the 1967 war, which forced Nasser to a more agreeable interaction. And the National Iranian Oil Company was rapidly becoming an experienced and effective organization. All of this meant that his relative power and influence had significantly improved, putting him in a more advantageous position.

All, of course, was not rosy. By now the shah had dropped his earlier reticence and developed a tendency to push, to overextend. That meant that by 1969 government costs had exceeded revenues practically everywhere, leaving the shah in a perpetual bad mood. "What can I do when there is no money coming in?" he complained to his court minister, Amir Asadollah Alam.[22] The shah grumbled to Alam about overspending, but his eye was always on getting more money rather than on spending less. He had concluded that it was impossible not to overspend if one was serious about development. In February 1969, he had received the representatives of the Consortium in St. Moritz and told them in no uncertain terms that Iran needed a guaranteed income of at least $1 billion, that is, $100 million above what it was getting, and that he expected them to come up with what he needed. The discussion was tense and unproductive. The companies refused to commit themselves. In Iran, Armin Meyer and Denis Wright, the U.S. and British ambassadors, respectively, expressed their disenchantment to Alam—Meyer more understandingly, Wright more belligerently, complaining that the Consortium was "tired of [the shah's] threats."[23] On his return to Iran, the shah lambasted the Consortium to the NIOC board on 7 March, calling the Consortium's behavior toward Iran "unjust and unwise."[24] Two days later, on 9 March, he ordered Alam to talk to the ambassadors and "stress to them the seriousness of our intent." To Alam's warning that "they know we are in a financial quandary" and "one cannot wage economic warfare without money," he answered: "We are not yet quite so poor as you like to make out." The next day, on the 10th, Meyer told Alam that Iran could expect "no more than $900 million so long as the increase in the Middle East oil production is set at below 6.5 percent," which Alam reported to the shah on 11 March. "He can think what he likes, but the Russians will come to our assistance, and then the whole region will be thrown into even greater turmoil" was the shah's response. No doubt he meant to impress Alam so that in his conversations with the ambassadors and the oil representatives he would convey the threat as the shah meant it to be conveyed, that is, as a conclusion Alam had reached on his own from the shah's remarks. But as they were talking, the current NIOC chairman, Manuchehr Eqbal, called in to report that the Consortium had asked for more time to try to come up with a scheme to satisfy the shah's demands. Eqbal told the shah they were proposing to raise Iran's income to $950 million and provide for an interest-free loan to bring it up to $1 billion.[25]

■

Early in 1969, the shah told Alam in confidence, "we should take the oil in our own hand and sell it ourselves. The companies should become our clients. Then we will not have to fight any longer."[26] The shah had already won a bout by forcing the companies to pay him a renewable annual advance without interest, which in four years would come to about $300 million. This, however, was not satisfactory to him. He now dreamed of something bigger—a nationalization of oil in fact, which this time would bring Iran the advantages the earlier nationalization struggle had strived for but failed to achieve. Alam was proud of the monarch's determination to take control of oil but feared the consequences. He was worried about the direction the shah's vision was leading him. In late March and early April, while in Washington, D.C., to attend former President Eisenhower's funeral, the shah urged President Nixon to buy more Iranian oil. He argued that it was unfair to offer the same terms to countries with vastly different populations and economic needs. Kuwait, Libya, and Abu Dhabi did not have the same needs as Iran, he told Nixon, and he would fight for what he considered Iran's legitimate right. He wished to sell oil to the United States independently of quotas, to be stored as strategic reserves for rainy days. Iran, he argued, was a true friend of the United States because it was on the American side as a result of its own interests. In fact, it was in the interest of the United States, he told Nixon, to pull out and leave the security of the Persian Gulf area to Iran. This kind of talk between Nixon and the shah, which unbeknownst to Alam had actually begun in 1967 during Nixon's visit to Tehran, now worried the loyal counselor. Four years before, in Yalta in 1965, where he was negotiating gas for steel mills with the Russians, the shah had told Alam he was thinking of signing a twenty-five-year nonaggression pact with the Soviet Union. Alam had called it a political masterstroke, but warned against its risks. "As far as the Americans are concerned, Iran's raison d'être is to be anti-Soviet." This measure, he said, would be dangerous. He now told the monarch the same: the matter needed to be studied; the proposition was risky; without the American presence, Iran would be left defenseless, at the mercy of the Soviets. The shah rejected Alam's points.[27] Contrary to the courageous way he had faced off Khomeini in 1963, Alam was rather cautious in his approach to Western powers, including the oil companies. He was even wary of Iraq. He thought Shatt al-Arab a nuisance and claimed that he had begun plans to transfer the refining of oil from

Abadan, which was at the tip of the Shatt, to the port of Mahshahr (Ma'shur) farther to the southeast. In April the Iraqis again interfered with Iranian ships that raised the Iranian flag as they passed through the waterway. The Iranian armed forces went on the alert. Alam sent a cautionary telegram to the shah, then on an official visit to Tunisia. The shah answered back curtly that Alam was uninformed.[28]

Clearly, the shah had other ideas, which had gelled in his mind over several years. On oil, he was now for attack. Without steady pressure nothing would ooze out of the companies, he said.[29] The international mood had changed significantly since the 1950s. He felt certain of the understanding he had reached with the new American president and more secure in his relations with the Soviets. Now that a gas pipeline was being built to the Soviet Union, he played with the idea of laying an oil pipeline to take the Persian Gulf oil, from both Iranian and Arab sides, to Russia. The project, he thought, would make the Soviet Union a stakeholder in the security of the Persian Gulf and the transit rent from the pipeline would benefit Iran. The interest thus kindled in the security of the oil would transcend East-West rivalries in the Persian Gulf to everyone's advantage.[30] In late May, he broached the idea to Nixon's secretary of state, William Rogers. "Perhaps such an idea has been talked about in the State Department," the shah told Rogers. "It has not," answered Rogers, apparently forcing the conversation to a different subject.[31] A few days later, in June, Alam brought to the shah what he considered to be good news: "In the talks between Nixon and [British Prime Minister Harold] Wilson it was decided that in no probable future agreement between the West and the Soviet Union would Iran's interests be sacrificed." To Alam's surprise, the idea made the shah furious. "How dare they say such a thing? Do they think we are dead? Do they think we cannot take care of ourselves? Do they think we cannot make our own deals with the Soviets? Well, we are now strong enough not to be a *rahat-ul-holqum* [a soft sweet], to be swallowed easily." The outburst meant that Iran needed more arms. "Israel buys $600 million worth of arms annually. Now they fault me for buying too much arms. If we did not have the arms, even a puny state like Iraq would turn us into dust."[32] All of this pointed to more oil at a higher price.

Jamshid Amouzegar was considered one of the brightest civil servants Iran possessed. He had studied in the United States, received a doctorate in hydraulics from Cornell, and by 1965 had served in several high positions, including minister of agriculture in Eqbal's cabinet and minister of health in Mansur's. In

May 1965, he was appointed minister of finance, which also made him Iran's representative in OPEC and other international oil meetings. He proved an exceptionally able delegate, a force to contend with, both in OPEC and in negotiations with the oil companies. He presided over several OPEC conferences between 1965 and 1975 in which historic decisions were made, including the Twenty-Second Conference, in Tehran in 1971, when the first decision to raise oil prices was made, and in 1974 in the Thirty-Eighth and Thirty-Ninth Conferences, in Vienna, where the second significant price hike occurred.[33]

Amouzegar became the shah's right hand in implementing his oil policy. Two parallel and interconnected paths were chosen, with Amouzegar playing a central role in both. One had to do with negotiating with the companies to increase production and raise prices; the other with taking over the oil operations, as the shah had confided to Alam. By 1970, the companies had been put on notice about both aspects of this two-pronged movement. They naturally fought back but were ultimately forced to give in on both.

For Iran actually to take over its oil, the Consortium Agreement had to be renegotiated. The Consortium structure, as mentioned in chapter 9, allowed only minimal Iranian control. The two operating companies in which Iran had some supervision rights by law—the Exploration and Production Company and the Refining Company—were registered in Holland and in practice carried out decisions made in another structure—the Iranian Oil Participants—in which Iran had no presence. Over the years, NIOC had developed a roster of complaints about the Consortium's undermining of Iran's interests.

First, according to NIOC, the Consortium did not employ appropriate secondary recovery techniques, damaging Iran's long-term capacity to draw oil. Its actual practice would make only about 20 percent of the oil in place, that is, the existing reserves, recoverable. With proper methods of exploitation, including injecting gas back into the fields, recovery could be increased to 40 or possibly 45 percent.[34] The Consortium refused to implement secondary recovery operations because they involved additional expenditure, the profits from which would likely not be realized during the Consortium's life span.

Second, the gas escaping in the production of oil was mostly burned or otherwise wasted, or, when liquefied, considered as "oil" belonging to the Consortium.[35] In the late 1960s some two billion cubic feet of gas oozed out daily with the oil, most of which was allowed to burn with no functional utility. After 1970, when the pipeline for exporting gas to the Soviet Union came online, the waste was reduced, but the Exploration and Production Company neither gathered and exported the remaining gas in liquid form (LNG) nor injected it into the fields for secondary recovery, nor did it place the gas at NIOC's disposal for refinement and sale.

Third, the Consortium refused to provide the government with adequate funds for its development needs. Nor would it yield control of the production volume to the Iranian government, arguing that increasing production in Iran interfered with its members' operations in states such as Saudi Arabia and Kuwait.

And fourth, agreements based on the 1957 law had rendered the fifty-fifty principle obsolete. Furthermore, based on the Iranian experience, several of the Persian Gulf states had renegotiated part of their agreements with the oil companies at better terms, making the Consortium Agreement untenable.[36]

Thus it seemed that the Consortium as set up in 1954 could last only as long as Iran could not muster the power to challenge it. By the early 1970s the shah's power had increased both domestically and internationally, and he was now also armed with several UN resolutions that he could call on for moral support, as evidenced in his speech on 23 January 1973, at the tenth anniversary of the White Revolution, announcing to the Iranian people the reasons he was about to challenge the 1954 Consortium Agreement:

> We have been negotiating with the companies that form the Consortium for some time now. The negotiations continue but so far they have borne no fruit. That is why I must talk to you about them, not in detail, but in their broad outline. One of the articles of the agreement we signed in 1954 (which perhaps was the best we could have gotten at the time) obligated the operating companies to protect the Iranian interests in the best way possible. We have reasons to believe that this has not happened. The 1954 agreement foresaw three five-year renewals [beginning in 1979], assuming that Iran's interests had been satisfied. We now have evidence that forces us to refrain from renewing our agreement with the Consortium in 1979, even if we were to decide on the basis of the 1954 Agreement itself.
>
> You know, of course, that the United Nations Charter and several specific resolutions state clearly that countries own their wealth and the agreements made with foreign companies cannot be used to exploit these resources without the approval of the country that owns the resources. Now, the oil industry is a complex operation. If you take more oil out of a well than is technically safe, you actually may kill that well. If you don't attend to secondary recovery, that is not protecting the nation's interests. If you don't inject the gas back into the well using sound scientific methods, this is not protecting the nation's interests. These have not been done for our country.
>
> Two roads remain open to us. Because we are the kind of people that honor their signature, we say to the companies that one option is that you can go ahead until 1979, six more years, provided the revenues to us from each barrel of our oil are not less than the revenues that accrue to any state in our oil fields. If this is what they choose, the present oil companies will be buyers of our oil [after 1979] without any special privilege; they will have to stand in line like all other companies. The other

option is this: we sign a new agreement that returns to us all the responsibilities and all that today is not in our hand, and based on that the present companies become our long-term customers, receiving oil at a good price with discounts sellers usually offer their good customers, whereby the companies will receive oil during the period stated in the agreement, twenty or twenty-five years. We must know which way we are going and we must know it soon. If we opt for the second alternative, we must develop our industry, for which we need to get the best foreign specialists, employ them collectively or individually, and we must pay far greater attention to protection, preservation and exploration.[37]

The companies flocked to St. Moritz, Switzerland, where the shah spent his winter vacation. After several meetings, the operating companies offered a preliminary set of proposals, later dubbed "The St. Moritz Document," which the shah found acceptable for further discussion. Immediately, negotiations were launched in Iran, leading to a Purchase and Sale Agreement, to be implemented for twenty years beginning 21 March 1973, the first day of the Iranian year 1352. Based on the new agreement, signed in July 1973:

1. The National Iranian Oil Company as owner of the oil reserves and installations took over the administration and control of all activities pertaining to the oil industry in the area of the agreement, including exploration, development, investment, production, refining, and transportation of crude, gas, and oil products. The Consortium companies were transformed to privileged buyers of Iranian oil.

2. The Consortium's two operating companies—the Exploration and Production Company and the Refining Company—were dissolved. In their place the Consortium established an Oil Services Company to provide for the NIOC the technical services it needed during the first five years of the new agreement. NIOC would approve the Oil Services Company's budget and operations.

3. The NIOC would sell to the Consortium companies for export the crude not needed for internal consumption and for its own independent export. The latter would begin at two hundred thousand barrels per day in 1973 and was estimated to reach 1.5 million in 1981. (In practice, the NIOC's lift for export exceeded 1.5 million before 1978.)

4. Investment was the responsibility of the NIOC. However, the companies agreed to provide 40 percent of the investment for exploration and production during the first five years of the new agreement.

5. Against the investment and services the companies offered through the Oil Services Company, the oil sold the Consortium members for export was discounted at 22 cents a barrel.

This law stipulated only service-type agreements, according to which a foreign oil company acting as a contractor for the NIOC incurred exploration costs at its own risk. If oil was found, the field would be developed in partnership with the NIOC. Once production began, the contractor's work ended. The Iranian oil company would take over the production but would sell the contractor oil for export at a discount for a specified period, ordinarily fifteen years, computed so that the contractor would retrieve its capital plus a fair return. The shah was proud of the accomplishment, especially after 1975, when the companies began to complain about the conditions of the agreement and asked for its renegotiation, the first time in the history of oil that companies rather than producer states initiated measures to renegotiate an agreement. (The resulting talks continued until the revolution of 1979.) The shah boasted that finally in 1973 Iranian oil was truly nationalized.[38]

When negotiations on the price of oil began in 1970, the shah had an unexpected and unwitting ally in Libya's Mu'ammar Gadhafi, a low-level officer who on 1 September 1969 led a coup d'état against King Idris, who at the time was in Turkey for medical treatment. The new Libyan regime, headed by the Revolutionary Command Council (RCC), abolished the monarchy and proclaimed a Libyan Arab Republic. Gadhafi emerged as the leader of the RCC and eventually as de facto chief of state. A self-defined revolutionary, he was erratic and unpredictable, apt to throw many calculations off course. Naturally, the oil companies inclined to more reasonable leaders who allowed them to calculate their interests with some degree of dependability. The circumstances made the shah a model of rationality. Everyone, even his enemies, preferred to deal with him rather than with the likes of Gadhafi.

At their Twenty-First Conference in Caracas in December 1970, OPEC ministers chose Iran, Saudi Arabia, and Iraq to represent them in preliminary talks on prices with the oil companies in Tehran in January 1971. The three representatives were empowered to decide on a price unilaterally if the oil companies refused to attend; however, the companies did attend, and the conference began on a note of unity on the part of the producers. Iraq's oil minister, Sa'doun Hammadi, nominated Iran's representative, Jamshid Amouzegar, to chair the conference, despite the tensions that existed between the two nations. But the friendly gestures came to naught. The companies refused the OPEC proposals, the conference ended in failure, and oil share prices tumbled in the world markets. "These gentlemen think they give us alms," the shah told Amouzegar as he instructed him to call a press conference "to explain to the world in detail what we demand and why." Amouzegar did what the shah had ordered, and the next day his words were headlined in major world newspapers. In the evening Amouzegar received messages from several senators, "ancient in years," he recalls, advising him to go slow on locking horns with the oil companies. "British Petroleum owns the largest share of the Consortium, and opposing the British never ends well," he was advised.[39]

Shortly, the company representatives returned to Tehran, seemingly more accommodating, but once again they refused to raise prices. Amouzegar, who was authorized to decide on behalf of OPEC, refused their terms and closed the meeting for a pause. He received a call from Alam, asking him to an early breakfast. "We should not insist too much on raising the price of oil," said Alam. "It is not to our interest. You have the authority to speak on behalf of the OPEC and for this very reason you should not be unbending."

Amouzegar was surprised. "Your Excellency, our demands are stated very objectively, and they are based on very precise figures and undeniable facts. Why shouldn't we defend our right? Besides, I am the Shahanshah's loyal servant. If he is not happy with what I have done and orders me otherwise, I will agree with the companies' proposals this very day."

"He will not," said Alam. "The Shahanshah is too fond of and too committed to the country's rapid progress and development, and naturally he wishes to have the oil income as high as possible as soon as possible. But you are his counselor. It is incumbent upon you to tell him that obduracy in this matter is not to our advantage."

Amouzegar was now totally perplexed. "Why is the shah's trusted court minister and friend giving me advice that is so contrary to his avowed policy?" he wondered. He asked to speak to the shah. "Well," said the monarch, "you know the source where he drinks his water. Do not listen to him. Do your work."[40]

Alam was reputed to be close to the British. Indeed, the British government acknowledged as much in eulogizing him at his death in 1978. The "source of water" is a Persian idiom suggesting the place to which one is beholden. If this is what the shah meant, it was an unkind statement. Alam was close to the British, but the closeness did not vitiate his loyalty to the shah or to Iran.[41] Alam's advice to Amouzegar suggested his fear of repercussions in the same vein as the worries expressed to Amouzegar by the senators "ancient in years." To older Iranians the British came with occult powers. This was one of the reasons the shah was inclined to the younger generation of Iranians, mostly technocrats and a few politically savvy men, most of them trained in their youth in the bosom of the Tudeh Party. Many Alam cronies, for example, were former members of the Tudeh.

Despite the warnings, Amouzegar kept on the pressure as the shah had instructed. At the January 1971 OPEC conference it was agreed that the price, then $1.80 per barrel, should be raised, but no firm figure was reached. Studies at the NIOC suggested a price hike of 40 to 42 cents feasible. The shah, hearing the pros and cons in a meeting with Prime Minister Amir Abbas Hoveyda, NIOC Chair Manuchehr Eqbal, Finance Minister Jamshid Amouzegar, NIOC Director of International Affairs Reza Fallah, and Fallah's deputy Parviz Mina, agreed with the figure as the starting point for talks with other OPEC members. The figure was debated and approved by an OPEC steering committee in Tehran, which presented it to the conference of the oil ministers and representatives. They agreed to raise the base price 38 cents a barrel, making the new price $2.18 per barrel, plus 2.5 percent to compensate for inflation and 5 cents to adjust to the price rise of petroleum products in oil markets. This agreement did not last more than a year, however, as a result of inflation running at over 8 percent in the industrial countries and the fall of the dollar against other currencies.[42] In October 1973, in Kuwait, OPEC once again raised posted prices unilaterally to $5.119 per barrel and in December, in Tehran, to $11.65, bringing the price of oil to a semblance of parity with that of liquid coal, and government take to $7 per barrel.[43]

The shah was the pivot in the price hike in 1971 and again in 1973 and 1974. But he was not the hawk the Western press made him out to be. He believed that the oil companies, which lifted oil cheaply, and Western states, which taxed oil exorbitantly, profited inordinately at the expense of the producer countries. This was unfair and needed to be corrected. He also believed Iran deserved to be treated differently than other Persian Gulf producers because of its larger population and because of the eventual responsibilities it would have to shoulder to keep secure oil so badly needed by Western industry. Furthermore, by 1970 he had come to believe that Iran's oil reserves would not last long and therefore they had to be put to the best use for the country. He began to speak of the oil as a "noble substance" with multiple uses—too valuable to be wasted as a source of energy when other substances good only for producing energy were available. As we shall see in chapter 15, he had already launched a potentially vast petrochemical industry to produce added value and soon would embark on atomic energy to provide a partial alternative to oil. The West, he was satisfied, would not look to alternative sources as long as oil was obtained cheaply. Over the years he had argued that the price of oil in fact had fallen relative to the cost of other commodities. In the late 1960s, Western experts also voiced the same concern, though not as pronouncedly or systematically as they would in 1970 and after, when the demand for oil began to rise precipitously. In September

1970, for example, the authoritative *Oil and Gas Journal* observed that the price of oil and gas was far lower than it should be. Since 1958, the article said, crude prices had fallen at least 20.2 percent relative to comparable products.[44] This was in line with the shah's statements, though his were considerably starker. Several Western statesmen, including then U.S. national security adviser Henry Kissinger, also had come to believe that the oil prices should be raised, albeit in frameworks they could control. Control proved difficult as the rising demand for oil and the political turmoil in the Middle East pushed prices up beyond control.

The shah took the lead in the price war at a time when the nature of the West's dependence on Middle Eastern oil had qualitatively changed. Western Europe and Japan had always depended on Middle Eastern oil. The United States, however, had not. In 1950, the United States was an oil exporter. By the early 1960s it imported 16 percent of its annual consumption, though it did not produce at capacity for strategic reasons. By 1973, it was importing 35 percent of its domestic consumption and was producing at full capacity. The situation had made the West vulnerable to OPEC pressure. The shah, conscious of the dangers involved, would not venture price hikes quixotically. He understood Western priorities better than other OPEC members did. His relationship with Nixon was excellent, the two understanding each other perfectly. Kissinger called him "enlightened" partly because he insisted on conservation. The shah balanced his position by letting the more belligerent leaders, the perennially quixotic Gadhafi of Libya in this case, spearhead the price hike, and by keeping Iranian oil separate from the exigencies of Arab-Israeli politics. Nobody in the West liked his raising of the oil prices, but if a price hike was inevitable, his position was the one the West could live with. He emerged as a reasonable intermediary between the states such as Libya and Iraq on one side and the oil companies, the United States, and Europe on the other.

Western acquiescence to controlled price hikes was facilitated also by another factor: the discovery of oil in non-OPEC regions, especially the North Sea and Alaska. Western governments and companies reasoned that since eventually they would lose control of non-Western oil, they should increase supplies in the West or in areas controllable by the West. However, as long as oil could be obtained inexpensively, exploring and producing oil from the new fields would not be cost-effective. It was therefore necessary to establish a price floor to make investment in Western fields feasible. This kind of thinking led to the establishment of the International Energy Agency (IEA), initially suggested by Kissinger, in November 1974 within the framework of the Organization for Economic Cooperation and Development (OECD), with headquarters in Paris. The idea was for the developed nations to present a solid front to OPEC. But the effort was not as successful as hoped for. The OPEC members managed to deflect the dialogue to include other members of the Third World as well as other issues of interest to them. This was in some degree also the work of the shah.

■

The International Energy Agency sponsored the North-South Conference of 1975, based on a suggestion that French President Valéry Giscard d'Estaing made in November 1974 for a dialogue between developed countries and developing countries without oil on one side and the OPEC members on the other. The shah was displeased. Over the past few months he had been especially vexed by the West's efforts to put the blame for the rise in the price of Western commodities, including agricultural products, on the oil-producing countries. He instructed Amouzegar to lead the Iranian delegation to the upcoming UN World Food Conference in Rome because, he said, "Amouzegar knows how to counter Western efforts" to blame him and other OPEC members in order to hide their own selfishness. On 1 November, a few days after the French president's proposal, the shah stressed the injustice of blaming countries like his for world inflation to Kissinger, who, given the shah's satisfied mood after the talks, apparently did not challenge him.[45] To the international press accompanying Kissinger to Tehran, he took a rather belligerent attitude, not only on the price of oil and food security, but also on Iran's intentions about regional security: "We want to assure peace in the Indian Ocean region. . . . But we will not wait for others. We are obligated to protect our national interest in any way we can. We hope others will cooperate with us in this effort, but if they don't, we will do this alone."[46] Kissinger, of course, had heard this before and acquiesced to the shah's leading role in the security of the Persian Gulf. The Indian Ocean, however, was a different matter. Nonetheless, he would not contradict the shah publicly.

A tripartite meeting held in Paris in April 1975 to prepare an agenda for the North-South Conference failed because the industrial countries, led by the United States, preferred the conference to focus on energy, whereas the Third World countries insisted on a broader agenda suggested by the OPEC summit in Algeria in March. In September, the UN General Assembly adopted the Resolution on Development and International Economic Cooperation, to which the United States government had reacted favorably. The resolution paved the way for the industrial nations to agree, albeit reluctantly, that the conference would include other issues, especially raw materials, development, and finances. The conference began at the ministerial level in Paris in December 1975, then convened at work levels off and on, ending with its last summit 31 May to 3 June 1977. It ultimately failed because the differences separating developed and less developed countries could not be reconciled.[47] It also showed why the shah's position was basically one that both sides might covet as a political meeting place.

Third World radicals attributed the existing malaise in the world to deep "structural imbalances" and "lopsided interdependence" that were essentially consequences of colonialism. In this view "the bulk of value-added in world production, processing and marketing" went to the developed world and only a small fraction to the developing nations. The existing structures, such as the international monetary system, compounded the disadvantages less developed countries suffered, because as products of the existing dominant regime they were by nature structurally and operationally arbitrary and inequitable. "The new world order must thus result from a complete institutional overhaul of the existing system."[48]

At the other end of the spectrum, the conservatives—that is, most of the industrial states—dismissed the radical position as "impractical and unrealistic" and thus irrelevant. Change had to come gradually, step by step and "case by case," to achieve "needed marginal adjustments." Required was a "new deal instead of a new order."

The shah's position was in between, in line with a moderate approach that held that the "new order" should give less developed countries a fairer share of world income and a greater voice in international institutions.[49] In August in a speech to a university audience in Prague, the shah put his thinking this way:

> Today's world is marked by interdependence and close sharing of problems. Our basic problems are universal and can be solved only in a universal framework. What I would like to point out is this: our world is blessed with the most advanced science, industry, and technology the world has ever known. It has the wherewithal and the resources to provide a fair and acceptable life for every human being. But it has become a place of injustice and deprivation because of the existence of an unjust and irrational order that favors neither human rights nor moral and social good nor humanity's true economic interest. If the world persists in this path, it most likely will face a destructive explosion.[50]

Playing the intermediary was not easy. The shah had problems not only with the West, especially the United States, but also with Saudi Arabia, the balancer of the oil market. He and King Khalid disagreed on oil policy, the Saudi king wanting to keep the prices down while the other oil exporting countries wished to link the price of oil to inflation in the industrialized world. Khalid, on the advice of his oil minister, Zaki Yamani, argued in favor of taxing the oil companies rather than raising the prices. "Saudi Arabia believes that raising oil prices at this time will reduce demand and consequently weaken the relative position of the oil-producing countries because, clearly, increasing demand is the foundation of the latter's ability to maintain price stability." The price hike in January 1975, he argued in a letter to the shah in August of that year, might well have been the cause of the fall in demand that led certain oil-producing countries to lower the price of their oil. "If we raise the price, others may also follow the same path." Moreover, raising prices would affect both the industrial and the developing countries, causing the developing countries that received financial aid from the oil exporters to ask for more loans and aid when several exporting states needed the money for their own development projects. And needless to say, Khalid wrote, this was a bad time to raise prices because the producers and consumers were trying to reconvene the Paris conference and such a policy did not seem politically propitious.[51]

The shah was not convinced. Iran and Saudi Arabia viewed oil from different perspectives. The Saudis had vast oil reserves, and their policy was organized around the principle of maintaining flexible demand into the distant future. The Iranians believed that their oil reserves were limited, that oil could be used to produce a variety of finished products that yielded far higher returns, that it was necessary for the industrialized countries to switch to other sources of energy if oil was to be preserved, and that the only way this could happen was if other energy sources became competitive. "The oil-producing countries," the shah wrote back to Khalid, "must gear the price of oil to the cost of producing energy from other sources to create an incentive for producing energy from other sources and to prevent this God-given but irreproducible resource from being exhausted in a short time; otherwise the industrial societies' insatiable appetite for energy will soon use all our oil resources and then the oil-producing countries will have to extend their beggar's hand to the industrial states for everything, even their energy needs." On the effect of higher oil prices on the advanced economies the shah was also unmoved. "The industrial countries may have paid more for oil, but they have sold, and are selling now, their industrial products and even their raw material at far greater prices to the oil-producing countries. The evidence for this is overwhelming," wrote the shah. "It would be a great mistake for the OPEC countries to fix the prices of their oil once again," the shah said, "because (1) the industrial countries will not take the matter of inflation as seriously as they should; (2) they will try, as they have stated on numerous occasions, to lower our oil's purchasing power as they have done in the past year by raising the price of their goods; and (3) they will forget about investing in other sources of energy, increasingly using our cheap oil in the service of their own economic progress. For these reasons, keeping oil at the present price is a very dangerous proposition. Moreover, it encourages the industrial societies to think we are incapable of defending our national interest."[52] He sent Amouzegar to Khalid and Crown Prince Fahd to explain Iran's position in more detail. Khalid sent Yamani back to him, but to no avail. Yamani concluded that he could not change the shah's position and apparently fell in line. The shah wrote Khalid that since December 1973 the purchasing power of income from oil had declined almost 35 percent and therefore Iran would propose a price hike of 15 to 20 percent in the upcoming OPEC meeting.[53]

The tension, however, did not end here. Khalid's position had its inner logic insofar as it concerned Saudi Arabia, but it also reflected the U.S. interest. On 9 September 1975, the shah received a letter from Gerald Ford in which the U.S. president mingled friendship and threats in order to cajole the shah to pull back from a price hike. Since the April preparatory meeting in Paris, Ford stated, the United States had worked very hard, particularly with Iran, to establish a productive dialogue between the industrial and developing nations.

> As you can appreciate, the support of the American public for the new United States position must be based on an awareness of the concerns of the oil producers and other developing countries and the need to seek cooperative solutions to our common economic problems. I am concerned, however, that this necessary support will be jeopardized should the member countries of OPEC increase the price of oil this fall.
>
> I am also concerned that such action could raise serious questions among the American public regarding the close cooperation we seek and are actively developing with your country in several fields of our bilateral relationship. I value this relationship greatly and sincerely wish to continue to broaden and deepen it.

Another oil price increase, continued the president, "would have a significant negative impact on the economies of all the oil importing nations — both developed and developing," and "would impose shocks on the United States economy, on the more vulnerable economies of Europe and Japan, and finally on the highly fragile economies of the developing world." He concluded:

> It is because I am aware, Your Majesty, of your sensitivity to the interdependence of the world economy and your commitment to a successful economic dialogue that I am asking you to weigh heavily the adverse effects — both psychological

and real—which a price increase would have. It is my hope that you will use your considerable influence among the producing countries to urge restraint on oil prices and to argue that our long-term mutual interest in a more rational global economic structure should prevail over short-term economic advantage.[54]

The shah's response was immediate and stern. He was all for dialogue between developing and developed nations, he wrote back, and it was at his suggestion that OPEC had agreed to freeze the price of oil until the end of 1975, "although we were subject to the continued inflation exported to our countries." The oil-producing countries, he said, could no longer tolerate "a decrease of 35 percent in our purchasing power" or an increase of 300 to 400 percent compared to eighteen months ago in the price of commodities they needed to buy from the United States. Oil prices in the West could be brought down by adjusting the taxes governments imposed on oil products, "which on average nearly equals the government take of the oil producing nations," or by "lifting the two dollar tariff" in the case of the United States, he wrote. Furthermore, he again argued that an increase in the price of oil was "imperative to create sufficient incentive for the development of alternative sources of energy," which would certainly be beneficial to the industrialized countries, "the sound economic growth of which directly affects the industrialization of OPEC nations." In relation to the non-oil-producing developing countries, he had "in mind a plan of assistance for these nations in the form of grant-in-aid," which with the support of the OPEC countries could be put into effect immediately. And, he protested, inflation in the West began "well before we increased the price of oil" and, at any rate, the price hike "was responsible for only 2 percent of the world inflation which was running between 12 and 17 percent." He then concluded: "I also appreciate very much and greatly value the special relationship that exists between our two countries, which as you fully realize, Mr. President, is not only in favor of Iran but is mutually and equally beneficial to both sides. If in defending our legitimate interests, we might raise serious questions among the American people, we would be very sorry to ascertain that the real facts have not been set before your public."[55]

This was a tough-minded turning of the table, with the shah now telling the president how to deal with the problem of the price hike in oil in the United States. Ford and Kissinger accepted the inevitable price hike but not the shah's theory that in the long run it benefited the West because it would make looking for alternative sources of energy more feasible. Two years later, with Jimmy Carter on the horizon, that prospect could have changed in favor of the shah, but it did not.

13

Commander-in-Chief

On the eve of the Islamic revolution, Iran's armed forces were composed of the Imperial Iranian Army, which included ground forces, air force, and navy; the Imperial Guard; and two national law and order organizations: the gendarmerie in rural areas and the police in urban areas. The gendarmerie and police were formally under the authority of the minister of the interior; however, functionally and structurally they followed the military's rules and regulations concerning personnel, command, planning, weaponry, and logistics. Practically, then, they were constituent military organizations.

At the time of the revolution, the Imperial Iranian Army was considered a formidable force, unrivaled in the Middle East except by Israel and vying to become a world-scale power. This army was the creation of the Pahlavi dynasty,[1] and the shah's hold on the army transcended the constitutional provisions that defined his role as commander-in-chief with supreme authority over the military. Both Pahlavi shahs advocated military strength and acted as a lobby for the military interest. They were also a buffer that separated the military from the domestic political environment. During the Pahlavi era, the officer corps became involved in politics only twice. The first time catapulted Reza Khan to power and subsequently the throne. Immediately afterward, however, Reza Shah reined in the military and turned it into a professional organization under his personal command. The second occurred after the Allied invasion, Reza Shah's exile, and the onset of a fractured pluralism—during the period 1941–53. This was a time of frantic competition among political factions—including some within the armed forces—for the military's loyalty. The officer corps, the NCOs, and the soldiers, however, remained by and large loyal to the shah, playing a pivotal role in bringing him back in 1953. After 1953, the military was sent back to the barracks and was substantially cut off from the nation's everyday politics.

In the Pahlavi military culture the shah was at once symbol and commander. As symbol, he represented the nation's past, present, and future, its sovereignty, dignity, and meaning. The shah was nation and nationalism combined. The military's motto was "God, King, and Country," the king being the point of convergence. The symbolism was reinforced by the command structure. A minister of war was responsible for budget and procurement but had no command function or responsibility. Planning and coordination were the responsibility of the Supreme Commander's Staff (SCS), whose chief was in practice the shah's military chief of staff. The line of command led directly from the force commanders — ground, air, and sea, the Imperial Guard, gendarmerie, and police — to the shah as the supreme commander. In routine matters, the shah's orders were transmitted to commanding officers by the Supreme Commander's Staff.[2] This direct liaison with the shah was a point of honor for the commanders and was jealously guarded. General Samad Samadianpur, the chief of police, asked to be retired when early during the Azhari government in the fall of 1978 the police and gendarmerie chiefs were directed to report to the minister of the interior. General Ahmadali Mohaqqeqi, the gendarmerie commander, thought Azhari's order represented a conspiracy to neutralize the gendarmerie as a fighting force.[3] For the generals, it was the shah that counted. The cadets took their military oath on the Koran and the flag to remain perpetually loyal to their commander-in-chief, in whom the nation was personified. All revered national values were thought to inhere in the shah as symbol, man, and commander. This mode of thinking was continually stressed and reemphasized through systems of reward and punishment. On the one hand, the idea that the shah embodied military loyalty was so well entrenched in the military psyche that it had become a fact of life; on the other hand, alleged systems of intelligence and counterintelligence pervading the military organization also made it prudent to shun ideas or actions that might suggest disloyalty. "The result was that for the most part the Iranian military universe received its light from the shah. Without him, bearings were lost, command structures were debilitated, and decisions were left unmade."[4]

This military establishment was largely shaped along U.S. organizational, procedural, logistical, strategic, tactical, and weapons guidelines. Over the years, it became increasingly disciplined and professional, though, ironically, this professionalism, in stressing respect for the line of command, strengthened the ties between the military and the shah. And the shah's exceptional aptitude for grasping military hardware, structure, and strategy made questioning his command redundant.

U.S. involvement with Iran's military dated from the middle of World War II. Most of the war material transferred to the Soviet Union through Iran was American, and once the United States entered the war, Americans took over the management of the transfer. The first contingent of American troops, the Iranian Military Mission, arrived in Iran in December 1942 and took over from the British the administration of the railroads and the transfer of munitions. By 1943, the number of U.S. troops in Iran had reached thirty thousand, and the name of the operation was changed to the Persian Gulf Command.

Interestingly, U.S.-Iranian cooperation in military matters was initiated by the British. In January 1942, the British ambassador Sir Reader Bullard recommended to the Iranian cabinet that it take advantage of the Allied military presence in Iran to reorganize the Iranian armed forces. Bullard's idea met with the approval of both the shah and the cabinet, but given Iran's history with the British and the Russians, the Americans turned out to be the natural option for the process. Approached by the Soheili and Qavam cabinets, the United States government agreed to assign two groups of advisers to Iran to help with the reorganization of the army and the gendarmerie.[5] Major General C. S. Ridley and Colonel H. N. Schwarzkopf arrived in Tehran in September 1942, and the two advisory groups — the United States Military Mission with the Imperial Iranian Army (ARMISH) and the United States Military Mission with the Imperial Iranian Gendarmerie (GENMISH) — were formally announced on 27 November 1943.

The coming of U.S. military advisers to Iran put pressure on the structure and functioning of the Iranian armed forces. The Iranian officer class then was of two types. There were the old Cossacks, Reza Shah's colleagues, who had learned soldiering under the Russians by fighting tribes and other rebels in the Iranian mountains. And there were the modern, more aristocratic types, who had studied in Europe; a few of them had been in Russia, Austria, or Germany before World War I, but most of them had gone to France, particularly after the rise of Reza Shah. The latter had brought with them the French system copied from the military schools of Saint-Cyr and Saumur. Their military preference was reflected particularly in the Officer Cadet College, the War University, and other military schools in Iran. The Americans were an unknown, and the American system did not always appear to them logically superior to that of the French. Indeed, the American missions in Iran at the time, except possibly Schwarzkopf's, did not seem to work well at all. Arthur Millspaugh, twice a financial adviser to the government of Iran, accused the U.S. government of assigning the missions and then forgetting about them, leaving a bad image in Iran. Millspaugh went so far as to claim that the ineffectiveness of these missions made some Iranians question the value of allying with the United States.[6] However, the Americans had one great, unchallengeable advantage: they had won a war in which the French had failed miserably. The relationship between the advisers and the Iranian military thus was cordial but tense. To the Americans the Iranian military was in shambles: divisions were ill equipped, scattered about the country with no logistical support, most of their equipment "antiquated, worn, and in need of replacement," and the "few existing military schools had deteriorated during the war years resulting in an inadequately trained officer corps," according to an ARMISH-MAAG (Military Assistance Advisory Group) memorandum.[7]

The U.S.-Iranian military relation gave the Soviets an excuse to accuse Iran of becoming a U.S. military outpost. As a result of Soviet pressure the United States changed the terms of the agreement establishing ARMISH to state clearly that U.S. advisers would not be involved in "tactical and strategical plans or operations against a foreign enemy, which is not related to the duties of the Mission" (Article 8 of the revised agreement) and that members of the mission would "assume neither command nor staff responsibility in the Iranian Army" (Article 9 of the revised agreement).[8] The GENMISH contract was also changed. In January 1948 General Mohammad Sadeq Kupal was given the sole command of the gendarmerie, eliciting a complaint from Ambassador George Allen, who offered either to withdraw U.S. advisers or to renegotiate their terms of contract to make their duties purely advisory.[9] By June, Allen had been replaced by John Wiley, and Schwarzkopf was given a new assignment out of Iran; and by September a new GENMISH agreement was signed, according to which the Americans assumed a purely advisory function vis-à-vis the Iranian gendarmerie.

The Iranian armed forces were formally reorganized after the U.S. model in August 1955. The structure, however, was adjusted to the shah's constitutional position as commander-in-chief. It was at this time that the Supreme Commander's Staff was established, and three separate commands—ground, air, and sea—were formed. War Minister Lieutenant General Abdollah Hedayat, soon to become Iran's first four-star general, was appointed chief of the newly established Supreme Commander's Staff. In December, the ground forces were organized into five army groups. By the 1960s a new crop of officers was replacing the old guard. The shah's classmates at the Officer Cadet College had reached top positions by 1970, and the army command passed to a new generation—Fereydun Jam, Gholamali Oveisi, Fathollah Minbashian, Gholamreza Azhari, Hossein Fardust, Abbas Qarabaghi, and others who were more or less the shah's age. The newcomers were better educated and, unlike their predecessors, who had been reared in a French-Iranian military culture, more at home with the Americans. By the time they reached top command, they were also socialized in the shah's superior military-strategic knowledge. The older generation had been dedicated to the shah affectively, morally, and nationalistically; they obeyed him as a matter of moral and professional duty, not for his superior military knowledge. The younger generation looked at him as *bozorg arteshtaran farmandeh,* the supreme commander who knew everything and whose judgment could not be wrong. The last one to question the shah's judgment, his erstwhile brother-in-law and his father's favorite, was General Jam, the first of his age group to reach the highest post in the armed forces, chief of the SCS, where he did not last long. He served for two years and was replaced in 1971 by General Gholamreza Azhari, a much milder personality, who lasted until 1978, when he was appointed prime minister. He in turn was replaced by General Qarabaghi, also the shah's classmate at the Officer Cadet College.

To the Soviets the presence of U.S. advisers in Iran and American control of Middle East oil and the Middle East alliance system were components of a unified "aggressive and adventurous military-political plan" that threatened the security of the Soviet Union.[10] When in 1955 the shah emerged as the prime personage in Iran's foreign and domestic politics, the Soviets focused their attacks on him, especially after Iran joined the Baghdad Pact in October of that year.

The shah, for his part, thought that the Baghdad Pact did not satisfy Iran's security needs. Rather, the pact was a device the United States employed to contain the Soviet Union, to protect the oil resources of the Persian Gulf, and to control Arab-Israeli tensions.[11] Iran and other constituent regional states only partially shared these objectives. Pakistan, for example, was mainly concerned with India; containing communism was secondary to its security interests. Turkey and Iran's primary worry was the Soviet Union, but they had other concerns as well. Iran especially felt threatened by the rise of Arab nationalism, whose Islamic component created domestic strife and also affected Iran's relations with the West. For the shah, confronting Nasser, who increasingly symbolized the emergent Pan-Arabism, was nearly as important as defending against the Russians. Worried about U.S. intentions, he sought understanding with the Soviets. He was thus happy to receive an invitation from Marshal Kliment Voroshilov, chairman of the Presidium of the Supreme Soviet, to visit the Soviet Union in the summer of 1956.

In Moscow, the Soviets gave the shah a royal reception but also a hard time. Khrushchev scolded him for joining the Baghdad Pact (he called it the American pact) now that the Soviet leader had declared peaceful coexistence to be the foundation of Soviet foreign policy. Against the shah's review of a history of Soviet-Iranian relations, Khrushchev conceded that some mistakes may have been made, but that was in the past, before he and his friends had taken the helm. Now, he said, the time had come for the shah to trust him. He knew that Iran did not contemplate aggression against the Soviet Union, but it was always possible that some great power might force her to make her territory available for such aggressive moves. Perhaps this was why Iran has been forced to join this pact, he said. "Iran joined the pact by its own volition," countered the shah. "No one has forced us to join, and had anyone tried, we would have resisted." He promised Khrushchev that Iran would not be used for aggression against the Soviet Union. "I give you my soldier's pledge: As long as I am on Iran's throne, my country shall never acquiesce to any demand for aggression against the Soviet Union and shall never be a party to such an action."[12] Khrushchev and his colleagues welcomed the shah's promise made seemingly in good faith. The Soviet press — *Pravda* and *Izvestia* — deemed the visit a success for producing initial agreements on a joint project to develop the rivers that bordered the two countries; the Western press praised the shah especially on his firmness vis-à-vis his giant neighbor.[13]

The shah considered his visit in the Soviet Union successful but not reassuring. He felt threatened by Khrushchev, whose designs he was not sure he could adequately discern. Stalin had been easier to fathom: whoever was not with him was against him. Khrushchev was subtle, clever, and at once pliant and hard. Stalin frowned, Khrushchev smiled, but the force that drove one also drove the other. He worried especially about the role Khrushchev played in the non-aligned movement and the effect of the Bandung Conference, held in Indonesia two months before his trip to the Soviet Union, on the relative power of Nasser's regime in Egypt and consequently on the stability of his regime. He had invited Nasser to visit Iran on his way back from Bandung, but Nasser had politely refused.[14] Bandung would not come to much, he thought, if Khrushchev did not give it weight. But now, it seemed to him, it had become a means of tilting the world eastward, and the thought discomforted him.[15] Still, when in July Nasser nationalized the Suez Canal, the shah declared Nasser was within his rights, and he denounced territorial aggression after Israel, encouraged by Britain and France, invaded Egypt on 29 October. Again, after Britain and France invaded Egypt, ostensibly to enforce peace, he condemned Israel and in a joint statement with other Muslim members of the Baghdad Pact demanded that the British and French withdraw.[16] However, much to his chagrin, the spectacle of the two major European powers being forced to withdraw, even though by the United States, made a veritable hero of Nasser in the Middle East and throughout the developing world.[17]

The Suez crisis also engendered the Eisenhower Doctrine, which the shah welcomed. The doctrine, announced on 5 January 1957, committed the United States to defend the countries of the Middle East against Soviet incursions, and to that effect stated that the United States would cooperate with and assist "any nation or group of nations in the general area of the Middle East" dedicated to the "maintenance of national independence" economically and militarily, including "the employment of the armed forces of the United States to secure and protect [consonant with treaty obligations of the United States] the territorial integrity and political independence of such nations, requesting such aid, against overt armed aggression from any nation controlled by International Communism."[18]

Eisenhower's statement of commitment to the defense of the Middle East led Khrushchev to seek accommodation with Iran as a way of derailing Iran's relations with the United States. As a result, relations between the two countries appeared to improve. Between April 1957 and July 1958 several agreements on commercial, transit, and border relations, river dredging, and the use of railways were signed between the Soviets and Iranians. In October 1957, Iran's council of ministers formally recognized the Soviet Union as a most-favored nation. On 26 November Khrushchev told a news conference that the border disputes between Iran and his country had been solved, that relations with Iran had palpably improved, and that now they were based on mutual respect.[19] He sent feelers to the shah about a nonaggression pact to last for centuries, guaranteeing neighborly relations, independence, and territorial integrity in perpetuity.[20] Indeed, the shah's worries about the events that shook the Arab Middle East in early 1958 and the American reluctance to enter a bilateral treaty with Iran might have brought Iran and the Soviet Union together in a treaty of alliance had the Soviets not conditioned their final agreement on Iran's quitting the Baghdad Pact.

On 1 February 1958, Egypt and Syria joined to establish the United Arab Republic under Nasser, a move that was popular in the Arab world but opposed by King Faisal of Iraq and his prime minister, Nuri al-Said. Said's long-standing association with England, accentuated by Iraq's recent membership in the Baghdad Pact, had made him unpopular among the Arabs. In July, the monarchy in Iraq was overthrown in a bloody coup and replaced with a radical nationalist-leftist regime led by Abd al-Karim Qasim and Abd al-

Salam Aref. Though the shah had some inkling of trouble brewing in Iraq and, according to his then special adjutant Ardeshir Zahedi, had warned Said,[21] he was devastated by the coup and disappointed by the seeming ineffectiveness of the Baghdad Pact to confront the new regime. "What is the use of this Pact if something so horrendous occurs and it does nothing about it?" he asked Prime Minister Eqbal, Foreign Minister Ali Asghar Hekmat, and Foreign Ministry Political Bureau Chief Amir Khosro Afshar.[22] He wondered aloud about the value of his attachment to the West. He directed Eqbal to inform the upcoming annual ministerial meeting of the Baghdad Pact in London, scheduled for 29 July 1958, that Iran would pull out unless the United States agreed formally to join the pact. The Iranian delegation consulted the Turks and the Pakistanis and found them agreeable to the proposition. In the closed session, Eqbal, supported by Turkey and Pakistan, made the announcement that unless the United States joined the pact, Iran would have to consider other options. Secretary Dulles, representing the United States, tried to trivialize the issue but, seeing that the other members were serious, said that he would have to speak to Eisenhower before he could make a decision and that he would announce the U.S. position the next day. In the morning, Dulles said that the United States would not join the pact formally but was prepared to sign bilateral agreements with each of the member countries. Two months later in Tehran the American ambassador handed the Iranian foreign minister a draft of a proposed bilateral agreement. The shah ordered the Ministry of Foreign Affairs to prepare an Iranian draft and charged Amir Khosro Afshar, director of the political bureau, with the task.

Afshar began his work by conferring with his Turkish and Pakistani colleagues in Ankara, the three having agreed to work in unison on the proposed plan. After several drafts of the proposed bilateral treaty had been traded with the Americans and a preliminary agreement on the basic points seemingly reached, Afshar suddenly found himself faced with a wholly new circumstance:

> I just had returned from Ankara to Tehran confident that we had reached agreement with the Americans. Hekmat called me to his office and told me, "I must inform you of a new development, but it is top secret and must not go beyond this room. We have begun negotiating with the Soviets to sign a nonaggression treaty in which the Soviets will formally renounce Articles 5 and 6 of the 1921 Treaty."
>
> I said, dumbfounded, "Why should we do this? We have already announced that we consider the two articles invalid, and everybody else sees it that way. Besides, who can trust the Soviets, regardless of what they sign?"
>
> "This is what he wants," said Hekmat, pointing to His Majesty's picture on the wall.[23]

Hekmat told Afshar the Soviets would sign the treaty provided Iran did not sign the proposed bilateral agreement with the United States. "You must stall the Americans," he said.

The shah apparently was serious, and something extraordinary might have happened had the Soviets not caused the shah to have second thoughts by their initial reactions to the bilateral treaty. As the shah stated it:

> The Russians sent us a very harsh note once they learned about [Iran and the United States negotiating a bilateral defense treaty.] However, contrary to diplomatic norms, they broadcast their opposition in the media and ordered their ambassador in Iran to take their protest directly to the Iranian parliament. We told them as sincerely as we could that their behavior might easily lead to a repetition of the past mistakes that had caused a deterioration of our relations. And we brought to their attention that given their extraordinary military might, it was ludicrous to fear any threat from small defensive organizations. And we told them that it was in the interest of our two nations to continue our friendly and brotherly relations.
>
> Concomitantly, the Russians sent us intermediaries with promises of long-term nonaggression treaties and large economic aid. The first drafts of the [U.S.-Iran] bilateral treaty did not satisfy our needs, because they lacked the guarantees we needed and therefore did not match our goals. The military hardware Iran received was meager, and we felt militarily very weak. We did not have the security guarantees that NATO nations enjoyed. We therefore felt we were justified in engaging in negotiations with the Russians about a nonaggression treaty.
>
> The Soviets now made an error by procrastinating two weeks before sending their representatives. During this period, the text of the proposed bilateral treaty changed to our satisfaction. The Soviets made another mistake asking us to get out of the Baghdad Pact. Later they conceded our staying in the pact but insisted on our withdrawing from the bilateral treaty. We now realized that the Russians wanted to sever us from our allies. Not only did they insist that we turn away from the bilateral treaty, but the text of the treaty they proposed contained material that seriously weakened our relations with our friends. This was not acceptable. Though we were not happy with our military forces, their preparedness, or the aid we received from our allies, nevertheless we decided it was better for us not to cut our relations with our friends and not to risk a venture that would undermine our independence and sovereignty.[24]

On 2 March 1959, Iran formally notified the Soviet government that it did not recognize Articles 5 and 6 of the 1921 Treaty, the articles the Soviet government claimed gave it the right under certain circumstances to bring troops into Iranian territory.[25] On 5 March, Iran, Pakistan, and Turkey each signed a separate bilateral defensive agreement with the United States. "These agreements," announced Iran's foreign minister, "are defensive in nature and no threat to the Soviet Union unless she plans to invade our countries."[26] The Majlis ratified the agreement on the 8th, the Senate on the 11th. On 19 August, the Baghdad Pact was renamed the Central Treaty Organization (CENTO), which the United States joined as an adjunct member.

The shah considered the Bilateral Agreement pivotal in Iranian-U.S. military and defense relations. He insisted on calling it a treaty and interpreted it as obligating the United States to intervene militarily if Iran was attacked by the Soviet Union or its proxies. According to Ahmad Mirfendereski, Iran's longtime ambassador to the Soviet Union and the last minister of foreign affairs under the shah, the shah believed there was a letter from the United States supporting his understanding of the treaty, although a search of the documents in the ministry failed to produce such a letter.[27] The United States, on the other hand, considered it an agreement and interpreted it vaguely as obligating the United States to take necessary measures, including military action, to help Iran. In other words, the United States saw the agreement as little more than a restatement of the Eisenhower Doctrine.

Two and a half years later, when the shah visited Washington in April 1962, he and President Kennedy agreed that from a purely military point of view Iran could never defend itself against the Soviet Union if the Soviets made a major effort to invade Iran. They also agreed that Iran ought to be strong enough not to be a tempting target for the Soviet Union. According to Kennedy's secretary of state, Dean Rusk, "The location of Iran . . . made it a [critical] country from a geopolitical point of view. That whole Middle Eastern area could have collapsed like a stack of cards if Iran fell under hostile domination of another country, from the point of view of the United States. So we were not interested in a weak Iran, but we did not think [the shah] should have such bloated military forces as to undermine the economic and social fabric of the country and weaken him so from within that he would not be able to run a successful government."[28]

The shah countered that cooperation and defensive military pacts with the West reduced Iran's military budget to the lowest possible minimum, allowing him to continue with economic and social progress. The cost per capita of population of maintaining the Iranian army, he argued, was only one-fifteenth that of those of two neutral countries, Sweden and Switzerland.[29] He worried that Kennedy and his administration might be ambivalent about the 1959 U.S.-Iran Bilateral Treaty. Rusk thought the shah might want a more formal treaty of alliance to give him a surer basis when he bargained for more military aid.[30] The impression he had was that the shah decided what money he needed and if the revenues fell short, he first pushed for more oil money and, when that venue was closed, turned up the pressure on the United States for military aid.

Rusk and Defense Secretary Robert McNamara wondered whether the shah needed the weapons he asked for within a militarily reasonable concept of legitimate defense. "He did not need any outside military help against any other neighbors he had except the Soviet Union. Turkey and Pakistan were no problems. Iraq was not a serious problem in those days. And it was simply . . . infeasible for him to think about any kind of armed force that could defend Iran against a major onslaught by the Soviet Union. So, basically, we felt that his armed forces were largely there for purposes of internal security rather than for external defense or attack."[31]

But Rusk also thought that the shah was different from some of the other leaders the United States dealt with. U.S. military aid to Latin American countries was tied to a scaling down of their military budgets. The administration tried to do the same in Iran, but, according to Rusk, "it was somewhat rougher going with the shah than it had been in Latin America, because, you see, he was influenced by the dreams of Persian Empire. He had a very lofty view of what Persia had been and perhaps could be again someday. The sense of glory in the shah was at least equal to President de Gaulle's views about the glory of France. [This] led to a failure of the meeting of the minds in a great many matters of detail in trying to work things out with the shah."[32] This line of thinking, of course, contradicted the idea that the shah wanted a strong military for internal security.

Shortly after the Washington negotiations, Kennedy and McNamara dispatched a team headed by Brigadier General Hamilton Twitchell to survey Iran's equipment needs and make recommendations about the military hardware to be provided under the U.S. military assistance program, especially in the areas on which the shah and McNamara had not reached agreement.[33] Twitchell, who would become ARMISH-MAAG chief in Iran in 1968, recommended that the military procurement program be coordinated with Iran's training program and only such equipment be supplied as the Iranians could operate and maintain themselves. Although the shah accepted the idea—known in Iran as the "Twitchell doctrine"—in theory, in fact he pushed it beyond the limits Twitchell suggested in order to gain the optimal balance between technical capability and best possible weapons system. In effect, he reversed the Twitchell doctrine: whereas Twitchell advocated adjusting weapons to capability, he pushed for adjusting capability to weapons.

After the assassination of President Kennedy, the shah found an easier relationship with his successor, Lyndon Johnson. The shah's political stature also improved as the 1960s moved on. His economy took off. The White Revolution reshaped urban and rural political structures. His relationship with the Soviet Union became friendlier. Slowly his tone assumed an authority it had not possessed before. He even intimated that if the Americans rebuffed him, he might turn to the Soviets for arms, a threat that, though never explicitly made, nonetheless registered with U.S. Ambassador Armin Meyer.[34]

The Americans factored the shah's distrust of the Russians into their calculations, but they also realized that military cooperation was the pivot that held U.S.-Iranian relations together. Meyer thought the military side of the relationship was essential to maintaining the rest and tried to communicate this to President Johnson, who, especially in his first term, depended on Kennedy's people in foreign policy. Meyer found himself in an ongoing debate with the Departments of State and Defense about the shah and the future of U.S.-Iranian relations. Rusk, advised by his department, had written to Johnson that the shah's demand for an extra $200 million in arms would strain Iran's economic development. McNamara worried that if the shah failed to find a source for these funds, the United States, recently freed from making aid grants to Iran, might have to come to his aid. Both, for their different reasons, advised Johnson to emphasize economic priorities when communicating with the shah.[35] Meyer thought this was not the right path to win and influence the shah.

The trip the shah made to the Soviet Union in 1965 boosted his morale. He was received with honor and respect and maybe for the first time in his career on a semi-equal footing as an important head of state. Again, he felt more self-assured and in control. He had found a way to keep the Soviets happy without putting himself in danger, as he believed would happen if he invited the Soviets into his military programs. To his credit, he thought, he had noted before many others, including the Americans, that the rift between the Soviets and the Chinese was serious, that it signified more than ideological conflict, and that it was rooted in history, geography, race, and ethnicity. He told the Russians that if Vietnam fell to the Chinese, the rest of Southeast Asia, including Indonesia, would also fall under Chinese control. He told them the Chinese were everywhere, including at the nonaligned meeting in Algeria, and scolded Soviet president Leonid Brezhnev for helping Egyptian President Nasser to make trouble in Yemen and elsewhere in the Middle East. Brezhnev made little effort to defend either himself or the Chinese. The Russians, the shah concluded, were ideologically on the defensive; they needed friends on their southern borders.³⁶ It was a good time to begin working on a new deal between Iran and the Soviet Union.

He summoned Ambassador Meyer on 31 August and, according to Meyer's report, spoke with him for two and a half hours. The shah said he had spent many sleepless hours meditating about reorienting Iran's policies. The Soviets did not want "escalation to major confrontation"; rather, they wanted "a friendly cordon of states around the Soviet Union so [it could] get ahead with its major task of developing its economy." There was also the "added incentive for the Soviets of rallying as many non-yellow countries as possible behind the Soviets in its long-term struggle with the Chinese Communists." When it came to Iran's maintaining its independence vis-à-vis the Soviet Union, "no one (not even Americans) could be more patriotic than Iranians." But the time had come for Iran to stand on its own feet militarily and economically, "because intervention by outsiders [had become] increasingly outmoded." Brezhnev had proposed to him "an unregistered nonaggression pact for two hundred years." The shah had redirected the conversation at that point, but perhaps it was not such a bad idea. "Such a treaty might serve Iran's purposes by assuring that the Soviets would spare Iran if world tensions [broke] out in hostilities." In fact, in 1959 the shah had rejected a similar proposal because the United States and the United Kingdom had urged him to turn it down.³⁷

He trusted in the United States, he told Meyer, but he found it strange that Nasser, Nehru, and other leaders critical of America received aid on more generous terms at a time when aid to Iran was being curtailed. "Meanwhile," the shah said to Meyer, "while Iran [had] virtually no air defense equipment, even Afghanistan [had] SAM sites and MIG-21s, which, by the way, the Soviets had offered to give him but he had not yet accepted. And wasn't it interesting that Lincoln White stated publicly that US refused to join CENTO, as the Baghdad Pact was now called, in deference to the Arab world sensitivities, by which, it was clear to [the shah], he meant in deference to Nasser."³⁸

Meyer read the shah as having been impressed by what the Soviet leaders had told him and thought that he was probably paving the way for a possible shift in policy.³⁹ His concern prompted a Defense Intelligence Agency study on the state of an Arab threat to Iran. The study, dated January 1966, concluded that the arms inventory of the Arabs was increasing in quantity and quality, but mainly for use against Israel. The report stated that Iran was not in real danger for the next five or six years and that its oil resources, though a target that had to be watched and defended, would produce enough income for Iran to eventually afford to catch up with her Arab neighbors' armaments.⁴⁰

The shah, of course, was not privy to such secret reports, but he received their gist and intent through the American press as well as U.S. emissaries. He found unconvincing the argument that he should not fret about arms because the Arabs had their own problems and were therefore unlikely to attack him. The premise of the argument, he believed, was ludicrous, because it assumed he should be content to receive hits and to fight non-Soviet enemies on Iranian territory. This he would never accept. In March 1966 he told the Majlis deputies that Iran would not be ruled by foreigners' whim. Since the White Revolution, Iran had made great strides forward: GDP had grown 10 percent during the year that was just coming to an end, farmers were working hard, and labor was content. All this pointed to the inborn Iranian genius. The negativists abroad and naysayers at home had been proven wrong, and from now on only Iranians would determine what was best for Iran. "We will move forward simultaneously economically and militarily," the shah told the Majlis. The country needed a strong military to defend against enemies who, mired in war and stagnation, might pose a real threat to Iran's increasingly pronounced economic prosperity. "We cannot subject our destiny to the decisions of others who may decide one day to help us and another day not to help us."[41]

While the speech contained nothing new, the tone was sharper and the sense both of self-satisfaction and of grievance somewhat stronger. Meyer cabled Washington that the shah especially resented the "papa knows best" attitude of the United States toward Iran's military requirements.[42] By August 1966, the State Department was talking about a near crisis in U.S.-Iranian relations as the shah "attempted to bargain with the U.S., lessen his dependence on us, and diversify his military procurement—and in doing so moved in the direction of inviting a significant Soviet military intrusion into the arms supply picture." The shah, as a State Department secret memorandum summarized, saw diversification as a means of securing more independence in foreign policy. This attitude was "in keeping with Iran's currently booming economy, the shah's greatly improved internal posture, and the general success he has had with demonstrations that he is less dependent upon the United States." This, noted the document, might have some advantages for the United States.[43]

Americans were feeling insecure because of Vietnam and somewhat guilty because of their failure to help Pakistan, an ally and member of SEATO and CENTO, in the Indo-Pakistan war. The shah used this failure to impress on them that a militarily strong Iran was good not only for Iran and the region but also for the United States because, among other things, Iran might save it from the embarrassment of failing to help allies when they needed help. Meyer, almost constantly in contact with the shah, sensed the changes that had occurred in him since the White Revolution. The assumption "that the US government can compel the shah to obtain only such equipment as we decide he can have . . . is altogether unrealistic in 1966," Meyer wrote President Johnson. If the United States pressed the shah too hard, "then we would be faced with a showdown in our total relationship here."[44]

By 1968, the shah's relationship with Lyndon Johnson had fundamentally changed. In 1964, the first time the shah met with him as president, Johnson had treated the shah kindly but somewhat patronizingly, complimenting him on his reform program and calling Iran "the brightest spot in the Middle East."[45] Johnson had promised to accommodate the shah's needs for military moderniza- tion but instructed then Ambassador Julius Holmes "to emphasize US concern that the program be kept within proper bounds in order not to jeopardize Iran's economic development and to make it clear that the US Government intended periodically to examine jointly with the Government of Iran the overall eco- nomic effects of its military expenditures."[46] Johnson, however, realized that the passing of the Status of Forces legislation in October 1964, which exempted U.S. military personnel stationed in Iran from Iranian legal jurisdiction (see chapter 16), was a heavy burden, which the shah had accepted, and that in some way it placed a moral obligation on the U.S. government. An attempt on the shah's life on 10 April 1965 enhanced the sense of U.S. obligation as it served to underline the shah's vulnerability on the one hand and his indispensability for American interests on the other. This dependence became even more evident when the United States was forced to seek alternative facilities in the region for the spying installations it had in Pakistan. Iran was cited as technically the most suitable place, which gave the shah additional bargaining power. In the meantime, in part as a result of the shah's trip to Russia, Soviet-Iranian rela- tions improved dramatically, giving the shah a seeming alternative to procure arms. As noted above, when the shah complained that the United States had no real understanding of Iran's needs, Meyer came to believe that he would almost certainly begin to shop for military supplies elsewhere, even perhaps in the Soviet Union.[47] In 1966, Johnson was still trying to control the shah's requests, though by now it had become difficult and, from the American point of view, politically hazardous not to accommodate the shah. On 30 May Johnson signed National Security Action Memorandum (NSAM) No. 348, "Alternatives to U.S. Facilities in Pakistan," approving a State-Defense-CIA recommendation to establish contingency alternatives in Iran for U.S. facilities in Pakistan, so the United States could be in a position to move them on short notice with little intelligence loss if necessary.[48]

Mollifying the shah now became an imperative pushed by the U.S. Joint

Chiefs, the CIA, and Meyer. In a meeting in Tehran with Meyer and Townsend Hoopes, of the Department of Defense, on 10 August 1966, the shah promised he would not allow Soviet technicians in Iran nor buy Soviet SAMs, but in 1967, despite U.S. protests, he announced he would buy less sophisticated Soviet military equipment. In mid-1967, when he visited Washington, he was able to extract an assurance about his military needs from Johnson, who now lavishly praised him for Iran's economic and social progress under his rule.[49] In late 1967, the shah informed Johnson that he was in the market for $800 million worth of equipment to reorganize the military and that he would prefer to buy it from the United States if the U.S. government offered the necessary credit. In April 1968 Rusk, McNamara, and Walt Rostow supported an interdepartmental recommendation for a six-year (FY 1968–73), $600 million military credit sales package for Iran, with a U.S. offer of a military credit sales program for the first year between $75 million and $100 million. Rostow reminded Johnson that such a package would be uppermost on the shah's mind when the two men met in June. Johnson gave his approval on 1 May.[50] The shah in fact was not happy with a package that offered only three-quarters of what he had sought, and when he met with Johnson in June he asked for and received another commitment from the president to do his best to get the full amount that he had wanted through Congress. As the Johnson administration drew to a close, the president told Prime Minister Hoveyda that although he himself would only be in office a short time longer, he believed that U.S. interests were such that a close relationship between the United States and Iran would continue.[51]

In early January 1965, General Fereydun Jam was chosen as the first chief of a newly formed Iranian organization named "Combat Development," a term that had no equivalent in Persian. Moreover, according to Jam, nobody knew what it was supposed to do. The idea behind the new organization, which the American advisory group had proposed, was that the time had come for the Iranian ground forces to develop their own structures, procedures, weapons systems, and plans according to their requirements rather than copy U.S. patterns.[52] Jam asked for an experienced consultant from a similar organization in the United States, in response to which a Colonel Park was commissioned to him for three months. Within a short time, "combat development" became an important component of planning in the Iranian armed forces. By the time General Twitchell was appointed head of ARMISH-MAAG in 1968, the relationship between the Iranian army and the U.S. advisory mission had significantly changed. When the missions began in Iran, their work was mostly in weapons training, individual training, small unit training—squads, platoon, companies, and battalions. By the late 1960s, the focus was more on policy and guidance, according to Twitchell's successor General Ellis Williamson. "We did not have what you would generally refer to as trainers; we were more advisors than trainers. We did not conduct any specific classes, except periodically they would ask us to gather their leaders and explain a type of subject."[53] The advisors' influence "depended in a large measure on their professional competence and their relationship with their counterparts." Indeed, the curriculum of the Officer Cadet College had been extended from two to four years and, according to Twitchell, upgraded considerably, triggering "a tremendous change between the time I was there in '62 and the time I left at the end of '71." The military officer corps' education had now come almost to par with civilian higher education and "there were plenty of capable people who were being brought along." Twitchell added, "The Iranian soldiers that I observed would be very good in combat."[54]

Some of the improvement in the Iranian military was due to help from Israel with planning, intelligence, and counterespionage. Much of this relationship occurred unbeknownst to the Americans except in very general terms. MAAG was not in the picture, Twitchell observed; the Israelis maintained a low profile; and the Iranians "did not talk about it."[55] Additionally, according to Williamson, the American military missions kept clear of intelligence work in Iran. "We had a bilateral agreement with Iran that was very specific. It was burned into my brain before I left Washington: 'The MAAG is not an intelligence agent.' We were absolutely forbidden to participate in intelligence activities."[56] Military intelligence, to the extent that it existed, was mostly the province of the U.S. military attaché at the American embassy in Tehran. The liaison with Israel was primarily a product of the tensions between Iran and the Arab states. Although after the 1967 war and Nasser's political demise the relationship between Iran and Egypt improved, the shah was still concerned about the combined forces of Iraq and Syria and the possibility that the tensions and actions along the Shatt-al-Arab border might get out of hand and lead to an all-out war.[57]

"The Nixon Doctrine germinated when Nixon visited Iran in 1967," argues Armin Meyer, who served as U.S. ambassador in Iran at the time of the former vice president's visit. The shah was then seriously thinking about Iran's strategic role in the Persian Gulf and gradually beyond. He had two interrelated strategies: first, to gain free access to military weapons, technology, and the command

and control he needed; and, second, to keep the superpowers as far from the region as he could. He believed his position was geostrategically sound. He was convinced that, given a chance, Iran would be the most powerful country in the region. And he believed that, given Iran's economy, geography, population, and history, his claim to leadership was not as far-fetched as his domestic and foreign enemies made it out to be.

He was, however, undermined on several fronts, especially in the Persian Gulf by the British, who disliked him and loathed the thought that Iran might take their place once they pulled out.[58] "We should not pull our punches in explaining that, while we intend to modernize our position there [rethinking the British future in the Persian Gulf], it is illusory to think that there is any chance of Iran eventually inheriting our role," the British ambassador to Iran Sir Denis Wright advised British Foreign Secretary Roger Stewart, who in turn relayed this view to Prime Minister Harold Wilson as the latter prepared to receive the shah on an official visit in London in March 1965. England, Wilson told the shah, would maintain her military and political presence in the Persian Gulf and honor her commitment to Kuwait and other Trucial states. In the meantime, he said, the shah was to lower his ambitions and expectations, try to get along with his Arab neighbors, particularly Iraq and Kuwait, and accommodate Nasser. England did not welcome Nasserite influence in Iraq, "in particular the presence of some United Arab Republic troops," but neither did it "see the situation as posing the threat to Iran that the shah suppose[d]."[59]

The shah was not moved. He saw clearly that England would have to withdraw for a variety of economic, political, and strategic reasons.[60] The issue for him was how to protect Iran in the bipolar power play, especially against the threats posed by Nasser and the Baathists in Iraq and Syria, which in his mind were client states in the global system. Iran therefore needed to buy protection, and the only viable, if not totally reliable, protection came from the United States.

Fortunately, as noted above, his relationship with the United States had improved considerably since Johnson had become president. His thoughts now were first and foremost bent on keeping that relationship solid. He was therefore initially reluctant to receive Richard Nixon when the latter passed through Tehran in April 1967. However, his foreign minister, Ardeshir Zahedi, and Richard Nixon were friends. Zahedi had kept in touch with Nixon in the years after Nixon lost his bid for governor of California and was seemingly a spent force in U.S. politics. He had been attentive when Nixon's father died, which had touched Nixon greatly. In 1967, still unsure of his plans for the future, Nixon paid a visit to the Far East and on his way back passed through Iran on Zahedi's invitation. The latter asked the shah to receive Nixon. The shah, remembering that his troubles with the Kennedys had been partly caused by allegations that he had made financial contributions to Nixon's 1960 presidential campaign, demurred at first but finally yielded to his foreign minister: He would see Nixon for half an hour, he said. The meeting between the two lasted several hours. The two men found that they agreed on most things.[61] The world had changed. The communist bloc was no longer as monolithic as it used to be. The Sino-Soviet rift was real and permanent. The United States could not fight everywhere. Iran, if given the means, would be able to defend herself and the Persian Gulf, protecting Western interests by assuring a free flow of oil. Meanwhile, great powers would not be directly involved, which meant the probability of catastrophic conflict would be substantially reduced. In the special case of Iran, if the Soviets were to aggress, they would most likely do so through proxies, and since such a war would likely be stopped before it deteriorated into a global conflagration, one would not want to see it stopped with the enemy in Iranian territory. Iran, therefore, had to be strong enough militarily to take the war across the enemy's borders.

Meyer reconstructs what the shah might have told Nixon based on his own repeated conversations with the shah:

> "Look, if I get into a quarrel with Iraq, which is backed by the Russians, I want to take care of it myself. You're my friends; you're my allies. If the Russians come cross the border, sure, I expect your help. But if I get into a regional quarrel, I want the equipment for self-defense. [The] Iraqis are getting all those MIG planes; I need to be able to take care of myself. I don't want another Vietnam here. In Vietnam the Russians get behind one side, you get behind the other. In the end there is a negotiation—and in Iran I lose part of my oil resources. No, thank you; let me do the job myself." That was the essence of the Nixon Doctrine. Let our allies take care of their own problems. Give them the equipment to do it. Why should American boys fight for Iran? In my judgment the Nixon Doctrine germinated when Nixon visited Iran in 1967.[62]

Clearly Nixon was impressed with the shah. In a foreign policy address at the Bohemian Club in San Francisco in July, he chose the shah as the first leader to quote in support of his point.[63] And in an October 1967 article in *Foreign Affairs,* Nixon wrote:

> If another world war is to be prevented, every step possible must be taken to avert direct confrontations between the nuclear powers. To achieve this, it is essential to minimize the number of occasions on which the great powers have to decide whether or not to commit their forces. These choices cannot be eliminated, but

they can be reduced by the development of regional defense pacts, in which nations undertake, among themselves, to attempt to contain aggression in their own areas.[64]

In 1967, when the shah and Nixon discussed the importance of alliances between the United States and selected regional countries, neither, of course, knew that their conversation would become a principle of U.S. foreign policy. To the shah, Nixon was still on the margin of American politics. He remembered him mostly by the memorable but less than admirable words Nixon had uttered to the press after he had been defeated in the 1962 California gubernatorial elections: "You won't have Nixon to kick around anymore." He was not too far off. Though most Republicans still admired Nixon, many felt he had not conducted a tough enough campaign against Kennedy in 1960. By the 1964 presidential campaign, conservatives wanted a man of their own, thus seemingly bidding Nixon farewell. Nixon, however, made a good showing in 1964, first maneuvering between Barry Goldwater and Nelson Rockefeller, hoping to emerge as a compromise candidate, and when that failed, casting his fortunes with the Goldwater wing. Conservative Republicans remembered him, but this was neither known nor of interest to the shah, whose friends in the Republican Party were more of the liberal Rockefeller type. And given Johnson's routing of Goldwater in 1964, the shah thought Nixon was a bad bet for a resurrection. Indeed, in early 1968 when Ardeshir Zahedi told him he had understood from a dinner conversation with William Rogers, Nixon, and several other Republican heavyweights that Nixon might have a good chance of becoming the Republican candidate in the coming election, the shah good-humoredly wondered aloud if his foreign minister had had too much to drink.[65]

With Nixon at the helm, however, things turned out exactly as the shah wanted, although the two were hardly friends. The relationship between them was based mostly on geopolitical agreement rather than personal affinity. Neither man displayed much propensity for personal relations. The shah was formal in his demeanor and behavior and except in certain very controlled circumstances never allowed trespass over a line that separated and probably separated him from others. Nixon too was never known for intimate friendships. Richard Helms, a former director of the CIA and ambassador to Iran, thought the idea of affinities between chiefs of state or chiefs of government was a myth. "I can promise you," he said, "that in the case of Richard Nixon, even in the United States of America he had no close friends or associates." As Helms saw it, Nixon and the shah "were certainly not bosom buddies. They simply saw an identity of interest. They were both good geopoliticians. They were pragmatic. And they made arrangements of mutual interest."[66] This pragmatism was also true of the relationship between the shah and Nixon's national security adviser and subsequently secretary of state, Henry Kissinger. Kissinger opposed the moralists who wanted to put pressure on the shah to reform his regime as a matter of U.S. foreign policy. It was not, he thought, the business of the United States to tell other leaders how to run their country. This, of course, suited the shah well.[67]

The relationship between Nixon and the shah was, as said, quintessentially geopolitical. It became a partnership in which the shah assumed primacy in determining the strategic dimensions of security in the Persian Gulf. In May 1972, Nixon visited the Soviet Union to sign SALT I (the Strategic Arms Limitation Treaty) and to negotiate superpower interactions in the Third World. From Moscow he went directly to Tehran to visit the shah—according to Gary Sick, an expert on Iran in Jimmy Carter's White House, not a chance occurrence.

> Tehran was in fact the showpiece of Nixon's emerging global design—the Nixon doctrine—which was an attempt to find regional powers that would protect American interests at a time when American capabilities were stretched much too thinly throughout the world. The meeting between Nixon, Kissinger, and the shah of Iran was extraordinary. In a couple of days in Tehran, Nixon and Kissinger struck a bargain with the shah which, in effect, relinquished responsibility for U.S. security interests in the region to the shah and told the shah that we would look to him for guidance. We would look to his judgments about what kind of arms he needed, and we would not second-guess him. Underlining that, at the end of this rather remarkable set of meetings, President Nixon looked across the table to the shah of Iran and said, simply, "Protect me." Now, this was the president of the United States speaking to the shah of Iran. And I would argue that those two words summarize better than I can the nature of the relationship between the United States and Iran over the next five or six years, until the time of the revolution.[68]

In military terms, the Nixon Doctrine had led to the "total force" concept, developed under Nixon's defense secretary, Melvin Laird, according to which an organic relationship was to be established between active and reserve forces in the United States, on the one hand, and between the U.S. forces and the forces of regional powers in Asia, Europe, and the Middle East, on the other. In the Persian Gulf, the concept meshed with the "twin-pillar" idea joining Iran and Saudi Arabia, although, as far as the shah was concerned, this was a nonstarter. Nixon's understanding with the shah, however, permitted the shah to move forward regardless and strengthened the shah's position vis-à-vis his critics in the U.S. political and military establishment. Buying weapons from the United States, however, was almost always a hassle. The shah, in principle, could have any military hardware he pleased. In practice, his demands never sailed smoothly. Many in Congress and the administration remained critical of Nixon's largesse toward him and did their best to delay if not derail the arms-buying process. Usually when Iran wanted to buy an item, it fell into the mire of bureaucracy: a message was sent for a "P and A" (price and availability), an estimated price and an approximate time at which the item might be available. "Since Nixon had told the shah 'yes,' no one told him 'no.' There was that group of people in Washington that was dedicated to delay," complained General Williamson, the MAAG chief in the early 1970s. "A few could say 'yes,' a few could say 'no,' but there are zillions who can say 'wait.'"[69]

◼

General Twitchell was a staff officer—an organizer and planner. At about the time Twitchell's term of service in Iran ended, U.S. Chief of Staff General William Westmoreland had stopped in Tehran and had an audience with the shah. The shah told him he wanted a MAAG chief with broader military experience than Twitchell. They discussed the sort of officer needed for the shah's purpose and came up with five criteria: an advanced degree in foreign affairs, the ability to think strategically, army experience, qualified as a pilot, and a National War College graduate.[70] Westmoreland chose Major General Ellis Williamson, an officer whose background satisfied the shah's conditions. Williamson found the shah challenging and in many ways extraordinary.

> In my initial briefing at every turn, whether it was at the Department of Defense, Department of State, CIA, everywhere I went for my preparations, I was told what a brilliant man the shah of Iran was, just the smartest man that ever lived. . . . After being over there just a very short time, and half a dozen or so private meetings with the shah, I became a total convert. I became thoroughly convinced that he was probably one of the most brilliant men I have ever met. He had as near total recall as any person I know of. He could understand the essence, the meaning, of a group of facts very quickly, and on top of that, he was an extremely nice person.[71]

The shah liked Williamson, perhaps because Williamson thought so highly of him. Their conversation gave Williamson a window into his thinking closed to most others. The shah used him as a sounding board, knowing that he reported what he heard to his superiors. He talked to him about nonmilitary matters, including the historical meaning of the White Revolution. He encouraged the American general to travel across the country and report to him on what he saw.

Williamson, a pilot with four airplanes in his command, flew all over Iran, often taking his wife with him, and he was able to land on the smallest, most primitive runways. He reported to the shah, who often followed up on the report through appropriate governmental channels. He also reported what he saw and what the shah said to his superiors at the State or Defense departments and, according to Williamson, "it would be considered and worked into the overall mill." The explanation Williamson gives for the shah's behavior, which he must have received from the shah, reveals much about how the shah viewed the relationship between the U.S. ambassador and the U.S. president.

> The shah talked to me not because of my personality, not totally anyway, and not because of my knowledge. . . . If the shah asked a question of the ambassador, that technically was the equivalent of his personally asking the President of the United States. The ambassador is representative not just of our government; he is the representative of the President. The shah recognized it as that. He said, "There are some questions that should not be asked or answered by the top man. The same question can be answered at a working level, thrashed out, all the innuendos, all the technicalities, all the problems considered, and if the answer is no, you can say no, and then you can tell General Azhari or General Tufanian that through your channels, the answer comes out no, and I don't have my nose out of joint. But if I ask President Nixon and he says 'no,' then just diplomatically I have to say 'Why?' And a lot of times I don't care why."[72]

Williamson thought Rusk and McNamara were wrong to believe the shah was building his army to protect himself against domestic foes. In the mid-1960s, when the drive for military development turned earnest, the shah felt quite safe and self-assured. His enemies, the shah believed, could at best engage in terrorist acts, as in the assassination of Prime Minister Mansur and the attempt on his own life in 1965. This, however, was a matter of law and order and could not be warded off by strengthening the armed forces. By the end of the 1960s, it became clear, at least to those who paid close attention to what he said, that the shah was after something else, though it was not easy to discern exactly what. "He did not—I can absolutely guarantee you this—he did not use his military for internal security." If not for internal security, then for what did he need it? Iranians, said Williamson,

> thought of themselves as bringing their country back into, as they called it, the community of advanced nations. They thought in terms of coming back into this community by a parallel improvement in twelve different fields [the now expanded Principles of the White Revolution], and surprisingly enough, [the] military was

not one of them. The first question the Westerner has: "If the military was not one of them, what caused this fantastic military buildup?" The military buildup in their mind—and I discussed this personally with the shah time and time again, and with many of his assistants—the military in their mind was 100 percent designed to permit the 12 elements of the White Revolution to succeed without outside interference. That's the way they looked at it.[73]

In the mid-1970s, the time period Williamson alludes to, the shah was reasonably certain that in case of war with neighbors other than the Soviet Union no cease-fire line inside Iranian territory would result. But he had also decided that if the Soviets were to invade Iran, nothing of value would be left for them. He told Williamson he did not want any of his neighbors' territory, but he "absolutely refused to surrender any of [his] territory to a neighboring country." In the case of a Russian invasion, he wanted to make sure that he "had the ability to delay them long enough for a scorched-earth policy and prevent them from getting anything of value. That we will do and are prepared for. . . . We will not lose to a neighboring country, and we will not let the Russians have anything."[74] Iran, the shah repeated in the 1970s, would never again be caught by surprise: "We will fight to the end. We will destroy our country before we will give it up to others."[75] This was more than rhetoric. It was communicated not only to the military command but also to civilian institutions. Several organizations, including the National Iranian Radio and Television Organization (NIRT), had taken actual measures to implement it.[76] It pointed to a new nationalism meant to discourage would-be aggressors.

"Never in the seventeen years that I reported to him directly did he initiate any specific policy on organization or strategy. After I explained my proposed plan, he sometimes made suggestions based on his vast knowledge and experience," recalled Lieutenant General Mohsen Hashemi-Nejad, the shah's adjutant general. According to Hashemi-Nejad, on every important military decision, the commanders of the forces—ground, air, sea—depending on the issue, would study the proposal and report their findings to the Supreme Commander's Staff. There, the findings were reviewed, coordinated, and adjusted within the global strategic framework before being reported to the shah. The shah, for his part, studied the reports he received carefully and chose the best option presented. Sometimes he suggested other options to be studied, but this was rare. "He was a true organization man. Once an officer was given a command, he was also given authority commensurate with responsibility."[77]

Williamson thought the commanders had some influence on the shah. "The most marvelous thing that I observed about the shah was there was a man who had been a king for thirty-five years and still had the ability to listen. When he had a subject or when General Azhari or General Khatami or General [Hassan] Tufanian—General Tufanian was the most outspoken of them all—when he had them come in, he asked them to tell him, and they would speak. They would talk and he would listen. He wouldn't interrupt them. He would listen to them. So yes, he got ideas from them on that, but any time there was an indication that the shah was ready to express himself or the shah had come to a conclusion, the discussion was terminated right then. Not because the shah said it was terminated, but because they thought he was ready. They thought he had the information—all that they were going to be able to give."[78]

The force commanders considered the shah the commander-in-chief constitutionally and their direct commander militarily. In that capacity, said General Reza Azimi—who rose through the ranks to become commander of ground forces, the shah's adjutant general, and the minister of war—the shah "personally and through inspectors in the general staff and special military inspectorates kept tabs on leadership, training, organizational and operational preparedness as well as legal and MP functions of the field and staff units in the imperial armed forces. He also determined the general strategy of the Iranian armed forces and oversaw tactical decisions and operations and complemented them based on the projects presented by staff and line units."[79]

The shah was a hands-on commander. He was on top of strategy, tactics, organization, and procedure. A lot of information that he did not need was brought to him. He could have demanded not to be bothered by all the minutiae, but he did not. Queen Farah thought it had become a routine that was hard to stop.[80] The shah's motives, however, were more complex. The military was devoted to him—but he lived in a dangerous region. "He had reason to be concerned with the security of the regime and with the military," observed General Karim Varahram, a military commander, governor, and senator. "There had been a coup d'état in every country in the neighborhood—Turkey, Egypt, Iraq, Syria, Afghanistan, Pakistan. So, he was careful." But, Varahram concluded, in Iran, given the cadre's devotion to the shah and the system of checks and balances established, the probability of a military coup was nil. The shah insisted on receiving reports, but he also moved with the flow. He was committed to the rules, and generally he deferred to expert opinion, though not always. This was true in both military and civilian fields. Varahram held that the shah always listened to reasonable and logical argument.[81] For Amin Alimard, secretary general of the State Organization for Administration and Employment (SOAE), the allegation that the shah meddled in the minutest of decisions was a bit of an exaggeration.

> My experience during the three and a half years I was SOAE secretary general was the following: in every case we prepared a report and gave it to the prime minister or alternatively to Moinian [chief of the shah's special bureau] to bring it to the shah's attention, the report was accepted and what we suggested was implemented. That was my experience also the times I was present at the High Economic Council, where the shah presided. Whenever a decision taken on grounds of expertise was reported, the shah invariably approved. Whenever two or three ministers disagreed on a point, he told them to sit together and work their problem out. In most cases, Safi Asfia [former head of the Plan and Budget Organization, serving as minister without portfolio called upon by prime ministers to troubleshoot] was the arbiter, and in most cases he helped them solve their problem.[82]

Nonetheless, the queen also had a point. The shah had fallen into a trap partly of his own making. He feared that if he ordered his commanders not to bring him reports that he did not need to see, he would also be deprived of material he needed to see. It was a matter of control, which in his mind, required direct contact with the commanders. However, in this also he abided by the rules. Despite his enthusiasm for detail, he rarely gave audiences to those below the top level of command.

One officer may, however, have become a favorite as a result of just such an audience. Hassan Tufanian was called in when the chief of the Supreme Commander's Staff, General Abdolhossein Hejazi, needed him to clarify to the shah a plan that Hejazi had failed to explain satisfactorily. Hejazi was soon replaced by General Bahram Ariana, and Tufanian was set on his way to become, as he put it, His Majesty's chief adviser on arms. In the 1970s he became a powerhouse in the Iranian military.

In fact, Tufanian impressed the shah in a number of ways. The shah, being religious, preferred his top officers also to be religious (though, according to General Hashemi-Nejad, not in a bigoted or show-offish way). Tufanian was unique among the officer corps in that he had also formal religious training.

In his youth, he had attended the Haj Abolhassan Mosque, where he studied traditional Islamic subjects. After he finished high school, he studied medicine but, finding it not to his liking, he volunteered for military service. He was one of the first officer cadets to join the fledgling Iranian air force and in time became an ace pilot. When the shah decided to take flying lessons in 1944–45, Tufanian was chosen to be one of his instructors. In 1955, he was appointed as one of Iran's representatives in a planning committee for the Baghdad Pact. In that capacity, he also helped draft an air defense project for Iran. The project, presented to the shah by the then chief of SCS, General Abdollah Hedayat, caught the shah's eye and helped launch Tufanian's career. Hedayat's successor, General Hejazi, as we have seen, was not adept at explaining plans to the shah's satisfaction. Gradually, Tufanian was called upon to help in briefings. It was the beginning of a relationship that ended in Tufanian's becoming chief of Iran's military industries, Iran's chief weapons procurer, and a shaper of the form and substance of Iran's military establishment.

Tufanian was appointed head of military weapons procurement in 1966 and held the position until the Islamic revolution in 1979.[83] Over the years, he learned how to relate to the shah and eventually became his main staff man on weapons and weapons development. "I told His Majesty my job was to study the weapons systems and to bring the results of my studies to His Majesty's attention. He was the commander-in-chief, and he made the decisions."[84] The shah was the final arbiter, but much thought and research went into the selection process, beginning with the needs generally stated by the three branches and collated at the SCS, and specified through research mainly done under Tufanian; the results would then be communicated to the shah. In later years, the shah became an expert in his own right, often initiating the research process. Tufanian, as one of his military confidants, was usually considered by international military observers to be one of Iran's five top general officers, together with the chief of SCS and commanders of the three forces.[85]

The shah, an avid reader of military journals, followed keenly new technical advances in military hardware. He was almost always after weapons systems that were still in the development stage. This put him in conflict with the U.S. government, which, as a matter of policy, assigned newly developed weapons first to the U.S. armed forces. It also made his advisers' work difficult because they did not have referents for judging the relative utility of such new weapons for Iranian purposes. However, despite his appetite for technical novelty, the shah was also deliberate when he chose. He studied the options, invited opinions, and acted on them within the constraints of his general strategy. In the case of the F-14 and F-15 fighter planes he was interested in, he had Tufanian bring the manufacturing companies to Iran and present their products to him jointly. Still, he did not decide. He sent Tufanian to make further studies in the United States and ultimately chose to wait until the United States made a final decision as to which plane was to be manufactured for what purpose.[86]

■

After the rise in oil prices in the early 1970s, Iran became a major market for arms where American and European firms, supported by their respective governments, competed for as large a piece of the pie as possible. The competition produced graft on all sides but, according to most counts, more on the foreign than the Iranian side. The Americans, according to Williamson, had what the U.S. military rank and file derisively called "the five percenters."[87] Twitchell thought that there was a climate of concern about arms agents and that "the arms sales people with the industrial firms bore an important responsibility for it." That, said Twitchell, was one of the reasons "Tufanian preferred to deal through the Pentagon, with the idea that that would reduce such a possibility."[88] The shah insisted that every contract Iran signed be "wire-brushed," checked carefully to make sure there was no inappropriate commission paid.[89] He called foreign companies corrupt, charging too-high prices. "If we find corruption at the highest level [in Iran], heads will roll. And don't doubt that this will be pursued. Other countries may be willing to live with corruption as an existing fact, but not in our case," the shah told *U.S. News & World Report* in 1976.[90] "The oil companies were thieves," he had said to Ambassador Meyer in the 1960s.[91] He was now saying the same about arms salesmen in the 1970s. Prime Minister Amir Abbas Hoveyda picked up the theme in a banquet audience in Tehran in March 1976 that included David Rockefeller, chairman of the Chase Manhattan Bank; William McChesney Martin, Jr., former chairman of the Federal Reserve Board; Peter G. Peterson, chairman of Lehman Brothers Inc. and a former secretary of commerce; and Donald C. Platten, chairman of the Chemical New York Corporation. "When we opened our doors to the international business community to meet our growing development needs, we seemed to have obtained more than we bargained for. For in some instances, along with goods and services, it appears we have imported a business morality — or more accurately, lack of morality — as well. . . . Now I am not claiming that Iranians are all angels, but, at least, in two cases that we investigated, it seems that certain operatives of these companies pocketed the money themselves and told their shareholders that they had been paid out to Iranians as bribes. Some crumbs may have been distributed to Iranians, but the meat went back overseas."[92]

The shah ordered Tufanian not to pay commissions for the military hardware he bought. Tufanian was able to have the U.S. government add a note in the Armed Services Procurements Regulation forbidding companies that sold arms to Iran to add to the price of their product the fee they paid agents under "recurring expense."[93] The "fees" were far from trivial: "When Senate investigators disclosed that Northrop paid $2.1 million for the F-15 sales and Grumman put up $24 million in such fees on the F-14 deal—both amounts added to Iran's bill—the shah forced both companies to make restitution."[94] Williamson interpreted the shah as saying: "We have taken our rightful position in the community of advanced nations. We are now talking to advanced nations on a coequal basis. We don't have to pay anybody a tax to get through the door. We don't have to pay for permission to talk to anybody. We don't have to pay any improper undercover bribe to anybody, whether it is Iranian, American, or Russian. We have arrived. We don't have to grovel anymore. We don't have to beg. We don't have to bribe."[95]

Problems, however, persisted; the lure of money was simply too strong to resist. Tufanian, Williamson, and Twitchell refer to the cases of Northrop in retrofitting tanks and Grumman and McDonnell-Douglas in the sale of F-14s and F-15s. In all cases, individuals, both Iranians and foreigners, with special claims to connection with the companies, the Pentagon, or the Iranian royal family, presented themselves as agents, middlemen, or facilitators. They ranged from Kermit Roosevelt and Eric Pollard, claiming that they had saved the Iranian throne in 1953, to Gene Farnab and James Zand acting on behalf of the companies, to Iranians—according to Tufanian, "Mahvis, Lavis, and others," the kind who claimed to have access to the royal court or high government officials.

All of this was exacerbated by congressional intervention brewed from domestic U.S. politics. U.S. senators and congressmen all seemed to have their own ideas about how the shah should go about improving his military. It is possible that each department within the government had its own collective judgment about what the shah did as opposed to what he should be doing with his armed forces. But all pressed for a deal when it affected their constituents. And there never was a comprehensive American position that could be discerned because of the variety of interests and forces that came forth whenever there was a chance to sell. U.S. military advisers were invariably instructed that they were not in Iran to sell arms. Every one of them was told at least by some superiors in the Pentagon or the State Department that the Iranians were buying more arms than they could handle and that an imbalance existed between the material purchases and available human resources. On the other hand, there was a strong commercial and industrial interest in selling arms. And when the price of oil was raised, there developed a commensurate interest in selling arms as extensively and expensively as possible.[96]

There was too much greed for things to turn out exactly right. For example, the shah hesitated about the AWACS airborne surveillance system for some time but finally chose it over fixed radar installations, based on several studies, including a recommendation made by Richard Hallock, a Pentagon expert suggested to the shah by Defense Secretary James Schlesinger in 1973.[97] Hallock had been at the RAND Corporation with Schlesinger and subsequently had worked with the Turkish general staff. Everyone, including Schlesinger, however, was later surprised at how Hallock had managed to become simultaneously an adviser to Iran, a partner with U.S. companies, and a consultant to the Pentagon. According to Barry Rubin:

> [Hallock] quickly proposed sharp cuts in the billion-dollar Iranian air defense electronics program and was able to build close relations with the shah. He made such a good impression that Intrec, his consulting company, signed a multi-million dollar contract with the Iranian government in July 1974 to advise it on research, planning and training. The programs he advocated to the shah, however, were not necessarily those backed by the MAAG and the Defense Department. There were also rumors that Intrec had among its clients a number of companies seeking Iran's business, including Northrop, E Systems, and Teledyne-Ryan.
>
> This seemed to put Hallock in the enviable position of advising the shah on what to buy, advising the United States government on what to recommend to him, helping the arms supply companies close the deals, and overseeing the program under which all these transactions were being made.[98]

According to Tufanian, Hallock saved Iran millions on AWACS. The shah considered the choice excellent: "7 airborne radar systems, reaching to at least 35,000 feet, which would have meant that we could economize on 30 ground systems; and other electronic look-out devices."[99] Tufanian considered Hallock a great asset—intelligent, knowledgeable, and "a force at the Pentagon resembling Oliver North in the White House in later years."[100] Hallock's advisory group brought experts to assist Tufanian, balancing the congregation of former MAAG chiefs employed by American companies — Major General Harvey Jablonsky (Northrop), Major General Harold L. Price (Philco-Ford), Navy Captain R. S. Harward (Rockwell International) — and higher luminaries, including Admiral Thomas Moorer, former chairman of the Joint Chiefs of Staff, then a consultant for Stanwick International Corporation, a firm managing Iranian ship repairs.[101]

The clash between commercial interest and military prudence invariably produced suspicion and led to doubt and hesitation, causing tension and delay. The shah spent a good part of his energy overcoming American doubts by playing on perceptions of both commercial and strategic interest in the United States. To be effective, he had to negotiate from a high moral ground and, again, that was one of the reasons why early on he insisted that purchases from the United States be done through the Pentagon rather than directly from the companies. Still, the pull of the money was too much, and the process was not always clean, though it was never as bad as the shah's enemies made it out to be. In the 1970s, military and atomic energy were two of the most expensive projects Iran followed. In both cases, the directors responsible — Hassan Tufanian and Akbar Etemad, president of the Atomic Energy Organization of Iran — testified in private and public that whenever they stood up to powerful interests who pushed for buying a particular product, the shah stood with them. Both stated in almost identical terms that "they were extremely powerful because the shah invariably supported them against everyone, from members of his own family to heads of state."[102]

This was the way the shah maintained authority over his people, by remaining personally above the financial fray. No one could ask him outright to order a purchase that his experts in the government opposed. Nevertheless, unscrupulous individuals found ways of achieving their goals. The lobbying, however, had to be subtle to be effective. It happened on several levels. The most common and least problematic was the case of a friend of the official in a position to decide, a call asking the official to hear a man with a project or proposal, usually representing a firm, domestic or foreign. The recommendation, of course, made an impact, but it was never decisive. It was of a kind inescapable in any business culture. Then there was the subtler and potentially sinister intervention, limited in scope, always effective, sometimes determining. An individual, usually a courtier who had the ear of the shah or the queen, made a comment about how difficult a particular government department was making life for a company that was offering something very important and useful for the country's development at an incredibly good price, and wondered what the reason behind the sabotage or procrastination might be. The shah or the queen would naturally want to know if something was remiss and would order a study of and a report on the case. The shah's decree would be issued through his office, in itself imposing and forbidding. There was never an explicit order and rarely an intimation of a preference, but the process was daunting and in some cases it was enough to move the decision in the direction the instigator sought. Nothing happened to the hardy soul that explained his or her position to the shah either orally or by written report. But the atmosphere created favored repositioning, the official who had before opposed the purchase now opting for the path of least resistance, walking with power, which was more often than not defined in terms of proximity to the court. Actually, there was a method to the subterfuge, perfected by some but never quite understood by others. The best operators had read the shah well and knew how to play to his idiosyncrasies, particularly his urge for unencumbered development. Their approach was to pose the question in terms of the shah's general policy, which invariably moved the sovereign to seek explanation. Behind all this, however, lay an incontrovertible fact: the shah knew that there was a limit to what was possible and that, given the acquisitiveness the culture of development had created in Iran and abroad and the power of money now moving at high volume and velocity within Iran and between Iran and the West, there was no way to establish absolute probity in financial matters. But his country had become far better over the years and, despite the accusations, innuendos, and crass propaganda to the contrary, was relatively better than most countries engaged in the arms race — developed or underdeveloped.

The manpower issue was more serious. The weaponry the shah wanted was technologically complex. It could be operated efficiently only on a foundation of modern education and specialized training. A critical mass needed to be created before the system could reach an acceptable level of efficiency. The shah acknowledged the crucial question of manpower but believed Iran could achieve what was needed if it was prepared, over the short term, to sacrifice other social and economic goods in order to assure a solid infrastructure of industrial modernity protected by a strong military. In Iran, he maintained, the sacrifice would never be as harsh as in other countries, democratic or totalitarian. The issue, in his mind, was not one of guns or butter. Iran had money for both. The issue was how much of the available infrastructure, including human resources, was to be allocated to building his priorities. His answer was: as much as needed. One had to push to the edge of the possible if one was to become competitive on a world scale. The difference between his vision of Iran's future and that of the West was precisely this: He saw Iran as a contender, while the West was not prepared to see Iran as a contender, not then, possibly not ever.

14

Development and Dreams

By the early 1960s it was clear to the shah that his development vision could not be realized with the older men who in the past had managed the country's economy and finances. Ebtehaj had been an exception, but he was a raging bull with little political acumen. In addition, the experts at the Plan Organization were too identified with the Harvard Group and, at any rate, not all of them wanted a ministerial position. As prime minister, Ali Amini had sought an economist to head his Ministry of Finance, and on the advice of Khodadad Farmanfarmaian offered the position to Reza Moqaddam. Moqaddam, however, would not accept the position but proposed Jahangir Amuzegar, another first-rate economist, whom Amini appointed.[1]

Amir Asadollah Alam had the same problem when he assumed the premiership in 1962. He had to find a modern-educated economist acceptable to himself and the shah. He asked his friend Jahangir Tafazzoli, a sometime adviser to Iranian students in Europe, who suggested Alinaghi Alikhani. Alikhani was French educated, nationalist, and anti-communist, an uncommon intellectual who as a young student at the Sorbonne in the 1940s and 1950s had been more impressed by Gide and Koestler than by Sartre.[2] He had returned to Iran in 1957 as an economic analyst in the foreign bureau of SAVAK, then served as adviser to the head of the Non-Basics at the National Iranian Oil Company and, concomitantly, to the chairman of the board of Tehran chamber of commerce. Because of these associations, he had gained experience in several important fields — Israel and the Persian Gulf sheykhdoms, development possibilities associated with his work in the Non-Basics at the NIOC, and the private sector through the chamber of commerce.

Alikhani had no prior acquaintance with either the shah or Alam and had no expectation that he might be asked to join the government. But the shah was not happy with the way the economy was being managed. He had scolded

Amini for calling the country nearly bankrupt, but he knew Amini was not totally wrong. Alam had tried to stimulate the economy but had not succeeded. His minister of commerce, Gholam Hossein Jahanshahi, and his minister of industry and mines, Taher Ziai, did not get along, the former supporting the merchants, the latter the industrialists, and neither having a well-founded idea about what was to be done. Moreover, Jahanshahi had lost favor for criticizing the administration of the land reform measures. The shah told Alam he wanted to unify the two ministries and have an economist who had not been educated in the United States run the new organization. It was then that Alam appealed to Tafazzoli and the latter came up with Alikhani's name.

Thus Alikhani was utterly surprised when Alam told him he had been chosen to head and unify the two ministries. "What should we call the new ministry?" Alam asked.

"Ministry of Economy," answered Alikhani, half-thinking that Alam had a definite plan but needed a scapegoat to hedge against things going wrong and that he, an inexperienced, ambitious thirty-four-year-old, would make a perfect scapegoat. "Do you, sir, have a plan you want me to implement?" he asked.

"No, young man, we don't have a plan," said Alam in his Khurasani accent. "We want you to give us a plan." Alikhani asked to be given a free hand in appointments and dismissals. Alam agreed, indifferently it seemed to Alikhani. He was presented to the shah that afternoon — 19 February 1963.

On 20 February, Alam announced the government's program as, above all, intended to implement the shah's six principles that had just been approved in the referendum. He took Amini to task for misreading the economy in pronouncing it bankrupt, a fable having nothing in common with reality, he said.[3] Meanwhile, the government was in the process of preparing an economic congress to debate the ways and means of bringing the nation out of the recession Alam would not admit existed. Indeed, on the day the new cabinet was presented, the shah told Alikhani his job was to take measures that would bring the factories out of bankruptcy and end the recession. He ordered Alikhani to be present when he examined the speech Finance Minister Abdolhossein Behnia was to deliver at the congress. The shah received the two in a small cottage in Ab-e Ali, where he was skiing, "tremendously impressing" Alikhani, in this first close encounter, with his "friendly, kind, and unaffected demeanor," and his willingness "to listen to what you had to say."[4]

The opening of the economic congress fell on 27 February, which had been declared International Women's Day. The shah used the occasion to speak about the future of women in Iran, their right to vote and to be elected to office, and their role as citizens and mothers. This, he said, will be "a nation of free men and free women." To bring the women's issue up in an economic congress was meant to assure the nation that he was serious and his program was there to stay. It worked. Women marched before his palace in droves to thank him for his support. So did workers for his support of the profit-sharing scheme in industries, and peasants for his support of land reform.[5] Even the left had been impressed with the audacity of the measures, and many among them had voted for the six principles. The shah prodded the congress to move quickly to accelerate development. He would support the process and he expected others to do their best. The aim, he said, was to achieve an economy vibrant enough to produce goods and services that moved the society forward independently of the revenues it received from the sale of crude oil.

One of Alikhani's first tasks was to regulate exports and imports as a means of fighting the recession. No meaningful export-import statistics existed, the latest available figures being at least five years old. There were also no reliable statistics about domestic production or trade. "We had no idea of what our inventories were, not only on the national but also on factory level. Our economy was truly primitive. We did what we did under these conditions."[6]

The shah, however, was not averse to pushing forward immediately, even if partly in the dark. He considered the general economic contour and the goals of the government as given. The White Revolution provided the framework for equity and justice within which economic growth was to take place. In the countryside, the shortage of water and fertile land limited development possibilities. For him it was clear that farming needed to be industrialized. Thus, the land reform project would progress gradually, passing through three stages, at the end of which, except for orchards and land farmed by mechanized means, all land was to be distributed to the peasants who worked on it. A system of agricultural support would eventually be devised, with several components: education, cooperatives, and farm corporations, the last resembling the Soviet *Kolkhoz*. Although these had been a failure in Russia, the shah would argue, given his socialist notions of equity, that an Iranianized Kolkhoz could be a successful marriage of industry, modernity, and equality. Once in Poland he boasted to the Communist Party Secretary Wladyslaw Gomulka that Iran had embarked on establishing kolkhoz-like collective farms. "What made you take that path?" asked Gomulka. "We have had so much trouble with them." The shah explained that Iran had the necessary resources to make the project a success and, besides, he moved slowly and cautiously.[7] The communist leader's warning did not have much effect on him. The idea, he believed, was sound. The Poles may have failed, but the Iranians would not.

The same bias affected the shah's thinking about labor relations. He sought a symbiosis of labor and capital. It was not enough to raise the worker's income or to guarantee him a secure retirement. Future productivity belonged to the technology contained in capital; for labor to share in it created not only a more just and equitable society but also a more productive and efficient industry. A laborer who was also an owner worked harder to make his property prosper.[8] The shah would push to give workers in certain industrial firms a share in the profits. In practice, however, the scheme did not work as he had envisioned; in most cases, workers ended up being paid annually an equivalent of a month's pay in extra wages. Still, their condition palpably improved, though not equal to their expectations.

The White Revolution, soon to be called the Revolution of the Shah and the People, raised the general morale and changed the country's mood. The fight for social and economic justice excited a majority of the people despite opposition from the bazaar, clerics, and landlords. The reactionary backlash even empowered the shah and his supporters in the government and among the public. The White Revolution also coincided with the coming of age of a considerable number of professionals who had grown up during and immediately after the Reza Shah period and who were now in a position to influence governmental decisions. They agreed on the fundamentals the shah proposed: land reform, women's suffrage, workers' rights, industrialization, modernization, and the like. Many years back the shah had said there was no honor or pleasure in being the king of a poor, illiterate, and sickly people. They too would not accept Iran as it was. Somewhere deep in their psyche there reigned a nebulous notion of empire. Many of them had studied abroad in the United States and Europe and naturally wished for a democratic system. But few would have been ready to accept democratically determined outcomes they did not agree with, including the positions taken by the clerics, the bazaaris, or the landlords, who wanted Iran to remain as it was and who would likely win democratic elections. Democracy, therefore, came down to a framework in which the professional elite argued the issues and made decisions. The people were the objects of, not the participants in, the arguments. The professionals also did not like the idea of power being concentrated in the shah. On the other hand, if the choice was between the people and the shah, the past and the future, they invariably chose the shah, and the future he articulated, because they agreed with him far more than they did with the people, whose will, at any rate, would not be known unless articulated by others.

In the Plan Organization, the last effort to keep the independence Ebtehaj had so fiercely staked out and defined as "plan discipline" had been made by Khodadad Farmanfarmaian during the premierships of first Sharif-Emami and then Amini. It did not work for several reasons, not the least of which was Farmanfarmaian's association with the Harvard Group. Safi Asfia, who had been appointed managing director by Amini, realized how things had changed and attempted to rationalize and articulate in the Plan Organization the shah's views of national development. His advantage was that he was a *Polytechnicien,* a French-educated university professor, an old hand at the Plan Organization, endowed with considerable wisdom, and a political and professional healer. He had the gift of bringing people together. He became a pivot around whom the development crowd argued their positions, tested their mettle, measured their chances, and made their peace.

Asfia prepared the Plan Organization for supervision and follow-up of the projects that since the fall of Ebtehaj had been gradually turned over to the ministries. He took the first steps to decentralize planning by creating technical bureaus in the provinces to perform as "mini–plan organizations" that would oversee and follow the provincial projects. He also established formal rules for assessing and engaging project consultants. More important, he became a main pillar on which Prime Minister Alam leaned to jumpstart the economy.

Changes were also introduced in the monetary system with the establishment of a Central Bank in the spring of 1960. The idea of a central bank grew out of several roots, including a report within the Plan Organization in which a Belgian economic consultant named François Craco advocated the importance of separating Bank Melli from the functions usually performed by a central bank.[9] This launched a formal debate in the cabinet, though, in the end, it was the issue of the need to regulate the nation's commercial banks that forced the establishment of a central bank.[10] The new bank took on all the functions then considered appropriate to a central bank: printing money; acting as the government's bank; managing the monetary and credit functions; supervising the banking system; and managing the nation's exchange reserves, policies, and operations. A Monetary and Credit Council composed of several ministers and chaired by the president of the Central Bank was established to determine the bank's policies. This governmental character differed from Craco's notion of a bank more fully separated from the government, an option that was rejected. The council's composition was meant to give the bank and its president muscle and legitimacy. Although having cabinet ministers in a council presided over by a non-minister might have been problematic, the issue remained moot because Ebrahim Kashani, the first bank president, was himself a former minister and thus his status was deemed legitimate. The bank had also a general assembly, where the minister of finance, as the shareholder, presided.

One of Kashani's first communications as president of the Central Bank was to the managing director of the International Monetary Fund (IMF) asking for funds to redeem part of Iran's foreign exchange commitments. The negotiations with the IMF would likely be successful if Iran's monetary policy could be shown to be rational. Iran's relations with the IMF were managed by the deputy director of the Central Bank, Reza Moqaddam, a man of considerable influence on the future of banking as well as development policies in Iran. Assisted by Manuchehr Agah, another first-rate economist who headed the newly established Economic Research Department, Moqaddam launched an economic stability policy aimed at controlling inflation by rationalizing foreign exchange reserves, bank notes, and the credit system, and by generally reducing the government's overdependence on the bank.[11] Not long after this, however, Sharif-Emami's cabinet fell, and Amini made his statement calling the system practically bankrupt as the country was not able to pay its foreign debts and had had to appeal to the IMF. The result, among other things, was Kashani's resignation.

The next Central Bank president, Ali Asghar Pourhomayoun, was a university professor and according to his students a good one. But he was not much of an administrator, leader, or decision maker. He never really associated himself with the bank, and at the end it was as if he faded away.[12] He was succeeded by Mehdi Samii, a certified accountant by education and a man of considerable dedication and backbone. Samii had a program, knew what he wanted, and was principled enough to condition his taking the job on the prior approval of his program. He appointed Khodadad Farmanfarmaian, the veteran of the Plan Organization, as his deputy, an appointment that significantly eased the relations between the Central Bank and the Plan Organization.

Under Samii the bank became more independent and increasingly a critical interlocutor in governmental debates. Samii found ways to come to terms with others whose interest conflicted with his, including Finance Minister Jamshid Amouzegar, an intelligent and ambitious technocrat with an eye for protecting and expanding his ministry's turf. Coming from the Industrial and Mining Development Bank, Samii brought with him a development outlook. This was not only crucial for establishing a banking culture that favored development policies but also important for his interactions with Safi Asfia at the Plan Organization and Alinaghi Alikhani at the new Ministry of Economy, the other legs of the development tripod. Asfia was the senior member and often the arbiter as the three became a synergic force for development—Asfia managing the governmental projects, Alikhani the private sector, and Samii the flow of credit and money, especially in the private sector.

These three officials—Alikhani, Asfia, and Samii—were not chosen by any well-thought-out, deliberative process; they simply all happened to be in the right place at the right time. Yet their synergy would help Iran's economy to take off in a way that was unprecedented in the Third World. Alikhani called the relationship between his ministry and the Plan Organization "lucky." A man could have one or two meetings with Asfia and feel he'd known him for years, Alikhani thought. He found Samii "principled" and "reliable." He later described the relationship:

> Samii, Asfia, and I understood each other. We kept each other informed of what we did and sought each other's advice. Consequently, we were almost always in agreement not only about general policy but often also about what went on in our individual bailiwicks. Once, the head of an IMF mission to Iran came to my office to discuss some economic issues. He asked me some questions, which I answered. He said he was amazed at my answers because he came from the Central Bank and there also he had heard exactly the same answers. He, an Englishman, told me he found the harmony among the Iranian governmental organizations just as good as in England and better than in Washington. He was surprised at the way we, a developing country, had achieved such coordination at the highest levels of decision making; for us, however, close cooperation had become the natural condition.[13]

Clearly, this triumvirate was aided by other changes in the economic sphere and by other competent individuals moving into critical spaces. By the time the three men came together, the economy had already begun to turn for the better. However, as Alikhani had quickly realized, information about economic indicators was scant. His most critical need was to get a handle on national income by establishing a center to study the nation's economy.

> There was no one who could give me the most basic information on the nation's economy, the industrial or trade sectors, or our industrial production. If we wanted to develop our textile industry, we did not know how much of it we were producing or what kind, where, at what price or quality. We had no idea of the industrial relations between the different productive units, or the primary material they needed. Or what should be our priorities and why. Or what was the rhythm of our growth, or the efficiency of our work.

Alikhani needed someone who not only knew the field but also believed in what he was doing. In 1963, there were still many who told him he was dreaming. But he was lucky. Jahangir Amuzegar suggested Mohammad Yeganeh, a Columbia University graduate who was at the time working at the United Nations. Once he had Yeganeh, Alikhani needed a team. He asked Asfia and the Plan Organization to help organize a Center for Economic Research at the Ministry of Economy based on the Plan Organization's personnel policy. Yeganeh's work with the center proved indispensable. According to Alikhani, it was he who taught the statisticians at the Central Bank and Plan and Budget Organization how to compute national income by using the input-output matrices, among other things. "He was," said Alikhani, "a crucial factor in our progress, qualitatively as well as quantitatively."[14]

Others also came to the rescue. Reza Niazmand, managing director of the Industrial Management Organization, Qasem Kheradju at the Mining and Industrial Development Bank, and his colleagues Reza Amin and Fereydun Mahdavi, and Alinaqi Farmanfarmaian at the Industrial Credit Bank all became important levers of Iran's development over the years. These and others like them, Alikhani would observe, had grown up and had been schooled under the Reza Shah system. They had a sense of what Iran could become and strived to achieve it.

The Third and subsequently the Fourth Plan channeled a huge amount of public funds — 204.6 billion rials ($2.73 billion) and 506.8 billion rials ($6.75 billion), respectively — into the various sectors of the economy.[15] The economy began to show extraordinary vigor. Industrial growth reached 15 or 16 percent annually, matched only by that in South Korea and surpassed only by that in Singapore. New management and organization ideas evolved, rehabilitating old productive units and launching new ones. Helping the private sector to become more rational and to grow became the official policy. The Ministry of Economy developed standards and asked for feasibility studies before it would entertain requests for financial aid, both of which served to rationalize thinking about technology, markets, and profitability. Horizontal and vertical linkages between industries were recognized and were gradually introduced into development planning.

Privatization, a concept that would wait some decades to gain currency in the world, became an accepted policy of the Iranian government, although the trend led to tensions, as this was still the era of Nassers and Nehrus and Sukarnos. There were charges of pampering the private sector as certain well-known individuals pulled out of the pack as a result of extraordinary business acumen and insight. To many people outside of the industrial milieu, it seemed such people became rich on government money, suggesting an unholy symbiosis of government officials and businessmen. Accusations of corrupt practices, always rampant in Iranian culture, kept cropping up, though they did not fit the new generation of Iranian technocrats, such as Alikhani, Amuzegar, Samii, or Asfia. The private industrialists too were now of a different brand. Some—mostly sons of former landlords, the traditional aristocrats—came to the field from agriculture, after it was clear that traditional farming no longer paid. Many of these men were educated outside of Iran and familiar with the Western world. Others, hailing from the more traditional Iranian merchant classes and beginning from scratch, were also extraordinarily successful.

The Khayami brothers, Ahmad and Mahmud, were examples par excellence. According to Alikhani, they and many like them were futurists, with visions that superseded not just the past but the present. Early in Alikhani's tenure, the Khayami brothers went to his office and asked for permits to build buses. "What experience do you have, and what makes you think you can build buses?" Alikhani had asked. They had replied that they had auto-repair shops in Mashhad and had learned how to make bodies for cars and buses. They were certain they could make buses to compete with those made in Europe or Japan. They did not want to import buses; they wanted to build factories to make buses. "Do you have the capital? Can you produce two hundred to three hundred buses annually in order to make a profit?" Alikhani asked. They knew what it would take for them to get started and to make a profit. They had some capital, but they also needed a loan from the Industrial Development Bank. Alikhani was impressed. He studied their request and agreed to it mainly on faith, since his system for evaluating proposals had not yet taken shape. The two brothers began their work, and shortly thereafter they invited Prime Minister Alam to visit their factory. "It was not much yet," Alikhani observed. "But they had begun."[16] By 1977, Iran National, the Khayami auto complex, was making more cars than Hyundai did and exporting cars to Russia, Eastern Europe, and the Arab countries. "Montage was the beginning," Mahmud Khayami explained many years after the fall of the regime. "The Japanese began with montage. As you make the car other industries develop around it: electrical, rubber, steel, and a host of others. This is what was happening in Iran. In a decade [by the mid-1980s] 90 percent of the components of our cars, buses, and other products would be designed and made in Iran. This was the program approved by the government."[17]

Khayami's understanding of "montage" seconded Alikhani's.

Every complex product is, in one sense or other, a montage. No one builds every component that goes into his final product. Every part of a car, for example, is built by a specialized factory. A diesel engine has on average about 40 percent of its cost made in the diesel factory workshops and the rest is purchased from other producers. . . . The issue is how the montage is related to your general industrial policy. Surely, if the net result of the process is money in one individual's pocket, it is not good economic policy. But if the aim is to build industry around industry, that is the only way to promote industrialization. When you make enough cars, then it makes sense for other industries to develop to supply the parts that the cars need. Correct policy encourages production interlace and industrial linkage. This is what we did; it was a logical program in which each piece complemented the others.[18]

The shah was fully behind the industrial development program, including its support of the private sector, despite his socialistic proclivities. "The shah," said Khayami, "was always helpful. He became delighted when he saw something had been built—almost as if he had witnessed a child of his be born or grow. He wanted Iran at the top. Progress made him feel proud. He expressed his joy, seemingly unable to contain his happiness."[19] He met with industrialists, often at industrial fairs. He would visit every showroom, ask questions, and remember the answers. His interest excited the producers and the inventors. "They came invigorated [for] the next year, looking forward to telling the shah what new product they had come up with."[20] Alikhani speaks of an engineer named Abolfathi, a designer of complicated metal containers. The shah was impressed, asking questions and welcoming the young man's answers. He was especially elated to learn Abolfathi's story. Because he had been in the Tudeh as a student, he had had to leave government service. He had then, however, begun his own private business, borrowing money from his family and building the containers that represented a cutting edge in the nation's technical prowess. "Now," Alikhani told the shah, "it has become our responsibility to defend his money and interest."[21]

This was the beginning. The shah's dreams of far more affluent conditions for his country were yet to be realized. For this, the axis would be the Plan and Budget Organization, run by Khodadad Farmanfarmaian in the latter part of the 1960s and by Abdolmajid Majidi from 1972 to 1977. The Fifth Plan, prepared under Farmanfarmaian, was to begin in March 1973 and was the most comprehensive of the plans so far. Its philosophy, content, and process were debated before the shah in Persepolis near Shiraz, and as far as Farmanfarmaian was concerned, the shah not only liked and approved the plan but was so pleased with it that his confidants concluded that Farmanfarmaian would be the next prime minister. Indeed,

Farmanfarmaian believed that this was what led Prime Minister Hoveyda to maneuver Farmanfarmaian's resignation.[22] By contrast, Majidi thought that the shah did not in fact agree with the plan because he was about to take measures that would increase Iran's income from oil significantly and therefore he knew the plan underestimated revenues by a large margin.[23] Indeed, within a year the shah repealed the Consortium Agreement while raising the price of oil to $11.65 a barrel (see chapter 12). This signified a hundredfold increase in Iran's annual income from oil since 1957 — from $200 million to $20 billion.[24]

Majidi's task then was to revise the plan to bring it in line with the new revenues — an unprecedented challenge, since traditionally planning in Iran had been constrained by a scarcity of funds. Now the issue was how to accommodate the funds' enhanced buying power in the face of scarcities of other factors, including specialized manpower; actual and potential capacity in infrastructural facilities such as ports, roads, and railroads; energy supply in all its forms; construction material, especially cement and iron; and agricultural products. As stated in the revised plan: "As the economy has rapidly grown, the nation's productive capacity has not increased commensurate with the growth of domestic capital and foreign exchange. Consequently, the public sector's investment capabilities and the private sector's purchasing power have far outweighed the domestic production capability while international inflationary pressure and domestic port and road bottlenecks have curtailed the nation's capacity to use foreign markets to alleviate internal shortages."[25]

Ultimately, the challenges posed by these shortages in absorptive capacity were too daunting to overcome. During the Fourth Plan, GNP had increased from 686 billion rials ($10.2 billion) to 1,165 billion rials ($17.3 billion) in fixed 1972 prices, registering an annual growth of 11.2 percent. The Fifth Plan foresaw an annual growth of 25.9 percent, increasing GNP in fixed prices to 3,686 billion rials, or $55 billion (actually by 1978 GNP had risen to above $80 billion). Assuming a 2.9 percent annual population growth, GNP per capita would be raised from 37,523 rials ($556) in 1972 to 102,665 rials ($1,521) in 1977 (actual GNP per capita was about $2,400 in 1978). Consumption expenditure had been 77.1 percent of the GNP in 1972; it was to fall to 58.8 percent of GNP and 66.1 percent of GDP in 1977. The influx of high oil revenues affected the balance of the growth sectors. From the end of the Fourth Plan in 1972 to the end of the Fifth Plan in 1977, for example, the value added in the oil sector was 51.5 percent, in industry and mines 18 percent, in services 16.2 percent, and in agriculture 7 percent, significantly altering the share of the sectors in the GDP. From 1972 to 1977 oil's share of GDP rose from 19.5 percent to 48.7 percent, while all others fell: agriculture, which had a 34.5 percent share at the end of the

Third Plan and 18 percent at the end of the Fourth, was reduced to 8 percent at the end of the Fifth Plan; industry and mines fell from 22.3 percent in 1972 to 16.1 percent in 1977; services fell from 40.1 percent to 27.2 percent. Oil and gas revenues, estimated at 6,628.5 billion rials ($98.9 billion), constituted 79.8 percent of the government's income during the Fifth Plan, nearly twelve times the receipts during the Fourth Plan. This compared with 14.6 percent of revenues from direct and indirect taxes, 1.8 percent from foreign loans, and the remaining 3.8 percent from other incomes, including the sale of Treasury bonds.[26]

Despite these anomalies, the transformation of the economy and the society was impressive. By 1976, Iran's GNP had grown 700 times compared to 1925, when the first Pahlavi was enthroned, per capita income 200 times, domestic capital formation 3,400 times, and imports almost 1,000 times. Most of this happened during Mohammad Reza Shah's reign. Between 1963 and 1976 the average annual industrial growth exceeded 20 percent and the size of the industrial workforce doubled. The GNP increased thirteen times, from $4 billion in 1961–62 to $53.5 billion in 1975–76. Per capita income rose eight times, from $195 to $1,600 in the same period and would pass $2,400 in 1978.[27] And not all of the growth was due to oil. Between 1960 and 1972 all members of OPEC enjoyed significant oil income but none except Iran had a brilliant development record; experts agreed that Libyan and Saudi growth, though extraordinary, was, unlike Iran's, due only to oil.[28] And Iran's growth was expected to continue. By 1985, Prime Minister Hoveyda predicted to *Le Monde* in 1975, half of Iranian families would own their own cars. Per capita income would reach $4,500. Iran would produce annually twenty million tons of steel, one million tons of aluminum, one million cars, three million television sets, and one million tons of paper, and its chemical industry's income would amount to $7 billion. Within the next five years, he boasted, Iran would train twenty-one thousand engineers, and the work potential of women would be tapped, whereas previously they had played only a minor role in economic activity.[29]

The contradictions in Iran's economic development were also recognized in three other plans: the Twenty-Year Perspective, the National Spatial Strategy, and the Sixth Development Plan. The Twenty-Year Perspective, 1972–1992, produced at the Plan Organization in 1976, reflected the shah's determination to take Iran to the gates of a "Great Civilization." Iran was one of the very few countries in the Third World that had the chance to break out of the vicious circle of underdevelopment, and therefore it had to assume the necessary order and discipline to achieve the feat, the study proclaimed. Iran had the money, the requisite natural resources, the leadership (now termed command), and the potential manpower. Modern technology would hurl the nation across time and space to the desired realm. What was needed was education on one hand and discipline on the other. Iranians needed to become socialized in the norms of modern industry: order and discipline, rules and regulations, attentiveness, diligence, and readiness to accept new standards and procedures.[30]

The Twenty-Year Perspective was, in fact, based on a rather pessimistic view of the world. The shah talked about peaceful coexistence, sharing of resources and technology, and global cooperation. But nothing he had seen encouraged him to think that any of these would materialize. Rather, the powerful would likely continue to ride roughshod over the weak, and justice would remain identified with the interests of the stronger. There would be a population explosion, mostly in poor countries where poverty, hunger, and hopelessness prevailed. The industrial nations' appetite for wealth and growth would most likely deplete the sources of fossil energy. The environment would likely diminish under reckless exploitation and misuse. This future necessitated that Iranians move forward with speed, discipline, steadfastness, and vigor; if the nation failed to gain self-sustainability before its oil was depleted, the window of opportunity that oil revenues had opened for them would close. Then they would be condemned to remain poor and backward and dependent on others for the foreseeable future.

The Twenty-Year Perspective was deeply concerned with the development problems the shah's vision created. Per capita consumption expenditures in urban areas, which had been 2.14 times those of rural areas in 1962, were 3.24 times greater than in rural areas in 1972. A parallel imbalance existed between public- and private-sector expenditures, with the ratio of government expenditure to GNP rising from 10.4 percent in 1962 to 21 percent in 1972. The Perspective concluded that the 1960s had seen a fundamental transformation in the role of the public sector as the government's investment and consumption had risen almost twice as fast as corresponding investment and consumption in the private sector. "Thus the considerable increase in GNP was connected to the changing role and rising share of the public sector, which in turn was affected by the rise in the price of oil during this period." Since the price of oil had risen significantly between 1971 and 1974, the imbalance between the private and public sectors as well as between urban and rural areas had increased even further. But as the share of oil in the GNP decreased, clearly so would the share of the public sector. If the mixed character of Iran's economy was to be maintained, it was imperative to do one's best to help the private sector to take over the engine of development as oil income decreased. This, said the Perspective, should be the mission of the public sector in the next twenty years.[31]

The Twenty-Year Perspective clearly endorsed a scenario that saved a part of the projected oil revenues as a strategic reserve to be used as those direct oil revenues progressively diminished. It did not foresee a situation in which non-oil exports would significantly impact the balance of trade by the end of the period, in 1992, though they were expected to increase significantly in absolute terms. Hence Iran would need more time to achieve non-oil-based sustainable development. To create the reserve would help reduce inflationary pressures in the early years, lower investment to a level the economy could absorb, help with the balance of payments, and facilitate economic growth in the years after 1992. Besides, if the imbalance between urban and rural regions was to be reduced, rural industry and services would have to develop as fast as possible, since not much could be achieved beyond a 4 percent growth in the traditional farming sector, given Iran's limitations in water and arable land.[32]

The Twenty-Year Perspective was supported by an ambitious study of population, space, and resources called the National Spatial Strategy Plan. The idea was of French origin, made popular under the de Gaulle presidency in the early 1960s, though it had begun as a project of the French government as early as 1950. It was defined as the art of optimal deployment of the population in relation to natural resources and economic activities for both national and regional development—at once a process and a condition aimed at achieving spatial justice, balanced economic development, and territorially defined functional specialization. It added a spatial division of activities to the notion of social division of labor, which the state would define and administer as the "spatial determinant" of its planning functions. The policy in France was complex but at its root it sought to move the industrial firms congested in and around Paris out to other development zones.[33]

The shah learned of the idea from President de Gaulle and Olivier Guichard, de Gaulle's old companion, who was appointed minister of what was called *aménagement* under Pompidou in 1968 and again in 1972–74 in Pierre Mesmer's cabinet. Guichard was also a friend of Prime Minister Hoveyda. These relationships encouraged the Plan Organization to engage a French-core advisory group, SCETIRAN, to draft the National Spatial Strategy Plan, which turned out to be more ambitious than comparable plans in France or any other country.[34] At the same time, the spatial strategy was a warning to the regime that incongruities in social, economic, and demographic fields would become even starker if the development trends of the past decade were allowed to continue.[35]

Economic development, said the strategists, was not in itself "an adequate response to the aspirations of the individual and of society." Nor did the efficiency of the economy depend on technical, quantitative, and short-term factors alone. And finally, the "manner in which individuals were spatially distributed played an important role in their well-being." For the spatial strategy to succeed, it needed simultaneous support from two quarters: "from the supreme authority of the country, first and foremost, but also from the very numerous decision-makers involved." The shah's support, said the planners, was the sine qua non of success. Only the "highest authority" was in "a position to arbitrate, particularly in conflicts between short- and long-term considerations." There was also a need for a general theoretical and behavioral consensus, a necessary condition if the decision makers were to "integrate a spatial planning approach into their assessments and decisions." Spatial planning was to be centralized based on "a nation-wide approach to major decisions and options and a decentralized concept of implementation via the use of tools and methods designed centrally but close to the ground, properly adapted to the problems and capable of changing along with the problems." Although this was not the only way to approach a spatial strategy, the planners argued that a framework such as described was best suited to Iranian conditions. Moreover, a national spatial planning policy was a matter of particular urgency because of the rapidly changing economic, population, and social conditions, and also because of the will and the means that existed at that moment but might not exist ten years hence.[36]

The assumptions on which the National Spatial Strategy Plan was based paralleled not only the Twenty-Year Perspective but also the Sixth Plan, which was being prepared at about the same time. The central government remained predominant; economic growth strategy aimed at providing a modern production apparatus that would supplant dependence on oil; national unity and identity were to be maintained in the face of the development shocks the society would receive; environment, natural resources, and the national heritage would be protected; socioeconomic disparities would be controlled and their effects on the individual mitigated as much as possible; management tasks would be decentralized, and individuals were to be taught to better comply with "the choices made by the society"; urban growth, especially the growth of Tehran, would be curbed; and migration would be controlled, with appropriate account being taken of the requirements of a modern economy and proper living.[37]

The spatial strategy was elaborate, dealing with every sector and region in detail. It identified two south-north axes, one to the east and one to the west of an already recognizable central axis formed by Shiraz-Isfahan-Tehran-Tabriz. The eastern axis ran from Chah Bahar on the Gulf of Oman through Zahedan to Mashhad and the border city of Sarakhs; the western axis began in Khoramshahr on the Persian Gulf and extended through Mehran, Ilam, Kermanshah, and Sanadaj to Rezaieh (Ormieh). Investments would be directed to these parts of the country, which were relatively less developed, thus bringing a better balance to the nation, according to Majidi.[38]

The shah embraced the spatial strategy, especially after 1976, when the economic and political situations both took a turn for the worse and many capital-intensive projects had to be scrapped. The plan suited his policy and temperament. It moved in the direction of his developing thoughts on the Great Civilization. And the strategy was politically centralized in its options and decisions, assuring his final control. The population pressure on cities such as Tehran and Isfahan was overpowering. Migration to the cities not only strained resources but also increased cultural and political tension. By 1977, he too had come to realize that there was a limit beyond which the country could not be pushed.

The Sixth Plan, which was never implemented, was at once inspired and constrained by the National Spatial Strategy Plan. It adopted the same spatial criteria and norms. It identified the critical strategy for sustained development as using revenues from oil and gas to develop the non-oil sectors. It assumed that unless new fields were discovered, the role of oil as the engine of development would reach a climax during the span of the Sixth Plan and begin to fall by the middle of the Seventh, that is, by about the late 1980s. "We must conclude that the era of effortless economic development will soon end," said the plan. "The ensuing normal economy will have to depend on domestic financial resources; that is, the government will depend increasingly on taxes and the private sector on private savings and profits. This in turn requires high efficiency." The Sixth Plan identified the industry and mine sector as the only possible alternative to oil as a source of foreign exchange. Agriculture was not promising, and "it was farfetched to expect that like Switzerland Iran also could satisfy its foreign exchange requirements by offering services." Rapid industrial growth, on the other hand, would naturally increase the tempo of already widening urban-rural disparities, unless critical attention was paid to appropriate spatial strategies. As did the Twenty-Year Perspective and the Spatial Strategy Plan, the Sixth Plan saw the proper role of the government as providing the private sector with the wherewithal to gain a comparative advantage in the international market. This would take time but could be achieved if the planning process, methodology, and philosophy were streamlined and adapted to future requirements. Waste had to be minimized and inflationary pressure reduced. More important, local individual participation in policy planning and administration had to be increased. All of this was related to the success of administrative revolution. "Thus, present bottlenecks in the government bureaucracy must be construed as an obstacle to the achievement of Iran's long-range objectives."[39] Quality of life could not be guaranteed or measured by the growth of the economy, technology, or any one sector. Indeed, one had to take care not to harm the environment in the process of developing the economy, lest the losses in one sector loom larger than the gains in the other.

The Sixth Plan envisaged a holistic development frame that would closely follow the prescriptions of the spatial strategy, stressing human and social development. Rapid growth, it said, leads to imbalance between groups, regions, and economic sectors. In balanced growth, social structure is protected, and those left behind benefit from a fair allocation of resources so that basic human needs are satisfied for all. Investment in health, education, housing, social welfare, culture and the arts, and rural and urban development have high priority.[40] All this was a means to an end, the fulfillment of the shah's dream of the Great Civilization.

In 1978, as his throne was about to be overturned, the shah published a book called *Toward the Great Civilization,* which described the dream that had guided his labor all his life—a vision of a tomorrow constructed on Iran's cultural heritage, as he imagined that heritage. "The Iran of today, architect of that tomorrow, is heir to the Iran of yesterday," he wrote. The Iran of yesterday contained imperishable values that had supported the nation through twenty-five centuries of tumultuous history—terrible invasions and massacres, blows "each sufficient to annihilate a lesser country"—that had become no more than "painful memories in our history." No change could take root in the Iranian psyche unless it was in harmony with these "eternal and creative values," the core of which was light, "the source of creativity that reaches its zenith in Iran," enveloping "the whole material and spiritual being of every individual, enabling him to distinguish between beauty and ugliness, purity and impurity, [relegating] all non-creative phenomena to the domain of darkness and non-existence."[41]

In the Iran of tomorrow there would be no poverty, ignorance, illiteracy, corruption, exploitation, or discrimination. Public health services would secure "for each Iranian maximum health and stamina"; education would bring them "the greatest possible degree of mental and intellectual well-being"; social insurance would provide security "from birth to death" and wages and income sufficient to satisfy all basic needs. Every individual would have suitable lodging, and none would know hunger. All human potential would have an opportunity to develop, all talent would flourish, all work would be done "under the protection of maximum human, social and economic rights in cooperation and participation with others, not in a spirit of hostile confrontation."[42]

This Iran was not a distant future, the shah believed. By 1990 Iranians would reach the level of progress western Europe had in 1978; it would catch up with France, England, and Italy by the end of the century. Economic development now would occur at the height of efficiency. Inflation would be harnessed and controlled. A highly humanitarian and democratic social order would come into being, "with individual freedoms, social justice, economic democracy, decentralization, informed public participation in all affairs, and productive national culture as its general features." Order and discipline would prevail and "the right of every person [would] be respected." Bureaucracy, centralized and politicized during the first decade of the White Revolution, would now be decentralized and made responsible and accountable to the public at all levels of government. Government and society would become truly complementary, and workers and farmers would occupy the first rank in reaping the advantages of the new era.[43]

All this was hinged on education, culture, and "the spirit and essence of the exalted teachings of true Islam," which had nothing to do with the "malicious, demagogic or reactionary abuse of its principles," which now, as in the past, threatened to victimize the nation. And it was destined, the shah believed, because Iranians had the requisite potential: invincible energy, humanity, a sense of justice and rights, a gift for science, literature, and the arts, a universal outlook, and a deep-seated patriotism that protects Iranianness in any adversity.[44]

15

Gas, Petrochemicals, and Nuclear Energy

Iranian-Soviet relations took a turn for the worse after the Bilateral Agreement was signed between Iran and the United States on 5 March 1959. The Soviet press and radio began a protracted attack against Iran and the shah. On the day the agreement was signed, Khrushchev called the shah a weakling who was afraid of his own people. A few days before the signing, on 2 March, Iran informed the Soviet Union it did not recognize that part of the 1921 Treaty which the Soviets contended gave them the right to send troops into Iranian territory. The Soviets called the statement immaterial. The Iranians maintained that the Bilateral Agreement was defensive, entered into only to protect against aggression. The Soviets installed giant loudspeakers at the border for calumniating the shah and his government; Iran retaliated by setting up loudspeakers on the southern side of the border. The Soviet attacks continued unabated over the next year, with Khrushchev calling the shah an American lackey who was turning Iran to an American base. Once that base was established, the Americans would not leave, as they refused to leave Cuba, he said.[1]

This was a difficult time for the shah, being attacked simultaneously by the Soviets and by the Arabs, led by Nasser, whom he considered a Soviet surrogate. He sent Khrushchev a letter through Tahmouress Adamiyatt, his ambassador in Moscow, explaining Iran's position, but Khrushchev was not pleased. The tone, Khrushchev complained to Adamiyatt, reflected American and British intervention. "I can even show you where they have put their mark."[2] But in the course of the conversation he hinted that he could live with both Iran's membership in CENTO and the Bilateral Agreement with the United States. By January 1960, it is likely that neither of these actions bothered Khrushchev any longer because by then he had switched to nuclear deterrence as the main element of Soviet defense strategy.[3]

The shah suspected Khrushchev was facing other troubles and might soon be amenable to a more reasonable relationship with Iran. In particular, by 1961 he had come to see the difficulties posed for Russia by the Chinese, who, he believed, pursued an agenda ethnically, nationally, and ideologically contrary to that of the Soviets. The Soviets therefore would eventually have to move to accommodate the West in order to play it against the Chinese, and these tactical necessities would affect Soviet-Iranian relations as well. But he had to play his cards cautiously. Tactical maneuvers were time-bound and might soon change as conditions changed. While strategic imperatives demanded that the Soviets move southward toward the Persian Gulf, the Chinese provided a hiatus he could use to fashion a workable system with the Soviets. He was lucky, he thought, because the Chinese also might wish to have better relations with Iran because of their conflicts with India. The entente between Iran and Pakistan and Pakistan's security problems with India made it natural for the Chinese to eye Iran's friendship. Conditions were not yet ripe and threats to Iran persisted, which made it imperative for his country to become militarily strong. But the future seemed promising.

He proved right. Khrushchev's attitude toward both Iran and him changed significantly in 1962, partly because of Khrushchev's problems with China and the United States and partly because of the shah's adroit diplomacy. He reiterated the "soldier's promise" he had given in 1956 not to allow Iran to become a base for aggression against the Soviet Union. A note, worked out between the Soviet ambassador, Nikolai Pegov, and the Iranian foreign minister, Abbas Aram, was exchanged in Tehran on 15 September 1962, assuring the Soviet Union that Iran would not grant foreign nations rocket bases on Iranian soil.[4] In late October, Khrushchev sent a "very warm personal" message through Mahmud Foroughi, Iran's deputy foreign minister, inviting the shah to come to Sochi in the Caucasus on the Black Sea, the Russian version of the French Riviera, whenever he felt like it; he also invited the prime minister and the foreign minister to pay formal visits to the Soviet Union.[5] Khrushchev had also suggested that the Soviet president might pay a return visit to Iran. The shah was gratified at the change of tone but remained suspicious of ultimate Soviet objectives, especially their energetic drive for joint works on dams and hydroelectric installations on the border rivers, the Atrax and the Araxes, as well as dredging operations along the southern shore of the Caspian, fish conservation projects, the construction of silos, and the supply of farm tractors, all to be paid for, as far as possible, by Iranian exports. The Soviets would have liked to do even more, but the shah did not wish to have them in "a position where they could bring economic pressure to bear for political purposes." On the other hand, he believed he could use the Russians to encourage the West to give him what he wanted. He told British

Ambassador G. W. Harrison he was "anxious to maintain and increase Iranian exports to the west; but the Common Market countries must recognize that they had a responsibility to buy Iranian wares and should avoid forcing Iran into the arms of the Soviet Union." In the same vein, he argued that Iran was in a category different from the Arabs and complained that the oil companies did not take into account Iran's economic and financial needs.[6] And he communicated to the oil consortium that Iran was determined to go ahead with plans for using its gas reserves and that he expected goodwill and increased cooperation.

Soviet President Leonid Brezhnev, invited by the shah on Khrushchev's suggestion, arrived in Tehran for an official visit on 16 November 1963. Just a month before his arrival, Charles de Gaulle had visited Iran and had lauded the shah for his great accomplishments. Although personally the shah could not accord Brezhnev the same warm and cordial reception he had accorded de Gaulle, whom he genuinely admired and looked up to as a role model,[7] he went out of his way to come as close as he could. He congratulated Brezhnev on the limited nuclear test ban treaty that had been signed in Moscow in August, and as a compliment to his guest he made a point of saying that "Iran had signed [it] immediately after its initiation in Moscow." He "hoped it was a first step the world was taking in assuring world peace" because Iran "believed in and needed peace so that she could take confident steps toward progress and development she deserved."[8]

Brezhnev left Iran satisfied; he did not insist on political or military realignments, and the shah did not deviate from his stated positions. Shortly after Brezhnev's visit, Iran and the Soviet Union signed a series of technical and economic agreements in Tehran on the projects Khrushchev had suggested to Foroughi in Moscow: the dams on the two rivers, dredging operations along the southern shore of the Caspian, fish conservatories, and silos.[9]

The shah reciprocated Brezhnev's visit in June 1965. His talks with the Soviet leaders, among whom Brezhnev was by then supreme, yielded an agreement in principle to provide natural gas in return for steel and machine tool factories. This was a great accomplishment, considering that, since the shah and Brezhnev had last met, Iran had signed the Status of Forces Agreement with the United States, and Iraq had become increasingly close to the Soviet Union. For Iran, the gas barter provided not only needed expertise and matériel for building steel mills and machine tools but also an outlet to use gas economically to produce energy within the country. Having its own steel mills had been a fundamental Iranian desire, a signature of the nation's independence, since the Constitutional Revolution and the first Majlis.

Some experts in Iran and abroad criticized the move on economic grounds, arguing that Iran could get better and cheaper iron and steel buying it on the international market. The shah considered the argument largely irrelevant because the primary drive for having the steel mill was nationalism and the exigencies of national security rather than economics, as he explained to his ministers. However, building steel mills, he argued, was also defensible on economic and technological grounds. Alinaghi Alikhani, his minister of economy, who negotiated the gas-for-steel deal, explains:

> Beyond the emotional factor, steel works in a country like Iran can be justified on economic grounds as well. We have significant iron mines. The new technology allows us to substitute gas for coal as a source of energy. We can make steel using electric rather than blast-furnace methods. Our steel consumption at the time and its rate of growth for the foreseeable future allowed us not one but several steel production units in the country. Generally speaking, at the time a blast furnace above one million ton capacity was considered economically justifiable. The Isfahan Steel works began with a capacity of 550 thousand tons and would expand to 2 million tons.[10] The question then is the unit cost of the raw material and the efficiency of the labor force. Clearly, you need to begin the industry and work at it for some time to learn the technology before you could compete with American or Japanese labor.[11]

Soviet technology was not as good as Japanese or American technology, the critics complained. Not so in the first stages where a blast furnace was used, Alikhani responded.

> Soviet technology was as good as any country's for melting iron. The problem arose when you wanted to build plates, sheets, or rolls. And the control chambers, where you needed sophisticated electronic technology. Soviet instruments were three to four times larger than those manufactured in the West. We had accepted this because we bought them with gas [which otherwise would be wasted]. On the other hand, building the steel works was a great stride in learning the metallurgy and other technologies of iron and steel. In the 1970s, Iran embarked on producing steel using direct reduction, which was almost as efficient as comparable production units in the West.

The same criticism was addressed to the machine tool factories built in Arak, a city on the eastern slopes of the Zagros. Units were oversized and under par, it was said, but Alikhani countered that they were adequate to the task for which they were used. "The machinery was for heavy work, from boilers to steel bridges and the like. It did its work. What was important was the design, which determined whether your end-product was marketable. We made them marketable by using Western designs."[12]

For Alikhani, the gas trunk line to the Soviet Union made it possible for Iran to use to good effect the gas that had been wasted for more than half a century. In that sense it was a "recovered" fortune, he said. Moreover, the pipeline created a potential for gas-based industry in a hundred-mile-wide corridor along the thousand-mile-long pipeline. "We expanded the possibility of gas-based industrialization from the south to the rest of the country." This was also the shah's position: "Expand the gas network as much as possible" was his directive to Taqi Mosaddeqi, general manager of the National Iranian Gas Company (NIGC).[13] Over the years most of the industries that used oil were expected to convert to gas, and many of them did, making the oil saved available for export.

On 28 October 1970, the shah met Soviet President Nikolai Podgorny on the newly built bridge over the Araxes, one of the rivers separating Iran and the Soviet Union, and escorted him to the city of Astara by the Caspian, where the trans-Iranian gas trunk line was to be opened. It was a soft autumn day, a good omen the shah intimated to Podgorny. "In this happy day, which nature seemingly has also celebrated, I would like to recall once again the friendship and the important spirit of cooperation that exist between our two countries. I would like to remind you that we for our part will follow our independent national policy. And I am certain that the rational policy we have chosen will yield us increasingly better results."[14]

When the agreement on gas was signed with the Soviet Union in October 1965, no infrastructure was yet laid. There was no gas available for export, no gas company to manage the gas, and no structured understanding of how to manage the development, transition, and exchange processes. In the Consortium Agreement of 1954 it was stipulated that the Exploration and Production Company, one of the two operating Consortium companies, would assess the amount of gas, including gas used in producing derivatives, needed by the National Iranian Oil Company (NIOC) for domestic consumption and determine the amount it would provide NIOC after assessing the gas required by the Consortium and its operating companies, provided that Iran paid for the capital equipment needed for transfer of gas. The Exploration and Production Company retained control of the new equipment and the processes of gas production and transfer. Additionally, it was not quite clear how Iran would export its gas. The Consortium considered liquid gas, such as butane and propane, a component of the crude and maintained that it had the sole right and power to export liquid gas from the areas where it controlled the oil. It would not relinquish that right to any third party, and because gas liquids were potential oil substitutes, it would count any amount exported as a part of Iran's quota, thus requiring a comparable reduction in the export of Iranian oil. To clarify Iran's rights, NIOC entered protracted negotiations with the Consortium in 1965 and soon ascertained Iran's right to its natural gas, though not yet its gas liquids. The new dispensation allowed Iran to claim potential control over its natural gas and provided a legal basis for negotiating with the Soviets—but it still had no actual gas or gas pipeline.[15]

The shah pushed the process forward, believing that unless deadlines were set, nothing serious ever happened. The NIOC was charged with preparing the ground for the agreement. Ultimately, the gas that was Iran's payment for Soviet goods and services was made available on time: it was refined in the Bid-Boland refinery in the south and traveled 1,106 kilometers in the 42-inch Iranian Gas Trunkline I (IGAT I), built and installed by NIOC, over the Zagros Mountains to Saveh near Tehran and from there in a 40-inch line installed by Russian contractors to the Soviet border near Astara by the Caspian. Along the way 667 kilometers of secondary lines carried gas to Shiraz, Isfahan, Qom, Kashan, and Tehran, later to be expanded to other western towns and villages. Ten compressor stations producing 457,200 horsepower pushed the gas on its way.[16] The Soviets also provided consultants for these compressors; for reasons not technically clear, they insisted on having fifty-two consultants for each station but finally agreed to two. The cost of the pipeline was recovered in eight years. The price of gas was pegged to the price of crude and as a result was raised in steps from an original 18.7 cents per 1,000 cubic feet to 80 cents by 1978. In fact, the price was kept low relative to the rise in oil prices because the shah wanted good relations with the Russians. For him, the gas he bartered with the Russians was worth several armed divisions at the Soviet border.[17]

IGAT I had a capacity of 16 billion cubic meters of gas per year, of which 10 billion was exported to the Soviet Union and 6 billion were used domestically. As mentioned above, initially Iran received for its gas several infrastructural investments in kind, including the Isfahan steel complex and Arak machine tool factories. However, once these purchases were paid for by gas, it was not clear how long Iran could continue exporting to the Soviet Union on barter, largely because Iranians did not consider Soviet products worth buying. The reverse was true of the flow of Iranian goods to the Soviet Union. By 1970, most of Iran's imports from the Soviet Union were primary goods, and most of its exports were finished goods, from razors and washing powders to shoes and refrigerators.[18] Iran needed international exchange that the ruble did not provide. This problem led to the idea of a second pipeline to Europe through swapping oil with Russia, a common practice today but a first in the early 1970s.[19]

Negotiations over the second trunk line began between NIGC and Ruhr Gas in the fall of 1973—about the same time the price of oil quadrupled—then gradually grew to include France, Austria, the Soviet Union, and Czechoslovakia, and eventually led to an agreement signed in Tehran on 30 November 1975.[20] Based on a rather complicated formula, Iran was to transfer gas to the Soviets at Astara, while the Soviets transferred an equivalent amount of gas to Weidhaus on the German-Czech border and Baumgarten on the Austrian-Czech border. The new pipeline, Iranian Gas Trunkline II (IGAT II) began at Kangan, an important gas field and refinery, and ran for a total of 1,364 kilometers. The last 480 kilometers of the pipeline, from Kuh-e Namak to Astara, were contracted out to the Soviets. The pipeline, scheduled to open in January 1981, had the dual purpose of providing 11 billion cubic meters per year of gas for domestic consumption and 17 billion cubic meters per year for export. A floor price of 80 cents per thousand cubic feet was set that guaranteed a capital rate of return of 14 percent. Had the project been continued and the pipeline utilized as planned, the capital would likely have been returned in five years. IGAT I and IGAT II together constituted a transfer capacity of 44 billion cubic meters of gas per year, the biggest gas corridor in the world after the Soviet Union's.[21]

The revolution stopped the export function of the trunk lines, but after a hiatus of several years domestic capacity building was resumed, and by 1997 some 2.45 trillion cubic feet of gas were produced in Iran, of which some 68 percent was consumed domestically and the rest burned or used alternatively in the oil fields. Had Iran continued its export projects, even at the prerevolution level, it would now hold the fourth place in production (after the United States, Russia, and Canada) and sixth place in exports (after Canada, Russia, Holland, Norway, and Indonesia).[22]

Taqi Mosaddeqi was charged with managing the gas industry in Iran once the agreement with the Soviets was signed, first to supervise the construction of the pipelines and then, after 1969, also to manage the National Iranian Gas Company. He was action oriented, a go-getter, a no-nonsense man, the kind the shah liked in production projects. He was in charge of negotiating IGAT II and making NIGC into a worthy interlocutor for the Soviets and the Europeans. He negotiated the right for NIGC to develop the gas fields directly, which freed it from the legal and practical limitations that applied to the gas at oil wells. He also negotiated several liquid gas production and exportation deals, including the Kangan Liquified Natural Gas Company (KALINGAS), a partnership with a consortium of Japanese, American, and Norwegian companies, in which NIGC and the consortium each owned a 50 percent share, and the consortium incurred the cost of expanding the field, and in case of sales, paid taxes to the Iranian government. Close to the revolution, the Americans and Norwegians withdrew, but an agreement was drawn up with the Japanese partner for exporting 2.4 million tons of LNG per year for twenty years to Japan, for which the Japanese partner would pay 55 percent taxes, making the Iranian share 77.5 percent. This was in line with the deals made by Iran in oil but almost unprecedented in gas. The agreement, like many others, was terminated by the Islamic regime.[23]

"The shah was adamant on the gasification of the country. We made gasifying the industrial plants our priority," said Mosaddeqi. In the 1970s, Iran's oil resources were estimated to last thirty to forty years, its gas resources about six hundred years. The shah pushed Mosaddeqi to move as fast as possible. However, neither the Russians nor the oil companies liked Iran's gasification project. The Soviets thought that domestic plans would reduce the amount of gas available to be exported to or transited through Russia. The oil consortium believed that Iranian gas exports to Europe and other areas would eventually reduce the need for oil. Mosaddeqi noted, "We unfortunately had neither the acumen nor the will to advertise the importance and profitability of what we did. But contrary to the other oil-rich countries in the region, which spent money mostly on nonproductive endeavors, we in Iran invested in factories, plants, and other productive projects. My answer to our critics is that the world considers any project that redeems its capital expenditure in 10 years valid and economically desirable. IGAT II cost $2.2 billion. We would have made on it $640 million annually. Count for yourself."[24]

The shah began to speak of petrochemicals in the early 1950s and discussed the subject rather extensively in his 1960 book, *Mission for My Country*. Oil, he maintained, was exhaustible and too precious to be used only for producing energy when it could be used to produce such a variety of useful goods human beings needed and wanted. Oil, he said, was "a noble substance" because it had so many uses. Other substances with little other utility could be used to produce energy; oil, he argued, should be employed for much more. He was also concerned about gas, part of the nation's patrimony, being wastefully burned since D'Arcy's time; it would be forever burning unless measures were taken to change the practice.

By 1963 he was planning "to make the products of the petrochemical industry . . . [Iran's] most important future source of revenue."[25] In this, as in most fields, he thought big and looked for individuals who thought as he did. Baqer Mostowfi, an NIOC board member and head of the Non-Basics, had written that the petrochemical industry in Iran could be made to play the same central role in the world market as that played by the Abadan refinery; Iran, he said, could take advantage of her vast gas reserves to become the world's petrochemical "balancing tank."[26] This, of course, matched the shah's dream. In 1964, following the initiation of the White Revolution, the cabinet had approved a charter for the development of petrochemical industries, and a small budget had been approved to establish a National Petrochemical Company (NPC) within the NIOC. The shah asked Prime Minister Ali Mansur, NIOC Chair Manuchehr Eqbal, and Plan Organization Managing Director Safi Asfia to come up with some names for who might head this enterprise and among them was Baqer Mostowfi's. In early 1965 the Majlis passed legislation for developing petrochemical industries, and the cabinet approved the structure and bylaws of the new organization in the summer of 1965.

The new organization began work within the NIOC. According to Mostowfi:

> You can't begin an efficient petrochemical industry on small scale. We needed large investment capital and for that we needed to partner with big international companies. These companies, however, did not know Iran's fledgling petrochemical company, but they knew NIOC very well. It was in our interest to grow within the NIOC until we were recognized in our own right. But it happened sooner than we thought. We grew rapidly. The NIOC's cash capital was $5 billion. Suddenly we found that we had $10 billion while still within the NIOC. I talked quickly and consecutively with Allied Chemicals, B. F. Goodrich, Mitsui, and Mitsubishi, among others. They came in, each with one, two, three billion, more or less. We all borrowed some money and began to build. When you added up all this, it came to approximately $10 billion.[27]

Mostowfi believed that unless Iran was in a position to export her petrochemical products, the enterprise would not be cost-effective; that is, the cost was too high and could not be redeemed at competitive prices if sales were confined to the domestic market. Alinaghi Alikhani, then minister of economy, agreed:

> We were at a crossroads. We either manufactured enough to satisfy our domestic needs, which meant our production would be relatively low and our cost per unit high, and therefore we would never be able to compete and to find our way to the world market, which meant we would have to import even if our domestic demand rose; or we had to produce on a scale that allowed us to fight it out on the international market, even if, for a while, we would sell our goods through others

at lower prices, until, gradually, our domestic market expanded or we learned how to penetrate the world market.[28]

Mostowfi determined that his best bet was the Japanese, who had expressed a wish to be involved in Iranian oil. The Japanese would bring with them not only money and technology but also a large established market in Japan and around the world. Conversely, Iran was good for the Japanese because its gas reserve was vast, its workforce promising, its market reasonably good, its political system stable, and its attitude businesslike. As it turned out, by the mid-1970s, it was pretty much agreed that the output of Iran-Japan Petrochemical Company (IJPC) would be just about enough for Iran's domestic consumption, given Iran's rapid economic growth.

The IJPC partnership agreement between Iran's National Petrochemical Company (NPC) and Japan's Mitsui, representing a consortium of Japanese companies, was approved by the Majlis in 1971. According to the agreement LPG (liquefied petroleum gas) and other light petroleum products would be transferred to the port of Mahshahr, where a sizable city and a giant petrochemical complex were to be built. This was a phenomenal undertaking, thirteen or fourteen units that would convert gas into chemicals used to manufacture a variety of products. Specifically, olefins were to be produced from ethane and used for a variety of intermediate petrochemical products, such as polyvinyl chloride, plastics, and fibers, that could be more readily exported than the olefins themselves, which needed to be liquefied and were therefore expensive to transport. "Startup was scheduled for the early 1980s, with 19,000 persons involved in construction and 3,500 technicians in actual operation."[29]

The city and the complex were 85 percent complete by 1978, the year of the revolution. The shah saw the complex for the last time as it was being constructed in 1977. Mostowfi would later comment:

I am very happy I did not wait for the complex to be completed before I took His Majesty to see it. He was beside himself with excitement. He could not wait to see everything. . . . We were to become the world's largest center for manufacturing petrochemical products. The goal was to pay off the cost of the complex in ten years, that is, by 1990, and to begin another complex, just as big, next to the first one. The Japanese would probably come in for the second complex also. But even as we were constructing the first, we were studying other alternatives, and two years before the revolution, I began to negotiate with several French, German, and British companies to begin new projects, not in competition with the Japanese, but for manufacturing different products and selling them in different markets.[30]

For the shah money was no object; that was the government's problem. Hoveyda had learned to joke about it. "Ask His Majesty to go a bit slower on spending on the army, and I will give you the money you want," he would tell Mostowfi. "Make me prime minister, and I'll do it," Mostowfi would joke back. But everyone understood the problem and tried to come up with a solution. "The truth is the government helped as much as it could without much fuss," according to Mostowfi, but partners also helped, usually paying 50 percent of the expenses, but not more than 20 percent of the cost was ever paid in cash. "The government thus launched a [5-year] $1 billion project with $20 million. This is because, of the $200 million [annual share], Iran put up $100 million over five or four or three years, depending on the project. And in some cases, such as the joint project with the Japanese, which would pay up ten times over, one would be wise to put up his home as collateral."[31]

Things, of course, were not always so simple. Costs might exceed the estimates, particularly if the schedules could not be maintained. The total petrochemical project, that is, the two Japanese complexes at Shahpour, the Abadan refinery, and the Abadan, Shiraz, and Ahvaz chemical fertilizer projects, was planned on a ten-year schedule at an estimated cost of $8 billion. The whole project was moving almost according to the timetable, despite the 1977–78 setbacks created by the political disturbances. Mostowfi surmised the cost would have remained below a $10 billion ceiling. More important, the Japanese brought the most advanced technology to Iran, and Iranians were good at absorbing the new technology, not only learning to work with the machines, but assuming the culture of the new technology.[32]

The shah followed Mostowfi's work with interest because it fulfilled his belief that oil should be used to produce added value, and that the best way, perhaps the only way, to do so was petrochemistry, which for him was a core industry. It would help develop downstream industries, where the private sector played an important role providing the commodities people needed and used. It would also produce foreign exchange when sold on the international market. According to Mostowfi, the shah believed transforming oil into rubber, plastic, or fiber would fetch higher income by at least a factor of six. With petrochemicals, said Mostowfi, one wove into the social fabric an industry — the oil — that historically had stood largely aloof from the society. It was Iran's destiny. The shah read Mostowfi's reports, underlined the parts he found interesting, unclear, or questionable, asked questions, and demanded answers. "He was the only person who ever read them," recalled Mostowfi.[33]

In the heyday of Iran's development in the 1960s and 1970s, two models of technological development were entertained. One, exemplified by the Chinese, began with lower-level techniques and moved slowly upward as one learned. The other took the best available (that is, borrowed from the West, as the Japanese had done) and did with it the best it could. The shah clearly favored the second. Followers of the Chinese model, among them many Iranians, found fault with the option of going with the best from the West. They pointed out the liabilities of this approach: it was hard to master, and often by the time a project was set up for use, it was no longer the best or the most advanced. If the country were not equipped to improve on it, to build the next best thing, it would forever have to run after the countries that produced it. To be scientifically productive, one needed research, and research resulted from need. "As long as you send a 707 to import eggs from Romania, nobody will go after developing ways and means of producing more and better eggs," the sociologist Ehsan Naraqi told Hoveyda in a meeting on technology.[34]

The shah rejected the argument. He wanted the best technology and insisted that the technocracy import the best. His point was that it was not necessary for Iran to go through the whole cycle of the industrial revolution. Iranians did not need to reinvent the wheel. Japan was the example to follow. It brought in the technology at its zenith but—and here was the point—it deconstructed as well as reconstructed it. To copy was not wrong if it was taken as the point of departure. To wallow in imitation was unforgivable. Iranian drivers with no education took apart a car that anywhere else in the world would be junked and reconstructed it into a usable vehicle that would work for many more years. Why wouldn't well-educated Iranians learn to do the same and more with the best education? We must train our people as fast and as thoroughly as possible. We must train them to unlearn, learn, build, and create, he argued.

The shah interpreted this as a "consensus on the principles" and as sufficient reason to spur the government and the private sector to adopt it. He forced Iran to opt for the most advanced digital phone system available, against advice from Siemens that the existing system in Iran should be improved and continued. He forced the military to go for the most advanced weapons systems on the same theory. And in the 1970s, after he had helped quadruple oil prices, he pushed the government to go for the best in nuclear energy. In his New Year message on 21 March 1974, he told Iranians: "We shall, as fast as we can, enter the age of using the atom and other sources of energy in order to save oil for production of chemical and petrochemical products. We shall not use oil, this noble substance, as common fuel."[35] This had become the mantra he repeated incessantly.

Akbar Etemad was in his teens when World War II reached Iran. He was attracted to the Tudeh Party and for some time wrote for Tudeh organs before leaving for Europe to pursue higher education. He received a doctorate in nuclear physics from the University of Lausanne, specializing in nuclear reactors. He worked in several private and public organizations, including the Swiss-based, U.S.-incorporated Brown Boveri Electric Company and the Swiss Federal Institute for Reactor Research, where he was appointed head of the office responsible for nuclear reactor shielding. He returned to Iran in 1965 and joined the Plan Organization as a technical consultant on reactor research. Over the next few years, as the responsibility for nuclear energy was moved from one organization or ministry to another like an unwanted stepchild, Etemad served both in and out of the government, as deputy minister for science and research, as head of the Institute for Research and Science and Education Planning, and subsequently as chancellor of the Bu Ali Sina University in Hamadan, in western Iran. In 1974, he was invited to organize and head the Atomic Energy Organization of Iran.

The shah had been pressing the government for some time to begin working on atomic energy, but no real progress had been made in all the bureaucratic shuffling. He was anxious for something to happen and pushed Prime Minister Hoveyda to get on with it. Hoveyda's excuse was that the right man was not in Iran. Reza Qotbi, who was present by chance once when the issue came up, suggested Akbar Etemad, whom the shah knew and liked. Qotbi and Etemad had worked together at the Plan Organization and had come to know each other well. Qotbi told the shah and Hoveyda that Etemad's specialty was shielding reactors and that he was known in the field in Europe. "Ask him if he will accept the position," the shah told Qotbi.[36] Qotbi did so; Etemad asked for forty-eight hours to decide—and accepted the offer with some trepidation.[37]

In a month's time, Etemad presented the shah and Hoveyda with a detailed report on the purpose and structure of the new Atomic Energy Organization of Iran (AEOI). As Hoveyda looked on silently, the shah read the report several times, asked Etemad a number of questions on the place of the proposed organization in the government, and decided that it was what he wanted. Hoveyda suggested that Etemad be appointed a deputy prime minister, but the shah was not convinced that this was a good idea. He wanted the organization to be as autonomous as possible. Hoveyda explained that being his deputy would help Etemad's work with other government organizations. The shah relented—though, as it turned out, Etemad's contact with the prime minister, nonexistent in the month he had worked to prepare the program, remained minimal to the end.[38]

It may be that Hoveyda was not anxious to get involved. Many government officials, especially in the oil and gas industries, did not approve of Iran's plunge into the nuclear field. Fathollah Naficy, a highly respected director at NIOC, argued in an official report against Iran's venturing into nuclear energy. "We have the gas, we have the people who can work with gas, and if we need more electric power, we certainly can get it cheaper and safer using gas."[39] The argument was off the mark as far as the shah was concerned. It did not comprehend the dimensions he had in mind.

Not much else was asked about the new organization in the government or in the Majlis, which passed the bill establishing it without much ado. The Senate was more interested and inquisitive but not for Naficy's reasons. The chairman of the Senate Water and Power Committee, Mohammad Sajjadi, an old hand in government and politics, worried about the authority, responsibility, and place of the proposed organization and its president in the general governmental scheme. The charter gave the president of the organization inordinate power, as the shah had wanted, and Etemad had no satisfactory explanation for Sajjadi. Etemad asked the Senate president, Sharif-Emami, to find a resolution. Sharif-Emami spoke with the shah and Sajjadi and the issue was resolved, Etemad's powers remaining largely intact.[40]

When Etemad began to work at his new assignment, there were, in fact, not very many Iranians schooled in nuclear energy, and of those who were, few were in Iran. Of the latter, most were in academe and a smaller number in NIOC and other like organizations. The academics did research on a small 5-megawatt swimming pool reactor that had been installed at Tehran University following President Eisenhower's Atoms for Peace proposal in 1953, which had aimed to transform nuclear energy from an agent of destruction to a force for peace and development. Eisenhower proposed an Atomic Energy Agency to impound, store, and protect fissionable and other materials from countries with nuclear capability and "to devise methods whereby this fissionable material would be allocated to serve the peaceful pursuits of mankind. Experts would be mobilized to apply atomic energy to the needs of agriculture, medicine and other peaceful activities. A special purpose would be to provide abundant electrical energy in the power-starved areas of the world."[41] These were brave and optimistic words. Etemad repeated them—atoms for energy, agriculture, medicine, and so on—as the mission of the new organization.

By 1974 history had proved Eisenhower's statements utopian. But they still resonated with Iranian experts, enticing them to flock to the new organization and to volunteer their services. Others showed up by chance. Argentinean experts, pushed away from their country by Perón, had joined the International Atomic Energy Agency as consultants. One of them, Oscar Quihillalt, a navy admiral and former head of Argentina's Atomic Energy Commission, had been scheduled to be in Iran to view the Tehran University reactor. He stayed to become the first foreign expert to join the fledgling atomic effort. Other Argentineans joined him, and soon the Atomic Energy Organization of Iran was a hub of activity. The leadership was with the Iranians; and although the Argentineans worked as consultants for two or three years, by 1978 there were essentially no non-Iranians working on the projects other than in special cases where exceptional skills were needed.[42]

The new agency acquired scientific and technological cadres in four ways: Iranian experts who had been working in various organizations in Iran; Iranian experts who transferred to AEOI from the Center for Atomic Research of the University of Tehran; Iranian experts who had been studying or working abroad; and the cadre that AEOI itself trained in Iran or abroad.[43] The fact that Iran could provide these cadres in such a short time testifies to the country's rapid development since the late 1950s. When Ebtehaj at the Plan Organization embarked on the project to develop Khuzistan, the American advisers David Lillienthal and Gordon Clapp had to bring their own experts and managers for work that ranged from agriculture to building dams, where the expertise required was ordinary, run-of-the-mill, unremarkable. In less than twenty years, Iran could manage a whole nuclear development project, an endeavor immeasurably more sophisticated, essentially with Iranians. Indeed, in the early 1970s Lillienthal wrote Alikhani, who was by then in private business, about a possible partnership. "When I first began working in Iran," Alikhani recalled Lillienthal writing, "there were hardly any skilled individuals. Today, however, you have many who have the best training the world offers. The capacity you now have is fundamentally different from what existed in Iran in the late 1950s." He was asking Alikhani to be the principal party in the partnership because "of the change that had happened in the quality and quantity of the expertise in Iran."[44] According to Etemad, when the first nuclear plant in Bushehr became ready to go online in 1980, "a hundred percent of the workforce would be Iranian."[45]

Building nuclear plants in Iran was a complicated proposition, not only because of technical requirements intrinsic to nuclear science and technology, but also because of geography. Several conditions necessary for locating a reactor were difficult to meet in Iran. The plant had to be near considerable water, connected to transport systems able to accommodate the weight and volume of the needed industrial machinery and structural components, close to the nation's electrical grids, and far from population centers. Most important, the location had to be free of earthquakes, to which a good part of Iran was prone. It was soon apparent that there were probably no more than ten suitable sites in the country. Bushehr by the Persian Gulf, Darkhwin along the Karun River, and an area southwest of Isfahan near Zayandeh Rud were initially selected. (Other possible locations were spotted for future activity along an imaginary line extending from Isfahan through Arak and Zanjan to Azerbaijan.) Before the revolution, construction began in Bushehr and Darkhwin, and studies were made on the Isfahan possibility. The project for Bushehr was prepared by Kraftwerk Union, a subsidiary of Siemens, and consisted of two 1,200-megawatt units that were to be completed by 1980 and 1981, respectively. Etemad estimated that the two would have been finished on time, "possibly with a few months delay."[46] Kraftwerk also began building a water desalinization plant with a 200,000-cubic-meter-per-day capacity, which was to use the energy derived from the nuclear plant. The two units in Darkhwin, each with a 900-megawatt capacity, were designed and built by Framatome, a French company. They were scheduled to begin production in 1982 and 1983. No definite decision was made about specifications for the plant in Isfahan before the revolution, except that because of Zayandeh Rud's meager water flow it would likely be cooled by air (called dry cooling).[47]

The deal with the Germans was straightforward, based on technical considerations. With the French there were complications arising from a rather close though formal relationship between the shah and the newly elected French president, Valéry Giscard d'Estaing.[48] Giscard had met the shah several times as finance minister, and the shah was pleased when Giscard was elected president. In response to the shah's felicitations on his assumption of the presidency, Giscard sent him a warm telegram asking him to set a date to visit France. "We must make this visit as soon as possible. Nuclear energy will be the core of our discussions. Make sure we know precisely what we want from him," the shah told Etemad.[49] The shah made a successful visit to France in June 1974, and Giscard in turn visited Iran in October 1976.[50] In Iran Giscard asked the shah to expedite the signing of the agreement to work with Framatome, but the AEOI was not ready and Etemad prevailed on the shah to postpone the deal. According to Etemad, the postponement won Iran two to three billion francs.[51]

The shah was familiar with the history of the atom — well beyond Einstein, relativity, Hiroshima and Nagasaki, and the American hegemony on decisions about nuclear issues. He knew about and generally agreed with the Baruch Plan, the initial American proposal in 1946 to renounce nuclear weapons and promote the peaceful use of the atom. He had impressed Ebtehaj with his knowledge of David Lillienthal's involvement in that plan.[52] When Eisenhower announced the Atoms for Peace Program in 1953, the shah was especially excited, though, given the state of Iran's technology, the program affected Iran marginally, if at all. As the Cold War continued and the world became increasingly bipolar, his attention focused mostly on survival — the ways and means of mobilizing U.S. support while simultaneously improving Iran-Soviet relations. He was consistently for disarmament. He hailed the 1963 Test Ban Treaty and immediately joined the Non-Proliferation Treaty (NPT) of 1968. At the time, Iran had no atomic energy program of any import and signing the treaty seemed to him no great matter. He believed the NPT eased international tensions, and he was happy to please President Johnson, with whom he had developed an understanding. In 1974, when he embarked on his new atomic energy policy, he had the advantage of being not only America's indispensable partner in the Middle East but also the leader of a progressive, rich, and powerful country that was a showcase of economic and military development. Indeed, when in the midst of the oil crisis, U.S. trade administrator William Simon called him a nut in April 1974, President Nixon found it necessary to apologize officially both in public and through a letter to him dissociating himself and the United States from the statement.[53]

Simon's remark, however, represented an undercurrent of tension between Iran and the United States that was rooted in more than the shah's role in raising the price of oil. Nixon's apology and his vows of deep friendship and camaraderie camouflaged a real and serious strain that would persist in great part because the shah saw himself as the rightful leader in the Persian Gulf area, among the oil-producing nations, and possibly in the whole Indian Ocean basin. To all this was added the issue of atomic energy, which now, in 1974, sprang anew as a universal problem with India's testing of its first atomic bomb in May, making the United States especially nervous.

In the mid-1970s when Iran embarked on its nuclear adventure, Americans and Europeans used mostly water-cooled nuclear reactors using uranium enriched to 3–4 percent U-235. (Weapons were made with 93 percent enriched uranium or purified plutonium.) After generating power for three years or more, the spent fuel would contain about 1 percent U-235 and 1–2 percent plutonium. The plutonium could be saved as fuel for breeder reactors, that is, reactors that produce more plutonium as a by-product. The United States led the world in numbers and efficiency of nuclear power plants and had already designed experimental breeder reactors. England, France, Germany, and Japan were building nuclear power plants and were planning breeder reactors for the future. The United States was concerned about the dangers of weapons proliferation because as early as 1962 it had exploded a device made of "reactor-grade plutonium" at its Nevada test site and now, in 1974, India's successful testing of a plutonium device proved that a preindustrial country's scientists and engineers could match those of the six nuclear nations, if there was sufficient will to achieve the needed concentration of resources.[54]

At the same time the United States was facing several other political and economic problems, as President Ford informed Congress in his 1975 State of the Union speech.[55] The country was still coping with the repercussions of Vietnam and Watergate, as well as the quadrupling of oil prices, in which the shah had played a role. But the United States also depended on the shah to help keep a balance not only in OPEC but also generally in the Middle East. The 1973 Yom Kippur War and the Arab use of oil as a political weapon had further increased the shah's weight in American calculations. Ten days before Ford delivered his State of the Union message, the shah made a trip to Egypt. Kissinger sent him a secret letter on behalf of the president to inform him of "the status of negotiations between Israel and Egypt and the longer term orientation of Egypt itself." The shah was to be privy to the president and his secretary of state's latest views, wrote Kissinger, "given our great confidence in Your Majesty."[56]

Given the shah's prestige—and his money—in late 1974 and early 1975 Ford and Kissinger decided to accommodate him on his nuclear policies, though they remained uncertain about his ultimate goals. U.S. companies, including Westinghouse and General Electric, scrambled to do business in Iran.[57] Ford and his team initially endorsed Iran's plan to build "a massive nuclear energy industry" essentially so that they could sell U.S. hardware worth billions of dollars. Ford "signed a directive in 1976 offering Tehran the chance to buy and operate a US-built reprocessing facility for extracting plutonium from nuclear reactor fuel. The deal was for a complete 'nuclear fuel cycle'—reactors powered by and regenerating fissile materials on a self-sustaining basis."[58] This, critics in Congress and the media complained, placed Iran in a position potentially to make nuclear weapons. In 1976, the Ford administration concluded, in relation to operations in the United States, that "reprocessing and recycling of plutonium should not proceed unless there is sound reason to conclude that the world community can effectively overcome the associated risks of proliferation." He had reached this conclusion, said Ford in October 1976, because he believed "avoidance of proliferation must take precedence over economic interests."[59] Ford's statement was forced by the exigencies of the campaign in response to Jimmy Carter's strict construction of anti-proliferation policy. Carter maintained that reprocessing should not proceed anywhere in the world because it was not essential either economically or technologically and, since it added to proliferation risks, "it just didn't make any sense" to allow it.[60] Both Ford and Carter, however, seemed to exempt Iran from the proliferation argument, though not from the strict rules inserted in the bilateral agreement the United States proposed to Iran.

The shah considered the American position on nuclear technology both unfair and untenable. The talks with the Americans during the Ford administration continued, but as far as Etemad was concerned, never seriously.

> For example, I was a member of the Iran-U.S. Joint Committee on Economic Cooperation. When this committee met, a joint communiqué stated that Iran will purchase eight nuclear power plants within the framework of the U.S.-Iran economic cooperation project. But we had no plan of any sort to buy eight power plants. I had not signed anything and had not agreed with it. Iran could not possibly buy eight nuclear power plants. It could not buy even one from the United States. This was something put into the statement by Hushang Ansary [Iran's minister of economy and finance] and Henry Kissinger [U.S. secretary of state] each for his own purposes. Look, eight nuclear power stations is simply shooting for the moon.

To Etemad the Americans were bossy, "acting as if it were natural for us to listen to what they said." He rebelled against it. "I did not object to the minutes of the Committee meetings because I knew neither Ansary nor Kissinger was on top of the issues involved technically and that each was after atmospherics for his own political purpose. The minutes did not oblige me in any sense, and I knew that the shah was with me."[61]

The Americans, eager to sell, pushed Iran to sign the bilateral agreement. In early 1976, Ford sent a letter to the shah through Robert Seamans, director of the U.S. Atomic Energy Commission, and Carlyle E. Maw, undersecretary of state for security affairs, asking him to expedite the signing of the bilateral agreement. The shah gave Etemad the letter to read and asked his opinion. "We have differences with the United States, and unless we resolve them, we cannot give them a positive response," Etemad said. The shah ordered Etemad to prepare the answer. After the usual diplomatic niceties had been added, the letter read:

> As you, Mr. President, are no doubt aware, the Non-Proliferation Treaty has two important aims that consist of preventing the spread of nuclear weapons and at the same time facilitating the exchange of nuclear technology, equipment and

materials for peaceful purposes. As you yourself know so well, Iran has initiated an important nuclear programme in order to support its rapid economic development which necessitates the widespread and increasing use of energy. In order to assure the successful implementation of our nuclear programme, we will have to be assured of a flow of nuclear technology and transfer of equipment and materials based on sound economic considerations. I would therefore very much hope, Mr. President, that your non-proliferation policy would remain flexible enough to allow a fruitful and meaningful cooperation to prevail between our two countries in the field of nuclear energy.

In keeping with the special relationship between our two countries and the importance that you and I attach to this matter, we look forward to continuing our discussions in this regard which I trust will lead to the conclusion of the cooperation agreement in nuclear energy.[62]

The shah accepted Etemad's position. "He did not bargain with me on even one word. His support gave me the power to stand firm not only in relation with the United States but in all else. The clear evidence of His Majesty's support is that the bilateral agreement with the United States was never prepared to be signed because the United States had conditions we could not accept."[63]

Thus it was that the AEOI negotiated primarily with the Germans and the French, although the United States needed to be pacified for the nuclear program to proceed systematically and confidently. In the 1970s only the United States and the Soviet Union enriched uranium and fabricated fuel. Iran neither wanted to nor could get it from the Soviet Union. Getting it from the United States required signing the onerous bilateral agreement. Iran opted instead to build an indirect fuel provision into agreements with the European countries. The German company signed an agreement with the Soviet Union to provide enrichment services for the Bushehr plants for ten years. The shah, however, looked at the arrangement as a stopgap. He was after a more solid foundation to guarantee the supply of fuel over the long run.

This was still a touchy proposition, however. The nations with nuclear capability had come to it as a result of war. The United States was especially concerned about proliferation and had been a mover in promoting the Non-Proliferation Treaty, which Iran had signed on 1 July 1968, the same day the treaty was presented for signature simultaneously in Washington, London, and Moscow, as the shah had proudly told Brezhnev. Iran had joined the treaty in good faith, though at the time of signing, neither the shah nor his government was particularly focused on possible future problems. In fact, as we shall see, the shah saw no contradiction between the treaty and his nuclear program.

To Etemad and his colleagues, providing nuclear fuel and mastering and controlling the nuclear fuel cycle were the most complicated, and critical, part of their work. The fuel cycle was at the heart of atomic science. But, of course, because fuel technology was closely related to nuclear weapons technology, acquiring it was difficult. Etemad told the shah "it was simply not practical to manage the nuclear power stations without full information on the fuel component."[64] The shah agreed that Iran should have as much independence and technical mastery in this field as possible. Iran therefore aimed for control over all stages of the fuel cycle: mining and milling uranium, conversion, enrichment, fuel fabrication, nuclear reactor, and spent fuel storage, the latter a matter still far in the future.

The first stage was gaining access to uranium. AEOI contacted every country or company that mined uranium; none had any available for sale. In the early 1970s all uranium had been pre-purchased for years to come. There were two ways left to Iran: gaining access to existing sources of uranium on a world scale and looking for uranium within Iran. Iran bought shares in a recently discovered huge mine in what was then Southwest Africa (now Namibia), belonging to a British-owned company, Rio Tinto Zinc, and in Uran Gesellschaft, a German firm with extensive uranium discovery operations across the world. Efforts were also made to enter participatory agreements in Niger and Gabon, but to no avail because France opposed Iran's gaining a foothold in her former colonies. On the other hand, Zambian President Kenneth Kaunda, who visited Iran in late November 1974, sent a message to the shah that Zambia had uranium and he was happy to discuss terms of trade as part of general Iran-Zambia economic relations. The shah was pleased to hear this and ordered Court Minister Alam to see to it that the matter was followed up.[65] AEOI also contracted with Uriran, a private Iranian company formed solely for the purpose of finding uranium within Iran, to determine if Iran possessed uranium ores. Uriran determined that it did, though time did not permit actual ascertainment by digging or exploitation.[66]

For enrichment, Iran bought into Eurodif—a French dominated consortium in which Italy, Spain, and Belgium also held shares and which would become one of the largest and most sophisticated uranium enrichment enterprises in the world. Iran's success in this endeavor was not cheaply obtained. The French were cautious initially and not immediately responsive to Iran's interest, but Eurodif was a colossal endeavor, needing four 900-megawatt nuclear power stations just to provide it with electricity. Iran's trump was France's need for money. The shah, however, was not immediately in favor of offering funds. Etemad convinced him, and he agreed to extend to the French a loan of $1 billion, to be invested in Eurodif in exchange for Iran's partnership. A protocol was signed in Paris during the shah's visit in June 1974, and the deal was made in principle in December 1974 during then prime minister Jacques Chirac's visit to Iran. It took some time before a mechanism was agreed on for Iran to have 10 percent of Eurodif without the French losing their majority in it. A company, Sofidif, was formed in France in which Iran held a 40 percent share to France's 60 percent. Sofidif, in turn, owned 25 percent of Eurodif, which gave Iran a direct right to 10 percent of Eurodif's enriched uranium.[67]

On the fabricating, using, and spending of fuel rods, the regime never had a chance to move seriously forward. The shah, however, was accused of subjecting Iranians to great danger by making Iran a storage dump for international spent rods. Although spent rods are highly radioactive, they can be safely stored in special ponds, which are usually located at the reactor site, or in specially engineered air-cooled facilities. Both kinds of storage are intended only as an interim step before the spent fuel is either reprocessed or sent to final disposal, but the longer it is stored, the easier it is to handle, due to the decay of radioactivity.[68] In the 1970s there was little concern about the ultimate disposal of nuclear waste and much faith that the matter would be solved in the future. At the time, Iran seemed to face a choice between two options proposed by nuclear-rich countries: the U.S. option, which treated the spent fuel in the reactor as waste, or the European option, which reprocessed it further to get additional enriched uranium or plutonium. Iran, according to Etemad, belonged to a third category of nations that were new to nuclear energy and would wait to see the final resolution of the issue before they made a choice.

AEOI intended to build a plant for fabricating fuel rods, but planning for it was still in the preliminary stages when the revolution occurred. Nonetheless, there was a hubbub caused by a statement the shah made about storage possibilities for the spent rods. The shah liked to boast that Iran was in this respect in a better position than the Europeans because of its vast desert spaces and its mountains. An Austrian reporter asked him if Iran would allow waste from Austrian reactors, which the Austrians were then debating whether or not to build, to be buried in Iran's central deserts. The shah answered he did not know and, more as an afterthought, added "Why not?" The statement—both offhand and purely speculative—became a cause célèbre, picked up by his foes as evidence that he intended to turn Iran into an open dump for foreign countries to bury their nuclear waste. Austria never built a nuclear power station, but the damage was done.

The shah considered nuclear science and technology indispensable components of the Iran of the future he proposed to build. Without them, he believed, Iran would not be admitted to the elite society of advanced nations. He was aware that the project was not favored by everyone, and he knew that it would further constrain the nation's increasingly pressured economy and finance. But he would not countenance serious cuts in the financial or other resources made available to nuclear energy development. Etemad gives an example:

> The government was pressed for money and wished to save by reducing development expenditures. Prime Minister [Hoveyda] talked to me, and I told him that I was at his service and would cooperate with the Plan Organization to the best of my ability. If the government decides to cut the funds earmarked for atomic energy, I will go along; indeed, I will show where best we can make the cuts. I was invited to attend the next High Economic Council to debate the issue in the presence of His Majesty. The Council debated appropriations for various departments, but when it came to atomic energy, His Majesty was adamant: the funds would remain as previously decided. . . . When the meeting was adjourned, members stood in line to shake His Majesty's hand.
>
> When my turn came up, His Majesty told me to follow him to the other room. He closed the door and said to me: "Make sure the government does not touch any of the atomic energy projects."
>
> I said the government had budget shortfalls.
>
> "That is not your problem," he said.
>
> I said, "Yes Your Majesty, it is not my problem, but isn't it yours?"
>
> "No, it is not my problem either." he said. "I am not the finance minister. Government must find the necessary funds for the projects that have priority. Energy projects have the highest priority and among them atomic energy has the highest."[69]

The Twenty-Year Perspective, prepared in 1972, had identified worldwide energy shortages as a threat to Iran's development and attributed this essentially to faulty policies pursued by industrialized nations, especially their one-dimensional and "unreasonable use of inexpensive fossil fuel as a basis of world technological development." In Iran, then, the long-term energy policy would include a significant reduction of the share of oil in favor of nuclear energy, gas, and hydropower. Coal was available only in quantities sufficient to feed the steel industries. In 1992, at the end of the projected eighth development plan, 22,100 megawatts of nuclear power produced would account for 15.5 percent of total energy consumption, compared to 44.2 percent from oil, 35 percent from gas, and 5.3 percent from hydropower. Total energy consumption would increase from 156.8 trillion kilocalories in 1972 to 1,908 trillion kilocalories in 1992.[70]

The shah insisted that Iran should have a powerful and productive nuclear industry within two to three decades, a goal that could not be achieved except in the framework of a program of considerable size and moment.[71] Etemad agreed and on his behalf traveled around the world, trying to convince others of Iran's right and need to have a productive energy policy and engaging in negotiations to enlist cooperation and support in taking Iran's nuclear enterprise forward. In addition to Germany and France, Iran established close contacts with England, Pakistan, India, and Japan. The British connection might well have been productive had the world interest in nuclear energy not abated. Although the British had relied on a technology that was not compatible with what Iran pursued, in early 1977 they were considering a technology shift. This opened a window for Iran to partner with England, essentially exchanging funds for technological know-how. Despite much enthusiasm and negotiations at the highest levels about forming a joint venture, the idea lost steam as political problems in Iran grew and the nuclear ethos slackened in the late 1970s.[72]

By 1977 Communist China also wished to engage Iran in nuclear transactions. The Chinese possessed a significant cache of nuclear bombs, but their technology was mostly Russian and geared specifically to making weapons. They wanted an opening to the West in their search for nuclear energy for civilian use, which would require complicated political, economic, social, legal, environmental, and safety considerations that had not concerned them in their military nuclear programs. By 1977 Iran had gained enough experience to advise them on German and French nuclear power stations. The dialogue between Iran and China continued even to the latter part of 1978, when the Chinese leader Hua Kuo-feng visited Iran.[73]

■

The nuclear Non-Proliferation Treaty had been initially proposed, not for countries like Iran that were far from nuclear knowledge or for industrialized countries that had the knowledge but posed no threat of becoming militarily nuclear, but for Third World threshold countries that already had a foot in the nuclear circle. These countries, however—among them Brazil, Argentina, India, Pakistan, and Israel—had refused to join. At the beginning, therefore, NPT did not seem very successful. But it did not take long for it to become a factor decisively affecting the policies of the nations that embarked on peaceful pursuit of nuclear energy, as Iran did in 1974.

The shah considered the non-proliferation regime, NPR, oppressive. He demanded "right of way" within what he considered the spirit of NPT, that is, complete access to the theory, process, and mechanisms of nuclear energy as long as it was used for civilian use. He was not after the bomb; however, given his appetite for military hardware, many believed he was.

Etemad had to make sure he understood what the shah was after. Since he was not familiar with atomic energy as science and technology, Etemad reasoned, might he not think that once he had nuclear power plants he could have a bomb whenever he wished? And could he not therefore say he was not after the bomb when in fact he was, though the nuclear energy regime followed did not lead anywhere close to having a bomb? Etemad asked Prime Minister Hoveyda and demanded a yes or no answer, but Hoveyda did not know. "I cannot possibly know the boss's *arrière pensé*. You have to find another way," he told Etemad. Etemad decided the only way he could be sure of the shah's intentions was to teach him the difference between what he was doing and what making a bomb entailed. "Once he knew the difference, I would know from his directives what he really wanted." He told the shah that what he did had significant technical ramifications and the only way he could have a meaningful dialogue with him was for the shah to know what atomic and nuclear energy and nuclear power plants were about. The shah was delighted and gave him one afternoon a week for this learning project; the program went on for six months. Etemad prepared material in Persian, English, or French as feasible for the shah to study and to discuss. The shah followed the program diligently, according to Etemad, "with remarkable discipline." By the end of the six months he knew

> [the] complex of information someone in His Majesty's position needed to know in order to make the final political decision. The program contained information about nuclear energy for producing electric power as well as the ways and means of making and using it for military purposes. When I explained to him that the reactors that we were constructing were of no use for making bombs and he reacted favorably to my choice of reactors, it showed me he had no sensitivity in the matter. Often I led His Majesty to discuss several alternatives, and the result showed me that he was not after nuclear weapons.[74]

In the end, this dialogue reached a point where the shah told Etemad why he did not believe atomic weapons were useful for Iran at that point:

> I do not see any place for nuclear weapons in our defensive system. We have built for Iran the kind of conventional military power that none of the countries that surround us — Afghanistan, Pakistan, the Persian Gulf Sheykhdoms, Saudi

Arabia, Iraq, and Turkey—can match. And we are increasing this power daily. Against these countries we are the superior power and therefore we do not need atomic weapons for our defense. Against the Soviet Union, we cannot defend ourselves with one, two, or even ten bombs. Thus, making atomic bombs for us today only increases our headaches and places inordinate pressure on our nonmilitary programs. If the favorable balance we have established today changes in ten or fifteen or twenty years, if Iran loses its comparative superiority, well, the question will take a different form. What form? I cannot tell now. Possibly, we may have to go the atomic way. Possibly, we may have to go some other way. We have to sit down and see which way to go then. Today, however, we do not need atomic bombs.[75]

It must be acknowledged, however, that nuclear research going on at AEOI was largely a function of the researchers' interests and fields of specialization and did not always fully correspond to the program's immediate needs. The military option was never talked about in the organization. On the other hand, no research project was ever forbidden because it might have some relevance to the military option. But this was a natural by-product of the learning process and in no way suggested specific determinations. It was dictated by the exigencies of science and testified to the ambivalence of all nuclear research.[76]

Not being after the bomb, the shah was overly sensitive to the conditions the NPR forced on him. Particularly annoying was the policy the have-countries adopted in London in 1975 and after, to make unilateral decisions regarding the dissemination of nuclear technology. The Americans tried to keep him informed, even under Carter, hoping he would bring some of the others into line. Practically, however, a nebulous entente was growing among the nations seeking nuclear technology that opposed the restrictive position of the United States, and in this the shah played a critical part. This relationship came together at the Persepolis Conference on the Transfer of Nuclear Technology in Shiraz, held 10–14 April 1977 and convened by AEOI in cooperation with the Japanese Atomic Energy Society, the American Nuclear Society, and the European Nuclear Society.

The Iranians had been in touch with these three organizations (among others) since the beginning of Iran's nuclear program in 1974 and found them—especially the European and the Japanese—sympathetic to the shah's point of view. In Europe, the French and the Germans, who had been totally dependent on the United States for nuclear fuel in the 1960s, had begun programs in the 1970s to gain the ability to enrich uranium. The Japanese had ongoing problems with the Americans over their Tokai nuclear processing facility near Tokyo and looked for ways of negotiating a solution. The issue had threatened the relationship between the newly elected U.S. president, Jimmy Carter, and Japanese Prime Minister Takeo Fukuda, who accused the American president of treating Japan differently than Germany or France. The Japanese were concerned that Carter's nuclear reprocessing policy, enunciated during the presidential campaign, would seriously hamper their nuclear energy program. Japan maintained that it had "signed the NPT to obtain benefits under Article IV for peaceful development, which the U.S. now seems about to deny; and that Japan had developed its nuclear program, including the Tokai facility, following U.S. guidance and stimulus." A sudden change of mind by the United States "would cause distrust and suspicion."[77]

The Persepolis Conference put AEOI on the map. Carter sent a message to the shah stating, "All nations must share in the responsibility to bring the benefits of nuclear science and technology to mankind within a framework which assures that its destructive potential is never unleashed." The shah answered that he shared the president's interest in nuclear energy and was "profoundly conscious of the potential dangers and harm to mankind that can arise from an irresponsible attitude to it." But, he pointedly added, he was convinced that "the result of the Conference will contribute to a better understanding of the problem of nuclear energy both by the suppliers of nuclear energy and also the recipients of nuclear science and experience." To the conference he said in his message, "our will to integrate technology with the basic values and foundations of Iran's culture assumes even greater significance in relation to the utilization of nuclear technology. Iranian culture and its historical evolution rest on principles of harmony and peaceful coexistence and, as such, they have persistently helped to promote cross-cultural understanding." Surely, he said, integrating nuclear technology and Iranian culture could only imply "its humane use for the resurgence of our nation." The NPT, however, had not achieved "its expected universality." He hoped non-signatory nations would join in the near future:

> We should, however, not forget that NPT has two other paramount and complementary goals, namely, transfer of technology and general disarmament. Undoubtedly, the single most important determinant of non-proliferation is a fundamental breakthrough toward general disarmament and what we can collectively achieve in this vital domain. The ideal of non-proliferation should indeed be ultimately viewed and assessed in this context. Otherwise, it is doubtful whether mankind can successfully achieve its non-proliferation ideals through negative and discriminatory attitudes.

Picking up on these words, Etemad stated in his address to the conference:

> The most disturbing damage to the institution of NPT is the growing divergence of the policies and practices of the exporters of nuclear technology from the spirit and letter of the Treaty. The suppliers of nuclear technology are imposing

ever-increasing stringent and distortive terms for the transfer of this important technology. . . . The fault of the supplier nations does not lie only in their distorted interpretation of NPT; the way in which they try to enforce their views and policies is even more alarming. . . . In 1975 they again disappointed the world community by resorting to "club diplomacy." We want to make sure that the higher ideals of NPT are not used to preserve and promote technological monopoly.[78]

The conference praised the shah as a great leader, who, in the words of Lord Walter Marshall of the U.K. Atomic Energy Authority, speaking for the participants, reminded everyone of three facts: that people everywhere "have taken it upon themselves to have a better standard and quality of life"; that oil "is too valuable a resource to continue to use it in the profligate way now common in the Western world"; and that while nuclear power must be used safely and wisely, an essential feature of NPT "calls for technology transfer for the benefit of mankind."[79] The shah was exhilarated by the intimations that he was now a leader in the fight for fairness in nuclear technology transfer. Iran was slated to host the next meeting of the conference in four years, which meant he was in a position to mobilize the American and European nuclear professional societies in support of his policies. The conference also brought him closer to India and Pakistan, two major Indian Ocean nations, and he felt his chances to implement his Indian Ocean basin dream of keeping the major powers out of the region improved. He was giddy that in only three years since the inception of its nuclear energy program Iran had become a voice in the international nuclear field.

With Queen Soraya,
Farahabad Royal Equestrian
Center, Tehran, 1952.

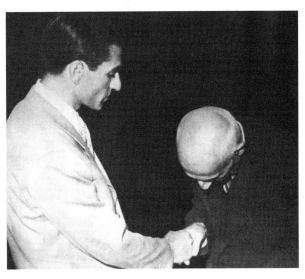

With Prime Minister Mohammad Mosaddeq, Tehran, 1952.

With President Charles
de Gaulle, Élysée Palace,
Paris, October 1961.

With Crown Prince Reza, Saʿdabad Summer Palace, 1963.

The coronation, Golestan Palace, Tehran, 26 October 1967.

With President Richard M. Nixon, Oval Office, Washington, July 1973.

With Queen Farah and their children, Reza, Farahnaz, Alireza, and Leila, Kish, 1975.

The Carter family with the shah's family, Niavaran Palace, Tehran, December 1977; from left to right, Princess Farahnaz, Crown Prince Reza, Queen Farah, Amy Carter, President Carter, the shah, Rosalynn Carter.

Last day in Iran, Mehrabad Airport, January 16, 1979.

With Chinese President Hua
Kuofeng, second from left, and
Queen Farah, Golestan Palace,
Tehran, August 1978.

With President Anwar Sadat, Kubbah Palace, Cairo, June 1980.

PART IV

REVOLUTION AND IRONY

16

Politics and Terror

"Teheran's Mosque of the Shah is getting to be no refuge for Premiers of Iran," wrote *Time Magazine* in its 28 November 1955 issue.

> In 1951, Premier Ali Razmara, one of Iran's ablest men, was assassinated there by a member of the fanatic Fadaiyan Islam (Crusaders of Islam). Last week 72-year-old Hussein Ala, the ablest of Razmara's successors as Premier, arrived at the mosque for a memorial service. Entering, he shucked his shoes, started across the carpeted floor. He was stopped by a thinly bearded man who drew a revolver and shouted: "Why are there so many prostitutes in the city?" The bearded man fired a single shot, but one of Ala's bodyguards, with quick presence of mind, jolted his arm just in time, and the shot went wide. As the assailant grappled with the bodyguards, he managed to get one hand free, and to hit Ala on the back of the head with the revolver before he was dragged away.[1]

Scraps of notes found on the assailant, Mozaffar Ali Zolqadr, led to several other members of the Fadaiyan Islam, including its leader, Seyyed Mojtaba Navvab Safavi. The attempted "revolutionary execution" of Prime Minister Ala was one in a series of assassinations and assassination attempts by the Fadaiyan dating from its inception in the early 1940s. And it was not the last, although with the execution of Navvab Safavi in January 1956 the killings would stop until the mid-1960s, after the Fadaiyan merged in 1963 with the movement led by Ruhollah Khomeini, to form the Allied Islamic Groups *(hay'at haye mo'talefeh-ye eslami)*. As members revealed after the Islamist victory in 1979, the Fadaiyan had had close relations since the early 1940s not only with Khomeini and his followers but also with the more traditional ulama, getting from them *fatwa*s for "Islamist assassinations" or, as they sometimes called the killings, "revolutionary executions."[2]

Information about the modus operandi of the Fadaiyan is based on their own statements and writings about their creed and activities, official investigations of the assassinations, and, after the victory of the Islamist revolution, the reminiscences of surviving members, especially Mohammad Abd-e Khodai, who was first recruited at the age of fourteen and in 1952, at the age of seventeen, was tasked to assassinate Hossein Fatemi. (He did not succeed, and Fatemi subsequently became Mosaddeq's minister of foreign affairs.) Though intellectually limited, the Fadaiyan preached in the burlesque the seemingly more sophisticated discourse of the learned ulama on apostasy, the corrupting of the earth, the war against God and Islam, and the reasons that killing might be justified. Indeed, most Fadaiyan insisted on obtaining a religious *fatwa* from an established Mujtahid before they set out on an assassination. They were the first in Iran after World War II to advocate and to strive to establish an Islamic government and the first to employ assassination as politics by other means. Their first assassination, of the historian Ahmad Kasravi in 1946, was religiously motivated. Subsequent assassinations and assassination attempts between 1946 and 1955 — two prime ministers and one minister of education killed and a prime minister and a foreign minister wounded — were primarily political, though justified on religious grounds. In the 1960s, the Fadaiyan would murder another prime minister and attempt to assassinate the shah, this time in association with movements devoted to Khomeini.[3]

Reza Shah's resignation and exile in 1941 lifted the lid off the religious forces he had kept under control during his reign, including the clerics in Qom, Mashhad, Tehran, and the two major holy cities of the shi'a in Iraq — Najaf and Karbala — allowing new Islamic groups, associations, and organizations to sprout across the nation. As a rule, these groups were attached to one or more of the established *marja*'s, or sources of emulation, some of whom, including the Ayatollahs Abolqasem Kashani, Haj Hossein Qomi, Mohammad Taqi Khwansari, and Seyyed Sadr-ud-Din Sadr (the father of Musa Sadr), encouraged Islamist activism.[4] Others, most influential among them the Grand Ayatollah Mohammad Hossein Borujerdi, did not support clerical intervention in politics. Borujerdi reminded his followers of the fate of his teachers — the Ayatollahs Khwansari and Naini — whose involvement in the 1906 Constitutional Revolution and after had ended in the anti-clerical Pahlavi regime. The clergy, he advised, would serve Islam better by attending to their own moral and educational requirements. All the clerics, however, agreed on a common goal: to reestablish the honor of Islam and to cleanse the nation and the government of anti-Islamic influences, especially communism and Baha'ism.

Communism was treated mainly as an aberration. Falling outside the zone of godliness, communism was unfit to be discussed on the merit of its arguments. Intellectual dialogue on communism was impractical in any case because most Islamist activists were not conversant with socialist ideologies, especially the Marxist-Leninist variety. Communists were therefore attacked as godless, materialist, and immoral (the last punctuated by accusations of sexual permissiveness), and also as a fifth column for the Soviets. Consequently, the Islamists and the government saw the politics of facing the communist threat more or less eye-to-eye.

Baha'ism was a different matter. When the creed emerged from the bosom of the shii faith in the mid-nineteenth century, it was considered a heretic tendency to be suppressed but, at the same time, to be confronted rationally and refuted on epistemological and eschatological grounds. Despite the pressures brought on the sect by the ulama and the Qajar state, Baha'ism grew, eventually finding its way out of Iran to Europe and to Palestine, where it established its first center outside of Iran. The Baha'is in Iran were generally protected under Reza Shah, but once the king's authority vanished, the religious community resumed the attacks, this time also on political grounds, accusing the Baha'is of serving foreign interests — Russia's before the Bolshevik revolution, England's after the Bolshevik revolution, and Israel's after 1948. Systematically, the original, organic connection between shiism and Baha'ism was spiked; instead, a new discourse was developed in which the Baha'is were represented as separate from and alien to both Iran and Islam. Fighting Baha'ism now was advocated as necessary not only on Islamic but also on national grounds.[5] This evolutionary process from religion to politics empowered the radical Islamists and put the traditional ulama on the defensive on most political issues, even those that had nothing to do with Baha'ism or communism. The fruits of this development were later picked by Khomeini and his movement.

The most violent group in this transformative process was the Fadaiyan Islam, organized initially in response to the anti-shi'a writings of the historian and critic Ahmad Kasravi. The Fadaiyan, the originary nucleus of political Islam in late-twentieth-century Iran, was led by a few young zealots and helped, sometimes grudgingly, by the established ulama. The Fadaiyan leader Seyyed Mojataba Navvab Safavi was a young man who had had only one year of formal religious education in Najaf, Iraq, when he was sent back to Iran to confront Kasravi in 1945. He was, however, in close contact with Ruhollah Khomeini, then a middle-aged Mujtahid in Qom and deeply concerned with the problems Islam faced in a society he believed had strayed from the teachings of the Prophet. Khomeini had just finished writing *Kashf al-Asrar* (The Revealing of

Secrets), a treatise he published anonymously in 1944, in which he criticized the de jure secularism of the West that formally separated church and state as well as the de facto secularism of the Muslim societies, specifically Iran's since the Constitutional Revolution, where Islam was officially recognized but the mosque had been progressively driven to the margins. Reza Shah's rule epitomized this de facto secularism, Khomeini claimed. Whereas the Constitution had a clause (Article 2, Supplementary Basic Law) that plainly said that the laws were to accord with the Islamic *shari'a* and had stipulated a council of ulama to assure the injunction, in practice the clause had never been observed. Ironically, the more liberal post–Reza Shah society provided the freedom to promote an Islamic state, which Khomeini and Navvab Safavi would skillfully employ to their advantage.

Kashf al-Asrar became the Fadaiyan's bible, a model on which Navvab based his declarations of 1945, which were published in book form in the fall of 1950 under the title *Ketab-e rahnemay-e haqayeq* (Guide to the Truth). In Khomeini's volume, as in Navvab's, law making is the province of God, and, as God's perfect, final, and unalterable religion, Islam contains the most perfect and comprehensive eternal and universal laws. Government, though at this point not necessarily of the ulama, must be guided by the ulama, and the Majlis should be composed of the *fuqaha* (theologians) who understand God's injunctions, who are morally and emotionally unblemished, and who are able to choose the right person as the just sultan to oversee the operations of the government. The Fadaiyan did not beat around the bush on this point: "These gentlemen [the Majlis deputies] should be made to realize that the Majlis does not make laws; it is only a national Islamic assembly, and they have only the right to consult in order to find the best way of implementing God's Holy Law." Khomeini's justice also derived directly from the *shari'a*. Manmade law was wrong and useless. *Dieh, qisas, hudud,* and *ta'zirat,* as defined by the *shari'a,* contained the essentials of criminal and civil justice — if societies implemented them crime would immediately disappear.[6] "Modern prisons are dream palaces for criminals," wrote Navvab. "The laws of Islamic punishment must be implemented in absolute detail: the thief's hand must be cut; the fornicator must be lashed in public; every criminal should be punished according to the holy writ of Islam. Only then will the root of crime and corruption be burned and eradicated."[7]

The ulama's power grew significantly during the Allied occupation. Many who had been exiled by Reza Shah or had migrated on their own now returned. The shii practices of breast-beating and self-flagellation in the passion of Hussein, the Third Imam's martyrdom in Karbala, which had been banned by Reza Shah, were resumed, much to the dismay of modernists. Kasravi gave voice to this dismay in his book *Shi'igari,* whose title connoted that shiism had become a business and in which he lambasted this "inhuman and uncivilized behavior" as "nothing but abject superstition." The clerics took arms. Khomeini called on the government to burn all copies of the book, accusing Kasravi of apostasy: "He is a corruptor of the earth and should be hanged in public."[8] But Kasravi would not drop the banner. In 1944, Haj Hossein Qomi, a grandee of the shiis who had been exiled by Reza Shah, returned from Iraq and announced he was back to fight the nefarious influence of communism by reinvesting the society and schools with Islam. Prime Minister Ali Soheili went out of his way to mollify the ayatollah, assuring him the government, acting on his demands, was promoting the hijab, allocating endowment funds to religious instruction, separating girls and boys in schools, and repairing shrines. "You'd think this gentleman is a hero of Stalingrad returning from a host of victories in the battle," Kasravi wrote in disgust. "Why is Iran's only radio eulogizing him so? Has anyone asked what profit this nation will have from the return of a Mujtahid? Except that the bazaar hajis, who have been busily enriching themselves at the expense of the poor, can now go to him, pay their Imam's share, pacify their conscience, and purify their loot." Kasravi took the leaders of the governments—"the Sa'eds, the Hazhirs, the Sadrs"—to task: "What is the secret behind your wish to empower the Mullahs, to bring back to this country the breast-beating, self-flagellating, self-stabbing, and the like? You pretend to be religious. Is this religion?"[9]

It was not only the government that went out of its way to accommodate the ulama. The young shah also tried to be on the right side of religion. The clerics accused his father of being anti-Islam, decapitating the organization of Islam in the country—according to several Mujtahids, worse than what Ataturk had done in Turkey. "My father was very religious," the shah protested meekly. "Perhaps not as religious as I am, but nonetheless deeply religious."[10] The son wanted to show he was committed, but it was harder for him than it had been for his father. Reza Shah was tough yet ordinary, familiar, one of the masses. The son was not. He was different in demeanor, vision, ideology, and behavior. And contrary to his own belief that he was a good Muslim, he was not one in the sense that the ulama demanded. Whatever he believed in religion he had come to independently of them, and they knew it. They had read his hand, as the Persian saying goes, and viewed him with suspicion, even though for most of them monarchy was still the preferred form of government.

On 13 June 1945, one day after he was appointed prime minister, Mohsen Sadr, a shii adept, ordered his minister of justice to indict Kasravi. The next day, Majlis President Mohammad Sadeq Tabatabai, also a shii adept, accused Kasravi of insulting Islam and, in a letter to the minister of justice, he also demanded his indictment. Questioned by the secular court, a religious judge *(qazi-e shar')* affirmed Kasravi's guilt. It took several months to bring Kasravi to trial, during which time Sadr fell and Ahmad Qavam became prime minister. Meanwhile, Kasravi's books were taken to Najaf in Iraq, the site of the Mausoleum of Ali, the First Imam of the shiites, to seek the ulama's ruling. Several of the ulama ruled Kasravi an apostate. It was at this point that Navvab Safavi was sent to Tehran to confront Kasravi. In Tehran he sought a ruling from Ayatollah Shahabadi, Khomeini's teacher, who confirmed Kasravi's apostasy. He then, according to Mohammad Mehdi Abd-e Khodai, debated Kasravi in person, after which he concluded Kasravi was incorrigible. Confronting Kasravi in the street, he shot and wounded him. Navvab was arrested and spent some time in jail, where he determined to start a formal organization to promote Islam's injunctions. The organization was called Fadaiyan Islam because, Navvab explained to a group of followers, "I saw in my dream the Lord of the Martyrs [Hussein, Third Imam of the shi'a] putting on me an armband on which was written 'Fadai-ye Islam [devotee of Islam].'"[11] The new organization voted unanimously that Kasravi must die. On 20 March 1946 Kasravi, as instructed, appeared in the Seventh Branch of the Tehran Tribunal. There he and his secretary were assassinated by two brothers, both members of the Fadaiyan Islam.

Kasravi's assassination launched a heinous practice that would last for decades. Over the next several years the Fadaiyan Islam assassinated Minister of Court and former prime minister Abdolhossein Hazhir, Prime Minister Haji Ali Razmara, Education Minister Abdolhamid Zanganeh, and Prime Minister Hassanali Mansur and made unsuccessful attempts on Foreign Minister Hossein Fatemi and Prime Minister Hossein Ala; they were also probably responsible for two attempts on the shah. They brought to Iranian postwar politics a culture of violence that lurked incessantly behind political and ideological debate, fed also by the pronouncements and decisions of complicit governments and political actors, beginning with Sadr's cabinet in 1945 and continuing off and on at least until after the oil nationalization conflicts in 1955.

Following Kasravi's assassination, the ulama pressed the Qavam government to release his killers on the theory that Kasravi had been an apostate who deserved to be executed. The demand was discussed in the cabinet, and, according to one participant, the Tudeh member Iraj Eskandari, Abdolhossein Hazhir, who was then finance minister, called the killing just, agreeing with the apostasy thesis.[12] Justice Minister Allahyar Saleh, however, refused to entertain the idea, but soon Qavam reshuffled the cabinet, and the next justice minister, Ali Akbar Musavizadeh, released the assassins. Ironically, Hazhir became the Fadaiyan's next victim. He was appointed prime minister in late spring 1948 but was soon forced to resign in the face of vociferous attacks by the clerics, especially Ayatollah Kashani and Navvab Safavi.[13] He was then appointed minister of court. The Fadaiyan, however, had decided that Hazhir was to be eliminated. He was shot in the Sepahsalar Mosque on 13 November 1949 by Navvab Safavi's collaborator, Seyyed Hossein Emami, and died the next day. Emami explained that he had concluded that Hazhir was dangerous and therefore decided to execute him.[14]

Hazhir's assassination was followed by Prime Minister Haji-Ali Razmara's on 7 March 1951. The man who killed Razmara, Khalil Tahmasebi, was a carpenter devoted to Navvab Safavi; he claimed he acted to avenge Islam and Iran. "There is no fear [in killing] an individual whom you have determined has committed treason against religion and country. Those who enter *Jihad* [holy struggle] in God's path, slay God's enemies, and are slain in striving, are alive, enjoying God's bounty in paradise. Yes, we are shiis and we believe in these truths. Razmara created the war in Azerbaijan when he served as chief of staff of the armed forces. He made the people fight against the people's opinion and God's laws. He blemished the six-thousand-year-old honor of the Iranian nation before other countries—Russia, England, or America. Anyone who trespasses against Islam, saying Iran is not able to make ewers or build a cement factory . . . I determined that Razmara was a treasonous and disloyal man, and I set out to rid Muslims of his evil."[15]

Navvab wrote Tahmasebi in jail, encouraging him to remain steadfast and to reject the structures and procedures of the state. "Oh, my dear brother Khalilullah, do not forget your religious duties. With God's assistance, we also shall do what God has commanded us to do. The desires of this-worldly men have reached the boiling point; therefore remember to execute Islam's enjoinments according to the Book. Do not agree to have an attorney—none of such things, for it is like thinking effective that which is other than God and this is *shirk* [deviating from believing in the unity of God]. You are now closer to God; take care not to fall away from Him." Navvab sermonized when he himself was interrogated: "Governments are legal and may legitimately interfere in the affairs of a Muslim nation only if they administer the laws of Islam. [Razmara's] government deviated from Islam and therefore had no right to meddle in the affairs of the Muslim nation of Iran."[16] Tahmasebi, he said, had done what the National Front and the people wanted, which was also what God had ordained. He referred to the articles in the National Front press and Mosaddeq's speeches in the Sixteenth Majlis, which, he argued, had encouraged killing Razmara in no uncertain terms. Later, after Prime Minister Hossein Ala had been attacked by a member of the Fadaiyan in 1955, the Fadaiyan's accusations against Mosaddeq and the National Front became specific and were made in the presence of Front members.[17]

Tahmasebi was freed on 15 November 1952 by a bill of the Majlis, endorsed by Mosaddeq and his cabinet. Tahmasebi's guru, Navvab Safavi, was released in February 1953 under pressure from the government, a strange fusion of politics and law with a deleterious effect on justice. Despite the official deference they received, the Fadaiyan had a tortuous relationship with Mosaddeq during the oil nationalization process. Mosaddeq was politically and culturally secular. Navvab and his followers sought an Islamic government. They cooperated with Mosaddeq on the issue of nationalization but opposed him on all others. Navvab thought Mosaddeq's idea of "negative equilibrium," a balancing of the great powers against each other, was misguided and ineffective in the 1940s. According to Abd-e Khodai, Navvab Safavi believed "Mosaddeq had learned the idea of negative equilibrium from the politician-cleric Hasan Modarres in the 1920s, at a time when there existed an objective contradiction between England and Russia in Iran. This contradiction did not exist between England and the United States in the 1940s. Mosaddeq wished to employ U.S. assistance to expel England, not grasping that times and conditions had changed. He still lived in the 1910s and 1920s. Navvab's position (and Khomeini's)—neither east nor west—rejected all the powers."[18] In fact, the Fadaiyan had a far closer relationship with Ayatollah Abolqasem Kashani than with Mosaddeq. Indeed, Khodai's attempted assassination of Hossein Fatemi in 1952 (ordered by Navvab from prison) was justified with the claim that Fatemi was the liaison between Mosaddeq and the shah. "During the events of 30 Tir 1331 [the popular uprising against Qavam in 1952 that brought Mosaddeq back to power] Fatemi was in the hospital, unable to play the liaison between Mosaddeq and the shah. Our friends had concluded that stifling the national movement and keeping Martyr Navvab Safavi and Martyr Khalil Tahmasebi [in jail] were the consequences of this unholy relationship. They reasoned that if they eliminated Fatemi, the revolutionaries would have a better chance. They were right. After Fatemi was hit, the relationship between Mosaddeq and the court was significantly curtailed and both Navvab and Tahmasebi were released."[19] This, though a specious interpretation, nonetheless does open a window on the Fadaiyan Islam's priorities. They were concerned with colonialism and East-West relations, but their primary goal was to defeat secularism.

With the attempt to assassinate Prime Minister Ala in 1955, the Fadaiyan's dormant police files were reopened. The subsequent investigation (and interrogations) implicated some members of the National Front and other groups as well, mostly on political grounds, but few indictments were issued. Four top members of the Fadaiyan, including Navvab Safavi and Khalil Tahmasebi, were tried, condemned to death, and executed. After Navvab's death, the Fadaiyan organization ceased operation until it merged with Khomeini in the 1960s.

■

On 19 March 1962, the U.S. embassy in Tehran sent Note 423 to Iran's Ministry of Foreign Affairs stating that the United States agreed to extend the United States Military Advisory Mission for another year. Similar notes had been sent every year since the original agreement to establish the missions on 27 November 1943. Note 423, however, contained new demands. "The existing arrangements," it read, "do not adequately cover the question of the status of the United States Advisory Mission personnel in Iran." To rectify the problem, it suggested "such personnel shall have the privileges and immunities specified for 'Members of the Administrative and Technical Staff' in the Convention annexed to the final act of the United Nations Conference on Diplomatic Intercourse and Immunities signed at Vienna, April 18, 1961." The note suggested that certain senior personnel be accorded the status of "diplomatic Agents" as specified in the Vienna instrument. Also, "in the interest of uniformity and ease of administration," the foregoing principle, said the note, was to be "made applicable to any other United States military personnel or civilian employees of the United States Department of Defense and their families forming part of their households whose presence in Iran is authorized by the Imperial Iranian Government."[20]

This "status of forces" demand put the Iranian government in a dilemma. The proposal smacked of "capitulation," a system of extraterritoriality that revived memories of colonial relationships to which Iranians were particularly sensitive. "Capitulation" was a signature of shame; it represented weakness and serfdom. Originally, it had been accorded from a position of power by the Ottoman caliph Soleyman the Magnificent to Francis I of France because of the religious foundation of the law and the differences that existed between Christian and Muslim systems of jurisprudence. In Iran, however, it had resulted from the Treaty of Turkmanchai of 1828, which formalized Iran's political and territorial losses to Russia. The privilege was subsequently extended to England after Iran's defeat in Afghanistan in 1858 and then, by applying the most-favored-nation principle, to France and several other European nations. The new Soviet government had rescinded the privilege in 1921, and Reza Shah abrogated it in 1928. The term and the idea were never taken lightly by Iranians.

The government naturally balked. The proposal was submitted in the last months of Amini's premiership, and he took no action on it. Alam, coming to office in July 1962, was acutely conscious of the political sensitivity of the

U.S. demand and tried to postpone dealing with it as long as possible. The shah abhorred the idea, but after his trip to the United States in April 1962 he had come to believe that Iran had no choice but to go along. Not only did Iran need U.S. military assistance, but other countries, including Germany, had granted U.S. forces immunity. The U.S. government was aware that the "status of forces" issue would cause the shah and his government egregious loss of face and support. The Pentagon, however, was adamant. They had done it around the world and they would do it in Iran. "It was a standard thing," said Stuart Rockwell, the U.S. chargé responsible for pushing the agreement with the Iranian foreign ministry and through the parliament. "The feeling has always been that not only in Iran but in other foreign countries the system of justice is so different that the possibility of what we would consider unsuitable treatment was very strong. So we tried for a long time to get, particularly the Pentagon was interested in it, a status of forces agreement with Iran which would permit military personnel accused of crimes against Iranians to be tried in U.S. military courts rather than the Iranian civilian ones."[21]

It took Alam's administration almost a year to reply to the U.S. embassy's constant pressure. On 11 March 1963, the foreign ministry sent the embassy a note stating that Iran had agreed to give "the high-ranking members of the Advisory Mission who hold diplomatic passports . . . diplomatic status until they can enjoy the relevant immunities and advantages — and concerning the rest of the staff of the American Advisory Mission also some studies are under way in order to provide them too with more advantages and facilities, and the Embassy will later be informed of the results."[22] In November, the Alam government advised the embassy that it believed the Vienna Agreement did not apply to high-ranking members of the Military Advisory Mission who were in the employ of the Iranian government and there must therefore be a different protocol to apply to them. This question in turn led to a series of communications that, as far as Iran was concerned, were equally irrelevant and problematic. Iranian foreign minister Abbas Aram, shunning the issue, pronounced it useless. Ahmad Mirfendereski, the undersecretary of foreign affairs for parliamentary affairs and the official who would be responsible for guiding the Status of Forces bill through the two houses, asked the embassy to bring instead a list of the people to whom it thought necessary for Iran to accord diplomatic immunity.[23]

Nonetheless, Alam's government submitted the bill to the Senate on 15 January 1964, less than two months before Alam was replaced by Mansur. The bill passed the Senate on 25 July 1964 without much debate and was sent to the Majlis. There it was made a cause célèbre by the opposition Mardom Party leader Holaku Rambod and his supporters, who took Prime Minister Mansur and his government to task. In contrast to Alam, Mansur had personally defended the bill and was guiding it through the legislative process, often preempting Mirfendereski. In October, the bill authorizing the government to "extend to the chief and members of the U.S. advisory missions in Iran, who according to agreements signed are in the employ of Iranian government, the immunities and exemptions provided to administrative and technical employees as defined under paragraph F of Article One of the Vienna Convention" was put up for final vote in the Majlis. According to the relevant articles of the Convention, the immunities extended to civil and administrative personnel did not cover affairs other than administrative and technical duties assigned to them. "Therefore," stated Mirfendereski in the Majlis, "the immunities extended to such personnel unlike those fully extended to diplomatic personnel [were] limited." To further sweeten the bill, Mirfendereski tried to explain that what the government was proposing to the Majlis was not unique to Iran; that American military advisory groups carried out duties in thirty-eight countries "and in all those countries they availed themselves of the immunities extended to diplomatic staffs according to their respective agreements." He outlined the varieties of such agreements—bilateral as with Greece or multilateral as in NATO and SEATO. The point was that, as he had now argued so many times "and as mentioned in Article 37 of the Vienna Convention, this waiver of jurisdiction in penal matters [did] not in any way impair the competence of the authorities of the host country to look into civil responsibilities, payment of compensations, redress of losses in cases where their acts are beyond the limits of their duties."[24]

The bill was passed on 13 October 1964 after a rancorous debate with a vote of 74 to 61,[25] an inordinately high number on the opposing side. Rockwell attributed the close vote to ruling party Iran Novin leaders' loss of control over their rank and file in the Majlis. Despite the heated debate, Mansur and other leaders had been overconfident and thus failed to whip up deputy support. Some fifty Iran Novin deputies did not even show up. Of those who did, at least twelve voted against the government—an option that had been made easy when the opposition maneuvered to make the ballot secret. Furthermore, the opposition Mardom Party as well as independents argued that the bill was unconstitutional; one of the deputies cited Article 71 of the Constitution and Article 11 from the Bill of Rights in the Supplementary Basic Law. According to Rockwell, the rumor in Iran Novin circles was that former prime minister Alam's friends were behind the opposition. Hasan Arsanjani, former minister of agriculture, was supposed to have written the speech on the Constitution delivered by the independent deputy Sartip-pur, and Mohammad Baheri, former minister of justice, was said to have helped as well.[26] Such rumors could not be corroborated, but they were spurred on the one hand by the opposition deputies' vigorous citing of precise items and instances where the bill contradicted previous law or political positions and on the other hand by the government's lukewarm defense. Mirfendereski, the man in charge of leading the bill through the parliament, did not have his heart in what he said. The opposition introduced several amendments that were voted down but provided repeated occasions to denounce the bill. The government's case was further weakened by a report in the press the day before about an accident in which a U.S. serviceman had gravely injured a taxi driver.[27] Where would the taxi driver receive justice if this bill were to become law? Would an American non-com then be able to "slap the face of an Iranian general with impunity"?[28]

Prime Minister Mansur later explained, in response to a query from Rockwell, that he had asked the shah and the shah had agreed not to interfere in the activities of the opposition parties in the Majlis,[29] which Rockwell reasoned had emboldened the opposition. It was a bad day for both Mansur and the shah, he wrote Secretary Rusk.[30]

The bill made both Mansur, who never seemed sure of what exactly it meant,[31] and the shah targets of attack. On 26 October, the shah's birthday, Khomeini used the shah to attack the bill: "Even if the shah of Iran runs over an American dog, he will be asked questions. But if an American cook runs over the shah of Iran, the highest personage in this country, no one has the right to complain." It was all because of a miserable $200 million loan, he said—"A $200 million loan to be paid to Iran in five years and $300 million to be received from Iran in ten years—that is $100 million profit. Still, Iran was sold for these dollars, our independence was sold, we became a colony, and the Muslim people of Iran became in the eyes of the world less [worthy] than the savages." All of this happened because the clerics were not there to defend the honor of the people, he said. He warned the army, the politicians, the merchants, and the ulama that this government was dreaming up much else to destroy Iran. He begged Muslim leaders to come to Iran's aid, and the shah to help himself. "Today," he said, "America is the source of our problems; Israel is the source of our problems; and Israel is America. These ministers are also of America. All are American lackeys. If not, why do they not stand and loudly object?" The laws were all unconstitutional, he claimed, as were the governments because, since the adoption of the Constitution, Article 2 of the Supplementary Basic Law, stipulating that a group of five Mujtahids was to rule that every law must agree with Islam, had never been honored. He finished by praying to God to destroy individuals who made treason against "this land, Islam, and the Koran."[32]

Khomeini was arrested on 4 November 1964 and exiled to Turkey. SAVAK announced that his exile was necessary because his presence threatened "the interests of the people, and the nation's security, independence, and territorial integrity."[33] The effects of Khomeini's activism and exile lingered in a series of assassinations and assassination attempts, in particular those against Mansur and the shah; the man himself, however, receded from the public's consciousness until late in the next decade. The years that followed, tormented and replete with risk, nevertheless belonged to the shah and the successes of the White Revolution. The shah was now significantly more confident of his position and policies. The status bill might have been controversial, but it could not damage his position, he told his ministers, even before the bill was passed.[34]

As had Navvab Safavi's Fadaiyan, Khomeini's followers also routinely asked one or more *marja*'s for a ruling before they attempted an assassination. After Khomeini was exiled for speaking against the Status of Forces Law, the new "capitulation" as he put it, his followers decided to go beyond distributing tracts and pamphlets. The revolutionary Islamic associations *(Jamiyathaye mu'talefeh-ye eslami)* in which they were organized were expanded; each association consisted of ten members, one of whom joined a higher rung, which then selected one of its members to join a central council. The council looked for members in lower associations who were willing to accept difficult assignments, even risk their lives for the cause. These individuals were organized in a special group and assigned one or two senior members as liaisons. In the case of Mansur, Haj Mohammad Naraqi and Haj Sadiq Imani were designated the council representatives. The assassination squad, composed of Mohammad Bokharai, Reza Saffar Harandi, Morteza Niknejad, and Ali Andarzgu, received special training in paramilitary techniques and use of weapons. According to Imani's brother, "When Imam Khomeini explained to the public that to fight the regime successfully it was necessary to act beyond the ordinary, the members concluded that armed struggle was the appropriate response to the call. But others were not yet familiar with the concept of armed struggle and thought it unwise; some even thought it un-Islamic. We answered that we never acted unless we received authorization from a *marja* and *vali faqih* [guardian jurist]." Asadollah Badamchian, another Khomeini follower and activist during the revolution, stated, "In the case of the revolutionary execution of the shah or Mansur also the ulama's authorization was sought. The Imam [Khomeini] was asked before he was exiled, but he advised that the time was not yet right. Imam had assigned the Ayatollahs Beheshti and Motahhari to speak for him in his absence. They were asked and they approved.

Finally Ayatollah Seyyed Mohammad Hadi Milani, a well-established *marja' taqlid*, authorized the act."[35]

Such rulings were not extracted from the ulama easily. Most of them refrained from making a definite statement endorsing an assassination, though they generally lauded the intention and, as a rule, did not forbid the act. To kill Mansur, the martyrs-to-be asked Ayatollah Milani to be specific: "Please tell us plainly that if we embark upon this act, first, will we be recompensed in the presence of the Almighty and, second, will we be burdened with a responsibility for which we will have to answer in the next world?" Milani answered: "This is indeed the correct act in the case of Mansur and a worthy act in the eye of the *shar'* [religious law]." Taqi Khamushi, Milani's interlocutor, concluded that once they received this definite answer, they "became duty-bound to act, given also the word of the Imam."[36]

Mansur was killed in front of the Majlis on 21 January 1965, about three months after the Status of Forces bill passed the Majlis. The assassins had debated three possible locations—the Majd Mosque, the armed forces co-op, and the Majlis. Though they considered the mosque safest, they decided on the Majlis to underline the connection of their act to the law for which Mansur was to be killed. On the morning of the assassination they set out from their safe house, walking toward the Majlis, led by Sadiq Imani, the liaison from the central council. The prime minister's official limousine stopped in front of the Majlis at 10 A.M. Mohammad Bokharai approached the limousine, a petition in his hand. Mansur emerged, his hand extended to receive the letter. The assassin shot him thrice—twice in the stomach, once in the throat. Mansur fell to the ground. Bokharai attempted to escape but was captured. An address on a piece of paper in his pocket led the police to two of his companions—Niknejad and Saffar Harandi—who were arrested the same day. The others were rounded up later.[37]

Stuart Rockwell, whose job it was to promote the "status of forces" proposition on behalf of the U.S. government, thought Mansur was naïve to endorse it. "We had particular difficulty in getting the Iranian Government, successive Iranian governments, to agree. It was not until Ali Mansour became Prime Minister that the Government did agree. And I have a feeling . . . that [it] cost him his life because . . . the traditionalist element . . . felt that Iran had given up part of its sovereignty to a foreign power and that he as the instrumentality of that was responsible." Mansur, according to Rockwell, had neither read the Vienna Convention nor quite understood that under the agreement if an American military person killed an Iranian national, whether intentionally or accidentally, he would not go before an Iranian tribunal.[38]

The morning of 10 April 1965 was to begin as usual. The shah was supposed to drive from his private home, located to the northwest of Kakh Square, across the small square and arrive at his office in the Marble Palace at the square's southeast corner exactly at 9 A.M. There, as usual, he would be met by his adjutant general, Lieutenant General Morteza Yazdanpanah; the commander of the Imperial Guard, Brigadier Mohsen Hashemi-Nejad; his protocol chief, Hossein Ali Loqman Adham; and his military adjutant of the day. In addition there was an honor guard present that saluted him every morning as he exited his car. It was also his custom to receive Hashemi-Nejad's report first thing, before he entered his office. The hour of 9 passed but the shah, habitually punctual, was late. Hashemi-Nejad walked to the residence palace on the other side of the square to see what had delayed the king. As he entered the gate, he saw the shah descending the stairs in front of the house. He approached the shah and was ordered to present his report there. The shah then drove through the gate toward his office; Hashemi-Nejad walked behind the car to his own office, which was situated near the gate inside the Marble Palace. As he entered his office, he heard several rounds of shots. He ran out toward the main building and entered through the half-open door. There he saw Master Sergeant Babaian on the ground, shot but still alive, holding his gun in his hand; a few yards beyond, Master Sergeant Lashgari lay dead next to the door to the shah's bureau, and Private Reza Shamsabadi was also dead on the ground, with his machine gun by his side. Hashemi-Nejad ran inside the shah's office, but the shah was not there. He then rushed into the adjacent room, a pantry, where he found the shah standing near the boiling samovar, shaken but in control.

The shah was lucky that day. His tardiness, out of character and unexpected, confused his assailant. As he arrived, General Yazdanpanah called the honor guard to attention, but the shah, having already received Hashemi-Nejad's daily report, instead of pausing, went straight toward the building. Shamsabadi, a private in the honor guard and the chosen assassin, opened fire when the shah was already halfway through the door but missed him. He ran after him, firing his submachine gun, and was shot by Master Sergeant Babaian, who had managed to get into the building before him. Babaian fired eight bullets, six of which hit Shamsabadi. Inside, Shamsabadi also exchanged fire with Master Sergeant Lashgari; he was hit twice more but succeeded in killing Lashgari and mortally wounding Babaian before he fell dead himself. In the meantime, the shah, hearing the sound of gunfire ever closer to his office, had moved to the pantry next door.

The attempt on the shah came less than three months after Mansur's assassination. It therefore could have had significant political reverberations. The imperial court announced the shooting as the work of a soldier gone mad. In fact, Shamsabadi had been groomed by the Fadaiyan Islam as part of the same Islamic fundamentalist groups that had masterminded Mansur's killing. The two slain sergeants were part of a group of special agents in the Imperial Guard trained to protect the shah, the queen, and the royal children. The episode could also have had tremendous repercussions for the Guard, especially its commanding officer, Hashemi-Nejad. The shah's adjutant general, Lieutenant General Yazdanpanah, called Hashemi-Nejad to task. How could such a thing happen, he asked? The queen wanted to know who was at fault. Hashemi-Nejad expected to be dismissed, at least reprimanded or demoted. The Guard's main duty was to protect the shah, the queen, and the rest of the royal family. Now, within the royal compound, in front of the royal office, a member of the Guard had attempted to assassinate him. "We have this rule in the army that says the commanding officer is responsible for his units' activities and operations—good or bad. I was in charge; I was responsible."[39]

The day, however, was not as catastrophic for Hashemi-Nejad as he had feared. The shah resumed his day's schedule after a half hour of rest, receiving Abbasali Khalatbari, Iran's minister of foreign affairs in the 1970s, but then secretary general of CENTO, and Pakistan's chief of staff, who was in Iran on a military visit. Manuchehr Gudarzi, then in charge of the State Organization for Administration and Employment (SOAE), was scheduled for an audience at 11 A.M. He learned of the attempt when he arrived at the palace and asked Hormoz Qarib, the court's master of protocol, to reschedule his audience, assuming it had been cancelled. Qarib reported the matter to the shah and was told to ask Gudarzi to go in. "I was surprised to see His Majesty so calm," Gudarzi later recalled. "He described what had happened as if the event had nothing to do with him and then proceeded to discuss my report."[40] At around noon, Hashemi-Nejad was informed that he was to present himself to the shah at 2 P.M. "I was certain His Majesty would scold me for what had happened," he later said. But the shah asked him about the Guard's organization, and as he was dismissing the general, he said, "Well, our guard performed its duty quite well today." For Hashemi-Nejad, this was a godsend. "I believe His Majesty knew instinctively that everyone was now calling for my head. He complimented the guards to make known that he still had confidence in me and the Guard."[41] The general owed his good fortune to the two sergeants who gave their lives to save their king.

17

SAVAK

The idea of a modern central intelligence agency for Iran was brought up a year or so after the fall of Mosaddeq in conversations with the Americans and the British and subsequently the Israelis. But it took several years before the idea gelled and finally became law. The Americans stationed in Iran were not initially involved. Indeed, the G2 officer in MAAG, Colonel Walker, protested to the Iranian G2 chief, Brigadier Vali Qaranei, about the Americans being left out of the establishment of a civilian security organization despite the contributions they had made to the development of Iran's military intelligence. Soon, however, an American colonel named Giroux was assigned to help with the new organization.[1]

American and British intelligence operations were divided into domestic and foreign—FBI and CIA in the United States and MI5 and MI6 in Great Britain. The Iranian organization, however, took Turkey as its model, where the two functions converged in one encompassing institution. In the original concept the proposed organization was only to gather information relevant to domestic and international security, sift and convert it to intelligence, and then convey it to appropriate military or civilian institutions for implementation. The bill to establish SAVAK—*Sazeman-e ettela'at va amniat-e keshvar,* or State Organization for Intelligence and Security—passed the Senate on 20 January 1957 and the Majlis on 14 March. Under its provisions, SAVAK's chief was to be one of the prime minister's deputies. The shah's first choice to run the new organization was Nasser Zolfaqari, a civilian. Zolfaqari, however, declined, arguing the job demanded extensive counterespionage experience, which he lacked, and was better suited to a military officer with intelligence background.[2] The shah then appointed Major General Teymur Bakhtiar, commander of the Imperial Guard and administrator of martial law, as head of SAVAK, and Hasan Pakravan and Hasan Alavi-Kia, two officers with security experience, as deputy chiefs; Pakravan was to head the foreign intelligence operations, Alavi-Kia the domestic. Bakhtiar was presented to the Majlis in his new assignment on 4 April 1957, in Manuchehr Eqbal's first cabinet. Under Bakhtiar, Pakravan, and Alavi-Kia, SAVAK was able to bring in a group of highly intelligent military and civilian officers. Colonel Gratian Yatsevitch, stationed in Iran from the late 1950s to the mid-1960s as the CIA country director, observed that "it was generally recognized that SAVAK actually managed to have assigned to it some very superior and quite intellectual officers." Earnest R. Oney, who instructed SAVAK personnel in foreign counterespionage and dealt with very high-level civilians in the late 1950s, was of the same opinion.[3]

The SAVAK organization developed gradually into nine bureaus. The two major fields of activity — domestic and foreign — were kept separate, though they were served by the same support groups. Foreign operations were initially concentrated in the second bureau, which both gathered and analyzed information. The responsibility for analysis was subsequently transferred to the seventh bureau, which became a repository for the organization's brainier members, looking into a wide array of subjects, including such matters as the probable effect of trends in the world economy on Iranian society. The eighth bureau was responsible for counterespionage. Over the years, it grew into a superb organization with significant information on the Soviet bloc as well as the regional countries. It predicted the Soviet designs in Afghanistan before any other intelligence organizations, including the Israeli Mossad and the CIA. As early as 1976, it advised the shah that Iraq was building and stockpiling chemical and biological weapons.

The third bureau was responsible for domestic security. It became the emblem of SAVAK, the bureau most people actually mean when they think and speak of SAVAK. Like most of the security agencies that preceded it, this bureau was also mainly concerned with the left and its operations in Iran. Though the Tudeh had very much diminished in power and membership by the time SAVAK was instituted, it still was considered the main Soviet agent in Iran and remained a focus of attention for both Iranians and Americans. The bureau's functions, however, were not limited to the surveillance of the left; they encompassed all domestic activities that SAVAK assumed might threaten the country or the regime. As time went on, this function branched out to cover a much wider array of individuals, including some who served in high positions, and measures, including gathering information on personal habits and behaviors, which were repulsive to many supporters of the regime. It may be said with some justice that this bureau was more successful in antagonizing the supporters of the regime than in neutralizing its enemies.

When SAVAK was established, the records and relevant personnel of the G2s in the army and the martial law administration were transferred to it. (The national police, then under General Mehdiqoli Alavi Moqaddam, refused to surrender its documents and after some argument prevailed. Thus, the police kept on doing what they had always done in the field of political unrest, independent of SAVAK.) At the beginning, each bureau maintained its own records. In due time, however, a ninth bureau was established to keep and secure all the organization's records. It became SAVAK's archives, from which other state organizations received the information they needed. Interestingly, this bureau failed to destroy the records it held, as it should have done according to its bylaws, during the revolution. As a result, the Islamic Republic's security organization, VAVAK, received intact most if not all of SAVAK's records. (The remaining bureaus were responsible for administration, budget, and training.)

SAVAK's relationship with Israel soon blossomed. Israel had had some contact with the army's G2 before Iran's armed forces were reorganized along U.S. army lines. This connection, which grew rapidly after the Supreme Commander's Staff was established with a reorganized G2 under Lieutenant General Haj Ali Kia, had been initiated because of a mutual interest in containing the Arab influence as well as Iran's belief in Israeli prowess in the intelligence field. The shah directed General Bakhtiar to inquire discreetly if the Israelis would train Iranians under conditions stipulated by Iran. After several secret contacts, an Israeli-Iranian intelligence connection, especially for training in surveillance and clandestine listening, was worked out. Although the direct training role ebbed after a while, the relationship was formalized in a joint committee of representatives from Iran, Israel, and Turkey, which met annually in one of the member countries.

The Iranian intelligence community believed that the Israelis had better accord with Iran than with Turkey because of a mutual history that looked back to when Cyrus the Great liberated the Jewish people from their captivity, and also because the Turks were overly sensitive about the Armenian and Kurdish questions, whereas the Iranians were more or less on the same wavelength with the Israelis about where threats lay. Furthermore, Iranians considered the Israeli intelligence superior to that of the Americans. "The American intelligence operation and method," observed Major General Mansur Qadar, an early director of intelligence at SAVAK, "were superficial and lacked depth. The Israelis, on the other hand, looked for and found the roots and therefore the sources that nourished the enemy and the danger it represented."[4] Iran and Israel agreed that Iran might face threats in a 150-kilometer radius around its borders, essentially on the Arab sides. Russia was out of reach and the shah forbad any activity in Turkey.

Formally, SAVAK's chief was the prime minister's deputy for intelligence. In practice, prime ministers received information from SAVAK on a need-to-know basis. They were regularly informed about the activities of the left, the religious community, and the other organizations SAVAK followed but knew little about the technical means SAVAK used or its methods of operation. They were generally not informed about cases of espionage until after the fact, when they would receive appropriate information on the shah's order. Always, the quantity and quality of the information received was colored by the SAVAK chief's personal relationship with a particular prime minister.

The shah received SAVAK's chief twice a week and heard his report. The men he appointed chief of SAVAK over the years were all loyal to him but conspicuously different in character, demeanor, and intellectual endowment. Bakhtiar was a smart but rough soldier, brave but callous in the genre of the *luti,* tending to help friends and destroy enemies, a womanizer, thinking himself at once irresistible and unable to resist. He had fought bravely against the Firqeh demokrat, showing, according to those who fought at his side, "a penchant for danger and cruelty."[5] He was self-confident and overly ambitious, and he believed he merited the highest political office Iran offered, with the shah preferably, without him if necessary.

Bakhtiar was succeeded on 15 March 1961 by his deputy, General Hasan Pakravan, who was in many ways his opposite—intellectual, politically moderate, temperamentally humane, family oriented, and nonviolent. These qualities are attested to in most accounts of Pakravan's personal as well as professional life. His tenure as chief of SAVAK made a difference. The organization became more rational, law-bound, and fair. He was succeeded by General Nematollah Nasiri, the third SAVAK chief and the last before the chaos of the revolutionary period. Nasiri stood at a third point, equidistant from Bakhtiar and Pakravan. He was the deaf-and-dumb, do-or-die man, neither intellectual nor ambitious, neither good nor evil, only loyal—the sort that would willingly part with life to protect or just to please his king. He was appointed chief as Hoveyda formed his first cabinet in January 1965 and ran SAVAK for thirteen years.

The *Kubark Manual,* a 1963 CIA handbook of interrogation, documents a plethora of torture and other coercive methods for making prisoners talk. According to Mark Bowden, writing in the *Atlantic Monthly* in 2003, it remains "the most comprehensive and detailed application in print of coercive methods of questioning—given the official reluctance to discuss these matters or put them in writing, because such things tend to be both politically embarrassing and secret." The manual tells interrogators, among other things, that fear of pain is more potent than pain (an unfrightened prisoner makes an unlikely informer) and that sensory deprivation and solitary confinement are among the more successful methods of obtaining information. According to Bowden,

> The history of interrogation by US armed forces and spy agencies is one of giving lip service to international agreements while vigorously using coercion whenever circumstances seem to warrant it. However, both the Army and the CIA have been frank in their publications about the use of coercive methods. The *Kubark Manual* offers only a few nods in its 128 pages to qualms over what are referred to, in a rare euphemism, as "external techniques": "Moral considerations aside, the imposition of external techniques of manipulating people carries with it the grave risk of later lawsuits, adverse publicity, or other attempts to strike back." The use of the term "strike back" here is significant; it implies that criticism of such unseemly methods, whether legal, moral, or journalistic, would have no inherent validity but would be viewed as an enemy counterattack.[6]

We are not sure if an actual copy of the *Kubark Manual* was ever given to SAVAK. It is clear, however, that the gist of what it contained was conveyed to the Iranian organization, probably before or about the time Nasiri succeeded Pakravan as its chief. The manual distinguishes between physical torture, the traditional method of applying pain by means of crude instruments of producing pain, and coercive methods, the more subtle deprivations produced by psychological means. By the late 1960s, SAVAK mostly used the subtle methods it had learned from the CIA and from Israel's General Security Services, or Shabak. The shah saw the change to the "subtle methods" as another proof of modernity and was prompted on several occasions to dismiss allegations of SAVAK atrocity, offering as evidence the modern techniques that in his judgment had rendered obsolete the crude old ways of torture. It is likely he was never told the details of SAVAK's methods and probably never seriously sought to know, as the following excerpt from his 1980 television interview in exile with David Frost suggests.[7]

FROST: In retrospect, with all the troubles it has caused you, do you wish SAVAK had never happened?

SHAH: Well, I can't say that, because every country has [its] intelligence organization. The United States has it, the UK has it, all other governments have it, not mentioning the KGB.

FROST: How many members of SAVAK were there? Full-time?

SHAH: At the end of 1978 around four thousand.

FROST: How many part-time informers?

SHAH: This you never know. How can I know that? Maybe if SAVAK asked a shopkeeper a question, he would answer.

FROST: Did they have paid part-time informers?

SHAH: Probably.

FROST: How many of those would there be?

SHAH: I wouldn't know. I would not know.

FROST: There was one case where a SAVAK official not wanting to deal with anything attacking the crown banned all Shakespeare's plays that dealt with the death of a king.

SHAH: I heard that. [The shah smiles.]

FROST: I imagine that was not what you had in mind?

SHAH: That was stopped, obviously. There might have been cases of exaggeration. The question is that, O.K., as I said, maybe we should have started before. But, they [the mullahs] had their revolution one year ago. Where is the freedom of the press? Freedom of the people? Where are they now? Do they have more freedom? Can they express themselves? We have never seen such repression in the whole history of our country.

FROST: How did the torture start? Not with an official order, but with individuals, would you say?

SHAH: Probably. You know, you can see films, for instance, you can hear stories that even in the police precincts the police officer or a detective gets so mad at the behavior of the fellow he has arrested that he loses his head, and he just punches that fellow or breaks a chair on his head. These are some kinds of human reaction that are almost beyond control.

FROST: When did people first tell you that torture was going on in Iran?

SHAH: In matter of fact, we heard it mostly from the outside. In the inside they would never come to me and say Sir, we have tortured this fellow to make him talk. No. That was not my business; that was not my job. The reports I received from these intelligence services were very top reports for the high stakes of the security of the state.

FROST: Do you, as the king of kings who in a sense gets all the credit and therefore all the blame, accept in your concept of kingship a sense of responsibility for those tortures although you did not know about them?

SHAH: Well, that must be either some kind of a sense of self-sacrifice or masochism, because how could I take that responsibility if I did not know about it?

FROST: You don't have responsibility for everything that goes on in the country when you are the king of kings?

SHAH: I was receiving the head of security, say, twice a week for 20 minutes, 25 minutes, and he would have his reports on important things to me, not just petty details like that. He would come with reports on Afghanistan, for instance, deep penetration, or at least trying to penetrate deeply of the students' or Mullahs' organizations outside, this or that, but he wouldn't come to tell me that today we have tortured this fellow or that fellow.

FROST: I agree when you talk about global and geopolitical things like Afghanistan. The word "petty" about one incident or group of incidents or whatever could be called petty if one looked only at global scene. But given the damage it did to the image of your country and given the fact that I don't know any defense of it, I don't think, with respect, that it turned out to be petty or was petty.

SHAH: Yes, you are right in that sense that the slightest thing that is not good is bad. But this is in a perfect society. Torture had stopped absolutely in my country since 1976.

FROST: In the period before . . .

SHAH: In the period before, those who were tortured, if they were telling the truth or not, they have been exposed and they have been receiving investigations and their numbers were counted for.

FROST: When you heard the reports from abroad you investigated, you were able to form an estimate of what had gone on in the previous 18 or 20 years?

SHAH: Sure.

FROST: You put the figure in the hundreds or what?

SHAH: Oh, yes. Maximum. Maybe even not that.

FROST: The point I wanted to make is that obviously we have been talking about the figures from the ayatollah and your figures, and your figures are much lower, and we ought to add, I think, that we have been talking in numbers in your answer to history, but that obviously in this area one is too many.

SHAH: Yes. Yes. For our code of principles and approach to civilization, that is quite true. The question is that they say anything. First, they say one thousand, then they say ten thousand, then they say a hundred thousand. We never had more than three thousand two hundred political prisoners, as they were called. Most of them were terrorists. And even international organizations like Amnesty International sometimes talked of ten thousand or twenty thousand or one hundred thousand prisoners—absolutely irresponsible figures.

Frost catches the shah at his slip, the word *petty*. The shah was exasperated at the accusations of torture and atrocities hurled at him over the years. His relationship with SAVAK was formal. During Pakravan's tenure, he received both Pakravan and his deputy, General Alavi Kia, but only those two. After Pakravan became minister of information in Hoveyda's cabinet, he saw General Nasiri and, in Nasiri's rare absences, SAVAK's deputy chief, General Hossein Fardust, his childhood friend and chief of his special bureau and after April 1973 also of the Imperial Inspectorate. He never received Parviz Sabeti, the head of SAVAK's third bureau, which was responsible for domestic security. He cross-checked the information he received from one organization, for example SAVAK, with the information he received from other organizations, for example the Inspectorate, the special bureau, or the police. The queen grumbled to him incessantly about the rumors that SAVAK tortured the prisoners, but he remained convinced the allegation was exaggerated. He was told by his security officers that they had to balance priorities—the rights of the prisoner against the rights of the state and the public—and that they used mainly psychological means of getting information, in the CIA parlance coercive methods as opposed to torture. Besides, he was told, most of the prisoners they interrogated were terrorists, not political dissenters. These explanations satisfied the queen for a while, who concluded, "His Majesty had better sources of information and was in a better position to know the truth."[8]

SAVAK was established as the Tudeh was evanescing as a political force. By the end of the 1950s the communist movement in Iran was at its lowest ebb. The 1960s, however, rekindled hope on the left, bringing together the nationalists and the leftists, at least for a while. Kennedy's presidency rejuvenated Mosaddeq's old followers, while Castro's victory in Cuba, romanticized by Che Guevara, inspired the youth. The result was a Second National Front, but it did not last long as a force. By 1962, the Bay of Pigs, Kennedy's confrontation with Khrushchev in Vienna, and the Cuban Missile Crisis had dampened the U.S. administration's enthusiasm for new democracy. In 1963, the shah's White Revolution and Khomeini's ability to wage war in the streets effectively contained the Second National Front, bringing it nearly to an end as an active force in Iran—but not abroad.

The counterculture movements in the United States and Europe, charged and invigorated first by the French experience in Indochina and Algeria and subsequently by the American action in Vietnam, impressed the more than sixty thousand Iranian students in Europe and America. The economic boom in Iran had by now significantly changed the social composition of Iranian students. Many came from families in small towns and villages and now found themselves in the world's most advanced metropolises. Culture clash, homesickness, and loneliness combined to make them more susceptible to utopian ideologies. The hard science of Marxism gave way before romantic dreams excited by Latin American heroes and the North American and European student movements. Stalin and Khrushchev yielded to Castro and Mao. The *khalq,* the people, became an object of imagination, molded to fit the dream. One had to move from talk to action. *Jang-e mosallahaneh,* armed struggle, was the way. The people were ready; what was needed was a spark. Everywhere youth gathered to provide the spark—the United States, Germany, Italy, Japan, and, of course, France, where students almost toppled the system in 1968. In that same year, in America, President Johnson was forced to withdraw from running for a second term. By 1968, the Confederation of Iranian Students had become the hub of the romantic left, nourished ideologically and materially by the supportive environments of Berkeley, Cambridge, Munich, Bonn, London, and Paris. It had also made contact, through several of its component groups, with international terrorist groups, and at least one of its leaders, Parviz Nikkhah, had been accused of attempting to assassinate the shah.

Parviz Nikkhah was a charismatic young man, destined to become a leader of the Iranian students in Europe. He was informed, rational, and as a political leader quite effective. He was the intellectual star of the Confederation of Iranian Students' second congress in London in January 1961 and the next year in the meeting of the congress in Paris. He became a leader of the Tudeh Revolutionary Party, an offshoot of the Tudeh that accused the old party of lethargy and promoted a more active policy based on armed struggle. Nikkhah met a Chinese delegation when visiting one of the leftist student organizations in Africa in 1964. The Chinese invited him to go to China to become acquainted with their work. Back in London, he arranged instead for several other Iranian students to go to China, where they received instructions and training in Maoism and guerrilla warfare. In the meantime, Nikkhah traveled to a number of European cities, inviting students to break away from the traditional Tudeh Party and to adopt armed struggle as the primary principle of revolutionary action.[9]

Nikkhah returned to Iran later in 1964. From Iran he initiated a series of discussions in Europe, which changed fundamentally the future of the student left by substituting China for the Soviet Union as the ideal example — and in time supplanting both with Cuba and Algeria. At the same time he made several trips to the countryside to test and, if possible, implement his theories in the Iranian context. His theory suggested that Iran was ripe for revolution, and given the existing social structure, especially the nature of peasantry, an alliance of workers and peasants, formed and led by the revolutionary party, was its appropriate instrument. The responses he received from the peasants he met, however, were not reassuring. Later, when he became a supporter of the shah's regime, he would explain that these peasant reactions were the key to his eventual ideological transformation. At this time, however, they became a reason for him to conclude that "cutting off the head of the regime" might be a shortcut to political salvation.

Nikkhah was arrested in relation to the attempt on the shah's life on 10 April 1965, although the man who made the attempt, Reza Shamsabadi, was, according to General Mohsen Hashemi-Nejad, a member of the Fadaiyan Islam.[10] Shamsabadi knew a certain Samad Kamrani, who was in contact with a man named Ahmad Mansuri, who in turn was in Nikkhah's political circle. That apparently was the line that connected Nikkhah to the assassination attempt.[11] In his trial, Nikkhah denied his participation in the plot, though not his Maoist ideology. He was sentenced to life but was pardoned by the shah, as were the other conspirators, and subsequently his sentence was reduced to ten years. Before he was pardoned, he had asked for and was granted an audience with the shah. He was taken before the shah in handcuffs, which the monarch found repulsive. He ordered the cuffs off. Afterward he said one look into the young man's eyes and he knew that he was not a murderer.[12]

Some years into Nikkhah's incarceration in the Falak-ul-Aflak prison, his brother, who worked in the state Bank Saderat (export bank) told Jahangir Tafazzoli, a board member at the bank and a friend of Court Minister Alam, that he sensed that his brother had undergone an ideological transformation. He asked Tafazzoli to look into the matter and, if he found Nikkhah had indeed changed, to see if it would be appropriate to review his case. Tafazzoli took the matter to Alam and his deputy Mohammad Baheri, who, like several of Alam's other friends and underlings, was a former communist and consequently politically tuned to the left and leftist movements. Baheri sent Nikkhah several documents about the White Revolution, including documents on land reform, asking him to write an article on one of them. Nikkhah submitted a positive article on land reform and agreed to have it published provided no part of it was changed. Baheri added an introduction of his own referring to Nikkhah as an "independent thinker" and had *Kayhan,* one of Tehran's two major evening dailies, publish it. Subsequently, Nikkhah gave several impressive lectures broadcast on television, as a result of which SAVAK recommended his release. Out of prison, Nikkhah chose to work with Reza Qotbi at the National Iranian Radio and Television (NIRT) as a political analyst. To Baheri he submitted a project for reorganizing the three revolution corps (education, health, development) into a system designed to achieve the moral purpose of the shah's White Revolution. The shah was so impressed that in the summer of 1977, when Baheri replaced Amouzegar as secretary general of the Rastakhiz Party (see chapter 19), he advised Baheri to avail himself of Nikkhah's counsel on the organization and management of the party.[13]

Nikkhah's brave words in the court and then his incarceration in a rough prison initially made him a hero of the student confederation in Europe and the United States. His imprisonment prompted the confederation to organize more tightly to defend him and others who might now be charged with rising against the constitutional regime. The confederation believed that Nikkhah's relatively light sentence was a result of its agitations.[14] Iranian records do not support this claim, though the event undoubtedly energized the organization and directed it to establish better connections with the liberal and leftist political groups in the West. According to Kurosh Lashai, Nikkhah in prison became an idol in the student movement. His picture was hung in most student homes. "When I was in Kurdistan on behalf of the Revolutionary Organization of the Tudeh Party to organize the Kurds for armed struggle, I had Nikkhah's picture hung on the wall of my room," said Lashai.[15] The honeymoon, however, ended when in one of his televised lectures Nikkhah offered a critique of his own theories, asking students to stop fighting the shah and to begin working for Iran's development. Now various theories of physical and psychological torture were offered to explain Nikkhah's change of mind; whatever had happened, he could no longer be the hero of the student movement.

Kurosh Lashai also descended from leader to "traitor." Lashai hailed from a family that worked for the government and had no particular gripe against the regime or the shah. His father was in the Ministry of the Interior and in the 1940s and early 1950s held governorships in medium-sized administrative divisions. In high school Lashai was for both the shah and Mosaddeq. After Mosaddeq's fall he was pro-Mosaddeq only. In Germany, where he studied medicine in the latter part of the 1950s, he gradually moved to the left and finally in the early 1960s he became fascinated with Parviz Nikkhah. When the latter established the Revolutionary Organization of the Tudeh Party based on the Maoist idea of armed struggle, he joined in. He became a leader of the movement, received ideological and practical training in China on several occasions, went to Iran to sway the Kurds, went back to Europe and back again to Iran in the fall of 1972, where he was recognized and arrested. By that time he had already developed serious doubts about the relevance of his theories or the political efficacy of his actions.

Lashai's discourse in this respect opens a window on the question of *shahadat* (martyrdom) in secular revolutionary movements. He had begun with Nietzsche and Kierkegaard, moved to Marx, Lenin, and Mao, and ended up by trying to learn from peasants in Dubai and Kurdistan. "Focusing on practice and action does not leave you much time for study," he told his interlocutor many years after the revolution. This was the lesson he had learned from Mao's teachings: simple, unsophisticated, but irresistibly revolutionary, each step leading to the next, as if fated.[16] Still, in the beginning he thought that his group had serious potential because members had received military training in China, Cuba, and Palestine. Mao's teaching had led him to believe that Iran was a semi-feudal, semi-colonial society that was ripe for becoming an ideal communist society by way of a violent revolution. But, somehow, the Iranian people neither resembled such a picture nor responded to it; instead, they presented a version of reality he hardly comprehended.[17] Bahman Qashqai, for example, a scion of tribal khans in Fars province and, according to Lashai, burning with ideological commitment, had joined an uprising against land reform in what he and the confederation dubbed the "Southern Revolt," but the revolt fizzled out over time. Bahman was captured on 15 April 1964, tried, and executed in November of that year because the attack he led had left five gendarmes dead.[18] The idea of fighting the shah by way of tribal khans and landlords in the hope of mobilizing peasants and workers seemed bizarre, though the irony escaped the Tudeh Revolutionaries. Later, on his trips to Iraqi and Iranian Kurdistan, Lashai was faced with widespread peasant indifference. He began to change ideologically after he left Iraq and Dubai for Europe and subsequently as he returned to Tehran to transfer the leadership of the movement to Iran. In Tehran, he decided he and his colleagues "had no roots in the society." His co-ideologists, however, could not accept this reality. They were, he would later say, "in denial." And it was not practical to bring up the issue with them at the time, because the movement was especially censorious of "pessimism," considering it "a sure sign of ideological corruption."[19] In Tehran, Lashai's revolutionary struggle shrank to teaching history and philosophy to his landlord's daughter. He began to doubt the rationality of his actions. The question now became whether he should die in order to kindle the revolutionary fire. At the same time, however, he began preparing a document that invited the organization to reconsider its strategy and tactics; the paper, still unfinished, fell into SAVAK's hands when he was arrested.

Lashai's account of his arrest differs from that of SAVAK. According to

"Hossein Zadeh," who was one of the SAVAK agents Lashai mentions in his interview, Lashai was caught when Hossein Zadeh went to his office pretending he needed an injection. The agents had been tipped off, presumably by Cyrus Nahavandi, a revolutionary friend who had been arrested, agreed to go to work for SAVAK and then "escaped" in a stage-managed operation during which he was actually shot in one arm to make the attempt seem authentic. Lashai soon realized that he had been recognized and made no effort to dissimulate or resist arrest. He was then taken in and interrogated, in this version with some psychological pressure but no physical torture.[20] In Lashai's account, he was caught in the street after he had visited several real estate agencies while searching for an apartment. He was slapped in the face with each question and flogged by a well-known torturer in the Evin prison. The interrogators suggested they knew who he was but never mentioned his name. Instead, they insisted that he identify himself voluntarily as he was being slapped. He came to believe that they did not know his real identity but thought, wrongly, he might be Hamid Ashraf, a member of the Fadaiyan Khalq, another Marxist group that was also involved in armed attacks against the regime. He was tortured for three or four days before he identified himself, at which time the torture stopped. He rejects the suggestion that Nahavandi had betrayed him because "it did not make sense for him to tell on me and not on the others. And I do not believe they beat me for tactical reasons. They just did not know who I was, and stopped beating me when I introduced myself."[21]

It is hard to believe that Nahavandi, who had been allowed out of prison in order to inform on cases precisely such as Lashai's, would fail to warn SAVAK and, more curiously, escape the failure unscathed. The important point, however, is that Lashai had concluded it was not possible to transfer the leadership of a revolutionary movement from Europe to Iran successfully and that for the movement to succeed it would have to develop inside the country. Once arrested, he contemplated whether by committing suicide or dying under torture he should become a martyr, feeding the heroic veneer that helped the revolutionary cult or, alternatively, should tell the truth and thereby refuse to become an accomplice to falsehood.[22] As Nikkhah and several others had done before him, he chose to challenge the beliefs he once held to be true, which he now believed to have been wrong.

Lashai did not spend as long a time in jail as Nikkhah. His sister was a chief of protocol at the imperial court, and once he recanted his revolutionary commitment, she was able to expedite his freedom by appealing to Court Minister Alam. Out of jail, he initially joined Ali Rezai, a major Iranian industrialist, as manager of an important steel operation. Later he found solace in the Lejion-e khedmatgozaran-e basher, Iran's answer to the American Peace Corps. The legion was established in Iran following a proposition the shah had made at Harvard on 13 June 1968 as he was receiving an honorary doctorate. "The roots of the sickness that engulfs our contemporary world," said the shah, "are in the deprivation, prejudice, discrimination, poverty, hunger, ignorance, and oppression that afflict human beings across the world. Whether in the north, south, east or west, today hundreds of millions of people await a helping hand to reduce their pain. That is why I propose the formation of an international Human Services Corps in which individuals from all nations, races, genders, and socioeconomic classes dedicate a part of their life to the service of humanity."[23] Four years before, in 1964, he had suggested that each country give a day's worth of its military budget to a fund to be used for the eradication of illiteracy around the world. Every country had hailed the idea then, but only Iran did anything about it. This proposal too fared well only in Iran, where, to announce its establishment Court Minister Alam invited to an open house a large number of people who, according to Baheri, flocked to it thinking a new political movement was being launched. Alam placed his friend Rasul Parvizi, a man of some literary erudition but no drive, at its head. Soon it was clear that the new organization needed an infusion of energy if it were to take off. Baheri had seen Lashai on television criticizing his former colleagues as "antirevolutionaries" and was very impressed. He asked Alam if Lashai might be recruited to work with the project as secretary general or, if political considerations made that impossible, would he, Baheri, be willing to take the position and have Lashai, for whom Baheri would vouch, manage the legion as his deputy. The options were presented to the shah, who, according to Baheri, insisted that Lashai be appointed as secretary general. Thus, the revolutionary became the head of an organization of which the shah was honorary chair and Alam head of the board. Later, according to Baheri, the shah would receive and compliment Lashai on a job well done, an "honor" he was not known to bestow often.[24]

Nikkhah and Lashai represented an aspect of the European left that developed in the mid-1960s and early 1970s. The postwar left in Europe was based on scientific Marxism, expressed as either social democracy or Leninist communism. Each of these manifestations identified itself and the other as part of the left, distinct from nonleft political and ideological organizations, groups, and movements. This orthodoxy was broken by the mid-1960s. The left, thus far mainly a European phenomenon, was now significantly influenced by American developments. Party and established ideology were gradually overshadowed by intellectual groupings and political romance. Che Guevara, Ho Chi Minh, and even Joan Baez achieved a saliency as great as, and sometimes even greater than, Marx's or Lenin's. (It is interesting that the German social democratic leader Joshka Fisher would recently admit that he was influenced by Bob Dylan more than by Marx.)[25] Vietnam and Algeria made a more immediate imprint on the young intellectual psyche than the memory of Stalingrad. Concepts of progress began to change, and success was defined differently. Whereas in the past progress was associated with growth, construction, and development, now individual space, the environment, justice, and "small is beautiful" became the vogue. Results were no longer as important as will and intent. Power relations were abstracted to mental exercises, and armed struggle became a value in itself, independent of the context. The romantic idealization of the struggle made the struggler largely impervious to measures the states, the object of the struggle—whether the United States or Iran—took. There was nothing that the shah and his government might reasonably do that would mollify the students who opposed them in the United States or Europe. Many of those students, now middle-aged in the early years of the twenty-first century, admit as much, among them Mehdi Khanbaba Tehrani, a pioneer confederation leader, though, unlike with Nikkhah and Lashai, the admission does not intrude on his description of his past. However, asked about the confederation's view of the "reforms" undertaken under the shah, he states:

> I believe the student movement had gradually fallen far afield from Iranian society's realities or real issues. The movement held a petrified image of poverty left from Ahmad Shah or Reza Shah's times, of the farmers in Baluchistan eating date pits, as an *Ettela'at* article had painted some thirty years before. In our mind, reform and revolution could not possibly mix. We believed, for example, that when the shah's regime accepted women's liberation, what it really was after was to turn them into bourgeois dolls, and we argued how could women be free when men were not? This kind of analysis drove us unconsciously to an alliance with Khomeini and Montazeri rather than to a position where we would say that even the superficial rights the shah had given were good but not enough; that we must go further.... The confederation was an organization built on absolute denial.... Members of the confederation did not belong to a deep-rooted social organization possessing profound revolutionary ideas. They were, first and foremost, idealists who had revolted against social inequities and whose picture of the enemy was the person of the shah.... [They] had no knowledge of Iran and we were afraid that if questions of reform were seriously raised, the picture of the enemy might fade from the members' minds. In intellectual parlance, we were model-tuned and dry-brained.[26]

Most major assassinations and assassination attempts in Iran — Hazhir, Razmara, Fatemi, Ala, Mansur, and the shah, among others — were the work of Islamic fundamentalists, mostly the Fadaiyan Islam. SAVAK, however, was concerned mainly with the left, primarily because of the left's liaison with the West. Nikkhah's and Lashai's defections, therefore, were considered a great victory, though, in the end, insofar as it concerned the student movements in Europe and the United States, they proved more symbolic than practically effective. These movements commanded considerable material, psychological, and strategic support and were fed too much ideological and emotional fire by the struggles in Cuba, Vietnam, Algeria, Palestine, and Latin America to be overcome by sporadic effusions of idiosyncratic behavior. There was no possibility of dialogue, even if the shah's regime had been open to one, which it was not. The attacks on the regime therefore took on a surreal character — a general stance against the shah that was energized by the efforts of the shah and his government to increase Iran's economic, military, and diplomatic capability to challenge both the West and the East. The shah's perception of this stance tended to see cause and effect in parallel events that might or might not in fact constitute cause and effect — for example, an increase in attacks on him and his regime whenever he tried to raise the price of oil or took the West to task for interfering with his notion of Iran's economic or military development. Thus it was that he considered pointless any attempt at dialogue with people who seemed to him not really in control of either their beliefs or their actions. Just as important, dialogue was unnecessary because the leftist opposition had no real political commerce with the masses of Iranians, no base. The opposition, therefore, metamorphosed in this conceptualization to a tool of terror, an image that was propagated by SAVAK and kindled by the theory and praxis of armed struggle.

In the late 1960s and the 1970s, the most active and representative exponents of armed struggle inside Iran were the Mojahedin Khalq and the Fadaiyan Khalq, two revolutionary organizations that significantly affected SAVAK's evolution strategically and tactically. The Mojahedin were especially interesting and effective because of their effort to produce a theoretical link between Marxism and Islam. Both organizations advocated armed struggle, clandestine action, and terrorism.

The Fadaiyan Khalq's theory of guerrilla warfare was stated in two basic tracts — *The Necessity of Armed Struggle and the Rejection of the Theory of Sur-*

vival and *Armed Struggle as Both Strategy and Tactic*—written by Amir Parviz Puyan and Masud Ahmadzadeh. These two leaders argued that the left had been decimated by the Tudeh Party's failure and the regime's growing power and so no longer enjoyed any prestige among the masses. There was thus no longer a possibility of organizing a mass movement by ordinary means. Only through sacrifice could the left achieve the prestige it needed to gain the respect of the masses. It was necessary to show the masses that the regime was vulnerable. To do this, the revolutionaries had to learn to move among the masses like fish in water. Armed struggle would provoke the regime into reacting forcefully and violently against the people in order to confront the terrorists. Thus, the regime would become the best promoter of the revolutionary cause. It would do for the left what the left could not do for itself.

Accordingly, the Fadaiyan robbed banks, attacked police and gendarmerie stations, and assassinated the security agents. But the Maoist parable of fish in water never materialized. In Siahkal, a mountainous area by the Caspian in Mazandaran, where they attacked several gendarmerie outposts, they were discovered and overwhelmed with the help of the local people. They later argued that the idea was never to win militarily but to show the regime's vulnerability. If so, they succeeded, not by proving the state was vulnerable, but rather by the validity of sacrifice as a prestige principle. Siahkal did make of them romantic heroes among some of the youth in Iran and abroad. Nonetheless, by 1976 the Fadaiyan Khalq organization had practically ceased to exist.[27]

The Mojahedin Khalq organization was established in the summer of 1965 by six former Tehran University students—Mohammad Hanif-Nejad, Said Mohsen, Mahmud Asgarzadeh, Rasul Meshginfam, Ali Asghar Badi'zadegan, and Ahmad Rezai. The Mojahedin's early beliefs are contained in their first ideological statement, *Mobarezeh chist?* (What Is Struggle?). The strategic goal in the first stage of the struggle was to train cadres capable of future leadership. The main enemy was world-devouring imperialism, led by the United States. Imperialism was by nature exploitative; therefore, no humane relationship could exist between the imperialists and the world's oppressed masses; what could exist was either serfdom or wars of liberation. The good news, however, was that imperialism was a "paper tiger," vulnerable internally and externally. The Mojahedin, said the tract, would carefully develop their theoretical work, especially in the realm of ideology, which was the prerequisite for success. They would engage in heroic acts only when they were ready. They would move through the masses armed with revolutionary theory and knowledge. They would be disciplined, secretive, and professional.

This Maoism was soon complemented by *The Profile of a Muslim,* a booklet written by Ahmad Rezai, in which he drew parallels between Marxist-Leninist ideas and Shii-Islamic texts. Verses from the Koran were eclectically cited to show that the primordial society had been a peaceful, homogeneous community which the coming of private property had subsequently turned into antagonistic classes and nations. The Koran, Rezai wrote, looked to the establishment of a classless society and called on oppressed Muslims to fight to achieve it. In this class struggle Hussein, the martyred Third Imam of the shia, was the model. Classless society was the same as the promised society of the Mahdi, the rightly guided Twelfth Imam, wherein divine justice prevailed—a "society of *tawhid,*" of unity and plenty, where "each contributes according to his ability and each receives according to his needs." There would be no exploitation of man by man in this society, no social, economic, and ethnic contradictions, and no human conflict. To achieve this society an all-out war must be waged on all exploiters and oppressors who, at this moment in history, were being led by the American imperialists.

Parallel to the development of ideology, emphasis was also placed on training the cadres. Candidates were chosen from among the youth deemed tuned to terrorist and clandestine acts. The point of training was, according to the manuals, to produce dedicated cadres able to sacrifice everything to the cause—family, love, independent thinking, friendship, and other "bourgeois" attachments. The leaders received their terrorist and paramilitary training in the Palestinian camps that had sprung up in Jordan, Lebanon, Syria, and Libya after the 1967 Arab-Israeli War. Whereas in 1967 the Mojahedin had barely sixteen members, by 1970 they had recruited close to two hundred, most of them living in secure houses. The Mojahedin claim that their members fought alongside Palestinians against King Hussein's army during the 1970 "Black September" conflict, an activity that they say gained them considerable military experience.

The 1970s were the years of terrorist attacks by the Mojahedin along with other Marxist groups. In 1970, the Mojahedin attempted to kidnap U.S. Ambassador Douglas McArthur but failed. In May 1972, they tried to assassinate Air Force Brigadier General Harold Price, chief of US MAAG in Iran. In 1973, they assassinated Army Lieutenant Colonel Lewis Hawkins of the U.S. Military Mission. In 1975, they "executed" Lieutenant Colonel Jack Turner of the U.S. Air Force. In 1976, they killed three civilian employees of Rockwell International—William Cottrell, Donald Smith, and Robert Krongard. But, like the Fadaiyan, the Mojahedin also had their setbacks. SAVAK succeeded in infiltrating their organization in 1972, identifying their leaders and arresting most of them, including Masud Rajavi, who would reassume control of the movement after the revolution.[28] The assassinations, however, continued, leading to an atmosphere of violent struggle. The guerrillas saw themselves at war, expecting to kill and be killed. By 1975 SAVAK had in fact killed or incarcerated most of the guerrilla leaders. In April 1975, it claimed it had killed nine members of the Mojahedin and the Fadaiyan being held in Evin prison as they were attempting to escape. It was later shown that they had in fact been executed for inciting others to riot. A few days later, Catherine Adl, daughter of one of the shah's closest friends, and her husband, Bahman Hojjat Kashani, son of one of the shah's favorite generals, killed a gendarme colonel in Qazvin during an attack on a gendarmerie station. Both of them were subsequently killed in gunfights as they were being pursued—Catherine in a cave, Bahman on a Tehran street.

The shah defended the Evin killing, arguing to Court Minister Alam that it was inevitable, for otherwise the terrorists would have escaped and once free they would kill other innocent people. Clearly, he had bought SAVAK's version. But he was more than vexed on hearing the news of Adl and Hojjat. He was baffled. "They have everything. What moves them to join in with adventurers and terrorists? What is it they want?"[29] The general had already disowned his son. The shah did not know how to console his friend Adl, whom he knew to be totally devoted to his daughter and thoroughly devastated. He did not know whom to blame, or how, or why. Yahya Adl believed it was a problem of the times, of romantic idealism, of confusion, of reaching for the unreachable.[30] The event, however, could not be dismissed philosophically. The shah's household was up in arms. Shahnaz, the shah's elder daughter, now in her thirties, had turned religious and was not on good terms with her father; she pushed him on the subject while he tried to defend the action of the security forces, though not wholeheartedly or successfully. Finally, Alam came to his defense. "The first principle on which the world's religions have come into being is to protect human life. The insane individuals who wish to subvert this principle by personal *ijtihad* [religious ruling] should either be committed to an insane asylum or taken to the military barrack and given a daily regime of a hundred lashes until they regain their sanity. The matter is beyond debate." Princess Shahnaz apparently found this adversary too formidable to continue and let the discussion drop. The shah, according to Alam, was visibly relieved. "This great man," Alam recorded in his diary, "is an icon of patience, greatness, and gentleness. I could never have such discussions with my daughter."[31]

Alam obviously was into his usual hyperbole, eulogizing his sovereign's virtues. But others, even those who hated what had happened, believed that the shah could not have known of the deliberate murder in the prison and was truly sorry about the youngsters' fate. Lashai, the erstwhile revolutionary, was asked about a meeting he had with the shah, how he read him, and what in him he found interesting. He answered:

> My sense was that he did not have much information about what was going on. I mean he did not know whose word to accept. He seemed a kind person to me. I saw nothing of the bully or tyrant in him, of the kind who would order imprisonment, beating, and killing. He was different from the mental picture I had of him. . . . What especially got to me was his hesitation, as if he did not know what is right and this told me that he sought to make the right decision for otherwise he would not be hesitant. He did go through the routine of equating his words with decisions that were made but, at the same time, he seemed worried about the fate of the country. Who was telling him the truth, he asked. I think, despite the SAVAK and the [political] suffocation we talked about, the shah had forgiven many of his opponents. When SAVAK declared that several prisoners were killed as they were escaping whereas it had executed them or it claimed Mahvash Jasemi and Masumeh (Shokuh) Tavafchian were killed during an armed skirmish whereas the Revolutionary Organization believed they were killed being tortured, the anomaly resulted from the fact that SAVAK did not report to the shah that it tortured the prisoners. . . . SAVAK did not tell only the people that it did not employ torture; it said the same to the shah.[32]

The shah never had the whole truth. What he told Frost about the police officer or detective who "gets so mad at the behavior of the fellow he has arrested that he loses his head, and he just punches that fellow or breaks a chair on his head," was not something he remembered only from American movies; he knew it was a part of the reality in his own country. SAVAK and torture, however, belonged to a different category. Torture implies deliberate, secret infliction of pain to elicit information or recantation, whereas police brutality may be a spontaneous act of anger. In either case, the prevailing "security culture" affects the expression of rage depending on the values and mores the culture contains and expresses. It may be that the SAVAK agent's war against the radical revolutionary who might kill him became also a personal war. Depending on the exigency of the circumstances, he might have moved from "coercive measures" to torture, but this excused neither the agent, nor the organization, nor the shah. On the other hand, none of this was easy to ascertain or codify, because the opposition indiscriminately accused SAVAK of torturing prisoners and because, as Frost made the point, one case of torture was "one too many." The shah was frustrated because he could not defend torture and yet torture occurred, and because he could not tie the hands of his men and yet expect them to fight against those who wished to destroy him or what he had built or what he still might build, regardless of the merit of what he did. In the end, he made a point of not asking.

The most exasperating aspect of SAVAK was its attitude toward the organizations and individuals that served the regime. It stifled much that needed not to be stifled, as, for example, in the media. The culture of reporting in Iran was not investigative. Government officials were usually not challenged, though often the tenor of the report depended on the reporter's disposition toward the official. Sometimes the managers or chief editors did ask for a more aggressive approach and got results, and individual ministers were not immune from criticism. The shah, however, was sacrosanct, because he symbolized the nation. The Constitution declared him "non-responsible," above the fray, representing the state, which presented an insoluble problem for journalism as it did for the political parties, since in fact he now managed the country's politics. Where he was directly involved, for example, with the military, where he was the commander-in-chief, the media were not allowed to tread. Foreign policy too was rarely touched on, except as the explication of the government's decisions. Whatever leeway might have existed for creative and aggressive reporting in other matters was also largely stifled by self-censorship resulting from ubiquitous fear—the true major weapon of control in SAVAK's arsenal. When he was informed of specific cases, the shah usually intervened on the side of fairness, though not to lasting effect, as the following episode shows.

Once, around 1970, there was a student strike in Tehran University. The National Iranian Radio and Television (NIRT) management decided to report on student grievances. It proved difficult to get the students to publicly voice their demands, partly because of the pressures brought on them by the student leadership and partly, of course, because of SAVAK and the possible repercussions their complaints might produce. After much bargaining, the reporters succeeded in putting together a group of students angry enough to voice their grievances in public and nonpolitical enough not to tread beyond the accepted bounds. NIRT general manager Reza Qotbi thought that the best man to talk to the students was Iraj Gorgin, a high-level NIRT official with enough seniority and knowledge of high policy to withstand SAVAK pressure and enough experience to handle the students satisfactorily. Gorgin managed the job with professional skill, which included an ability to engage in political give-and-take with the students. Somewhere in the midst of hot debate, he said he understood what the students were saying and agreed with much of what they said, but there were other points involved in the issue that must be addressed. SAVAK did not appreciate the phrase "I understand and I agree with some..." and let him know in no uncertain terms.[33]

The treatment of Gorgin was symptomatic of SAVAK's suspicion that NIRT was infiltrated by the left. His sister had been married to Khosrow Golsorkhi, a member of the Fadaiyan Khalq who had planned to take the shah, the queen, and the crown prince hostage. Golsorkhi remained adamant in his beliefs and outspoken throughout his trial in open court, which was broadcast in its entirety over the television. SAVAK clearly did not trust Gorgin and did not approve of the way NIRT was run.[34] Soon after the government took over television, around 1968, SAVAK prepared a very negative report for presentation to the shah, an important part of which was that the organization had become a nest of leftist agitators. The shah wrote at the report's margin "Qotbi: Explain." Qotbi discussed the report with his colleagues, including Mahmud Jafarian, at the time his deputy for administration. Jafarian had previously been a member of the Tudeh Party and had later recanted and worked with SAVAK; he knew both the left and SAVAK. He told Qotbi that this report meant prison. The way it is put together and the allegations it makes suggest treason. "He put God's fear in me," Qotbi later remembered.[35]

Qotbi prepared a counter-report, explaining the organization's policy and why they did what they did—the decision process, the news, the newsreels and the films, the critiques, and the employees who may have belonged to some leftist organization in their student days and may have even been arrested for their activities but had now changed politically. Assisted by Jafarian, Qotbi went through the files of the employees who were connected with the production of news and commentary. There, he came across an employee who had once been arrested for having in his possession Maxim Gorky's *Mother.* This gave Qotbi a good excuse to hit at SAVAK's report. "I have this book in my library and many more like it; should I be arrested?" he wrote in his report to the shah. The report ended with a counterstrike, suggesting that those who prepared the original report attacking a young organization that employed bright young men and women in the service of king and country had themselves done a great disservice to king and country.

Co-opting former dissidents, particularly on the left, in the service of the regime was a routine policy, ironically more frequent in the organizations nearer to the shah. Qotbi argued in his counter-report that there was a spectrum of ideas in the country. Individuals saw events and explained them on the basis of their position on this spectrum. It may be that in NIRT the spectrum was somewhat heavier on the left than on the right. But every member there had opted to work for an organization that was committed to the regime strongly, openly, and clearly. Would it have been better if the talent now working in this institution instead worked for Radio Peyk-e Iran, a communist-inspired and communist-assisted radio broadcasting to Iran from East Germany? It should not be our policy to push people away from us, nor to bribe them into silence, Qotbi stated. There are those who sell their pen in the daytime and say the other thing when they are in their private circles. Such individuals and such pens we do not want. On the other hand, we should do our best to help those who come to us openly and sincerely to become productive for the country and themselves.

The shah was touched and wrote at the margin: "Those who prepared the erroneous report on NIRT should be identified and punished." This was too much. When the news reached NIRT, Qotbi's colleagues begged him to do whatever he could to put a stop to what they considered a dangerous development. "No punishment, please. They may single out one person there for punishment, but the organization will surely take it out on all of us," they pleaded.[36]

Qotbi complied with this request.

18

A Celebration and a Festival

The celebration of the anniversary of twenty-five hundred years of Iranian monarchy in October 1971 was meant as a tribute to Iran's history, an affirmation of Iran's progress under the Pahlavis, and a testimony to the shah's achievements during his reign. Instead, the event became a rallying point for his enemies, who used the celebration's glitter and gaudiness — glamour, to some — to launch a widespread attack on him and his policies. The same was true of the Shiraz Art Festival, designed to promote "the arts and the appreciation for traditional Iranian art forms," to elevate "the standard of culture in the country," and to bring to Iran the best, newest, and most avant-garde art of the world. The festival, though artistically successful, became politically an issue of considerable consequence for the regime and a strain on the dynamics of art and politics in the country.

The idea of celebrating the twenty-five-hundredth anniversary of the founding of the Persian Empire (henceforth referred to as the Anniversary Celebrations) was suggested in 1958 by Shoja'eddin Shafa, a prolific writer and translator who then served as cultural counsel at the imperial court. The Anniversary Celebrations, originally scheduled for the year 1961, when neither Iran nor the shah was impressively strong, were conceived as belonging to both Iran and the world and were therefore to be implemented with the help and participation of other countries. According to Mehrdad Pahlbod, a subsequent minister of culture and arts, "we wanted to tell the world who we are."[1] To launch the program, a committee, or council, soon to be replicated in other European, Asian, and American cities, was established in Paris. In August 1960, Senator Javad Bushehri, the Celebrations Council vice-chairman, presented a report to the shah, estimating an initial cost of 250 million rials (approximately $3.5 million), which was to be borrowed from the government. The loan did not materialize. A few days later Prime Minister Manuchehr Eqbal, with whom the loan had been negotiated, resigned; his successor, Ja'far Sharif-Emami, faced new elections and financial shortages; and by the time Ali Amini was appointed prime minister in 1961, the government had been declared nearly bankrupt. On 7 January 1962 Court Minister Hossein Ala wrote Amini that the shah had agreed that the government's financial condition forced a delay in the Celebrations, provided the government forwarded to the Celebrations Committee half of the required loan in the winter of 1962 and the other half in the winter of 1963. This also came to naught; under Alam's premiership the Celebrations were once again put off, this time until the fall of 1967.[2] By that year Hossein Ala had passed away, Amir Abbas Hoveyda was prime minister, Alam was minister of court—and the work of the Celebrations Council still was not moving forward.[3]

The shah seldom talked about the Celebrations, but when he did, he complained, mostly to Alam, about the slow pace and lack of initiative and demanded something be done to get it going. In the meantime, planning for the Celebrations slowly underwent a metamorphosis. Initially, the activities as contemplated by Shafa were to be mainly cultural, designed to present to both Iranians and the world the meaning and contribution of Iranian culture, especially Iran's pre-Islamic civilization as reflected in its imperial heritage. There was not much money available, and consequently the intellectual and political designs were bounded by that scarcity. Shafa had made several trips abroad and consulted with major Iranologists around the world. By 1970, he had received enough negative reports from committee members in Europe and elsewhere to write a memo complaining to Alam, who, because Senator Bushehri was now chronically ill, had basically taken over the program. Shafa identified himself as the originator of the idea and faulted the Celebrations Council for failing to provide appropriate leadership and guidance. He suggested that the authority for the international aspects of the program be transferred to the Imperial Cultural Council, which he supervised.[4]

The planning for the programs inside Iran also continued to advance only slowly. A decision had been made to begin the program in Persepolis and end it in Tehran. Alam's deputy for internal affairs, Amir Mottaqi, had argued that the hotel that was to be built in Persepolis would not handle the heads of state and their entourages and suggested that several tents be set up on the site to accommodate the guests. The suggestion was taken to the shah, but he dismissed it as surrealist and impractical. In July 1970, Mottaqi wrote a formal letter to Alam proposing that the program be carried out in Tehran because the facilities in

Persepolis and Shiraz were simply not adequate to the task. There would most likely be more heads of state than the thirty projected, he said. A hotel that was scheduled to be finished just a month before the festivities began might not in fact be completed on time and even if it was, it would most likely be full of problems, as all new buildings are. The attendants would not have enough time to become acquainted with the hotel's internal structure and geography. The outside landscaping would probably leave much to be desired. If the number of top guests exceeded thirty, there simply would be no room for all of them in the same hotel. If it did not, still the inadequacies in the size and structure of the hotel would present all kinds of protocol headaches. And, he said, this was too grand and important an affair for Iran's history and kingship not to be done in the best manner possible.[5]

In 1970 Abdorreza Ansari was Princess Ashraf's deputy for economic, social, and cultural affairs. Ansari had had a successful public career beginning at the Point IV program and becoming successively treasurer general, minister of labor, managing director of the Khuzistan Water and Power Authority, governor of Khuzistan, and finally minister of the interior. In 1968 he had been dismissed from the ministry for a principled position he had taken, about which there were many rumors but not much fact. He had then been asked by the princess to help her as her deputy, a position he had accepted.

Sometime in late October 1970, the princess asked Ansari if he was familiar with the Anniversary Celebrations. He had heard about them when he was serving in Khuzistan, but neither he nor his deputies had given the matter much thought. He was aware of a council headed by Bushehri, but that was the extent of his knowledge. She said the shah wanted a decision about the proposed Anniversary Celebrations—ten years had passed since the idea was first broached, and the time had come either to set a date and get on with it or, if the idea was no longer feasible, to abandon the plan. Javad Bushehri had been ill for some time and was out of the country, and Mehdi Bushehri, the princess's husband, who was slated to head the council, would be traveling abroad a good part of the time. Thus, said the princess, she would like to ask Ansari to take over as Mehdi's deputy, at least until Court Minister Alam returned from his European trip and a final decision was made.

When Ansari met with Alam before his departure, he was told the same: the shah definitely wanted a decision and wished to know as soon as possible if the Celebrations were to take place and if so, exactly when and where. Ansari got the impression that no firm decision had yet been made. A few days later, however, Alam told him the shah had decided that the Celebrations would indeed take place and the date would be the 23rd of Mehr the following year (15 October 1971), when the weather was likely to be just right. He wanted to know what was to be done. "This is not something that the present council, as established, can do by itself," Ansari answered. "This is a national affair requiring the participation of all national organizations. You should play a leading role, and if possible those responsible should meet intermittently with His Majesty."[6] Alam agreed. He would be involved in his capacity as minister of court and would see to it that others actively participated. He would ask the queen to be the honorary chair of a new Celebrations Council to be established for the purpose and to be composed of nine members under Alam's chairmanship. The council would meet every two weeks, and its work would be performed independently of the government.[7]

The initial projection assumed that no more than thirty countries, mainly monarchies, would attend. Council members thought socialist countries would not participate and doubted that nonsocialist republics would. The initial program foresaw a two-day event in Persepolis, including a day of parades representing the historical evolution of Iran and the monarchy, a light and sound program, and two dinners. Traditional festive programs were to take place in other Iranian cities. Development projects were to be speeded up to finish, when and where possible, by the Celebrations date.

In the meantime, Alam made his trip to Europe and was gone for some time. Once back in Tehran, he told the council that he was troubled by the thought of receiving, lodging, and feeding the heads of state coming to Iran. "We have nothing in Takht-e Jamshid [Persepolis] and no appropriate hotels in Shiraz." He had consulted with his staff and concluded that the only remedy was to import thirty prefabricated apartments to be placed near Takht-e Jamshid. Plastic covers placed on them would give them the sense of a tent. "It replicates our kings' historically setting up tents on their travels in the desert and conforms to our nomadic traditions," he observed.[8] He had talked about the idea with Jansen of Paris, who had done work in Iran, and they were prepared to undertake and finish the job on time, provided the Iranian government transported the furniture to Iran by air. Using Iranian chefs was also dangerous, said Alam, because they had no experience with serving appropriate food to so many heads of state, and it would be disastrous for Iran if anyone became ill. He had talked with Maxim's, the well-known and highly experienced culinary establishment in Paris, and Maxim's proprietor had said he would be honored if given the responsibility and if commissioned would render the service at the lowest possible cost because it would also be great publicity for his business.

The Anniversary Celebrations, said Alam, reflected the blossoming of the Iranian economy. Therefore, it was only natural that those who had gained most by Iran's economic development should share in its cost. Iranian industrialists and entrepreneurs, he said, had announced that they would gladly share the expenses and that they were ready and willing to support the celebrations in any way they could. Thus, the expenses of the Anniversary Celebrations would not have to be defrayed by the government. Alam would supervise this private-sector participation and would see to it that everything moved smoothly. The council took up the matter in the presence of the queen and approved its broad outlines after a long debate about food and lodging.

Money turned out not to be as much of an issue as feared. The original council, headed by Senator Bushehri, had existed now for approximately ten years. Each year the government had allocated it a small budget, which Bushehri had put in an interest-bearing account, using part of the income to defray salaries and other expenses the council incurred. By the time Ansari was recruited, this reserve had reached about 450 million rials (approximately $6 million). The money was allocated to building the Shahyad Monument in Tehran, organizing the light and sound project in Takht-e Jamshid, and reimbursing Sangway Publishers for a book it was to prepare on the history of ancient Iran.

One of the major events of the Anniversary Celebrations was a proposed symposium of Iranologists to be convened in Iran at the time of the festivities. Shafa, charged with the project, traveled to Europe to consult European Iranologists. When he returned to Tehran, he asked to see Ansari on an urgent, disturbing matter. In Europe he had encountered several Iranians and non-Iranians who had objected strenuously to the idea of the tents by Jansen and the meals by Maxim's. They could not understand why the guests, celebrating Iran's history, would not accept Iranian lodging or Iranian food. Shafa said he had heard of "irregularities" and did not know whom else to talk to. They agreed to bring up the matter in the next council meeting in the presence of the queen.

As Shafa talked about the matter in the next meeting, Alam became agitated, his face turning white, his demeanor increasingly bitter and angry. He told the queen that what Shafa said pointed only to him. "I have made the decisions and followed them up. These are my responsibilities. If, for any reason, my integrity is in doubt, I will now offer my resignation from this council and from the ministry of court." Then, visibly shaken, he left the room. The queen, placed in an awkward situation, adjourned the meeting, leaving members uncertain about the future of the council and of the Anniversary. Alam, however, went straight to the shah, who managed to calm him down. He did not resign, and the council continued its work with no change of plans.[9]

The shah received regular progress reports from Alam and the queen. He told Alam that as far as he could see, a part of the work was being done by the government and a part by the council. What, he asked, was the people's contribution to the project? Alam posed the question to the council. Ansari suggested building twenty-five hundred new schools in the villages across the country to correspond to the twenty-five-hundredth anniversary of the founding of the Persian Empire. The council was to declare that in each area individuals willing to participate in the building of the school might contribute to a local account set up for that purpose. There was to be no pressure; it would be a testimony to the people's commitment to the cultural development of their towns and villages. There were questions about the proposal's feasibility, given the extent of responsibility each member had and the short time remaining before the guests were to arrive. Ansari, however, explained that he had done this on a smaller scale in Khuzistan and assured the council that if they approved the project, he would see to it that it was done on time and properly.

The plan for a four-grade school was quickly designed. The cost for each school was estimated at 300,000 rials (approximately $4,000). Rural areas where schools were needed were quickly determined by the Ministry of Education. The plans were then sent to local functionaries, accounts were opened, and it was announced through radio, television, and the press that contributions would be accepted from interested individuals. Money was to be deposited in the school's account, and the school was to be named as the contributors directed. The project was well received, though a few individuals were unhappy because the school they had contributed to could not be erected on the spot they wanted. Altogether, however, in most places participation went beyond monetary contribution; people helped with the actual work of building. On the day the Celebrations began, 15 October 1971, 3,200 schools had been built, and an education corps person was present and ready to teach. According to the Ministry of Education's statistics, on that day 120,000 new students began studying in these schools.[10]

As news of the Celebrations spread around the world and the names of participating heads of state became known, more countries expressed interest, especially among the African states. Originally fifty tents had been ordered, thirty for the guests and twenty for the Iranian royal family and dignitaries. In the end, sixty-nine heads of state wished to be present, creating a huge problem of protocol and priority. In August, Hormoz Qarib, the imperial court's protocol chief, asked Ambassador Peter Ramsbotham of Britain informally and confidentially about the British system of assigning precedence, following a general consensus that the British were best in these matters. Ramsbotham, disavowing any "responsibility in a matter which it is only proper for the

Iranian Government to decide," nonetheless gave Qarib certain general principles identified by the British protocol department: "Monarchs who are Heads of States take precedence according to the length of time that they have been on the throne. A similar rule applies to the Presidents of Republics. Similarly, the order of precedence of Crown Princes depends on the length of time that they have been heirs to the throne, which may be from birth or at a later date. Presidents, being Heads of State, take precedence after Monarchs, but before Consorts and Crown Princes." The problem, however, was not as simple as it sounded. Ramsbotham informed Qarib that Prince Philip, the Duke of Edinburgh, took precedence over Prince Charles. "Although he is not officially called 'the Consort,' Prince Philip is in fact the Consort. Assuming, therefore, that Prince Bernhardt of the Netherlands has been Prince Consort longer than Prince Philip, the former takes precedence over the latter. They both, of course, take precedence over the Crown Prince of Sweden."[11] And, of course, there were also prime ministers and ministers of foreign affairs and others whose precedence had to be determined.

Two months before the Celebrations, Alam invited Prime Minister Hoveyda and the council of ministers to the meeting of the Celebrations Council. Ansari had kept Hoveyda abreast of what was being done, though the government was not directly involved. This meeting formally put the government in the picture, and Hoveyda, approving of what had been done, asked his ministers to lend their utmost support to the success of the undertaking. Thus, during the last two months before the Celebrations, the ministers regularly informed the council of any programs their ministries were pursuing to promote the Anniversary. In one of the meetings, Alam said that it had been put to him that since Iran was celebrating the twenty-five-hundredth anniversary of its monarchy, it was proper to have the beginning of the history of kingship as the base of Iran's calendar. This was a surprise that would turn into a problem difficult to tackle politically and culturally, but most individuals present, having no idea of the proposal's political ramifications, received it rather enthusiastically—except Ansari, who had a history to fall back on.

When he had been minister of the interior in 1967, his director of legal affairs at the ministry, a man named Mohammad Farahmand, had given him a written statement arguing that the calendar Iranians used was an Arab calendar and thus a disgrace; Iranians, he insisted, should have their own. The most appropriate event to be designated as the beginning of a truly Iranian calendar was the ascent of Cyrus the Great to the Iranian throne. The world would understand and applaud the choice because Cyrus was not only a great king but also the first king to bring forth a concept of human rights. Ansari was not familiar with the idea; he did not have anything in particular against it, but he did not feel comfortable with it. "We had too many problems and worries as it was. Why would we want to add another?" he thought. Farahmand was insistent, and Ansari promised to discuss his project with Prime Minister Hoveyda. Hoveyda, however, dismissed the proposition as irrelevant and odious. "We have more problems than we can handle," he said. "It is not at all a good thing to bring up something like this. Make it go away."[12] Ansari told Farahmand that the time was not right for such an idea and that he should attend to his responsibilities in the ministry.

Hoveyda had understood well the turmoil such a proposition would generate. When Alam put the idea of changing the calendar on the table, however, Ansari did not object. "I thought I was one against many, and my opposition to the idea would not change anything. Maybe I was afraid. I don't know. At any rate, I said nothing."[13] The council approved the suggestion, and Alam reported it to the shah. No doubt the excitement of the time also encouraged the council members to agree to a matter of such import without much reflection, especially since the proposal would need to be approved by the government. Whatever the reason, the decision became a cause célèbre, playing an important part in the fall of the monarchy less than a decade later.

The Twenty-Five-Hundredth Anniversary Celebrations of the Iranian Monarchy were carried out seemingly with great success. Much of the event was directly televised in Iran and around the world, and its outward show inspired awe. The officer who reported to the arriving heads of state and led them in the review of the honor guard was superb. The shah's speech at the grave of Cyrus, assuring the memory of the great king that he could sleep in peace because the shah and the Iranians were awake, was moving. His leading so many important heads of state through the various functions in the celebrations was emblematic of the change that had occurred over the years in his personal stature and, just as important, in the stature of his country. The Parade of History, the work of two brothers, Fatollah Minbashian and Mehrdad Pahlbod, the one a general and commander of the ground forces, the other an artist and minister of culture, was uplifting. The sound and light presentation of the story of the Achemenid kings told in the ruins of the lofty palaces built by the great king Darius could not but elicit admiration. Everything seemed to come together nicely. Everyone had worked as hard and as heartily as possible. Public and private institutions came together to make the affair a success. The queen and other members of the royal family, even the children, did their share of physical labor, moving tables and furniture to get everything prepared in time.[14] And the shah was pleased. The setting and the honors his peers accorded him validated what he considered his rightful place among them. The fact that he had been seen on television and movie screens around the world as he led sixty-nine heads and near heads of state in so many different functions was not to be taken lightly. He was pleased and showed his pleasure by acknowledging and thanking everyone according to his or her rank with promotions, medals, and pecuniary rewards.

The event, however, did much damage to the shah and the regime. The Celebrations were ill-conceived, not because the time was not ripe for extolling Iran's history or monarchy but rather because they became too foreign dominated, both politically and culturally. Instead of bringing the shah and the people together, it gave ammunition to the shah's enemies to separate him from the people. Alam may have been honest in his fears of botching the reception, given, as he put it, "the singularity of the occasion." But he and other participants were remiss in not recognizing the contrary effect the foreign tinge would have on the whole occasion. Shafa had the right instinct, making a case out of what he had heard, or possibly feigned to have heard, from the Iranologists in Europe. Why should the world not feel honored being served the fruits of the Iranian culture when it was honoring the Iranian culture?

The harshest attacks on the Celebration events were issued by the Islamists, especially the Ayatollah Khomeini. In his statements, subsequently picked up by the shah's other critics, the Celebrations were anti-Islamic and those who participated in them were enemies of Islam. The Celebrations were to be disparaged for the "exorbitant expenditure" that otherwise could have been spent to improve the lives of children who "were taken to the pastures to be fed." The treacherous system robbed the Iranian people to feed its decadent debaucheries, said Khomeini. But the real sin was that it extolled the kings rather than the Prophet, the imams, and the ulama. "Let the world know that these festivities have nothing to do with the noble people of Iran, and that those who organized and participated in them have committed treason against Islam and the people of Iran."[15]

The left attacked the regime with equal vigor. The Confederation of Iranian Students in Europe considered the exposing of the regime's sins on the Celebrations the apogee of its struggle. "The shah's regime spent an enormous amount of money to organize the festivities," said Manuchehr Hezarkhani, a Confederation leader, "and a great deal of energy to advertise the occasion and to attract the world leaders to Iran. In truth, the propaganda battle the Confederation waged against the regime was one of the brightest moments of its struggle. In most countries, the Confederation set out to bring to the attention of the leaders and the people the shah's crimes, Iran's poverty, the wide chasm separating economic classes, and the regime's militarism. It disgraced the regime and its propaganda carnival through extensive contact and communication with not only European and American politicians and statesmen but also literary, cultural, and political circles."[16]

The Western press picked up on this criticism and bloated it beyond recognition. The issue of Jansen and Maxim's was extended to other parts of the ceremony—the shah's moving speech at the tomb of Cyrus, the superb parade, the sound and light show, and the dinners. Glitter, appropriate to celebrations, became gaudiness, inappropriate to all things.

William Shawcross, presumably a friend but quintessentially British, wrote only of "the party": top hairdressers coming flying in from "the Paris salons of Carita and Alexandre," Elizabeth Arden creating a make-up named Farah "to be given in kits to the guests," Baccarat designing the goblets, Maxim's preparing food "aided by other leading French chefs and caterers," and a host of other bad things, including the Iranian history, or its representation, for which soldiers were "forbidden to shave for the last month so that their faces would more nearly represent those of warriors of old." The cost, Shawcross divined, was anything up to $300 million. This was a Cecil B. DeMille production, a Technicolor epic "projected onto the screen of the vast plain," as Shawcross approvingly quotes an Iranian ambassador. More ominously, he points out, "by celebrating the Iran of Cyrus and Darius, the Shah completely and deliberately ignored a part of Iran's history that was far more relevant to the twentieth century A.D.—the teachings of the prophet Mohammad."[17]

Marvin Zonis qualified the Celebrations as "Pahlavi Grandiosity" and the shah as *nouveau arrivé*. "For the Iranian people," he wrote after the revolution, transforming an event of the moment to a historical prophecy, "the institution of monarchy in Iran was not significant." Suddenly, an ayatollah's criticism of land reform assumed grand moral clarity and the shah's "tentative steps" to land reform became purely "material," and thus "offensive to the deeper moral sensibility at the bedrock of Iranian culture." If the shah offered financial assistance to other nations, this was also a sign of his moral limitations, seeing the world in the same material frame in which he saw his own country. And if he said, "I have known the most dark hours when *our country* was obliged to pass under the tutelage of foreign powers, among them England, [and] now I find that England has not only become *our* friend, *our* equal, but also the nation to which, should *we* be able, *we* will render assistance with pleasure," according to this view "no mention was ever made of Iran." The shah's narcissism had no bounds; it "was expansive to the point of grandiosity."[18]

These accounts — echoed by innumerable others — find nothing praiseworthy in the Celebrations. Indiscriminate objections were hurled, the kind always available to the demagogue — money spent on festivities when so many people are poor and hungry. Alam declared the cost of the festivities to be $16.8 million.[19] Ansari estimated the cost at 1.6 billion rials, about $22 million. According to Ansari, "One third of the money was raised by Iranian industrialists to pay for all the festivities. Another third was from the budget of the Ministry of Court and went to pay for the Tent City. The rest of the money came from the original budget under Senator Amir Homayoun Bushehri, which he had invested in 1960, and was spent on the building of the Shahyad Monument. The remaining funds [left over after the Celebrations], amounting to $1.6 million were by order of HIM [His Imperial Majesty] allocated towards the ongoing construction of a mosque in Qom, which on completion was to be named after the late Ayatollah Borujerdi, in his time the most prominent shi'a leader in the world."[20]

There is nothing in the accounts the shah's detractors give of the Celebrations about the roads and airports, communications networks, tourist resorts and hotels, schools, health clinics, and other facilities of social and economic worth built in Shiraz and across the country. More important, there is no mention of the hundreds of committees of Iranologists established across the globe to collect work of value on Iran's history or to identify Iran's influence on the evolution of culture in other countries. Even less is there of the effect of the Celebrations on the development of new capacity in Iran for transferring the study of Iranian history from Europe to Iran, including the establishment of the Pahlavi Library, an Iran-UNESCO project chaired by the shah and slated to become one of the grandest specialized libraries in the world. The library, in which, according to Queen Farah, "the shah showed intense interest,"[21] was to become home to the collection of Iranian studies undertaken around the world over the past two hundred years and a center for future studies about Iranian history and culture. An important component of the Celebrations was the articles prepared by the foremost Iranologists of the world on the occasion of the anniversary of the establishment of Iran's monarchy by Cyrus the Great and published in more than a hundred books and brochures in Germany, France, the United Kingdom, the Soviet Union, Italy, Spain, Austria, Portugal, Sweden, Norway, Denmark, Finland, Romania, Hungary, Czechoslovakia, Bulgaria, Yugoslavia, Greece,

Japan, India, Pakistan, Turkey, Egypt, Tunisia, Morocco, the United States, Canada, and New Zealand. These publications were collected and archived in the library, as were the many other special publications on the influence of Iran's culture on specific countries around the world.[22]

Early in the winter of 1967 Queen Farah discussed with her cousin Reza Qotbi, recently appointed head of the National Radio and Television (NIRT), the idea of an art festival, the kind she had seen in places like Nancy, Aix-en-Provence, or Royan when she was a student in France. She had talked about the idea with the shah, who had left the decision up to her, somewhat indifferently. The queen, however, thought having an art festival a capital idea and talked about it with considerable excitement. A committee under her patronage was formed, headed by Qotbi and managed by Farrokh Ghaffari, Qotbi's deputy for culture at NIRT. It was a foregone conclusion that the festival would not be in Tehran, since, as a matter of general policy the government preferred to take as many activities as possible to the provinces. Several cities, including Kashan and Isfahan, were considered, but the choice fell on Shiraz because, according to the queen, it was close to Persepolis and the desert and it was also the city of Saadi (1213–91) and Hafiz (1324–89), "the two favorite poets of the Iranian people," whose tombs were also there. "We could already imagine what the theatre people could do with that."[23]

Actually, Persepolis was problematic as a site. Several members of the committee, including Ghaffari, were apprehensive about possible damage to the invaluable ruins. The place, however, was majestic and certainly, as the queen had said, enticing to artists, especially thespians. And Shiraz had a first-class university and other facilities that made it perfect among Iranian cities for the purpose. As for the ruins, it was agreed that maximum care would be taken to protect them.

A more immediate question about the festival concerned the organization responsible for its execution: Why NIRT and not the Ministry of Culture, where, by law, the responsibility for the preservation and development of culture lay? The queen, of course, was closer to her cousin, Reza Qotbi, and more at ease dealing with him. On the other hand, the minister of culture, Mehrdad Pahlbod, who was married to the shah's older sister Shams, could have put up a fight. He did not, partly because the idea of a festival was sudden and as yet undefined and partly because Pahlbod was not into "newfangled" modern art. He would later express his opinion of such art in a critique of the shah's concept of the

"Great Civilization." "We had some people who returned from Europe and wanted to have and do exactly what they had had and done in Europe," Pahlbod recalled. "We could provide this only under the 'Great Civilization.' Until then, we needed teachers. Under Reza Shah a college of fine arts was established. They trained artists. This, in my judgment, was a mistake. They should have trained teachers. We had individuals who wanted to do Cubism. Why should we use government money to help Cubist artists?"[24]

Pahlbod's ministry was also not sufficiently motivated to assert a claim, whereas NIRT was a new organization, populated by new blood and led by a young, dedicated, and charismatic director eager to move. According to Ghaffari, Qotbi moved so fast that by the time the culture people realized what was happening, the basic structures had been laid.[25] This was the norm in Iran in the 1960s and 1970s. Much of the progress occurred because eager individuals picked certain causes and ran with them till they were absorbed by the regime in a combination of osmosis and natural selection. There were, of course, people who were given positions because of their proximity to power. But unless they possessed sufficient ability, motivation, and know-how, they usually failed to compete and consequently fell by the wayside. Qotbi was a supreme example of the eager and successful go-getter. Under his leadership NIRT expanded in all directions, exceeding the energies of his first deputy, Farrokh Ghaffari, who asked to be reassigned as deputy for culture. This made him the point man for the Shiraz Art Festival.

Like most other events of this sort, the Shiraz Art Festival developed a character of its own over its short life. The program for the first year, 1967, was haphazard and mainly European, despite the presentation of an inspired Iranian play by Bijan Mofid, *Shahr-e qesseh* (City of Fables), and the Persian classical music performed at the tomb of Hafiz. The patrons, in Ghaffari's words, "were too elegant."[26] The programs, the intellectual climate, and the mood changed during the next years to include modern Iranian theater, religious-traditional theater (especially the form called *ta'zieh*), Western theater, including Western classical theater, Iranian music, international traditional music, ballet, traditional dance, Western dance, and films of all sorts, among others. The clientele also changed. The programs provided a unique opportunity for Iranians, especially youth, to learn about the art forms of other countries, in particular, countries beyond Europe and North America. For the first time, the Iranian public, especially artists and literary groups, saw what until then they had only heard about: Kabuki, No theater, traditional and modern music of countries such as Malaysia, Indonesia, China, and Vietnam, and India's dances and music and theater, including the Katakali, with its magical movements, signs, and sounds, from which so many other musicians, playwrights, and choreographers had received inspiration. Two of those so inspired, Peter Brook and Jerzy Grotowski, put on performances in Shiraz. Brook directed *Orghast at Persepolis,* by Ted Hughes, in 1971 in Naqsh-e Rostam, the tomb of Cyrus. In 1972 Robert Wilson, described by the *New York Times* as "a towering figure in the world of experimental theatre and an explorer in the use of time and space,"[27] put on *Ka Mountain,* a production that extended along the slope of a hill and lasted some 168 hours without interruption. In 1974 in Takht-e Jamshid, Maurice Béjart created and directed a special ballet named *Golestan,* after the poet Saadi's masterpiece, using the traditional music of Baluchistan. This was one of the rare productions the shah attended.

More important was the opportunity for Iranian artists to present their work next to the work of the best in the world. They did this with gusto, and in many cases their creativity excited interest and admiration. Arbi Ovanessian's recasting of Camus' *Caligula* to a purely oriental frame competed favorably with some of the best drama in the world, including a Japanese production directed by Terayama that mixed Kabuki and Nogaku, two modes of Japanese traditional theater. As noted, Mofid's *Shahr-e qesseh,* one of the most successful Iranian theatrical productions ever, was first shown at the Shiraz Festival. Other writers and directors—among them Manuchehr Yektai, Parviz Sayyad, Bahram Beizai, Ali Nassirian, Mahin Tajaddod, and Ashur Banipal Babella—presented significant works that later were taken to other countries. Especially interesting and innovative was the presentation of *ta'zieh,* which Peter Brook called the highest form of theater. In 1976, for the first time in history a group of scholars from Turkey, France, Italy, Germany, and the United States joined Iranian scholars in Shiraz in an international forum to discuss *ta'zieh* as ritual and art form. The 1977 festival included a seven-act *ta'zieh* that played several nights in Hosseinieh Moshir in Shiraz and also in a village near the city; some seventy thousand viewers attended these performances.

The Shiraz Art Festival, one of its organizers said, brought art, particularly theater, out of closed quarters into the open air, allowing an organic relationship between music, lyrics, action, and setting. The directors chose their spaces as they saw fit and created a harmony between art and nature. According to the authorities, in its last several years some seventy thousand people paid money to attend the festival.[28] Most of the patrons were students who attended because they were interested in the arts and could see all programs at each festival on a ticket costing approximately $20. Some programs were free, and most of the rest were considered easily affordable for those likely to be interested in what was presented. Many entry permits were issued gratis. Farrokh Ghaffari believed that the Shiraz Art Festival was unique for its time.

> No festival has done what the Shiraz Art Festival did during its lifetime. The 12 to 15 days of the Shiraz created an exceptional cultural and human environment for the artists to learn of each other's accomplishments, to establish contact and friendship with each other and with their public. The Festival brought together the performing arts of the nations possessing ancient cultures with those of Europe and North America. Sometimes the two were combined as in the works of Peter Brook and Maurice Béjart. The Shiraz Art Festival was the only one of its kind that offered these two opportunities. A third contribution of the Festival was that it helped the third world artists overcome their complexes vis-à-vis western art. Conversely, it brought the western artists face to face with the extraordinary works created by non-western traditional as well as modern artists.[29]

Most of the people who attended the festival appreciated the effort. Many who condemned the festival did so without ever seeing it. Those who attended and yet disparaged it as artistically wanting were mostly the few who had either been invited for their official position or had paid to attend because it was the chic thing to do. The Shiraz Festival was also attacked for its high cost and elitist exclusivity. Neither charge is persuasive. The cost for the festival was reimbursed partly by the sale of tickets and mostly by NIRT, which in return recorded and showed the programs it wanted on its radio and television network throughout the year. Thus, everyone who had access to radio and TV could see the programs. Some of the cost was for buying material and for building infrastructure that remained for future use. The sites built in Takht-e Jamshid and Naqsh-e Rostam, for example, are still being used for a variety of private and public functions. And most of the patrons, as already mentioned, were students.

On the other hand, some programs in Shiraz were too modern and cutting edge even for the arts aficionado in Iran or elsewhere. In 1977, the last year of the Festival, *Pig, Child, Fire* was staged by a Hungarian troupe originally from Budapest but in exile since 1976, first in Western Europe and subsequently in the United States. In 1977, the troupe, calling itself the Squat because it had squatted in Rotterdam after leaving Budapest, produced the play and staged it in France, England, and Holland. The Squat then moved to the United States, debuting the play in Baltimore and subsequently moving to New York's West Twenty-Third Street, where the troupe then made its home. *Pig, Child, Fire* won an Obie Award, making the Squat an important part of New York's avant-garde theater. Don Shirley of the *Washington Post* described the play after the Baltimore showing:

> The incredible "Pig, Child, Fire!" uses words, but most of them were written by Dostoyevsky and Antonin Artaud and never intended to serve as a script. . . . It's difficult to describe these events without sounding like a gibbering fool; let's just say they utilize a goat, masks, flour, a giant puppet, a noose, a knife sharpener, a dinner, an automobile, three TV screens, broken glass and several more unmentionable items. Plus the devilishly witty actors from the Squat Theater who thought all this up. The piece is in four acts, largely unrelated, and the second, "Nous Sommes Les Mannequins," is clearly the highlight of the show — an unendingly surprising "film noir" that occurs on two stages and videotape rather than film and combines comedy and suspense with the flair of a Hitchcock.[30]

Ghaffari's exegesis of the play, which he first saw in Paris and thought suitable for the festival, is as symbolic rape, specifically the rape of Hungary by Russia. Briefly, "a soldier wearing a Soviet-type uniform enters a town, where the Soviet military commander has ordered all male children to be killed. A woman dresses her son up as a girl to save him from being murdered. The soldier realizes that the child is a boy and signals the woman he is wise to her stratagem and to keep her secret she will have to submit to his will. To assert his will, he takes the woman violently in his arms. There is no nudity in the Iranian version and no exceptionally lewd movements."[31]

The play was staged in a storehouse by a street, with room for approximately a hundred viewers to sit inside. The last scene, where the soldier drags the woman into his arms, took place close to the door and moved partly to the street, where several passersby standing at the front rows on the street also saw it. The play was shown three or four nights. To protect the players and keep the street safe, on the later showings several police officers in plainclothes and their families populated the street so that, according to Ghaffari, not very many ordinary people could see the play. Ghaffari estimates the number of the people who saw the play at 300–350.[32] Qotbi estimated the number was probably higher, but not by much. The play was discontinued because a respected ayatollah in Shiraz called to complain about the lewd acts reported to him. When it was explained to him that there was no nudity in the play, he nevertheless suggested that the intimation of the act, even if rape and not sexual pleasure was meant, harmed the public.[33]

Pig, Child, Fire became yet another cause célèbre, picked up by the shah's foes. The clerics and the left portrayed it as an act of nude copulation performed in the street, witnessed by thousands if not millions of innocent men, women, and children. Others in Iran and abroad mimicked what they heard and repeated the same. It was touted as more evidence of the regime's depravity and natural urge to corruption. The play had its detractors in Europe and the United States as well, who criticized it as tasteless and artistically corrupt. But these came mainly after the showing in Iran. Mel Gussow of the *New York Times,* for example, called it "reprehensible," derived from "the Theatre of Cruelty," its movements "violent, lewd, and tasteless," more "revolting than revolutionary."[34] Clearly the Squat adjusted its presentation to the environment. The New York showing was undoubtedly more daring than the presentations in Baltimore or Shiraz. However, as a French-educated sociologist told Qotbi after seeing the play, the Shiraz version was also "vraiment osé"—truly audacious.[35] In hindsight, it would have been politically wise not to have shown it.

Whatever the case, the shah had no real idea of this or any other program performed at the festival and certainly not of any nudity. Semi-nude dances had been performed in a Senegalese ballet and in Maurice Bejart's second ballet, where several women appeared with their breasts showing. According to Ghaffari, "no one protested,"[36] probably because in the earlier years, before the advent of Carter in the United States and what would be called the opening of political space in Iran, there was neither much meaning nor any political profit in such moralistic protesting.

Pig, Child, Fire was unique; other cutting-edge programs were simply avant-garde. Iannis Xenakis, famous for pioneering electronic and computer music and for the use of stochastic mathematical techniques, game theory, and Boolean algebra in his compositions, performed at the festival annually beginning in 1968 and in 1971 premiered *Persepolis* at the ruins of the palace of the Achemenid kings at Takht-e Jamshid. The work was declared "a landmark in the evolution of one of the most speculative and general philosophies of our time, especially by its annexation of vast acoustic and visual spaces and by placing living human presence within a mechanism that is dominated by musical logic."[37]

Xenakis continued his association with the festival for several years. He fell in love with the setting—the mountains, the desert, and the ruins, as the queen had foretold—and was even more excited than others because of his Greek heritage. A great postmodern composer like Xenakis, however, had to be rescued by the shah's opponents from the sin of associating with the dictator shah. Asphodel, an international online music company headquartered in San Francisco, extolling Xenakis and his work *Persepolis* more than a quarter century after the work was performed in Shiraz nevertheless found it necessary to apologize on behalf of Xenakis for having composed the piece and performed it under "Iranian dictator Muhammad Reza Shah," who, according to Asphodel, commissioned Xenakis to write a piece of music exalting "ancient

Persia's aristocratic pre-Islamic religious culture." *Persepolis* was performed in the same year, though not at the same time as or in relation to the Anniversary Celebrations. Nonetheless, according to Asphodel, "Selecting Xenakis to author such a work could not have been more symbolically appropriate. A central figure in the development of computer composition, this half-blind former architect, WWII resistance fighter and associate of Le Corbusier evolved a new approach to music, most notably one that employed mathematical probability functions as a compositional methodology." Why computer composition, mathematics, and association with Le Corbusier were especially relevant to the celebration of "aristocratic pre-Islamic religious culture" remains a mystery. However, Asphodel continues:

> Titled *Persepolis,* in honor of the location in which it was to be performed, Xenakis composed a fifty-six minute, eight-track tape piece of musique concrète for the occasion. A noisy, apocalyptic-sounding work distinguished by rising waves of intensity, *Persepolis'* debut must have been quite an experience for those lucky enough to be in attendance. *Persepolis* takes on an even greater significance when listened to as a musical work whose purpose was to serve a failed secularist ideology overtaken less than a decade later by a fundamentalist Islamic revolution.
>
> In light of the events that have consumed the world since September 11th, 2001, the notion that a radical composer would align himself with a political figure like the Shah shows how very few places such a brilliant artist could go to receive support for their work. Creative modernism is left with choosing between authoritarianism and religion.[38]

The shah probably had never heard of Xenakis before. He did not commission the work.[39] Nor did he attend his program in Persepolis. Had he attended, he probably would not have liked it—many who attended did not. The common people, unfamiliar with classical music, seemed to connect with cutting-edge modern music more easily than those initiated in the classics. After listening to Karlheinz Stockhausen in the same ruins, an Iranian violinist-composer wondered aloud how Beethoven's *Eroica* would have sounded if played over so many loudspeakers amplified in such a majestic site. He clearly preferred the classics but nonetheless appreciated listening to a postmodern electronic composition issuing, in this case, from the German school. To him Stockhausen was a bright star in the history of the festival, though not as luminous as Xenakis.

The festival also featured music genres that were mainstream, indigenous, and traditional. These, such as the Persian music and poetry played and recited at the tombs of Saadi and Hafiz, or traditional Iranian comedic shows, the so-called *Ru-howzi,* or, alternatively, the *ta'zieh,* were ignored by the shah's critics, whereas the postmodern works were singled out and criticized as too daring and at odds with the popular culture. The clerics were anti-art on religious grounds, the leftists on ideological grounds; the one attacked it as a signature of infidelity, the other disparaged it as bourgeois and anti-people. Still, it was not primarily the programs that led to attacks on the festival, the shah, or the regime; rather, the shah's foes seized on the festival as a means of attacking him and his regime. Xenakis was moved by the pleas of the Confederation of Iranian Students in Europe and the United States to write to the directors of the Shiraz Art Festival in 1976, after ten years of cooperation with them, that although he was dedicated to the festival he could no longer attend because of the repressive policies of the shah and his government against the youth of Iran.[40] He had his wife telephone on his behalf to assure the festival directors further that his heart was still with them, despite his inability to continue his work at Shiraz.[41] Ironically, 1976 was the year the regime adopted the policy of "open political space." The work of the confederation and its supporters, however, had by then borne fruit. It had become decidedly easier to attract artists from the Eastern and Iron Curtain countries than from Europe.

19

The Rastakhiz Party

In the early 1960s there were several attempts to organize young professionals for political activity, led by various political hopefuls, including Ali Amini and Jaʿfar Sharif-Emami, and largely inspired by the changing political climate in the United States. Of these only one, the Progressive Circle, survived. The circle was the work of Hassanali Mansur, an ambitious young man who was then secretary of the High Economic Council, and it provided the nucleus around which the Iran Novin party would form.

The Progressive Circle had played an important role both in organizing the Congress of Free Men and Women, where the shah had declared the principles of the White Revolution, and in the 1963 referendum whereby the principles had been approved. Mansur and several members of his group were then elected to the Twenty-First Majlis, where Mansur declared the formation of the Iran Novin Party on 16 December 1963, with himself as the leader and Amir Abbas Hoveyda, his friend and then a member of the NIOC board of directors, as deputy leader. Iran Novin quickly established itself as the majority party in the Majlis; the Mardom, led in the Majlis by Holaku Rambod, became the minority. In an unprecedented move, prompted by the shah's desire to bring a new and younger group of technocrats in, Mansur and several of his colleagues were invited to meet with Prime Minister Alam and several of his ministers in the presence of the shah to discuss the program and policies of a new government that would be formed under Mansur's leadership.[1] Alam could not be said to be happy about the turn of events, but he dealt with it in good humor.[2] On 7 March 1964, when the newly appointed Prime Minister Mansur presented his cabinet, the shah made a point of thanking Alam for his services in helping to bring about the White Revolution. The Mansur government's task, he then said, was to prepare the government and the people for making the revolution a success.[3]

As prime minister, Mansur was clever but not judicious. He was admired for gumption, drive, and self-assurance, but not for intellect or leadership. He also was not lucky. He inherited the decision on the "status of forces," granting legal immunities for American forces in Iran, which had been made by previous governments and which in the end proved his undoing. He was shot on 21 January 1965 and died on the 26th.

The shah knew that certain measures the government had taken, including the Status of Forces bill, were severely opposed by the clergy and others. But he had not expected assassinations, after almost ten years of relative political calm. As was his way in such circumstances, he fell into silence, which others respected by keeping silent also. In the hospital his fallen prime minister, sedated and half-comatose, tried to move his head, looking at the shah as if he recognized him. "This was a very painful moment for us," said Queen Farah, who had accompanied her husband to the hospital from Ab-e Ali, a ski resort near Tehran, as soon as they had heard the news. "I am certain that he recognized us and tried to pay his respects to His Majesty."[4] Soon it was clear that Mansur would not recover. On 26 January, the anniversary of the White Revolution, Mansur's friend and second in command, Amir Abbas Hoveyda, informed the shah of Mansur's death. On the 27th the shah appointed Hoveyda prime minister.

Hoveyda's appointment was initially regarded as temporary, honoring Mansur and providing the shah time to appoint a more experienced statesman. At first no one took Hoveyda seriously, although everyone who knew him thought him intellectually and temperamentally superior to Mansur. He was well read in history and philosophy, spoke Arabic and French perfectly, and English quite well, and he was self-effacing and outwardly humble. He had been devoted to Mansur, yet was also conscious of Mansur's defects, including a haughtiness that tended to drive people away. He told the shah he was not ready for the job, knowing the sovereign would assure him that with his help he would soon learn. He said the same to his colleagues, asking them for guidance. But when his friends told him the time had come for him to act as prime minister, he proved ready. "Well, the next day, much to everyone's surprise, he became a prime minister who manifestly knew the issues, what needed to be done, how to respond to his ministers and their problems, and how to manage the cabinet, in fact elevating the level of the government's work," observed his minister of economy, Alinaghi Alikhani.[5] The shah is reputed to have said that all his life as a king he had searched for a prime minister like Hoveyda. The temporary became permanent; Hoveyda remained in office for the next twelve and a half years, the longest-serving prime minister in Iran's constitutional history.

Hoveyda became a favorite of the imperial court. Queen Farah liked him: "I was involved with him more than with any other prime minister. I often had to ask for his cooperation and support. I felt we had an easy, friendly relation." He was received at royal family gatherings with warmth and affection. There were others as well who were close to the shah, Alam being one of them. To the queen, however, Hoveyda appeared "more honest, less devious." Alam spoke in parables, which to her seemed as if he did not want to commit himself outright. "But Hoveyda was straightforward, said what was in his mind." And he could converse about subjects that had universal import. Alam was knowledgeable about Iran, but not much more than Hoveyda. "Alam had a more profound knowledge of Iranian society—the tribes, clerics, politicians, and the people in general. Hoveyda also knew about these matters, but he was, perhaps, more of an intellectual as well as a better technocrat."[6] Hoveyda, for his part, was partial to the queen and went out of his way to keep her happy. The queen's responsibilities being mainly social or cultural, she rarely created a major problem for him. On the other hand, her good graces were essential to his smooth relations with the shah, especially in the later years when she had become a power in her own right. And Hoveyda, perhaps the most politically astute official of his time, was alive to the evolution that had occurred in her and her position over the years. By contrast, he did not much like the shah's twin sister, Princess Ashraf, though one could never tell by his behavior when he was with her. According to the princess's bureau chief, Reza Golsorkhi, their relationship "was extremely good. Hoveyda could charm a snake out of its hole. He was always gracious. On many occasions, for example private dinners at [the princess's lady-in-waiting and sometime sister-in-law] Minoo Dowlatshahi's where Hoveyda and Princess Ashraf often met in very small company, they had a great time. I never sensed any tension between them. I suppose Hoveyda was too masterful at the game to show tension even if it existed."[7] Most important, the shah was fond of him. "Hoveyda," said the queen, "had His Majesty's ear; the shah trusted him. They were comfortable with each other. There was team work. To him, Hoveyda was an interesting person. He knew his business. He was popular; people liked him and that was an asset, especially because he followed the shah, saw issues very much as he did, and he did not have any ambitions other than serving him as prime minister."[8]

These were important assets. Hoveyda came to power when the shah was transferring the management of the country from the old guard to a new generation of technocrats. Mansur was instrumental in bringing together a constituency of technocrats to take the helm of the government, but it is unlikely that had he lived, he could also have managed the political tensions the transfer produced. The technocrats were mainly Western-educated—a majority in America—politically inclined to democracy, but professionally committed and confined to the fields of their expertise. Most of them shunned politics despite their coming to power on the wings of the Iran Novin Party. However, the politics of the Iran Novin, as for politics generally at this time, was largely determined by another group, mostly reformed communists, who though protesting to be democrats were temperamentally totalitarian. The regime sought to expand its support base or, alternatively, to neutralize the opposition by co-opting any individual in any opposition group who appeared amenable to co-optation. Some members of the National Front, for example, were paid for no work at all or were helped to set up lucrative businesses; others in the opposition pursued their professions and succeeded, often with the help of the regime; and still others, of various political persuasions, were inducted into politics once they recanted their adversarial ideology. Among the latter category the rehabilitated communists were instrumental in giving shape to Iranian politics in the 1960s and 1970s, adapting totalitarian methods of governance to constitutional monarchy. After the demise of the Tudeh Party in the mid-1950s, they moved to the regime, placing their substantial political skills at its disposal. They made their way into the imperial court, higher bureaucracy, political parties, and the mass media. They set the style and tone of allegiance to the monarch, extolling obedience to the shah at the expense of the institutional constraints of the crown.[9] The effect was that gradually politics was sublimated on one end in eulogies of the shah and on the other end in "bureaupolitics"—professional bureaucrats fighting for turf and their respective points of view among themselves and before the monarch.

There would have been little communication and even less political commerce between the politician and the professional bureaucrat had it not been for Hoveyda's ability to relate to both and to maintain peace between them. Intelligent, erudite, cosmopolitan, self-effacing, and philosophically cynical, he was suited to the part. He was at once earnest and flippant, a good friend and a dangerous enemy, affable and on the lookout for competitors, open and enigmatic. Philosophically, he was a believer in absurdity, a world where men and women strove to extract meaning from the meaningless parts they were assigned to play, each for a price. For some the price was paid in money, status, position, or praise; for others, an opportunity to serve, to create, or to build; but all at the mercy of clever manipulation by fate, God, or other human beings. He would not deny that he too was a player on the same stage, a disarming quality that made him unique among Iranian politicians. His cynicism embraced himself as well as others, a major reason why he lasted as long as he did.[10] Others would have failed to keep the pace or the balance without either exceeding the mark or falling short; they would have failed to negotiate successfully the tensions entailed in maneuvering between the shah, their colleagues, and the public. Hoveyda's success was helped also by the fact that he was not encumbered by memories of high political office when the shah was not yet the near-absolute power he had become in 1965. He arrived when the shah was already the "Aryamehr," the light of the Arians, though not yet totally assimilated in the myth. He would help the process of assimilation by succeeding where others were likely to fail.

The Iran Novin ossified over the years as it became increasingly an adjunct of both the bureaucracy and the crown. Most organizations across the country became associated with the Iran Novin, most votes were cast for Iran Novin, and most ministers and their deputies and assistants were also Iran Novin members, though many of them never participated or voted in party affairs. The Mardom Party, the loyal opposition, was invariably stifled. Its function was to criticize the government, but the task was well-nigh impossible because the government had managed to maneuver itself out of responsibility. Prime Minister Hoveyda first accepted and then promoted the idea that policy was the shah's, development was the shah's, and consequently all the progress the nation made was the shah's. The monarch, he insisted, was the boss, the final arbiter, the supreme decision maker. Gradually, the shah became the leader of the governing team, a position manifestly unsuited to his office—both tradition and constitutional law designated him as the majesty of the state to whom all should be loyal, the symbol of the nation's identity, inviolate, inviolable, and beyond reproach. Under Hoveyda, Iran Novin became a rare device, in theory a party constituting the majority on which the government stood, in practice an adjunct of the crown and hence irreproachable. This was democracy stood on its head. Nonetheless, things moved on, and the shah moved from one victory to the next. By 1971, the year he celebrated the twenty-five-hundredth anniversary of the Iranian monarchy, the shah had achieved what no Iranian had achieved in recent memory. He was in a position to challenge the West and win. By 1975, the year of the Resurrection Party, the "Rastakhiz," he seemed invincible.

Things were not moving as smoothly as the shah imagined or had hoped, however. It was not that his grand projects were not working. He had already won on the economic front and on oil. Gas, petrochemicals, atomic energy, a naval base at Chah Bahar, railroad electrification, the communications network, and other mega-projects had begun and were being run effectively. The people were living far better than before: per capita income had grown significantly; inflation was under control, although it had risen disturbingly after the rise in oil prices; and the troubles he had had with the clerics and landlords now seemed only a memory. Iran's relations with neighboring countries had improved and with both the Soviet Union and China had become quite friendly despite the rivalry marring relations between the two communist giants. Nixon's political demise in the United States had been disconcerting, but in 1975 the shah felt President Gerald Ford's troubles actually gave him an advantage. He was in the best of relations with European countries, despite his ongoing criticisms of their leaders' policies. Awash in money, he had become a magnet attracting practically every government, businessman, politician, ex-king, or potentate from around the world. And he was magnanimous with the money, both within the country and without. It was difficult for him to see where trouble might lie. But he sensed it in the grumblings of his economists, though he dismissed them as nags, and in the attacks against him in Western media, though he dismissed them as oil company–instigated and pangs of repressed colonialism. He also sensed it in the complaints of his trusted friends, Alam and Adl and others, who seemed to be saying that his two-party system was not working, though he dismissed them as grievances born of envy.[11] And there was the increasingly leveled charge that he was a dictator, though he dismissed that as coming from individuals who forgot he was a king or did not realize that being a king made a difference. He would show those who doubted him that Iran was a democracy and that he, as king, was even-handed between the two parties.

On 27 May 1974, Prime Minister Hoveyda announced a change in his cabinet, introducing several new ministries and two super-ministers: Hushang Ansary as minister of economy and finance with supervision over the Ministry of Commerce and a newly established Ministry of Industry and Mines; and Jamshid Amouzegar, formerly minister of finance, as minister of the interior with supervision also over the State Organization for Administration and Employment (SOAE), which was charged with administrative reform. Ansary had had a meteoric rise in the government. He had begun his career in the private sector, working in Japan, where he made a fortune. He then returned to Iran, increased his fortune many times over, served as a deputy in the Tehran chamber of commerce and as ambassador to Pakistan, and joined the Hoveyda cabinet as minister of information in the summer of 1966. He was appointed ambassador to the United States in May 1967 and served till July 1969, when he was called back to take the helm at the Ministry of Economy. The shah believed he was a genius in financial matters, especially equity markets. Once at a dinner at Princess Ashraf's, he had observed that Ansary, though small in physique, was weighty in mind.[12] The observation had rendered Ansary practically untouchable.

Amouzegar was not happy with his new assignment as minister of the interior, though he was mollified once assured that he would continue as the shah's representative at the Organization of the Petroleum Exporting Countries (OPEC). The interior ministry was the repository of all the decisions made in other ministries but in fact had little to do other than conducting elections. In theory, the minister of the interior was responsible for law and order across the nation; however, that function had been practically taken away since the police and gendarmerie had become de facto adjuncts of the military, their commanders reporting directly to the shah. The ministry also acted in lieu of a council for cities and localities that lacked local councils. It was responsible for the general organization of the provinces and the appointment and dismissal of provincial governors, though for the major provinces this function also had devolved for all practical purposes on the shah. Amouzegar's major function at the ministry therefore was the coming national election, scheduled for 20 June 1975.

On 22 October 1974 Amouzegar presented to the monarch his deputy ministers, none of whom was drawn from the Ministry of the Interior and or had any experience in elections.[13] The shah made a point of telling them he was indifferent to which party won in the coming election. "They will tell you I prefer this man or that woman, this party or that party. This is false. What I want is a clean election." Now the first task of the group was to learn the nitty-gritty of managing elections. An opportunity was presented when the deputy from Shahsavar, a town by the Caspian, was appointed to the cabinet and consequently resigned his seat in the Majlis as the law required. Because the Majlis had passed beyond the halfway point of its term, an election was no longer mandatory, but Amouzegar and his deputies decided to use the occasion to gain some acquaintance with the electoral process.

The ensuing election in Shahsavar was not only instructive but surprising. Amouzegar's appointment to the Ministry of the Interior had had the tinge of a new political dispensation. Most people in the government and beyond thought him to be independent of Hoveyda, directly in contact with the shah, and Hoveyda's likely competitor. Placing him at the helm at the interior suggested something different was on the horizon, though the Shahsavar voters neither knew nor probably cared exactly what. His presence motivated the Mardom

Party and its secretary general Nasser Ameri to campaign seriously for the next general election, beginning in Shahsavar, a little town that was a microcosm of the nation. Almost all organized communities dispensing general services to the people were associated with the Iran Novin Party. The idea of a free election was difficult to impart, but once imparted it led to hectic activity, though no issue of any import to the people was involved. In the end, each party sent several of its leaders to campaign, realizing that the Iran Novin candidate might actually lose. Shahsavar exemplified the observation that all politics is local. Over 60 percent of the eligible voters participated simply because there was an election and they wished their side, the candidate they knew or had been wooed by, to win. At the end, the Iran Novin candidate did win, by about two hundred votes, 50.1 to 49.9 percent of the ballots, because it was still the better organized party.[14] In the previous election in Shahsavar the Iran Novin candidate, who had now become a cabinet minister, had won by an overwhelming majority. In the upcoming June election the Mardom candidate would carry the vote by a large margin.

The Shahsavar election was a booster for the new leadership in the ministry, for the Mardom Party, and for the people. The shah declared afterward that the June election would be absolutely free and serious, and that the candidates of both parties would have to prepare to labor for votes.[15] Ameri's campaign for the Mardom focused on criticizing the government's ability to implement efficiently the shah's intentions *(manviat-e shahaneh),* but even this would not be countenanced. Alam, the high priest of the Mardom Party, later complained that Ameri then reached the end of his rope, begging to be either allowed to work as befitted an opposition leader or let go.[16] He was replaced in January 1975 and died in a tragic car accident a few days afterward. Hoveyda, meanwhile, was elected secretary general of the Iran Novin Party in a grand party congress, the pageantry giving Alam, who was always looking for a reason to disparage Hoveyda, an excuse to insinuate that Hoveyda might have "diabolic machinations" in mind.[17] All of this, however, came to naught on 2 March 1975, when the monarch suddenly declared the formation of the Rastakhiz.

■

The shah had just returned from his regular winter stay in St. Moritz, Switzerland. The previous month had been quite productive for his foreign policy. Before going to St. Moritz, he had visited Egyptian President Anwar Sadat. Knowing of his plans, U.S. Secretary of State Henry Kissinger had written to the shah, asking him to reason on behalf of the United States with Sadat about the upcoming Egypt-Israel negotiations and, as Kissinger put it, "the longer-term orientation of Egypt." Kissinger asked the shah to prevail on Sadat not to put the United States in a position of having to choose between Egypt and Israel.[18] Given Sadat's future politics, including his relationship with the shah, the Iranian sovereign was apparently successful in convincing Sadat that Egypt's future lay with the West and that he should remain constant in the West-leaning position he had already adopted. In St. Moritz, the shah had received President Giscard d'Estaing of France, and he subsequently met in Zurich with Kissinger, discussing oil, among other subjects, all discussions ending to his advantage. So did Alam's meeting in Tehran with a representative of the Algerian president, Houari Boumedienne, with whom the shah's relations had improved significantly in recent months and who was about to play a vital role in helping the shah achieve an entente with Iraq.

Back in Tehran, however, Alam found the shah preoccupied, "tapping the table with his forefinger," as he habitually did when about to make an important or controversial decision. In the past, he had pulled at his hair, "but now that thank God power was in the Shahanshah's hand, [tapping the table with his forefinger] is the manner of his thinking," Alam wrote in his diary.[19] The next day, 24 February, the shah ordered Alam to summon the cabinet, the Majlis presidium, and the media representatives to be present for an important announcement on 2 March. Nobody knew exactly what he would say, though some members of the government, including Hoveyda and his plan and budget chief, Abdolmajid Majidi, probably guessed. Majidi had had an audience with the shah in St. Moritz on the budget. When he was about to take his leave, the shah informed him he intended to introduce some changes in the political system. "I feel there is not enough criticism of the government and therefore the government does not have an incentive to correct itself," said the shah. "We need a system in which the government can self-correct from within." Majidi assumed that the shah was talking about a one-party system. "We had talked about this in the Iran Novin's political bureau. Mr. Hoveyda had remarked that there was no alternative to a one-party system."[20]

Majidi's position agrees with that of Yahya Adl, who was secretary general of the Mardom Party several times and a close friend of the shah. "There are those who say that Rastakhiz was the shah's idea. I believe it was Hoveyda's," Adl later recalled. According to Adl, Nasser Ameri had been made secretary general of the Mardom Party in August 1972 on Hoveyda's suggestion. "Ameri was told the party was a serious matter and he believed it," Adl said. "He began to do serious stuff but in vain." After they "kicked [Ameri] out," Adl took over the position once again because "There was no other way." Adl had come to believe the existing party system was a joke. "But even if it is a comedy, you should play it well. If you don't, you will look ridiculous," he said. He asked Hoveyda sometime before the announcement of the Rastakhiz why he did not simply dissolve the other parties and stop the charade. Hoveyda, according to Adl, agreed that this was what needed to be done.[21] Many years later, after the fall of the regime, it was suggested that the shah got the idea of a one-party state from Sadat during his trip to Egypt. The idea, however, was never aired at the time. The queen had heard nothing about the shah discussing the subject with Sadat. "My recollection is that His Majesty thought that in Iran everyone follows the party whose leader is prime minister. Thus the other party never gets a chance," Queen Farah said later.[22]

On 2 March 1975, the shah told his audience at the Niavaran Palace that the parties were not working as he had hoped they would. The country had accomplished much under his leadership, but the credit had gone mostly to the ruling party. The minority parties, though as patriotic, knowledgeable, and efficient as the majority, had not shared in the honors and rewards equally. He was introducing a system in which everyone would have a chance to participate and everyone would partake of the credit for the service he or she rendered the nation and its progress. The proposed system would be based on three principles—the Constitution, the Shah-People Revolution, and the imperial order. By far a majority of Iranians believed deeply in these principles, he said, and these would be fully engaged in all aspects of Iranian life, including the political. There were those who might not support the three principles, but they were good citizens doing their work and making a living in peace and dignity. They would benefit from everything the country offered in the economic, social, and cultural fields, but they should not expect to participate also in the governance of the country. And finally, there was that small minority of misguided individuals who acted against the nation's vital interests, "like our own Tudeh" *(tudeh-i ha-ye khodemun),* whose place according to the law was in jail. However, if they wished to travel to any of their "promised lands," their passports were ready.[23] The shah's enemies subsequently changed this last sentence to apply to all Iranians: join the Rastakhiz or take your passport and leave.

No one knows exactly how the shah got the idea of the Rastakhiz. His vow to have free elections and the expectations excited by his placing Amouzegar at the interior ministry had highlighted for him the implications of a free election. He now wished to make the impossible possible. He had helped maneuver

Mansur and the Iran Novin into power to administer his White Revolution. He had hoped that the two parties that existed then would act not as adversaries on policy but as vehicles for negotiating a more efficient way of implementing policy. This had not worked politically. He had tried again in the early 1970s, sensing a change was needed. Another group of professionals, this time led by Mehdi Samii, formerly president of the Central Bank and the shah's financial inspector of Iran's military purchases, was invited to discuss with him the possibility of an alternative to Hoveyda's government. This also did not work, partly because the shah would not deviate from the political routine developed over the years, partly because the country had made significant progress with that routine, partly because, according to Adl, the shah habitually defended the individuals he appointed to office,[24] and partly because his affection for Hoveyda made it excruciatingly difficult for him to dismiss the prime minister.

Rastakhiz was a stream many tributaries fed. One tributary may have been an analysis of Iran's political conditions made in late 1971 and early 1972 for the queen, and by extension for the shah, by a group of relatively young intellectuals drawn from the universities and mid-level government, who acted as an unofficial think tank for the queen.[25] The analysis and ensuing recommendations stated that, realistically speaking, only the monarch had the power to redefine and reshape the political system and it was to his advantage to do so. The White Revolution had been overly successful. Its first decade had achieved significant changes in relation to Iran's natural resources and in the condition of its peasants, workers, and women. The government had implemented the change essentially by legal and administrative measures. Except for an initial outbreak of violence consequent to clerical and landlord opposition, the changes were effected with relative ease and little political tension. But over the past few years society had changed significantly, and everything suggested that the tempo of change would pick up in the future. Unless measures were taken to convert to political capability the economic, social, and cultural capabilities the White Revolution had created and would increasingly create, the political system would become dangerously underdeveloped relative to other social subsystems, and consequently increasingly vulnerable. To achieve this conversion, ways and means would have to be designed to make it likely for the evolving social and economic power groups to participate in the political system. Political participation, on the other hand, could be mobilized only if the process was genuine, that is, only if it led to meaningful political decisions. However, this would be impossible if the decisions were made by a hegemonic bureaucracy attached to the person of the shah, which in fact was the case, the two parties notwithstanding. Given the shah's supreme power, it was objectively necessary for him to take measures to break this vicious circle. The measure he was reasonably expected to take was to use his power to establish a different pattern of relationship between the bureaucracy and its social environment, not by separating himself from the government completely, which was neither realistic nor wise nor productive, but by embracing popularly elected organs as well.

To achieve a nexus between the shah's actual power on one hand and the problems of cultural fragmentation and institutional weakness on the other, it was assumed that to be successful a consensus was needed on the boundaries of political process and content. The signposts on which both the shah and a vast majority of the people agreed were the Constitution and the general principles of the White, or Shah-People, Revolution. This would leave out the Islamists and, at least for a while, the communists but include all others, who once empowered would interpret the Constitution and the legal and political procedures that followed from the Constitution. "To this end," the think tank suggested "a political movement, not a party, called the Resurrection Movement of the Iranian Nation, or Rastakhiz, be announced within which individuals would be free to join associations, unions, cooperatives, and political parties of their choice. Simultaneously, steps would be taken to decentralize the bureaucracy and empower local councils through appropriate legislation."[26] The monarch's power was the catalyst; without it, there would be chaos and an uncertain future. If the project was efficiently managed, the shah would gradually move from being the captain of a team to becoming an umpire, seeing to it that the rules of the game were respected. For some time, he would remain closely involved with the military, foreign policy, oil, and national security, but other matters—economic, social, cultural, and judicial—would be determined by the political give-and-take within the evolving consensual framework. In the early phases certain groups, mostly the intellectuals, might remain skeptical, but if the system behaved honestly and efficaciously, they would gradually join the process.

After some discussion, the queen took the proposition to the shah, who, as the queen informed the "think tank," had appreciated the thought and the effort but had observed that with the people he had around him he could not implement the idea at the time. And then a caveat: Iran was a democracy and the prevailing two-party system, as explained in his book *Mission for My Country,* would remain the appropriate frame of reference. To the members of the group it was evident that the idea had been rejected.[27]

In his March 1975 discourse on his "Rastakhiz," the shah was not clear about the structure of the system he proposed. He appointed Prime Minister Hoveyda as secretary general of the Rastakhiz for two years and charged him with developing for it the appropriate constitution, organization, by-laws, membership, and rules for electing officers. Nonetheless, despite the confused picture he drew, the public reacted to the Rastakhiz positively. Many individuals who had never before participated in the political process, including some among the intelligentsia, were drawn to the possibilities the release from the Iran Novin impasse offered. The question was whether the shape the Rastakhiz took would encourage or stifle participation. Would Rastakhiz become a movement, as the 1972 project had suggested, or a party, as many in the government assumed?

Soon, it became clear that the Rastakhiz was to be a party. The task of preparing its structure was given to one of Hoveyda's deputies, Manuchehr Azmun, a former Marxist who had received his doctorate in social studies from Karl Marx University in Leipzig, East Germany.[28] The decision to organize the Rastakhiz as a party cut short the activities of individuals within and without the government who were striving for a movement along the lines originally proposed. Azmun came up with a perfectly fascist plan, according to which each profession—farmers, workers, teachers, students, shopkeepers, doctors, and so on—was organized internally and joined at the top by the party's command organs. This, argued Azmun, was the only way the Rastakhiz could be organized quickly and controlled under the country's leadership structure.[29]

This conception of the party, a hybrid construct of the Italian and Spanish schools of fascism, met with widespread opposition and was withdrawn once the queen sided with its opponents. But then fascism yielded to communism. The organizing principle became democratic centralism, though the term was not mentioned. Two parallel vertical lines—a command line from the top down and an elective line from the bottom up, joined at determined hierarchical rungs—were to be established. The command line was supervised by a Rastakhiz secretary general elected by the party congress; he then appointed a hierarchy of secretaries who in turn organized and led the participatory line at each organization level. The participatory line began at the grassroots level with the party's primary organizations, called *kanuns,* whose representatives would join together in a series of hierarchical elections at town, county, and regional levels, culminating in a central committee, which, in turn, elected an executive committee, the highest party organ acting in the name of the central committee between its sessions. A political bureau, chaired by the prime minister and composed of representatives from the executive committee and the cabinet, the latter selected by the prime minister, was to ensure coordination between the party and the government. To secure the primacy of the party in the political bureau, the executive committee had a slightly higher representation than the cabinet.[30]

The Rastakhiz as conceived and organized could have worked in a totalitarian state but not under the monarchy in Iran. Every step in its development highlighted the contradiction between the institutional requirements of kingship and the party as the instrument of generating and managing political power. The king by definition belonged to the whole people. Accordingly, the Rastakhiz, being the shah's party, was declared to encompass the whole people, thus made indistinguishable from the "political society" and meaningless as a political party. A single party in a modern totalitarian state, the Soviet Union for example, was a party of the political elite and cadre theoretically acting on behalf of history (defined as ideology) to prepare for and usher in the golden age. Such a mission logically limited the party membership to the initiated. In Iran the single party was bastardized as no party and in the process vitiated the traditional position of the king, though it would take time and many missteps before the damage became irreversible.[31]

Rastakhiz was initially received enthusiastically. Alam reported to the shah a few days after the party was announced that two thousand students and faculty had registered as members at Tehran University and that former prime minister Ali Amini had written a letter applying to register.[32] Joining the Rastakhiz, of course, was not a problem; everyone above the age of eighteen was a member by decree unless he or she declared otherwise. The immediate test of the new party was the upcoming national election, which now was to be reformulated to agree with the new political conditions. In the past, the Iran Novin and Mardom parties fielded candidates, albeit with the prime minister's and ultimately the shah's approval. Now the candidates, of which there was no dearth, were selected by the party's executive committee, chaired by Jamshid Amouzegar. The rule was to field in each electoral district approximately three times as many candidates as the parliamentary seats apportioned by law to the district. Almost two-thirds of the Majlis deputies were elected in single-member districts. The rest came from districts with different allocations of representatives, depending on their respective populations, Tehran having the highest at twenty-seven, followed by other large cities such as Tabriz, Mashhad, and Isfahan, among others. In these districts voters voted for as many candidates as the district was allotted deputies, and candidates were elected according to the number of votes they received. In Tehran, for example, the twenty-seven who received the highest number of votes would be elected, in the order of the number of votes they received. In the multi-candidate districts a coalition of workers, guilds, and women fielded a joint list of candidates negotiated among them, for which they pooled their resources and campaigned. In the single-member districts the party fielded three candidates for the single seat, one of whom was the district's present deputy in the Majlis, usually a member of the Iran Novin. To assure impartiality, governors were instructed to select members of the supervisory electoral boards in equal proportion from a roster of names suggested by the candidates. In the end, approximately 60 percent of the eligible voters voted, an impressive ratio considering the country's sociopolitical and geographic conditions. Success in the election, a study commissioned by the Ministry of the Interior showed, was determined by three factors: affiliation with the Iran Novin Party, residence in the electoral district, and availability of campaign funds. Candidates who had no association with the Iran Novin, were actual residents of their district, and had a richer fund chest had on average a better chance of getting elected.[33]

Once the Rastakhiz Majlis was opened on 8 September 1975, a decision had to be made about how to manage it, debate issues, make decisions, and legislate. Two wings, dubbed the Rastakhiz "thought basins" to distinguish them from political parties, were established, one called the Progressive Wing, led by Jamshid Amouzegar, the other the Constructive Wing, led by Hushang Ansary, the two super-ministers. The Amouzegar wing emphasized social welfare, economic equity, decentralization, and political participation; the Ansary wing, economic growth, technology, and industrialization. Despite an effort to diminish the wings' political dimension, Majlis deputies recognized them as the only available vehicles for political activity within an otherwise functionally apolitical Rastakhiz. Accordingly, about two-thirds of the Majlis deputies joined Amouzegar's wing, one-third Ansary's. Now the question was how to make sense of a single party with two voices. The wings, it was argued, were channels for arriving at political decisions; they should not be allowed to reflect divisions in decision making. The single party was to legislate with a unanimous voice and the wings were to be represented in equal numbers in the Majlis leadership, as a result of which the minority's opinion received a far greater weight relative to its size than that of the majority, making the parliament's operations manifestly irrational. The deputies complained with considerable justice that because they had been approved beforehand by the party, they should be presumed to be loyal to the regime; and because they had vigorously campaigned for their seats and won honestly, they should be presumed to have some political influence in their districts. Why should they be reduced to a rubber stamp and seen as such by the people?[34] The élan created initially by the promise of popular participation soon yielded to despair.

Rastakhiz was gravely mishandled, and in the end its failure launched Iran's tragedy by depoliticizing the regime. The demise of the wings in the Majlis diminished and in time ended whatever influence the deputies had in their regions. Unlike the old guard, whose local power depended on land, money, or family, the Rastakhiz deputies' claim to legitimacy depended on their influence with the government. Once it was shown that they were no more than puppets, they had nothing left on which to stake a political claim. Rastakhiz became the only thing it could have become — an appendage of the bureaucracy, this time clearly and inevitably recognized as an agency of the shah. Its failure, unlike the Iran Novin's, directly touched the monarch, who had staked his prestige on its success. And it failed despite the fact that the people liked the shah, were ready to become politically involved, as both the Shahsavar and the subsequent national elections showed, and supported the regime by actually rallying to the party the shah had established.

The Rastakhiz's failure exacerbated the tensions created by other issues — inflation, power shortages, and transportation bottlenecks. The regime's immediate reaction to each of these structural problems was to use the shah's power of command. On 9 September 1975, the shah announced price stabilization and a campaign against profiteering as the fourteenth principle of the Shah-People Revolution. The man in charge of the campaign was by law the minister of commerce, Fereydun Mahdavi, who had also been serving as deputy secretary general of the Rastakhiz since May 1975, shortly after the party had been announced. Mahdavi had used the commerce ministry as a springboard to whip up enthusiasm for the party. He now called on university and high school students to act on behalf of the Rastakhiz to help the ministry control prices and profiteering. However, inflation caused by too much demand and too little supply could not be harnessed by fiat. Instead, the policy corrupted the students and alienated the bazaar and the shopkeepers. By the fall of 1976, Mahdavi, who had been hailed just a few months earlier as the government's mover and shaker, became the prime scapegoat, blamed not only for the inflation but also for alleged corruption in his ministry and for the bottlenecks the government's shopping abroad had produced. Everyone now braced for a cooling down of the economy. In November, a grand congress of the Rastakhiz elected Jamshid Amouzegar as secretary general, separating the party's leadership from that of the government, and an Imperial Commission was formed under the chief of the Imperial Bureau to look into the reasons for the government's failure to meet production schedules, especially of electrical power, which had become a political embarrassment.

The Imperial Commission was intended to demonstrate the shah's determination to act on the people's behalf to keep the government on its toes and answerable for its deeds. Instead, the commission's proceedings, broadcast directly on radio and television, impressed on the public mind the connection between the shah and an indicted government, now also saddled with an enervated bureaucracy.[35] Clearly the government faced a dilemma. Several ministers, including Hoveyda's minister of plan and budget and close ally, Abdolmajid Majidi, thought the cabinet should resign. Hoveyda would not hear of it. "Resignation has no place in the reign of the Shahanshah Aryamehr," he told Majidi.[36] Amouzegar as the Rastakhiz secretary general and Hoveyda's senior minister, Majidi at the Plan and Budget Organization, and a few others addressed the structural problems and supported the need for decentralizing the decision-making process and empowering elected councils, but they were in a minority and not on the best of terms with each other.[37] Others were either indifferent to the issue or, like the agriculture minister Mansur Rowhani, otherwise a competent administrator and a powerful voice in the cabinet, were against it.[38] Thus no effective decision on the subject was made when the shah's power and prestige might have helped maintain balance and order, allowing democratization from a position of strength.

By the time Amouzegar was elected secretary general in 1976, the Rastakhiz had lost much of its original promise, but the nation was still moving forward on other fronts. GNP had risen nearly 38 percent in the budget year 1975 and would rise another 18 percent in 1976.[39] The bureaucracy, though clearly failing to keep up with the demands the shah had placed on it, nonetheless seemed reasonably energetic and on the whole operative. The regime was attacked here and there but not on a grand scale. Iran's military involvement in defeating a rebellion in Dhofar, by now successfully concluded, had occasioned intermittent student demonstrations against the shah in the United States and Europe and occasional altercations with leftist guerrillas within Iran. One such was SAVAK's encounter with a group of Marxist Fadaiyan Khalq in June 1976 in southwest Tehran, where nine Fadaiyan members were killed. Such events, interpreted as the domestic inflections of covert battles fought in a bipolar world, were not seen as cause for worry. The real worry was the effect on Iran of "stagflation" in the West, a novel phenomenon caused by a combination of recession and inflation, and the turn the presidential election campaign was taking in the United States. Some Americans in the U.S. administration and Congress had always opposed the shah's politics and policies. But the shah's relationship with U.S. presidents had been traditionally based on a "realist" definition of national interest. The American presidential campaign in 1976 suggested the possibility of a significant change in the foundations on which U.S. national interest might be assessed if the Democratic nominee, Jimmy Carter, won. For the shah the thought that a president of the United States would privilege human rights over the Soviet threat was simply bewildering. He did not know Carter, but he was reasonably certain that the sort of Americans who were close to him would likely not favor the shah or his policies. The thought prompted him to speed up democratization when the economy was stressed. For the past several years he had been speaking of the need "to turn the people's business over to the people." In 1975, he had declared administrative decentralization and political participation the official policy of the state. Rastakhiz had been explained as a vehicle for enabling participation. By late 1976 he was convinced that to ensure sustainable development he would have to moderate the tempo of growth and to negotiate successfully the processes needed for decentralization and participation. These, however, he could still see as "options" he could take. If Carter became president, he might be forced to make choices that until that time he believed were his to make at will.

20

The Gathering Storm

Jamshid Amouzegar was appointed prime minister on 7 August 1977. The shah had finally become convinced that the nation could not absorb the vast inflow of money, goods, and services the rising oil income had made possible and that a reining in of national expenditures had become necessary. He believed Amouzegar was the man to do the job. He had wanted to replace Hoveyda for some time, but, according to the queen, he could not bring himself to dismiss him.[1] Now, however, he could appoint Hoveyda court minister because his trusted friend Alam had had to resign the position due to a blood illness that would soon end his life.

Amouzegar was known for honesty, integrity, intelligence, wit, and a sharp tongue. His superb performance as Iran's delegate to OPEC had set him apart from his other colleagues. But unlike Hoveyda, who was by nature warm and gregarious, he was reticent, structured, uncommunicative, and hierarchy-bound, which was reflected in his relationship with others, including the shah. The shah, of course, was no one's friend in the ordinary sense of the word. Nonetheless, Alam, Ardeshir Zahedi, and Hoveyda, each in his own way, was allowed an intimacy that Amouzegar was denied. But he understood what the shah wished him to do: cut expenses, balance the budget, harness inflation, control land speculation, lower rents, and get the bureaucracy moving, all of which he did rather well, as the balance sheet of his one year in office showed.[2] During his watch, there were no significant layoffs despite the recession that had begun in 1976; employers still hired workers from other countries, especially Afghanistan, Pakistan, and Bangladesh; and wages did not show negative seasonal fluctuations.[3] Nor did workers in construction or elsewhere seem willing candidates for promoting the revolution. In fact, in most cases, especially in large industrial firms, they were willing to demonstrate against the revolution if they were allowed to do so.[4] Amouzegar has been blamed for cutting government subsidies that prime ministers had made to the clerics out of their secret budgets, thus making them receptive to the revolution. But Amouzegar denies that he ordered such funds to be cut or even knew they existed, and he argues rather persuasively that in any case the revolution could not have occurred or succeeded in a regime such as the shah's simply because some funds were denied certain mullahs.[5] Overall the records suggests that in normal times his tenure would have registered considerable success.

But these were not normal times. Amouzegar took the helm when Iran needed a prime minister good at politics, one who could communicate, cajole, threaten, and mobilize. Instead, he proved good at further sublimating politics to bureau-politics and political issues to moral, financial, or managerial questions. His success in fighting inflation by lowering land and housing prices, intrinsically virtuous, alienated the bazaar, which held considerable investments in specula-tive land, and the bankers, who held land as collateral. Lowering the rate of construction made available to the opposition contingents of unemployed and disgruntled rural migrants it used to great advantage. Though cut off from the decision process in the best of times, the Rastakhiz deputies in the Majlis had had access to Hoveyda; Amouzegar cut his meetings with them to a minimum, making them seem even less effective to their constituents. He remained distant from the political storm that was gathering during his tenure. It should be noted that over the years a de facto division of labor had placed the responsibility for containing violence largely outside the civil government's purview. The police and gendarmerie, for example, as has been noted, though formally under the civilian government, were practically adjuncts of the military. Previous cabinets also had remained relatively aloof from the issues of insurgency, terrorism, armed or organized attacks on the regime. In 1963, Alam's cabinet was substantially uninformed about the preparations made for confronting Khomeini's followers, although Alam did then become closely involved and personally managed the counteroffensive that suppressed the revolt. Conditions, of course, had changed since 1963; the shah and the armed forces were far more powerful and seem-ingly in control, making comparisons between Amouzegar and Alam unfair. Still, the year Amouzegar was at the helm saw a transformation in the anti-shah forces and their strategy that required political response. The opening of the political space had enabled the left, hitherto engaged in sporadic armed struggle, and the Islamists, more or less contained since the attempt on the shah in 1965, to achieve a political mass based in universities and mosques, respectively. All this had an evolutionary history that remained mostly nebulous and seemingly marginal. In 1977, however, what the shah called the alliance of the red and the black began to gel, moving from the shadows into the open.

In 1962, Jalal Al-Ahmad published *Gharbzadegi* in Tehran. The title, commonly translated as "Westoxication," had been coined by Ahmad Fardid, an Iranist philosopher and one of Iran's first Heideggerians, whose idea of the fall of man included both Iran and the West and was esoterically ascribed to a Hellenism that first alienated being from consciousness.[6] The Orient, argued Fardid, had to recapture the ethos it had lost to a worldview that had already tainted the West by placing man at the center of the universe and by separating him from the cosmos of which he had been, and was meant to be, an integral part. The school to which Fardid and his colleague Zabihollah Behruz belonged had developed their own history of the fall of the Achemenids based on the technological and geographical hurdles that they argued made Alexander's conquest of the empire improbable. Their argument intimated that a Western conspiracy had robbed Iran of the ethical and political grandeur that had been hers and that the time had come for Iranians to reconceive and reappropriate the spirit that had once made their country grand. Spirituality was an indispensable ingredient of such a reconception. Their position, never taken up seriously by either the intelligentsia or the government, nonetheless appealed, often surreptitiously, to the Iranian nationalist ethos, and Iranians of different political and ideological persuasions used it in different forms and contexts to prop their respective position. Concepts such as indigenous culture, national identity, and return to the origin became the stuff of which new orthodoxies were woven.

Al-Ahmad hailed from the left, but by 1962 had adopted a nebulous idea of "authentic culture," identified by a strong Islamic element, which he claimed was about to be lost under the influence of Western values and mores. Government, intelligentsia, modernists, and the new entrepreneurial crowd contributed to the loss of authenticity by embracing the West uncritically. Al-Ahmad and his followers extolled authentic indigenous culture, but their treatment of the concept remained murky. If culture was a prism of facts, values, and aesthetics through which individuals and communities interacted with their world, how would societies progress without undergoing cultural change? And how would Third World nations remain culturally authentic if to develop economically and to achieve freedom politically they had to learn the worldview that had empowered the West? Neither the government nor the opposition ever seriously debated the meaning of authentic culture. Consequently, ideology trumped sociology, many intellectuals became "orientalists in reverse,"[7] and complex issues marked by gradations of substance, form, and hue were posed and accepted as black-and-white absolutes.

Gharbzadegi became the vogue, and its cultural diagnosis a line that everyone dealing with social and cultural issues felt obliged to toe. A generation or two before, the intellectuals who had helped modernize the country had assumed modernization involved a good dose of Westernization. However, they were more pragmatic than ideological and better grounded in the indigenous culture. For them, the clergy was anti-progressive because it opposed concrete options such as modern education, women's admission to society, and specific efforts at secularization and rationalization. Rejecting the clerical stance, however, did not seriously affect their relationship to religion. Most of them believed in God and his Prophet, but they also believed that worship was a personal matter. The clergy had interests and power that had to be reckoned and dealt with politically. Modernizing forced them to oppose the clergy but not Islam. However, the new patterns they introduced, though of much significance later on, at the time affected a relatively small layer of society. The rest of the society went its way and behaved as it always had. The weight of what Reza Shah accomplished did not hit the clerics until after the fact. World War II changed the equations by opening up much of society not only sociologically but also intellectually. The Tudeh's teachings, the nationalization experience, the beginnings of economic development, and the appearance of women in public demanding social and political rights affected the relationship between modernist thought and religion. Modernity was becoming internalized. Colonialism was no longer the British coveting Iran's oil; it now was the West stealing Iran's culture.

With *Gharbzadegi,* the left willy-nilly made religion intellectually respectable. Now, suddenly, Islam was being flaunted by non-clerics as well. This Islam was not the same as that of the clerical leaders. It was more akin to what the shah also preached. Let us believe but let us not imitate like monkeys. The shah's Islam was half superstition, half secularism. It was religion in the sense of believing in God but refusing to define God in terms of some revealed scripture: religious chic. Now the "indigenous culture" became another version of religious chic: undefinable, but ideologically anti-West, anti-colonial, and anti-shah. And here it was that the foundations were laid for the future political convergence of the secular left and the religious right, an amalgam that in later years Morteza Motahhari, Khomeini's disciple, and after him the shah, would call "Islamist-Marxist," the unholy alliance of the red and the black. In the 1960s, the movement received its political energy from Third World wars of liberation fought in such places as Indochina, Algeria, and Cuba. The underdeveloped countries were no longer underdeveloped because they had slept while the West had gone through the rigors of renaissance, reformation, industrial revolution, and the rest. They were underdeveloped because they had been kept backward—*aqab-*

negahdashteh in the suddenly à la mode Persian intellectual vernacular. The thing was to rediscover self, which could be done by rejecting the West. Frantz Fanon and Aimé Cesaire, among others, became the gurus of choice. Fanon's interpretation of the role of "indigenous culture" in the anti-colonial struggle and his insistence that the road to national consciousness passed through the intellectual community's reappropriation of its past and rediscovery of its inherent value particularly impressed the new "nativist" intellectual elite.[8]

In the 1970s, Fanon and Cesaire were picked up by others as well, notably Ali Shariati, an eloquent and charismatic speaker, a good politician, extremely intelligent but not correspondingly learned. He had received a *doctorat d'université* from the Sorbonne in hagiology, based on translating to French a part of *Faza'el-e balkh,* a book of biographies of Balkh notables that had been translated into Persian and edited by an Afghan scholar several years before. He was employed as an assistant professor of history at the Ferdowsi University of Mashhad, according to Jalal Matini, dean of the university's College of Literature and Humanities and subsequently president of the university, evidently after some machinations, including maneuvers to have the degree recognized as a doctorate in history by the Ministry of Education.[9] In Mashhad he was a popular teacher, students flocking to his classes even from beyond the College of Literature and Humanities. In 1971, he was appointed to the Ministry of Science and Higher Education in Tehran, where, possibly with a nod from the government and SAVAK, he became a popular speaker at the Hosseinieh Ershad, a nontraditional Islamic organization established and funded by two bazaar leaders, Nasser Minachi and Mohammad Homayun.[10]

Shariati was a superb eclecticist. His forte was bringing together elements of Islam and socialism, mixing chiliastic Marxism and shii eschatology (classless society and the advent of the Twelfth Imam heralding the end of time) to produce a unitary classless society *(jame'eh-ye bitabaqeh-ye towhidi),* that is, a society whose members were anti-imperialist, believed in the primacy of the community, and were ready to die for their common goals.[11] To Shariati, the essence of shiism was to defend the *mustaz'af,* the disinherited, and as such shiism was nothing if it did not address basic political issues of the time. The Safavids (the dynasty that had made shiism the official religion of Iran in the sixteenth century), he said, had vitiated this fundamental obligation by turning Islam into prayer, mourning, and self-flagellation. Even "George Gurvitch, a Jew and former communist who [spent] his life fighting fascism, Stalinism, and the French colonialism in Algeria [was] closer to the spirit of shiism than Ayatollah Milani, who [had] never been a part of any struggle."[12] It was necessary to return to the origin, the Koran, which offered the schema for the perfect society and, as one scholar noted, in Shariati's teachings also a radically populist theology of revolution: "In a manner reminiscent of Shatov in Dostoevsky's *The Possessed,* Shariati equate[d], as regards matters social, God and the people."[13] Rather than the preacher, one needed the revolutionary, an Abu Zarr, an early companion of the Prophet who loved, believed, and fought. And the best way to train the youth to become Abu Zarrs was to ideologize Islam and society.[14]

Shariati became exceptionally popular among religious and lay students because despite the fuzzy logic of his sermons and writings he seemed to offer them an option other than either the crass materialism of growth politics or the spiritual staleness of traditional religion. And he had an advantage: government allowed him leeway because he was thought to diminish the influence of the traditional clergy, several of whom, including the Grand Ayatollahs Abol-Qasem Kho'i, Mohammad Kazem Shari'atmadari, Shahab-ud-Din Mar'ashi Najafi, Mohammad Hadi Milani, and Haj Hossein Qomi, ruled formally against his books and lectures.[15] The Ayatollah Ruhollah Khomeini's followers, especially Morteza Motahhari, accused Shariati of deviations; Motahhari went as far as to declare Shariati guilty of flagrant *bed'at*, or newfangledness, in religion.[16] Khomeini, on the other hand, treated Shariati gingerly, careful not to alienate his followers.[17] Whatever the intrinsic virtue or vice of his preachments, Shariati was singularly effective in kindling the revolutionary fire, which facilitated the convergence of Islamism, nationalism, and Marxism, begun in the 1960s, and consolidated under the Khomeini flag in the late 1970s. The aim was to establish an Islamic state. Khomeini and his followers, however, neither knew nor probably cared about statecraft. Just as Al-Ahmad and Shariati had written and preached careless of practical politics, Khomeini and his followers assumed things would go right once the shah was overthrown. According to Abdolkarim Soroush, one of the more thoughtful of Khomeini's followers, they had little to offer beyond slogans. "The founders and rulers of the revolution were, and still are, mostly professional orators. To many of them success means delivering an impressive sermon, attending an elaborate ceremony, and so on."[18]

When Amouzegar became prime minister, the opening of the political space was already the declared policy. In 1976, prodded by criticism in the foreign press and prospects of radical change in U.S. policy, the shah ordered SAVAK to clean up its act. In May and June 1977, the government invited the International Red Cross to inspect Iranian prisons and held talks with the head of Amnesty International and the International Commission of Jurists, assuring them that torture had been stopped, prison conditions would be improved, and judicial rights would be respected.[19] Late in July, Hushang Ansary, leader of the Constructive Wing of the Rastakhiz, told the press that the right of the Iranian people to be informed was absolute and the press was a mirror to public opinion. "Let the pens write and the tongues speak so that the exchange of thoughts and experiences paves the way to the achievement of the aims of the [Shah-People] revolution. Criticism is the flare that saves the executives from the perils of treading in the dark."[20] "Henceforth, no one should be afraid of criticizing the government," declared Dariush Homayun, Amouzegar's minister of information and government spokesperson.[21] Democratization was the mantra, but democracy, said the shah in August on the anniversary of the Constitutional Revolution, was not an imported good. It had to emanate from within Iranian conditions.[22] He declared two new principles of the Shah-People Revolution, the first forbidding annual increase in land prices to exceed annual inflation and the second directing government employees to declare their individual wealth as well as the wealth of their wives and children at intervals determined by law.[23] "No one should use government high office to amass wealth," the shah told *Kayhan Daily*'s chief editor in September on the anniversary of his ascending the throne. "There were still terrorists in Iran, but they had received new orders, now striving to create chaos by means other than assassination. They talk of freedom, but they do not tell us what kind of freedom they seek. Iran is the envy of the world. They want to take us back to the stone-age. This, however, [will] not be allowed as long as I, the armed forces, and patriotic Iranians are here to protect the country." He would not settle for a second-class Iran, he said, and he would not tire of fighting until Iran achieved the place it deserved in the world.[24]

The shah believed that Iranians appreciated what he had done for them and that now they would respond positively to his invitation to them to participate in the political process within the framework he set. But the responses were not what he had expected. Student activism in the universities increased. Charges of dictatorship against him were now more acute. National Front leaders Karim Sanjabi, Shapur Bakhtiar, and Dariush Foruhar wrote him an open letter demanding absolute compliance with the Constitution — except presumably, he chuckled to his queen, the article that enabled the clerics to control the law. Poetry readings, especially the one at the Goethe Institute, metamorphosed into abusive language against the regime. A group of fifty-four members of the Lawyers Association issued a public letter criticizing the proposed changes to judicial procedures, though these were certain to improve the rule of law. An obviously studied campaign was underway to accuse the shah of complicity in the apparently natural deaths respectively of Ali Shariati in London in June

1977 and Khomeini's son Seyyed Mostafa in Karbala in November of the same year. And most important at the time, the Confederation of Iranian Students intensified their activities against him and his regime significantly in Europe and the United States just before his scheduled visit to the United States on 14–18 November 1977.

When Jimmy Carter was inaugurated as the thirty-ninth president of the United States, the shah was certain he would survive him, though the road he would have to travel would be uneven and bumpy. Carter was ambivalent about the shah, a feeling that was reflected in his administration. However, he did not hold any particular animus against him. Indeed, as his energy secretary, James Schlesinger, observed, "the public expression of that ambivalence grew less as the Shah got into greater trouble." Carter would "let things sort themselves out." He believed in reconciliation and negotiation: "If you put [Egyptian President Anwar] Sadat and [Israeli Prime Minister Menachem] Begin in the same room, they hammer out a reconciliation of sorts. If you put Energy and Environment in the same room, they hammer out the reconciliation," said Schlesinger. Carter was deeply concerned about human rights, which made him quite different from Nixon, who scoffed at the idea, or Ford, who paid little attention to it and was easily deflected from it by Kissinger, who, as Schlesinger also tells us, "was not known to be a crusader on human rights."[25]

The shah picked up on this difference and was prepared to deal with it when he met Carter on 15 November 1977 in Washington. U.S. Ambassador William Sullivan had mentioned to him several matters of interest to the United States, including the price of oil, the scale of Iranian arms purchases, emerging nuclear weapons capabilities in India and Pakistan, and Arab-Israeli relations. He was familiar with U.S. worries and was confident he had appropriate answers for them. He, however, had a different set of interests: a reliable source of military equipment for his air force and navy, free of political interjections; license for the export of American nuclear power equipment to Iran; and getting the United States to agree with him about the threat that Soviet actions in Aden, Yemen, the Horn of Africa, and other approaches to the Indian Ocean posed to the oil in the Persian Gulf. Most of all, according to Sullivan, "he wished to size up the new administration, to understand the new president, and to assess how significant the obvious political differences we had in domestic terms would be for the strategic alliance that he felt was essential for the well-being of both Iran and the United States."[26] What he could not foresee was the scene at the White House when he and President Carter were exchanging diplomatic niceties.

He arrived in Williamsburg, Virginia, as was his custom, in a plane he was piloting. He would spend the night in one of the town's celebrated historic houses before he and the queen were helicoptered to Washington to meet the president and the First Lady the next morning. Sullivan, who was in Williamsburg to receive him, had been warned to expect anti-shah demonstrations. At dusk, as he was preparing to walk over for an informal dinner with the royal couple, he saw a gathering on the sidewalk across from his residence, "a composite of Iranians and Americans," many of whom carried banners with signs of hammer and sickle and slogans directed against President Carter and the United States and another group of banners bearing a portrait of Ayatollah Khomeini, describing the shah as a puppet of the United States and demanding, "U.S. hands off Iran." Though he had heard of Khomeini before, this was the first time Sullivan had seen Khomeini's "name and portrait evoked in the struggle by the Iranian students against the shah's regime."[27] The sight of students carrying Khomeini banners was surprising not only to Sullivan but also to the queen, who had seen this once before, a few months back in the summer when she was attending a meeting of the Aspen Institute. "I saw a student carrying Khomeini's picture. It struck me as unnatural. I had always thought of students as young, idealistic, liberal, progressive individuals seeking freedom. Why would a student in America demonstrate for Khomeini and carry his picture as an emblem of his belief?"[28]

What Sullivan especially noted in Williamsburg, however, was the care with which the police, the FBI, and the Secret Service representatives had "cleverly" separated the shah's supporters and opponents, placing supporters across from the shah's residence, opponents next to the residences of his American hosts. In Washington the next day, as Sullivan and the royal couple were driving on the National Mall near the reflecting pool, where their helicopters had landed, across from the south-portico entrance to the White House, he noticed two large groups of demonstrators with the same kinds of banners he had seen in Williamsburg, but this time separated only by a light collapsible fencing and "a space of no more than twenty yards" and "a mere scattering of park police [moving] in that twenty-yard stretch of no-man's land."[29] But the shah and the queen arrived at the White House without incident and were warmly greeted by President and Mrs. Carter.

This was the shah's first visit with the president. The queen had met Carter once before, in July after the Aspen Institute meeting. The conversation, however, was not what she had expected. "I had just left Aspen where the talk was about such things as the meaning of development, unified approach, balance between political and economic change, justice and the like. The first thing President Carter told me was 'You look more beautiful in person than in your pictures.' I am sure he meant that as a compliment. But I found it insulting. I felt that he obviously did not think that he could have an intelligent conversation with me."[30] But on this day the weather was good, the hosts otherwise gracious, and the beginning seemed to her auspicious. The royal couple was led to the receiving stand, a twenty-one-gun salute boomed out, and the band played the national anthems of the United States and Iran. Then, suddenly, there was a commotion outside. The shah's opponents had overcome the police and the separating fence and had set on his supporters. As the president began his welcome, the park police used tear gas to disperse the demonstrators. The gas flowed in with the wind, causing eyes to tear, forcing the shah and many others to use their handkerchiefs to dry their eyes. The spectacle was seen around the world. The shah and the queen apologized to the Carters for causing embarrassment. The Carters reassured them that everything was under control and no harm had been done. The harm done, of course, was enormous, the wind providing an unexpected windfall for the shah's enemies. The day was an "augury," wrote President Carter, of "real grief in our country because of Iran."[31]

Carter found the shah "a likable man — erect without being pompous, seemingly calm and self-assured in spite of the tear gas incident, and surprisingly modest in demeanor." He knew that the shah was experienced in dealing with American presidents — Carter was the eighth American president the shah had known since he had met President Franklin Roosevelt in Tehran in 1943. In the Cabinet Room with Vice President Walter Mondale, Secretary of State Cyrus Vance, National Security Adviser Zbigniew Brzezinski, and Chief of Staff Hamilton Jordan, Carter was impressed with the shah's "excellent analysis of the troubled situation around the Persian Gulf area." The shah, wrote Carter in his memoirs, spoke "quietly and proudly" about the changes that were taking place in Iran, quoting "improving statistics on employment, education, housing, transportation, and healthcare, obviously pleased with the fruits of his leadership."[32] Jordan later observed that "of all the people we had seen during that period — Sadat, Schmidt, Callaghan, Giscard, and scores of others — the shah was easily the most impressive." The shah conducted "a *tour d'horizon* of the world," Jordan continued, "describing with great accuracy the problems facing the West, the strategic importance of Iran, and the critical nature of US-Iran relations. He spoke for almost an hour without notes. It was more than a presentation — it was a performance."[33]

The shah judged Carter a good man but naïve on global strategy, especially about the Soviets. In July, he had written the president a letter complaining about the delay in presenting to Congress the proposal he had submitted on purchasing AWACS, threatening to withdraw his offer if the president did not move. Carter had managed to secure congressional approval by September, and now he was eager to mobilize the shah's support for Sadat's impending visit to Jerusalem. He was also anxious to get the shah not to raise the price of oil at least for a while, which the shah agreed to, and to Carter's delight he announced it at a press conference shortly before attending the president's dinner in his honor. Thus, it appeared that the shah would have no great problem with the United States, except on human rights, which the president felt obliged to bring up, albeit as gently as he could. Carter told the shah he realized that much of the trouble came from the mullahs who did not want things to change, students who wanted things to change too fast, and the new middle class that sought more political influence. Their complaints, however, damaged Iran's reputation in the world, he said. "Is there anything that can be done to alleviate this problem by closer consultation with the dissident groups and by easing off on some of the strict police policies?"[34]

To the shah, who thought he had already done much to improve the police situation, Carter was on the wrong side of the issue. He appeared sad to Carter as he spoke. His problem, he explained, was the communists and the laws. Iran, and indeed the region, was seriously threatened by the communist presence, mostly clandestine, often disguised in front organizations that on the surface appeared benign. The laws in Iran were made to prevent mischief by such groups and organizations. He was obligated to implement the law. Someday, perhaps, the menace might be removed and the need for such laws would no longer exist. He did not think that day was near. But the troublemakers were few, marginal, with no support among the vast majority of Iranian people. Carter was not convinced but thought that it would be useless to pursue the subject since the shah obviously believed in the truth of what he was saying.[35]

In Washington the shah invited President and Mrs. Carter to visit Iran. The Carters accepted the invitation in principle; however, the president's schedule being full, it was assumed the visit would not take place anytime soon. The shah therefore was pleasantly surprised to hear in mid-December that the president wished to spend the last evening of 1977, New Year's Eve, in Tehran, between trips to Poland and India. To the shah this meant Carter had made a special effort to demonstrate his friendship for him and the value he placed on U.S.-Iranian relations. He reciprocated by having King Hussein of Jordan come to Tehran on a private visit to discuss Jordan in relation to the Camp David agreement, which stipulated that Jordan would at some time in the future associate itself with the talks. In the event, not much came out of this trilateral meeting, Hussein being reluctant to commit himself in the face of opposition from the Palestinians in Jordan and by his neighbors, especially Saudi Arabia, Iraq, and Syria.

The shah and Carter reached several agreements in principle, including one on nuclear nonproliferation related to the sale of U.S. nuclear power plants to Iran and one on a list of Iran's anticipated military needs for the next five years.[36] The most surprising event of Carter's visit, however, was the toast the president offered the shah at the dinner the shah gave in his honor at the Sahebqarabieh Palace:

> Iran, whose destiny is so well-guided by the shah, is an island of stability in one of the most troubled regions of the world. That is a great tribute to you, Your Majesty, and to the great task that you are accomplishing in Iran, and to the respect, admiration, and love that your people bear you.
>
> Driving through the beautiful streets of Tehran today with the shah, we saw literally thousands of Iranian citizens lining the streets to show their friendship. And I also saw hundreds, perhaps even thousands of American citizens who had come to welcome their president in this nation that has adopted them, and where they feel at home....
>
> No other nation of the globe is as close to us in the military organization of our mutual security. No other nation is in such close consultation with us on the problems of the regions that concern us both. There is no other head of state with whom I feel on friendlier terms and to whom I feel more gratitude.

Reproducing the toast in her memoir, Queen Farah wrote, "No American president had ever paid such tribute to a sovereign."[37] The statement was extraordinary in substance and tone, confusing most Iranians, including the shah, who assumed Carter would not make such statements unstudied. Later, James Schlesinger observed that Jimmy Carter was prone to hyperbole to please friendly audiences. He should not have been taken as seriously as he was.[38]

◾

Iranians, however, habitually took the president of the United States very seriously. Many among the shah's opponents, for example, took the intrusion of tear gas into the White House not as an accident but as a sign that the United States had lowered, if not withdrawn, its support for the shah.[39] Consequently, the event prompted them to expand their anti-shah activities. Khomeini, abandoning all limits, called the shah a "filthy and inefficient element" who has "trampled this noble people's honor, self-respect, independence, and economy" at the altar of "his and his pilfering family's caprice." On 30 December, the day Jimmy Carter was in Tehran, Khomeini called the Iranian government illegitimate and illegal.[40] These statements embarrassed the shah so much as to prompt him to order Court Minister Hoveyda and SAVAK Chief General Nasiri to launch a public attack against the ayatollah. The result was an article published in the *Ettela'at Daily* on 7 January 1978, in which Khomeini was vilified as a reactionary Indian-born British lackey of colonial powers.

Titled "Iran and the Red and Black Colonialism" and written under the fictitious name Ahmad Rashidi Motlaq, the article became a *casus bellum* for the opposition. Who wrote it and why have been subject to much speculation, despite the fact that most of the people who were in a position to know something about it have commented on it.[41] The facts about the article are as follows:

On 5 January, Court Minister Hoveyda called Information Minister Dariush Homayun at the congress of the Rastakhiz Party—which had just elected Prime Minister Jamshid Amouzegar secretary general for a second time after a hiatus of several months when the party leadership had passed to Mohammad Baheri—to inform him he would receive an article that was to be immediately published in the press. Soon, Homayun was handed a yellow envelope with the markings of the imperial court containing the promised article. He took the article out of the yellow envelope and handed it to Ali Bastani, the *Ettela'at* assistant editor covering the party congress, and ordered it to be published. The *Ettela'at* editors, however, balked at printing the article once they learned it contained virulent attacks on Khomeini, fearing a backlash and possible danger to themselves. The publisher, Farhad Masudi, called Homayun, who called Amouzegar, who called the imperial court, but once it was learned that the shah had ordered the article to be published, everyone fell in line. The article was printed on Saturday, 8 January, three days after it had been handed to the paper, appearing on page 7 as an opinion piece under the Motlaq pseudonym.[42] On the 9th, demonstrations began in Qom and Mashhad.

While these events were occurring, the shah was in Aswan, meeting with President Sadat, and later in Saudi Arabia, visiting King Khalid. His meeting with Sadat smoothed the way for the latter's eventual meeting and understanding with Israeli Prime Minister Begin, prompting Sadat to observe: "The Shahanshah has demonstrated that Iran and Egypt have close and real cooperation in establishing peace." And the shah also came to an understanding with Khalid on behalf of Sadat.[43] Back in Iran, however, tensions intensified. Demonstrations in the shrine cities of Qom and Mashhad led to altercations with the security forces that resulted in deaths and damage in Qom. Several ulama, including Grand Ayatollah Shari'atmadari, the leading *marja'* in Qom, denounced the government for insulting the clergy. The *Ettela'at,* which had published the anti-Khomeini article, now published a declaration by the Grand

Ayatollah Mar'ashi Najafi objecting to the article for "insulting Ayatollah Khomeini" and holding the government responsible for the killing and beating of "religious students and others" in Qom.[44]

Forty days after the events in Qom, Tabriz became the scene of one of the most violent demonstrations in recent times. As a prelude to what was to come, banks, cinemas, government offices, and a Pepsi-Cola factory were burned, and several demonstrators were killed or wounded. The provincial governor, Lieutenant General Eskandar Azemudeh, a relative of Prime Minister Amouzegar, was caught completely off guard. Not only had he taken no effective measures to prevent violence, he failed to alert the prime minister after the riots broke out. Asked on the day of the riot by NIRT Director Reza Qotbi about the ongoing violence, Amouzegar answered that Tabriz was quiet. He called Qotbi after a few minutes to confirm his previous statement, which surprised Qotbi, whose reporters in Tabriz were keeping him constantly informed of the bloody events.[45] Seeing that he was getting nowhere with Amouzegar, Qotbi called the palace to speak to the shah, but the shah was in a meeting and he was able only to exchange messages. He told the aide-de-camp to inform His Majesty that Tabriz was in a state of turbulence, that what was happening was politically important, and that something needed to be done about it immediately. The shah instructed Qotbi to inform and stay in touch with the government. Azemudeh was sacked the next day, and Amouzegar went to Tabriz personally to take charge of the affair, after which things quieted down. The government explained away the disturbances as the work of a few agitators coming in from beyond the borders. Ayatollah Shari'atmadari, foremost religious leader in Azerbaijan, cautioned the people against violence, which, he said, harmed religion, the *shar'* (religious law), and the clergy. Khomeini, on the other hand, celebrated the heroic Tabriz people and encouraged them to march forward. "The dear people of Tabriz with their grand movement have brought their iron fists on the mouths of the regime's dim-witted propagandists who call the bloody colonial revolution, which the noble Iranian people oppose a hundred percent, the Shah-People Revolution. But I bring you good tidings: I bring to the people of Azerbaijan the promise of final victory."[46]

In January 1978 the government saw Khomeini as irrelevant. Such a statement sounds bizarre, given Khomeini's record over the preceding quarter-century and his intellectual, religious, and political presence among a good portion of the *tullab,* the religious students, in Qom, Mashhad, and the shrine cities of Iraq. But 1963 was largely forgotten, an aberration that the White Revolution had corrected. For Qotbi and the NIRT leadership, for example, Khomeini was history, a pseudo-claim spent. Now, because his name was mentioned here and there on the margin of the demonstrations, they showed interest in who he was, what he said, and what he had written. They began to gather his tapes and writings in an archive, initially more as a curiosity than a source for learning about a real threat, but eventually for developing a strategy to counter him. But it did not occur to them to put the idea of the *wilayat-e faqih,* the rule of the religious jurist, on the board for public discussion. Qotbi explains:

> It was not in the government's agenda to confront such ideas. It was not in our agenda that because we were against communism [we had] to expose the contradictions in its doctrines and practices and confront it in public. On several occasions the general question of the regime's ideology was discussed. The shah, for example, proposed that we should develop our dialectic against the communists' dialectic. But the idea of the rule of the religious jurist was so alien to our historical thinking, so absurdly farfetched, that we did not think it would catch fire, and when we realized that it had, it was too late.[47]

The regime interpreted the opposition as following two trends. One was the Carter effect — the intellectuals, the left, and the liberals, who did not seem inordinately dangerous. The liberal wing of the regime, in fact, supported, if not the regime, the ideas they propounded. Qotbi, for example, as we have seen in chapter 17, thought there was no reason why SAVAK should suspect people on the basis of what books they read. It was of course unpleasant to see individuals who until recently had gone out of their way to show their loyalty to the regime now suddenly change color. Nonetheless, the demands made by the man in the street were not outrageous and therefore merited respect; thus the more open the system, the better it was. So, the regime's liberal wing was not unhappy about the forces that they thought were seeking a more participatory political system.

With the religious groups it was different. The security elements as well as former leftists in the regime believed that some of the seemingly religious partisans were actually leftists of various ideological hues. This was their main and persistent worry. The coming together of the revolutionary left and the Islamic fundamentalists suggested to them that the left was using religion as a decoy to gain control of the system. No one in the winter of 1977–78, when the Tabriz revolts occurred, thought, much less believed, that the Islamists might be the real enemy.

Tabriz was the beginning of a strategy aimed at shattering the shah's image. The radical Islamists, Khomeini's followers, still small in number and less endowed than the followers of the major ayatollahs, such as Kho'i in Najaf and

Shari'atmadari in Qom, set out to conquer the mosques and use them to mobilize the higher clerical establishment in the service of their cause. Their initial tactic was to use the time-honored *arba'in,* the fortieth day of mourning for the dead, traditionally a purely religious ceremony, but now susceptible to politicization by the theory of shii activism advanced in the 1960s and 1970s. In Tabriz radical young seminary students were able to use the ceremony—mourning for those who had died in Qom—to riot and attack the regime against the wishes of Azerbaijan's highest religious authority, Shari'atmadari. The success of this event convinced the movement's strategists that they could easily force the major ayatollahs to support their cause by making it costly for them to remain on the fence. Thus, in Tabriz, Shari'atmadari first counseled caution but, seeing that events had taken a different turn, felt compelled to take the side of the radicals. He was beseeched by his own students—his field force—as were the other ayatollahs by theirs. The younger clerics, following the directives of Khomeini's field commanders, invited confrontation with government forces, which invariably placed them at the center of the stage, giving them an advantage over the high clerics.[48] In time, the radicals succeeded in achieving for their cause a semblance of unity among the ayatollahs, many of whom did not really favor Khomeini's ideology or cause. The appearance of support by otherwise moderate clerics, in turn, made an in-depth study of the ideological foundation of the movement, the radical theory of Islamic government, seem less critical for lay intellectuals and the public, who did not learn what Khomeini was after until after the fact.

Over the next months, Khomeini's followers succeeded in taking control of the mosques, which became the focus of their organization and command structure. They controlled demonstrations at will and decided where and how to confront the regime. Demonstrations for the *arba'in* of those who died in Tabriz were centered in the desert city of Yazd, but also took place in Qazvin, Isfahan, Babol, and Kashan. The subsequent *arba'in* for the Yazd demonstrations returned to Qom, where cars, banks, and stores were put to fire and more people killed and wounded. Security forces entered the homes of the Ayatollahs Shari'atmadari and Golpayegani, who had scolded the government on the occasion of the fortieth-day mourning for the Yazd victims. In late May, Khomeini berated the shah for promising false freedom to the people. "What freedom is this that he speaks of? Freedom is not his to give. God has given the people their freedom. Islam has given them freedom."[49] The shah in Mashhad repeated what he had said before—that he, the armed forces, and Iranian patriots would not allow foreigners to take hold of Iran, and if it were to happen, it would be the communists who won.[50] Clearly Khomeini was trying to neutralize the shah's trump card—democracy. By July, the shah was wondering how the situation had come to the state it had. And the government, including SAVAK, for its part, was wondering what the shah was up to.

■

In a select meeting in Court Minister Hoveyda's office in the summer of 1978 General Hossein Fardust, the shah's childhood friend, head of the Imperial Inspectorate and deputy head of SAVAK, known as the shah's eyes and ears, expressed concern about the political turmoil that seemed to him to be method-ically expanding across the country. "If His Majesty knows what is happening, if he is playing a game with foreign powers, he should tell us. He should put our minds at ease. If he does not know, then I must say that things are bad. Something must be done or we shall all be lost."[51] It is bizarre that Fardust did not know exactly what was happening and thought that such events might be political or diplomatic games the shah was playing to make a point. More bizarre was Amouzegar's position that the chaos was deliberately concocted to weaken his government in order to get him out of the picture. It was the work of the Freemasons and the Hoveyda clique come together in an unholy alliance against him, he said. Once he was gone, so would be the turbulence. Like most others, he could not believe at the time that such a chaotic situation would be permit-ted to continue if the shah or some other force did not wish it. No one took the matter seriously enough to take a stand. No one had the gumption to take it up with the shah, who was indeed worried. He was the one who knew that this was not his doing and that he was helpless to do anything about it.

In early August, the demonstrations gained a new momentum. Ramadan, the month of the fast, began on the 6th, bringing new opportunities to the Islamist opposition. Future Islamist leaders—Javad Bahonar, Mohammad Mofatteh, Seyyed Ali Khamenei, Mehdi Bazargan, and Yadollah Sahabi—chose the Qaba Mosque for regular evening sermons to attack the regime. On 5 August, Constitution Day, the shah announced the advent of responsible democracy in Iran:

> This is a new chapter in our country and we shall enjoy a maximum of freedoms allowed by the law. . . . In the political realm, we shall have as much freedom as the European countries, and the limits of our freedoms will be defined as in Europe. . . . That means, we shall have freedom of association, but our associations must be peaceful, free of arms. . . . We shall have freedom of speech and freedom of press according to a new press law that may be adopted from any of the world's freest nations. Certainly elections will be a hundred percent free, everyone will have the right to vote and have his vote read. . . . But we must know that no nation, least of all democratic countries, allow churlishness, violence, provocation, and outlawry.

Senate President Sharif-Emami followed the sovereign, promising that the "open political space" would usher in a new era for free expression of opinion. Prime Minister Amouzegar promised that the elections the next year would be completely free and that the open political space would expand even further. A day later, he declared the opposition also would be allowed to participate in the elections.[52]

These promises made some impression on the liberal opposition but none on the Islamist activists. On 9 August, a mob invaded Hotel Shah Abbas, a beautiful establishment in Isfahan, and set a part of it on fire. Two days later, on the 11th, the Isfahan mob attacked and burned movie theaters, liquor stores, banks, government buildings, and the Rastakhiz Party headquarters, forcing the government to declare martial law. "A group of hooligans with no aim other than to kill and to destroy . . . threatened to put the whole of the city to fire and ruin," said the newly appointed military governor of Isfahan, Major General Reza Naji. But, said Information Minister Dariush Homayun, this was a by-product of the march to democracy, greater political freedom, and open political space.[53]

From Isfahan the demonstrations spread to Shiraz, this time ostensibly to denounce the Shiraz Art Festival, which usually took place at the end of the summer. Arson was again the weapon of choice, forcing Governor Manuchehr Azmun to declare he would do his duty with whatever it took. Shiraz and Isfahan now became the excuse for mobs in Ahvaz, Qazvin, and Abadan to burn and loot. On the 13th, Khomeini called the events of Isfahan and Shiraz "another example of the shah's crimes." "The people should know," he said, "that nowhere in the world have the seekers of freedom been offered it on a silver platter." That same day, a bomb in the Khansalar Restaurant in Tehran, a favorite of Americans, exploded, killing and wounding several patrons. In Qom, the young *talabehs,* students of religion, pressed the grand ayatollahs to support the Islamist movements and succeeded in getting the most exalted among them — Shari'atmadari, Golpayegani, and Najafi-Mar'ashi — to issue a joint declaration condemning government policy in Isfahan and Shiraz. On the 15th, the Shiraz Festival Organization announced it had cancelled both the Shiraz Art Festival and the Isfahan Cultural Festival due to the conditions in the two cities. On the 17th, the shah told the press a few hooligans and others belonging to the unholy alliance of the red and the black wished to take the country back to the Middle Ages, but would fail. "I, the Iranian nationalists, and the armed forces will not allow Iran to fall in the hand of foreign agents."[54]

On 19 August, the twenty-fifth anniversary of the fall of Mossadeq, twenty-eight cinemas across the country, the number corresponding to 28 Mordad, the date in the Persian calendar, were set on fire. In Abadan, in a deliberate act of terrorism, the doors were locked from outside when the Cinema Rex was set on fire. Three hundred seventy-seven men, women, and children out of some seven hundred watching the popular Iranian-made film *The Deer* perished. Clearly, as the perpetrators admitted after the revolution, this was an act of sabotage, calculated to create fear. The shah pronounced it "the great terror," contrasting it with his own promise of "the Great Civilization." But no action was taken. No one from the court, as custom dictated, visited the city. The government took no measures to seek, identify, or confront the culprits. The queen volunteered to go to Abadan, but was dissuaded.[55] The government reasoned it was better to keep the matter as quiet as possible because the opposition would ridicule what the government said. The regime had internalized the "credibility gap" proclaimed as a propaganda device by its enemies. In the next few days Khomeini, Bazargan, Sanjabi, and others accused the government of the most heinous crimes to eager listeners, among them the international press. Sanjabi told the Reuters news service that his sources confirmed that government agents had set fire to buildings and banks and that they had broken the windows to make the opposition look bad.[56] Anti-government demonstrations now spread to almost all of the major cities, especially those circling the central deserts. The government, failing to take the lead, now was placed on the receiving end, accused of the most odious of barbarisms. In Germany, Belgium, Denmark, the Netherlands, and several other countries Iranian and non-Iranian students invaded the Iranian embassies. On 26 August, Tehran became a focus of demonstrations, some slogans demanding the shah's resignation. On the 27th, Amouzegar offered and the shah accepted his resignation, a decision he would later regret.[57]

Ja'far Sharif-Emami had not volunteered for premiership and had not campaigned for it. He was a reluctant inductee. The shah chose him because he thought the act would assuage the mullahs. His chief of SAVAK, General Nasser Moqaddam, brought him a message from a major ayatollah (probably Shari'atmadari) saying that, given the prevailing unrest, he should do something "spectacular." He thought of changing the prime minister.[58] Sharif-Emami, however, was a surprising choice if the shah wished, as he claimed, to devolve power on a reasonably independent prime minister. Sharif-Emami was deputy president of the Pahlavi Foundation, a former prime minister, for many years president of the Senate, and considered very close to the monarch. He was a Grand Master of Freemasonry, an organization that in Iran was thought to be connected to foreigners, especially the British. He was reputed to be corrupt, dubbed "Mr. Five-Percent," drawing salaries from a large number of government and private sources. But he also had family ties with both the clerical establishment and the National Front.

The choice of Sharif-Emami proved to be unpopular. On the 25th, two days before Amouzegar resigned, Moqaddam had asked Houchang Nahavandi, the queen's chief of special bureau, to arrange an immediate audience for him with the queen. Moqaddam had just come out of his regular Thursday meetings with the monarch, where he had learned that the shah had decided to appoint Sharif-Emami prime minister. He had suggested to the shah that he reconsider, but seeing the sovereign determined, he had, as army protocol demanded, refrained from insisting. He now thought perhaps the queen might prevail on her husband to change his mind. He asked Nahavandi to be present as "witness to history" as he told the queen the appointment would be a "catastrophe . . . the worst possible choice for this critical moment and for the future of the nation . . . a falling into the abyss" and begged her "to plead with the shahanshah to reconsider his choice."[59]

Touched by the general's intensity, the queen called the shah as the general stood on attention. "Your Majesty," she said, as she always addressed her husband when others were present, "your Chief of SAVAK is here with me. He asks me to throw myself at your feet to beseech you not to appoint Mr. Sharif-Emami head of government. He has a terrible reputation, he says, and to make him prime minister is the most dangerous thing one could do at this time." She listened for a few minutes as her husband explained to her why he had made the choice. She put back the phone and said she believed there was, unfortunately, nothing that could be done. The general, disappointed, begged Nahavandi to keep pressing the point.[60]

It was not easy for Sharif-Emami, either. He had accepted the post as a matter of patriotic duty, a "sacrifice," he told Nahavandi, who thought joining the cabinet was "political suicide" but would become Sharif-Emami's minister of science and higher education under pressure from the shah and the queen.[61] He had come to make peace, or rather to appease, because no one had understood the meaning of Khomeini's demands. He was the culmination of the choices the shah and his government had made until then, systematically misreading the challenge they faced. Over the past year they had neglected the organizational underpinning of a movement that by now had form, substance, and vigor. The shah's moment of truth was at hand: he could wear his military uniform and charge against his enemies in the name of honor, nation, and history, accepting the consequences; or allow a man or a group of men able to forge an independent following to take the reins of government and be a political buffer between him and those intent on deposing the monarchy. Instead, he chose Sharif-Emami, an act that was both a denial and a negation. The new prime minister began by denying himself: this Sharif-Emami is not the old Sharif-Emami, he proclaimed to the parliament and the nation. His "government of national reconciliation," he said, would heal the wounds, respect the Constitution, and guarantee the people's basic freedoms by implementing the clerics' wishes. He would stop corruption and fight frill and mendacity in government. He would have government agents who had transgressed the law brought before the courts and punished. And to show he was serious, he rescinded the imperial calendar and ordered all the cabarets and casinos closed.[62]

The plea for reason merely whetted appetites. "We will not make peace at the expense of our martyrs' blood," replied Khomeini. "Closing the casinos and cabarets in a brothel is nothing but a ruse to deceive the people and their religious leaders," he said. "No party, front, or movement will or may make peace with this government, for making such a peace is to enslave the people and to commit treason against the nation."[63] Others followed. The National Front demanded the dissolution of SAVAK. Opposition and pseudo-opposition leaders announced the formation of political parties, fourteen in one day, ranging from the Pan Iranist, led by Mohsen Pezeshkpur, to the Toilers, led by Mozaffar Baqai—activists in the political heydays of the 1940s reemerging in late 1978 as leaders with few or no followers. Names such as Sanjabi, Foruhar, Hassibi, Bakhtiar, Sadr, Saleh, Azar, Maleki belonged to the past. But they were important for giving the anti-shah movement a liberal tinge, deceiving the foreign press as well as the shah and his regime.

Sharif-Emami's major encounter with the opposition occurred on the *id al-fitr*, the end of Ramadan, on Monday, 4 September 1978. According to the most comprehensive report on the subject to date,[64] the Islamists tricked the liberal opposition at the bazaar into arranging for them the largest venue at an open field in north Tehran. In exchange, they promised the meeting would be similar to such gatherings in past years and would not develop into street marches or demonstrations. On this understanding the bazaar leaders negotiated with the government for official permission. At the appointed hour, on the hills of Qaytariyeh in north Tehran, some fourteen thousand people, according to the security police, gathered carrying banners with Khomeini's picture. After the ceremony, a speaker directed the audience to follow the designated marshals and to cooperate with them. On the street leading to the middle of the town the crowd was joined by smaller gatherings at other quarters of the city according to a precise and calculated plan. By the time the column reached the middle of the town, it had become between one and two hundred thousand strong, according to the newspapers, stronger according to the opposition. They shouted anti-shah and pro-Khomeini slogans on cue. The bazaaris tried to disperse the crowd, but could not. On their way the marchers passed contingents of soldiers and armored vehicles that had been ordered not to intervene, which, of course, the marchers could not know for certain. "Soldier, my brother, why do you shoot your brothers?" shouted the marchers, offering the soldiers flowers, handshakes, and kisses.[65]

The security forces were struck by the organization and discipline of the marches. The shah was especially affected by what he heard. In the morning he had held a special *salam* ceremony, receiving in audience among others the ambassadors from the Muslim countries to honor the *id al-fitr*. In the afternoon, he personally surveyed the demonstrations from a helicopter and subsequently listened to a recording of the slogans. He was shocked. Never since the Mossadeq days had he heard such negative voices against himself. He had always been told that his people were devoted to him, and he had never heard in person anything other than expressions of respect, love, and appreciation. To Reza Qotbi, who talked to him afterward, he sounded devastated: "We heard what they said with our own ear," he kept repeating.[66] How could that be? He had launched democratization on the assumption that his people would rally to him. Now, he was no longer sure. Something was there that he did not understand, some force creating a condition he could not control, some diabolical intrusion about to undo what he had laboriously built over the years. This could not be a communist plot, even though he kept talking about the unholy red and black alliance. Just a few days back, on 29 August, the Chinese leader Hua Kuo-Feng and a large retinue of statesmen and experts had paid him a visit and offered homage in glorious terms. The official Soviet press, unlike its Western counterpart, had not attacked him in the past and was not attacking him now, even though he was hosting the Soviets' nemesis. The left, he thought, could not manage so much subtlety. Increasingly, he suspected the West, especially the oil companies. He had been harsh on them. They had been begging to renegotiate the terms of the Purchase and Service Agreement of 1973, the first time international companies had asked such a thing of the producer countries. But would the Americans and the British embark on such a mindless policy, he asked himself.[67]

The demonstrations continued. On 6 September, Khomeini warned his followers not to let up. "The passing of the holy month of Ramadan does not alter God's injunction." The shah's words were deceptive, he said, Satan's guile to buy time.[68] Khomeini's prodding was essential for mobilizing his lieutenants. The *id al-fitr* event marked a qualitative shift in the Islamists' movement. They now knew, and they assumed the government also knew, that they were able to mobilize large groups of people, supply their slogans, and control their movements according to their strategic and tactical needs. They assumed the government would launch a counteroffensive. So did the major ayatollahs, the National Front, and Mehdi Bazargan's Liberation Movement, all of whom were against provoking the regime. The rumor was that the shah was about to appoint as prime minister General Gholamali Oveisi, commander of the ground forces, and that he had ordered the police and the army to shoot to kill.[69] Khomeini's message mobilized the militants. They had agitated on the 5th and the 6th without encountering any serious reaction and now they pushed for more demonstrations on the 7th, arguing that it was necessary to test the government's mettle. They did not know yet how right they were. The regime, studying the liberals and the traditional ayatollahs, was hoping that the revolutionary fervor would subside with the passing of Ramadan.[70]

On the 7th marches were organized in Tehran and several other cities. The soldiers were ordered not to carry arms to prevent the possibility of their being provoked to fire, according to transcripts of a cabinet meeting. The police, armed with tear gas, confronted the marchers on several routes to Shahyad Square, the marchers' final destination, but soon pulled back. As it became clear that there would be no killing, the number of marchers grew, by some estimates again to one to two hundred thousand. Gradually, Tehran's ulama as well as lay leaders also joined, some, it was said, arriving at the head of the column in taxicabs.[71] At Shahyad a declaration was read by the militants, demanding freedom, independence, release of political prisoners, dissolution of SAVAK, and an Islamic government led by Khomeini. Other than the Khomeini militants, few in that large assembly knew what an Islamic government meant. For the first time, the demands suggested the idea of doing away with the monarchy. Later in the afternoon at Zhaleh Square near the Majlis several thousand Khomeini followers shouted "Death to the shah," the first such organized and coordinated slogan since the beginning of the turmoil.

Thursday, 7 September 1978, was the first day of the first weekend after Ramadan and therefore considered a good day for celebrations and weddings and jollity, despite all the demonstrations and the slogans. As the anti-shah crowd did its thing, the queen visited Dr. Eqbal Hospital at the University of Tehran and subsequently the Cancer Foundation associated with the university. People in the area, on learning she was there, gathered to get a glimpse of her; seeing her walking to the foundation, they shouted hurrahs and "Long live the shah," a spontaneous expression of their sentiments, according to Houchang Nahavandi, who escorted the queen on her visit.[72] But much to his surprise, he was reprimanded by the prime minister for having let the queen visit the hospital and, further, for having accompanied her. Later in the evening, Nahavandi and other ministers were called to a joint meeting of the National Security Council and the cabinet to decide on the course the government was to take. At the council, Sharif-Emami said his information, corroborated by the chiefs of SAVAK, the police, and G2, was that the Islamists had decided to gather at Zhaleh Square early the next morning, move to the Majlis, occupy the Majlis, and proclaim an Islamic republic. Consequently, said the prime minister, the council should proclaim martial law. In the ensuing discussion General Gholamreza Azhari, the chief of the Supreme Commander's Staff, explained that, because it was Thursday, the Sabbath eve, military personnel were not present in full at their posts and those who were on duty might not be trained in mob control, but if martial law was to be declared it should be announced immediately so that the greatest number of people could be informed. This was important because the practical effect of martial law under the circumstances was that it limited the number of individuals who could gather together in public to no more than three. It would still be possible to get the word out since television stations broadcast until twelve midnight, and the radio throughout the night.

Sharif-Emami called the shah for permission to declare martial law and to appoint General Oveisi military governor. The shah was noncommittal at first. He was discussing the situation with Ardeshir Zahedi, his ambassador to the United States, who was back in Iran ostensibly to report on the embassy finances but actually to prop up the shah. Zahedi was against martial law. He also thought the shah could not afford to appear weak or indecisive. And he did not like Sharif-Emami. In the few days he had been in Tehran, several people from the universities, government, business, the bazaar, and the political crowd, including former Prime Minister Ali Amini, had told him Sharif-Emami was a bad choice. Zahedi agreed with this opinion, though he thought the shah could not change the government every day. "Tell Sharif-Emami to do it himself," he advised the sovereign.[73] Now, of course, all the shah could do was to go along with his prime minister.

Sharif-Emami gave the task of informing the media about government policy to his minister for executive affairs, Manuchehr Azmun. No one knows exactly why the proclamation failed to be broadcast that night by either television or radio. NIRT's general manager, Reza Qotbi, had resigned when Sharif-Emami was appointed prime minister, but his resignation had not yet been formally accepted. Meanwhile, Azmun and Qotbi had been at loggerheads since the formation of the Rastakhiz Party. In any event, the martial law proclamation was not broadcast until 6 A.M. on the 8th, though police and military units had announced it on loudspeakers across the city throughout the night. Clearly, the Islamists were determined to push on, and by early morning a sizable crowd had already gathered at Zhaleh Square. They needed blood to keep the revolution-ary fervor kindled, and by now they had transcended the fortieth-day stage. In Shiraz, during Ramadan, they had coined the phrase "Ashura in Ramadan."[74] The Third Imam's death had its *arba'in,* the fortieth-day mourning, but Ashura, the pageant of Karbala, the essence of Hussein's martyrdom, transcended time and space: its moral impact was infinite and eternal. Ashura in Ramadan there-fore became "Every day is Ashura."

The 8th of September became a tragedy for the regime. The Islamists had scored a coup with the Cinema Rex arson in Abadan. They had succeeded in denud-ing the regime of all moral standing. They, on the other hand, had gained in moral and political authority. In the media, former "hooligans" became peace-ful protesters, the government the oppressor-killer. The events at Zhaleh Square provided another opportunity for the Islamists to claim evidence of the regime's bestiality. The troops available to be sent to disperse the crowd had no training in mob control, as General Azhari had explained to the prime minister the evening before. Their number was inadequate. They did not have time or they simply did not think of asking for reinforcements, from either the anti-riot police units or the military. They were up against professional agitators, some of them trained in Palestinian and Libyan camps.[75] Faced with mob agitation, they were ordered to fire in the air. According to military reports, the troops then were fired at. They responded by firing into the crowd. According to official reports, the number of dead was eighty-six. The opposition put the number at hundreds and sometimes thousands. In the cabinet, it was declared that seventy police and soldiers were also killed, which the military preferred not to make public.[76]

The government figure is closer to the truth. The Iranian revolution had relatively few casualties. Immediately after the revolution an organization called Bonyad-e shahid (The Martyr Foundation) was established by Khomeini's order for the sole purpose of ascertaining the identity of those killed during the revolution in order to honor and compensate their families. According to Emadeddin Baghi, then a young revolutionary assigned to research the martyrs, the total number of victims killed in clashes with the regime's forces of law and order was 3,164, of which 2,781 were killed in nationwide disturbances during 1977–79. The figures published by Baghi for 8 September speak of 64 killed in Zhaleh Square, among them two females—a woman and a young girl. On the same day in other parts of the capital a total of 24 people died in clashes with martial law forces, among them one female. Therefore, according to Baghi, the number of people "martyred" on Black Friday is 88.[77] These statistics are very close to the figures announced by Mohammad Reza Ameli Tehrani, minister of information in Sharif-Emami's cabinet; the shah's officials repeatedly spoke of 86 people dead and 205 wounded in clashes. Other post-revolution studies also agree with these numbers. One study puts the number of martyrs the Martyr Foundation found for Tehran for the whole revolution at 744. The coroner's office put the figure for Tehran at 895, and Tehran's main cemetery, Behesht-e Zahra, put it at 768.[78] Even when one allows for miscounting or undercounting, these figures are fundamentally different from those generally cited in the West or in Iran itself.

During the next two months, the opposition moved from demonstrating on the outside to attacking the regime from within its paraphernalia of governance. The main instrument was strikes by government personnel, used increasingly in September and October. Strikes usually began with demands for higher wages and benefits to compensate for inflation. Initially, the government encouraged them as a means of deflecting attention from politics to economics. However, as the strikes spread, demands metamorphosed from economical to political: repeal of martial law, dissolution of the parliament, dissolution of SAVAK, unconditional freedom for political prisoners, and the return of all exiles. By the end of October, the strikes were disrupting much of the government's routine, bringing some vital operations in the oil, communications, energy, and banking industries to a near standstill.

The confrontation tactics also evolved. The charm offensive—flower bouquets, kisses, and brotherly love offered to the soldiers in the streets—was rounded out by cruel and unusual punishment inflicted on military and SAVAK personnel caught in the revolutionaries' dragnet. They were not simply killed; they were maimed to set examples. The practice terrified soldiers' families, especially because the units had orders not to shoot. Sometimes, as in Zanjan or Ahwaz, individual NCOs challenged the revolutionaries by threatening to retaliate. In Zanjan, the bazaar opened and was quiet for several days, until the sergeant who had driven his tank to the gate of the bazaar because his family had been threatened was ordered court-martialed for disobeying orders. The policy emboldened the revolutionaries and caused the military units in the streets to appear ludicrously helpless—castrated giants behind grotesquely large Chieftain tanks harassed by youngsters who shouted anti-shah slogans, stopped traffic, burned banks, cinemas, and liquor stores, obstructed streets with cars, tires, and other obstacles, shouted obscenities at the soldiers and officers, and dispersed, only to regroup in another part of the town. Soon these same youngsters on the roof-tops would shout "Allah Akbar" (God is the greatest) and "Begu marg bar shah" (Say death to the shah) in the evenings at predetermined hours that were syn-chronized with prearranged power blackouts, creating the impression that the whole city cried in supernatural unity. The word *say* in "Say death to the shah" would point to a conscious effort at achieving a psychological breakthrough: most ordinary people neither conceived of nor thought it possible to utter the phrase. To say it broke a taboo, demystified a myth.

21

"I Heard the Message of Your Revolution"

On 2 November 1978, at 6 P.M., President Carter's National Security Adviser, Zbigniew Brzezinski, called to order an "urgent" meeting of the Special Coordination Committee (SCC). Ambassador William Sullivan had sent a cable from Tehran reporting that the shah had indicated he might either abdicate or go for a military government. Clearly, the political conditions in Tehran were reaching a boiling point and demanded an urgent decision. The United States, having been simultaneously engaged with the SALT talks, China, and recently the Israeli-Egyptian negotiations at Camp David, had until this point put Iran on the back burner. Sullivan had never indicated that things were getting out of hand. The State Department was satisfied that the shah was implementing a liberalization policy that would soon bear fruit, turning Iran more or less into a democracy. The shah had said on several occasions that he had expected turmoil as the price of liberalizing, but it was a passing political spasm and the country would soon return to calm and tranquility. The Americans had generally encouraged the shah along these lines.

Political conditions in Iran, however, had not evolved as expected. The Americans had monitored the gradual increase of violence since 1 January 1978, when President Carter was last in Tehran. By September, after the tragedy of Cinema Rex in Abadan, they were becoming more focused on Iranian events. In late August, Brzezinski had a private dinner with Iran's ambassador to the United States, Ardeshir Zahedi, and found him candid about the problems the shah was facing. Brzezinski's National Security Council (NSC) assistant, Commander Gary Sick, had told him that the situation in Iran was deteriorating, that the religious and social forces would not be easily placated, and that the U.S. government should probably pay greater attention to what was happening in Iran. The CIA reports to the president in August, however, gave no cause for alarm. Iran, according to one report, was "not in a revolutionary or even a prerevolutionary situation." The military, said the report, was loyal to the monarchy and the opposition was basically a nuisance, not a serious threat.[1]

As Brzezinski tells it, the 8 September violence at Zhaleh Square prompted Carter to call the shah on 10 September to express his support. The shah told Carter there was a diabolical hand guiding the plans for the disturbances but he was intent on continuing with his liberalization policy. He asked the president to "endorse his efforts as strongly as possible because otherwise his enemies would take advantage of it. The interests of America and Iran were so identified that such an action would be much appreciated. The President promised to do just that."[2] Neither Carter nor Secretary of State Cyrus Vance report in their memoirs on the content of this call, though Vance states that on the suggestion of his deputy, Warren Christopher, he had urged Carter to make a call to the shah.[3] The shah denies he ever had a call from the president at this time. "Sadat called me late on the night of September 9 and we talked for a few minutes. As always, Sadat offered his encouragement and his help. I have no way of knowing what he said to President Carter later that night. But I do know that reports widely circulated in the West about a Carter telephone call to me later that night are false. President Carter never called me—except once at Lackland Air Force Base in December 1979."[4] Why would Carter say nothing about this call? Why would the shah so vehemently deny it was ever made? Possibly, Carter was urged by his staff as well as Sadat to call, but the business at hand in Camp David had not afforded the time. And the shah, expecting a call from Carter, interpreted his failure to call as lack of political support. Two days later Brzezinski saw a report from Tehran that in an interview with *Time Magazine* the shah had looked "like a shattered man on the verge of nervous collapse" and "had mused out loud to the effect that the United States perhaps had conceded Iran to the Soviets or at least to 'a neutral sphere of influence.'" To Brzezinski it was clear that "the shah felt our human rights policy had aided his opponents and that he was not certain of American support."[5] At about the same period, when Vance was at Camp David, Christopher met with Ambassador Zahedi to reaffirm U.S. support and to urge "moderation in enforcing martial law." Zahedi voiced the suspicion, called absurd by Vance, that the United States "was plotting with the opposition to overthrow the shah." Christopher, of course, denied the allegation emphatically, but the suspicion persisted. Early in October, for example, Foreign Minister Amir Khosro Afshar confided in Vance that the shah was determined to continue with liberalization, but the rumor in Iran was that the United States was surreptitiously supporting the opposition.[6] The shah was conflicted, to say the least, but none of this led his administration seriously to reassess its approach to the issue.

In the meantime, according to Brzezinski, Sullivan reported to Vance that on 22 October he and British Ambassador Anthony Parsons had told the shah that in their view "a military solution was a nonstarter." As far as Brzezinski knew, "this important judgment was not approved by the White House."[7] But it was not at variance with the U.S. State Department's view of the Iranian situation, which, though still formally supporting the shah, insisted that "the Iranian military had been discredited by recent events,"[8] and that the United States "should maintain steadfast opposition to a military regime."[9] The position, contained in a document prepared at the State Department, was supported by Sullivan, who on 27 October sent a message stating that "there was no current need for more public statements by the president or visits by high emissaries, that the Embassy opposed any proposals for U.S. assistance to the Iranian military for crowd-control purposes, that there should be no contact with Khomeini, and that 'our destiny is to work with the Shah,' who is prepared to accept a truly democratic regime if it can be achieved responsibly."[10] According to Vance, the "candid" views of his colleagues were known to the White House. But, said Vance, "Zbig [Brzezinski] concluded that the State Department had given up on the shah and was 'soft' on a military solution to the crisis. In a situation quite different from the close and harmonious cooperation on the Middle East—although some of the same people were involved in both—an estrangement grew up between the White House and my key advisers."[11]

On 2 November Sullivan sent another cable, based on two audiences he and Parsons had had with the shah, on 31 October and 1 November. The two ambassadors saw the shah jointly on the recommendation of Ardeshir Zahedi, who thought this would lessen confusion. In practice, things did not work as Zahedi had hoped. Parsons accentuated Sullivan's doubts about the shah's survivability. According to Lord George Brown, a former British foreign secretary, who met both the shah and Parsons at around this time, Parsons placed the probability of the shah's survival at less than fifty-fifty. Lord Brown confided in Iran's ambassador to Britain, Parviz Radji, that Parsons's impending departure from Iran would help the shah's circumstances, though the shah was not inclined to take the rough measures that the circumstances required, including "the offer of scapegoats 'like Hoveyda and Nasiri'" and "more frequent use of the military," both of which Brown had offered as appropriate policy options.[12] The shah did both half-heartedly.

Before opening the 2 November NSC meeting, Brzezinski told Carter that "the shah is losing his will while we continue to push him more and more for liberalization." He wrote in his diary, "In my judgment, I told the President, (he was sitting there with Charles Kirbo [Carter's long-time friend and adviser] having a chat), . . . unless the Shah can combine constructive concessions with a firm hand, he will be devastated." Brzezinski also consulted with Sullivan in Tehran, Ardeshir Zahedi in Washington, and Jean-François Ponçet, his counterpart in Paris. Brzezinski called Vance and "obtained his concurrence in the line that [he] wanted the SCC to adopt."[13]

The group assembled in the Situation Room that day—consisting of Warren Christopher (representing Vance), Secretary of Defense Harold Brown, General David Jones, Admiral Stansfield Turner, and David Aaron and Gary Sick, both of the NSC, the latter responsible for Iran—agreed that the shah should be sent a strong message of support but that the United States should not assume responsibility for decisions that only the shah could and should make. Carter associated himself with the message and suggested also that Brzezinski call the shah. It was agreed that to stress the importance of the matter, the message should go from the White House under Brzezinski's signature. That evening the following message was sent to Sullivan: "On the highest authority and with Cy Vance's concurrence you are instructed to tell the shah as soon as possible that the United States supports him without reservation in the present crisis; that the US has confidence in his judgment regarding the government he decides to set up and recognizes the need for 'decisive action and leadership to restore order and his authority'; and that 'once order and authority have been restored we hope that he will resume prudent efforts to promote liberalization and to eradicate corruption.'"[14]

On the following day, 3 November, Brzezinski called the shah to reassure him personally on those points:

I told the Shah that "the United States supports you without any reservation whatsoever, completely and fully, in the present crisis. You have our complete support. . . . Secondly, we will support whatever decision you take regarding either the form or composition of the government that you decide upon. And thirdly, we are not, and I repeat, not encouraging any particular solution." I then went on to say, bearing in mind Sullivan's report that he and [the] Ambassador of the British Labor government had advised the Shah against a military government, "I hope that is very clear and the Ambassador has been instructed to make it very clear that we are not advising or urging you to go in any particular direction." The shah responded to the effect that he was very appreciative of the message, "but it is a very peculiar situation," and went on to suggest that he was made to feel that "extreme measures, if at all possible, should be avoided." I then responded by saying, "Well, you in effect, it seems to me, have the problem of combining some gestures which would be appealing in a general sense with a need for some specific actions which would demonstrate effective authority." The Shah simply said "Yes." I went on to add, "It is a critical situation in a sense, and concessions alone are likely to produce more explosive situations." The Shah then asked me to repeat that last sentence, and I did so. Curiously, though of course subsequent events have made clear what the Shah meant, he then asked me, "Is your Ambassador briefed?" I assured him that he had received a message to that effect and that I would call him after this conversation to reaffirm it.[15]

On 5 November 1978 Tehran was on fire. Rebellion enveloped the city. Major companies, cinemas, liquor stores, buses, and cars were vandalized and burned, but banks were the primary targets. By one account some four hundred branches of public and private banks were totally or partially burned or otherwise destroyed.[16] Clearly, the Sharif-Emami cabinet would not survive. The government of national reconciliation had seen anything but reconciliation. Tehran Mayor Javad Shahrestani, sensing the inevitability of change, fired a letter to the prime minister demanding his resignation.[17] The previous day's violence at Tehran University had been broadcast in full on television that same evening; now Shahrestani used the event to ingratiate himself with the stronger wave.

In the palace the mood was grim. The shah's adjutant general, Lieutenant General Mohsen Hashemi-Nejad, commander of the Imperial Guard Lieutenant General Abdolali Badrei, commander of the airborne forces Major General Manuchehr Khosrodad, and Brigadier Javad Moinzadeh begged the shah's grand master of ceremony, Amir Aslan Afshar to speak with the shah. "I am the protocol chief," Afshar objected. "You are the generals. Why don't you speak with him? You command all the military in Tehran. Why don't you stop this nonsense?" Nonetheless, he told them he would initiate the subject with the shah provided the generals pursued it to conclusion. The generals promised they would. As the shah descended the stairs of the Jahan Nama building to enter the car to drive up the compound to the Niavaran Palace, Afshar fell on his knees and clasped the shah's feet. Aghast, the shah tried to pull back but could not. "What is it?" he asked.

"Your Majesty, the city is on fire. The banks have been burned. The citizens' possessions have been destroyed. Civil documents have been cast away. No one is safe. It is no longer clear what remains to the people or of the authority they can turn to. Please, Sire, something must be done."

The generals were now all on their knees. "But the army is attending to the matter," retorted the shah.

Khosrodad then stood at attention, raised his hand in salute, and, as tears ran down his face, implored: "Your Majesty, your army has become an object of scorn, contempt, disrespect. They spit on your soldiers. No honor remains to the imperial forces. Your Majesty must order us to defend you, the country, and ourselves."

The shah was visibly shaken. "Of course; we shall take measures," he said, turning back from the car.[18]

Back in his office, he called Afshar and ordered him to telephone General Oveisi and tell him to stay in his office and await his call. The thought of Oveisi taking the helm of the government rejuvenated the generals. He was the one with a reputation for courage and toughness. "Thank God," said the generals. "It was Oveisi who wished to strike from the outset, but he was not allowed. Now, he will become prime minister and things will be in step again."[19] Afshar ordered tea to celebrate the good news. The shah called Afshar once again and told him to summon Sullivan and Parsons. He then took a helicopter ride to survey the burning city. "Destruction everywhere, hardly a clear spot, nothing but devastation and ruins," he later lamented to his wife.[20]

Sullivan received the shah's summons at dusk as he was visiting a friend in the north of town. He had no problem reaching the court. The British embassy, however, had been on the rioters' route and had been attacked and severely damaged; Parsons himself had taken refuge in the French embassy. An armored personnel carrier was sent to fetch him to the court. Sullivan arrived at the Niavaran Palace just after dark, an hour before Parsons. He found the place quieter than usual and emptier. He saw no aides-de-camp in their accustomed stations. He went into the main drawing room. No one was there, either. As Sullivan puzzled what to do next, the queen came in through a door to one of the small rooms to the side. She was surprised to see Sullivan in the room. Sullivan explained that he had been asked there for an audience with the shah. The queen went out into one of the adjoining rooms and, according to Sullivan, rounded up an aide-de-camp, who came in shortly followed by two or three more aides. They told Sullivan the shah awaited him in his study and led him there without delay.[21]

The shah, striking Sullivan as "strangely calm," told Sullivan the destruction wreaked on the city during the day left him no choice but to institute a military government. Sullivan assured him that the U.S. government supported his decision. Then he recounted what he had heard all day—that the arson was the work of SAVAK—and asked whether the shah thought that this might be true. "Who knows? These days I am prepared to believe anything," answered the shah to Sullivan's amazement.[22]

Sullivan then recounts, seemingly in passing, an event that may be the key to understanding a part of the enigma surrounding the ensuing choice of General Gholamreza Azhari rather than Oveisi for prime minister.

> It was nearly another hour before the British ambassador arrived, and during that period the shah rehearsed once again his familiar arguments about the options open to him. In the middle of this he received a telephone call from the shahbanu. Although my understanding of Farsi was less than adequate, I could make out that he was telling her of his intention to instill a military government and answering some of the reservations she was expressing about such a decision. It was a gentle, patient sort of conversation with nothing peremptory in its tone. He informed her at the end that the United States government had agreed with the wisdom of this course of action. Once this conversation was concluded, he picked up the phone and called General Azhari, the chief of staff, asking him to come to the palace as soon as he could get there.[23]

Almost everyone expected Oveisi to be named prime minister. Everyone in the military agreed that Azhari was too mild a person for the job, given the prevailing chaos. The shah had instinctively picked Oveisi as his initial choice. Afshar and the generals had already celebrated the event. By the late afternoon the city was abuzz with the news of Oveisi's appointment. Sullivan apparently only learned Azhari had been selected after the shah called for the general. The queen, on the other hand, seems to have been left out of the loop in the early hours before a final decision was made. She was surprised to find Sullivan in the palace and apparently did not know what had passed or was passing. She learned about the decision to install a military government with Oveisi at the helm after Sullivan had arrived for his meeting with the shah. She did not like the choice. She called the shah in the middle of his conversation with the American ambassador to make sure she would have her input. She proved convincing, though only because her husband was inclined to be convinced. She explained later:

> General Oveisi was the military governor of Tehran. After what had happened in Zhaleh Square, the Black Friday, I felt that General Oveisi was not the right man if we were after understanding with the opposition. But it was not like my point of view prevailed. I did not know the military in a way that I could influence the events. I had seen General Azhari in formal occasions as His Majesty's adjutant. Other events had transpired. His Majesty had confidence in Azhari. It is not true that he was chosen on my recommendation.

Actually the queen thought Oveisi was not as tough as he was reputed to be. As military governor, Oveisi constantly asked for directives from the shah. "Well, if you have a job to do, do it, as Alam did in 1963. Why must you ask for directives all the time?" observed the queen.[24]

The shah was surprised at the depth and spread of popular dissatisfaction. He could not understand why what he considered service to the people was rewarded by expressions of dislike and seeming hatred. All around him he sensed negativity, emptiness, and squalor, as when rats abandon a sinking ship. His enemies, he said, marched on the streets of Tehran, his supporters on the Boulevard des Champs-Élysées. He was caught between his military commanders, who advised him to show an iron fist, and civilians whose sense of guilt foreshadowed and encouraged his, advising him the opposite. As early as September he had said that if it came to shedding blood, he would leave the country rather than kill his people.[25] He would later write that he could not order his people killed because he was a king and not a dictator. A king, unlike a dictator, is the custodian of an office; he holds it for a time and passes it on to an heir, if he is lucky, in better shape than when he received it.

Others, however, could only guess at what he might do. His enemies, having forever maligned him as the Attila of the age, expected him to strike at a time of his choosing. The idea of a military government put the fear of God in their hearts and they waited anxiously to see what the new government would do. His hardliner friends, especially those whose association with the shah had come after he had assumed the pomp and power of the title Aryamehr, thought almost to the end that he was playing a game. He was showing the Americans that the only way to run Iran was his way. No more nonsense about democracy and human rights. Look what would happen when you offered the people an "open political space." And there were those who thought how great it would be if the mayhem led to a balance between freedom and authority, individual and community, man and government. One of them told the queen that the shah would be remembered as one of the greatest kings in Iranian history if he could negotiate the change from authoritarianism to democracy in a country such as Iran, beating the menace of the red and the black. In fact, the generals had already lost their ability to strike, though as yet they did not know it. They, but not General Azhari, who had been put in charge, pleaded with the shah to use the iron fist.

In the preceding weeks, as the hawks and doves battled over policy, an idea had begun to take shape—a hope more than an idea—that perhaps a workable middle way could be negotiated. The people wanted change. They were making a revolution. Fine; but must the revolution be violent? What if the regime agreed to everything the people wanted short of regime change? What if a distinction were made between *enqelab va shuresh,* revolution and revolt? The shah, after all, had launched a White Revolution, which—the present turmoil notwithstanding—had been astonishingly successful. He had even ordered the revolution's dialectic to be written. But his was a peaceful revolution. Why not make a distinction between revolution and violence? Why not consider what the people demanded a corrective to, if not a continuation of, his revolution and give it to them if they agreed to be peaceful? What if he became the leader of the new revolution? After all, for almost two years now he had adopted a strategy meant to create in his people's mind a perceptual disconnect between him and his government. He had wanted always the best for his people and they knew it. They had shown their approval in countless ways. They had poured into the streets whenever and wherever he appeared, shaking with excitement. They had filled the papers with their ceaseless expressions of gratitude. "*Sepas, Sepas, Sepas*—Thank you. Thank you. Thank you." How many times had they shouted and written how glad they were to have him as their leader? After all, who could be against a more prosperous life, security from womb to tomb, the Great Civilization he had promised? If things had gone wrong, it was not he who had caused them to go wrong. He meant the best for his people, and his people had appreciated it until this unholy alliance of the red and the black, propped up by those foreign forces bent on clipping his wings, had succeeded in perpetrating this vile trick.

The shah's efforts to separate himself from his government had failed, but having foregone use of the military, he had very few choices left. Besides, the proposed strategy would appeal to the Americans. That's in essence what Sullivan pushed, though most likely not knowing it was flawed and useless. It represented a profound misunderstanding of the nature of the revolt and of Khomeini as cleric and man. The revolution was anything but spontaneous. It was meticulously planned and led. Long before General Azhari was appointed prime minister on 6 November, Khomeini's people had taken over the revolutionary movement's ideology, strategy, and command structure. It was no longer (if it ever had been) the "people" who decided how the process unfolded. It was Khomeini and his followers who mapped the revolution's path. Khomeini as cleric and man was different from the others. His theory of Islamic government separated him from the other ulama in Iran. So did his personality, which could be designated a Hofferian "true believer," an ideal type totally committed to a mission. Such a man saw himself as put on earth for a purpose, the achievement of which was his only goal. For him, compromise was anathema and moderation no virtue. His opponents' efforts at compromise only proved to him that he was right, binding him further to his purpose. But the shah neither understood this nor could have done much about it if he had.

On the evening of 5 November, Reza Qotbi's home telephone rang.[26] Qotbi, the queen's cousin, picked up the receiver and immediately recognized the shah's voice on the other end. He was surprised. He had resigned as the head of the National Iranian Radio and Television (NIRT) over two months ago when Sharif-Emami had been appointed prime minister. Since then he had often seen the shah at court, but there had never been a matter so urgent as to require a direct call. His surprise did not last long as the sovereign came quickly to the point. He had decided to appoint a military cabinet, and he wanted to address the nation. He wanted Qotbi to write the speech. Qotbi now was more than surprised; he was perplexed. "I cannot write my own speeches. How will I be able to write such an important speech for Your Majesty?" he said.

"We have seen and read some material you have written and we think you will do quite well." the shah replied. "At any rate, I have some notes that I will send to you. They contain what I intend to say. I will have to appoint a military government. But I would like to tell the people that this is a temporary necessity. Soon, we will replace it with a *melli* [nationalist] cabinet."

"But a military government is also a melli government. How can we imply that it is not?" Qotbi said, now really puzzled.

The shah, somewhat flustered, said, "I mean a democratic government," which suggested to Qotbi that "in the past also whenever he talked about a *hokumat-e melli* [nationalist government] he meant a democratic government."

Then, the shah said, "I will have to talk on television; however, they tell me that the television people are refusing to come to the Palace."

"This is impossible," said Qotbi and mumbled to the effect that he was no longer the head of NIRT, thinking that under the strain of circumstance the shah might have forgotten. But he added, half-incredulously, "I will talk to them."

Qotbi called the NIRT and asked Amir Mekanik, the man in charge of mobile units, to prepare to go to the palace the next day, to which Mekanik readily agreed. Later that evening Qotbi received from the palace an envelope containing material relevant to the proposed speech. "Some of the material, essentially the notes on the margins, was the shah's; the rest was prepared by others. The 'I heard the message of your revolution' piece was part of the material and seemed to have been jotted down by [the shah] himself." Qotbi telephoned Seyyed Hossein Nasr, an Islamic philosopher, former chancellor of the Aryamehr Technical University, and at the time chief of the queen's special bureau. Nasr had also been contacted by the shah and expected to go to the court the next morning. They arranged to go together. Qotbi suggested they consult the queen before they took the speech to the shah, and Nasr agreed. Qotbi worked late into the night on the speech, arranging and rearranging the material. He prepared three versions, reasoning that the shah should be provided with some options to choose from. In the morning he took the three versions to Nasr, who also had prepared a version. They chose and corrected a version they both preferred. When they arrived at the Niavaran Palace, the queen told them that she had had a difficult night, had stayed up late, and could not help them much with their task. They went from the residence down the compound to the Jahan Nama building to meet the shah in his office. Qotbi gave him the different versions of the speech, indicating the one he and Nasr preferred, and left to help arrange the set for the television recording. At this time he was told that the shah wanted the speech to be written in larger letters so he could read it more easily. In the past, the shah had used notes that prompted him on the points he wished to emphasize. This time he seemed tired and wished to have the whole speech written out. Qotbi rewrote the speech, a version of his preferred arrangement with the shah's final corrections, in large letters.

Seyyed Hossein Nasr's recollection is somewhat different, though he agrees with Qotbi on the essentials of the speech. According to Nasr, the shah called both Nasr and Qotbi into his office.

> He had a large notepad on which he had jotted down a number of topics, more like talking points, perhaps twenty. He said he had a very important speech to deliver the next day and wanted us to prepare it for him. 'You have always told me I should speak with the people. I will tomorrow.' Qotbi and I retired to my office and then to my home. We worked hard on the notes and came up with a text; it was essentially what His Majesty had written down, which contained the sentence 'I have heard the voice of your revolution.' His Majesty had instructed me to take the text to him that evening no matter how late. He would stay awake and wait for the text. I called in after we had finished writing the text and told [Major] General Ali Neshat [commander of the Immortals, the king's special guard unit of the Imperial Guard], I was bringing the speech. Neshat received me at the door to the Niavaran Palace, the building. We both went in, I insisting that Neshat

personally deliver the speech to His Majesty. I waited while Neshat took the text to His Majesty in his bedroom. When he returned, Neshat said His Majesty had received the text, thanked me for my labor, and said I could go and rest.[27]

From that point Nasr's version is almost identical to Qotbi's. The problem with Nasr's account is that it also does not agree with that of Aslan Afshar, the shah's protocol chief, which suggests that the shah had not seen the text before it was handed to him in the morning. This, however, is not materially important and may be a matter of confusing two different occasions. There is no doubt that both Nasr and Qotbi worked on the text and that the text essentially contained what the shah had indicated in his notes.

That morning the shah was tense and short-tempered. His speech was scheduled to be broadcast on the 2 P.M. news. It was near noon, and the speech was not yet ready. Earlier, when he had been told that Nasr and Qotbi had taken the speech to the queen, he was quite angry. "Why have they taken the speech to Her Majesty?" he shouted to Afshar. "Is she the one who reads it on television? Am I not to read it at least once to know what it contains before I deliver it?" But the visit to the queen had not taken long, since she was indisposed. The shah had several questions, and according to Afshar both Nasr and Qotbi told him that if he were to give a speech of this sort, he might as well put himself squarely on the side of the people and say what the people wanted him to say.[28] The advice did not sit well with Afshar. He was surprised at the tone. To him it did not suit the idea of a military government. He gave the speech to Kambiz Atabai, who read it perfunctorily. As far as Atabai remembers, neither he nor Afshar brought the matter up with the shah. "We thought there must be some virtue in it that we did not discern," said Atabai.[29]

The fact was that military government meant different things to different people. The hawks around the shah believed it meant enforcing Article 5 of the martial law code, as now in effect, which said any grouping of more than three people would be forcefully dispersed and the offenders arrested. "You wouldn't want to make a joke of the military government," observed Afshar.[30] The doves, however, thought differently. They wanted to buy time, hoping to come to terms with the opposition. According to the queen, this was already a thankless task:

Individuals who came to me seemed obsessed with the idea that we should satisfy practically everybody. Ayatollah Shari'atmadari complains that meat is not prepared according to the Islamic rules; we must find out who the culprit is and assure him that the problem is rectified. There are reports of a shooting near the shrine in Mashhad; we must look into it and assure the ulama nothing of the sort has happened. We had fallen into the habit of appeasement. In the meantime things got worse. Some people suggested that His Majesty send a message to calm the people down.

I remember Dr. Nasr and Reza Qotbi brought the message. I now believe that this was not the right option. At the time, when I read it, I did not find anything wrong with it. But I don't know what had transpired before. Dr. Nasr says that the basic ideas came from His Majesty. Who was involved in drawing up those ideas I do not know.[31]

The doves and the hawks vied for the shah's ear, which the speech showed belonged to the doves, a fact that the hawks found difficult to accept. They blamed those who prepared the speech rather than the shah who read it. The shah, on the other hand, was pleased with the speech and his performance. Later that afternoon he called in person to thank Nasr and Qotbi for the speech. Nasr recalled the conversation:

I was Her Majesty's chief of bureau and she had called me many times. Indeed, I had taught my little girl, who often answered the phone, to speak with reverence when the queen was on the phone. "Address her as Your Majesty," I said. "Say, '*ta'zim arz mikonam*'" [please accept my salutations]. This afternoon she came to me and said His Majesty was on the phone. I thought she was mistaking the queen for the shah and kidded her about her confusion. I took the receiver and lo and behold it was His Majesty. "I thank you very much for the good work you did on the speech," he said. I replied with a few nondescript sentences such as it was my duty and that the basic ideas were His Majesty's. After the revolution I met His Majesty several times—in Morocco, Mexico, New York at the hospital, and in Lackland. His Majesty talked about many things, including the mistakes he thought he had made. But not once did he complain about that speech.[32]

■

General Gholamreza Azhari was the same age and rank as Generals Oveisi, Qarabaghi, Fardust, Jam, and others who were of the shah's generation, and he had moved up the ranks in parallel with them. In 1970, as a lieutenant general, he had been retired and had thought of living the rest of his life in the United States. When Jam moved up from acting chair to chairman of the Supreme Commander's Staff (SCS), the shah asked whom he would appoint acting chair in his now-vacant position. Jam left it to the shah, but it was not the shah who chose Azhari. General Reza Azimi, then the shah's adjutant general, asked Jam to return Azhari to active service and appoint him his deputy chief. Azimi was full of praise for Azhari, who had been his chief of staff when Azimi commanded the ground forces. Jam was deferential to Azimi. "I thought I owed the general for his unfailing friendship and support as I moved through the ranks from the time I was appointed commandant of the Officer Cadet College to the time I commanded the Second Army Group. I could not turn him down. I took the proposal to His Majesty, who said he had not been impressed with Azhari as commander of the First Army Group, but I could call him back and give him the job if that [was] what I wanted."[33] But Jam soon fell out with the shah, and the shah, foreseeing closer military interaction with the Americans in planning, weapons, and logistics, and wanting a chief able to do his bidding with as little friction as possible on either side, then made Azhari, who was U.S.-educated, spoke English well, and was on good terms with the U.S. military advisers, his SCS chief. Azhari didn't have much to do with the line commanders, who reported directly to the shah. But he was good at staff work and at getting everybody to work together. He did in the military what Hoveyda did in the world of the civilians.

Azhari's appointment as prime minister was welcome news to Sullivan. "Civilized," Sullivan described him to General Khosrodad and Kambiz Atabai as he and Parsons were leaving the shah's presence the evening of 5 November.[34] By this time Azhari had also arrived, apparently guessing that he was to be prime minister. To Sullivan he appeared dejected as he climbed the stairs to the shah's study to receive his appointment. The next day as Reza Qotbi came across him unexpectedly in the hall to the shah's bureau, he thought Azhari looked sick, and asked if he was ill. "I wish I were," Azhari replied, "but what has befallen me passes illness. I am ruined." Qotbi was surprised, not yet knowing what had caused the general's melancholy. Perhaps he had been dismissed for some failure associated with yesterday's mishaps, he thought. He asked again what had happened, this time with more sympathy in his voice. "His Majesty has appointed me prime minister," said the general in a tone more apposite to an officer about to be court-martialed.

"God help us all if the top-ranking officer of the realm, now appointed prime minister, sees his appointment not as honor and opportunity but as a calamity," Qotbi thought.[35] But Azhari was the preferred general for the royal advisers who advocated negotiating with the opposition. No one in the opposition would talk to Oveisi, the butcher of Black Friday, as the queen had observed. Azhari, on the other hand, was mild and, as Sullivan had said, civilized. All he wanted was for the turmoil to go away so he could go back to the barracks, where everything was orderly and disciplined. This was not what he had asked for.

Clearly the general was not prepared for his new assignment. As he was leaving the palace after receiving his appointment, he called on General Khosrodad and asked him to give him names of military officers for various ministries — any names. Then he spotted Major General Ali Neshat, commander of the Immortals. It was Neshat's turn then to provide names. But Azhari could come up with no better than the names of the commanders of the forces and his own staff, appointing them to various ministries more or less at random. The next day, 6 November, he presented to the shah his incomplete cabinet, which included three civilians: Amir Khosro Afshar, foreign affairs; Mohammad Reza Amin, industry and mines; Ezzatollah Homayunfar, minister without portfolio. Two events dominated that day: in his speech the shah made the fateful statement, "I heard the message of your revolution," probably the first time the word "revolution" was used; and the new government, invoking Article 5 of the martial law, detained several of the regime's major political personalities, including former SAVAK chief General Nematollah Nasiri and former minister of information Dariush Homayun, for security reasons. The action caused one general, the head of Iran's national airlines, to commit suicide before the martial law officers reached his home.

Nonetheless, the idea of a military government scared the opposition. All activity subsided, as everyone waited to see what a military government might mean. Azhari's first encounter with the Majlis was triumphant. The deputies, awed as everyone else by the idea of a military government, were largely compliant in their reactions, which helped boost the new prime minister's morale. The next day at the court he boasted to Abolfath Atabai, then the oldest hand with the shah and a deputy court minister, about his mastery of the Majlis. The old man had suggested he dissolve the parliament and rule by decree until new elections were held. "You are a military government. You should not be hampered by a Majlis that could very well oppose some of the more difficult decisions you may have to take," said the elder Atabai.

"Didn't you watch me in the Majlis yesterday? I can handle these people. Woe on him who dares oppose me. He will face my MPs."[36] This bravado proved more fantasy than fact. In the succeeding days the new government fell in line with the appeasement routine. Azhari kept on reciting from the Koran and recoiling before the opposition's advances.

On 5 October Ayatollah Khomeini had been taken by the Iraqi government from Najaf to Kuwait, but the Kuwaiti authorities turned him back at the border. He was returned to Baghdad and flown to Paris on the 6th. The shah believed that Saddam Hussein had seized on Prime Minister Sharif-Emami's request to curb

Khomeini to get rid of the troublesome cleric. The French asked the shah if they should let him in. The shah said yes. "I said: What is the difference? If he was not in Paris, he would be in Hamburg. So, what's the difference?"[37] Paris, of course, made a real difference. France was culturally closer to Iran and thus more accessible. From a cleric in a confined space in Najaf, Paris turned Khomeini into an international personality able to communicate globally. Cassettes were now only a small component of the system of communication established in Paris. International radio became an instrument of Khomeini's informal directives. The BBC became a most effective channel of communication as it regularly broadcast the plans of action of the opposition, the center of which by October had become a semi-insurgency. The Iranian government repeatedly complained to the British government, but the answer was always that the BBC was an independent organization dedicated to broadcasting the news impartially and that the British government had no influence on what the BBC reported. The BBC, for its part, denied that it was a "mouthpiece" or "tribune" for Khomeini.[38] In Iran, however, everyone, including the shah's foes, believed that the BBC was instrumental in promoting the cause of the rebellion. The National Front leader Shapur Bakhtiar, for example, was struck by the influence the BBC exerted on the Front's affiliates. "My years in the opposition taught me . . . [that the] BBC, serving the interest of its country, and applying its policy, supported Khomeini well before he arrived in Iran and even before he arrived in France." Often he had heard people tell him about a future date for a demonstration they had heard on the BBC, when he still had no knowledge of it. Bakhtiar deduced from his own experience that British policy favored Khomeini.[39] More likely, the BBC, like many other media establishments in Europe and America, was anti-shah not because of formal directives from the British government but rather because of the liberal proclivities of the reporters and analysts who had formulated the shah as a tyrant and Khomeini as an ascetic sage seeking freedom and dignity for his people. On the other hand, it seemed politically irresponsible for the British government to allow an enormously powerful organization, which it financed, to be free to manage Britain's foreign news (some argued, its foreign policy) as it pleased, given the fact that much of the reporting was generated by non-British sources. In other words, while most Iranians found the British government's claim of noninterference with the BBC a possibility they could accept for constitutional reasons with respect to domestic news and commentary, they found the same claim ludicrous when applied to the BBC's reporting of foreign news, especially when directed to the foreign country in local vernacular.

While the BBC was the most effective tool for transmitting the Islamists' activities, including their tactical instructions, there were other respectable organs of the Western media and press that also placed themselves at the service of the anti-shah movement. *Le Monde* and the *Guardian* are examples of otherwise reasonable liberal press in Europe maligning the shah and extolling Khomeini with absolute moral and intellectual conviction. The same was happening with the liberals in Iran. By October, the Khomeini movement began to invade the liberal mood, which then overcame the liberal intellect. Part of this transformation may have resulted from the stark difference that had begun to show between the shah's seeming lack of conviction and Khomeini's ineluctable, passionate intensity. The liberal press projected the shah, whose major worry was to avoid bloodshed, as the Attila of the age and Khomeini, for whom bloodshed was just a means to a desired end, as the ascetic saint. No one in Iran or in the West took the trouble of reading what Khomeini had written in his treatises or listening to his lectures on tape, which were available to all. Soon Khomeini's persona would become transcendent, even be claimed to be reflected on the surface of the moon, seen not only by the illiterate devout but also by the learned and the literati, scientists and philosophers alike.[40] This kind of abandonment of reason could come about only if there was a predisposition to see just one dimension of a multidimensional reality. By the beginning of November, when Sharif-Emami yielded to Azhari, the liberal middle class in Iran was about to lose all sense of proportion.[41] And the shah and his men, even those who advocated the iron fist, were at a loss as to what exactly had caused the madness.

Holding court in Neauphle-le-Château, the Paris suburb where he was ensconced, Khomeini had concluded that the shah was on his way out, and that he, Khomeini, was the only force that counted. It was essential to maintain the unity of command and purpose, as he let his interlocutors know. On 28 October Karim Sanjabi, the titular head of the National Front, flew to Paris for a meeting arranged by Khomeini's disciple (and the Islamic Republic's first president), Abolhassan Bani-Sadr, and Bani-Sadr's friend Ahmad Salamatian, with whom Sanjabi was in contact. Sanjabi was on his way to Vancouver to represent the National Front at the Socialist International. According to Shapur Bakhtiar, the Front leadership had told him he could visit Khomeini and listen to what he had to say, but he was not to make any commitments.[42] According to Ebrahim Yazdi, an adviser to Khomeini in Paris, Sanjabi was cowed by Khomeini even before he saw him. During their first meeting Khomeini would not allow Sanjabi to speak with him privately and instructed him to speak loudly so he could be heard by everyone present. Sanjabi did as instructed. He had been scheduled to visit Khomeini again in the afternoon but was advised the ayatollah would see him after he returned from Canada. Sanjabi cancelled his North American trip, thinking he would lose the chance to see Khomeini if he continued with his trip. Khomeini now demanded that Sanjabi put on paper his views about the shah's regime before he would decide on giving him an audience. Sanjabi wrote down what Khomeini wanted him to: that the present monarchy lacked a legal and religious foundation; that as long as the present illegal monarchical regime existed, Iran's national Islamic movement would not accept any government as legal regardless of its composition; and that Iran's national governmental regime, based on Islam, democracy, and independence (independence added by Khomeini), should be determined by a national referendum. Khomeini was satisfied. He told Sanjabi the shah had been weakened, was politically dying, and should not be given a chance to regain power, "for if he does, he will take revenge on all of us. We must not give him time, for if we do, the people will lose hope." Was he permitted to announce in Tehran the points he had submitted to Khomeini, asked Sanjabi. "You can announce it anywhere, even as soon as you go out of this door," Khomeini instructed. Sanjabi did just that.[43]

Those who met with Khomeini in Neauphle-le-Château invariably did so on Khomeini's terms. There was never any give-and-take, advice, or consultation. The demand for submission was total. Men like Sanjabi or the Liberation Movement's Mehdi Bazargan could not have failed to realize after their first meeting with Khomeini that he was not what the world said he was. But in knowing that, they also realized that he was not a man to be crossed or trifled with. They were emotionally cowed, made to behave as would a disciple, even as they knew that the man stood for thoughts, actions, and political structures that were far from their ideas of justice, freedom, or fair government. On the day after Sanjabi was admitted to his presence, Khomeini was asked in several interviews if he had entered a coalition with any political party or movement, such as the National Front, now that he had conferred with Sanjabi and Bazargan. There was not and would never be a common front, he answered clearly and unequivocally: "The present Islamic movement includes all the people and shall proceed in the same way. We remind you that we have no relationship with any group or front and shall receive no one or group that does not accept our [terms]."[44] He would not countenance coalition with anyone. On his talks with Sanjabi he observed: "I told him what was on my mind. There is no coalition. All the people are with us and we are with the people. Whoever accepts our position, which is independence, freedom, and an Islamic Republic replacing the monarchy, is of us and of the people. Whoever does not accept our position walks against Islam and the people and is not of us nor are we with him. We will speak with those who are with us, but we have no special relations with anyone."[45] And on the day General Azhari was named prime minister, Khomeini told his followers this was much ado about nothing: "the tanks, machine guns, and bayonets are all rusty; they will not withstand your iron will."[46]

Azhari's behavior proved Khomeini's point. Azhari took away the shah's last defense — the idea of an invincible fighting force. The military government continued the policy of freeing enemies and imprisoning friends that the Sharif-Emami government had begun — this time with a vengeance. At a special council before the shah and the queen during Sharif-Emami's premiership, held to brainstorm about the deteriorating situation, Manuchehr Azmun, the minister for executive affairs, had suggested that the shah place himself at the head of a revolutionary council and among other things arrest and execute a few of his former civilian and military officers. The SAVAK chief, General Moqaddam, had cut him short, stating that if that were to be the nation's policy, by right Azmun would be the first to hang.[47] Now, indeed, Azhari soon began arresting the former ministers, among them Azmun; many of those arrested, including both Moqaddam and Azmun, would be executed by the Khomeini regime. The shah, much to his later regret, went along with the decision, by this time no longer able to guide policy. When the decision was made to arrest Hoveyda, he was heard to say: "How hurriedly we are putting nails to our own coffin."[48]

On 1 December, the first day of the month of Moharram, Khomeini ordered soldiers to desert their barracks as a religious duty. That evening, for the first time, youngsters invaded the rooftops and began shouting, *"Allah Akbar,* God is the Greatest." The Islamists prepared for the ninth and tenth of Moharram, the anniversary of the martyrdom of the Third Imam, the most celebrated tragedy of all time in the shii lore. Aware of the criticalness of the event, the government also prepared, negotiating with the revolutionaries along the lines of the *id al-fitr* agreements in September. The result was a reasonably bloodless two days in which the opposition gained the right to claim that the revolution was catholic, comprehending all social strata. The claim was true, though the opposition and the international press exaggerated the number of the marchers. The BBC placed the number at two million, which stuck; though the actual number was likely below one million, even that was massive and convincing.[49] In Tehran, on the Ashura, a significant number of the participants, including women, hailed from the middle class. Many of them walked as families, some with babies in strollers. By their presence, they endorsed the Islamists' demands — the abrogation of monarchy and the institution of an Islamic Republic with Khomeini at its head—though not many of them knew what in fact they were endorsing. They voted with their feet, as Khomeini later claimed.

This was not a good day for the shah. As the people were marching against him in the streets, he was hit by an unexpected, harrowing event in the mess hall of his special guards, the Immortals, at their headquarters in Lavizan, reminiscent of the Marble Palace attempt on his life in 1965. At 12:30 P.M. on 11 December 1978, Private Salamatbakhsh and Corporal Abedi, both of the anti–air artillery, took positions on opposite sides of the dining hall and fired their G-3 semi-automatics at the officers and the NCOs as they were having lunch in their appointed sections. A young communications officer and twelve NCOs and soldiers were killed; thirty-six more were wounded. The attackers were gunned down by the Guard personnel. In the private's pocket was a letter he had written to his father, telling him he was about to kill the Guard's personnel and was on his way to heaven. Later it was learned that the Islamists had swayed two more soldiers to help in the killing, but they had lost their nerve just before the action was to begin. Several members of the airborne units were among the casualties. Since their headquarters were on the route of the marchers, they had been ordered to move their helicopters to Lavizan for safety. When their commander, General Khosrodad, visited them that afternoon at the Guard's headquarters, he found them in a state of shock. It was unthinkable to them that such an event might occur in a military organization most loyal to the king. Was this a prelude to an anti-shah coup? Khosrodad gave them a pep talk, assuring them that there was no plot in the military to sabotage and kill them. Later that evening the queen visited the wounded to offer them her solace.[50]

By now it had become clear to everyone that Azhari would not do. Three days before the Ashura, on the 7th, the Associated Press reported that President Carter was doubtful about the shah's ability to control the events but had made clear that the United States did not intend to interfere in Iranian affairs. The American position was now moving, ever so imperceptibly, from saving the shah to saving Iran, which suggested a growing readiness to negotiate seriously with the opposition. The shift in mood was punctuated by an invitation extended to former Undersecretary of State George Ball by Brzezinski to advise the NSC on Iran policy.[51] Ironically, Ball's position was significantly different from that of Brzezinski and far closer to that of Vance, although, according to Brzezinski, Vance had been singularly unenthusiastic about inviting Ball. Ball suggested that the shah yield his authority and power to a "Council of Notables," which Brzezinski considered "a political pastiche that would represent the various feuding elements of Iranian politics."[52] The idea, supported by Vance and Sullivan, was further endorsed by a conversation between Sullivan and the shah on

13 December. There were three choices, the shah had told Sullivan: a national coalition, surrender to the opposition, and the iron fist. Sullivan had advised a coalition government as the only logical alternative.[53] In Washington, opinions were divided, the president agreeing with Ball that U.S. involvement in the Iranian crisis should not appear excessive. "The shah," Carter wrote in his diary on 14 December, "must share substantial governmental authority with civilians, including the opposition, in order to prevent having to abdicate." The NSC debate led to a series of questions for the shah to answer, which, according to Brzezinski, helped the shah to clear his thoughts and, according to Carter, worked since the shah "responded well to them."[54]

Much of the debate in Washington had little to do with what was happening in Iran. The shah clearly did not favor the iron fist. Even his mild military prime minister complained about the shah tying his hands. The army was permitted to fire only in the air, no matter how badly bruised, Azhari told Sullivan on 21 December. Azhari, who had suffered a mild heart attack, received the ambassador lying in bed in a small room next to his office. According to Sullivan, Azhari asked him to tell his government that "This country is lost because the king cannot make up his mind."[55] The shah for his part was looking for an alternative to Azhari, but could not find takers who also satisfied his conditions. By this time, however, he had basically decided that he would leave the immediate future of the country to a *hokumat-e melli,* a government by the nationalists as he had defined it to Qotbi and others on the occasion of preparing the "I heard the message of your revolution" speech.

Toward the end of November, the CIA submitted a psychological analysis of the shah to the NSC that, contrary to Brzezinski's intimations, described the shah in relation to his environment rather accurately. "It continues to be our judgment," read the report, "that the [shah's] mood is not inappropriate to his situation, that he is not paralyzed by indecision, by his emotional reactions, and that for the most part he is in accurate touch with reality. . . . Reports of discouragement or transient depression should not be read as difficulties with leadership. That he moves first in one way and then in another should also not be considered surprising. It is his way of grappling with pressure from all sides in a situation that has no clear solution."[56]

The shah realized that since he had chosen not to give his military a free hand, he in fact had no solution. This reality severely limited the choices available to Sharif-Emami and Azhari as prime ministers. Sharif-Emami realized it a week or so after he had been appointed; Azhari knew it before he took on the job. This status weakened their authority and lowered their own expectations. It also encouraged individuals of different backgrounds and political persuasions to offer themselves as replacements. The first and most sensible candidate was Ali Amini, the former prime minister and in his own words *rajol-e siyasi,* a political personality. Amini had certain positive qualities: he supported the Constitution, was not associated with the White Revolution, had considerable experience of governance, was friendly with the Americans, and had some support in the bazaar and among the clergy. More to the point, in September he was willing to accept responsibility when most others in his category were not. The shah and his family, however, did not trust Amini, though his son had been for some time a protégé of Princess Ashraf. The shah thought Amini's real aim was to undermine his throne. Princess Ashraf herself believed Amini was more dangerous than Mosaddeq.[57] Amini wanted the job, but he was not willing to fight for it. He believed that to stop the turmoil he needed the army's support, which he could receive only if the shah so ordered. The order, however, would be only for appearances. To succeed he had to be seen as being his own man, which would be unlikely if he could not demonstrate that he was independent of the shah. He faced a catch-22. Only political novices believed that the Iranian military organization was a machine whose key could be handed to whomever the shah pleased. The intricate relationship between the military and the shah made a separating of the two well-nigh impossible. The army might obey someone else for a while, but only on the monarch's sufferance. Amini did not know how to frame his position in order to satisfy both the shah and the shah's opponents; the shah, in the meantime, procrastinated until Amini became irrelevant.[58] When consulted in early November, Amini advised the shah that only a military government might now be able to do the job.[59]

Despite the shah's appointment of Azhari, his "I heard the message of your revolution" speech implied a search for a civilian government capable of taking the nation to the free parliamentary elections he had promised for 1979. However, beyond Amini, not very many eligible candidates were available. Karim Sanjabi and Mehdi Bazargan, the leaders of the National Front and Freedom Movement, respectively, had already met with Khomeini and accepted his leadership. In mid-December the shah approached Gholamhossein Sadiqi, a former National Front member and Mosaddeq's minister of the interior, a highly reputable sociologist now an emeritus of Tehran University. Sadiqi, recognizing that he would need the army's support, accepted the challenge but posed two conditions: the shah would remain in Iran, though not necessarily in Tehran; and Sadiqi would have to succeed in securing the support of the National Front. On the first condition opinions vary, though it is unlikely that the shah had any problem with it. It was the second that mattered, for Sadiqi was not able to mobilize his colleagues' support. On the 24th, he reported to the shah that he had failed.[60]

Other candidates surfaced, most of them quixotic and inconsequential. By November Iranian politics had become utterly confused. Individuals who previously would not have dreamed of being in the presence of the shah now had a tête-à-tête with him. Some who were hardly eligible for office now aspired to the highest. Yet, ironically, they did not wish to be seen when seeking the shah's favor; they would ask to be taken to the palace incognito. Shortly after Azhari was appointed, Kambiz Atabai, the shah's adjutant and master of the horse, received a call from a General Pezeshkpur telling him that his brother, Mohsen Pezeshkpur, leader of the recently resurrected Pan Iranist Party, wished to have an audience with the shah. "He had something important to say," said the general. Atabai relayed the message to the shah. "What could he possibly have to contribute?" retorted the monarch. Atabai had no idea. All he knew was what he had heard from the general, whom he respected. The shah reluctantly agreed. Pezeshkpur, however, required elaborate camouflage to pass through the gates unrecognized. Atabai obliged. He arranged with the guards to allow his car to pass through the gate unchecked; Pezeshkpur, a top hat on his head, lowered himself to hide in the backseat. Pezeshkpur saw the shah three times and the queen once over a period of approximately a month. He had a plan to save Iran, he told Atabai after his third and last visit to the shah: "We need to detain and hang a good number of the regime's high functionaries, beginning with Amir Abbas Hoveyda, and I should be made prime minister to do it." He was, of course, a constitutionalist, Pezeshkpur said, and wished to retain the monarchy, which necessitated the sacrificial killing he proposed.[61]

Killing the regime's leaders, beginning with Hoveyda, was a favorite recipe offered by friend and foe alike. As we have noted, Manuchehr Azmun, a favorite of Hoveyda, openly advocated it, though by any reasonable account he himself would, and eventually did, end up on the scaffolds. Others who had not received what they considered their due during Hoveyda's tenure also advocated the same, purportedly in order to save the country. Many among them were not vicious, or known to like harming others. But killing had become the preferred ritual, a paganism to assuage a raging beast's appetite for offerings. A respected lawyer, a friend of many venerable high-placed officials, suggested to the shah that a hundred gallows be erected across Tupkhaneh (Artillery) Square, where criminals were hung in the olden days, to hang a hundred of the regime's leaders, headed by Hoveyda, whose rope he would personally pull. He was extremely dismayed when the shah turned down his suggestion. He too thought that a chance to save the country was lost.[62]

A more serious contender seeking the shah's audience through Atabai was Mozaffar Baqai, an old hand in Iran's politics. Baqai had been one of the foremost oil warriors of the nationalization era and was a founder of the National Front. Like several other of Mosaddeq's initial allies, he had fallen out with him during the last year of his rule and had helped in the efforts that led to his overthrow. In the succeeding years Baqai had kept mostly to his principles, which were not always honorable, and had paid for it by being forced out of politics. But he still had a respectable following, particularly in Kerman. He approached Atabai through a mutual friend. Atabai reported to the shah, and this time the monarch was more interested. He only asked if Atabai knew what the old man wanted to talk about. Atabai did not; he had never seen the man.

The same charade was repeated. Baqai also insisted on going to the court incognito. No one was to know. His problem was Shapur Bakhtiar. "He is not to be trusted," he told the shah. "It would be calamitous for the country if the shah left under any circumstance but particularly if Bakhtiar were prime minister." This should not happen. It was possible to find a middle way. If he himself were appointed prime minister, Baqai told the shah, who reported it subsequently to Atabai, he would invite Khomeini to come to Iran. He was the only man who could handle Khomeini. By his third meeting with the shah, Baqai was clearly dismayed. "His Majesty does not pay proper attention to what I propose," he told Atabai. "I am afraid his way shall lead to unfathomable disaster."[63] The next day, 28 December 1978, the shah asked Shapur Bakhtiar to form a government.

Bakhtiar was in many ways the bravest of the National Front leaders. He hailed from a line of Bakhtiari tribal chiefs who had ruled their area some hundred miles southwest of Isfahan with considerable authority for generations before the advent of the Pahlavis. His maternal grandfather, Najafqoli Khan Samsam-Saltaneh, had twice been prime minister after the Constitutional Revolution. His father had risen against Reza Shah in one of the campaigns by the central government to bring the tribes under control and had surrendered under an amnesty, but a military tribunal had nonetheless found him guilty and had him executed in 1934, when the son had just arrived in Marseille, France, to begin his university studies. Not unnaturally, the event had made Shapur bitter against the Pahlavis. He was culturally a Frenchman when World War II broke out. He had been impressed by Hitler's political sway in France, especially over the youth—at least until he invaded France. Bakhtiar then joined the French army and fought in the war on the side of the Allies, resisting the French authorities' insistence that being a foreigner he should join the Foreign Legion. The fascist appeal for the French, however, sensitized him to the emotional logic behind the intellectually illogical choices men sometimes made. In 1978 Khomeini's appeal for the Iranians appeared to him to fall in the same frame.[64]

After the war, Bakhtiar returned to Iran and joined the Iran Party, a group of professionals and intellectuals politically inclined to social democracy. On the advice of a family friend, he joined the newly established Ministry of Labor, where the chances of promotion would be better because there were fewer entrenched interests there than in the older ministries. He rose in four years to the position of director general, was stationed in Khuzistan, and by the fall of 1952, during Prime Minister Mosaddeq's second term, he had become a deputy minister. During this period, his relative Soraya was queen, and the Bakhtiaris were politically and socially in vogue. As a staunch supporter of Mosaddeq, however, he kept away from the court.[65] After the fall of Mosaddeq, he remained in the leadership of the National Front, though he was never the top man, as he was preceded by more senior colleagues.

Bakhtiar admitted to the dislike he held for the Pahlavis over his father's execution only by indirection—misstatements and misrepresentations that cannot be explained except by a visceral dislike of the shah. In his representations, Reza Shah was an illiterate bully created by the British to help them overcome the multiple points of resistance, and thus freedom, that the tribal chiefs provided. Mosaddeq was an epitome of a democrat; he could do no wrong. The shah had done nothing right. Even returning Azerbaijan to Iran had nothing to do with the shah. Not much had happened in the economic realm, either, he maintained, and what had happened was due to the mandate of history. And the military too had done nothing to merit any accolade. All of this pushed him to positions that would work against what he bravely set out to achieve. His war became focused on the Pahlavi regime rather than on Khomeini.

■

Bakhtiar's first contact with the shah was through Jamshid Amouzegar, "five or six weeks" after Amouzegar's resignation. Bakhtiar was a good friend of Dr. Manuchehr Razmara, the brother of the slain prime minister, who taught at the National University's medical school and in that capacity knew Ahmad Ghoreishi, the university chancellor. Ghoreishi, in turn, was Amouzegar's friend, political ally, and successor as head of the Rastakhiz Party's executive committee. Razmara and Bakhtiar met with Ghoreishi and asked him to arrange a meeting for them and Karim Sanjabi with Amouzegar. They had something to say that they believed would interest the former prime minister. Ghoreishi conveyed the message to Amouzegar, who reluctantly agreed to the meeting. They were to go to Amouzegar's house in Tajrish the same week, on Thursday at 6 P.M. The day was 26 October, the shah's birthday.[66]

Bakhtiar and Razmara arrived late, explaining that Sanjabi had had a meeting with the Ayatollah Shari'atmadari in the holy city of Qom and that they had waited for him, but when he did not return on time, they decided they could not keep Amouzegar waiting any longer. So, here they were without Sanjabi. However, they had something important to say to Amouzegar that could not wait, said Bakhtiar. The country was in grave danger. The people did not trust Sharif-Emami, the situation had become worse after Black Friday in Zhaleh Square, the nation was speeding toward disaster, and the momentum increased daily with Sharif-Emami at the helm. They asked Amouzegar to tell the shah to dismiss Sharif-Emami and turn the government over to the National Front before it was too late. "Why don't you convey your message through the Ministry of Court?" Amouzegar asked. They did not trust the people at the royal court to convey the message truthfully, Bakhtiar answered. They trusted Amouzegar. As they prepared to leave, Bakhtiar left a number for Amouzegar to call him if needed.

Amouzegar agreed that Sharif-Emami was not the right choice, but he had been reluctant to interfere, fearing he would be misunderstood. In the past, as noted, he had seriously believed that some conspiracy was at work and that at least some of the trouble was concocted by his enemies to disparage him and his government—some combination of Hoveyda and the Freemasons, whose interests lay with individuals other than him. But a few weeks had passed since his resignation, and the situation now appeared to him much more serious than he had imagined. He now felt he must act precipitously. Though it was somewhat late in the evening, he telephoned the shah and told him he had news he could not deliver on the telephone. The shah asked him to go to the court the next working day—Saturday—at 9 A.M.

When Amouzegar delivered the message to the shah, verbatim as was his custom, he was met with absolute silence "for a few deafening seconds," as he put it, before the shah started on his familiar walk across his office. "Do you know what they are after?" the shah asked.

"No, Sire, this is the first time they have approached me," answered Amouzegar.

"They want to establish a republic in this country, and they want me to do it for them," said the shah.

The shah's tone and conversation were novel and surprising to Amouzegar. "If you wish me, Sire, I will ask them," he said.

"Yes. Ask them," said the shah.

The shah's statement apparently did not surprise Bakhtiar. "We are about twenty-three people in the National Front, and I cannot answer for all of them. I will bring up the matter in our general meeting tomorrow and will let you know," he said. Two days later he told Amouzegar the National Front was not against the monarchy. What the Front wanted was to take up the responsibility for the government and the country, hoping to deflect the dangerous crisis the nation faced. "We are ready to declare our support of the monarchy unambiguously, transparently, and directly," Bakhtiar stated.

Amouzegar reported what he was told to the shah, who directed him to ask whom they had in mind for prime minister. Amouzegar called Bakhtiar with the shah's query. Bakhtiar's voice appeared to him trembling with excitement: "I think we will propose Allahyar Saleh. But the decision must come from everybody. We did not think His Majesty would decide so expeditiously. The trouble is Sanjabi and Bazargan are out of the country in Paris and London. We cannot decide in their absence. I will try to contact and ask them to return immediately." He added: "Dr. [Houchang] Nahavandi called yesterday and stated that he was to be the conduit for the National Front's communication with His Majesty. But we do not consider Nahavandi the right person. He acted badly as university chancellor. We do not want to have him as our contact. What is to be done?" Amouzaegar said he would ask the shah.

The shah was at dinner when Amouzegar called. He was manifestly satisfied with Allahyar Saleh. "Great, let them tell me as soon as possible," he said. Still on the phone, Amouzegar heard the shah address someone else: "They say Nahavandi does not have a good reputation."

"Who says this?" Amouzegar recognized the queen's voice.

"Bakhtiar," said the shah.

"Nonsense," said the queen.

The shah now returned to Amouzegar: "You shall be our sole conduit with the National Front. Tell them."

No call from Bakhtiar. In three or four days the shah called Amouzegar for news. He had none. Realizing his sovereign was disappointed and unhappy, he called Bakhtiar. "You have put me in a very awkward position. It was you who came to see me. It was you who asked me to take your message to the shah. Now that His Majesty has agreed with your proposition, you play coy, causing me to lose face [man ra sang-e ruye yakh kardid]."

Bakhtiar sounded unhappy and disturbed. "You can't imagine how difficult it has been for me," he said. "Contact with Sanjabi and Bazargan is almost impossible. I was finally able to speak to Sanjabi today. He said he has something to attend to after which he will return to Tehran."

"Give me a time frame I can report to His Majesty," Amouzegar shot back.

"I will try to contact him again," answered Bakhtiar.

Bakhtiar called the next day saying Sanjabi's business in Paris was finished but he was unable to find a seat on the flights to Tehran. Amouzegar was astonished. "We will send him a government plane," he said.

"I will let him know," said Bakhtiar, sounding happy.

Realizing he had made the commitment without authority, Amouzegar telephoned the shah and informed him of what had transpired. "You did well. Ask them the date he wants the plane to be sent," said the shah. Amouzegar informed Bakhtiar.

Three days passed, again with no news from Bakhtiar. Unbearably dismayed, Amouzegar called Bakhtiar for the last time. "What happened?" he queried.

"I don't know," answered Bakhtiar. "Sanjabi and Bazargan are not prepared to return and to negotiate. I am sorry."

Amouzegar reported what had happened to the shah. "I told you they have a different purpose in mind," said the shah.[67]

Bakhtiar had not been honest with Amouzegar. He knew Sanjabi would meet with Khomeini, and on 31 October, soon after Sanjabi reached Paris, he learned that his colleague had capitulated to Khomeini.[68] The shah also knew what Sanjabi was doing. The day he told Amouzegar the National Front was after a republic, he already had information about Sanjabi's meeting with the Ayatollah Shari'atmadari and Shari'atmadari's subsequent statement that he and Khomeini wanted the same things.[69] And by the time Bakhtiar had begun playing hide and seek with Amouzegar, Sanjabi had declared himself on the side of Khomeini, of which the shah was certainly aware. Nonetheless, the Allahyar Saleh proposition opened for him a new window of opportunity, which he was determined to follow. Amouzegar, on the other hand, was the innocent in the charade.

Unsuccessful with his colleagues, Bakhtiar nonetheless pushed on. Sanjabi's capitulation to Khomeini ripped the National Front apart. Bakhtiar resigned from the executive committee, claiming he now was the only true and rightful heir of Mosaddeq. He no longer needed to defer to his more senior colleagues. He approached his cousin Reza Qotbi, whose mother was Bakhtiar's aunt. He said he wished to speak to the shah but preferred not to go to the court, at least not before he knew how he stood with the shah. The queen agreed to see her cousin's cousin at Qotbi's mother's home. In their first meeting, about the end of November, Bakhtiar was full of complaints, making the queen somewhat impatient. "Look," she said, "the country is in deep trouble. We now must concentrate on saving it rather than harping on the past." Bakhtiar agreed. He wanted to speak to the shah, but he had certain conditions, one of which was to have Sanjabi's arrest rescinded.[70] The shah's departure, however, was not one of his conditions.[71] The queen reported the meeting to the shah, who instructed General Moqaddam to pursue the matter, including Sanjabi's release.

Moqaddam, of course, knew about the queen's meeting with Bakhtiar. According to the queen, he and General Oveisi had in fact suggested Bakhtiar as a possibility after General Azhari's heart attack on 21 December.[72] Moqaddam had also already discussed Bakhtiar with Reza Qotbi, who had told him Bakhtiar was brave, respected the Constitution and the monarchy, but held grudges against the Pahlavis.[73] Bakhtiar was placed on the short list. Asked to name a contact, he named Qotbi, but Qotbi excused himself. Instead he suggested the shah's special bureau chief, Nosratollah Moinian, or, alternatively, General Moqaddam. Bakhtiar chose Moqaddam.

Bakhtiar's first meeting with the shah went surprisingly well. According to Qotbi, with whom Bakhtiar spoke immediately after this meeting, the shah listened to what Bakhtiar said with patience and equanimity: "Your father killed mine, and you put me in jail. I ought not to have any personal loyalty to your line. But I do believe that Iran is not ready for a democratic republic, not for at least another fifty years. And when the nation becomes ready for democracy, a constitutional monarchy will do just as well. But at the moment, our first task should be to stop these barbarians." As Bakhtiar rose to leave, the shah said something about his leaving the country. Bakhtiar did not quite understand what the shah meant. He said that he wished for the shah to stay at least until the Majlis would make known its preference for him to be appointed prime minister, and then until after he received a vote of confidence. "His Majesty might then leave, if he wished, until Bakhtiar pacified the country for him to return," Qotbi understood Bakhtiar as saying.[74]

Like Sadiqi before him, Bakhtiar failed to receive his colleagues' support at the Iran Party and at the National Front. His strong personality, however, made him a favorite of the Imperial Guard. Sadiqi had made his acceptance of premiership contingent on the shah's staying in Iran. He had also said he would not take office under martial law, but as things got worse, he realized that no one could govern without martial law and therefore, he concluded, he could not take office. His position had frustrated the Imperial Guardsmen. General Abdolali Badrei, commander of the Guard, asked Qotbi if Bakhtiar was as wishy-washy. "Perhaps you should be worried about his becoming more of a dictator than you'd like," answered Qotbi. Badrei had a talk with Bakhtiar after the latter's second meeting with the shah, in which he had informed the monarch that the National Front would not join his cabinet but he was ready to proceed with non-Front members. As Badrei recounted to Qotbi, Bakhtiar told him he would fight to the end; he would kill if necessary even if blood rose up to his elbow. He used the archaic term *marfaq* for elbow, which Badrei pronounced *mafraq,* meaning the place where hair is parted on the head.[75] Badrei was clearly impressed, finding in Bakhtiar a man who spoke his language. On 29 December 1978 the shah asked Bakhtiar to form a government.

22

"Melting Like Snow"

By mid-November 1978 most experts at the U.S. Department of State had come to believe that the United States should be bracing for a post-shah Iran.[1] On 9 November Ambassador Sullivan had sent a message suggesting that the United States begin to "think the unthinkable." What would the United States do if the shah was shown to be unable to rule? The cable painted an optimistic picture of a post-shah Iran: both Khomeini and the Iranian armed forces were anti-communist and anti-Soviet; the officer corps was pro-West; the clerics would likely maintain the armed forces; the military, in turn, would protect Iran's national integrity; economic relations with the West would continue; Khomeini would return to Iran and assume a Gandhi-like role; and the elections would produce an Islamic republic with a strong pro-Western tilt.[2]

Sullivan had received these ideas mostly from those affiliated with the National Front, especially Mehdi Bazargan's Iran Freedom Movement (IFM), with minimal input from the Khomeini core. Bazargan was a moderate Islamist, in contradistinction to a moderate Muslim, a university professor, and a moderate activist, who had initially joined the National Front and subsequently in the 1950s and 1960s the National Resistance Movement and in the 1970s the IFM. He had also founded the Islamic Students Society and the Society of Engineers.[3] Sullivan had reasoned that if Azhari's government did not succeed in regaining control over Iran's key economic and production sectors, the revolution would likely win. And if that were the case, why not focus on the bright side. Khomeini's supporters such as Ayatollah Seyyed Mahmud Taleqani and Ayatollah Seyyed Mohammad Hossein Beheshti were educated men: "Beheshti, in particular, who had a degree from the University of Tübingen in Germany, appreciated the more secular aspects of the revolution," and Bazargan and his associates Abbas Amir-Entezam and Nasser Minachi, who were connected with Khomeini and his friends, were well disposed toward the United States. "They seemed to recognize that the prime threat to the future of Iran came from the Soviet Union and that the United States, despite its close association with the shah, had long been a force for social, economic, and political improvement for the people of Iran," Sullivan concluded. What he thought was needed was an accommodation between the military and the religious that was accepted by the latter. This could be achieved, he thought, if the present military commanders, who were largely unacceptable to Khomeini and his followers, could be persuaded to yield to younger ones the revolutionaries would accept. Talking to Bazargan and Minachi, he was assured that the idea would work. In fact, Bazargan intimated that the top brass might be allowed to leave with their families and property if they agreed to go peacefully.[4]

Sullivan's ideas exerted considerable influence on the thinking at the State Department. According to Secretary Vance, some of the advisers "were beginning to doubt that the shah could remain even as a figurehead in a parliamentary democracy." Once the likely outcomes of the crisis—a military junta with the shah or without a shah, or a civilian government supported by the military in an Islamic republic, or complete collapse and chaos—were recounted, most advisers believed that the United States should immediately position itself to adjust to an Iran without the shah. "In addition," wrote Vance, "echoing arguments urged with increasing force by Sullivan, they suggested that if the shah could not bring himself to deal with the moderate opposition, we should seek an accommodation between the military, as the strongest pro-Western force, and the Islamic clergy, as the dominant political force in the country."[5]

President Carter believed he should support the shah, but was unable to define a policy for his administration to follow. He too did not understand the structure of the insurgency that supported the façade of the revolution. He went along with the contradictions that were increasingly marring the information that reached the shah and the Iranian military.[6] The shah believed that since Ambassador Sullivan represented the president of the United States, his word was the only authentic representation of the president's intent. This put him in a quandary. What Sullivan conveyed to him, by word and by demeanor, seemed to him to withhold straightforward support, which led him to think that the United States was being duplicitous when on the one hand it claimed to support him and on the other hand such claims were constantly vitiated by the communication he received through the ambassador. Carter's national security adviser, Zbigniew Brzezinski, was told that "the shah found the situation baffling, incomprehensible, and almost overwhelming."[7] He tried to assuage the shah's doubts, but to little effect. The shah's reasoning about communications between states made him give Sullivan precedence. His own ambassador to the United States, Ardeshir Zahedi, confirmed Brzezinski's assurances of support, but the monarch dismissed his arguments as uninformed.[8]

Carter also was unhappy with Sullivan. He decided to send a military person to Tehran to maintain correct relations with the Iranian military, since Sullivan "seemed unable to provide [him] with adequate reports." Based on recommendations by his secretary of defense, Harold Brown, he chose General Robert E. Huyser, the deputy commander of U.S. forces in Europe. Huyser, who arrived in Iran on 4 January 1979, was to keep him informed about the Iranian military's needs and to encourage the Iranian commanders to support Prime Minister Bakhtiar and in any case to stay in Iran to maintain stability if the shah left. Surprisingly, neither he nor General Huyser informed the shah or the Iranian commanders that Huyser was being sent to Iran.

The shah knew Huyser and respected his military credentials, however. Huyser had worked with the shah's military staff and line commanders over the previous three and a half years on various military issues of mutual interest. In April 1978 the shah had commissioned him to prepare an automated command control system for the Iranian armed forces. In August Huyser had presented a hand-written draft of the plan to General Azhari, then chief of the Supreme Commander's Staff, and to the key members of his staff and the force commanders. Azhari and his colleagues had approved the plan and subsequently presented the document to the shah, who much to Huyser's surprise also approved it without any alteration. The interesting point about the document was that it sought to wean the military from depending overly on the shah's mind for planning and operations by arming it with a more integrated system of intelligence, logistics, command line, and operation.[9]

Huyser's mission, however, became controversial. His immediate superior, General Alexander Haig, was solidly against his going to Tehran. He believed U.S. policy was faulty, the administration was divided, the terms of the mission were at best "murky," and Huyser would likely end up as a fall guy covering for other people's mistakes.[10] Sullivan objected to Huyser's mission on the grounds that it was not needed and that it interfered with his work. The Iranian generals were suspicious of his purpose and considered his being in Iran insulting. The shah was astonished by Huyser's clandestine arrival, which was unprecedented and contrary to established protocol. The cloak-and-dagger subterfuge, however, proved useless since, only a few hours after his arrival, Huyser's presence was announced in the press, which had just begun publishing after several weeks of strike.[11]

On 4 January 1979, the day Huyser set out for Tehran, President Carter met with the leaders of France, Great Britain, and Germany in Guadeloupe to discuss the Iranian crisis. According to Carter, there was "little support for the shah among the other three leaders. They all thought civilian government would have to be established, and were unanimous in saying that the shah ought to leave as soon as possible."[12] Prime Minister James Callaghan of Britain, who was asked to open the discussion, concluded that the shah was lost and that there was no workable alternative to replace him. He was repeating the reports he had received from Sir Anthony Parsons, his ambassador in Tehran.

French President Valéry Giscard d'Estaing, the host of the meeting, also felt that there was not much support for the shah. His own ambassador had sent pessimistic reports based on contacts with the government and mostly the secular opposition, but not with the shah or his close advisers. Consequently, the French government, including Giscard d'Estaing, had remained relatively uninformed about Khomeini, his role, and his intentions, until the ayatollah arrived in Paris. Giscard felt he had been stuck with Khomeini largely because the shah had urged him not to antagonize the cleric. Nonetheless, in October and November he had warned the ayatollah that, according to French law, his sojourn in France was conditioned on his refraining from advocating violence in Iran. The ayatollah, however, had continued sending cassettes to Iran doing precisely that, the ones in late December, according to Giscard's own sources, encouraging his followers to murder the shah. Giscard ordered his interior minister, Christian Bonnet, to arrange for Khomeini's departure from France to Algeria. He then informed the shah of the decision. To his surprise, the shah would not associate himself with the idea. "Expulsion of the Ayatollah is a French decision; Iran will not accept responsibility for it," said the shah, according to Giscard. The French president concluded that this was not a risk France should take unilaterally. He ordered Bonnet to stop the eviction process. In late December, just before the Guadeloupe meeting, Giscard sent Michel Poniatowski, a former interior minister and at the time his personal troubleshooter, to visit with the shah and report back to him on his condition. Poniatowski met the shah on 27 December and reported to Giscard that the monarch was finished: ill, helpless, alone, and determined not to allow his army to shoot at his people under any circumstances. Giscard concluded that "for better or worse, the die had been cast." He attributed this partly to the American attitude, which he found "incomprehensible." The Americans had a unique political and military relationship with Iran, which made them treat the Iranian issue largely independently of European interests.

On the other hand, his information from Iran suggested that U.S. embassy and other American services were distancing themselves from the shah, looking instead to a "political" solution, for which they sought, but failed to find, the right man.[13]

This, however, was only partly true. Carter harbored more doubts than designs. He believed the intimate relations that existed between American and Iranian officers would enable the Iranian military to maintain the nation's integrity and stability.[14] Sullivan seemed to him to have become "obsessed with the need for the shah to abdicate without further delay" and for the United States to establish direct contact with Khomeini. When Carter asked Giscard d'Estaing to act as an intermediary with Khomeini, Sullivan, according to Carter, "lost control of himself, and on January 10 sent Vance a cable bordering on insolence." Carter asked Vance to "take Sullivan out of Iran," but Vance "insisted that it would be a mistake to put a new man in the country."[15] Carter reluctantly acquiesced.

Carter now increasingly relied on the reports he received from Huyser, who as far as the president was concerned "remained cool and competent . . . and always sent back balanced views."[16] Huyser reported that he was making headway with the commanders. He had got them to work together to prepare plans for taking over the oil fields and power plants and communications, and to break the strikes and to regain control. He reported that he was able to move them from depending on the shah to working as a team under Bakhtiar.[17] All of this was wishful thinking. What in fact was happening was a game that only Huyser took seriously. What the commanders asked of him was to appeal to his government to quiet Khomeini, to put pressure on Britain to moderate the BBC's "anti-shah vitriol," and to prevent the shah from leaving Iran. Otherwise, they humored him by pretending to follow his guidance about planning to take over various vital industries — oil, electricity, communications, water and food supply, among others. In fact, as attested by the conversations among themselves and with other high-ranking officers at the four meetings of "the commanders council" that would take place starting in mid-January — in which not once was Huyser referred to, directly or indirectly — the generals essentially argued that the armed forces were unprepared for facing a domestic war of the sort they now encountered.[18] Furthermore, it soon became clear to the generals that Huyser was falling in with Sullivan, whom they detested. According to General Abbas Qarabaghi, the current chairman of the Supreme Commander's Staff, in one of the discussions about the possible strategies for dealing with Khomeini's return to Iran, Huyser suggested that Qarabaghi meet with Bazargan and Beheshti as Khomeini's representatives. "And without waiting for my answer, he immediately asked [MAAG Chief] General [Phillip] Gast to bring us their telephone numbers. General Gast left the office and returned with several telephone numbers which he placed on the desk. General Huyser said, 'These are Dr. Minachi's telephone numbers. He will arrange for them to meet you at your convenience.'" The exchange astounded the generals. Qarabaghi reported it to the shah. "This is strange!" exclaimed the shah. "Does anybody know what they want?" He asked Qarabaghi what he intended to do. Qarabaghi reacted with the usual "whatever Your Majesty orders" routine, but, urged further, he said he did not think it would be of any use.[19]

■

The Iranian generals' view of their relationship with the United States military was shaped by two agreements: one gave the United States the right to make sure that the highly secret and classified parts of the weapons systems it sold Iran would not fall into unfriendly hands; the other, the 1959 bilateral treaty, obligated the United States to protect Iran's national independence and territorial integrity against any external or internal communist threat. The G2 estimates, which according to General Qarabaghi were normally coordinated with information secured by the U.S. military advisory group, had determined that the riots were being led by international communism, mediated by "Islamic Marxists." Since it had also been established that many opposition groups were armed, their activities were construed as a communist armed insurrection against the Iranian government and therefore, based on the bilateral treaty, a joint international communist threat against the vital interests of Iran and the United States.[20]

All this, however, had to be mediated through the shah, whose behavior toward the armed forces palpably changed during his last weeks in Iran. In the past he had always shown interest in military plans, operations, and appointments. In recent weeks, according to Qarabaghi, he seemed detached. He had appointed General Abdolali Badrei as the commander of the ground forces and acting commander of the Imperial Guard, but beyond that he had left everything else to Qarabaghi and others. He received the force commanders as in the past, but he had nothing specific to discuss.[21]

On 13 January, three days before he left Iran, he summoned his commanding generals—Qarabaghi, Badrei for the ground forces, Kamaleddin Habibollahi for the navy, Amirhossein Rabii for the air force, and Tufanian for armaments—and ordered them to support the Bakhtiar government. According to Bakhtiar, the shah told his generals: "As you well know, Mr. Bakhtiar has accepted to form a cabinet under very difficult circumstances. As I have decided to go abroad, you should know that you take your orders from him. If there are questions that relate specifically to my office, he has the possibility to convene the [newly established] Regency Council, which will relay the question to me and will communicate the answer to you. But for all matters that pertain to government, it is Mr. Bakhtiar who will decide."[22] Bakhtiar also maintains that on military matters such as issuing any promotion or retirement of general officers or the like, the shah ordered his generals "to refer to the prime minister through the minister of war," a contention that Qarabaghi denies as "an absolute lie."[23]

Qarabaghi's account of the meeting in fact differs significantly from Bakhtiar's. According to Qarabaghi, the shah said, "Since Mr. Prime Minister has formed a cabinet that supports the Constitution, the imperial army has the duty to support the legally instituted government." On behalf of the generals and himself, Qarabaghi responded: "The duties and the mission of the army are clear. We all are and shall remain loyal to the oath we have taken to protect the Constitution."[24]

Contrary to Bakhtiar's intent and subsequent understanding, Qarabaghi states that the form of the meeting and what was said in it suggested unquestionably that the shah wanted the generals to believe that nothing had changed as far as the military was concerned. For example, Qarabaghi says General Tufanian, who had been deputy minister of war for many years, asked the shah to allow him to retire now that General Jaʿfar Shafaqat (who was not present and who had no command function) had been appointed minister of war. The shah answered: "You have nothing to do with the war minister," and told him to continue with his work. The absence of the minister of war, Qarabaghi maintains, meant that the shah wanted to emphasize that, as in the past, the minister of war was not allowed to interfere in the affairs of the armed forces. And the presence of the commanders of the three forces individually conveyed to everyone that they were independent and were to carry out exclusively the shah's orders.[25]

The difference in nuance between Bakhtiar's and Qarabaghi's renditions of the meeting is both important and understandable. Bakhtiar did not wish to press for specifics. His government's life depended on the military's support, and obviously he sought its goodwill. Of all that the shah had said, he likely emphasized that which supported him best, namely, that the shah had ordered his officers to obey the prime minister unconditionally. However, Qarabaghi's insistence that the shah emphasized the Constitution agrees with the general tenor of the shah's statements at the time. The future of the monarchy in Iran depended on the survival of the Constitution. The difference between the two interpretations therefore was consequential. If the order was to obey Bakhtiar, it would be difficult for the military to engage in any planning and decision making without Bakhtiar's participation. If, on the other hand, the army was directed to support the government on constitutional grounds, then, under the prevailing circumstances, the interpretation of the relationship between the government and the Constitution had to be made independently. Assuming the ability to act, the military would support the government only contingent on its understanding of the government's motives and functions.

Other conversations between the shah and his chief of staff also support Qarabaghi's understanding. On several occasions before the shah's departure on 16 January the general had asked his commander-in-chief to clarify what was to be done if unexpected events occurred. The shah had remained generally noncommittal. But, according to Qarabaghi,

> After what had transpired between us during our last meeting, he now began to pace the room dictating orders, the summary of which was the following: "You know very well what the conditions of our armed forces were after Shahrivar 1320 [September 1941, the date of the Allied invasion of Iran], how much effort has gone into their development and perfection, and finally what status they have achieved today. You all have a share in this. This army is necessary for the preservation of the country's independence. Try to prevent factional divisions from developing in it and no matter what the price, protect and preserve the [integrity] of the armed forces." ... I asked again "... if after Your Majesty's departure unexpected events, contrary to the Constitution, occurred, what must we do?" After a moment of silent reflection, as he continued pacing the room he said, "We do not know what will happen. Do whatever you and other commanders deem appropriate."[26]

Evidently, the shah intended for his generals to be independent but to act in concert after he left. This was the only option that favored him, the armed forces, and the country. He refused either to give Qarabaghi an enabling *farman* to make command decisions in his absence or, alternatively, to establish a protocol by which Qarabaghi or other commanders could contact him in the future. He wanted them to decide and make choices on their own collectively, which went against their culture under the best of circumstances and paralyzed them under the prevailing conditions.

Once it was clear that the shah intended to leave, the commanders were faced with a dilemma: they had to do something but they had waited too long and now it was not clear to them what they were able to do. They met as a council four times in Chairman Qarabaghi's office to discuss the situation and to devise a strategy. As the record of these meetings, published in 1987, reveals, the commanders' discourse reflected the impasse they faced. They suggested action and immediately argued the futility of the action. Most of them agreed that Prime Minister Bakhtiar was brave, determined, and committed to the Constitution, but this was not a firm belief. No one knew what was to be done if Bakhtiar, for any reason, left or was removed. Everyone realized that steps to stop the mayhem should have been taken long ago, but no one would voice why such steps had not been taken. Everyone realized that Khomeini commanded the mob that invaded the streets and that facing him meant bloodshed, but no one was willing to suggest that therefore the army would not face the people. Everyone knew that the armed forces were being morally and structurally consumed from within, but no one was willing to say it outright. The discourse therefore was surreal, the generals moving across possible and equally unsatisfactory options. Nonetheless, there was a trend. During the first three meetings, which stretched from immediately before the shah's departure on 16 January 1979 to 28 January, statements became gradually less belligerent, inclining to what increasingly appeared inevitable, though as yet unutterable: Khomeini had triumphed and the shah would never return.

The first council meeting was convened on 15 January 1979, two weeks into Bakhtiar's premiership, the day the Senate gave its consent to his cabinet. Four days earlier, on 11 January, Khomeini had declared that the shah's exit from Iran would not change anything unless he abdicated. The regime, he said, was illegal, as were the government, the parliament, and the new Regency Council. All must be dissolved, he said.[27] On the 13th, the shah presided over the first meeting of a Regency Council he had announced the same day. The council—which would be routinely named whenever the shah and the queen were both out of the country—consisted of the prime minister, the presidents of the Senate and the Majlis, the minister of court, and the chairman of the Supreme Commander's Staff as ex officio members, and appointed members, including Seyyed Jalaleddin Tehrani, who was appointed chair of the council.[28] Also on the 13th Khomeini announced his Islamic Revolutionary Council to supplant the Bakhtiar government. On the 15th, as the Commanders' Council was being convened, Ayatollah Shari'atmadari, the nation's top cleric, admonished the army against firing on the people or otherwise committing violence "now that the nation was approaching the advent of a government of Islamic justice."[29]

The reason for the formation of the Commanders' Council was R-Day—the day of the shah's departure. The 15th, on which the council was first meeting, was thus "R minus one." General Qarabaghi had asked his colleagues to prepare a plan for R-Day, in which, he explained, the military would likely face awesome challenges in Tehran and across the country. The army, he said, was unprepared for the strikes, demonstrations, and violence that would be launched after the shah's departure. He had already been scolded on this by the new prime minister. "I cannot believe that this army does not have fuel reserve," Bakhtiar had exclaimed to Qarabaghi in their last National Security Council meeting. "I cannot believe that this army cannot take over and manage the nation's communications."[30] Qarabaghi directed his deputy, General Abdolali Najimi-Naini, to read a letter that Qarabaghi as minister of the interior had written on 28 October 1978 to then SCS Chief General Azhari. He had obtained the shah's permission to ask the military to draw up plans for securing manpower, technical requirements, and reserves and when necessary control of such commodities and services as water, power, bread, fuel, transport, post, telegraph and telephone, radio, and the rest. Nothing had happened because the military had been organized and trained to fight foreign enemies. The assumption had been that once such a contingency occurred the nation's resources would be mobilized for support. Now these resources were mostly out of reach because workers everywhere were on strike. "Well," said Qarabaghi, pointing to General Badrei, "this now is a burden for the commanding general of the imperial ground forces who, by the royal decree, also commands the Imperial Guard."[31]

The generals were especially concerned about the "flower tactic," the revolutionaries' way of gaining the soldiers' sympathy. To the generals, rebels' offering flowers to the soldiers on the streets was at the heart of the enemy's psychological warfare. Everyone knew that keeping the soldiers in the streets while ordering them not to fight was a recipe for demoralization. But this was an order they could not conceive of disobeying. Throughout the discussions, the more frustrated among the officers made obscure references to the shah as the source of the order, but never explicitly or retrospectively. Qarabaghi spoke as openly as he could: "The commanders were present, as was General Tufanian, when the shahanshah ordered the army to support the Constitutional government with all its might. In the past five months—we have had two cabinets, this one is the third—this has been the pattern. If we were to change [our policy] now, they would think that we do not want to support this government. Fortunately, the prime minister is very rational, strong and determined. Is it prudent for us now to pull the military back into the barracks?"[32]

The generals praised Bakhtiar for his firmness. Bakhtiar had told Military Governor Lieutenant General Mehdi Rahimi to act as he deemed appropriate, which was to keep the units out of the path of the demonstrators but close enough to engage when required. Rahimi had so ordered his units, though he thought flowers would be given and efforts would be made to gain the soldiers' sympathy. "You see General," Rahimi addressed Qarabaghi, "we must make a choice, to fight or to make peace *[ya zangi-ye zang, ya rumi-e rum]*."[33]

Opinion on how to encounter the flower issue differed. A long debate ensued until General Tufanian, the senior officer in the group, objected to the council's engaging in such details. He would rather hear what General Nasser Moqaddam, the SAVAK chief, had to say. Moqaddam agreed that this was no time to dabble in small details:

> Our goal must be to protect the imperial forces. The enemy's plan is to destroy the imperial armed forces after His Majesty's departure. Offering flowers, bring-ing down the statues, hurling insults, attacking the NCOs' homes, and other such acts are preludes to that end. Therefore we must plan for R-Day, the day the shahanshah will depart. In as yet normal conditions [when the shah is still in the country] we have witnessed huge demonstrations, 600 to 700 thousand people [in Tehran]—according to the opposition, 2 million people. In the holy city of Mashhad there have been demonstrations ranging from 500 to 700 thousand; in other cities, 200 to 300 thousand. These are the same people who brought down the statues, attacked the police stations, attacked the SAVAK, attacked the hospitals, attacked the military post exchanges, and threatened the life and limb of our sol-diers, NCOs, and officers. We must take measures, even if only to save ourselves. If this wave is so expansive when the imperial armed forces are powerful, tomorrow, when the shahanshah sets foot out of the country, the 1-million-strong crowd will become 3 million, and the flowers turn into violence, aggression, and the destruc-tion of the Imperial Army. General, this is why we have gathered here today.

There was no time to complain about the past or to assign guilt, Moqaddam warned. What the generals needed was "unity," or tomorrow "there would be no imperial army." The admonition was not effective. The discourse went back to the problem of the demonstrators, the soldiers, and the flowers. Now Lieutenant General Ahmadali Mohaqqeqi, commander of the gendarmerie, pleaded for the regime's proponents also to be allowed to demonstrate. "The army is part of the people; the people are not separate from the army. The soldier is the child of the people. . . . If the opposition is allowed to demonstrate, why can't the people on our side? Unless we mobilize these people, nothing else will work; after all we are a part of the people."[34]

Mohaqqeqi's proposal was put on the agenda for the next meeting. The dis-cussion then turned to the ways and means of reestablishing communications, at least in the army. The general in charge, Hasan Yazdi, was not optimistic. "France is one third [the size] of Iran," said Yazdi. "Its army was never able to work out its communications. Wasn't there a strike just a month ago? Could they do anything? General, our country cannot do anything either." Qarabaghi gave up. "Very well, we will do what we can."[35]

Bakhtiar had told Rahimi to prepare a place for incarcerating as many as one hundred thousand people if need be. The army had made a study and come up with a maximum capacity for five thousand prisoners. "After all," observed Lieutenant General Nasser Firuzmand, "a prisoner is a human being; he needs appropriate food, toilet, bath, blankets, and the like. At this scale [for five thousand], SAVAK has prepared an excellent plan and we have a copy of it in our [Supreme Commander's] G2." The generals were loath to tell the new prime minister, a man they considered foreign to their traditions, that they had not planned for all contingencies. "We can't tell him we cannot give him what he needs," said Qarabaghi. "He meant a lot of people. OK, the people we take might become somewhat uncomfortable for lack of space. They have made others uncomfortable. This is tit for tat."[36]

Tufanian, playing the moderator, wanted to hear from the police chief, the man "responsible for protecting the city." The police, said General Fazlollah Jafari, would make everything needed available and put all its personnel at the service of whoever was designated to carry out the generals' decisions. But, everyone should know that the police force could not by itself face turmoil of this size. "As I stated at the National Security Council, our police are organized to act as the arm of the judiciary, not to quell rebellions. . . . We have been accused of killing the people . . . [but] this is not true. We have been in the open and our officers have been killed. . . . But if you think our police in Tehran can stop 400, 500, or 600 thousand people marching, this is not at all possible, unless we operate within a larger organization." Everyone agreed.[37]

The focus now turned to domestic security—facing the rebellion in the streets and securing the sectors that critically affected the people's lives and the government's sustainability. On the first point, explained G3 Chief Lieutenant General Alimohammad Khajenuri, it was essential to define explicitly the level of violence at which the military would engage the rebellion. "It must be made clear," he said, "whether the encounter is serious and accepts high risks or not." The issue would have to be decided in the National Security Council (NSC), but the generals agreed that on R-Day all the country should be designated condition red and everywhere the military governors be given the authority and the responsibility for maintaining their regions' security. On the matter of risk, Khajenuri was pessimistic, but Qarabaghi would not let him speak. It was not a matter for the meeting and besides it was dispiriting, he said.[38]

By this time, Lieutenant General Ja'far Sanei, deputy commander of the ground forces, had come to the end of his patience. He asked permission to speak:

> This, general, is a historic meeting. It may be that, God forbid, we will never again be able to convene such a meeting. It may be that we shall achieve honors so as to obviate the need for such a meeting. . . . As an officer of the imperial armed forces, I feel obligated to say that all pertinent information has already been given to the Supreme Commander's Staff and to all security organizations. What now every individual, civilian or military, readily sees is that we are on the threshold of defeat. Everyone can see that if His Majesty the Shahanshah leaves the country, there will be war and bloodshed here. I think the chief of the Supreme Commander's Staff should ask His Imperial Majesty to postpone his departure until this staff is enabled to do the following:
>
> 1. Before His Majesty leaves, arrest the opposition leaders, regardless of their number;
> 2. Take over the country's electricity and fuel. We cannot do this by talking about it. We must do it with the power of bullets and bayonets. We are not a technical army. We must use every technical cadre we possess and the cadres we do not possess we must produce by the dint of our arms. We must put the technical civilian behind the machine and our gun behind his head. We must say, do the work or you shall be executed, and if he refuses to do his work, we must execute him. We shall have enough technicians to do the job after we have shot ten people;
> 3. Immediately take over the nation's propaganda organizations. Every member of this country in every corner of the nation ought to know about the new situation. Call it a coup d'état, call it supporting the Constitutional government, call it saving the country, I do not care. On R minus 1, we must take over the imperial country with military force based on what I just stated.[39]

"This is what every military man has thought about," said Qarabaghi, cutting Sanei short. "The Imperial Army," however, "does not interfere in politics. It supports the Constitutional government. This is a Constitutional government, taking office by His Imperial Majesty's decree, and seeking votes of confidence from the two houses of parliament. Our duty, therefore, is to support this government with all our might." Such talk, he said, was for when or if the prime minister ran or shed his responsibility.[40]

The meeting then turned to the meaning of condition red and its legal ramifications. At the end of the meeting, it was decided to delineate carefully the conditions under which the military was permitted to use arms.

The shah left Iran on 16 January 1979. Khomeini declared 19 January (29 Dey), which was the *arba'in,* the fortieth day of Hussein's martyrdom, as a day for a million people to march. The 19th witnessed a huge demonstration in Tehran, called by its organizers the "grandest religio-political march" in Iran's history. The marchers, uninterrupted by the military, converged on the Shahyad Monument, demanded the abrogation of monarchy, and declared that "God, Koran, and Khomeini" had replaced "God, King, and Country" as Iran's national motto.

On 20 January Khomeini declared he would return to Iran. Bakhtiar, inti-mating a military coup, retorted that if Khomeini returned and declared an Islamic Republic he, Bakhtiar, would be faced with only two alternatives: "either remain as the head of the Constitutional government, in which case there will be bloodshed; or leave my duties and inform the army that there is no longer a place for me here and you are free from your commitment to me." On the 21st, Khomeini said the future government of Iran would be Islamic, administered by a new set of laws derived from the Koran. On the same day, the chair of the Regency Council, Seyyed Jalaleddin Tehrani, who was in Paris seeking an audience with Khomeini, resigned from the council after Khomeini refused to meet with him as a council member and then, upon Khomeini's demand, called the council illegal. On 22 January Qarabaghi denied the rumor that a coup was imminent and vowed to continue to support Bakhtiar. On the 23rd, he con-vened the second meeting of the Commanders' Council to discuss supporting Bakhtiar, Khomeini's return, demonstrations in favor of the Constitution, and the possibility of a political solution. However, he had to explain himself before the meeting could pick up the agenda.

The issue was a statement by Qarabaghi to the members of the armed forces, which had been read the night before on the radio and in which the word *shah-anshah* was not used. The prime minister, said Qarabaghi, had suggested that the political climate was not favorable to the use of the term. Qarabaghi, on the other hand, had insisted on using the term *imperial (shahanshahi)* in reference to the armed forces, though this last point also was contested by NIRT employees and had taken some bargaining before his statement was finally broadcast. The intent of the statement, to reaffirm the military's support of the "Constitutional govern-ment," was also challenged. "Our war, more than anything else, is a political war," Qarabaghi told the council. The country needed to stop Khomeini from coming to Iran, and it needed to show the world, mesmerized by the recent marches, that there was more to Iran than Khomeini and his *hezbollah* (party of God).[41]

Qarabaghi and Bakhtiar had agreed that Khomeini's return to Iran was inexpedient. Rumor had it that the armed forces planned to hit Khomeini's plane in the air, divert it to a distant island, or find other ways of preventing it from landing in Iran. What was the army to do in case Khomeini actually arrived in Iran, Qarabaghi asked. Who would accept responsibility for his safety? These, according to Qarabaghi, were insoluble problems. The only solution, Bakhtiar had suggested and other NSC members had concurred, was to find a way diplomatically to dissuade Khomeini from returning to the country.

A second issue for the council to debate was how to demonstrate the so-far-silent support that nevertheless existed for constitutional monarchy. The NSC had decided on a "national demonstration" in favor of the Constitution to show the world that not everyone in Iran supported the Khomeini line. The generals had been upset when previous prime ministers had objected to pro-regime demonstrations. On several occasions industry captains had offered to bring out their blue-collar and white-collar workers on the streets but had been rebuffed. The generals' displeasure was directed primarily at Sharif-Emami and Azhari. Bakhtiar, despite his involvement with Mosaddeq, exhibited an innate courage that appealed to them. At the NSC meeting on the day before the shah left, Bakhtiar issued several secret directives to Qarabaghi, which Qarabaghi now, on Tufanian's suggestion, read to the generals with obvious relish. It was, said the directive, incumbent on the imperial armed forces to quell any move suggesting cessation from the imperial nation. The army was not to intervene in peaceful political demonstrations or anti-regime sloganeering, but this was for the moment. Once the government was in better command and relative calm prevailed, other appropriate decisions, consonant with the Constitution, would be made. To Qarabaghi, this was the height of political acumen. The army was not to confront the people on R+1, the day after the shah's departure, when most likely there would be large-scale demonstrations, but should be available and prepared to act if things got out of hand. After consultation with SAVAK, the government would immediately approve the arrest of instigators when needed, except for the ulama, who would not be arrested for the present. Bakhtiar also complimented the imperial armed forces on their "profound moral endowments and unswerving discipline" and asked Qarabaghi to pass the message to every officer, NCO, and soldier that he, the prime minister, "hailed the Imperial Iranian Armed Forces" whose support "cause[d] my government to succeed" and that he and his government "bow[ed] before Iran's tricolor standard and salute[d] the proud imperial army." He would do whatever practicable to support and strengthen the armed forces. These sentiments prompted Tufanian to exclaim: "This truly signifies."[42]

However, not everyone was pacified. Major General Changiz Voshmgir, the deputy commander of the ground forces, who was representing General Badrei in the meeting, complained about not knowing what was behind all this. "It is not acceptable that the country is in such turmoil and we do not know who is behind it. Are you telling us that the people are doing all this? We know enough to know that in all such situations there is some support from some source. Who has created the present condition? Why don't you tell us who it is that is hitting us? Who is it, that against him we just stand still, retreat, and yield? I as a general of this army must know the reason." Qarabaghi, exasperated, was about to explain, when Voshmgir hit him with another potentially lethal blow. "General, in your discourse, did I hear you say that the army is 'national'?"

"I never said anything of the sort," Qarabaghi retorted. "I only talked of our 'national duty.'"

"Is the army *melli* [national] or *shahanshahi* [imperial]?" snapped Voshmgir.

"Never in my life have I uttered *artesh-e melli* [national army]," pleaded Qarabaghi. "Good thing we have recorded all the conversations."

But this was a question that hit at the heart of the generals' faith. *Melli* in reference to the army was a devastating signal for separating the army and the shah—devastating because the term was blameless. General Mohaqqeqi now shouted, "Let those who say they want a 'national army' eat crow. We *are* the national army. The traitor who utters such nonsense is a communist lackey. We will not allow him to separate us from the people. The shahanshah is the head of the people and the most beloved of all." For Mohaqqeqi, this was the eleventh hour, the last chance to act. "Mr. Bakhtiar is just sitting there. Like a hundred prime ministers before him, he also shall leave when the time for action comes. We must force him to take action."

Qarabaghi tried unsuccessfully to cut Mohaqqeqi short, protesting, "We don't have to force him. He is a believer."

Mohaqqeqi retorted, "A believer, indeed; what does he have to do with the shahanshah? Bring in Mosaddeq's picture; that is what he is telling us. I am not telling him not to bring in Mosaddeq's picture. But how can we tolerate his telling us not to utter the name of the shahanshah? This for us is intolerable."

Mohaqqeqi was a hawk, forever advocating strong and decisive action, forever being rebuffed. "We have always fallen short, General," he said to Qarabaghi.

Qarabaghi, striving to appease him, said, "I have walked along with you, and I agree."[43]

Voshmgir's question still remained to be answered, however. Qarabaghi turned to SAVAK Chief Moqaddam, who began a discourse on how decisions were made in "the Imperial Iran."

The commanders acted independently, asked for orders [from the shah] and orders were issued. So no one person really could say he knew everything that was going on. But as a military officer with some political experience, I can say this: Foreigners have had and still have interests in this country. They have never been prepared to accept an independent Iran, an Iran whose sovereign declares we want to have a national independent policy; we want to be our own master within our land. This was too much for the foreigners, and it still is. They planned and, regrettably, we became the instrument of their plan, turning our country into what it is today. We are all Muslims, Twelver Shiis. Look into General Voshmgir's pocket and you find a Koran. It is not difficult for a [foreign-motivated] policy to use religion to split the regime and the people. These groups that march in the cities in the name of religion provide cover for other political factions, especially the communists. This stratagem has also cut a deep chasm between the imperial regime and extremist Muslims, who dispose of a great deal of power. . . . Khomeini has one leg on the communists, the other on the disaffected Muslims. This is what I can say as a general explanation.

Tehran's major daily newspapers—*Kayhan, Ettela'at, Ayandegan*—were in communist hands, continued Moqaddam. They went so far as to refuse to print a matter His Majesty wished printed. This was when the shah was still in Iran. One could deduce "our situation" now that the shah was no longer in Iran. "Why are we in this predicament? Because of the threats and interests that created them in the first place in order to diminish our national power, and succeeded in diminishing it. . . . The people now can count only on the imperial armed forces. Only the imperial armed forces can protect this nation. And the imperial armed forces can perform this duty only if they remain united and disciplined."[44]

But, according to Moqaddam, not every commander was brave or patriotic. In Mashhad and Shiraz military commanders were derelict in their duties. In Mashhad, on the first day of martial law, several individuals, "communists and other opposition groups," were allowed to climb up the tanks and hurl slogans against the regime. Moqaddam objected, but was accused of framing his colleagues. "Often we wanted to arrest those who committed treason, those who acted against our *moqaddasat-e melli* ["nationally sacred," a euphemism for the shah]. The military governor [General Oveisi] tied our hand. He even directed the Ministry of the Interior not to arrest anyone." General Oveisi, according to Moqaddam, did not let SAVAK do its duty either. He tied "our hands and feet," not letting the institutions that are the "shield" of the nation do their job. The day Oveisi was leaving "he told me 'Why don't you arrest five thousand people?' If we had arrested ten or twenty people the first day, we would not be where we are now." But, said Moqaddam, there was no use now. "When a million people, no matter how wrong their motives, march, there is no longer any use." He felt obliged to warn his colleagues: "If we procrastinate longer, we shall all perish."[45]

Qarabaghi did not want to discuss the past because in the end military paralysis had resulted from the shah's decision not to allow his army to use violence. The sovereign had reasons that the generals could not comprehend. But he was the king and neither Qarabaghi nor the other generals would contradict him in the presence of others.

A committee on pro-regime demonstrations had been established under the prime minister, in which Military Governor General Mehdi Rahimi and his staff participated. Rahimi, who had also been appointed police chief the day before, had told the prime minister he should appoint one of his ministers to manage the committee. "What minister? There is no one but him," said Qarabaghi. In fact, the revolutionaries barred most of Bakhtiar's ministers from entering their ministries. "It will not work," intoned Qarabaghi and Tufanian simultaneously. "What is to be done?" Qarabaghi asked Moqaddam. General Rahimi, as both military governor and police chief, was the ideal man for the task, insisted Moqaddam: "No one is more qualified to do the job than he." Everyone was to give Rahimi utmost support. His own organization could not give him much moral support, because "they have tied our hands." Materially, however, he was prepared to help as much as needed until the mission was accomplished.[46]

The issue was who would participate in the march. "No officers or NCOs," said Qarabaghi. "Not so," said air force commander General Rabii. "Without the army's participation this thing will fail. Everyone who is not absolutely necessary at his post must take part, or it will fail." Rabii's words met with general approval. "This, sir, is a matter of the Constitution, not politics. If I do not defend the Constitution, what else remains to me to defend?" continued Rabii. Qarabaghi was now clearly on the defensive. Of course he would give his life for the Constitution. On the other hand, it would not be wise to vitiate the efforts of the two hundred thousand civilians who might march. The statement led to another uproar, causing the Guard's deputy commander, Major General Beiglari Amin, once again to take Qarabaghi to task for speaking on the radio when he had been denied permission to use the word *shahanshahi* in his speech. Qarabaghi now threatened to close the meeting. "Nobody knows my pains. I have worked for six months to get this permission for a popular march, and now they say let's delay it. This will take place before Friday. That is a military order."

"Yes, sir," said Beiglari.[47]

In the end, Qarabaghi gave in to what the generals wanted for the march.

Everyone in the military family was to take part, men and women, in civilian clothes, except the security and the personnel needed at their posts. General Rahimi was to supervise and General Moqaddam was to take charge of the operations.

Six days later, the commanders met again. By then Khomeini had made clear his intention to return as soon as possible. Khomeini had received the former U.S. attorney general Ramsey Clark on 21 January, after which Clark had declared that the United States should begin negotiating with the religious leader because, as Clark put it, 99 percent of Iranians supported Khomeini and the same number opposed the shah.[48] On the 23rd, even as the Commanders' Council was meeting, the National Front issued a letter announcing Khomeini's return: "For once in human history the sun moves eastward from the west," the letter read. On the 24th, Bakhtiar, incongruously, offered bills in the Majlis on the dissolution of SAVAK and the procedures for putting on trial prime ministers and ministers who had served in cabinets in the fifteen years since the White Revolution, from 1963 to 1979. At the same time, he told the deputies, "This government will not be shaken and I will never leave the Constitutional trench." Mehdi Bazargan, Qarabaghi's interlocutor and by now widely known as the ayatollah's choice for prime minister, suggested that the Prophet's ten-year rule in Medina and Ali's five years in Kufa were the models for Iran's future Islamic government. The Islamic Republic, therefore, he deduced, was democratic.[49] The pro-regime demonstrations had taken place on 25 January, and though the turnout had not been as large as the opposition marches, it was nonetheless impressive. The government, claiming the rules of martial law, had then ordered the airports closed and declared all demonstrations illegal beginning at 5 A.M. on 26 January (6 Bahman), the day after the pro-regime demonstrations.[50] The declaration, however, did not prevent the opposition from jamming the streets. In the late hours of the 27th, Bakhtiar declared he was ready to fly to Paris in forty-eight hours to meet with "His Excellency Grand Ayatollah Imam Khomeini" to seek his guidance—or, according to some accounts, his directives. Khomeini, however, on the same day said he would not receive Bakhtiar unless he resigned his office.[51]

Thus this third meeting of the Commanders' Council, on 28 January, took place under heavy pressure. The generals knew there would be no political solution to their dilemma. Bakhtiar's government was likely to fall. And they had to decide how to preserve the military—by coup d'état or in some other way.

"What if His Excellency the Prime Minister resigns?" Qarabaghi asked.

"What are we to do if no one takes the helm, as no one would when His Majesty was still in the country? What are we to do when Ayatollah Shariʻatmadari, who is a source of emulation to a majority of the people, declares that the armed forces should come to terms with the oppositionists? Suppose, General Rahimi, we have no prime minister and the people decide to march on the airport, occupy it, and open it for Ayatollah Khomeini to land? What is the army's duty then? What is our duty? What must we do?"[52]

The top generals — Qarabaghi, Tufanian, Badrei, Rabii, Habibollahi, Rahimi — had discussed these matters earlier. Now, Qarabaghi wished to have everyone involved so that "we would not be surprised." The question, as far as he was concerned, was what must be done when no other responsible institution was around to make an authoritative decision. The discussion, however, was interrupted, because the prime minister had just announced to the press that the airport, occupied by the military since 24 January, was to be opened. The reason, Qarabaghi explained, was that the foreign press representatives in Iran who had been waiting for Khomeini wished to leave Iran now that he apparently would take some time to come. The generals were shocked. "Put them in a military plane and take them to Turkey, Iraq, or Kuwait, but don't open the airport" was the response. Qarabaghi agreed, but who would be held responsible for closing the airport, he asked. "The prime minister orders the airport open, but the airport remains closed. Who keeps the airport closed? The army, who else? Isn't this what they will conclude?" It was up to the generals to decide if it was to the army's advantage to close the airport. However, Qarabaghi said, "This is a Constitutional government — a government that believes it does not take its directives from His Majesty and therefore assumes all responsibility. I have directed General Rahimi to address all communication to the Ministry of War because martial law now means that we have given the government a military governor and a certain level of military force that acts at the government's pleasure. If the government so wishes, the military governor carries a stick; if the government wishes otherwise, the military governor acts otherwise. Nevertheless, we all know that everything the military governor does will be written on the military's account because it executes the order."[53]

Qarabaghi's discourse reopened the issue of the responsibility of the armed forces. What if Bakhtiar failed? What would the armed forces do? General Rahimi suggested a military prime minister. Who would appoint this prime minister, asked operations chief General Khajenuri, noting, "If we appoint him, it would be a coup d'état." The idea of a coup d'état was not well-received. "The Regency Council would appoint him," Rahimi corrected himself. If they were unable or refused to perform their duty, then, "maybe it will be a coup d'état," Rahimi concluded.

"Then we don't need a prime minister . . . ," Khajenuri responded.

"Then, perhaps the generals who have more experience than I will guide us to the right course of action," Rahimi said, clearly exasperated.

Qarabaghi now turned to General Badrei, the most powerful man in the group, commanding at once both the ground forces and the Guard. Badrei, who had just arrived, had not much encouragement for his colleagues:

> The prime minister will not resign. He may be assassinated but he will not resign. If he was going to resign, he would have gone to Paris, where he would decide whether to resign or not. However, my view is that whether he resigns or not, our aim must be to save the armed forces. The only way to save the army is to keep out of these altercations because we will be held responsible for whatever happens regardless of who issues the order—the government, someone else, or no one. The fact is the enemy creates conditions in which the soldier is forced to shoot so that someone is killed. We must do what we can to save the army and the only way to do that is to take our forces back to the barracks. Then at least we have an army. At the moment, we do not have an army. In the ground forces, our units are scattered across the smallest of the cities; they are no longer units under the command of their commanding generals. . . . Let us gather up the military and maybe if the opposition sees no army in the streets to confront, it will no longer shed blood, or commit arson, or engage in violent demonstrations.[54]

Qarabaghi found Badrei's discourse irrelevant. It was not likely that Bakhtiar would leave of his own accord; however, like his predecessors, he might have to because, for example, his ministers could force the government to resign as they almost had under Sharif-Emami. At any rate, the question was, said Qarabaghi, what were the armed forces to do if no other authority remained? "We must," said Qarabaghi, "formulate a plan together, top secret, for the generals to have if the day . . ."[55]

For General Mohaqqeqi, the gendarmerie chief, that day was now.

> I have been steady in my position, sir. If we are facing some strange political thing we do not know of, that is something else. If our problem is Khomeini and only Khomeini, then we cannot satisfy him. We have exacerbated our situation because we have been indolent, because we have refused to see, because we have woven ropes to hang ourselves. I have said this a thousand times and I say it again: tomorrow will be worse for us than today. . . . Things will get worse. Do now what you think you will do tomorrow. Why should we let the communist reporter write the lies he does? Why should we be afraid of Khomeini? Let this head of government

arrest all the corrupt elements, past and present, and put them in jail or hang them. Let us move fast, at revolutionary speed. No one will be able to confront us if we do. I tell you, you show power and everyone will turn to us. Do as we have been doing, no one will even dare to step forward after this one leaves. And we won't have a soldier, let alone an army, to command. It is now or never. We must do what we must do now.[56]

But Mohaqqeqi's outburst did not solve the generals' problem, either. The strategy, said Rahimi, required both military and political solutions. The French government must be prevailed upon to get Khomeini out of France to Libya, where he would not have such easy access to Iran. General Khajenuri now embarked on a rational discourse on the military's options, taking care to remind his colleagues that these were not necessarily his choices.

Assuming that the government was no longer able to decide, the army had two options: to let Khomeini in or not to let Khomeini in. If Khomeini was let in, the army would likely face one of two alternatives Khomeini might pursue: either he would form a temporary government until the situation calmed, at which time he would conduct a referendum, or he would form a revolutionary council and force a republic on the nation. But what if the army did not allow Khomeini in? In that case, persevering in the present course will harm the Imperial Armed Forces because the army will increasingly deteriorate and that is not acceptable. If we do not let him come in, then, as General Rahimi said, the only alternative for the army is to act in full force and take over the country. That means the army must accept the risk of a bloodbath.... But this is the only solution. Procrastinating will lead to the destruction of the army and a high probability that the communists will succeed and that will only exacerbate our problems.[57]

Now Moqaddam took the floor. The way conditions were unfolding, said Moqaddam, the prime minister would fall, despite his courage and commitment. The political situation was getting worse. The center could not hold. Yesterday, they did not dare attack a police station; today they attack the gendarmerie headquarters. They speak of individual assassinations. Revolutionary bands walk the streets unafraid and unchecked. There is no organization to stop them. Our reports tell us that even several of our generals are no longer at their posts. Finally, there is an unprecedented effort to bring Khomeini back to Iran and to mobilize forces in Iran and abroad to receive him. "This all points to one fact: there are elements, organizations, and forces that aim to overthrow Bakhtiar's government regardless of his will. The political strategy, to which several colleagues have referred, is clear — it is to bring 'that gentleman' to Iran as a prelude to further planning. For more than a month now we have been asking our friends to quiet Khomeini. The night before last, after several hours of negotiations with Khomeini's representatives, an agreement was reached for the prime minister to travel to Paris to meet with Khomeini. There was no talk of resignation. He [Mr. Bakhtiar] was to go as Iran's prime minister. This morning at 5 A.M. suddenly they announced Mr. Khomeini had decided differently. This is a proof that the root of our problem is not within the country; it is clearly outside."[58]

For Moqaddam, keeping the army intact under the circumstances was impossible and taking half-measures the worst option. The enemy intended to destroy Iran as a national power. The army was an important component of Iran's national power. The enemy had successfully pitted the army against the people. The army's duty was clear. As long as there was a Regency Council, the army was duty-bound to obey it. If, for any reason, that council was not able to function, then the army would have to take matters in its hands and to act forcefully, with all its power. That meant it had to kill the communists, destroy the printing presses, and arrest the clerics. It meant the military against the people. It meant the military and the people mutually destroying each other. But the army had sworn to protect the monarchical system, the Constitution, and the nation's independence. "This army must remain true to its oath—unless we found a political solution that relieved us of our oath, saying, in effect, we are no longer bound by the oath to which we were bound in the past."[59]

Moqaddam's discourse was eloquent, but like most other statements ultimately not very helpful. It proposed that the military was pledged to fight, but fighting meant destroying everything the military stood for. Logically, then, any alternative was preferable to fighting. But he had no alternative to offer, except an as-yet-unknown political solution. This alternative was halfheartedly supported by Admiral Habibollahi. Nothing else would work. "We must continue to resist in order that the other national organs get a chance to strive for a political solution," said the naval commander. There was no other way. The need for a political solution was further grounded in strategic imperatives by General Najimi Naini. The truth was, said Najimi, the armed forces had lost their material support base. The army was built on the assumption of popular support. The strikes, however, were about to paralyze its logistical base. "We have no fuel, energy, electricity, or money. Today we suffer from a scarcity of security; tomorrow, the army will have problems providing food for our soldiers."[60] It was true, said Najimi, that the army would have to take care of the situation, because the rest, including the Regency Council, was nothing but a soap bubble. The council was, in fact, Qarabaghi. But the trouble was that the army also could not do much. It was a stalemate, like a chess game in which there was no exit. The country was stuck in a vicious circle.[61]

The discussion returned to the specifics. Rahimi, the military governor, asked for a joint headquarters to make collective decisions. Qarabaghi agreed with the idea of a joint headquarters but not collective decisions. The military governor was the decision maker; other generals were his liaison officers. Rahimi was not satisfied but was not allowed to follow up. Najimi now picked up his speech about the army's sorry state. The situation was not to be compared with seemingly like conditions in other countries. The operating paradigm was the Passion of Karbala and the history of Imam Hussein. It was no longer possible to stop Khomeini's return to Iran because his followers had gone mad with passion. They were willing to die for their leader, in numbers that only a few weeks ago had seemed impossible. And Khomeini would not change; the old man was about to overthrow a history as old as twenty-five hundred years. Nothing would divert him from his path. "We must clarify our strategy, for otherwise we will melt like snow, melt like snow." His Majesty, said Najimi, had instructed everyone on the wisdom of finding a political solution. "How do we find a political solution to save ourselves and our country, gentlemen? That, I do not know."[62]

General Tufanian now recommended greater contact with the minister of war. "We are not political people," he said. "But one thing I know is that the prime minister is courageous and determined. He must be made to find a political solution" This, he said, was his definitive position.[63] Qarabaghi agreed.

> To summarize the generals' views: we must, as I stated the first day, strive to preserve the armed forces. . . . Military action is neither expedient nor possible. We must uphold the honor of the army. Our second task is to search for a political solution. . . . As long as the prime minister persists in his way, a political solution means that we support him. He is the responsible authority; we give him our advice; he finds the political strategy. At the end, if, God forbid, his political strategy proves ineffective, we must sit together, the generals, to see what political options are open to us. This is of the highest secrecy.[64]

PART V

EXILE

23

Trek to Nowhere

As December 1978 came to a close, pressure on the royal couple became almost unbearable. The shah and the queen saw the gloom spreading across the palace in the eyes of the people who served them. The men and women working in the royal palaces were invariably religious, torn between their loyalty to the shah and their belief in the religious leaders. They lived in co-op houses built by the court ministry and were known in their neighborhoods to work in the king's palace, an honor that in the past had brought them respect and deference. Now, the situation had changed. They were insulted, accosted in the street, and sometimes physically attacked. Not in their most pessimistic moments had they foreseen the calumnies they were now subjected to. As it gradually dawned on them that the sovereign was preparing to leave, they became anxious about their own fate and the fate of their families. Their gloom darkened the air in the palace further, punctuating the hopelessness that pervaded every interaction.

Behavior change was discernible also in the Guard, though camouflaged by military discipline. Occasional flares of rebellion told of the chaos that was on the horizon. Kambiz Atabai recalls one such story. One day in the midst of the demonstrations in Tehran a young soldier of the Guard went berserk during lunch and attempted to pull the shah's portrait down from the wall. The soldier happened to be a son of a man named Hassasi, who for many years had served as butler to the shah's offices in the Jahan Nama palace. Hassasi was devoted to the shah and had proved this in no uncertain way. On 10 April 1965, as the shah sought to escape an assassin's bullet inside the Marble Palace, Hassasi had placed himself between the assailant and the shah's office and, though shot in the arm, had held on to the doorknob to prevent the assailant from entering the office. After the canteen incident, Atabai said to Hassasi, who on occasion served him tea in his office, that he was sorry about what had happened in the canteen and, by way of sympathizing with the old butler, he had wondered aloud how anyone could think that a man like Khomeini would be able to rule a country like Iran. To his surprise, Hassasi was offended. He told Atabai to take care not to insult the ayatollah. "I am devoted to His Majesty, but I am also a follower of the Imam. I will not have anyone disparage the Imam in my presence," he said.[1]

Hassasi's reaction pointed to a profound change, not in the religious but in the political atmosphere. Hassasi had always been religious, a fact that was well known. But his religion had been private. A year before, his source of emulation most likely had been Shari'atmadari rather than Khomeini. If someone had then said in his presence that the clerics would not make good governors, he would not have been offended. Indeed, it would most likely have been his opinion also. Now, of course, everything had changed, inside the court as outside. The shah understood the change, which made him despair, knowing he had lost the game. The queen also suffered. "One day I stood by the window looking outside. It occurred to me that I could be dead within days. Then I thought death is the end of things and may not be as bad as all that. I then felt a calm I had never felt before."[2]

Still, the employees at the palace remained by and large loyal, although one or two were obviously working for the opposition. Anti-shah slogans were found on the dining table where the shah had his lunch, but the perpetrators remained unknown. Even after the fall of the regime, no one divulged any information from within the court. On one or two occasions, personal animosity assumed after the shah's death led to vicious attacks on the shah and his family, but this was the exception rather than the rule. Yet once he had decided to leave, the shah had become mistrustful of the people who served him. The only person among his servants he completely trusted was Mahmud Eliasi, an NCO in the Guard who was his personal valet. Contrary to all precedence, Eliasi was now the person who relayed the shah's orders to the others, including the commanders of the forces. This irked the generals. Rabii of the air force called Atabai, who had been charged since the days of Alam to arrange with the air force whenever the court needed airplanes, to complain about Eliasi's communication. "Why is it that rather than General Badrei or Mr. Afshar, or you, Sergeant Eliasi calls me to convey His Majesty's wishes?" Rabii asked. "Why would he tell me to keep it a secret? What is happening?" Rabii was obviously dismayed at the shah's attitude and suspicious of what might come next. So was Badrei, who did not know how to explain it to the others.[3]

The shah's decision to leave was hard on his friends and supporters, many of whom believed at the time that if the shah remained, Khomeini would not return to Iran. The decision disheartened the armed forces, said Ardeshir Zahedi after the revolution. "If the shah had not left, the army would not have given in. There might have been a need for significant change, but it should not have ended in the destruction of the country's economic and military might. His Majesty's leaving should not have been such as to result in so much hardship, misery, and bloodshed for the Iranians." But Zahedi put the blame on the shah's "chameleon friends" rather than on the shah.[4]

The royals' departure from the palace on 16 January was a horrendous experience for them and for the others who had served them over the years. "It was excruciating," observed Atabai, who was present at the scene. The servants lined up along the wall leading to the helicopters that would take the shah and the queen to the airport. There was moaning and crying everywhere, and beating of the head and chest in the traditional style of mourning. Others seemed in a trance, emptily looking into space. Some threw themselves at the shah's feet, begging him not to leave. The shah tried to comfort them as best he could. "No reason to worry," he said. "We are leaving for a long-needed rest and shall soon return." This was the official line given out for his trip, belied by his face and posture as he walked past the mournful line.[5] The self-confident, proud poise he had struck for so many years was gone. The defeat engulfed everyone. The servants, and the guards who stood at attention at a distance, knew this was their last glance at their sovereign; there would be no return.

It was the same at the royal pavilion at the Mehrabad Airport. The air was heavy. A detachment of the Imperial Guard standing by at random reflected the disorder that pervaded the nation. The shah's helicopter landed. He descended, followed by the queen. Two officers, commissioned to the airport and not part of the Guard, stood at a distance, inattentive to the shah and the queen. The royals waited for the prime minister to arrive, who was at the Majlis seeking a vote of confidence. The shah had been assured that the vote was forthcoming before he left the palace, but the process had taken longer than anticipated, and the prime minister was not yet at the pavilion. A second helicopter landed, but it carried only the remainder of the travelers from the palace. The monarch told his protocol chief, Amir Aslan Afshar, to call the Majlis to see if the prime minister had received the vote of confidence he sought, but Afshar found that the lines had been cut. At last, the prime minister arrived, alighting from his helicopter triumphantly, approaching the shah. They spoke alone for a few minutes. Then the shah moved toward the plane, no honor guard for him to review, no national anthem to herald his presence. His ashen face reflected the end. The Guardsmen fell at his feet for the last time, begging him to stay. He burst into tears, for an instant losing control. He reached the plane and hurried in, followed by the prime minister. According to Afshar, who witnessed the scene on the plane, the shah talked to Bakhtiar for a while, and as Bakhtiar was about to take his leave, the shah said: "You now have all the power and authority. I leave the country with you and you with God." The prime minister then kissed the shah's hand and descended the stairs.[6]

The shah took the controls during the take off, as was his custom. He enjoyed this plane, the *Shahin,* Iran's answer to *Air Force One* in the United States. He liked the accommodations, the service, and the food, especially the steak the caterer prepared. After an hour or so of flying, when they reached the Persian Gulf, he came out of the cockpit and asked Afshar to order lunch. But there was no lunch. The caterers had not allowed the food to be taken to the plane. The royal plates, glassware, and cutlery had been taken out. Only the guards had food, *baqali polo,* a traditional dish of rice and beans that the royal cook Kabiri had prepared. The pot was placed in the middle of the table, surrounded by small paper plates and tissues, with which the royal couple and their entourage ate—Afshar and Dr. Liusa Pirnia, who was the pediatrician for the royal children and who also served as the queen's companion. "It needs a Shakespeare to do justice to what Iranians did to their sovereign on his last day in his country," Afshar said.[7]

◼

The shah planned to go to the United States after visiting with President Sadat in Aswan, Egypt. He had an official invitation from the United States government, offered after rather tumultuous meetings of the Special Coordination Committee (SCC) and National Security Council (NSC) at the White House. On 28 December Zbigniew Brzezinski, supported by Secretary of Defense Harold Brown, had got the president as well as Cyrus Vance, Stansfield Turner, and Deputy Defense Secretary Charles Duncan to agree to send the shah, through Ambassador Sullivan, a firm message of support, saying, in effect, that the United States stood with the shah in whatever decision he made. But, the message emphasized, it was "essential to terminate the continued uncertainty." It is not clear how Sullivan delivered the message to the shah. However, it would not have made any difference. The shah had already concluded that the option of a military government was out and had turned to Bakhtiar. The decision led the Americans to conclude that it was in the United States' interest for the shah to leave and that the United States should send General Huyser to "assist the Iranian military in retaining their cohesion once the shah left." On 3 January, in a meeting of the SCC, arrangements were made "for exile for the shah in the United States" at the Walter Annenberg estate in California. It was also decided to inform the shah that the United States supported his decision to leave the country when Bakhtiar was confirmed and that "he will have hospitality in the

United States."[8] The shah told his protocol chief he was going to the United States to explain to the president, Congress, and the American people that they were making a big mistake in Iran.[9]

In Aswan, President Sadat and his family, Vice President Hosni Mubarak, and other Egyptian dignitaries received the shah and the queen warmly. Sadat was devoted to the shah. It was a friendship rooted in the help he had received in a most critical moment in his presidency. The Yom Kippur war was a gamble in which Sadat had bet stakes he could not afford to lose, a matter of life and death to him and to Egypt, and the shah had come through by providing weapons and fuel and by allowing the Soviets to fly through the Iranian airspace to bring him the supplies he desperately needed. The shah too had taken a risk, knowing it displeased the United States, his indispensable friend, and Israel, whose supposedly clandestine strategic support for Iran was well-known. Indeed, the liaison with Sadat had opened a new political and diplomatic vista in the shah's strategic thinking. The Persian Gulf littoral states, including Iraq, now appeared to him as a possible resource, still surely in need of development, but also potentially crucial to a different strategic design. Israel would be something of a dilemma—it was likely to remain a counterbalance in Iran's relations with the Arab countries, but the shah's increasing power and improving relations with the Arabs, the United States, and Europe would diminish Israel's critical importance to U.S. interests in the Middle East. This calculus of changing relative power ultimately augured ill for the shah and Iran, but the shah, basking in the praise he had received in Iran and abroad, pushed on, only half-aware of the dangers looming ahead.

The shah's friendship with Sadat, however, was based on more than strategy. It was personal as well. After Nasser, Sadat was a breath of fresh air. He was strong and intelligent but not bombastic and unpredictable. He had a keen sense of politics and power. Israel and the United States were fast becoming one, and no Arab strategy could defeat the combination. A deal, therefore, had to be made, but it could not happen unless a showing of courage and power preserved honor and created credibility. The Yom Kippur war had established Sadat's claim to honor, and the sheer bravura of the act had left an indelible impression on the shah. Whether directly or indirectly, he never ceased to repeat to his Israeli, American, and European interlocutors that here was a man willing to make an honorable peace defying insurmountable odds, and that he should be honored and supported.

There was also the chemistry. The two men hit it off well mostly because of Sadat's charm and wit. Sadat had known the shah since 1938, as he was fond of repeating to the shah. Crown Prince Pahlavi of Iran had gone to Cairo in

1938 to marry Princess Fawzieh, the sister of King Faruq of Egypt. Sadat, then a second lieutenant, had marched in front of the crown prince as he reviewed the parade from a raised platform. Sadat repeated the story with relish, making everybody laugh, to the delight of the shah and the queen.

The shah, of course, had never heard of Sadat until he had become Nasser's deputy. Their first political encounter occurred in 1969 in Rabat, Morocco, at an Islamic summit convened to discuss the arson that had damaged the al-Aqsa Mosque in Jerusalem and the ways and means of protecting the Islamic holy places in the areas under Israeli rule.[10] Sadat, representing Nasser, responded to the shah's speech harshly, accusing him of being soft on Zionism and making the shah angrier than he had intended. To defuse the matter, Sadat then addressed the meeting in Persian, reading from a text in his heavy Arabic accent. The shah was touched; according to Jehan Sadat, he rose to his feet, applauding Sadat with a big smile.[11] This was the beginning of a fateful friendship for both the shah and Sadat.

The shah and queen were now received with full honors. The regalia of the reception energized the shah. Sadat asked him to remain in Egypt. "Egypt is closer to Iran," he said. "It is a Muslim country. There is much that can be done from here. Move your airplanes to Egypt where a real resistance may be put up against Khomeini."[12] Sadat was a warrior. The shah was not. He thought the idea was unrealistic. The planes belonged to Iran. He commanded them as the shah of Iran. He could not order them to war against the Iranians. He was worried about the effect of his stay on Sadat—and perhaps of Sadat's influence on him. He knew the power the clerics had on the masses, and he thought it inevitable that his stay in Egypt would lead to trouble for his friend. Still, in the first hours he perked up emotionally.

Soon, however, the news from both Iran and the West, especially the United States, took him back to his former mood. Upon his leaving Iran, large groups of "his" people had poured out into the streets, celebrated his departure, and brought down the remainder of the statues that commemorated his and his father's reigns. Khomeini had said that neither the Majlis deputies nor the members of the Regency Council had legal standing; they must resign. The next day, on 17 January, the BBC quoted Khomeini as declaring the shah's belongings nationalized and charging the future Islamic government to retrieve and return them to the Iranian people. The following day the Associated Press reported that President Carter had said that Vietnam had taught the United States not to interfere in the affairs of other states, but he hoped that Ayatollah Khomeini would support Bakhtiar's government, which was established following the laws of the country. And on the 18th, the *arba'in,* a large number of demonstrators in

Tehran and other cities marched with no police or army in sight and declared, among other points, the end of the monarchy. On the 20th, the president of the Regency Council, Seyyed Jalaleddin Tehrani, who had traveled to Paris to have an "audience" with Khomeini, declared, upon the latter's demand, that the council was illegal and that he had resigned from it. These events could not but diminish the shah's hopes.

The shah stopped listening to the news while he was in Aswan. Instead, he asked Afshar to inform him if he heard something he thought the shah should know. The queen tried to talk to some contacts in Iran to get the news first-hand. But calling from Aswan was next to impossible. The telephones did not work, and connections had to be made via other countries. As she kept trying, it became clear to her that Egypt was not the best strategic place from the stand-point of communications, which was the single most important factor if a real fight was to be launched.

In Aswan, for the first time as far as the queen can recall, she and her husband talked to each other about their children's schooling. In the past, everything was assumed, determined, routinely managed. Now, suddenly, these matters had assumed extraordinary significance. The crown prince, Reza Cyrus, and Farahnaz, the older daughter, had already advised their parents not to go to the United States because of the unfriendly political atmosphere there. Surely, the hostility they seemed to engender everywhere would affect the children also. How would they protect them? Where would they be safe? Where would they get the schooling they deserved without the psychological pressures that would certainly exacerbate the shocks they had already received? Leila was only nine, Alireza twelve. They had been put in a C-130 military transport to Lubbock Air Force Base, near San Antonio, Texas, where their older brother, the crown prince, was enrolled in a fighter pilot course. They did not understand why all this had happened. When the queen called them from Aswan, Leila cried on the telephone, asking when she would return home. The queen answered her daughter—"soon," she said, as she saw the king's eyes fill with tears.[13]

The shah now wanted to leave Egypt to lighten Sadat's burden. "The man is busy, and he spends much of his time to see that we are cared for," he told Afshar.[14] But where would he go? He spoke of the United States with Afshar, but his friends, Sadat and King Hassan II of Morocco, told him he should post-pone the American trip if he could. Hassan also extended an invitation to the shah and his family. This turn of events relieved the president of the United States. "This suits me fine," Carter jotted down in his diary when he heard the news from Brzezinski, who in turn had been informed by Ardeshir Zahedi. "The taint of the shah being in our country is not good for either us or him."[15]

On 22 January the shah and the queen flew from Aswan to Cairo, where once again they were received formally by President Sadat, and from Cairo on to Marrakesh. Throughout their stay in Aswan, the shah had remained aloof, rarely speaking about Iran. On the plane, the queen and Afshar began a conversation about Iran and the possible strategies they might adopt. The shah looked at them, a smirk on his face, but refused to participate. "Perhaps he thought this was all folly, useless," the queen said later. "We failed when we were in Iran, had a government and an army. How can we succeed now?" But he did not stop them when they asked his permission to write letters or to telephone world leaders to ask for help. He would only say, do what you please, or go ahead if you think it is useful.[16]

In Marrakesh, King Hassan brought his wife, Lalla Latifah, to receive the shah and queen at the airport, a gesture that considerably buoyed their spirits. The Moroccan queen never appeared in public or participated in ceremonies. Hassan and the Moroccan dignitaries never called her by name in public but referred to her as "la mère des princes," or mother of the princes. Her presence was to the king and queen of Iran a sign of special friendship, a closeness denied others. They were received warmly and led to a beautiful villa outside Marrakesh in an oasis looking at the Atlas Mountains. The setting seemed to the queen to bring her husband some needed respite. But this would not last.

On 26 January 1979, in Marrakesh, the shah had a photo-op session with the media, among them ABC, represented by Pierre Salinger, who had served as press secretary under President John F. Kennedy. Salinger had been a guest at the 1978 New Year dinner reception for President Carter in Tehran, the last time he had seen the shah. Seeing him among the reporters, the shah called him over. Salinger was shocked by the change he saw in the shah. "As I approached, I was struck by how drastically his appearance had changed in the year since our meeting in Iran. His face was thin and sallow, and his expression suggested the existence of fierce struggle within him, as though the regal person he believed himself to be could not accept the ordinary mortal he had become." In the course of their short conversation Salinger asked if the shah had made any definite plans. "I am not going to the United States. I'll stay here for a while," the shah answered.[17]

It was not to be, though the shah did not yet know. Khomeini was still outside of Iran, and Bakhtiar gave the impression of being in charge—although his ministers were being barred from entering their ministries. Sullivan had met with Bakhtiar the day after he had been installed and had been surprised by the force with which he had spoken of his mission and his plans to salvage Iran's future; on balance Sullivan had determined that the new prime minister was a "quixotic" character.[18] The military was intact, looking invincible from the outside, though it had been inwardly decimated by the shah's departure and Bakhtiar's attitude. The luxurious, palm-shaded palace in Marrakesh, where the royal couple spent the first three weeks of their stay in Morocco, was pleasant and the shah and the queen, still officially royal, were treated with the pomp and ceremony their dignity required. Friends came to visit them and the invitation from the United States was periodically reaffirmed. The situation in Iran, however, was progressively deteriorating, leading to further confusion, both there and in the United States.

On 22 January, the day the royals flew to Marrakesh, General Huyser reported to Defense Secretary Brown that Khomeini's return to Iran "represented the greatest potential for complete disaster" and that it would cause "Bakhtiar to go down the drain." The report was certainly prompted by Qarabaghi and other generals, who demanded of Huyser that he encourage his government to take measures to keep Khomeini out. On 29 January, Duncan, the deputy defense secretary, reported to the president that Huyser believed Khomeini's return was imminent and that it would end in Bakhtiar's fall. This, Huyser said, would be the time for a military coup, though Sullivan did not agree with the idea.[19]

The conflict between Huyser and Sullivan mirrored the conflict between Brzezinski and Vance. Huyser was singularly inattentive to the civil dimension of the trouble in Iran: that the armed forces did not see themselves as different from the people, and that the idea of killing their compatriots was totally distasteful to them. His reports about the ability of the Iranian army to stage a coup were premised on force calculations germane to wars against foreign enemies. He confused the military's discipline and, given the circumstances, remarkable cohesion with indifference to the nature of the enemy it might face.[20] The Iranian generals, on the other hand, were keenly conscious of the difference between a foreign foe and a domestic insurgency, as reflected in the structure of the armed forces they commanded and the logistical prognostications they had made for possible armed conflicts.

Sullivan, on the other hand, had transferred his sympathy to the opposition and consequently tended to underestimate the potential for mobilizing the pro-shah civilian forces around the military. Before Bakhtiar took the helm, no attempt had been made to confront the opposition in the streets with pro-regime demonstrators. The shah had not pushed it, at first because he thought it unnecessary and in later stages because, he argued, it conflicted with certain articles of martial law. The effect was to give the opposition considerable moral advantage. Huyser, probably correctly, spoke of a silent majority for the shah. The idea never entered Sullivan's discourse. It also was never seriously considered at the State Department.

This kind of thinking led Sullivan to Mehdi Bazargan, the leader of the liberal Islamic Iran Liberation Movement, which, under the revolutionary halo, had attracted a following superior to that of the National Front. Bazargan had committed himself and his movement to Khomeini and therefore worked at Khomeini's pleasure, though he misread both Khomeini and his purpose. However, he seemed sincere in thinking that Khomeini would allow a democratic regime that respected Islam as he believed the 1906 Constitution had originally intended. This sincerity impressed others, including Sullivan. According to Sullivan, Bazargan told him, as Khomeini's presumed representative looked on, that "they wanted the military to remain intact and to work with the new government. They had a list of designated military officers who would be required to leave the country but they would take their possessions with them and escape any retribution. They wanted a continuation of the military associations and other security arrangements with the United States."[21] On 23 January Huyser and Sullivan sent a joint request asking Washington to change their instructions to "permit the possibility of a coalition between the military and religious elements."[22] The proposal exacerbated the contradictions in Washington, with Vance agreeing and Brzezinski strongly disagreeing.

In the meantime, the Iranian generals were having a hard time of it. When the shah was still in Iran, Sullivan had arranged for Eric von Marbod—a Pentagon expert on military sales programs, a friend of both Sullivan and Huyser, a "bureaucratic genius" according to Sullivan, and an "extremely brilliant man" according to Huyser—to come to Iran to collect the money Iran owed the United States on the military purchases Iran had made in the United States. According to General Tufanian, von Marbod, who had arrived in Iran on 18 January, was making life difficult for the military. Tufanian interpreted von Marbod's presence as a sign of U.S. duplicity: "On one hand they speak of support and on the other hand Mr. Eric von Marbod is consistently pressuring me about payments for our contracts and demands unpaid installments, which is impossible to meet at this time. General Huyser, also, says that the Iranian government should officially ask for any assistance it needs, but this also does not appear very serious, since, for example, in the matter of the fuel for the forces, which we have asked for, for some time, he refers to a tanker they have brought to the Persian Gulf, and not only persistently asks for money, but also insists that we should unload it immediately. Given the strikes on the docks and the political condition in the oil company, this is practically impossible. If they really wanted to help us, they would supply us with fuel by air route, as they did for the air force. You see, gentlemen, American support of the Iranian army is nothing but a lot of hot air."[23]

Part of the generals' problem was that they had no contact with the shah. One reason for that, the shah explained in exile, was an agreement he had made with Bakhtiar.[24] More likely, he did not talk to the military because he saw no purpose to it. For the queen, on the other hand, talking to Iran was very important. She, like most of her entourage, craved news of Iran. She talked almost every day with General Neshat, then the acting commander of the Imperial Guard, until one day King Hassan sent a message asking her to stop, which she did. "He was the king. I could not do otherwise than do as he had asked. In Morocco, when the king said something, he expected it to be obeyed."[25] She continued listening to the radio and was excited to hear reports of the demonstration in favor of the regime on 25 January. Bakhtiar had flown over the city by helicopter and had been surprised at the number of people. It had occurred to him that he could do this again and probably even more people would participate as time went on, cutting into Khomeini's sense of invincibility. He needed time, he thought, which he could have only if Khomeini was persuaded to postpone his return. He had hoped President Carter might do the persuading, but Carter had done little more than asking "the Saudis, Egyptians, Moroccans, Jordanians, and several other Moslem countries to give their support to [Bakhtiar's] new government and encourage Khomeini to stay out of Iran."[26] This had not helped.

On 1 February 1979, Ayatollah Ruhollah Khomeini returned to Iran, apparently in a stoic mood. On the plane he was asked what he felt, returning to his country after fifteen years of exile. "Nothing," was his answer. His plane was escorted by the Iranian air force once inside Iranian space. Of the various options the generals had discussed, they had chosen the one that made the military responsible for protecting Khomeini. Bakhtiar reasoned that he was an Iranian and therefore had the right to go to Iran whenever he pleased. Later he would muse that perhaps he was wrong: he had been Cartesian in his reasoning, but the time had gone mad and incoherent and the most elementary rules of law were disdained.[27]

In Marrakesh, monitoring Khomeini's return on the radio, the shah observed that the prime minister was still in his office and the army remained loyal to the Constitution.[28] He had himself turned down an offer to stop Khomeini from returning to Iran. He had flown to Morocco on *Shahbaz,* a plane assigned by the government for royal use. King Hassan advised him to keep the plane, but the shah insisted that it be returned to Iran. Colonel Kiumarth Jahanbini, commander of the shah's personal guards, had thought that he and Atabai should return with the *Shahbaz* and see what they could do to mobilize the military to prevent Khomeini from taking power. "What we need to do requires small military contingents, which we can suggest to General Badrei," Jahanbini told Atabai. "We can choose from three alternatives which do not require a large force. We can take a contingent of the Immortals and blast away Khomeini's airplane as soon as it stops at the Mehrabad Airport. Or we can divert Khomeini's plane to a secure air base, such as Shahrokhi, and in effect keep him hostage against the people's peaceful acquiescence to status quo. Or we can blast Khomeini's plane out of the air before or as soon as it enters Iranian air space."

After several hours of debate, Jahanbini and Atabai decided to take their project to the shah. Jahanbini explained it to the shah as he was taking his daily stroll in the garden. The shah listened attentively until Jahanbini finished. "I am grateful for your willingness to put your lives at risk for my sake. I must tell you, however, that you two are crazy." And he turned from them, continuing with his walk. A little later Ardeshir Zahedi called Jahanbini and Atabai in and told them that His Majesty had instructed him to tell them that if they even thought of such nonsense he would ask King Hassan to put them in jail.[29]

Khomeini arrived in Tehran to a tumultuous welcome. He went to Tehran's main cemetery, Behesht-e Zahra, to pay homage to the "martyrs." There he said the Pahlavi regime was illegitimate. Reza Shah had gained kingship by force. But even if he had not, decisions then made could not bind the people living now. Now the people were saying they do not want the shah. The parliament, the Majlis and the Senate, was also illegitimate and illegal. So was the government installed by the illegitimate shah and confirmed by the illegal parliament. The shah, he said, destroyed the country and developed the cemeteries. He destroyed the economy. "We must work years to return it to the state it was at the beginning." The United States, he said, took Iran's oil and instead gave it arms it cannot use. He would slap Bakhtiar and his government on the mouth. He would try in revolutionary courts whoever did not obey him. *He* would install the government. And to the armed forces he would advise: Join the people; we will not hang you.[30] Two days later he told the press that he was about to appoint a new prime minister and a revolutionary council to prepare for a referendum to approve a new constitution.[31]

On 5 February Carter received General Huyser, whom he had brought home "to give [him] a personal report." Based on Huyser's report, the president determined that there had been major incongruities in the interpretation of his orders by Huyser and Sullivan and, by extension, by the Pentagon and the State Department. As he compared Huyser's statements and what Sullivan had done and said, he "became even more disturbed at the apparent reluctance at the state department to carry out [his] directives fully and with enthusiasm." He asked the Iran desk officers and a few others to come to the White House and, as he put it, "laid down the law to them as strongly as [he] knew how." He told them that if they did not agree with his policy, they should resign, and "if there was another outbreak of misinformation, distortions, or self-serving news leaks, [he] would direct the secretary of state to discharge the officials responsible for that particular desk, even if some innocent people might be punished."[32] By this time, however, nothing he did made a difference in Iran. MAAG Chief Major General Phillip Gast, substituting for Huyser, still reported that Bakhtiar had the military behind him and though "the fight could get extremely bloody, there was no reason why he should not come out on top."[33] At that time, the military on whose prowess the shah, Bakhtiar, Huyser, and Gast counted was bewailing the "melting snow" of its own future.

On that same day, 5 February, Khomeini appointed Bazargan interim prime minister and charged him to hold a referendum toward the formation of an Islamic republic, to oversee the election of a constituent assembly to write a new constitution, and to elect a new Majlis based on the new constitution. Then the interim government would yield to a permanent government.[34] Bazargan's government, said Khomeini, was based on Islam, and obeying it was a religious duty. He asked the people to demonstrate their support for it. This they did on the 8th, coming out in droves. In the meantime, the commanders of the armed forces and Bakhtiar met with Bazargan and several ayatollahs, especially Mahmud Taleqani, a more modern cleric favored by the Mojahedin and other Islamist leftists. They were promised amnesty along the lines Bazargan had indicated to Sullivan and Huyser. Bakhtiar, speaking firmly, nonetheless began to intimate the possibilities for a republic based on free elections. The country, however, could afford only one government, he said, and at the time his was the only legally instituted one. The wobble was apparent, and the military brass, having become wobbly itself, fed it. On the evening of the 10th a riot broke out in the barracks of the air force technical cadets, most of whom had by now become pro-revolution. Inexplicably, a crack contingent of the Imperial Guard was defeated by the cadets and groups of armed revolutionaries that came to their assistance. A curfew the government declared almost completely failed. In the morning Qarabaghi called the Commanders' Council to order for what would be their final meeting to discuss the armed forces' policy, apparently unbeknownst to the prime minister, who had ordered the air force to bomb the rebel cadets the night before—an order that was never carried out. Having heard nothing, Bakhtiar had called Qarabaghi the next morning but was told that the general was in an important meeting. Bakhtiar knew nothing of these council meetings, which subsequently he would call baseless in law. At the time, the news only seemed to him to signal ill portent.[35]

In the council, one by one the generals declared that the units under their commands could no longer carry out the mission assigned to them. Summarizing the debate, Qarabaghi's deputy, Lieutenant General Hushang Hatam, concluded that based on the commanders' reports, the armed forces had lost the ability to act and that since according to the prime minister the sovereign would not return, since the people had demonstrated their support of Khomeini, and since Bakhtiar also intended to establish a republic, the reasonable thing for the armed forces to do was to remain neutral and in the manner of the Turkish army support the people while keeping out of partisan politics. After some further debate, the generals decided unanimously to declare the armed forces neutral on the proposition that the monarchy was lost, and that the struggle now raging was about the character of the future republic.[36] This was a logical conclusion to what SAVAK chief General Nasser Moqaddam had said in the last meeting of the commanders: "This army must remain true to its oath—unless we found a political solution that relieved us of our oath, saying, in effect, we are no longer bound by the oath to which we were bound in the past."[37]

Bakhtiar's fall and the army's declaration of neutrality essentially transformed the shah from a monarch to a former king, though no one made a point of it. He, however, was punctilious about the change in his status. Khomeini and his regime were no doubt illegitimate usurpers. He was the king. But not being in control of the government, he would not retain what he thought belonged to the government. It was at this point that he ordered his chief pilot, Colonel Behzad Moezzi, to fly the royal plane back to Iran. "It belonged to the Iranian Air Force," he said. According to Amir Aslan Afshar, he asked all his entourage to chip in with their rials, which he would reimburse in dollars once his money manager, Mohammad Ja'far Behbahanian, provided it, for him to reward the pilots and the crew as they returned to Iran. In order to save the men from being punished for serving the shah, he ordered Moezzi to say that they had been with the shah under duress and that they had taken the plane in the middle of the night against the shah's will. According to Farhad Sepahbodi, Iran's ambassador to Morocco, the shah paid for fuel with a personal check in the amount of $14,777, drawn to the order of Shell of Morocco because Moezzi's fuel card had expired.[38]

In Morocco, kings and queens from around the world still showed concern for the now deposed shah. Hussein of Jordan, Juliana of Holland, the king and queen of Belgium, and the king and queen of Thailand called, and former kings and queens—Umberto and Emmanuel of Italy, the comte de Paris, Constantine and Queen Anne-Marie of Greece—came to visit. The shah's friends not now in office also tried to help—especially Nelson Rockefeller, although he died before he was able to make an intended visit, Henry Kissinger, David Rockefeller (mostly on his brother Nelson's account), John J. McCloy, and members of the Rockefeller political organization, which became a great support during the shah's odyssey in exile. However, it was clear to the shah that the presidents and prime ministers who in the past had sought him were now keeping their distance. The comte de Marenche, formerly chief of the French secret service, the shah's old acquaintance, and the French president's special envoy, met with him in Marrakesh to inform him that Ayatollah Khomeini had instructed his people to kidnap the Moroccan king's family as a bargaining chip to exchange for him. Hassan II apparently had bravely refused to bow to the threat.[39] But the shah was made to feel embarrassed.

Just before the Iranian New Year, the first day of spring, the shah and queen moved from Marrakesh to the Moroccan capital, Rabat. Rabat was hard on the shah. King Hassan had his ways, which were different from his. The shah was punctual, precise, and committed to his word. Hassan was the opposite. Time did not bind him. He decided in the moment and assumed that everyone else would accommodate his whim. In the past, his behavior had occasionally irked the shah, who let it pass as royal idiosyncrasy. He criticized the malek (king) to his associates as more interested in women than in running his country. Now, however, the situation had drastically changed. The irony did not escape him, or, probably, the malek. Here was the king of kings, once many times his superior in power, riches, and aspiration, now without crown and country, helplessly staying in his palace by his grace. Hassan kept to his custom: made an appointment to visit the shah but failed to keep it; invited the shah to his residence, but kept him waiting; told him he would call, but did not. Oblivious to the shah's feelings, now he lectured that a king in a Muslim country should respect the ulama and follow tradition. The insults were mostly unintended, but they hurt. The shah also began to feel that his stay in Rabat might create problems for King Hassan. He now heard again from de Marenche, the French security chief, who told him that certain religious groups in Morocco were pressuring the king to ask him to leave. Hassan II was the head of the Islamic Conference about to be convened in Morocco. Several radical Arab leaders, among them Yasser Arafat and Mu'ammar Gadhafi, were to attend. It would have been awkward for the shah to be there. Hassan could not bring himself to tell the shah in person that his presence in Morocco was problematic. He asked the former Greek king Constantine, the shah's friend and protégé, who was on a visit in Rabat, to tell the shah of his predicament. The shah received the message with equanimity. "Things are not the same when one is no longer on the saddle," said the queen.[40]

The killing of the shah's military and civilian officers began when he was in Morocco. On the day the regime fell several of the officers already taken into custody by the shah's last three prime ministers were able to escape when the prison gates were opened. Others were not as lucky and were captured by the revolutionaries. Some presented themselves to the new regime of their own accord, among them Amir Abbas Hoveyda and Shoja'eddin Sheikholeslamzadeh, a former minister of health. Several of the shah's military commanders were killed on the spot—General Badrei in his office and General Boqrat Jafarian, the governor of Khuzistan, shot down in his helicopter. General Rahimi, the police chief and military governor of Tehran, was arrested in his office, and General Nasiri, the former SAVAK chief who, ordered by the shah, had returned from Pakistan, where he was ambassador, and was jailed, was arrested in his prison cell. Rahimi declared he had taken an oath and thus he remained loyal to the shah. Nassiri declared he would not have returned if he thought he had committed any crime.

That same day, 12 February, several ministers and generals were interrogated on television, among them Hoveyda, Manuchehr Azmun, Sheikholeslamzadeh, the minister of agriculture Mansur Rowhani, the former Tehran mayor Gholam Reza Nikpay, and Generals Rabii, Rahimi, Naji, and Ayat Mohaqqeqi. Hoveyda was told the shah had imprisoned him to save himself. Now that the revolution had triumphed, whom did he consider guilty? "The system," he answered. "I was arrested according to Article 5 of the martial law. I have come here of my own accord. There was no soldier or guard to stop me. It was my decision to come. I could have gone out of the country six months ago. But I did not. I stayed to respond to any accusation that might be brought against me."[41]

Hoveyda was telling the truth about refusing to leave Iran. When he resigned from the Ministry of Court, the shah sent his chief of protocol, Amir Aslan

Afshar, to ask him to accept a position outside Iran. "When I went to Hoveyda, he was sitting behind his desk in his library in his robe de chamber. His mother and wife were sitting on the floor. His friend Ali Ghaffari was in another chair. I told him what His Majesty had sent me to tell him. 'You have worked hard for thirteen and a half years. You are tired. Take a vacation or a position out of the country for a while.' He would not, Hoveyda replied. 'Thank His Majesty for his kindness. But if I leave, they will say Hoveyda ran. I see no reason for it.' I reported back to His Majesty in the morning. 'Did you tell him I am asking him to leave?' 'Yes Sire,' I answered. 'Does this man not know what might await him?' Next day His Majesty sent his chief of special bureau [Nosratollah] Moinian, thinking that perhaps I was not as clear as I should have been. Moinian did not succeed either. Of course, Hoveyda did not think a revolution was in the offing."[42]

On television, after Hoveyda spoke, Rowhani defended his work promoting Iran's agriculture, Rahimi reiterated his loyalty to the shah, and Rabii explained the military's declaration of neutrality as a catch-22: "Bakhtiar said he would declare a republic through the present constitution; Bazargan said he would declare a republic through a referendum. Since both pursued the same objective, to avoid bloodshed we declared our neutrality. Both Rahimi and Rabii denied the shah had ever ordered them to kill."[43] On 13 February Ali Asghar Haj Seyyed Javadi, a liberal writer and human rights advocate, wrote in *Kayhan*: "Military neutrality is meaningless. . . . Any pretension to surrendering by these people should be crushed with revolutionary cruelty *[birahmi-e enqelabi]*." Demands for the abrogation of the military and revolutionary trials of military officers were independently made by the Sazeman-e Mojahedin Khalq and Sazeman-e Fadaiyan-e Khalq, Islamic-Marxist and Marxist groups, respectively.

Two days later the killings began. Generals Nassiri, Rahimi, Naji, and Khosrodad were the first victims of Islamist justice. They were convicted as *mufsed fi'l arz* (corrupter on earth) and *mohareb ba khoda* (warring against God), the first time such reasons were adduced in modern Iranian jurisprudence. The killings had been approved by Khomeini, who later said that all that was needed was to ascertain the identity of the accused. Shortly after, on 20 February, four more generals were executed on the same grounds. And by the 22nd, the number of high-ranking officers dismissed or forced to retire from service reached 215. Clearly, the new regime sought a complete re-manning if not yet reconstruction of the shah's armed forces.

The shah heard the news and according to the people with him slumped into profound dejection. Prince Victor Emanuel, whom the shah liked and who had come forward to help like many other former kings and queens, came with a

French lawyer to help organize a media war to condemn the killings. The queen liked the idea but the shah remained noncommittal. He did not object to the effort, though he knew that given King Hassan's problems, no such project could be initiated from Morocco.[44] On 12 March several more officers, including a family friend, Lieutenant General Nader Jahanbani, were executed. Jahanbani was an ace pilot and for some time the leader of the air force Acrojet Team. When asked to offer his final defense, he answered he had no defense; he was ready to die. The people in jail with him later said he had put on his flight uniform, donning the special blue scarf. The queen called his wife and not knowing how to console her, wept with her.[45]

Just before the royal couple moved to Rabat—a few days before the Iranian New Year at the spring equinox, around 21 March—the children came from the United States to visit. This was a great boon to the shah. He especially loved his older daughter, Farahnaz, and enjoyed playing with Leila, the youngest. Also the shah's twin sister, Princess Ashraf, arrived, seeing her brother for the first time in six months. She learned now for the first time that the shah was ill with some type of cancer, though she was told no more than that. The information put her in a frenzy to find some way to save her brother's life. She felt that had she known he was ill, she would never have left him, despite his orders for her to leave Iran. In September 1978, she had made a trip to the Soviet Union on Brezhnev's invitation. Her return to Tehran had coincided with the grand marches of the *id al-fitr*. She had gone immediately to her brother, who told her there was nothing to worry about and asked her to leave the country. "Why?" she had asked. "I would feel better," he had answered. And she had left.[46] However, in the meantime, many people, including military officers, had gone to her and begged her to intervene with her brother to do something. The Imperial Guard deputy commander General Neshat and the air force's Lieutenant General Jahanbani had suggested that serious military action should be taken. "If His Majesty was sent to Kish Island and they had instruction, they could stop all this in two or three days. You order us; we will finish the job."[47] She sensed the danger and the need for action, but she knew nothing about what the shah thought or what he intended to do. "My brother was royal in his demeanor, on top of the situation, in command. I had no reason to doubt his ability to deal with the situation."[48] But now she set out to do what she could.

Ardeshir Zahedi also arrived in Rabat to consult with the shah about what policies the royal camp should adopt, particularly about where the royals should stay. Since his departure from Iran, the shah had picked up on the increasing reluctance of the Americans to have him in the States. In Morocco, some of his American friends and some members of the administration began to send him messages that sounded "strange and disturbing." "The messages although not unfriendly were very cautious: perhaps this is not a good time for you to come; perhaps you could come later; perhaps we should wait and see. About a month after my departure, the tone of the messages became warmer and they suggested that I could, of course, come to the United States if I were so inclined. But I was no longer so inclined. How could I go to a place that had undone me? Increasingly, I began to believe that the United States had played a major role in doing just that."[49] But where would he go? Switzerland, where he owned property, could not provide appropriate security. The British Labor government would not take him for political reasons, though Margaret Thatcher, the Conservative leader, had promised she would if she won the upcoming elections. France was now out of the question, but Monaco was still a possibility. Prince Rainier had left the door open, suggesting that they would be welcome. He was a friend, and Monaco was not a "political" state. Zahedi and Crown Prince Reza left for Monaco to speak with Rainier to arrange the conditions of their stay. Rainier, however, was forced to renege under pressure from the French government. This was probably the friendliest rejection the shah would receive; but it was also the first, signaling an ominous beginning to a tragic trek.

By mid-March, King Hassan had become quite nervous about the shah's stay. He sent word to President Carter, asking him to allow the shah to come to the United States. Carter now made it clear that he would not, fearing the mob in Iran. He asked Vance to find an alternative place for the monarch.[50] On 17 March the U.S. ambassador in Morocco, Richard Parker, informed the shah of the president's decision. According to Vance, the shah "reacted calmly and merely requested our help in finding another place of exile."[51] None was assured at the time. There was talk of Paraguay, which the shah would not entertain, and of South Africa, which had had friendly relations with the shah, but since it was an apartheid nation, he did not wish to go there. It was only at the last moment that the royals learned that they were going to the Bahamas for three months before a more permanent place could be found. Vance claimed that the U.S. government was instrumental in getting the Bahamian government to accept the royal couple. Given the events as the shah arrived in his new place of residence, more likely it was mainly the work of David Rockefeller and Henry Kissinger, as the queen suggests,[52] propped by the efforts of Princess Ashraf and Ardeshir Zahedi. Zahedi and Princess Ashraf had been talking to Rockefeller and Kissinger, seeking their help to find a reasonable residence for the shah.

Rockefeller assigned as liaison between the shah and the United States government Robert Armao, an energetic young man who had been Nelson Rockefeller's
labor adviser and who, having trained in the Rockefeller milieu, was well versed
in politics, negotiations, and uses of power. Through American mediation the
government of the Bahamas agreed to admit the royal family for a period of
three months, and Armao and his associate Mark Morse went to the Bahamas
to find an appropriate house. When the plane placed at the shah's disposal for
the trip by Hassan II landed at the Nassau airport, the first person he saw was
Robert Armao.

24

The Ayatollah's Shadow

The shah and the queen arrived in the Bahamas on 30 March 1979. They were accompanied by their children; the queen's mother; Dr. Liusa Pirnia; Colonel Kiumarth Jahanbini, in charge of security; Colonels Yazdan Nevissi, Siavush Nasseri, Hossein Hamraz, and Reza Mohammadi; Kambiz Atabai; Leila's governess, Ms. Golrokh; and the shah's valet, Mahmud Eliasi.[1] The group was taken by Armao and his associate Mark Morse to a place somewhat incongruously called Paradise Island, across from Nassau. "It was beautiful. Indeed, for most people the island was a paradise. For us, it was hell," recalled Atabai.[2]

The royals' residence was a small villa on a small lot with a small kidney-shaped pool in the middle, around which on the lot and on the veranda were piled, one on top of another, suitcases belonging to at least ten people—the shah, the queen, their children, and their personal guards. Other suitcases contained "small rugs, small boxes made of silver, trinkets that [the royal couple] usually gave as gifts to heads of states or friends [they] met."[3] The sight of the house irked the shah and the queen. The first two days, the queen, desperate, stayed in her room, rarely venturing outside. The shah maintained a trance-like decorum and never complained. He was bemused by the occasional small demonstrations against him even in the Bahamas. His American assistants counseled him to stay on the island, which made him feel imprisoned, helpless, and suspicious.

The Bahamian government and people saw him as a fat cat, a man with billions of dollars snatched out of the mouth of poor women and orphaned children, deserving no pity. The new government of Iran issued claims of his pecuniary perfidy as it pleased. In February, not yet two weeks in power, the interim government assessed the shah's money in Swiss banks at two billion Swiss francs and demanded its return from the Swiss authorities. The Swiss Central Bank replied that the total value of all Iranians' accounts in Switzerland was no more than several hundred millions. Earlier in March, when it was still unclear where the shah would go, the *New York Post* wrote, "the advantage to the shah of operating out of the US is access to much of his money, relative freedom of communications and the presence of the CIA. The shah's strength lies in his ability to maintain Iran's vast Mid-East intelligence network, paying the spies out of his own pocket." The paper repeated the estimates of the shah's money by Iranian authorities uncritically: "The shah shipped $24 to $30 billions out of the country in the last days of his reign. All told, he is believed to have $40 billion in gold and other assets secured around the globe, making him easily the richest man in the world—and potentially one of the biggest troublemakers."[4]

The shah had decided it did not help to tell the world how much money he did or did not have. In the past, he had never talked about money with his wife. Nor had Farah asked questions. Iran was for the most part so prosperous that she never thought she needed to have any reserves outside Iran. And she didn't think that the shah was particularly concerned with what he had outside. In the early years of their marriage, she sometimes thought of the possibility of change, revolution. On her first visit to the Soviet Union she had dreamed that the people had invaded the Sa'dabad Palace and she had rather content-edly agreed to become a laborer. But this was in the beginning. In later years, everything seemed to go so well that such thoughts never entered her mind, including the need to stash money for a rainy day. She advised her mother not to buy an apartment in Paris, though later she thanked God that her advice was not heeded. The shah, of course, was more experienced and practical; 1953 had left a strong residue of caution. But the 1960s and early 1970s had diluted his worries. He was a successful king, the second of his dynasty, and accord-ing to everyone around him fully intent on passing the throne to his son. For the most part, having money in some European bank was far from his mind, although others took care that his wealth grew. He helped deposed kings who came to him for aid and this gave him cause to think. The predicament of the ousted Mohammad Zaher Shah of Afghanistan was a wakeup call. He no longer thought of the possibility of a revolution from within; but some machi-nation from outside ending in foreign invasion or proxy occupation was always a distant possibility. It was always prudent to provide for all contingencies, no matter how distant or unlikely.

The shah's money was managed by a deputy court minister named Mohammad Ja'far Behbahanian. According to the queen, Behbahanian met with the shah in Morocco and told him what he had and where. As far as the queen was con-cerned, he had dealt honestly and fairly with the royal couple. "Behbahanian was an honest person. He accounted for everything His Majesty had. His Majesty, of course, did not know exactly what he possessed; I even less. But the man came and told us what was where."[5] Others say they heard the shah complain about his money manager,[6] but he is not known to have said anything negative about him in public. Behbahanian, for his part, had always been discreet about the shah's wealth. Several years after her husband's death, the queen said that she had thought much about revealing the shah's wealth in exile but was never sure if that was the correct course for her to take.

> It is amazing to me that almost everything else, matters of horrendous importance for the country, is subjugated to this question. It seems to me that for almost everybody money has become the most important of all issues at all levels — national, international, and personal. This saddens me. I mean, it is now established that the figures [of the shah's wealth] cited are invented. One of the people accusing us was asked how he had come by the figure he cited. He answered he had no idea: "Everyone quoted a number coming to his head; we chose the figure 26 billion." The truth is that despite the absurdity of it all, this has harmed us tremendously. It has harmed us politically and financially. Because everybody believes we have so much money, everybody expects us not only to do everything we do for saving the country on our own, but to help everybody else as well. Everywhere there are innuendos that what the shah had was gotten illegally. They compare Iran with other countries in the region, which is absurd. I resent it.

One problem, said the queen, was that

> for most people across the world even one million dollars is a lot of money. A bigger problem is that a good many number of people would not believe the truth whatever it may be — not only our enemies but also our friends. There is no escape route. We have tried to live in a particular way in order to maintain the honor of the position we hold. This has not been easy. They have brought lawsuits against us in Switzerland and England, which they lost, and in the United States, where we had not a penny. They lost all of them. But they have taken energy, caused anxiety, and cost us money.[7]

The shah had also once thought of suing the Iranians and others who accused him of plundering his country, citing his wealth in astronomical figures, but had concluded it was useless. He couldn't sue everybody, and those he did would likely draw endless financial support from the Islamic Republic. He could never sustain the fight. The experience of the past several years had also taught him that what he said would not make much difference to those who chose not to believe. In his interview with David Frost broadcast on the ABC program *20/20*, on 17 January 1980, he refused to tell how much he had, but offered to exchange all he had for a sum Frost suggested.

The shah had known he was ill since late 1973, but apart from his French doctors George Flandrin and Jean Bernard, he had kept this information from everyone except court minister Alam. Subsequently, Alam's specialist Paul Milliez, the shah's friend and household doctor General Karim Ayadi, and Alam's relative and the shah's doctor Abbas Safavian had been informed; and, finally, in 1977, the queen was also told. In late 1973 on the resort island of Kish in the Persian Gulf, the shah had noticed an enlargement of his spleen. According to his doctors he had himself diagnosed it as some sort of blood disorder. He asked Alam, who was being treated for a blood disorder, to request his French doctors to come to Tehran to examine him, but he wished it to be kept secret. Through Safavian, Alam contacted Flandrin and Bernard, who went discreetly to Tehran and visited the shah at the Niavaran Palace on 1 May 1974. They decided the shah suffered from "a chronic lymphocytic blood disease," or, according to Flandrin, "a slightly unusual form of chronic lymphocitic Leukemia with enlarged spleen." When Ayadi was told of this, of which apparently he only absorbed the term "leukemia," he told the doctors they should tell nothing of it to the shah. Back in Paris, when the doctors had all the results of the tests they had made, they settled on Waldenström's disease, a low-grade chronic lymphoma, which did not appear to be advanced. They decided this diagnosis accommodated Ayadi's worries. On a second visit to the shah on 18 September 1974, the doctors prescribed Chlorambucil and a monthly hemogram check. To preserve secrecy, Flandrin undertook to travel to Tehran to perform the tests and brought the Chlorambucil pills camouflaged in Quinercil containers. The treatment proved successful; the spleen returned to normal size and blood cells to normal. However, in his February 1976 visit Flandrin was shocked to see abnormal blood cells and an enlargement of the spleen, for which he had no explanation. Soon, however, it was discovered that the shah's valet, fearing the shah might run out and reading the medication label, had bought Quinercil, which the shah had used for almost two months. The proper treatment was begun again, and by September "a complete hematological normalization was achieved." The unexpected benefit of this mishap was that the shah became convinced of the efficacy of the treatment.[8]

After this episode, the French doctors decided that it was in the interest of their patient to inform the queen, though, apparently, the idea was not well received by some of their Iranian interlocutors. The doctors had tried to broach the idea to the shah in some of their previous meetings, but each time the shah had changed the subject. They had acquiesced because their patient was the shah and also because any patient was entitled to secrecy if he so pleased. However, they reasoned that the shah being who he was and "fearing a foreseeable deterioration of the disease," the queen did need to be informed. They enlisted Safavian's help and met with her in Paris in the spring of 1977. The information had bewildered the queen. As far as she was concerned, her husband had been in perfect health. Yet now she was told that he had a blood disease that was chronic and manageable but serious. Furthermore, he had been treated since 1974, but the shah had chosen to keep it a secret. She would later say that he did not tell her because he did not wish to worry her; but she knew better and she was hurt. The problem now was how to tell him that she knew. They had talked about each other's illnesses in the past but only casually. The shah had often discussed his spleen with her and sometimes asked her to examine it to see if it had grown larger. He had explained it in terms of platelets and red corpuscles and the like. She now tried to convince him that she needed to be present when the doctors came next to examine him. The shah finally agreed, and after that he was freer with her when discussing his condition. But the term *cancer* had never come up, and the queen did not know if her husband actually knew how seriously ill he was. Flandrin and Bernard tried to explain the situation to the shah, but they also never knew for certain what the shah knew or understood about his disease. To Flandrin's mind, the shah made a statement that "completely ruled out the assumption that he had not understood what we wanted to tell him: 'I am only asking you to help me maintain my health for two years, enough time for the Crown Prince to finish the year in the U.S. and spend another in Tehran.' (Why a year in Tehran? He told us, but I have forgotten.)" Alam had told Flandrin that the sovereign was in some ways naïve but also an expert in hiding his true knowledge or feeling. "That is why," Flandrin observed to Bernard, "I have always thought that we could not rely on our own impressions to know if the king had really understood what we were telling him about his health."

When a few months later the shah's illness became public knowledge, many observers would attribute his seeming lethargy and indecisiveness in the last months of his reign to his illness and the medicine he took for it. Some would say, had they known about it, they would have taken over and stopped the revolution. Some would say, had the people known he suffered from a terminal disease, they would not have risen against him. Some would say that those who knew of the disease but did not disclose it committed treason against the state and the dynasty. It is a moot point what would have happened if the shah had disclosed his illness. The chances are that nothing significantly different would have occurred from within the regime but the opposition would have become far more empowered by learning that the shah was incapacitated.

But the shah was not incapacitated, at least not as a result of his illness. Most people who knew him intimately saw nothing debilitated in his mental or physical agility. Her twin sister, Ashraf, believed he was in complete control. His government and those he consulted with never suspected he was ill. His generals saw some indecisiveness at the end but attributed it mostly to the pressures of the time. The two ambassadors—the American William Sullivan and the British Anthony Parsons—who met him several times a week saw in him mood alterations but nothing that would suggest illness. His friends who were with him almost daily during his times of repose never thought he was ill. "He was active; he did his exercises, and his demeanor was not changed," said Dr. Yahya Adl, his old friend from the time he was crown prince. "Surely, he sometimes seemed tired and more irritable, but who would not be under the circumstances." Adl was a witness night after night to the shah's orders to his generals not to be violent enforcing martial law. He was not surprised; neither did he attribute it to the shah's being ill or in any way not being himself. "He was always like this, since I have known him. He shunned violence, hoping some other way would be found to calm the situation."9

In the Bahamas, the shah's illness flared up, requiring chemotherapy, which was for the first time administered intravenously under the supervision of his French physician Flandrin. The treatment left him physically weak and mentally depressed. He spent most of his time listening to the radio with the children and the few friends who occasionally came to visit. His condition deteriorated. His depression, begun in Iran, progressively worsened. He took little interest in what went on around him. He hardly talked, drowned as he was in his own thoughts, trying to reason out why things had gone so unexpectedly wrong. His doctors had ordered him to exercise for physical and psychological reasons. The queen encouraged him to keep fit as she tried to keep fit herself. "This was the only way for us to remain alive—swimming untold lengths of the small pool, walking about, running. I needed to remain alive for my husband and children and for the fight that needed to be fought against our enemy that was also the enemy of our people. It was a vexingly difficult period."10 The shah listened to the doctor's advice and responded quietly to his wife's prodding.

On the day the shah left Morocco, a referendum was held in which Iranians were asked only one question: Should the government be changed to an Islamic republic? On 1 April it was announced that 98 percent of eligible voters had participated and 97 percent had voted yes. Therefore, Iran was officially an Islamic republic.[11] That evening, Khomeini declared Iran's now was the government of the disinherited, the Government of God, and that these "executioners" of the Pahlavi regime were not "accused"; they were "criminals." There followed a new rush of killings. First, on 7 April, Amir Abbas Hoveyda was executed—murdered, the shah would call it. Two days later his air force commander, General Rabii, and chief of planning, General Khajenuri, were killed. A day later the regime executed his SAVAK chief, General Moqaddam; his former chief of SAVAK, ambassador, and friend, General Pakravan; his commander of the immortals, General Neshat; his mild-mannered minister of foreign affairs, Abbasali Khalatbari; his Majlis president, Abdollah Riazi; and his minister of agriculture, Mansur Rowhani, among many others. They were all executed on the charge of corrupting the earth because they had worked with the shah. All of these weighed heavily on him, but none as heavy as the news of Hoveyda's execution.

Amir Abbas Hoveyda was tried by Sadeq Khalkhali, the man Khomeini appointed as religious judge, to try the Pahlavi regime's leaders. According to Khalkhali, it was not worth wasting time on any of the accused and therefore he was intent on conducting speedy trials. He could not see why Hoveyda needed time to prepare a defense since he had no defense except talking about the system. Hoveyda did not have a defense attorney, said Khalkhali, because no one would agree to defend someone who was already known to be a criminal. And anyway, Hoveyda had an attorney, because Khalkhali, as the religious judge, acted also as the attorney for the defense. Furthermore, there were some people who wished to buy time to save Hoveyda; it was therefore imperative to punish him before they could snatch him away from Islamic justice. And Khomeini, Kahlkhali said, might not have interfered in the minutiae of the trials, but he clearly believed the high officers of the shah were ipso facto guilty.[12]

Hoveyda's trial had moved many of his friends and acquaintances to intercede on his behalf. In France, six heads of government—Jacques Chaban Delmas, Jacques Chirac, Maurice Couve de Murville, Michel Debré, Edgar Faure, and Pierre Messmer, who all had been close to General De Gaulle—sent a telegram to Bazargan demanding respect for accepted law and international human rights. Faure proposed to go to Iran to defend Hoveyda before the court but was not allowed in by the regime. Many who praised Hoveyda also blamed the shah for leaving him in Iran. Jean d'Ormesson of the French Academy, for example, opened his eulogy of Hoveyda in *Le Figaro* with the phrase "abandoned by the shah."[13] These accusations devastated the monarch. He wished to say something, but the governments in Morocco and now in the Bahamas had forbidden him to engage in politics. The queen suggested they rent a boat, gain international waters, and send a message from there. But no ship was available.[14] Helpless, he shunned others and fell silent, confiding only in his wife and Ardeshir Zahedi when he came to visit him.[15] His expressionless gloom, however, could not be concealed. Could he have done something to save these brave and honest men? He felt guilty, though he never said a word. Shahriyar Shafiq, his nephew and a Navy commander, visited him to give him courage and to talk about the plans he had for fighting back, begging him not to give up. His presence buoyed his uncle's spirits, but only as long as he was there. Soon the shah was down again, succumbing to apathy.

Hoveyda's execution was hard on everyone. For the royals it was especially difficult, not only because they liked him very much, but also because many Iranians, some among their close friends and supporters, held them somehow responsible for his death. Others who bore no particular love for the fallen prime minister used him to attack the shah. The shah was accused of bringing out even his dogs while leaving Hoveyda in Iran to be butchered by the barbarians. One genuinely angry person was Hoveyda's brother, the former Iranian ambassador to the United Nations, Fereydoun Hoveyda. The queen took it on herself to offer the royals' condolences and to try to console him.

> Calling Mr. Hoveyda was one of the most difficult tasks I have ever undertaken. He was understandably angry and disappointed, thinking that His Majesty had not done everything possible to rescue his brother. I expressed to him our heartfelt condolences and how the news had devastated the shah. I explained to him that we did our best to make it possible for him to leave Iran. That His Majesty offered him, indeed asked him to accept, an ambassadorial position outside to get him away from Iran. It was his will, however, as a man proud of his service to his country to stay and defend his record. We had to respect his will. We could not have known that such a horrific event would or could occur. My words of sympathy and condolence seemed to mollify Mr. Hoveyda at the time. Later, understandably, he turned bitter.[16]

Fereydoun Hoveyda remained bitter for some time after this conversation. In his book *The Fall of the Shah,* when still reeling from Amir Abbas's death, he would write:

> The Shah and his family swam in the warm waters of the luxury seaside resort, and tanned themselves in the sun. A few days earlier they had let themselves be photographed with smiles on their lips by the international press. When the ex-sovereign learned of my brother's murder he said nothing. He went on minding his health and devoting himself to his favorite sports of tennis, water skiing, jog-

ging, golf, and so on. For weeks he remained silent. Then with the European press attacking him for not having lifted a finger to save Amir Abbas, he issued a statement on April 27 in an attempt to clear himself of the accusation.[17]

Paradise Island, where the shah's villa was situated, indeed summoned to mind an image of carefree mirth and so set the background for negative press and supplied ammunition to his enemies. When the shah was in the Bahamas, several articles were written about him in exile in the European press. One particularly searing article appeared in *Paris Match* with two pictures side by side — one of the shah swimming in the sun and the other of Amir Abbas Hoveyda lying slain on a gruesome, filthy sheet of linen. The pictures, meant to be self-explanatory, nevertheless misread the reality; Paradise Island was no paradise for the royals. Fereydoun Hoveyda, however, could not know that. He was close to his brother and naturally grieved his loss. But for him the bitterness was rooted in more than a man's hurting for a brother lost. He was a liberal leftist writer and film critic who happened also to be the prime minister's brother, Princess Ashraf's friend and protégé, and Iran's ambassador to the United Nations. He had served a country that was changing rapidly for the better economically and socially by accepted international standards and a political system that was not a democracy in the Western sense or a "progressive" state in the socialist sense. His dilemma, shared by many other high officials of the regime, was reconciling the contradiction between his intellectual leanings and his serving a government that went against his intellectual principles. He was, however, more eloquent than most and he wrote well.

The issue of the shah's residence became a matter of controversy within the Carter administration as well as between the administration and certain political and economic groups interested in the fate of the shah. Among the latter, the Rockefeller-Kissinger-McCloy group proved most persistent. Carter was particularly annoyed with the trio because their criticism was not confined to the United States' moral obligation to the shah; rather, it concerned the whole range of the administration's policy toward Iran, before and after the revolution. Their position implied that administration policy was faulty from the start and was partly, if not wholly, responsible for the debacle in Iran. Now that the revolution had occurred, it was incumbent on the United States not to yield mildly to the revolutionaries' demands, particularly the claims they made on the shah and the United States, citing U.S.-Iranian relations during the past thirty-seven years.

The group would hammer on this theme throughout the remaining history of the shah.

Early in April, Brzezinski received a call from Kissinger, who complained bitterly about the apparent U.S. reluctance to allow the shah to travel to the United States. Brzezinski related the message to Carter, whom Kissinger had also called the day before.[18] Carter, obviously irritated, asked what Brzezinski would do if he were the president. "This was not only a pragmatic question, which called for a careful assessment of the impact of our decision on Hassan or Sadat, but above all a question of principle," Brzezinski answered. America should stand by its friends.[19] Carter was not pleased with the answer and became more displeased later that day when David Rockefeller arrived at the White House to make the same points, asking him to let the shah in. "Rockefeller, Kissinger, and Brzezinski seem to be adopting this as a joint project," he wrote in his diary on 9 April 1979.[20]

Soon the pro-shah group realized that its major adversary was Secretary of State Vance, who, according to Carter, could not be convinced.[21] They apparently then deputed John McCloy to try to work on Vance. On 15 April McCloy telephoned Vance, who told him to remain in touch with the State Department through his deputy, Warren Christopher. In his memorandum of 16 April to Christopher, McCloy states he was asked by Kissinger about his views on "what position the Government should take if the former Shah of Iran sought residency in this country as a refuge from his revolutionary deposition in Iran." He had talked with former Secretary of State Dean Rusk, Brzezinski, and Vance, the latter suggesting that he communicate his views to Christopher. He wrote in the memorandum that he had known the shah for some time. The shah was a supporter of the United States and its policies on principle, as attested by every U.S. president since Roosevelt, and most recently by Carter only a few months ago. He had taken concrete steps in this support that had been risky to his popularity and position among his own people as well as his neighbors. This man now sought refuge in the United States, and the United States had no other option but to grant it. "I very much fear that failure on our part to respond to the Shah's request for permission to reside in the United States would take the form of a conspicuous and perhaps historical example of the unwisdom of other leaders affiliating themselves with United States interests." This was more than a matter of convenience or risk to property or personnel. "It relates to the integrity, the standing, and in a longer range, perhaps, to the security of the United States itself." It was also a matter for the government rather than private citizens to deal with and needed to be dealt with promptly so that "time and circumstance" did not interfere with the steps that must be taken. The situation required "action rather than more studies." An officer with general staff experience should be put in charge of the logistics of responding promptly to the shah's request. A good "planner" should also be appointed to help the shah. "The presence of such a person would have the added and important advantage of imparting, at least, a certain sense of confidence to the Shah by way of a symbol of our willingness to cooperate and within our capacity to help him in his present plight — an attitude which to date, I understand, has not been made apparent to him during his stay in the Bahamas." The foregoing might have "awkward consequences" but "by doing something along this line we would be meeting our responsibilities as well as making it clear to the Shah and to the world that we were acting in a forthright and appropriate manner as a nation of our standing should."[22]

Christopher was not impressed. Some of the points McCloy had made were not devoid of merit, he wrote back, but "we must be deeply concerned regarding the safety of official and unofficial Americans in the currently unsettled conditions in Iran. Now the risks to these Americans are great, but they could lessen over time, and we do not exclude the possibility of the Shah's coming here at a future time."[23] McCloy took what Christopher dished out stoically. Perhaps the department was doing what it could, but the matter could not be postponed indefinitely, he replied. At any rate, the idea of the planner he had suggested was to help find a solution to the shah's plight. And "the action would not seem to be at all inconsistent with your quite proper concern for the safety of our personnel in Iran."[24]

McCloy kept calling Christopher the next few days but to no avail. He then called Brzezinski, who asked for the material he had sent to Christopher.[25] Brzezinski, preoccupied with U.S.-Soviet relations and at the time not much involved in the State Department activities regarding the shah, nevertheless on 1 May suggested to the president they "should at least be flexible on the question of the Shah's wife and children."[26] Vance agreed and arrangements were made for the crown prince to study in the United States.

In the meantime, Princess Ashraf had consulted her legal adviser William E. Jackson, an associate of the firm of Milbank, Tweed, Hadley and McCloy, on going public, advertising in American media that her brother should be permitted to go to the United States. Jackson conferred with McCloy, who advised against advertising, but suggested that as a distraught sister the princess might write to the president and that he would be happy to help with the drafting of the letter. On 3 May, McCloy had a telephone conversation with the shah, during which he informed him of Princess Ashraf's intention. The shah said he would not be a party to such an action. McCloy then told the shah about his advising the princess to write to the president. The princess, of course, would not take any action without the shah's consent. The shah said he would not countenance such a letter. "People might misconstrue his own dignity and his own pride if she did so. He would not make such a request of the president."[27] The shah said the same to his sister, and for the moment the idea of the letter was put aside.

However, the shah's health and security conditions progressively worsened. On 13 May Khalkhali ruled that the shah, the queen, Princess Ashraf, the shah's brother Prince Gholam Reza, and several others, including Ardeshir Zahedi, Ja'far Sharif-Emami, Houchang Nahavandi, and Generals Azhari and Oveisi were *mahdur-ud-dam,* that is, individuals whose blood might be shed with impunity, and declared that whoever killed them would be acting on behalf of the Islamic court. The ruling clearly increased the dangers the shah faced. By the end of May the royal group had reached almost the end of the line. Their visas were expiring, and the government of the Bahamas was preparing for their exit from the islands by 10 June. Other venues were fast closing. They had thought it a possibility to go to their place in Surrey, England. When still a member of the opposition, Margaret Thatcher had vowed she would invite the shah to England. But now, as prime minister, she reneged on her promise. She sent Sir Denis Wright, a former British ambassador to Iran, to the Bahamas to inform the shah. Wright chose to arrive incognito, camouflaged in a strange outfit. He called Kambiz Atabai, refusing to identify himself by name until Atabai was able to guess his identity. Surprised, Atabai reported what he had seen and heard to the shah, who, in turn, was amazed at Wright's behavior and disappointed at Thatcher's.[28] Other potential havens, Mexico for example, were fading as friends disposed to help were met with one impasse after another.

On 31 May McCloy sent another memorandum to Christopher. As a private individual, he said, the former shah would not be able to communicate with the heads of government on whose decision alone such moves depended. Private individuals who wish to help "are frequently met by inquiries as to why the United States refuses entry," argued McCloy. "The fact is that neither the former shah nor, for that matter, any private individuals are in a position to conclude definite arrangements which would enable him to find and move to a suitable haven. . . . It is the United States Government which over the years has received his outstanding cooperation. . . . It is United States reluctance to take him in which in large part prompts others to hesitate and defer action." The time had come for the United States either to admit him or take charge of finding a suitable residence for him and his family, he concluded.[29]

The shah's health deteriorated significantly while he was in the Bahamas. Flandrin had seen the shah twice in Morocco; now he agreed to go to Nassau. The shah had found a mass above the clavicle and Flandrin, on the telephone, had diagnosed large cell lymphoma. On Paradise Island, he explained to the shah that his condition was dangerous. "Following normal medical practice," Flandrin wrote his colleague Bernard, "he should have gone to a well-equipped special medical center to have a biopsy of the lymph node that I had just tapped, radiological investigations, very probably a laparotomy with splenectomy even before additional chemotherapy followed by radiotherapy could be begun." The other choice, said Flandrin, was to forego investigations and do three series of additional chemotherapy over three months, without wasting any time. Then the state of the lesions would be assessed and most likely there would still be "splenectomy and radiotherapy on the site of the Richter's syndrome that had just been discovered."[30]

The shah asked about the risks of the second alternative and decided to take it. He told Flandrin: "At a time when they are killing officers faithful to me in my country, I cannot reduce them to complete despair by revealing my state of health." He asked Flandrin for those three months and promised that "after the three monthly series of chemotherapy [Flandrin] wanted him to have, secrecy would be abandoned so that the more normal medical practice could be resumed." To maintain secrecy, the queen was to serve as the only nurse.[31] The treatment began, and initially the shah responded well.

The government of the Bahamas refused to extend the visas of the shah and his companions. The shah suspected the British government was behind the decision. "With the U.S. distant and cool, and the British, as always, hostile, Bahamian Prime Minister Pindling wanted me out—despite the enormous sums I spent there for my ten weeks stay," the shah complained.[32] Finding the next residence remained a problem. Despite the efforts of the Rockefeller and other groups, the government of the United States did not involve itself actively in the shah's residency. President Carter had begun to think that the situation in Iran was stabilizing and that there was a good chance relations between Iran and the United States would improve. Nonetheless, he thought Khomeini was irrational, kept Iran in a state of turmoil, and blamed the United States for his own problems. "While the government was seeking in many ways to restore normal relations with us, Khomeini was identifying us to his followers in the streets as the source of all his troubles."[33]

Carter's reasoning logically led him to take measures to satisfy the demands of what he construed as the reasonable element in the new regime. The irrational, the erratic, the killings were traits suitably applied to Khomeini and his clerical followers. The government led by Mehdi Bazargan, Ebrahim Yazdi, Sadeq Qotbzadeh, Abolhassan Bani-Sadr, and the like, on the other hand, was sane and rational. And, as Carter saw it, the two elements "had apparently decided to avoid one another and, to a surprising degree, go their separate ways."[34] Khomeini's troubles in several parts of the country reinforced this thinking. Carter never grasped Khomeini's personal charisma, determination, and, especially, organizational strength, which always trumped the indecision of either governments or formless masses. He adopted the same policy of appeasement with Khomeini in power that the shah had followed with Khomeini in the opposition. To sell that policy, he also had to go along with the vilification of the shah and, by extension, of the United States as a supporter of the shah for the past thirty-seven years.

In the meantime, the shah's friends were frantically looking for a place of residence. Panama was an option, though the shah at the time did not wish to go there. In fact Zahedi and Crown Prince Reza had made a trip to Panama and had been received kindly by the Panamanian strongman Omar Torrijos. Mexico was also considered a possibility. President José López Portillo of Mexico had visited Iran when he was finance minister and had been treated with pomp and ceremony. He was the same age as the shah and was a friend of Ardeshir Zahedi. The shah had visited Mexico when Luis Echeverría was president and had liked the country. And López Portillo was not averse to having him in Mexico—in part, according to some accounts, because he had his eyes on getting the shah to invest in business with some of his friends.[35] Zahedi met with López Portillo, who asked for a few days until Fidel Castro, who was visiting Mexico, left the country.[36] Henry Kissinger also talked to the Mexican president and secured López Portillo's consent for the shah to visit. The queen thought that López Portillo might have wanted to teach the Americans "a lesson in political ethic." Robert Armao and Colonel Jahanbini made a trip to Mexico to find a suitable residence. Jahanbini was especially worried for the shah's safety since he had been condemned on religious grounds. They chose a villa in Cuernavaca, about eighty miles south of Mexico City, which satisfied the security requirements, and on 10 June the royal entourage moved in. The new villa was larger than the one in the Bahamas and more pleasant. "Coming from the Bahamas, where we had suffered claustrophobic accommodations and a host of other irritations, we were agreeably surprised at our new residence," wrote the queen. "A tropical garden hid it from the street, and it was large enough to lodge the people who were with us. However, as it had not been lived in for some time, it was damp and covered with mildew, and I had something of a shock to find scorpions on the walls. That did not worry the king, who exclaimed as he inspected it, 'We'll be able to come alive again at last.'"[37]

Cuernavaca was a place for the retired. It was quiet and the Mexicans were kind. "Even some families invited us to their home," recalled the queen. They were able to travel in Mexico, taking an outing to Mexico City and small trips to closer towns and historical sites. The guards here were Mexican. So was the secretary they employed to help them answer the mail. The couple thought of making their home in Mexico and began looking for a house. But it was neither easy nor happy. "His Majesty, I believe, wanted to occupy himself to take his mind off the terrible news coming out of Iran. He sometimes went out looking at houses. But it was extremely painful for both of us. Looking for a house is usually a joyous occasion; for us it was nightmarish. Imagine, the shah of Iran walking through the rooms, the basement, and the attic? It was horrible."[38] Nonetheless, the shah put on as good a show as he could, appeared interested, and commented on the architecture, design, brightness, or the price of the houses he saw.

The shah felt physically and mentally better in this new environment. The space here allowed him "time and solitude" to think again about the geopolitics of the recent events in Iran and its meaning for the west. And his friends now came to visit him. He especially appreciated Richard Nixon's visit. They talked about the past and the future, and as always they agreed on most things. The shah hinted at his meeting with Nixon in 1967, just before Nixon ran for president, and the ideas they discussed, which later became known as the Nixon Doctrine. And he praised Nixon for his "loyalty to old friends." Henry Kissinger was also welcomed for his steadfast friendship, superior intellect, and two other rare qualities: "an ability to listen and a very fine sense of humor."[39]

His family also was nearby. His mother and his older sister Shams and her husband had taken up residence in a villa next to his. Other Iranians could come more easily to visit with them. And there was room for the children to live with them. Once they came close to suffering another tragedy. The older son, Reza, had gone flying, unbeknownst to the guard. Suddenly a helicopter was seen zooming straight on the villa. Because of Khalkhali's license to assassinate the shah, the guard took the event for a commando attack and began shooting at the approaching helicopter. Suddenly the shah and the queen realized it was their son showing off his flying prowess. The queen ran out to the guards and was able to stop the firing before the bullets could find their target.[40]

Now that things were looking better, the queen thought that they should have the dishes from their residence in St. Moritz brought to Mexico. "We should have a better environment even though we may live for only another six months," she thought. She and her companion Liusa Pirnia set out to learn Spanish and live as ordinary a life as was at the time possible. But it was not to be. In Cuernavaca for the first time the shah talked of "cancer" to his wife. The queen habitually stayed with him, sitting on the side of the tub, when he was massaged and bathed. One evening, he turned to her and said in what seemed to her an inordinately normal tone: "You know I have cancer." She was speechless for a time, appropriate words escaping her. "You'll be fine," she finally said. "We will overcome it."[41] But soon the shah developed excruciating abdominal pains he had not previously experienced. His skin turned yellowish, and it was not known whether these were symptoms of his known illness or had a different cause. The Mexican doctors, who were kept in the dark and allowed only a cursory examination of the patient, thought that the pain and jaundice were the results of recurring malaria. With the shah's situation getting worse, Robert Armao talked to the U.S. government, and consequently Dr. Benjamin Kean, an American specialist in tropical diseases, was dispatched to Mexico to examine the shah. Kean ruled out malaria in favor of a pancreas problem and proposed a blood test, which the shah refused, much to his surprise. Dr. Kean then returned to New York to follow the case with American doctors.

Dr. Flandrin arrived in Cuernavaca just after Kean had left. He advised hospitalization and proposed the United States as the proper place for it. The shah refused at first, though further developments suggest he might not have been as adamant in his refusal as he seemed. Flandrin went to Mexico City and had a conference with the head of the medical department at the city's main hospital, a Dr. Garcia. He explained the condition but not the name of the patient and specified several requirements, including security. Garcia seemed to him unfazed by the information, taking him on a tour of the hospital. Flandrin found the medical facilities satisfactory. The next day, with the shah's permission, he asked Dr. Garcia to come to Cuernavaca to see and talk to the patient personally. Garcia did and agreed with Flandrin that "an etiologic diagnosis of febrile obstructive jaundice was to be done as soon as possible, certainly leading to surgery." Flandrin thought medically the situation was not complicated.[42]

What Flandrin did not know was that the debates had gone on before his arrival. Armao was determined that the shah should go to the United States for treatment on the premise that, given his station, "good enough," as Flandrin had called the Mexican facilities, was not good enough for the shah. Only the best would do. To Flandrin it seemed that now the shah was inclined to Armao's position. He attributed this to Mexico's social environment. Mexicans apparently had the habit of disparaging their own worth, a trait Iranians shared, and consequently gave the impression that wisdom demanded that anyone who was afflicted with a serious disease and who could go to the United States for treatment should certainly do so.

But the family was also pressing for treatment in the United States. Princess Ashraf, worried about her brother, insisted on it. She now returned to the idea of writing a personal letter to President Carter. She dispatched the letter in mid-August, asking for asylum for her brother in the United States because of the friendship that had existed between him and the United States and because his health was deteriorating and his family suffering. "My brother is a reasonably proud man and he certainly would not wish to seek the hospitality of the United States or any other country, for that matter, if he felt his presence would be unwelcome. In view of his long friendship with the United States and so many of its public and private citizens, I find it very difficult to believe this situation obtains in the United States." She finished the letter by saying she was aware of the argument that harm might come to the Americans in Iran but "she could not believe that means could not be taken by your country to assure the essential safety of United States citizens in Iran rather than to submit to any such type of blackmail."[43] Ashraf's letter was not received kindly. It was given to Deputy Secretary of State Warren Christopher to answer. According to Brzezinski, Christopher prepared a very cold response, addressing the princess as Ms. Pahlavi. Brzezinski moderated it a bit and brought it up to polite diplomatic standards.[44]

The shah had by now decided he should personally pressure President Carter to take an interest in solving the problem of his residency, if not in the United States, then in some other appropriate country. In September he asked to have a conversation with Rockefeller, Kissinger, and McCloy. Rockefeller's associates Joseph Reed and William Jackson were deployed to Cuernavaca on 5 September. In the course of the conversation, the shah expressed his "unhappiness, displeasure, and disappointment" about the treatment President Carter and Secretary Vance had accorded him, and wanted these sentiments forwarded to the president by Rockefeller, Kissinger, or McCloy. "I cannot ignore the fact that I have been mistreated by President Carter. I cannot accept this insult." The president, he said, had repeatedly given him assurances that he would be welcome in the United States, but that the "timing" was not right. "This has dragged on for days, weeks, months and there is no end in sight. My country is in chaos. There is no government. There is a spiral of confusion. . . . I need to settle my residency problems and to obtain appropriate travel documents so that I can have liberty of action. The President has an obligation to answer why I am not welcome. I am not asking the State Department . . . , I am asking the President of your country." Jackson and Reed concluded that the shah "appeared drawn and tired, with moments of pensiveness which bordered on melancholy." But this was mainly on the question of relocation. He was decisive on legal and financial issues.[45]

By October, the shah's cancer was no longer a secret. On 28 September the office of David Rockefeller informed Undersecretary of State David Newsom that "the shah was seriously ill and might ask to come to the United States temporarily for medical reasons." The news prompted the State Department to consult the embassy in Iran, which answered that admitting the shah even for humanitarian reasons "might provoke a severe disturbance." Early in October, Secretary Vance was asked by Iran's foreign minister, Ebrahim Yazdi, if the United States was contemplating admitting the shah. Vance answered that he did not rule out the possibility at some point but that the United States accepted the revolution in Iran and sought normal relations. Yazdi, according to Vance, was noncommittal. On 18 October David Rockefeller's office informed the State Department that the shah's illness was worsening and that "his illness could not be properly diagnosed or treated in Mexico" and that cancer could not be ruled out. The U.S. government sent a Dr. Eben Dustin to Mexico to examine the shah. He confirmed that the shah was suffering from malignant lymphoma. Vance, about to depart for South America, directed Christopher to inform the White House that he thought the shah should be admitted for humanitarian reasons if the Iranian government was first informed and did not vehemently object. The shah should keep his household in Cuernavaca, and the press should be informed that the shah was in the United States only for diagnostics and evaluation and "that no commitment had been made as to how long he can remain."[46]

Bruce Laingen, the U.S. chargé in Tehran, met with Bazargan and Yazdi on 21 October and reported that though the Iranians had expressed some concern about possible effects on bilateral relations of admitting the shah, they seemed to be confident that the U.S. embassy would be protected. Carter then decided to admit the shah. As Brzezinski observed, it may be that "he felt morally ill at ease over the exclusion of the shah . . . and that Vance's flat recommendation that temporary admission be granted on compassionate medical grounds clinched the matter."[47] On 22 October the royal couple entered the United States to seek treatment for the shah's cancer at New York Presbyterian Hospital.

■

The shah arrived in Ft. Lauderdale, Florida, on time but at the wrong airport — instead of flying as ordered to Executive Airport, they went to the executive jet section of Hollywood International Airport. The shah and the queen did not possess visas and were not allowed to exit the plane while it was inspected and foodstuffs, considered illegal by the airport authorities, removed. Armao, who was accompanying the royals, called Washington, and finally the inspectors who had been waiting at the other airport arrived to process their entry. The royal couple was to stop first at Princess Ashraf's apartment on Park Avenue to visit with their children, but they were told the news of their arrival in the United States had leaked and that there were photographers in front of the apartment. The shah decided to go directly to the hospital.

Until this time the children did not know that their father was most likely terminally ill. Now, doctors were about to examine the shah, and it was a foregone conclusion that the news of their father's illness would be immediately announced in the media to tell the world, especially the revolutionary government in Iran, that he had been admitted to the United States for humanitarian reasons and that he would be asked to leave as soon as he was able to. The queen now had the difficult task of telling her children the truth before they heard it on television but had also to comfort and reassure them that their father would recover. It was especially difficult to tell Leila, the youngest, only ten years old and already fragile and confused by the inexplicable transformation of her life.[48]

At New York Hospital the shah was assigned two rooms—one for him and one for his companions and visitors. The rooms were cordoned off from the rest of the hospital by a small corridor with a locked door at the end guarded by hired security as well as the New York Police Department. Outside the hospital demonstrations against the shah, begun as soon as the news of his admission to the United States had become known, were incessant, including collective prayers for his death, broadcast by the media throughout America and the world. The shah heard some of it, the queen all of it, though soon she decided to turn off the TV whenever possible to spare the children and herself the agony. But it proved impossible to escape the ferocity of the attack, its spread, or its inclusiveness.

On 24 October the shah was operated on by a team of doctors led by Dr. Benjamin Kean, who had examined him in Mexico and recommended the New York Hospital. The surgeons took out only his gallbladder and gallstones, leaving the spleen intact, on the theory that his obstructive jaundice was due to gallstones. The shah at the time was satisfied with the diagnosis and issued a statement to that effect.[49] According to Flandrin, this was an egregious mistake with mortal consequences. The operation had taken place without input from the shah's oncologist, Dr. Morton Coleman. The surgeon had "decided a priori not to do a splenectomy . . . and he had left an obstructive calculus [stone] in the common bile duct as he had not done the final radiography during the operation." This, Flandrin concluded, "was not the 'best' that American medicine could offer, but the worst, as can be found in any country in the world. . . . What followed was a string of consequences caused by this bad blunder."[50]

After the operation, the shah soon developed pains because of the remaining stone. Was it wise to take the spleen out so soon after operating on the gall bladder? It was decided that they should not operate on the spleen and should remove the remaining stone using endoscopy. Dr. Morton Coleman also began treatment for the cancer, which had to be done at the Memorial Sloan-Kettering Cancer Center. The two hospitals were linked by basement passages through which the shah was to be wheeled to reach the cancer center. There, he would meet doctors and nurses obviously unhappy about his being there and afraid of revenge by his enemies. For security reasons the timing was kept secret and was changed without notice. He would get himself ready for the appointed hour only to be told the appointment was cancelled because the doctor had not showed up. Some days he would be awakened at 6 A.M. to be moved across the street before the demonstrators gathered. To add to the indignity, the passage was full of dirty linen. The shah accepted his lot stoically, never complaining. The queen thought they were being harassed in order to force their departure as quickly as possible. "Several years later when [the shah's half-sister] Princess Fatemeh was expiring from cancer, I was told by a doctor who had attended my husband 'they pushed us to do what we did.' I never asked him what he meant by 'they.' I assume that they wanted to make life for us as miserable as possible to get us to want to get out of the U.S. the first chance we got."[51]

The shah went along with whatever course of treatment was devised and whatever changes were introduced. Once able, he received visitors. President Johnson's daughter Linda and her husband, Charles Robb, came to wish him well. Red Skelton visited. Frank Sinatra gave him a Saint Christopher medallion to protect him in his travels. Barbara Walters interviewed him. And loyal Iranians came in droves to visit him. But he received no calls from the president or any other person high in the administration.

While the shah was hospitalized in New York, a group of militant students calling themselves Students Following the Line of the Imam attacked the American embassy in Tehran on 4 November. Sixty-six Americans were taken hostage; fifty-two of them would be held for the next 444 days. For the shah and his family, this made an already very painful situation unbearable. Iran demanded the shah's return, and rumors about U.S. communications with the revolutionary regime began to spread. The hospital informed him that his room was needed and that he had to leave. He thought that they would return to Mexico, but soon he would learn that Mexico would not admit them.

The shah was still supported by Rockefeller, Kissinger, McCloy, and their assistants and colleagues, who mediated with the U.S. government on his behalf. On 8 November at David Newsom's request McCloy and others met with him in the Hotel Carlyle in New York. Newsom told McCloy he had asked for the meeting to inform him what the government policy was on the shah's stay in the United States. The government, said Newsom, had decided "it would not entertain any demand for the return of the shah to Iran against his will and further it would not attempt to induce or pressure the shah to leave the country." He wanted to know what McCloy thought. McCloy told him he agreed with the administration's decision and that he sympathized deeply with those in the administration who had to deal with the "ugly problems" the events in Iran had brought about. McCloy, clearly speaking for the Rockefellers and Kissinger also, said that "any negotiation with the Iranians must be preceded by the release of the hostages." Moreover, he told Newsom that the administration must now take charge of the matter and communicate directly with the shah. "Future Government involvement certainly will have to be assumed whatever the ultimate disposition of the shah may be. This is advisable quite apart from any consideration which might be due the shah by reason of his past record of effective cooperation with United States policy to which all recent presidents had attested."

The next day, McCloy visited the shah in the hospital and reported to him and the queen on his conversation with Newsom. The shah thanked him for his efforts and expressed "his great distress over the condition of his country." To McCloy, the shah's appearance gave "substantial evidence of the physical and nervous ordeal" he had gone through, but he also felt "that both he and she displayed considerable dignity in view of all the circumstances." That same morning Dr. Lew Thomas of the Sloan-Kettering Memorial Hospital had called McCloy to tell him that the shah's radiation treatment was about to begin and that he thought moving the shah under the circumstances was, from a medical point of view, "out of the question."[52]

The day before Newsom met with McCloy, the president had dispatched Ramsey Clark to Iran with a message for Khomeini. Clark was recommended to him by Secretary Vance on Warren Christopher's suggestion, though Carter apparently was not comfortable with the idea. Clark had been President Johnson's attorney general, but since leaving government in 1969 had moved precipitously to the left. He had been a powerful anti-shah voice in the United States, had had an audience with Khomeini in Neauphle-le-Château, and was in good standing with former student dissidents now holding important positions in the Islamic Republic. Carter's objection, however, was mainly about Clark's erratic behavior and his tendency to fault the United States for most problems in the world. But with the resignation of Bazargan and his government on 7 November Carter had few choices. Clark, accompanied by the Iran desk director, Henry Precht, and William Miller, a staff member of the Senate's Select Committee on Intelligence, both of whom were known for their anti-shah sentiments, set out for Tehran, but by the time they reached Ankara, Clark was advised by the Iranians that he would not be admitted to the country.[53] President Carter then took several punitive measures: on 9 November he ordered shipments of military equipment to Iran halted; on the 10th he ordered the deportation of Iranian students not in compliance with visa requirements; then he cut off oil imports from Iran; and on the 14th, he froze the Iranian assets in U.S. banks.

On the 8th the shah had issued a statement that he was willing to leave the United States in the interest of saving the hostages. He had received no reaction from the United States government. President Sadat, however, had sent Ashraf Ghorbal, his ambassador to the United States, to the hospital with a message for the shah "to return to Egypt for further medical treatment in Cairo." The shah had been touched but had replied that he would return to his house in Mexico as soon as his doctors allowed, believing that would still be possible.[54] A few days later, on 15 November, David Rockefeller told President Carter in a telephone conversation that the issue of the shah had become a matter of supreme national concern and that the time had come for the U.S. government to establish direct contact with him. The shah, he said, was willing to meet with Secretary Vance to review the current situation in Iran and if Vance found it awkward to initiate such a move, perhaps another special envoy of the president, for example, his legal adviser Lloyd Cutler, might take the initiative. According to Rockefeller, the president made it clear that "under no circumstances or conditions would he want it to appear that the USG was asking the shah to leave the United States."[55]

This, of course, was only partly true. Carter thought he could deal with Khomeini if he could also control tempers in the United States. On that same day Carter had talked tough at the AFL-CIO convention, holding Iran accountable for any harm done to the American diplomats being held hostage and vowing that "the United States would not yield to international terrorism and blackmail." Later, in the Oval Office he had explained to Hamilton Jordan that he needed to talk tough to give expression to the anger of the Americans, most of whom wanted him to "bomb Iran." "If they can perceive me as firm and tough in voicing their rage, maybe we'll be able to control this thing."[56] As things got worse, however, he became increasingly desperate. The hostage problem, the Islamic government said, could not be solved independently of other issues. The United States should give up the shah to Iran; return the shah's wealth; recognize all the harm it had done to Iran; and commit itself not to interfere in the internal affairs of Iran. On 18 and 19 November, thirteen American hostages, five women and eight African-American men, were released. Khomeini called all the hostages spies but said he was releasing the women because Islam did not incarcerate women and the African Americans because he knew that they and their kind were treated badly in the United States. He said Carter was helpless, "beating an empty drum," and did not have "the guts to engage in a military action."[57] He threatened to try the hostages as spies.

In the White House on 20 November, trying to find an appropriate answer to Khomeini's statements, Vice President Walter Mondale suggested that as long as the shah was in the United States, the hostages would not be released. Despite objections by Brzezinski, Carter agreed and ordered Vance to see when the shah was medically ready to leave, though a counterargument was made by the CIA Director, Stansfield Turner, that getting the shah out of the United States might cause the Iranians to "feel that the United States has denied them their prize, and they could take it out on the hostages, killing them out of a sense of frustration."[58]

The shah, for his part, deduced that by the end of November the United States would want him out "at any cost," and for that and other reasons he was eager to leave. By the 27th, his doctors told him that his radiation treatment had been completed, the stones in the bile duct crushed, and his fever brought under control. He was ready to leave. He sent his aides to Cuernavaca to prepare the villa. Everything was being readied. Suddenly, on 30 November, two days before the shah was scheduled to depart, Robert Armao received a call from the Mexican consul general in New York. "The shah can't come back to Mexico," said the consul. "Two or three days, okay, because he's got that much time left on his tourist visa, but that's all."[59]

This was unbelievable news. Armao had received confirmation from López Portillo's office that same morning, and he had been talking about it to the shah when he had received the consul's call. This, however, "supersedes all previous communication," said the consul. "The shah cannot stay in Mexico. You don't believe me? Let's get the ambassador on the phone. He is the one who received the message from Mexico." When the shah was told, he also was stunned. "But why?" he asked. There was no good answer.[60] He was scheduled to leave the hospital on 2 December. But where would he go? The only place immediately available to him was Princess Ashraf's townhouse in Beekman Place in Manhattan.

Armao called David Newsom at the State Department but was told Beekman Place was a bad idea. Armao blew up. There was only so much he could do. "We are now making an official request to the White House," he shouted. "You have to assist him in finding another place. You have to provide him with safe haven. You have to provide him the transportation there, and the medical care. Otherwise we are going to Beekman Place."[61]

"López Portillo is a liar," shouted Carter when he heard the news. He asked Vance to make earnest requests of "our friends to help us by providing a home for the shah." He received no firm responses except the one from Egypt. Meanwhile, he sent Lloyd Cutler to New York to see the shah and invite him to move to Lackland Air Force Base, near San Antonio, Texas, where, Cutler said, they had good medical facilities. He assured the shah that while he recuperated at Lackland, the president would do his best to find him a suitable residence.[62]

25

Almost Bartered

On the evening of 1 December the queen was having dinner at Princess Ashraf's when she received a call from the shah: "We are leaving tomorrow for Texas, but they have told us no one must know, not even the children." Keeping their departure a secret proved harder than expected. The queen had made several appointments for the coming days, including one the next day for lunch with a close friend who would not take no for an answer. But all that paled compared to not telling her children.

The shah was to go to the airport directly from the hospital, the queen from where she was staying at Beekman Place. She was meticulously careful not to let anyone in on the departure date, and as far as she could tell the only other person who knew was Kambiz Atabai, who helped her get her things together for the trip. In the morning, as they opened the door to the house, much to her surprise, they were faced with a host of TV cameras and an avalanche of questions. "I was flabbergasted," said the queen. "I kept our trip from my children while the entire world knew or soon would know about it. How was I to explain this to them?"[1] Later she and the shah learned that Leila had awakened calling to her mother and, not hearing her voice, had run to her bedroom only to find she was gone. Leila had cried, then fallen into silence, refusing to be comforted. Years later she would remember the event as a bad dream, "an impossible dream," she would insist.[2] To Sondra Phelan, who saw her twice a week on behalf of the Rockefellers during the period her parents were away, she would say: "I wish time would go backwards instead of forwards."[3]

The shah and the queen were escorted separately to LaGuardia Airport under "inordinately heavy security." The shah, dressed in a dark suit, was taken from his rooms on the seventeenth floor of the hospital in a wheelchair, to descend by elevator to the hospital basement and then to one of the exit routes. From there, he was led through a four-block-long tunnel to a garage, thence driven to the airport.[4] At the airport, soldiers had cordoned off the plane that was to take them to Texas, giving the scene the look of a place under siege. The queen wondered about all the sound and fury; once inside the U.S. Air Force DC-9 and close to the shah, she observed to him that all this was "to expedite our departure from this country. We already know we are not welcome here; why this show?"[5]

At Kelly Air Force Base in Texas they were received by Major General William P. Acker, the Lackland Air Force Base commander, who met the shah in the plane and escorted him and the queen to an ambulance that took them at high speed—jolting them against the sides of the ambulance along the way—to the hospital at Lackland, where the security was so tight that not a single reporter got a glimpse of the shah, let alone a chance to talk to him. San Antonio Congressman Henry Gonzales, who was at hand to welcome him, later reported that the shah looked fine "from the standpoint of physical composure," and that he "conveyed a heartfelt sense of gratitude to the American government."[6]

At Lackland a wing of the hospital had been evacuated to make room for the royal couple and their entourage. Later the shah and the queen learned that the wing was equipped to meet the needs of the air force's mental patients. General Acker had chosen this part of the hospital apparently for security reasons, because all the windows had steel bars. They put the shah in a windowless room with brick walls, the queen in a room where the door handle had been detached to prevent patients from exiting the room. On the ceiling, there was an instrument that to the queen looked like a combination camera and loudspeaker, presumably to allow the staff to observe the patients. She felt pressured and claustrophobic. She walked to the window to open it. On the other side a male nurse gestured to her with a shake of the head that it was not allowed. The fact that the nurse was a man scared her. She felt incarcerated. She did not know what to do. She turned to Liusa Pirnia, who asked the nurse to please let her open the window. The nurse at first refused, citing security needs, despite the bars on the window, but finally relented, and the queen opened the window, "regaining her breath." She called Atabai in New York, telling him that if he didn't hear from them again, he should know they were kidnapped. Later, of course, she thought what she said was silly, because obviously kidnappers would not supply their victims with a telephone.[7]

Clearly, the hospital would not do, though the shah never complained. Armao talked to the authorities, demanding a more humane place. The authorities protested that they were notified of the royals' arrival very late and there was no time to prepare a more suitable residence. Finally, they agreed to set up a few rooms at the Officers Club and they moved the royal group there.

Life changed for the better at the Officers Club. The air force was acquainted with Iran and the Iranian officers under the shah, many of whom had received their training in the United States. The American officers respected them as professionals and respected the shah, whose leadership they considered instrumental in developing the Iranian armed forces into an efficient force friendly to the United States. They did not like the Khomeini regime. Many of them believed that had the United States government acted more wisely and resolutely this catastrophe would not have occurred. They tried to make life as pleasant for the shah and the queen as possible despite the awkwardness of the circumstances. General Acker encouraged the senior officers in his command to visit with the shah, which they often did, bringing their families along. He found tennis partners for the queen, a kindness that significantly raised the quality of her life. The younger officers made derogatory poems about Ayatollah Khomeini and, innocent of the denotation of the term *ayatollah* or the connotation of their action, made toilet paper with Khomeini's face as the motif and called it "ayatoilets." Nevertheless, the shah was very much confined. Lackland was an open base, where hundreds of student cadets entered and exited every day. Security was always a problem. The royals had to remain very close to their compound, never allowed to go beyond a periphery the commandant had defined as a few yards from their building. At the same time, the shah needed medical attention, including the always critical, time-sensitive spleen operation. It was understood that they would have to leave the United States. But they did not know where they would be going. For a time they heard of South Africa as a possibility. But South Africa rejected the American inquiries, which in fact pleased the royals. Princess Ashraf contacted Canada to test the possibilities there and received intimations that an arrangement might be made if the shah helped Prime Minister Trudeau's campaign with a few million dollars. Finally, the search settled on Panama.

At Lackland, the shah received news of one of the saddest events he would encounter in exile. On 7 December 1979 his nephew, Navy Commander Shahriyar Shafiq, was assassinated in Paris. The Khomeini regime had murdered many of the shah's civil and military officers who had remained in Iran and now it had set out to eliminate systematically opposition leaders abroad. Khomeini had decreed that those who had worked with the shah were ipso facto guilty; all that was needed was to ascertain their identity. The Revolutionary Council had established an elaborate committee to determine the ways and means of implementing Khomeini's ruling and to prepare a list of the persons to be targeted. Shahriyar Shafiq was actively mobilizing the Iranian military in exile and, consequently, he was one of the first on the list. He was shot in the back of the head as he was carrying groceries to his sister's home in the rue de la

Villa Dupont. Sadeq Khalkhali, the "judge dread" of the Islamic Revolutionary Court, proudly claimed his part in the murder. "I take responsibility for this assassination. The Islamic Fedayeen are continuing their activities in Europe and the United States to identify these wrongdoers and punish them for their actions. This will continue until all these dirty pawns of the decadent system have been purged."[8] Later, when he himself came under attack for overstepping his authority, Khalkhali proclaimed that he had never killed anyone without Khomeini's express approval.

Shahriyar's death devastated the shah, who eulogized him as "a gallant naval officer who served his country with distinction." His sister Ashraf, Shahriyar's bereaved mother, was more eloquent. She called her son "a staunch patriot and a fine and dedicated navy officer who helped raise high the flag of Iran. . . . My heart, which grieves today the loss of a son, is also with all the American mothers and fathers who have their children captive in Tehran. . . . I pray for the American people and the Iran for which my son died."[9] The shah asked Ashraf to come to him in San Antonio. Just before she arrived, he observed to Hamilton Jordan, admiringly: "What a brave woman she is. I have lost my country, but she has lost her country and her son. I am sure you know that her son was killed by some of Khomeini's assassins. But her sole concern now is for my health." Princess Ashraf arrived at Lackland on 12 December. As she was entering her brother's room, she came face to face with Hamilton Jordan, who was leaving. Jordan extended his hand, but she refused to take it.[10] She entered the room, and brother and sister consoled each other as best they could.

"López Portillo is a liar," Carter had shouted when he heard on 30 November that Mexico would not renew the shah's visa. He was galled especially because López Portillo had made much of his magnanimity and grit in giving asylum to the shah when Carter had equivocated. He told Vance "to really lay it on the line with our friends to help us by providing a home for the Shah."[11] Vance went to work, but found no takers, except the once and ever loyal Sadat, who had gone out of his way to assure the shah of his welcome in Egypt. Carter, however, was worried about the Arab response, as was the shah, and petrified that if no other country except Egypt accepted him, the shah might have to remain in the United States. Vance and Brzezinski, not always in agreement on policy about Iran, had now concluded that the shah should not be allowed to go to Egypt. On Sunday, 2 December, Brzezinski called Carter at Camp David to tell him he concurred with Vance and Averell Harriman, who had also made the same point to Vance. Carter was furious. He accused Brzezinski of "conspiring with Kissinger and Rockefeller to get the Shah permanently into the country" and Vance of "sitting on his ass and doing nothing."[12]

Early in the morning of 11 December Vance informed Carter that he had failed to find a home for the shah. Now only one possibility remained to Carter—Panama. He recalled the friendship he had struck up with General Torrijos at the settling of the Canal Treaty. The general owed him one. Moreover, Panama did not depend on Iranian oil. As he recalled, Torrijos had been willing to take the shah when he first left Iran. Still, he had to be careful. Refuge for the shah was a difficult request for him to make to others. They always asked why he did not take him in himself—surely, no country owed the shah as much as the United States. A telephone call might do it, but now that Mexico had refused to let the shah come back, the risk had increased. What if the general said no? Someone must talk to Torrijos in person. He thought of Jordan, whom Torrijos trusted and liked. Jordan addressed Torrijos as Papa General and let him lecture him ad nauseam on fine points of diplomacy. Jordan was the man to go to Panama, as quietly as possible.

Jordan called Ambler Moss, the U.S. ambassador to Panama, and asked him to arrange for him to meet Torrijos that evening. Jordan had first met Moss during the Panama Canal Treaty negotiations, when Moss, a Spanish-speaking lawyer, was on the staff helping Ambassador Ellsworth Bunker in the negotiations. Moss had ably defended the treaty in the Senate hearings and was subsequently rewarded with the post of ambassador to Panama. He was on good terms with Torrijos and the rest of Panama's ruling elite. He guessed immediately why Jordan was coming to Panama and told him he had a good chance of succeeding, when he met him at the airport to take him to Torrijos "in one of his eight or ten places scattered about the city and countryside."[13]

Still, Jordan was unusually nervous. There was much at stake and Torrijos was somewhat unpredictable. When they met, Jordan tried to lighten the atmosphere, making small talk over a drink, but it did not work. The general abruptly asked him the purpose of his visit. Jordan asked to speak to him alone. He then explained the president's dilemma. It was impossible to resolve the hostage crisis as long as the shah remained in the United States. The shah wished to leave, but there was nowhere for him to go except Egypt. But his presence there would endanger Sadat, and therefore the president preferred for him to go somewhere else, with which the shah concurred. And "the president wanted me to ask if you would be willing to accept the Shah in Panama until the hostage crisis is resolved."[14]

Torrijos was not one to let such an opportunity pass him by. He leaned back in his chair, eyes closed, puffing on the cigar his friend Castro had sent him as a gift. After a few seconds that seemed inordinately long to Jordan, he began in a deliberate, studied tone:

> Hamilton, the crisis is first and foremost the problem of the United States, because those people are Americans and they represent your country and your government. But it is also the problem and the responsibility of the world community. As long as diplomats can be held like those in Tehran, no diplomat is safe anywhere. You can tell the President that we will accept the Shah in Panama. We are a small but proud country. If we can make even a small contribution to peacefully resolving this crisis, we will be happy to do so.

Jordan was elated. He called Carter and told him the good news. "Thank God!" said the president. "I am glad and very relieved. I have been worried all day about what we could do if he said no."[15] He then thanked Torrijos personally on the telephone.

Now someone had to inform the shah, who most likely would not welcome the new arrangement. Jordan asked Lloyd Cutler to be present when he broke the news to the shah and boarded his plane the same night for Lackland. The next day he and Cutler were met by Robert Armao, who briefed them on the shah's condition as they drove to meet him. Over the months he had been with the shah and his family, Armao had grown fond of the man, and protective. He told Jordan that the shah had been treated badly and taken advantage of everywhere since he had left Iran. He did not know Panama or General Torrijos. They should be careful. And please, "Be sure to refer to the shah as Your Majesty when you address him."[16]

Jordan and Cutler found the royal family's quarters at Lackland "drab," like "a $75-a-day Holiday Inn 'suite' in Peoria," with "awful blue and green curtains and carpet." It struck Jordan as anomalous, odd, unnatural. "You know Mr. Jordan, Your Majesty," Armao introduced Jordan in a formal tone. The shah said he remembered Jordan from his 1977 visit to the White House; Jordan had written of that encounter that of all the foreign leaders he had seen he had judged the shah "easily the most impressive." Now, scarcely two years later, the once-confident leader sat on a vinyl sofa, emaciated and gaunt, wearing a blue air force robe with "USA" stamped across the back, seemingly unaware of the attire in which he received his guests.[17]

On matters of policy, however, the shah remained acute. He rebutted Jordan's claim that the hostage crisis would not be solved as long as he was in the United States, though he would do whatever he could to help the United States resolve it. He did not want "to be blamed by history for this terrible thing."[18] Where would he go? he asked. At this point Cutler informed him that none of the countries the shah had indicated — England, Switzerland, Austria — had been forthcoming. (According to David Rockefeller, in the case of Austria, Carter had asked him "to call Chancellor Kreisky to encourage him to go through with his earlier offer of asylum for the shah in Austria," but to no avail.)[19] But it is not clear that the shah knew this. "I must admit that I am surprised and disappointed," the shah said in a low voice that to Jordan seemed loaded with grief. "It seems that no one wants me."[20]

At this point Jordan told him about Torrijos and Panama. Armao objected. The shah had had an invitation from Torrijos before, said Armao. The man was unsavory, not to be trusted. He would be low enough to entertain extradition for some profit. And the shah would not be able to receive the medical care he required.[21] Armao's outburst dampened Jordan's euphoria. But the shah came to his assistance. "I have to admit that I know very little about Latin America, or Panama, or this man Torrijos — and I would much prefer a European country," said the shah, to whom Torrijos was "a typical South American dictator." But Panama was the only country available save Egypt, and if the shah did not want to "burden his friend Anwar with his problem," as he had maintained, there was no other choice. He told Armao that he would go to Panama, and he told Jordan not to worry about disappointing him. "After what my family and I have been through, nothing disappoints me anymore."[22] The conversation then turned to the suitability of Panama for the shah's medical and security requirements, which Armao, disappointed at the decision, nonetheless undertook to study and report on to the shah.

The next day, 13 December, Jordan, Armao, and Colonel Jahanbini flew to Panama. There they agreed that the vacation home of Gabriel Lewis on Contadora Island was the most suitable place for the royals to stay — it was close to the hospitals in Panama City, the surrounding water was good for security, and it had the air of a resort area, which would be restorative for everyone concerned. Lewis had been Panama's ambassador to the United States during the debates in the Senate on the Panama Canal Treaty; he was Jordan's good friend and Carter's "secret weapon" in the Senate discussions and his "favorite ambassador." His house was clearly one of America's preferred places for the shah in Panama. The trio then met with General Torrijos, who wrote a letter inviting the shah to Panama and asked Armao to convey to the shah that if he accepted his invitation he would "be treated as an honored guest" and that if he heard "that anyone tries to take advantage of the Shah," he would "have that person thrown in jail."[23] The next day, at the Friday foreign affairs breakfast at the White House, Brzezinski asked what Torrijos would be charging the shah, but got the answer that Torrijos had given when asked: "I don't talk about costs of drinks when I have someone to dinner." "I am afraid he is going to skin the shah alive once he has him in his hands," Brzezinski observed.[24]

The shah's medical requirements still needed to be addressed. The air force doctors who had examined the shah had recommended that his spleen be taken out as soon as possible. The shah's New York Hospital doctors Kean and Hubbard Williams were summoned to Lackland, accompanied by the shah's lawyer, William Jackson. Kean and Williams agreed with the air force doctors and recommended immediate operation. It would take the shah two to three weeks to recuperate, they said. The shah thought it too long. Might Chlorambucil, the medicine he had been taking until his operation in New York, help speed his recovery, the shah asked. Kean answered that it probably would. Jordan and Cutler promised, on behalf of the United States government, "that the shah would be allowed to return to the United States in case of a 'medical emergency.'"[25] The shah then decided to leave and have the operation in Panama, at Gorgas Hospital at the U.S. base in the former Canal Zone, which had also been promised to be made available to the shah. "For the shah," Kean observed, "to agree to go with a major illness and with the need for a major operation to a strange country of limited medical facilities was a sacrifice."[26]

The shah and the queen flew to Panama on 15 December to an uncertain future of controversies, threats, and deceptions. At the time, however, the shah was not conscious of the travails ahead. He thought Hamilton Jordan was "nice," and Panama the logical choice. "Panama was the most logical decision to take in those days because we had a letter of invitation from the General. They had already once invited my son from the Bahamas to go to Panama. They treated him very well. What else, they did not have diplomatic relations with my country. And it looked like a very nice proposal. And it was not very far from the United States or Europe. In those days it seemed like a very good solution."[27]

Contadora is an island some thirty miles off Panama. The villa assigned to the shah was a modern house on a promontory overlooking a bay that opened to the sea, according to the shah, a "splendid view." It had three bedrooms downstairs and one upstairs with a balcony, the one the shah occupied. The queen stayed in one of the bedrooms downstairs; the shah's servant, Amir Pourshoja, in one of the others. Liusa Pirnia, Colonel Jahanbini, and Robert Armao and Mark Morse lived in separate quarters.

The shah did not feel well. The weather was muggy. The house was built for a tropical climate, but the shah did not tolerate well the air currents that flowed when the windows were opened, and it became extremely warm and humid when the windows were closed. Nonetheless, the shah said that the heat and the moisture soothed his throat, which the radiation he had received for his cancer had hurt badly. After the first week, he began to feel fatigued again. But he made an effort to swim a little, walk along the beach, and keep as active as possible. And though usually quiet, he tried to show a bit of humor when he could. "My wife cannot live without a telephone," he joked with the telephone company agents setting up a phone with international dialing capability. As they were installing the telephone, the queen observed in the installation room a voice recorder with two tapes, which she assumed was there to record the conversations in the house. In fact the shah's residence and those of his retinue were bugged. Colonel Noriega's men intercepted, translated, and transcribed everything said in person or on the telephone.[28]

Colonel Manuel Antonio Noriega, Torrijos's assistant chief of staff for intelligence, provided the shah's Panamanian security. At the beginning, the agents were friendly, willing to help in any way they could. Torrijos visited the shah, and once stayed overnight in a nearby hotel. Another time he invited the royal family to his house, where they met his family. President Aristides Royo also visited the shah. And when the telephone was installed, they could speak with friends around the world, and with the children in the United States. Several kings and leaders did call — the kings of Jordan and Belgium, the queen of Thailand, the king and queen of Spain, among others.

The children had a hard time of it, and their unhappiness made life even harder for the shah and the queen. Reza now attended Williams College, at first staying in a hotel. The charges at the hotel, paid by Armao, were sometimes in arrears, causing him trouble. Ordinarily this would not be a matter of great concern, but under the circumstances he felt embarrassed. The queen tried to keep the shah out of these hassles, but was not always successful. Farahnaz was in a dormitory at the Ethel Walker School in Connecticut and also felt she was not treated well. She was her father's favorite, and the shah always felt extremely sad when she was unhappy. "I now regret that we sent her to a dormitory," the queen said later. "We thought at the time that she would be insulated from all the problems we had and the dangers we faced. Around us, the talk was mostly of death and destruction. Now I think that was perhaps a mistake. It was too much of a shock for a young girl faced with the troubles she faced to be away from her family."[29] Alireza and Leila were at Beekman Place with their grandmother. During the Christmas holidays the children all came to Panama for a visit, staying in a nearby house that was rented for them.

The Panamanian government did not interfere with friends who wished to visit the royals. In fact, at times it was quite lenient with the passport and visa problems facing most Iranians of the type who wished to see the shah and the queen. Ordinary American agents were also helpful. Individuals who traveled from Europe usually had to change planes in Miami. U.S. immigration agents in the airport would let them pass through even when their documents were not in order once they learned they were on their way to see the shah of Iran. Professor Seyyed Hossein Nasr, for example, was stopped on the highway for speeding on his way from Boston to New York to visit the shah while he was in New York Hospital. He told the officer who stopped him he was in a hurry because he had to get to the hospital to see the shah at a given hour. The officer let him go without giving him a ticket. "Every letter we received was full with kindness. Only one, from a priest, asked if the shah would forfeit his life to save the hostages," the queen recalled.[30]

The shah received visitors on a covered veranda in front of the house. This was the place where he usually sat reading or listening to the news. The expressions of sympathy and understanding in the violent meanness of those days eased his suffering. And the shah appreciated it. The visit of Randolph Hearst and his daughter Patty cheered him, with Hearst recounting the services the shah had rendered his country and the friendship he had shown America. Hearst expressed sadness at his government's treatment of the shah and offered his apology.

In the early days the shah was still able to visit some other parts of the country. Somewhere to the north of Panama City, in a small suburban village, an Iranian family lived. The family invited him, his companions, and several villagers to a feast of Iranian food. The shah chuckled when the young Iranian host turned the local mayor's down-to-earth welcome into a long, elaborate, flowery speech in his Persian translation. Such things—little things—boosted his morale and cheered him up considerably. The kindness turned out to bring the village more than verbal gratitude. The shah donated $30,000 to a charitable organization there.

The shah was vulnerable, however—too many people and governments were against him; too few were on his side. Naturally, some individuals in business or government found him good prey. Armao and Morse told Lisa Myers of the *Washington Star* that "the Panamanian government ripped off the late shah by grossly inflating bills at the government-owned hotel and charging for washing machines, televisions, china, silverware and a host of other things that were never requested. . . . They put a man in our own house with a tape recorder to monitor all conversations and made me pay for it." The shah, they told Myers, had no choice but to pay. His only alternative was to go to Egypt, but he did not want to impose on Sadat, "unless it was absolutely necessary." It was no use complaining to the U.S. government. "The administration refused pleas for the White House to intervene with Panamanian strongman Omar Torrijos to stop harassment, extortion and other abuse of the exiled monarch during his three months at Contadora Island. 'In fact, every time we complained about something, including telephone taps, the Panamanians would say, "These are the orders of the United States,"' reports Armao, president of New York's consulting firm of Armao and Company." Myers also reported that Juan Materno Vasquez, the Panamanian lawyer who would represent Iran in the extradition proceedings that lay ahead, asserted on an ABC News report that the shah's arrest "was something desired by Iran, Panama, and the United States."[31]

The shah was aware but the queen remained mostly uninformed of such Panamanian underhandedness.[32] "I did not feel they were pressuring us for money," said the queen many years later. "I did not hear such a thing from His Majesty. If there were such pressures for money, nothing actually came out of them. Some time after this period, when Noriega, in trouble with the Americans, had been apprehended, US envoys asked me if he had tried to extort us. I told them our time in Panama was unpleasant, but this was not part of it."[33] That such pressures existed, not only from the Panamanians but also from the Americans, is indisputable. According to Morse, a few days after the shah finally reached safety in Egypt, he received a bill for $255,000 for the flight. When aides protested, "Lloyd Cutler said, 'You better pay this because, after all, it was the cheapest plane ride you could have ever had,'" recalls Morse. "I said, 'Why?' He said, 'Because if you hadn't gotten out Sunday night on that plane, Monday they were going to arrest you and you'd all still be in jail, including you and Armao.'" Armao received a bill of more than $100,000 for security at Lackland, "where the administration had invited him to go."[34]

After Mehdi Bazargan resigned on 7 November 1979, the Islamic regime embarked more seriously on attempting to have the shah eliminated, by assassinating him as Khalkhali wished or by bringing him back to Iran as the new foreign minister, Sadeq Qotbzadeh, preferred, which would yield the same result. For Qotbzadeh the hostage crisis provided an opportunity to design a strategy to exchange the hostages for the shah. This put everybody in a quandary, including several of Khomeini's nonclerical followers.

Bazargan and his foreign minister, Ebrahim Yazdi, had been forced to resign because they had talked with Zbigniew Brzezinski in Algeria. Since then the accepted policy had been that no Iranian would speak with an American. If communication was to take place, which was necessary in the case of the hostages and the shah's return, intermediaries were to be recruited. Two adventurous lawyers were soon found—an Argentine named Hector Villalon and a Frenchman named Christian Bourguet. The two worked together in France and had been associated with leftist movements in the past. They had become acquainted with Qotbzadeh and Bani-Sadr during the revolution. Based on the accounts they had heard from their Iranian revolutionary friends, they believed that the shah and his regime were the most cruel, horrid, and corrupt on the earth.

For Qotbzadeh and Bani-Sadr, getting the shah back in Iran was a serious matter, almost a life-and-death game. They charged Villalon and Bourguet with launching an extradition process with the Panamanian government. The object of the process was to use Article XX of the Panamanian constitution, which stipulated that if a state recognized by Panama asked for a citizen of that state residing in Panama to be extradited to that state, the individual named would be put under arrest. Extradition, however, was a different matter. Late in December Villalon and Bourguet arrived in Panama, unbeknownst to the shah or Armao, and met with Panamanian president Royo and Marcel Salamin, one of Torrijos's leftist political counselors, in effect trying to establish their bona fides with the Panamanian government. They argued that the shah's extradition opened up the possibility of solving the hostage crisis and therefore it was worth pursuing as an option. Royo stated that Panama did not have an extradition treaty with Iran; it did have its own laws on the basis of which action could be initiated and those laws governed the process. Royo then made a public announcement that Iran was in violation of international law and that he did not think Iran would be able to fulfill the requirements of the Panamanian constitution.[35] On 11 January 1980, Iran sent a telex to the government of Panama stating that a warrant charging the shah with a list of crimes was on its way. On 17 January the warrant was submitted to the Panamanian delegation at the United Nations in New York, and the next day it was passed to the Panamanian government. At 3 A.M. on 23 January in Tehran Qotbzadeh received a call from President Royo that the shah would be arrested at 7 A.M. An hour later, he received a call from General Torrijos, affirming the news. Qotbzadeh, however, had to leave for his presidential campaign in Mashhad at 6:30 A.M. He left a note to announce the arrest of the shah at 7:30 A.M. to make sure that the announcement was made after the act had taken place. But he had failed to take into account the time

difference between Iran and Panama and thus the announcement was made at
11 P.M. on 22 January Panama time, forcing the Panamanian leaders to deny that
they ever had made such a promise to Iran.[36]

In the meantime, Villalon and Bourguet targeted the United States as well.
Indeed, to them Panama was simply the way to reach the U.S. government.
On 11 January Hamilton Jordan received a call on behalf of Torrijos to visit
with him in Panama. Worried about the hostages, the president encouraged
Jordan to go to Panama. Instead, Torrijos sent Marcel Salamin and Gabriel
Lewis to meet Jordan on a military base in Homestead, Florida. Salamin had
just returned from a meeting with Qotbzadeh in Iran and now he was telling
Jordan that a line had been opened for him—Jordan—to be a conduit for talks
on hostages between Iran and the United States. He mentioned Villalon and
Bourguet and suggested that it would be helpful if the U.S. initiative at the
UN Security Council to impose sanctions on Iran could be postponed. Jordan
secured Carter's approval of the postponement and eventually was led, accompanied by Hal Saunders of the State Department, to a meeting in London with
Villalon and Bourguet on 19 January. The gist of what these two told them was
that while Khomeini had the supreme power, there was a difference of opinion
about the hostages. The group they represented, that is, Qotbzadeh and Bani-
Sadr, thought the hostages were a drag on Iran's standing in the international
community. The other side, mainly the mullahs, believed that taking the hostages was an affirmation of the revolution, which under Bazargan had drifted
away from the line of the imam. To get the hostages out safely, it was imperative
to help their group. And the way to do that was to return the shah to Iran.
To soften the blow, they painted a picture of the shah as one of the most evil
men in history, if not the most evil one. To impress Jordan with his connections in Iran, Bourguet called and talked to Qotbzadeh as Jordan and Saunders
watched.[37] Jordan was impressed.

Back in Washington, Jordan and other Americans heard the announcement of
the shah's arrest in Panama. Was Torrijos about to sell the shah to the Iranians?
The president was worried, especially about what the shah would do once he
also heard the news. And how was the United States to respond if he asked to
come back to the United States? Jordan called Lewis, who said matter-of-factly
that under Panamanian law when a request for extradition was received, the
person in question was put under arrest. Since the shah was being protected by
Panama's forces, for all practical purposes he might as well be considered already
under arrest, though he was on Contadora and nothing had changed materially.
Extradition, Lewis assured Jordan, was not being considered. Based on Jordan's
recommendation, the president decided that the only path immediately open

to the United States was to follow the Villalon-Bourguet lead. What now happened was that U.S. foreign policy with respect to the hostage crisis was for the most part taken over by, according to the CIA, these two rather questionable characters.[38]

⬛

Villalon and Bourguet flew to Tehran after their conversation with Jordan and Saunders. There they learned first that the Panamanians were going to arrest the shah and, soon after, that the Iranians had bungled the affair by announcing the arrest prematurely. They now had to establish their bona fides with the Americans in order to be able to proceed on surer footing. Qotbzadeh gave them a tape of UN Secretary General Kurt Waldheim's meeting with the members of the Revolutionary Council. Waldheim had gone to Tehran on 2 January, but had had a very difficult stay there, most of the time being attacked for his previous relations with the shah and Princess Ashraf and fearing for his safety. Vance had given him a five-point statement to discuss with the Iranians: the hostages were to be released prior to the institution of any international tribunal for the Iranian government to air its grievances against the shah and the United States; the United States would reach a firm understanding on airing Iran's grievances before an appropriate forum after the hostages had been released; the United States would not object to Iranian suits in U.S. courts to recover assets allegedly taken illegally from Iran by the former shah; the United States would affirm jointly with Iran to abide by international rules governing state relations and accept the present government of Iran as legitimate; and once the hostages were freed, the United States would be willing to seek in accordance with the UN Charter a resolution of all issues between Iran and the United States.[39] Waldheim was not able to convey much to the Iranians or to put forward the American position in his meetings with Qotbzadeh or, on the last day of his visit, with members of the Revolutionary Council.[40] The tape of that meeting told the story of Waldheim's failure to communicate with the council, contrary to Waldheim's claim; it further suggested that the hostages would not be freed unless the Americans acquiesced to the imam's demands and assured the Americans that the two lawyers were authentic representatives of Iran.

Villalon and Bourguet met with Jordan and Saunders on 25 January and with Jordan, Saunders, and Henry Precht on 26 January and came up with a "scenario" for the steps the United States and Iran would take to liberate the hostages. A UN commission would be established, in such a way as to appear to be in response to Iran's demand and against U.S. wishes, to look into the Islamic Republic's grievances and to meet with the hostages. The commission would have to be heavily tilted to the Third World. And it was to be made to understand the political and psychological conditions that prevailed in Iran. At the end of the day, a detailed five-page scenario describing the steps to take was prepared. The next day Villalon and Bourguet left for Panama and thence to Tehran to pursue the shah's extradition and to report to Tehran on their meeting with Jordan. Saunders flew to New York to talk to Waldheim about the proposed commission.

Soon after, Khomeini stated that he might approve a UN commission to come to Tehran to investigate the shah's crimes and to report on Iran's grievances. But he made no mention of the hostages. In early February, Jordan received a call from Villalon's secretary that Villalon was optimistic about the "scenario" but did not offer much more detail. Jordan was, however, called to a meeting with the two lawyers in Bern, Switzerland, on 9 February, which he, Saunders, and Precht attended. According to Pierre Salinger, it was agreed in the meeting that the shah would be arrested in Panama, tried, but not extradited, and that the United States would undertake not to interfere in Iranian affairs. The problem that remained was whether the United States would apologize to the Islamic Republic for past interventions in Iran. That, said Jordan, was not possible. In the end a compromise was reached: Carter would "express understanding and regret for the grievances of the Iranian people, including the widespread perception of U.S. intervention in Iran's internal affairs; affirm the right of the Iranian people to make decisions governing their political future and the engagement of the U.S. to respect that right; and to affirm a desire for normal relations based on mutual respect, equality, and the principles of international law." For the Islamic Republic, the newly elected president, Abolhassan Bani-Sadr, would "admit the moral wrong of holding hostages, express regret, and promise to respect international law and affirm a desire to establish normal relations based on mutual respect, and equality and international law."[41]

None of these statements is specifically mentioned in Jordan's account of the meeting. If true, they point to the lawyers' duplicity and the Americans' naïveté. It would have been impossible for Bani-Sadr to make such statements, given Khomeini's previous pronouncements on the subject. And the concessions made by Jordan and Saunders would certainly reinforce Khomeini's belief that the Americans were in retreat. Nonetheless, based on the reports made to Washington, President Carter gave Jordan the following written memo on White House stationary to take to his interlocutors:

The White House
Washington

February 15, 1980

To Hamilton Jordan

In your conversations this weekend with Messrs. Bourguet and Villalon, please ask
them to convey to President Bani-Sadr and Foreign Minister Ghorbzadeh the
following message:

"If, at any time, the Government of Iran desires to release the American hostages
at an earlier date than called for in the mutually agreed plan, the Government of
Iran has my personal assurance that the United States will abide by all the terms of
that plan."

Convey to Messrs. Bourguet and Villalon our continued appreciation for the
useful role they have played in trying to resolve the differences between the United
States and the Islamic Republic of Iran.[42]

On 20 February the newly established UN commission, composed of five
members from Venezuela, Syria, Sri Lanka, Algeria, and France, arrived in Iran
"to liberate the hostages," as one of them said to a surprised Villalon. He had
heard nothing of the "scenario" so painstakingly and meticulously prepared. The
commission was allowed to see the hostages after some debates with Qotbzadeh
and Bani-Sadr, often mediated by Villalon and Bourguet. In the meantime,
Ayatollah Khomeini announced that the fate of the hostages would be determined by the parliament, which was yet to be elected. President Carter, afraid
that the students might kill the hostages rather than release them to the government or the commission, sent a message through Mohammed Hasanayn Heikal,
an Egyptian journalist, a longtime editor of the daily *al-Ahram,* and a friend
and supporter of Nasser and his politics, to tell the Iranian authorities that "the
murder of the U.S. hostages would be a tremendous setback to stability in the
region, would put the U.S. and Iran at odds for some time to come, and would
blacken irrevocably the image of the Iranian revolution."[43] Heikal had been
received warmly by the students in the embassy in early December and treated
as a fellow revolutionary. He had found the students intent on getting the shah
and his wealth back in Iran and very much engrossed in themselves — "a closed
society, in its way as isolated and inward-looking as the hostages it had seized,
a community fully conscious of the power it was exercising, proud to have the
eyes of the world upon it." This community, according to Heikal, had respect for
only one person — Khomeini — and was prepared "to defy President Carter or
anybody else." Heikal told Saunders, who met him on behalf of President Carter,
that the students would not kill the American hostages and the Americans did

not understand them or Khomeini.[44] Nonetheless, he passed the message to Ahmad Khomeini, the ayatollah's son.[45]

The commission met with and received testimony from a large number of what the Iranian government identified as "victims of the SAVAK and the shah," in fact mostly victims of accidents, disease, and other mishaps, who had been assembled from around the country.[46] Negotiations on the transfer of the hostages from the embassy and the control of the Students Following the Line of the Imam to the Ministry of Foreign Affairs and control of the government, however, were not successful, though at times Qotbzadeh and Bani-Sadr assumed or pretended they were. On 8 March, Khomeini at one point said he would order the transfer if the commission made a statement describing and condemning the shah's crimes and U.S. interference in internal Iranian affairs. Anxious to have the hostages transferred, President Carter, in constant contact with Villalon and Bourguet through Jordan, Saunders, and Precht, said, "The United States is not opposed to the Commission doing its duty"; according to Salinger, this was "a clear signal to the Commission that it could accept the Iranians' conditions."[47] According to Jordan, however, "The president wanted [the commission] to remain and work on the scenario if they were willing to, but not if the scenario were to be changed."[48] This also did not work. Before the commission could make a decision, Khomeini's words were broadcast over the media. Realizing they were compromised, the commission decided to leave on 9 March 1980.

Back in January, when he still felt relatively well, the shah had shown some of his old vigor and enthusiasm. In particular he welcomed the opportunity of having a major interview with a well-known media person.[49] Several applications were made by both American and European networks. On Armao's recommendation, the shah chose David Frost, with whom he spoke in mid-January. Armao also brought to Panama Christine Godek and Tom Weir, who later would interview the shah in Cairo for the official version of *Answer to History,* to help the shah prepare for the Frost interview. This was probably the first time the shah had had such assistance. However, this exercise was not what the shah needed, though he later remarked that he had never been so well prepared. In the interview he said his thing but was, as usual, careless of the effect on the audience.[50] He enjoyed the give-and-take, he said. Frost had been tough with Kissinger in an interview for NBC news. Kissinger had objected that the interview had been unfair and subsequently, when informed of the shah's scheduled interview with Frost, had warned the shah not to go through with it. The shah, however, had welcomed it as a way of responding to what he called "exaggerated fabrications" about him, his rule, and his money. In the end, he had remarked that Frost had not been tough enough. The only thing he resented was the presence of Andrew Whitley, the BBC correspondent in Iran during the revolution, who, as far as the shah was concerned, had aided the process that ended in his fall on behalf of the British government. Frost commented after the interview that the shah was more honest than most other leaders, but somewhat out of touch with reality.[51]

It was at this time that the rumor about negotiations between Panama and Iran began to circulate, gaining increasing credence. The Panamanians did not deny it; they were only following their own law, but there would be no extradition, President Royo told the shah. "We will employ a Panamanian lawyer to defend you," he said. The shah was astonished. "They do not know where Iran is, let alone what is going on in the minds of these people," the shah told the queen. "Can you imagine a Panamanian attorney defending me against the lies these people will concoct? Amazing, isn't it!"[52]

In fact, it was frightening. The shah maintained a calm and dignified bearing, but inside he felt helpless, suspicious particularly of an American ploy. As events unfolded in Iran, the United States, and Panama, the royals became increasingly insecure. The Panamanians had their shenanigans mostly aimed at keeping him in Panama. The shah saw them essentially as intermediaries for the United States—executioners on their behalf. He had been forced out of the United States because of the demands of the new Iranian government and the hope that his departure would lead to the release of the hostages. Nothing had come of it. Now, the mullahs were asking for his extradition to Iran. Would Carter give in? Was the past the prologue? The idea that he might receive a fair trial in Iran was absurd. David Frost had asked him in his interview if he would go to Iran to stand trial in a court of law to acquit himself of the charges the new Iranian government was making against him. "I have been accused of many things, but so far not of stupidity," the shah had answered. His friends in Europe and America, including a few in the media, sent him messages urging him to leave immediately. "It is very dangerous for His Majesty to remain in Panama. You must do whatever you can to get him out as soon as possible," the French newspaperman Eric Desaunois, an old family friend, called to tell the queen. Such suggestions kindled a depressing debate between the shah and the queen. Someone suggested Santo Domingo. "What difference does it make where we go?" argued the shah. "Wherever we are, it will be at the behest of the U.S. government. They will do with me what they want."

"The difference is that any move will buy us time," the queen answered. "They can't just send us back. They'll have to devise a scenario to make it palatable to their people and the world. Such machinations take time."[53]

The air became tenser as suspicions about U.S. intentions grew, the shah's physical condition deteriorated, and the royals' vulnerability became palpably obvious to everyone around. Amid this confusion, General Torrijos's secretary called on the queen. "General Torrijos knows about your interest in architecture and wishes to invite you to visit the site the government is building in a nearby island," she said. The queen was both surprised and annoyed. "You know His Majesty's illness does not allow us to make the visit at this time. We will do so as soon as his condition will allow," the queen responded. "General Torrijos knows about His Majesty's condition. He wishes you to visit the sites alone." The queen refused, thinking at the time that they might want to take her away, possibly in order to kidnap the shah or otherwise harm him. Later she read that Torrijos might have had more personal designs. "It is truly appalling. I read some such thing in Shawcross's book and I found it distressfully sad. To what miserable depths had we descended for people such as this to entertain ideas such as that in their minds! Just think of it! How cruel life—how cruel politics—can be! It simply didn't occur to me at the time."[54]

The preoccupation with the hostages rather pushed back considerations of the shah's health in U.S. debates. The shah's spleen, however, was flaring up and his condition getting progressively worse. General Torrijos had assigned his own doctor, Carlos Garcia, to attend to the shah. Dr. Kean had arranged with Dr. Adan Rios, an oncologist trained in Houston, Texas, to follow the shah's cancer. Everything went smoothly as long as the shah's health held. Once the flare-up began, the issue of hospitalization and probable surgery also flared, not only between the Panamanians and the Americans, but also among the Americans themselves. In the meantime, the queen sent word to Dr. Flandrin to return to the shah.

In Panama, Flandrin and Rios, whom Flandrin considered a competent oncologist, recommended an immediate splenectomy and on Rios' recommendation decided to ask Dr. Jean Hester of Houston, Texas, whose reputation "in matters of transfusional resuscitation," according to Flandrin, "was beyond doubt" to help with the operation. Flandrin then called Benjamin Kean in New York to inform him of the decisions they had made. Kean and Hubbard Williams now flew to Contadora, whereupon Kean announced his opposition to an immediate operation, arguing the dangers involved. The issue was taken to the shah, who upon hearing the low probability of death, less than 1 percent according to Flandrin, reaffirmed his trust in the French doctor. Kean now relented and said he would get "the greatest living surgeon," Michael DeBakey. DeBakey, of course, was probably the world's most famous surgeon in the field of cardiovascular diseases. The shah took the suggestion in stride. Flandrin was obviously familiar with the name but did not know enough about American doctors to intervene. Hester and Rios, however, objected on the ground that DeBakey had no specialization on "abdominal cancer surgery." The objection, however, was overruled, since Kean was accepted as the shah's chief doctor.

But now the Panamanians were to be brought on board, which proved difficult, not only because of Panamanian pride but also because of the negotiations going on between the Panamanians, Iranians, and Americans. On the medical level, relations between American and Panamanian doctors went sour. No immediate agreement could be reached on the hospital to perform the operation—the Gorgas at the U.S. military base or the Panamanian Paitilla, where Dr. Gaspar Garcia de Peredes reigned. Days passed. Finally Dr. DeBakey and his retinue arrived, much to the Panamanians' dislike. A debate began about who would lead the surgery, DeBakey or Garcia. Garcia called DeBakey an "itinerant physician," which DeBakey, used to fanfare wherever he went, greatly resented. Kean, for his part, gave an interview in which he implied that the Panamanians were not competent to lead the operation. The controversy became acute. The shah had been taken to Paitilla, which was surrounded by soldiers monitoring non-Panamanian doctors' movements. Soon, the fiasco hit the media. The Panamanians, the Americans, and Dr. Flandrin had a roundtable meeting at Paitilla Hospital, where after much wrangling an understanding was seemingly reached for the shah's operation to be postponed because of a respiratory problem, but it would be performed at Paitilla with Dr. DeBakey taking the lead. They then met with the shah, who received them in his room, dressed in a blue suit. He listened dispassionately to the arguments, and as the Panamanians and the Americans were leaving, he signaled Flandrin to remain behind. Did Flandrin believe he should have his operation here in Panama, he asked. "Certainly not. I have no confidence in what might happen," Flandrin replied. "That's what I think too," said the shah. Apparently so did DeBakey. A day later, on 17 March, DeBakey called Jordan to tell him that "he had never encountered anything like what I saw over the weekend in Panama. . . . I have to tell you that I have qualms about operating in Panama after the experience of the past few days." Jordan encouraged him to stay firm.[55]

The Rockefeller group had informed the government of the United States of the shah's medical predicament and pressured it to do something about the situation. Probably under Armao's prodding, McCloy sent a letter to Vance on 11 March 1980 telling him about the shah's medical condition based on reports from Kean and Flandrin and what he called the consensus of "the medical opinion" that "a prompt splenectomy was essential; that such an operation had a level of mortality rate that could reach as high as 25% even if performed in a modern medical complex under the best conditions with up-to-date equipment and surgeons."[56] This assessment of the risk, though somewhat exaggerated, in the end proved closer to the truth than Flandrin's. McCloy insisted that the U.S. government take care to provide doctors and facilities, especially if the operation was to take place in Panama, probably helping mobilize DeBakey and others.

However, the events in Panama were taking their own course. On 19 March, the White House received an intelligence report that the shah was leaving Panama. For the past few days the Iranian king and queen had gone back and forth to Paitilla and Contadora several times. As the war of the doctors flared, they encountered a wall of silence. Nobody they wanted to contact was to be found. Torrijos was out of reach—he and his secretary alike. Royo did not answer them. Their friends, especially Armao and Morse, insisted that they should get out of Panama as soon as possible, not only for medical reasons, but also for the political calamity that awaited them if they remained in Panama. After the shah's decision at Paitilla that he would not undergo surgery in Panama, the queen called Jehan Sadat, telling her of their situation. "It was surreal. I told Jehan next time to call Princess Ashraf in New York. Here they listen to our conversation—not realizing that if they did, they probably were listening to the conversation I was having with her at the time."[57]

And it was a heartrending conversation, Jehan Sadat remembered. "You must come to Egypt immediately, Farah. I will call you back with the arrangements."

Jehan Sadat called her husband, informing him of the conversation she had just had with the queen. Was she right to ask Farah and the shah to come immediately to Egypt, she asked. "There is no question, Jehan. Tell Farah I will send the presidential plane for them immediately," answered Sadat. She called Farah with the news.

"You are sure?" Farah asked, not used to good news.

"Yes, Farah. Yes."[58]

Hearing of the shah's decision to go to Egypt, President Carter dispatched Hamilton Jordan to Panama to stop him. "We've got to try to keep the shah in Panama," he said. "It will be bad for Sadat in the Arab world to have the shah there now, not to mention the reaction of the militants against the hostages if he moves again." Jordan headed out for Houston to convince DeBakey to go with him to do the operation in Panama. But the doctor would not move. His first concern had to be for the patient, he said. The hostages were the government's problem. Jordan, however, was determined. Reaching Panama without DeBakey on the 21st, he nonetheless insisted to Ambler Moss, who asked what they would do if the shah insisted on leaving, "We can't let that happen. We've got to figure out a way to keep him here." Torrijos was accommodating. Over the past two months, he had been angered by the shah's American associates complaining that the Panamanians were fleecing the monarch and by the shah's refusal to invest in Panama in partnership with Torrijos's friends. Now he offered to hold the shah in Panama by force, leaving Jordan to mull the idea over for its practical political effect. Of the three options available — Panama, Egypt, the United States — Panama seemed the least problematic place to keep the shah. But, said Jordan, "Let's try to keep him here first, then worry later about what to do if he insists on leaving." When he next saw Torrijos in the latter's office that same day, he saw Christian Bourguet sitting next to Torrijos. He was there, explained Bourguet, to finalize the extradition papers. He advised Jordan not to let the shah leave Panama under any circumstances. And he insisted that if the shah was allowed into the United States, the students would kill the hostages, a baseless threat repeated ad nauseam to scare the Americans into yielding to Khomeini's demands.[59]

Lloyd Cutler arrived in Panama on the afternoon of the 21st to join Jordan in speaking with the shah. Jordan, however, decided not to attend the meeting, since he reasoned that the chances of success were slight. Cutler and Ambassador Arnold Raphael of Vance's staff then arrived on Contadora at 9:30 P.M. Cutler insisted on seeing the shah alone, without the latter's aides being present. The queen insisted on staying in the room. "I thought they would put pressure on His Majesty, harp on the plight of the hostages, bring in a false notion of noblesse oblige, and extract from him a promise to remain in Panama, which would surely end in his death. I was adamant that we should go to Egypt."

The four of them went into the room. Ambassador Raphael began with a recitation of the shah's service to his country, his sacrifices, and his achievements. "As he spoke," remembered the queen, "I waited for him to maneuver his speech to the plane where he would tell my husband, 'You who have been so willing to sacrifice for your country should now prove more of a man by sacrificing yourself to save the American hostages.' Well, I thought, surely it is a king's duty to do what he can for his country. But it is not incumbent on him to die for the sake of a barbarous regime or for the sake of the mistakes the United States government has made and continues to make." Raphael also praised the queen for all the good work she had done in Isfahan and other Iranian cities. The queen wrote in her diary: "Does this man think I am a child?"

But Raphael did not ask the shah to sacrifice himself for the hostages. That task fell to Cutler. The queen wrote in her notebook after the meeting: "He told the shah of the moral and political weight of the hostage crisis on the US government. President Carter, he said, was very keen on having the shah come to the US for treatment. But he is weighed upon by the hostage situation and the harm that would come to the captive Americans. Houston is in the United States and the shah's going to Houston would make our task very difficult by endangering the lives of the hostages. To remove that danger, would the shah abdicate the throne?" The queen wrote in Persian *"az taj va takht este' fa bedehid."*

At this point the queen told Cutler this would not work. "You see," she said, "even if the shah abdicates, the throne shall devolve on his elder son, then on the second son, then on any number of several members of the family." She thought they might do anything, go to any length to accommodate the Islamic Republic. "Why did you leave the embassy gates open?" she asked. "Is the shah the only venue to rescue the hostages?"

"Yes. We have tried different venues," answered Cutler.

"You approach the mullahs as if they are normal people. They are not. You see them in your own image; you should not," said the shah.

"When the Iranians were normal," the queen followed her husband's discourse, "they were different from you, and you did not understand them. How do you expect to understand the mad men who now rule the country?"

"How do we go about knowing them?" asked Cutler.

"Ask the British, perhaps," responded the queen.[60]

Cutler then turned to Egypt. The shah's stay in Egypt would produce much difficulty for President Sadat, he said. President Carter was worried about him and expected to speak with him soon. To this the queen responded that Sadat was a man who knew his own mind and what he must do. The shah said he preferred Houston on medical grounds; Egypt, however, was for him a psychological haven. It was then decided that everyone present should take the issue under advisement until the next morning, when a final decision would be made. Cutler undertook to inform the White House of what had passed. Raphael described to Jordan the last moment of their stay with the royal couple. "Just as we were ready to leave," Raphael added, "the phone rang. Lloyd glanced at his watch and asked who was calling so late. The shah hung up and reported it was one of his Panamanian doctors, drunk, calling to complain that he had not paid the $1,800 bill for his most recent 'housecall.' The shah smiled. Then he said, 'You wonder why I want to leave this place?'"⁶¹

That night, neither the shah nor the queen could sleep. "Houston," confided the queen to her notebook, "means *abdiquer.* It means that tomorrow Reza, now at the university, will be shah. The poor boy will be pulled every direction possible. We haven't assigned anyone to be with him. We will be away from him. How will he manage the situation? Perhaps the Americans want this so that those Iranians who may still have hopes would lose their hopes. Egypt? That's a long way. Who knows what will happen? Who knows how His Majesty's health will hold? Who knows whether we will be able to leave Panama? There is so much whispering here and there, so many messages, so much gossip, so much coming and going, so much uncertainty that only God knows what is about to happen. Our telephone is tapped. I don't know whom to consult. The situation is so uncertain and volatile that it makes me reluctant to assert my views. Tomorrow I will be blamed for having said thus."⁶²

The shah probably never knew how close he had come to being kept in Panama. A war had begun between the White House and the State Department over the shah's destination. Carter was dead set against the shah's going to Egypt; Vance and his people were dead set against his going to the United States; Torrijos was eager to carve his name in history by keeping the shah in his power. On Saturday morning, 22 March 1980, Cutler and Jordan called the president to inform him that the shah seemed determined to leave Panama. He would have to go to the United States if he did not go to Egypt, but, said Jordan, the State Department objected to the former and argued that Sadat was already isolated in the Arab world and that one other problem would not make much difference. All this frustrated Carter and led him to call Sadat himself. "Jimm-ee, don't you worry about Egypt. You worry about your hostages," Sadat told him.⁶³ Carter relented. Now Torrijos came to visit the shah and stayed, talking to him for some time. "You will go through the grand gate with all the respect due your exalted station," said the general. "We shall place a special airplane at your disposal," he said. The royals were scheduled to leave on Monday, the 24th. When they learned that, despite Torrijos's blandishments, extradition papers would be presented that day, their flight to Egypt was rescheduled for Sunday. They were told that it was better for them to travel in an American plane to the Azores and change to an Egyptian plane there.

26

Closing in a Dream

The royal couple, accompanied by the shah's guard Colonel Jahanbini, his valet Amir Pourshoja, the American advisers Robert Armao and Mark Morse, and the queen's friend Elli Antoniades, who was visiting when the trip to Cairo suddenly came up, left Panama on Sunday, 23 March 1980, at 1:42 P.M. local time aboard a chartered Evergreen Airline DC-8. "When we crossed the Panamanian border, we breathed easy," recalled the queen. But she did not dare to speak her mind to Antoniades, afraid that the plane was bugged.

The plane was not fitted for a sick man. The shah, feverish and weak, sat covered in a blanket in a regular seat, patiently enduring his pain. When they arrived in the Azores it was dark. A delegation of dignitaries, including a Portuguese general and the American consul, was at hand to welcome the shah. The shah received them formally, standing in the middle of the plane, despite his physical condition. They were told the plane was being serviced for the rest of the trip; this took some time. The queen was suspicious. The delay seemed to her extraordinarily long. She worried about the shah because it was getting too cold inside the plane, and about what might happen to them. Wouldn't they have cleared their flight route over the airspaces they would pass before they took off from Panama? She wished she could ask the shah. He would try to allay her qualms and she would pretend to accept his judgment, but she knew she couldn't bother him with her suspicions now. The shah had told her many times that she was very strong when a crisis struck. Now, she reasoned, was no time to disabuse him of his belief in her strength of character. She found a telephone in the airbase and called her childhood friend Fereydun Javadi in Paris and the shah's adjutant Kambiz Atabai, who was with the children in New York, telling them that she and her husband were in the Azores, so at least they would know where they were last if for any reason they disappeared from the map.[1]

■

In Panama, just a few minutes after the shah's plane left, Hamilton Jordan received a call from Christian Bourguet wanting to know what had happened. "It's over, Christian — the shah has left," Jordan said, feeling half-relieved. Bourguet was upset. He told Jordan he had just talked to Qotbzadeh, who told him the Revolutionary Council was in session and they were about to take the hostages from the student militants and transfer them to the government. Something needed to be done to stop the shah. Jordan said he could stop the plane in the Azores, but he needed hard evidence. Bourguet advised him to stay in touch.

Jordan now thought of all kinds of schemes to keep the shah from reaching Egypt. The plane could be kept for some time at the U.S. base in the Azores. Carter could appeal to the shah's sense of nobility. Vance could travel to the Azores to talk to him. On the plane back to Washington he called Secretary of Defense Harold Brown and asked him if he would keep the shah's plane in the Azores for a while, until he called him back. Brown agreed without asking any questions, assuming the idea had been cleared with the president. Jordan then called Bourguet to ask what was happening in Iran. Bourguet sounded excited: "It is about to happen, Hamilton — the Revolutionary Council is meeting this very minute. Ghotbzadeh just left the meeting to take my call and asked how much time he had to make the transfer public. It is about to happen."[2]

But in Iran events were not proceeding as Bourguet wanted Jordan to believe. In Washington, Brown informed Jordan that the shah's plane had landed in the Azores, had refueled, and was now awaiting Brown's permission to take off. Jordan frantically called Ambler Moss and Christian Bourguet in Panama. He was told that things in Tehran had fallen through. The scheme for holding the shah in the Azores, Bourguet told him, would not work. Jordan called Brown and "gave clearance for the shah's plane to leave the Azores."[3]

■

The plane carrying the shah from the Azores arrived in Cairo on the 24th of March. As it landed, the shah noticed President Sadat standing with the Egyptian dignitaries and an honor guard waiting to receive him. His eyes filled with tears. As he descended the stairs, Jehan Sadat noticed how thin, weak, and gaunt he had become, his suit looking two sizes too large. But he carried himself with dignity.[4] When he reached the last step, Sadat came forward. "Thank God you are safe," he said, and they embraced.[5] "I have done nothing for you," the shah said to Sadat as he was being taken to Maʿadi Military Hospital on the Nile, just outside Cairo, "yet you are the only one to accept me with dignity."[6] Sadat's unique sense of chivalry was indeed indisputable, though the shah was too modest: he had in fact done much in the past to help Sadat economically, politically, and militarily.

Four days after the shah was admitted to the hospital, Dr. DeBakey and his American team arrived in Cairo and, assisted by Egyptian doctors, removed the shah's spleen. It was the size of a football and weighed four and a half pounds, several times the size and weight of a normal spleen. The operation seemed successful and everyone in the operation room clapped as DeBakey finished and exited the room. But it was not flawless. According to an Egyptian doctor assisting DeBakey, the extremity of the pancreas had been injured. The basic problem, however, was that "the spleen was full of nodules indicating localizations of large cell lymphoma." This, according to Flandrin, suggested that "the liver was the site of periportal nodular lesions of the same kind."[7]

The shah, however, seemed to be recovering despite persistent pain in the lower left region of his body. He was allowed to move out of the hospital to the Kubbah, the kingly palace to the north of Cairo that Sadat had placed at the royal family's disposal. His children now also came to Cairo, and the younger ones were enrolled in school. Like most other patients in his situation, the shah also had his good and bad days. But he seemed to enjoy the quiet, the security, and the children, especially his older daughter, Farahnaz, whom he adored. "When she entered the room, his mind would turn to her, totally absorbed in her being there. That was the only time we could win from him," observed Fereydun Javadi, who played cards with the shah for chips.[8]

The children put on a good face, but they were deeply hurt. They knew this man for the loving, caring father he had been to them. They now heard things they could not believe. Their father was vilified beyond recognition, called names they did not recognize, accused of having committed crimes worthy of the worst people—the Attilas of this world. Why had this happened? Why are we in this situation? What have we done to deserve this? Whose fault is it? They loved their father for who he had been; they hated the conditions in which they lived. The older ones secretly blamed him for having been too despotic, too democratic, too hard, too soft. They did not know. They knew it was somebody's fault, and felt guilty when their thoughts turned on their father.

At the Kubbah, the shah received friends and some Iranians, including his generals, who were planning to put up a fight against Khomeini. In 1980, the situation in Iran was still fluid; many who had supported the revolution had not bargained for an Islamist society. Many of the officers and NCOs remained loyal to the shah and their former commanders. The fight against Khomeini was not devoid of logic; but the situation could not be reversed by using the same logic that had brought it about. And this remained the dilemma of the shah, who understood it, but did not know how to respond to it. Back in Panama, he had told David Frost with surprising honesty that he did not know why things had happened the way they had. And now, he could not advise honestly the Oveisis and Arianas and other former commanders who came once again to receive orders and guidance.

And there was the question of succession. Nobody had the heart to bring it up, but as his health deteriorated and it became increasingly clear that his liver also was becoming cancerous, the question assumed greater urgency. His older son, Reza, had told his mother he was ready to take his father's mantle when the time came and was proud to carry it forward in the same spirit of love for the country that his grandfather and father had harbored. For counsel on how to proceed, he and the queen sought President Sadat. "Ask the king," Sadat advised, "who are the men he would like to have around him today. For Reza, just naming these men will be like a legacy from his father. He will be able to call on them in the future; they will show him the way as his father would have done if his health had permitted."[9] The shah identified three men: his chief of protocol, Amir Aslan Afshar; his chief of special bureau, Nosratollah Moinian; and his minister of war, General Reza Azimi—none of whom was later approached by the young prince.[10]

In late May, when he felt better, the shah had a series of conversations on the final, authoritative edition of his book *Answer to History* with two editors provided by the Rockefeller organization—Tom Weir and Christine Godek.[11] He felt well enough to speak for hours, maintaining his composure and focus. Soon afterward, however, his condition worsened, his pain increased, and his body weakened. The Egyptian and American doctors attending him diagnosed pneumonia and prescribed high doses of antibiotics, to no effect. Late in June, the queen called Flandrin, who had been away from the shah's case since the operation in March. He was asked to go to Cairo with an internist. In Cairo, Flandrin and his companion found the shah still spirited enough to joke about Flandrin's age. However, he was clearly in bad physical shape, his pulmonary problems connected to "subdiaphragmatic infection." They sought a surgeon in Paris and were put in contact with Dr. Pierre-Louis Fragniez, who agreed to go to Cairo to perform the needed surgery. The operation was again declared a success as Fragniez drained a liter and a half of pus and necrosed pancreas debris.[12] The body reacted positively. In a day or two the shah began to feel better. People went in to see him and pay their respects. Others read books to him, which he greatly enjoyed, especially when Fereydun Javadi, who had been educated in France, read English books in his thick French accent to make him laugh.[13] After a few days more he began to walk, and everyone, including Princess Ashraf, who had come to Cairo at the same time, began to hope that he might survive. On 26 July the queen sent the younger children to Alexandria for a day or two to get them away from the depressing atmosphere of the hospital. That same night the shah lapsed into a coma. Apparently the cancer, untreated since Mexico, was reasserting itself.

July 1980 corresponded with Ramadan, the lunar month of fasting, and in the evening, the fast being strictly observed in Egypt, almost everyone, including the shah's doctors, went away for *iftar,* the breaking of the fast. When Flandrin, Fragniez, and their resuscitator arrived at the hospital a little after the *iftar,* they immediately realized that something was wrong. They rushed to the shah and found the queen, Princess Ashraf, and the others standing stunned around the comatose patient. They began to work, raising the blood pressure and restoring the heartbeat. But they knew it was the end. Flandrin advised the queen and Princess Ashraf that there was not much hope. The children, certainly the older ones, needed to be called back. The queen asked Flandrin to make the call. "I will never manage it," she murmured.

The shah was resuscitated for a few hours, during which time he was able to speak to the crown prince, his wife, his twin sister, and his other children. Flandrin wrote to Bernard:

> I remember in particular the poignant scene of the older girl, Farahnaz, kneeling close to the right side of the bed, holding her father's hand and kissing it, with a kind of ecstatic smile on her face as she repeated in Persian, "Baba, Baba." On the left side of the bed, we continued to watch the arterial blood pressure and to pump blood. We did only what was necessary, and the king passed away peacefully in the morning. While I was there, H.M. the Queen withdrew a little bag of Iranian soil from under the pillow of the deceased—they had brought it with them when they went into exile.[14]

The monarch died with his wife, his children, his sister, and his valet Amir Pourshoja around him. "He breathed quickly twice, then drew a long breath and stopped." It was 9:45 in the morning of 27 July 1980. Pourshoja began to cry. Others stood dazed. Then Princess Ashraf, standing next to the queen at the bottom of the bed, whispered "Close his eyes." The queen closed her husband's eyes and then took from under his pillow the little bag of Iranian soil Flandrin had noted and the cloth bag of prayers the shah had carried all his life. The queen then asked Dr. Liusa Pirnia to take off the shah's wedding ring and give it to her. Then all left the room, to return singly to say their last farewell.[15]

◼

The funeral was scheduled for the 29th. On the 28th, Ardeshir Zahedi and Amir Aslan Afshar attended a meeting at the office of the Egyptian president's chief of protocol at the Abedin Palace to discuss the details of the ceremony. It was decided that the sarcophagus would be carried on a caisson followed by detachments of a hundred soldiers each from the Egyptian ground, air, and sea forces. The two Iranians were asked how many officers were required to carry the king's medals ahead of the coffin. The shah's two valets—Eliasi and Pourshoja—had on their own initiative brought all of the shah's medals, forty-five in number, though initially the instruction had been that the monarch was leaving Iran only for a short time. But Zahedi and Afshar decided that only three decorations would be used: Egypt's Nile, carried in the center, with Iran's Zolfaqar and Pahlavi on either side. The shah's medals were the highest offered and came mainly from countries that had refused him in his hour of need. His loyal officers determined that they would not be carried in a place of honor.

It was three miles from the Abedin Palace, where the funeral march began, to the el-Rifa'i Mosque, where the shah would be buried. It was a hot summer day, but the funeral moved with pomp and grace. "No state funeral was grander," wrote Jehan Sadat. Students from Egypt's military academy led the procession, playing instruments and dressed in uniforms of white, yellow, and black according to their rank; then soldiers carrying wreaths of roses and irises; then officers mounted on horseback; then the shah's military decorations on black velvet pillows; then the coffin draped in the Iranian flag on a military caisson drawn by eight Arabian horses. Behind the caisson walked the procession: the shah's family, a handful of Iranians, Richard Nixon, former king Constantine of Greece, and a few ambassadors; the rest were Egyptians. The event was a signature of President Sadat's unique sense of personal honor. As Jehan Sadat wrote, "The music was louder than any they had ever heard. There were more flowers than anyone had ever imagined. It was the most spectacular funeral that any of us in Egypt had ever seen, and the last chance to show the world that the Shah deserved better than the way he had been treated. Egypt, at least, had not turned her back on a friend."[16]

IRAN'S PRIME MINISTERS UNDER THE SHAH
AUGUST 1941 – FEBRUARY 1979

ALLIED OCCUPATION AND THE AZERBAIJAN CRISIS
1941 – 1948

Mohammad Ali Forughi	August 1941 – March 1942
Ali Soheili	March – July 1942
Ahmad Qavam	August 1942 – February 1943
Ali Soheili	February 1943 – March 1944
Mohammad Sa'ed	March – November 1944
Mortezaqoli Bayat	November 1944 – April 1945
Ebrahim Hakimi	May – June 1945
Mohsen Sadr	June – October 1945
Ebrahim Hakimi	October 1945 – January 1946
Ahmad Qavam	January 1946 – December 1947
Ebrahim Hakimi	December 1947 – June 1948
Abdolhossein Hazhir	June – November 1948

NATIONALIZATION OF OIL
1948 – 1954

Mohammad Sa'ed	November 1948 – March 1950
Ali Mansur	March – June 1950
Lieutenant General Haji Ali Razmara	June 1950 – March 1951
Hossein Ala	March – April 1951
Mohammad Mosaddeq	April 1951 – July 1952
Ahmad Qavam	17 – 21 July 1952
Mohammad Mosaddeq	July 1952 – August 1953

PREPARING FOR SOCIAL AND ECONOMIC DEVELOPMENT
1954 – 1962

Lieutenant General Fazlollah Zahedi	August 1953 – April 1955
Hossein Ala	April 1955 – April 1957
Manuchehr Eqbal	April 1957 – August 1960
Ja'far Sharif-Emami	August 1960 – May 1961
Ali Amini	May 1961 – July 1962

GALLOPING FORWARD
1962 – 1976

Amir Asadollah Alam	July 1962 – March 1964
Hassanali Mansur	March 1964 – January 1965
Amir Abbas Hoveyda	January 1965 – August 1977

THE REVOLUTION
1976 – 1979

Jamshid Amouzegar	August 1977 – August 1978
Ja'far Sharif-Emami	August – November 1978
General Gholamreza Azhari	November – December 1978
Shapur Bakhtiar	December 1978 – February 1979

PRINCIPLES OF IRAN'S WHITE REVOLUTION

The original six points, announced by the shah on 9 January 1963 and endorsed by national referendum on 26 January 1963:

1. Land reform
2. Nationalization of forests
3. Sale of state-owned enterprises to the public
4. Workers' profit sharing in 20 percent of net corporate earnings
5. Voting and political rights for women
6. Formation of the Literacy Corps

Additional three points, 1964–65:

7. Formation of the Health Corps, 21 January 1964
8. Formation of the Reconstruction and Development Corps, 23 September 1964
9. Establishment of Houses of Equity, 13 October 1964

Additional three points, 6 October 1967:

10. Nationalization of water resources
11. Urban and rural reconstruction
12. Administrative and educational revolution

Additional five points, 1975:

13. Employee and public ownership (up to 99 percent in state-owned enterprises and 49 percent in private firms), 9 September 1975
14. Price stabilization and campaign against profiteering, 9 September 1975
15. Free education and daily meal for all children from kindergarten to eighth grade, 12 December 1975
16. Nutrition support for pregnant women and for infants up to the age of two, 25 December 1975
17. Nationwide social security for all, 25 December 1975

Additional two points, 17 October 1977:

18. Land price appreciation not to exceed inflation
19. High government officials to declare their own, wife's, and children's wealth

LOUIS G. DREYFUS (18 December 1940 – 12 December 1943). Dreyfus served in Iran during the Allied occupation. He and his wife were much admired, especially for Mrs. Dreyfus's charity work. He was removed under British and Soviet pressure.

LELAND B. MORRIS (21 August 1944 – 20 May 1945). Morris had been ambassador to Germany when Germany declared war on 11 December 1941. During his stay in Iran, Reza Shah died in exile, and the Soviets began pressuring Iran for oil.

WALLACE S. MURRAY (5 June 1945 – 18 April 1946). Murray was ill during most of his tenure and served with little effect.

GEORGE V. ALLEN (11 May 1946 – 17 February 1948). Allen served during the Azerbaijan crisis, a crucial period for Iran and the region as the Cold War was taking shape. He told the shah that the United States would not go to war with the Soviet Union over Iran but Iran could and should take advantage of the Truman Doctrine. Allen's unpublished manuscript detailing his service in Iran is held by the Truman Library in Independence, Missouri.

JOHN C. WILEY (6 April 1948 – 18 June 1950). Wiley had been ambassador to Colombia (1944 – 47) and Portugal (1947 – 48) before he was posted to Iran. During his stay in Iran, the shah escaped an attempt on his life (4 February 1949); a Constitutional Assembly gave the shah new power to dissolve the National Consultative Assembly, or Majlis, and the Senate (8 May 1949); a series of preliminary oil negotiations known as Gass-Golshaiyan was launched; Court Minister Abdolhossein Hazhir was assassinated (4 November 1949); and the first Senate and the Sixteenth Majlis, one of the most tumultuous assemblies in Iranian history, were convened (9 February 1950).

HENRY F. GRADY (2 July 1950 – 19 September 1951). Grady had served in India when it gained independence and then in Greece before he was posted to Iran. Grady's term coincided with the assassination of Prime Minister Haji Ali Razmara, nationalization of oil, and appointment of Mohammad Mosaddeq as prime minister. Grady, viscerally favoring the underdog, inadvertently conveyed his own disposition as that of the U.S. government to Premier Mosaddeq as the struggle for the nationalization of Iranian oil was gaining momentum.

LOY W. HENDERSON (29 September 1951–30 December 1954). Henderson served in one of the most tumultuous periods in Iran's recent history. He was the West's main interlocutor with Premier Mosaddeq during the nationalization struggle, especially after Mosaddeq severed relations with England in 1952. He is implicated in the events that led to Mosaddeq's fall in August 1953. The Consortium Agreement was made when he served in Iran.

SELDEN CHAPIN (19 July 1955–2 June 1958). Chapin had served as ambassador in Hungary, the Netherlands, and Panama before he was posted to Iran. Iran joined the U.S.-sponsored Baghdad Pact during the first year of his service in Iran.

EDWARD T. WAILES (19 July 1958–9 June 1961). Wailes arrived in Iran only a few days after the Iraqi monarchy was overthrown in a bloody coup on 14 July 1958. The Baghdad Pact, formally the Middle East Treaty Organization (METO), with headquarters in Baghdad, became the Central Treaty Organization (CENTO) in August 1959, with headquarters in Ankara, Turkey. The fall of the monarchy in Iraq exacerbated Iran's relations with the Arab Middle East.

JULIUS C. HOLMES (17 June 1961–13 March 1965). Holmes served in Iran soon after John F. Kennedy took office in the United States and the shah launched the White Revolution. He generally took the shah's side as tensions ebbed and flowed between Iran and the United States, mostly on defense and human rights issues. He was in Iran as the economy began to take off and the shah's power gelled. Also, it was during his service that the Status of Forces bill, passed in October 1964, was imposed on Iran, which became an issue endlessly haunting the shah and his government. Because of it, Prime Minister Hassanali Mansur was assassinated on 21 January 1965, and the shah narrowly escaped an assassination attempt on 10 April of the same year.

ARMIN H. MEYER (27 April 1965–30 May 1969). Meyer was appointed ambassador to Iran shortly after Lyndon Johnson, with whom the shah got along far better than with Kennedy, had won the presidency in a landslide. Meyer became an advocate for the shah, believing that the shah had become powerful and self-confident enough to maneuver between the East and the West and that a military relationship had become the linchpin of U.S.-Iranian alliance.

DOUGLAS MACARTHUR II (13 October 1969–17 February 1972). A nephew of General Douglas MacArthur and a senior diplomat, MacArthur was posted to Iran a few months after Richard Nixon had become president. By the end of his term of service in Iran, the shah and Nixon had become strategic allies. MacArthur became a devotee of the shah, relaying to his government mainly the shah's wishes. He narrowly escaped a kidnapping attempt by the Mojahedin Khalq as he was being driven in his car in Tehran in 1971.

JOSEPH S. FARLAND (21 May 1972–10 March 1973). A few days after Farland's appointment, President Nixon arrived in Tehran from Moscow, where he had signed SALT I and negotiated superpower interaction in the Middle East, to seek the shah's help.

RICHARD HELMS (5 April 1973–27 December 1976). Helms's appointment led to controversy in both Washington and Tehran. As a former director of the CIA, he was the highest-ranked American to be nominated as ambassador to Tehran. On the other hand, it was hard for Iranians to adjust to the idea of a career CIA person being posted to their country, especially when it was alleged that Helms had helped set in motion the coup d'état against Salvadore Allende of Chile in September 1973. (When he was asked later in congressional hearings about the CIA's role, he lied, for which he was eventually prosecuted and convicted, though he did not serve his sentence.) Nixon sent Helms to Iran to get him out of the United States, and the shah accepted him partly to please Nixon and partly to benefit from the vast body of secrets he assumed Helms possessed. Helms, for his part, tried to please the shah. The shah launched the Rastakhiz Party in 1975 and declared the "open political space" in 1976 when Helms was ambassador in Iran.

WILLIAM H. SULLIVAN (18 June 1977–6 April 1979). Sullivan was the last U.S. ambassador in Iran during the shah's reign. Previously he had served as ambassador in Laos (1966–69) and the Philippines (1973–77). His term of service in Iran corresponded with the presidency of Jimmy Carter in the United States and the Islamic revolution and the fall of the shah in Iran. He has documented his experience in Iran in a book titled *Mission to Iran.*

BRIEF CHRONOLOGY
OF THE PAHLAVI DYNASTY

REZA KHAN, REZA SHAH PAHLAVI

15 March 1878	Born in Tehran
1903	Married Tajmah (d. 1904)
1904	Daughter Fatemeh born; later titled Hamdam Saltaneh by Ahmad Shah
?	Second marriage; circumstances not known; no children
1916	Married Nimtaj; later titled Taj-ul-Moluk, the Queen Pahlavi
1917	Daughter Shams born (d. 1996)
26 October 1919	Twins born: son Mohammad Reza (later crown prince and shah) and daughter Ashraf
22 February 1921	Led a coup d'état
27 February 1921	Titled Sardar Sepah (Commander of the Army)
24 April 1921	Appointed minister of war
1922	Son Alireza born (d. 1955)
	Married Turan (Qamar-ul-Moluk) Amir Soleimani (divorced 1923)
1923	Son Gholamreza born to Turan
	Married Esmat Dowlatshahi (5 children)
26 October 1923	Appointed prime minister
1924	Son Abdorreza born (d. 2001)
1925	Son Ahmadreza born (d. 1981)
15 December 1925	Crowned king
1926	Son Mahmudreza born (d. 1999)
1930	Daughter Fatemeh born (d. 1989)
1932	Son Hamidreza born (d. 1992)

16 September 1941	Resigned and went into exile after the Allied invasion
26 July 1944	Died, Johannesburg, South Africa

MOHAMMAD REZA SHAH

26 October 1919	Born in Tehran, with twin sister, Ashraf
17 December 1925	Pronounced crown prince
1931–36	Studied in Switzerland
1939	Married Princess Fawzieh bint Fuad of Egypt
27 October 1940	Daughter Shahnaz born
17 September 1941	Took oath as king under Allied occupation
1948	Divorced from Fawzieh
4 February 1950	Survived assassination attempt
1951	Married Soraya Esfandiary Bakhtiari
1952–53	Challenged by Prime Minister Mosaddeq; left Iran under duress 16 August 1953; returned 22 August
1958	Divorced from Soraya
1959	Married Farah Diba
31 October 1960	Son Reza Cyrus (crown prince) born
26 January 1963	Launched the White Revolution
12 March 1963	Daughter Farahnaz born
10 April 1965	Survived assassination attempt
15 September 1965	Titled Aryamehr (Light of the Aryans) by the legislative houses in joint session
28 April 1966	Son Alireza born
26 October 1967	Crowned himself and the queen in formal ceremony
27 March 1970	Daughter Leila born (d. 10 June 2001)
October 1971	Celebrated anniversary of twenty-five hundred years of Iranian monarchy
1973	Replaced the Consortium Agreement on oil with Sales and Purchase Agreement
1975	Established Rastakhiz, the Resurrection Party
1976	Launched "open political space" policy
1978–79	Faced Islamic revolution; left Iran 16 January 1979
1979	Deposed in exile
27 July 1980	Died in Egypt of cancer

NOTES

CPUSEDD   Center for the Publication of the United States
Espionage Den's Documents. Established by the
students who took over the U.S. embassy during
the hostage crisis, the center has published a series
of reconstituted documents seized from the embassy,
collectively called Asnad-e laneh-ye jasusi, or Documents from the U. S. Espionage Den. Each collection
of documents has been published as a book with a
number and a title. In the present volume, each book
is cited in the following order: Students Following the
Line of the Imam, [number], title [italicized] (Tehran:
CPUSEDD, date), page.

FIS   Foundation for Iranian Studies

FISOHA   Foundation for Iranian Studies' Oral History Archives,
located at the Foundation for Iranian Studies headquarters in Bethesda, Maryland. English interviews
are available also at Columbia University's Oral History Research Office in New York and the Hoover
Institution in Stanford, California. Tapes of most
interviews may be listened to for research purposes
on the FIS Web site at http://www.fis-iran.org

FO   See PRO FO.

FRUS   Foreign Relations of the United States, located in the
Department of State and the National Archives and
Records Administration (NARA; www.archives.gov/
locations). The documents for the period 1964–68
(Johnson administration) are on the State Department's
Web site at http://www.state.gov/www/about_state/
history/vol_xxii/index.html

Gahnameh	*Gahnameh-ye panjah sal shahanshahi-e pahlavi* [Chronology of Daily Events of Fifty Years of the Pahlavi Monarchy] is a monumental work undertaken in the 1970s in the Pahlavi Library in Tehran by an editorial board headed by Mahmud Raja and supervised by Shoja'eddin Shafa, deputy court minister for cultural affairs. The work, recording the Pahlavi shahs' daily activities in political, military, economic, and social events from 3 Esfand 1299 (22 February 1921) to 30 Esfand 1355 (21 March 1977), was concluded in 1977; ten thousand copies of the 3-volume series were printed in the fall of 1978. However, in February 1979, shortly after the revolution, Islamists invaded the library and destroyed every copy of the *Gahnameh,* except the three volumes Shafa had taken with him to Paris for his own research. Shafa's series was reproduced in five volumes by Soheil Publications in Paris in 1985.
PRO FO	Public Records Office, Foreign Office documents, United Kingdom. The documents used in this volume are mainly from the political category identified by number 371. The number following 371 refers to the document's location. Thus, PRO FO 371/170381 EP 103138 refers to a political document in box/location 170381 related to Eastern Department, specifically Persia (Iran).
Ruzshomar	*Ruzshomar-e tarikh-e iran* [Chronology of the History of Iran], a 2-volume chronology of events from the signing of the Constitution Decree by Mozffareddin Shah Qajar on 13 Mordad 1285 (5 August 1906) to the declaration of neutrality by the military on 22 Bahman 1357 (11 February 1979), authored by Baqer Aqeli and published in Tehran by Nashr-e Goftar in 1372 (1993). Whereas *Gahnameh* focuses on the two Pahlavi shahs and the royal family, *Ruzshomar,* published after the revolution, is mainly concerned with nonroyal players. The one, therefore, complements the other.

ORAL HISTORY REFERENCES

Interviews conducted specifically for this book are identified as "Interview with [name]." When reference is made to transcribed interviews, the page number is cited; when reference is made to oral interviews that have not been transcribed, the tape number and side are cited.

WORKS IN PERSIAN

For most works in Persian, the Islamic solar calendar year (or in some cases the Persian Empire year) of publication is given, followed by the Gregorian year in brackets.

PREFACE

1. See Reinhold Niebuhr, *The Irony of American History* (London: Scribner, 1952), ix – xi, quote at x; and James H. Billington, *The Icon and the Axe: An Interpretive History of Russian Culture* (New York: Vintage Books, 1970), 590.

2. The "Documents from the U.S. Espionage Den" are documents that were seized during the occupation of the U.S. embassy in Tehran in the hostage crisis of 1979–80 by a group of young revolutionaries known as Students Following the Line of the Imam [Khomeini] and later reconstituted and published by the students in a series books or booklets. (See CPUSEDD in Abbreviations, above.) *Iranian Contemporary History* is a quarterly journal publishing documents retrieved from various Pahlavi- and pre-Pahlavi-era archives as well as articles based on these documents. The journal is a publication of the Institute for Iranian Contemporary Historical Studies.

1. THE FATHER

1. Mohammad Hasan Etemad-Saltaneh, *Tarikh-e montazam-e naseri* [Naseri History] (Tehran: n.p., 1298 HQ [1880]), 16. Seyyed Hasan Taqizadeh, "Qazzaq-e iran" [Iran's Cossacks], in *Kaveh,* collected issues 1916 – 22, 2 parts (Tehran: Offset Company, 1977), part 1, 25.

2. See Fereydun Adamiayat, *Ideolozhi-ye nehzat-e mashrutiat-e iran* [The Ideology of Iran's Constitutional Revolution] (Tehran: Entesharat-e payam, 2535 [1976]), chap. 5.

3. Nikki Keddie and Mehrdad Amanat, "Iran under the Later Qâjârs, 1848 – 1922," in *The Cambridge History of Iran,* 7 vols. (Cambridge: Cambridge University Press, 1991), 7: 174 – 212, quote at 187.

4. Edward G. Browne, *The Persian Revolution 1905 – 1909* (Cambridge: Cambridge University Press, 1910), 113.

5. Keddie and Amanat, "Iran under the Later Qâjârs," 203, give twelve thousand; *Ruzshomar,* 1:26, has twenty thousand.

6. The classes named by the shah were abolished by the electoral law of 1 July 1909.

7. Reza Niazmand, *Reza Shah as tavallod ta saltanat* [Reza Shah from Birth to Kingship] (Bethesda, Md.: FIS, 1996), 70.

8. Malek-u-Sho'ara Bahar, *Tarikh-e mokhtasar-e ahzab-e siyasi-e iran* [A Brief History of Iran's Political Parties] (Tehran: Amir Kabir, 1357 [1978]; orig. pub. 1321 [1942]), 16. Ahmadali Sepehr, *Iran dar jang-e bozorg* [Iran in the Great War] (Tehran: 1366 [1978]), 14.

9. Quoted in Aryeh Y. Yodfat, *The Soviet Union and Revolutionary Iran* (New York: St. Martin's Press, 1984), 6.

10. George Buchanan, *My Mission to Russia and Other Diplomatic Memoirs,* 2 vols. (Boston: Little, Brown, and Co., 1923), 1: 169; quoted in Yodfat, *Soviet Union and Revolutionary Iran,* 8.

11. See Cyrus Ghani, *Iran and the Rise of Reza Shah* (London and New York: L. B. Tauris, 1988), 164; Niazmand, *Reza Shah,* 158 – 62; Donald N. Wilber, *Riza Shah Pahlavi: The Resurrection and Reconstruction of Iran, 1878 – 1944* (Hicksville, N.Y.: Exposition Press, 1975), 12.

12. Letter to Reza Niazmand from Abbas Malayeri, Sheykh Abolqasem's son, July 1990; quoted in Niazmand, *Reza Shah,* 183.

13. The 1919 Agreement is an unhappy event in Iranian history, and much has been written about it. The most reliably documented account is Ghani, *Rise of Reza Shah,* chaps. 1–5.

14. Ath Thawra al Iraqiyya al Kubra, the Great Iraqi Revolution, as the 1920 rebellion is called, which was crucial in the British decision to withdraw from Iran, was also of course a watershed event in contemporary Iraqi history. For the first time, Sunnis and Shias, tribes and cities, were brought together in a common effort. In the opinion of Hanna and John Batatu, coauthors of a seminal work on Iraq, the building of a nation-state in Iraq depended upon two major factors: the integration of Shias and Sunnis into the new body politic and the successful resolution of the age-old conflicts between the tribes and the riverine cities and among the tribes themselves over the food-producing flatlands of the Tigris and the Euphrates. The 1920 rebellion brought these groups together, if only briefly, an important first step in the long and arduous process of forging a nation-state out of Iraq's conflict-ridden social structure. The revolt had been very costly to the British in both manpower and money, putting Whitehall under domestic pressure to devise a formula that would provide the maximum control over Iraq at the least cost to the British taxpayer, a condition Norman must have been familiar with as he tackled the Iranian question. See Hanna Batatu and John Batatu, *The Old Social Classes and the Revolutionary Movements of Iraq* (Princeton: Princeton University Press, 1982).

15. *Ruzshomar,* 1: 137–38.

16. Saffari's remembrances in Ebrahim Safai, ed., *Reza Shah dar ayeneh-ye khaterat* [Reza Shah in the Mirror of Remembrances] (Los Angeles: n.p., 1986; orig. pub. Tehran: Ministry of Culture 1354 [1975]), 250–57.

17. Niazmand, *Reza Shah,* 180.

18. *Pahlavan,* strongman or champion, is derived from the Old Persian word *pahlaw,* meaning *strong, brave,* or *champion.* Pahlavi, which Reza Shah took as his last name, and Pahlavan, which was assumed as a last name by certain of Reza Shah's relatives, are derived from the same root. In the Sasanian period (226 B.C.E. to 651 C.E.) the heads of several major families adopted this title. See Mohammad Moin, *Farhang-e moin* [Moin Dicitonary], 2 vols. (Tehran: Amir Kabir, 1353 [1974]), 1: 846–48.

19. Herman C. Norman to Lord Curzon, 24 June 1920, PRO FO 371/3874.

20. Norman to Curzon, 3 January 1921, in Rohan Butler and J. P. T. Bury, eds., *Documents on British Foreign Policy, 1919–1930* (London: HMSO, 1963), doc. no. 626; quoted also in Ghani, *Rise of Reza Shah,* 129.

21. Niazmand, *Reza Shah,* 197–99.

22. Richard H. Ullman, *The Anglo-Soviet Accord 1917–1921* (Princeton: Princeton University Press, 1972) 3: 388; quoted in Ghani, *Rise of Reza Shah,* 179.

23. Ahmad Amir Ahmadi, *Khaterat-e nakhostin sepahbod-e iran* [Memoirs of the First Lieutenant General of Iran, Ahmad Amir Ahmadi] (Tehran: 1373 [1994]), 164–71; see also Ghani, *Rise of Reza Shah,* 169–70; Niazmand, *Reza Shah,* 244–45.

24. Major General Sir Edmund Ironside, *High Road to Command: The Diaries 1920–22* (London: Cooper, 1972), 161; quoted in Ghani, *Rise of Reza Shah,* 154–55.

25. Gholam Hossein Mirza Saleh, ed., *Reza Shah: Khaterat-e Soleyman Behbudi, Shams Pahlavi, Ali Izadi* [Memoirs of Soleyman Behbudi, Shams Pahlavi, Ali Izadi] (Tehran: Sahba, 1372 [1993]), 46.

26. Seyyed Hassan Taqizadeh, "Doreh-ye jadid" [The New Cycle], *Kaveh* 5, 36 (22 January 1920): 2.

27. Malek-u-shoara Bahar, *Tarikh-e ahzab-e siyasi-e iran* [A History of Iranian Political Parties] (Tehran: Amir Kabir, 1357 [1978]), 12.

28. Jamshid Behnam, "Dowlat-mellat, huviyyat-e fardi, va tajaddud" [Nation-State, Individual Identity, and Modernity], *Iran Nameh* 18, 4 (fall 2000): 375–86, at 378.

29. Ali Akbar Siassi, *Gozaresh-e yek zendegi* [Report of a Life] (London: n.p., 1363 [1984]), 76.

30. See Shahrokh Meskoob, "Melli-gera'i, tamarkoz va farhang dar ghorub-e qajarieh va tolu'e pahlavi" [Nationalism, Centralization, and Culture at the Twilight of Qajarieh and the Dawn of Pahlavi], *Iran Nameh* 12, 3 (summer 1994): 479–508; at 499.

31. M. Farrokh, *Khaterat-e siyasi-e Farrokh* [The Political Memoirs of Farrokh] (Tehran: Sahami Press, 1348 [1969]; cited in Niazmand, *Reza Shah,* 388.

32. Mehdiqoli Hedayat, *Khaterat va khatarat* [Memoirs and Dangers] (Tehran: Zawwar Press, 1363 [1984]), 364.

33. Ghani, *Rise of Reza Shah,* chap. 13.

2. FATHER AND SON

1. Interview with Princess Ashraf Pahlavi, New York, 3 February 2001, tape 1, side 1.

2. "Khaterat-e Soleyman Behbudi" [Memoir of Soleyman Behbudi], in *Reza Shah: Khaterat-e Soleyman Behbudi, Shams Pahlavi, Ali Izadi* [Memoirs of Soleyman Behbudi, Shams Pahlavi, Ali Izadi], ed. Gholam Hossein Mirza Saleh (Tehran: Sahba, 1372 [1993]), 32.

3. In the 1970s in the royal court the rumor was that the CIA had produced a psychological profile of the shah based mainly on the information given them by Marvin Zonis and James Bill, much of it taken from their books. According to this profile, the shah lacked self-confidence because of childhood experiences with a disciplined, stern, and forceful father who had sapped his ability to stand on his own feet. Queen Farah's friends had never suspected before, even remotely, that the shah was indecisive. Indeed, they were struck by his grasp of every issue and his ability to decide and to dispose of it. Fereydun Javadi, the queen's childhood friend, brought this matter out in one of his conversations with the shah in exile. "This is what they are saying, Your Majesty." The shah made the answer quoted. Interview with Fereydun Javadi, Bethesda, Md., 9 November 2003, tape 2, side 1. In fact, Reza Khan could not help but yield to his son's whims, a soft spot his associates quickly detected and used to advantage. Soleiman Behbudi, Reza Khan's sometime secretary and chronicler, recalls the case of master builder Ali Mohammad Sanei, the architect overseeing the construction of a house intended for Mohammad Reza, ingratiating himself to the young boy by bringing him toys. According to Behbudi, a false accusation landed the architect in jail, but he was released by Reza Khan's order after his son interceded with his tears. "Khaterat-e Soleiman Behbudi," 7.

4. Interview with Princess Ashraf, tape 1, side 1.

5. Ashraf Pahlavi, *Faces in a Mirror: Memoirs from Exile* (Englewood Cliffs, N.J.: Prentice-Hall, 1980), 15–16.

6. Soleiman Behbudi tells the story of the illness and the cure: "Early in His Majesty

Reza Shah's reign, His Highness the Crown Prince caught typhoid. The shah and the queen naturally were extremely worried and unhappy. The prince liked me and often asked me to stay and talk to him. So everyday I spent some time with him. On one of the days his fever was very high, His Majesty came in the room and seeing his son so ill, he became desperate, the pain he felt showing on his face. After a while, when he returned to his personal residence, the prince's condition worsened, the fever increased, and he fell, it seemed, into a coma, unable to keep his eyes open. Some time passed. Then I saw that he was sweating profusely on his forehead and body. Then, suddenly, he woke, a smile on his face, and said: 'I have become well. I saw the Imam in my dream.'" "Khaterat-e Soleiman Behbudi," 275–76.

7. Mohammad Reza Pahlavi, *Ma'muriat baray-e vatanam* [Mission for My Country] (Tehran: Nashr-e Ketab, 1353 [1974]; orig. pub. 1961), 87.

8. Ibid., 87–89.

9. Mohammad Reza Pahlavi, *Answer to History* (New York: Stein and Day, 1980), 57–61; quote at 60.

10. "Khaterat-e Soleiman Behbudi," 253.

11. Interview with Princess Ashraf, tape 1, side 1.

12. FISOHA interview with Majid A'lam, by Ahmad Ghoreishi, Walnut Creek, Calif., 22 May 1991, 2.

13. Interview with Princess Ashraf, tape 1, side 2.

14. Ibid.

15. FISOHA interview with Abolfath Atabai, by Ahmad Ghoreishi, New York, 6 June 1982, 61–63.

16. Interview with Princess Ashraf, tape 1, side 2.

17. Pahlavi, *Ma'muriat,* 86.

18. Ibid., 66–67.

19. Interview with Princess Ashraf, tape 1, side 1.

20. Pahlavi, *Ma'muriat,* 84.

21. Ali Asghar Naficy, Mo'addab-ud-Daula (1873–1949/50), was the son of a famous and influential physician, Ali Akbar Naficy. Ali Asghar studied in Tehran, Brussels, and Lyon during the Constitutional Revolution, was a member of the Second Majlis and later head of the Office of Health and Public Welfare. M. Sadr-Hashemi, *Tarikh-e jaraed va majallat-e iran* [History of Iran's Newspapers and Journals], 4 vols. (Esfahan: Kamal, 1327–29 [1948/49–50/51]), 1: 221–23.

22. Interview with Princess Ashraf, tape 1, side 2.

23. Pahlavi, *Ma'muriat,* 99–100.

24. See http://www.rosey.ch/welcome.html.

25. Pahlavi, *Ma'muriat,* 100–101.

26. Ibid., 102–3.

27. "Khaterat-e Soleiman Behbudi," 352–53.

28. Told to Queen Farah by Princess Metternich, wife of Prince Paul Metternich. Interview with Queen Farah, Paris, 3 July 2000, tape 3, side 1.

29. Pahlavi, *Ma'muriat,* 104–5.

30. Interview with Princess Ashraf, tape 1, side 1.

31. Ibid.

32. Pahlavi, *Ma'muriat,* 106.

33. General Hassan Arfaʻ, *Under Five Shahs* (London: John Murray, 1964), 236.

34. *Ruzshomar,* 1: 291–92.

35. Mehdiqoli Hedayat, *Khaterat va khatarat* [Memoirs and Dangers] (Tehran: Zawwar Press, 1363 [1984]), 395. Hedayat was prime minister at the time.

36. Donald N. Wilber, *Riza Shah Pahlavi: The Resurrection and Reconstruction of Iran* (Hicksville, N.Y.: Exposition Press, 1975), 150.

37. For different views of the oil issue in this period see L. P. Elwell-Sutton, *Persian Oil: A Study in Power Politics* (London: Lawrence, 1955); Ronald Ferrier, "The Iranian Oil Industry," in *The Cambridge History of Iran,* 7 vols., ed. Peter Avery, Gavin Hambly, and Charles Melville (Cambridge: Cambridge University Press, 1991) 7: 639–701; George Lenczowski, *Russia and the West in Iran, 1918–1948: A Study in Big-Power Rivalry* (Westport, Conn.: Greenwood Press, 1968; orig. pub. 1949), 76–81; R. B. Stobaugh, "The Evolution of Iranian Oil Policy 1925–1975," in *Iran under the Pahlavis,* ed. George Lenczowski (Stanford: Hoover Institution Press, 1978), 201–52, esp. 201–6. And see Gholam Reza Afkhami, "Moruri bar qarardadha-ye naft oish az melli shodan-e sanʻat-e naft dar iran [A Review of Oil Agreements before the Nationalization of the Oil Industry in Iran]," in *Tahavvol-e sanʻat-e naft-e iran: Negahi az darun* [The Evolution of Iran's Oil Industry: An Insider's Assessment], An Interview with Parviz Mina, ed. Gholam Reza Afkhami (Bethesda, Md.: FIS, 1998), xv–xxxi.

38. Pahlavi, *Ma'muriat,* 106–7.

39. Conversation with Brigadier General Beiglari, former commandant of the Officers Cadet College, Bethesda, Md., 26 June 2003.

40. Conversation with General Fathollah Minbashian, Paris, 19 July 2003.

41. Pahlavi, *Ma'muriat,* 109.

42. Mohsen Sadr, *Khaterat-e Sadr-ul-Ashraf* [Memoirs of Sadr-ul-Ashraf (Mohsen Sadr)] (Tehran: Entesharat-e Vahid, 1364 [1985]), 311–15.

43. Ibid., 351.

44. Pahlavi, *Answer to History,* 53–54.

45. Interview with Princess Ashraf, tape 1, side 1.

46. Ibid., tape 1, side 2; also A. Pahlavi, *Faces in a Mirror,* 29–30.

47. Cyrus Ghani, ed., *Yaddashthaye doctor Qasem Ghani,* 12 vols. [The Memoirs of Doctor Ghasem Ghani], 12 vols. (London: Anchor Press, 1982), 7: 2.

48. Ibid., 2–3.

49. *Ruzshomar,* 1: 311.

50. *Gahnameh,* 1: 155; *Ruzshomar,* 1: 312.

3. THE MAN

1. Interview with Princess Ashraf, New York, 3 February 2001, tape 1, side 2.

2. "If there was time, I tried to put out two or three suits for him to give him a choice, but more often than not he would say go ahead and pick one, and I did. But then I always insisted on showing him more than one tie when I chose the suit; but I picked the tie if he determined which suit to wear," said his personal servant Amir Pourshoja. FISOHA interview with Amir Pourshoja, by Mahnaz Afkhami, Washington, D.C., 12 December 1990, 33.

3. Fereydun Javadi, a friend of Queen Farah and a frequent guest at the court, recalled: "In Noshahr [a Caspian resort where the royal family stayed in summers] he came out of his room at 10 A.M. every single day—not one minute to ten, not one minute after ten. He was at the lunch table at one. Not one minute after or one minute before. At 8 P.M., exactly, he turned on the radio to listen to the news. If someone had been given an appointment to see the shah, he would most likely be received on time. Nowhere else in Iran, and certainly in Muslim courts, was such punctuality maintained. The shah harbored a modern conception of life in mind." Interview with Fereydun Javadi, 9 November 2003, Bethesda, Md., tape 2, side 1.

4. Of his father, the shah wrote, "Apart from relaxation with his family, my father almost never devoted any time to recreation. Perhaps once or twice a year he would go hunting for two or three hours. Mainly he got his exercise through walking. In my memory it seems as if he were *always* walking, either pacing up and down in his office or inspecting troops or projects on foot or, in the late afternoon, taking long walks in his garden. Often he would hold audiences while walking; those whom he received were on such occasions expected to pace up and down with him." Mohammad Reza Pahlavi, *Answer to History* (New York: Stein and Day, 1980), 54–55.

5. Mohammad Reza Pahlavi, *Ma'muriat baray-e vatanam* [Mission for My Country], (Tehran: Nashr-e Ketab, 1353 [1974]; orig. pub. 1961), 71.

6. Interview with Queen Farah, Paris, 1 July 2000, tape 2, side 1.

7. Pourshoja interview, p. 40.

8. Interview with Queen Farah, 1 July 2000, tape 2, side 1.

9. See the account of Fawzieh's divorce in Cyrus Ghani, ed., *Yaddashthaye doctor Qasem Ghani* [The Memoirs of Doctor Ghasem Ghani], 12 vols. (London: Anchor Press, 1982), 7 (this volume is devoted to the marriage and divorce of the shah and Fawzieh).

10. Interview with Princess Ashraf, tape 1, side 2.

11. FISOHA interview with Majid A'lam, by Ahmad Ghoreishi, Walnut Creek, Calif., 22 May 1991, 13–19; FISOHA, interview with Professor Yahya Adl, by Gholem Reza Afkhami, Paris, 20 August 2000, tape 2, side 2.

12. A'lam interview, 18.

13. Interview with Princess Ashraf, tape 1, side 2.

14. Interview with Ardeshir Zahedi, Montreux, Switzerland, 5, 6, and 7 July 2001, tape 3, side 2.

15. Pari Abasalti and Hushang Mirhashem, eds., *Ardeshir Zahedi: Untold Secrets* (Los Angeles: Rah-e Zendegi, 2002), 75–78.

16. *Gahnameh*, 2: 933; *Ruzshomar*, 2: 85.

17. Notably, Court Minister Hossein Ala had an encounter with Prince Ruffo di Scilla and his wife, friends of the former king of Italy, Umberto II, at the Italian embassy in Tehran. The conversation turned to the possibility of a marriage between the shah and Umberto's daughter, Princess Maria Gabriella di Savoy. The ambassador suggested that di Scilla meet with Umberto in Lisbon and inquire discreetly if the king was agreeable to the marriage and, if so, would he and the princess be present in Cannes at about the time the shah was scheduled to be there. Ruffo di Scilla accepted the charge but reminded his friend the ambassador that a marriage between a Catholic Italian princess and a Muslim king might not be an easy proposition. The ambassador, however, thought

that it was likely that the pope would grant permission and even agree that the children be brought up as Muslims. Prince Ruffo, who appeared to enjoy the task he had been assigned, assured Ala that he also knew several German princesses who were not Catholic and therefore did not have the papal problem. If Gabriella did not work out, he could arrange for the shah to meet the German princesses in one of the castles in Bavaria. Hossein Ala, Ministry of Court, Daily Reports to the Shah, 21 May 1958 (31 Ordibehesht 1337), No: 10, confidential, *Faslnameh-ye tarikh-e mu'aser-e iran* [The Contemporary History of Iran Quarterly] 1, 2: 140–41.

18. Farah refers to her parents in her autobiographical book, *An Enduring Love: My Life with the Shah* (New York, Miramax, 2004); her comment about her cousin Reza is at 16.

19. Quoted in ibid., 45, 57.

20. Abasalti and Mirhashem, *Ardeshir Zahedi,* 79.

21. Farah Pahlavi, *An Enduring Love,* 68–69.

22. Abasalti and Mirhashem, *Ardeshir Zahedi,* 80–81. The shah learned during this time that Mohammad Mosaddeq's half-brother was a Diba, a discovery that bemused him for a while but that he let pass once he was reminded that in upper-class Iran anyone could be found to be related to anyone else.

23. Farah Pahlavi, *An Enduring Love,* 77.

24. Abasalti and Mirhashem, *Ardeshir Zahedi,* 85.

25. Farah Pahlavi, *An Enduring Love,* 78.

26. Ibid., 79.

27. Pahlavi, *Ma'muriat,* 457.

28. A'lam interview, 6.

29. This writer saw him several times in the late 1940s and early 1950s getting out of the car in the street and walking up the hill, his skis on his shoulder.

30. Interview with Kambiz Atabai, New York, 5 February 2001.

31. Interview with Queen Farah, 1 July 2000, tape 2, side 2.

32. Pahlavi, *Ma'muriat,* 90–92.

33. He behaved the same, maneuvering through the mountain passes, when he flew helicopters. On the other hand, he needed to fly a certain number of hours every month to remain qualified, and in these flights, which he performed under Air Force Commander General Khatami's supervision, he abided diligently by the rules, on which Khatami was quite severe. For a time the shah flew the helicopter without the headgears, arguing that it was enough that his copilot wore them. When Khatami was apprised of this, he forbad it and the shah complied. Interview with Queen Farah, Paris, 1 July 2000, tape 2, side 2.

34. As Gholam Reza Adl, Yahya's brother and a member of the shah's circle of friends, said about the royal family in those years: "Money is like a beast with horns that show; we never saw horns in the court." Yahya Adl interview, tape 2, side 2.

35. Interview with Reza Golsorkhi, New York, 14 May 2001, tape 1, side 1.

36. A'lam interview, 1, 7–9.

37. Adl interview, tape 1, side 1.

38. A'lam interview, 26–27.

39. Ibid., 27–28; Adl interview, tape 3, side 1.

40. Adl interview, tape 4, side 1.

41. Interview with Queen Farah, 1 July 2000, tape 2, side 1.

42. Shahrokh Amir-Arjomand, a physicist, entered the court in 1967 as a result of marrying a friend of the queen. He had been a member of a right-wing movement when a high school student in Iran in the late 1940s and early 1950s but had subsequently developed left-wing tendencies in the United States as a member and sometime president of the Iranian Student Association of Minnesota, where he studied physics. His first social encounter with royalty was at a reception at the home of Princess Fatemeh (the shah's younger sister), which did not go well for him. After he was married, he was invited regularly to the various functions the royal family routinely attended for dinner: twice a week at Princess Ashraf's, once a week at Princess Fatemeh's, once a week at Princess Shams's, and on Fridays all day at the shah's. He found these outings routine and altogether uneventful. "Before going to the court, I had imagined that there they did strange and unimaginable things. I was surprised to see that there was less of a strange nature there than in any party I had attended at the homes of my ordinary friends." FISOHA interview with Shahrokh Amir-Arjomand, by Mahnaz Afkhami, New York, 21 June 1988, tape 1, side 2.

43. Ibid.

44. Javadi interview, tape 2, side 1.

45. See Alinaqi Alikhani, ed., *Yaddashtha-ye Alam* [Alam's Diaries], 5 vols. (Bethesda: IBEX, n.d.), especially vol. 5.

46. Ibid., 3: 86–87, 111, 120–21.

47. See Ghani, *Yaddashtha,* 3: 156–73.

48. Ibid. They included Mohammad Qazvini, Seyyed Nasrollah Taqavi, Hasan Esfandiari (Haj Mohtasiem-Saltaneh), Ali Akbar Dehkhoda, Hossein Shokuh (Shokuholmulk), and Qasem Ghani. Later, General Yazdanpanah, the shah's military adjutant general, suggested Dr. Reza Zadeh Shafaq's name, which he approved, and then he ordered Yazdanpanah, Ala, and Muaddab Naficy, his erstwhile tutor, also to attend.

49. Ibid. Mohammad Qazvini was one of the great Iranian scholars of the twentieth century. The shah was the only person from whom he had accepted financial help—once toward paying for a house, and later monthly stipends as long as he lived.

50. Rumor had it that he called them "an-tellectuel," the French pronunciation used in Persian, "goh-tellectuel," the pun being that the first syllable in both terms meant "crap" in Persian. He had apparently heard this from Alam, who had learned it from his friend Rasul Parvizi. Interview with Reza Qotbi, Bethesda, Md., 20 June 2002, tape 1, side 1.

51. Ibid.

52. Ibid.

53. Ibid.

4. ASCENDING THE THRONE

1. Anne Lambton to Professor Rushbrooks Williams, 21 December 1939, No. 308/4/39, PRO FO 371/24570.

2. *Ruzshomar,* 1: 315–16.

3. *Gahnameh,* 1: 159.

4. "Remembrances of Mahmud Jam," *Salnameh-ye donya* [The Donya Yearbook], reprinted in Hossein Makki, *Tarikh-e bist saleh-e iran,* 8 vols. (Tehran: Elmi Publishers, 1364 [1985]), 8: 122–23.

5. Mohammad Reza Pahlavi, interview in exile on *Answer to History*, by Christine Godek and Tom Weir, Cairo, 27 May 1980, tape 4, side 2. Godek and Weir interviewed the shah over four days—27, 28, and 29 May and 1 June 1980. Altogether eleven full (both sides) and two half-full (one side) 90-minute tapes were recorded. The interviews are informal, covering a wide range of personal and political issues. Although terminally ill, the shah sounds lucid, in control, and confident, and for a man in his physical and political condition surprisingly resigned, almost stoic. Again, I am indebted to the office of Princess Ashraf, especially to Gholamreza Golsorkhi, for providing a copy of the tapes to the Foundation for Iranian Studies for my use.

6. Mohammad Reza Abbasi and Behrooz Tayarani, eds., *Khaterat-e Nasrollah Entezam* [Memoirs of Nasrollah Entezam] (Tehran: Sazemane Asnad-e Iran, 1371 [1992]), 2.

7. Sir Reader Bullard to Viscount Halifax, "Political Review of the Year 1939 in Iran," 10 February 1940, PRO FO 371/24531, EP 584/584/34, para. 4.

8. Bullard to Halifax, 4 January 1940, No. 3, PRO FO 371/24570.

9. Bullard to Halifax, "Political Review of the Year 1939."

10. W. Fraser, Anglo-Iranian Oil Company's Concession in Iran, 23 February 1940, PRO FO 371/24572, 2.

11. M. Moghaddam to Viscount Halifax, 19 June 1940, No. 1520, PRO FO 371/24572.

12. Bullard to Halifax, 20 June 1940, No. 181, PRO FO 371/24572.

13. Halifax to Bullard, 25 June 1940, No. 142, PRO FO 371/24572.

14. A. P. Waterfield (Treasury) to Sir Arthur Street (Air Ministry), 3 July 1940, PRO FO 371/24573.

15. Foreign Office to Bullard, 4 July 1940, No. 156, PRO FO 371/24573.

16. Sir Kingsley Wood to Halifax, 22 July 1940, PRO FO 371/24573.

17. Halifax to Wood, 26 July 1940, PRO FO 371/24573.

18. Final Iranian Government Reply, 21 August 1940, PRO FO 371/24574.

19. In 1921 the newly established Soviet Russia concluded a treaty of friendship with Iran reversing the tsarist policy toward Iran. The treaty ended all treaties and agreements formerly signed between Russia and Iran and declared null and void all Russian agreements with third parties that were harmful to the best interests of Iran. The treaty also voided all Russian concessions and returned to Iran most of Russian assets on Iranian soil. It also had two articles (5 and 6) according to which each signatory was to keep out of its country troops of a third power that threatened the security of the other. "But if a third power should create such a threat within Iran, or attempt to turn Iran into a military base for action against Russia, and if Iran itself should be unable to cope with this danger, Russia reserved the right to send its troops into Iran in self-defense." Donald N. Wilber, *Iran: Past and Present* (Princeton: Princeton University Press, 1958), 83.

20. Lacy Baggallay (Foreign Office) to A. P. Waterfield (Treasury), 25 August 1940, PRO FO 371/24754; emphasis added.

21. Leo Amery to Anthony Eden, 16 May 1941, PRO FO 371/27196, E 2583.

22. Eden to Amery, 18 August 1941, PRO FO 371/27197, E 4586/3691/G.

23. Anthony Eden to Harold Nicholson, 18 August 1941, PRO FO 371/27197, E 4594/3691/G.

24. Nicholson to Eden, 8 August 1941, PRO FO 371/27197, E 4594.

25. Abbasi and Tayarani, *Khaterat-e Nasrollah Entezam,* 8.

26. Foreign Office to Tehran, 14 July 1941, No. 382, PRO FO 371/27196.

27. *Ruzshomar,* 1: 326.

28. Anthony Eden to Government of India, 23 July 1941, PRO FO 371/27196.

29. Leo Amery to Eden, 31 July 1941, PRO FO 371/27196, E 4276.

30. *Gahnameh,* 1: 171–72.

31. Ibid., 173.

32. Secretary of State to Government of India, etc., 21 August 1941, PRO FO 371/27197, EXT 5074 1941.

33. Foreign Office to Moscow, 1 August 1941, No. 945, PRO FO 371/27196.

34. From Tehran to Foreign Office, 25 October 1941, No. 1037, PRO FO 371/27248.

35. See communications between Bullard and Foreign Office, numbers 523, 512, 524, 11 August 1941, PRO FO 371/27197.

36. Ali Mansur, "Khatereh," in *Reza Shah dar aineh-ye khaterat* [Reza Shah in the Mirror of Remembrances], ed. Ebrahim Safai (Los Angeles: n.p., 1986; orig. pub. Tehran: Ministry of Culture, 1354 [1975]), 387–88.

37. Ibid., 388–89.

38. Ibid., 389–90.

39. Javad Ameri, "Khatereh," in Safai, ed., *Reza Shah,* 278–80.

40. *Gahnameh,* 1: 174.

41. George Lenczowski, *Russia and the West in Iran, 1918–1948: A Study in Big-Power Rivalry* (Westport, Conn.: Greenwood Press, 1968; orig. pub. 1949), 281–83.

42. Mansur, "Khatereh," 391.

43. Lenczowski, *Russia and the West,* 283.

44. *Gahnameh,* 1: 174; Mansur, "Khatereh," 392; *Ruzshomar,* 1: 329.

45. Mansur, "Khatereh," 393–94.

46. Habib Ladjevardi, ed., *Khaterat-e Mahmoud Foroughi* [Memoirs of Mahmoud Foroughi], Iranian Oral History Project, Harvard University, 2003, 43.

47. Mostafa Alamuti, "Negahi be vapasin ruzha-ye saltanat-e Reza Shah Pahlavi and Mohammad Reza Shah Pahlavi" [A Look at the Last Days of the Reign of Reza Shah and Mohammad Reza Shah Pahlavi], *Rahavard* no. 58 (fall and winter 2002): 220–44, at 220.

48. Ebrahim Safai, *Khaterat-e Sa'ed* [Sa'ed's Memoirs], quoted in ibid., 228–29.

49. *Ruzshomar,* 1: 331.

50. Author conversation with Lieutenant General Karim Varahram, Washington, D.C., 8 August 1989.

51. *Gahnameh,* 1: 180.

52. Fereydun Jam, "In the Service of the Pahlavi Shahs," *Rahavard* 11, 36 (summer 1994): 239.

53. Ashraf Pahlavi, *Faces in a Mirror: Memoirs from Exile* (Englewood Cliffs, N.J.: Prentice-Hall, 1980), 42.

54. *Gahnameh,* 1: 181.

55. Ibid.

56. Ladjevardi, *Khaterat-e Mahmoud Foroughi,* 56.

57. Reader Bullard to Anthony Eden, 26 September 1941, Intelligence Summary, No. 132, PRO FO 371/27188, E 6869/268/34.

58. Ladjevardi, *Khaterat-e Mahmoud Foroughi,* 64. I have not seen any reference to a possible Iranian republic in the documents in PRO FO except in connection to what the Soviets might want for their own purposes. This, however, does not mean that such a possibility was never entertained.

59. Bullard to Eden, 26 September 1941.

60. See PRO FO 371/27197. The shah's telegram is in French. It ends with a formal closing—"Please accept the assurances . . ." No such valediction exists in King George's reply, dated 24 September 1941.

61. *Gahnameh,* 1: 181–82; *Ruzshomar,* 1: 333–35.

62. Bullard to Eden, 26 September 1941.

63. Anvar Khamei, *Khaterat* [Memoirs], vol. 2, *Forsat-e bozorg-e az dast rafteh* [Great Opportunity Lost] (Tehran: Entesharat-e hafteh, 1362 [1983]), 17–18.

64. Reported by the shah's friend and confidant Haj Aqa Reza Rafi'. Rafi' had arranged and was present at the meeting between the shah and Tudeh leaders, which included Fereydun Keshavarz, a pediatrician who later became a leader of the party. FISOHA interview with Professor Yahya Adl, by Gholem Reza Afkhami, Paris, 20 August 2000, tape 4, side 2.

65. Governor of Mauritius (Sir B. Clifford) to Secretary of State for the Colonies, 24 October 1941, PRO FO 371/27247.

66. Bullard to Foreign Office, 24 October 1941, No. 1037, PRO FO 371/27248, E 6943.

67. Ibid.

68. See PRO FO 371/27248, E 6943.

69. Gholam Hossein Mirza Saleh, ed., *Reza Shah: Khaterat-e Soleyman Behbudi, Shams Pahlavi, Ali Izadi* [Reza Shah: Memoirs of Soleyman Behbudi, Shams Pahlavi, Ali Izadi] (Tehran: Sahba, 1372 [1993]), 564–65.

70. For the account of bringing back Reza Shah's remains, see Mohsen Sadr, *Khaterat-e Sadr-ul-Ashraf* [Memoirs of Sadr-ul-Ashraf (Moshen Sadr)] (Tehran: Entesharat-e Vahid, 1364 [1985]), 502–11.

71. Ibid.

5. AZERBAIJAN

1. FRUS 1941, D.P. 3: 434–35.

2. Leland M. Goodrich and Marie J. Caroll, eds., *Documents on American Foreign Relations* (Boston: World Peace Foundation, 1942), 4: 681–86.

3. Ibid.

4. For a more general discussion, see Ruhollah K. Ramazani, *Iran's Foreign Policy 1941–1973: A Study of Foreign Policy in Modernizing Nations* (Charlottesville: University of Virginia Press, 1975), 45–69.

5. Quotations in ibid., 66–67. For the text of the declaration, see Husain Kuhi Kir-

mani, *Az shahrivar-e 1320 ta fajaye-e azarbaijan va zanjan* [From September 1941 to the Disasters in Azerbaijan and Zanjan], 2 vols. (Tehran: Mazaheri, 1950/51), 2: 646–47; cited also in Ramazani, *Iran's Foreign Policy.*

6. During the war, several oil companies had indicated interest in probing for oil in the remaining areas. In the fall of 1943 the British Shell Company approached the Iranian government for exploration in southeastern Iran. In the spring of 1944, two American companies, Standard Vacuum Oil Company and Sinclair Oil Company, also applied. At about the same time the Iranian government engaged two American oil geologists—A. A. Curtice and Herbert Hoover, Jr.—to survey Iran's oil reserves. George Lenczowski, *Russia and the West in Iran, 1918–1948: A Study in Big-Power Rivalry* (Westport, Conn.: Greenwood Press, 1968; orig. pub. 1949), 216.

7. Hossein Kayostovan, *Siyasat-e movazeneh-ye manfi dar majles-e chahardahom* [The Politics of Negative Equilibrium in the Fourteenth Majlis], 2 vols. (Tehran: Entesharat-e Mosaddeq, 1327 [1948]), 1: 158–60.

8. Prime Minister Saʿed's report to Majlis, 9 October 1944, in the *Official Gazette,* the Majlis Record, 17 Mehr 1323 [9 October 1944].

9. Lenczowski, *Russia and the West in Iran,* 217–18.

10. Kayostovan, *Siyasat,* 1: 162–63.

11. Lenczowski, *Russia and the West in Iran,* 219; *New York Times,* 30 October 1944, 5.

12. Kayostovan, *Siyasat,* 1: 166–67; Gholam Reza Afkhami, ed., *Siyasat va siasatgozari-e eqtesadi dar iran, 1340–1350* [Ideology, Politics, and Process in Iran's Economic Development, 1960–1970], An Interview with Alinaghi Alikhani (Bethesda, Md.: FIS, 2001), 6.

13. Kayostovan, *Siyasat,* 1: 182.

14. Lenczowski, *Russia and the West in Iran,* 221.

15. On the origins of the bill, see Jalal Matini, "Tarh-e Man" [My Project], *Iranshenasi* 16: 1 (spring 2004): 1–8.

16. Jalal Matini, "Mosaddeq, pishnahadha-ye nakhostvaziri, va engelishia, bakhsh-e dovvom" [Mossadeq Offers of Premiership and the British, part 2], *Iranshenasi* 12, 2 (2000): 242; Kayostovan, *Siyasat,* 1: 232.

17. Ahmad Qasemi, an important member of the party's political bureau in the 1940s, had been invited into the party and given the job of secretary for agitprop because party potentate Nureddin Kianuri had seen on Qasemi's desk at the Ministry of Finance a tract by Lenin in French. "I knew only a little French and read the tract with the help of a dictionary, a few pages at a time. But they recruited and gave me such an important position in the party," Qasemi reported to Tehrani. Gholam Hossein Forutan, a member of the party's central committee, had learned of materialism in Montpellier in his biology classes and of Marxism in French leftist newspapers. Hamid Shokat, *Negahi az darun be jonbesh-e chap-e iran: Goftegu ba Mehdi Khanbaba Tehrani* [Iran's Left, a Look from Within: Conversation with Mehdi Khanbaba Tehrani] (Paris: Vajeh Desktop Publishing, 1990), 19–20.

18. Anvar Khamei, *Khaterat* [Memoirs], vol. 2, *Forsat-e bozorg-e az dast rafteh* [Great Opportunity Lost] (Tehran: Entesharet-e hafteh, 1362 [1983]), 9–11.

19. Fereydun Keshavarz, *Man muttaham mikonam* [I Accuse] (Tehran: Entesharat-e Khalq, 1358 [1979]).

20. *Gahnameh,* 1: 330–41; *Ruzshomar,* 1: 377–80.

21. Mohsen Sadr, *Khaterat-e Sadr-ul-Ashraf* [Memoirs of Sadr-ul-Ashraf (Mohsen Sadr)] (Tehran: Entesharat-e Vahid, 1364 [1985]), 426.

22. *Kayhan,* 6 November 1945; *Gahnameh,* 1: 349.

23. *Gahnameh,* 1: 351–52.

24. *Ruzshomar,* 1: 381.

25. Lenczowski, *Russia and the West in Iran,* 292.

26. *Ruzshomar,* 1: 382, 383.

27. FISOHA interview with General Karim Varahram, by Seyyed Vali Reza Nasr, Washington, D.C., 9 April 1989, 11. General Varahram, who was at the time chief of staff of the Iranian division in Azerbaijan, has a copy of a map printed in 1943 in Baku but discovered in Tabriz after the Firqeh demokrat uprising that shows Iran partitioned into several "democratic republics": a Democratic Republic of Azerbaijan, composed of the Soviet and Iranian Azerbaijans; a Republic of Kurdistan, which included the area of the Iranian west down to Bushehr; a Republic of Arabistan, containing the greater Khuzistan territories; a Republic of Baluchistan, which included Kerman and Makran; a Republic of Khurasan, containing also Uzbekistan and Tajikistan; a Republic of Tabarestan, covering the Caspian provinces; and a Republic of Fars, including the central Iranian areas.

28. *New York Times,* 28 December 1945; quoted in Lenczowski, *Russia and the West in Iran,* 294.

29. *Gahnameh,* 1: 361.

30. Ahmad Qavam (Qavam-us-Saltaneh) was an old hand in politics, his career stretching back to the late nineteenth century and the court of Nassereddin Shah Qajar and subsequently the personal office of Chancellor Amin-ud-Daula. His political take-off, however, occurred after the Constitutional Revolution of 1905–6. Immediately after the 1921 coup d'état he was imprisoned by Prime Minister Seyyed Zia-ud-Din but then succeeded him as prime minister. After a short interval he was once again appointed prime minister on 17 June 1922. Reza Khan was his minister of war in both his terms. After Reza Khan ascended the throne in 1925, Qavam left the country but was allowed to return in 1928. When the old king resigned and went into exile, Qavam emerged as a contender for prime minister and succeeded Ali Soheili in August 1942. He was forced out in February 1943. Mehdi Bamdad, *Sharh-e hal-e rejal-e iran* [A Biography of Iran's Statesmen] (Tehran: Zawwar, 1357 [1978]), 95–99.

31. See Abolhassan Amidi Nuri, "Khaterat-e safar-e Qavam-us-Saltaneh be-mosco" [Memoirs of Qavam-us-Saltaneh in Moscow], *Sepid va Siah,* no. 1007, 18 Bahman 1381 [2002].

32. Tahmouress Adamiyatt, *Gashti bar gozashteh: Khaterat-e safir kabir-e iran dar shoravi* [A Promenade in the Past: Memoirs of an Iranian Ambassador to the USSR (1945–65)] (Tehran: Ketab Sara Co., 1368 [1989]), 16.

33. Amidi Nuri, "Khaterat."

34. Ibid.

35. *New York Times,* 20 March 1946; quoted in Lenczowski, *Russia and the West in Iran,* 296.

36. *Gahnameh,* 1: 371; *Ruzshomar,* 1: 385.

37. *Gahnameh,* 1: 371–72; *Ruzshomar,* 1: 387.

38. Harry S. Truman, *Memoirs,* vol. 2, *Years of Trial and Hope, 1946–1952* (Garden City, N.Y.: Doubleday and Co., 1956), 94–95.

39. *Gahnameh,* 1: 372.

40. See Mohammad Reza Pahlavi, *Ma'muriat baray-e vatanam* [Mission for My Country] (Tehran: Nashr-e Ketab, 1353 [1974; orig. pub. 1961]), 214.

41. *New York Times,* 5 April 1946; quoted in Lenczowski, *Russia and the West in Iran,* 299.

42. *Ruzshomar,* 1: 391.

43. *New York Times,* 15 June 1946, quoted in Lenczowski, *Russia and the West in Iran,* 302. The full agreement comprised fifteen articles and four notes. *Gahnameh,* 1: 381.

44. Khamei, *Forsat,* 313.

45. *Rahbar,* 19 Tir 1325 (10 July 1946).

46. Lenczowski, *Russia and the West in Iran,* 304.

47. Mohammad Reza Pahlavi, interview in exile on *Answer to History,* by Christine Godek and Tom Weir, Cairo, 27 May 1980, tape 5, side 1.

48. Lenczowski, *Russia and the West in Iran,* 308.

49. Pahlavi, *Ma'muriat,* 214–15.

50. Ibid., 215.

51. The text of the report is in Sarlashgar [Major General] Ahmad Zangeneh, *Khaterati az ma'muriatha-ye man dar azarbaijan: Shahrivar 1320-dey 1325* [Memoirs of My Missions in Azerbaijan: 1941–1946] (Tehran: Pip Publications, 1353 [1974]; 3rd printing, 1366]), 152–53.

52. Ibid., 153.

53. *Gahnameh,* 1: 398–401.

54. Zangeneh, *Khaterati,* 161–62.

55. Texts in ibid., 173–75.

56. *Gahnameh,* 1: 402–6.

57. Zangeneh, *Khaterati,* 179, 180.

58. Alikhani in Afkhami, *Siyasat,* 36.

59. *Ruzshomar,* 1: 400–402.

60. Ibid., 406–8.

61. Lenczowski, *Russia and the West in Iran,* 309–10.

62. *Ruzshomar,* 1: 408.

63. Lenczowski, *Russia and the West in Iran,* 309.

64. See Students Following the Line of the Imam, 70, *The U.S. Military Advisory Mission in Iran* (1) (Tehran: CPUSEDD, 1369 [1990]).

65. See Lenczowski, *Russia and the West in Iran,* 311.

66. *New York Times,* 12 September 1947.

67. Dean Acheson, *Present at the Creation: My Years at the State Department* (New York: W. W. Norton, 1969), 196–98.

68. Lenczowski, *Russia and the West in Iran,* 311–12.

69. *Gahnameh,* 1: 435–36; Lenczowski, *Russia and the West in Iran,* 312; *Ruzshomar,* 1: 409–10.

70. Interview with Princess Ashraf Pahlavi, New York, 3 February 2001, tape 2, side 1.

71. *Ruzshomar,* 1: 410.

72. See FISOHA interviews with Naser Zolfaqari, by Farrokh Ghaffari, Paris, 11 May, 9 and 23 September, 5 and 28 October 1989, 49–50.

6. NATIONALIZING OIL

1. Abdollah Mostowfi, *Sharh-e Zendegi-ye man ya tarikh-e ejtemai va edari-ye dore-ye Qajariyeh* [My Life, or the Qajar Social and Administrative History], 3 vols. (Tehran: Zawar, 1373 [1994]), 2: 322. See also Jalal Matini, "Dr. Mosaddeq, enqelab-e mashruteh, va tahsilate 'alieh dar orupa" [Dr. Mosaddeq, the Constitutional Revolution, and His Higher Education in Europe], *Iranshenasi* 11, 4 (winter 2000): 711–41, at 716.

2. Dr. Mohammad Mosaddeq, *Khaterat va ta'llomat-e Mosaddeq* [Remembrances and Sorrows of Mosaddeq], ed. Iraj Afshar (Tehran: Entesharat-e 'Elmi, 1373 [1994]), 13 (hereafter cited as *Khaterat*); Matini, "Dr. Mosaddeq," 722.

3. Jalil Bozorgmehr, *Taqrirat-e Mosaddeq dar zendan* [Mosaddeq's Statements in Prison], ed. Iraj Afshar (Tehran: Entsharat-e farhang, 1359 [1980]), 13; Matini, "Dr. Mosaddeq," 722.

4. *Khaterat,* 79–81; Matini, "Dr. Mosaddeq," 729. Interestingly, Mosaddeq had no idea that the method he employed to prepare his dissertation (in effect written by the two clerics) and have it translated to French (by a Frenchman) is not how doctoral dissertations are expected to be written. All this appears in his memoirs innocently and uncritically.

5. *Khaterat,* 341–42.

6. Hossein Kayostovan, *Siyasat-e movazeneh-ye manfi dar majles-e chahardahom* [The Politics of Negative Equilibrium in the Fourteenth Majlis], 2 vols. (Tehran: Entesharat-e Mosaddeq, 1327 [1948]), 1: 78–80; Jalal Matini, "Mosaddeq, pishnahadha-ye nakhostvaziri, va engelishia, bakhsh-e yekom" [Mossadeq Offers of Premiership and the British, part 1], *Iranshenasi* 12, 1: 12.

7. *Khaterat,* 152.

8. Kayostovan, *Siyasat,* 1: 194–95.

9. The reasons for Matin Daftary's arrest are not clear. Possibly, the shah wanted to show the British he was not pro-German by dismissing Matin Daftary, who had studied in Germany and was known to have pro-German sympathies. Haji Mehdiqoli Hedayat, *Khaterat va khatarat* [Remembrances and Dangers] (Tehran: 1377 [1998]), 416.

10. *Khaterat,* 338–39.

11. FISOHA interview with Professor Yahya Adl, by Gholam Reza Afkhami, Paris, 20 August 2000, tape 2, side 2.

12. Mohammad Reza Pahlavi, interview in exile on *Answer to History,* by Christine Godek and Tom Weir, Cairo, 27 May 1980, tape 4, side 2.

13. Mohammad Reza Pahlavi, *Ma'muriat baray-e vatanam* [Mission for My Country] (Tehran: Nashr-e Ketab, 1353 [1974]; orig. pub. 1961), 154.

14. Ibid., 155; Kayostovan, *Siyasat,* 1: 194–95; *Khaterat,* 358–59.

15. Kayostovan, *Siyasat,* 1: 184–86; Matini, "Mosaddeq, pishnahadha," 244.

16. *Gahnameh,* 1: 308.

17. *Salnameh Pars* [Pars Yearbook] (Tehran, 1329 [1950]), 145–46.

18. Ibid., 144–50.

19. *Kayhan,* 23 October 1947.

20. See Ruhollah K. Ramazani, *Iran's Foreign Policy, 1941–1973: A Study of Foreign Policy in Modernizing Nations* (Charlottesville: University Press of Virginia, 1975), 184–87.

21. Gavin R. G. Hambly, "The Pahlavi Autocracy: Muhammad Riza Shah," in *The Cambridge History of Iran: From Nadir Shah to the Islamic Republic,* ed. Peter Avery, Gavin Hambly, and Charles Meville (Cambridge: Cambridge University Press, 1991), 252.

22. Pahlavi, *Ma'muriat,* 92–94.

23. Mohammad Reza Pahlavi, *Answer to History* (New York: Stein and Day, 1980), 59.

24. Conversation with Cyrus Ghani, New York, 20 September 2004. Ghani recounted what he personally had heard from Amini in Washington not long after Amini met with the shah.

25. *Gahnameh,* 1: 470–71; *Ruzshomar,* 1: 420.

26. Sepehr Zabih, *The Communist Movement in Iran* (Berkeley: University of California Press, 1966), 161–65.

27. *Gahnameh,* 1: 476–77.

28. The amended article reads as follows:

Article 48. His Imperial Majesty may dissolve the National Consultative Assembly [Majlis] or the Senate, each separately or both simultaneously. When either both or one of the houses of parliament is dissolved by Royal decree, the same decree must state the reasons for the dissolution and order a new election. New elections must begin within a month of the dissolution decree, and the new house or houses shall commence work in three months. The new parliamentary house or houses that are elected subsequent to a dissolution decree shall be elected for a full term and they may not be dissolved again for the same reasons.

(See George Lenczowski, "Political Process and Institutions in Iran: The Second Pahlavi Kingship," in *Iran under the Pahlavis,* ed. Lenczowski [Stanford, Calif.: Hoover Institution Press, 1978], 434–75, at 437–38.)
The remainder of the article, which referred to disagreement between the Majlis and the Senate, was left mostly untouched.

29. *Ruzshomar,* 1: 422.

30. *Kayhan,* 27 January 1949; see also Ramazani, *Iran's Foreign Policy,* 184.

31. From the text of Namazi's letter appearing in *Eradeh-ye Azerbaijan* on 1 March 1952; English translation in PRO FO 371/98682.

32. *Gahnameh,* 1: 505. For a discussion of development planning, see chapter 10.

33. The non–National Front members of the committee were Javad Ganjei and Mir Seyyed Ali Behbahani, vice-chairs; Hasan Alavi and Khosro Qashqai, secretaries; and Jamal Emami, Javad Ganjei, Hedayatollah Palizi, Naser Zolfaqari, Javad Ameri, Khosro Qashqai, Abdorrahman Faramarzi, Hasan Alavi, Mir Seyyed Ali Behbahani, Nosratollah Kasemi, Abolhasan Haerizadeh, Mohammad Ali Hedayati, Abolqasem Faqihzadeh, and Ali Asghar Sartipzadeh. *Ruzshomar,* 1: 434. Ali Shayegan replaced Hadi Taheri after the latter withdrew. FISOHA interviews with Nasser Zolfaqari, by Forrokh Ghaffari, Paris, 11 May, 9 and 23 September, 5 and 28 October 1989, 10–36; on Shayegan, 14.

34. Ebrahim Safai, *Eshtebah-e bozorg, melli shodan-e naft* [A Grand Mistake? Nationalization of Oil] (Tehran: Ketab Sara, 1371 [1992]), 105–6.

35. Ibid., 108.

36. Matini, "Mosaddeq, pishnahadha," 256–57; *Ruzshomar*, 1: 434–42; Safai, *Eshtebah*, 106–12; Zolfaqari interviews, 91.

37. Matini, "Mosaddeq, pishnahadha," 257–258; Safai, *Eshtebah*, 116–17.

38. The *Official Gazette*, the Majlis Records, 26 Azar 1329 [17 December 1905]; also in Matini, "Mosaddeq, pishnahadha," 258.

39. Rahim Zehtab Fard, *Afsane-ye mosaddeq* [The Myth of Mosaddeq] (Tehran: Nashr-e Elmi, 1376 [1997]), 230; also in Matini, "Mosaddeq, pishnahadha," 259.

40. Safai, *Eshtebah*, 136–37.

41. George McGhee, *Envoy to the Middle World: Adventures in Diplomacy* (New York: Harper and Row, 1983), 321–23.

42. Ibid., 325.

43. Gholam Reza Afkhami, ed., *San'at-e petroshimi-e iran: Az aghaz ta astaneh-ye enqelab* [The Evolution of Iran's Petrochemical Industry], An Interview with Baqer Mostowfi (Bethesda, Md.: FIS, 2001), 13–14.

44. Interview with Princess Ashraf Pahlavi, New York, 3 February 2001, tape 1, side 1.

45. In the twenty days between the finalization of the committee's report and its formal submission to the Majlis on 17 December, a bizarre event occurred in Tehran, causing massive confusion. The Tudeh leaders had been tried and convicted of treason in military court. They appealed the ruling, and the Supreme Court agreed with their argument that they should be tried in the criminal court of Tehran province. On 15 December, a military truck, commanded by a man in lieutenant colonel's uniform accompanied by eight men dressed as NCOs arrived at the Qasr Prison where the Tudeh leaders were kept. The "colonel" told the officer of the guard, a certain Lieutenant Qobadi, that they were there to take the political prisoners to the civil court for arraignment. The truck was allowed to enter the prison courtyard, and the matter was reported to a Lieutenant Mohammadzadeh, the officer of the guard in charge of the prisoners. Mohammadzadeh fetched the prisoners, and together they joined Qobadi in the convoy and left the prison. After several hours, the other prison officers, now worried because the prisoners had not been returned, informed the authorities. But prisoners — Yazdi, Jowdat, Kianury, Shandermani, Qasemi, Nushin, Hakimi, Ruzbeh, Alavi — all top leaders of the party, managed to escape to the Soviet Union. It happened so easily that many people wondered if the government had been involved. By the time the committee was about to present its report in the Majlis, the Tudeh event had become another point of suspicion around Razmara.

46. Gholam Hossein Mosaddeq, *Dar kenar-e pedaram*, [At My Father's Side], ed. Gholamreza Nejati (Tehran: Rasa, 1369 [1990]), 156–57; also, see Mosaddeq's statements in his interrogation on the murder of General Razmara, in Mohammad Torkan, *Asrar-e qatl-e Razmara* [Secrets of Razmara's Murder] (Tehran: Rasa Cultural Institute, 1370 [1991]), 394.

47. *Khaterat*, 361–62.

48. *Ruzshomar*, 1: 443.

49. *Gahnameh*, 1: 524–43.

50. *Ruzshomar*, 1: 446.

51. Safai, *Eshtebah*, 146.

52. Ibid., 145–46, 148; Matini, "Mosaddeq, pishnahadha," 261.

53. *Official Gazette,* the Majlis Records, Record of the Debates, Sixteenth Majlis, 22 Esfand 1329 (13 March 1951).

54. *Khaterat,* 177–78, 361–62; Matini, "Mosaddeq, pishnahadha," 261.

55. *Khaterat,* 177–78.

56. Sir John Le Rougetel to Clement Attlee, 1 February 1950; PRO FO 371/82310, EP 1016/10.

57. George Middleton, Reports on Events in Persia in 1951, March 24, 1952, PRO FO 371/98693, EP 1011/1.

58. Stokes's notes on visit to Tehran; 3–24 August 1951, PRO FO 371/98674.

59. Ibid.

60. Ibid., 6.

61. R. R. Stokes, "To the Editor of the Times," *The Times,* 6 September 1952.

62. Henry F. Grady, "Mistakes in Persia," *Berlingske Aftenavis,* 11 August 1952; also FO 371/98694.

63. McGhee, *Envoy,* 393.

64. Text in ibid., 385–87.

65. Ibid., 398.

66. IBRD Press Release, 4 April 1952, World Bank, Washington, D.C., IB/322.

67. Anthony Eden to Francis Shepherd, 15 January 1952, PRO FO 371/98646, EP 1531/9.

68. Ibid.

69. Eden to O. Franks, 22 January 1952, PRO FO 371/98646, EP 1532/16.

70. Based on the fundamental point of nationalism, Mosaddeq asked the following pointed questions for the bank to clarify:

> 1. Who are "all concerned" for whose benefit large-scale oil operations in Iran would be restored? Iran has no obligation towards previous customers who have not taken advantage of priority given them.
>
> 2. What is Neutral Executive Group? Are these neutral persons who are not hostile to anyone?
>
> 3. Does "employment of non-Persians" apply to all nationalities?
>
> 4. Will the Bank's authority be restricted to technical questions or will it extend to economic matters?
>
> 5. Is "bulk export contract" to be made with the Iranian Government or with other Governments?
>
> 6. What does "division of proceeds of sale" mean? Purchasers may be accorded reduced price at the time of purchase with the approval of Iranian Government. Purchasers may not be assumed in any way to be entitled to "shares." According to the law of nationalization oil must be managed by the state. Consequently, the Government must refuse to give any concessions. The Bank, therefore, should fix commission rather than allocate proceeds.
>
> 7. The Bank should account for its expenses with fair profit or commission. The Iranian Government will assume no other obligation towards the Bank.

Mosaddeq concluded: "If these points are clarified and if the Bank agrees with our interpretation of what may be done, the Bank may proceed to inspect the installations in the south. Otherwise, the journey is pointless." Middleton to Foreign Office, 4 January 1952, PRO FO 371/98646, EP 1531/12.

71. Middleton to Foreign Office, 2 January [19]52, PRO FO 371/98646, EP 1531/4.

72. Foreign Office to Washington, 5 January 1952, PRO FO 371/98646, No. 70.

73. *Kayhan,* 19 Dey 1330 (10 January 1952); PRO FO 371/98618, EP 1051/2.

74. *Kayhan,* 21 Dey 1330 (12 January 1952).

75. Sir O. Franks to Foreign Office, 10 January 1952, PRO FO 371/98646, EP 1531/7.

76. Foreign Office to Franks, 12 January 1952, PRO FO 371/98608.

77. Francis Shepherd to Anthony Eden, 17 January 1952, PRO FO 371/98618, EP 1051/15.

78. Pahlavi, *Ma'muriat,* chap. 5.

79. Kingsley Martin, "Cold War Becomes Costly," *The New Statesman,* 12 January 1952, 27–28.

80. Ibid.

81. Ibid.

82. *Ruzshomar,* 1: 459, 464.

83. *Gahnameh,* 2: 570–80; *Ruzshomar,* 1: 457–66.

84. Middleton to Foreign Office, 11 March 1952, PRO FO 371/98651.

85. Talking Points, 10 June 1952, PRO FO 371/98691.

86. FO 371/98690, EP 15314/167.

7. TOWARD THE ABYSS

1. Francis Shepherd to Anthony Eden, 17 January 1952, PRO FO 371/98618, EP 1051/15, No. 24.

2. Eden to Anthony Nutting, 30 January 1952, PRO FO 371/98683, EP 16913/2.

3. See ibid.

4. De Courcy's letters in PRO FO 371/98683, EP 1015/438G.

5. De Courcy to Nutting, 13 February 1952, PRO FO 371/98683, EP 15313/2G.

6. Attachment to ibid.

7. Anthony Nutting to Julian Amery, MP, 19 February 1952, PRO FO 371/98683.

8. Julian Amery to The Rt. Hon. Selwyn Lloyd, 25 March 1952, PRO FO 371/98683, EP 15313.

9. Ibid.

10. Ibid.

11. Foreign Office to Tehran, 16 April 1952, PRO FO 371/98683, EP 15313/6G, No. 302.

12. Record of the meeting held in the Foreign Office, 14 February 1952, PRO FO 371/98608, EP 1022/q.

13. A. D. M. Ross to Eden, 23 June 1952, PRO FO 371/98690, EP 15314/167.

14. Minutes of meeting of 28 June 1952, PRO FO 371/98690, EP 15314/163.

15. *Ruzshomar,* 1: 466–67.

16. See ibid., 464–67; *Gahnameh,* 2: 586–89. Qavam had written a letter dated 17 March 1950 objecting to a constitutional amendment giving more power to the shah. This had led to an altercation that ended in the shah taking back Qavam's title of Jenab ashraf, which now he informally restored. The text of Qavam's original letter, Court

Minister Hakimi's response, and Qavam's response to Hakimi are in *Ruzshomar,* 1: 545–54.

17. *Ruzshomar,* 1: 468, 469.

18. George Middleton to Foreign Office, 25 July 1952, PRO FO 371/98691, No. 518.

19. Eden to Washington and Tehran, n.d., PRO FO 371/98691.

20. Oliver Franks to Foreign Office, 26 July 1952, PRO FO 371/98691, No. 1428.

21. Franks to Sir Roger Makins, 12 August 1952, PRO FO 371/98693, No. 1510.

22. Washington to Foreign Office, 24 August 1952, PRO FO 371/98694, No. 1611. The communications containing information on and leading to the joint proposal are contained in this file.

23. Tehran to Foreign Office, 27 August 1952, PRO FO 371/98695, No. 626.

24. Tehran to Foreign Office, 28 August 1952, PRO FO 371/98695, No. 628.

25. Middleton to Foreign Office, 1 September 1952, PRO FO 371/98695, No. 648.

26. Personal and Secret message to the president, Foreign Office to Washington, 28 August 1952, PRO FO 371/98695, No. 3581.

27. Foreign Office to Washington, 30 August 1952, PRO FO 371/98695, No. 1651.

28. Gholam Reza Afkhami, ed., *Tahavvol-e san'at-e naft iran: Negahi az darun* [The Evolution of Iran's Oil Industry: An Insider's Assessment], An Interview with Parviz Mina (Bethesda, Md.: FIS, 1998), 9.

29. Tehran to Foreign Office, 7 September 1952, PRO FO 371/98696, No. 671.

30. *Kayhan,* 3 Dey 1331 (24 December 1952).

31. See Loy Henderson's communications to the State Department, 31 December 1952 and 2, 4, and 8 January 1953, in PRO FO 371/104606.

32. Cited in confidential security information sent out by Roy M. Melbourne, First Secretary of U.S. Embassy, [February 1953], PRO FO 371/104561.

33. Henderson to Washington, 20 February 1953, PRO FO 371/104613, EP 1531/168.

34. Henderson to Washington, 23 February 1953, PRO FO 371/104613, EP 1531/173.

35. *Ruzshomar,* 1: 475.

36. For the law see *Vezarat-e dadgostari, Majmu'eh-ye qavanin, sal-e 1331, ruznameh-ye rasmi-ye keshvar-e shahanshahi-ye iran* [Ministry of Justice, Law Series, 1952–53, the Official Gazette of the Imperial Iranian State], 85–86.

37. *Ruzshomar,* 1: 478–80.

38. Hossein Ala, "Hossein Ala's Daily Reports to the Shah, No. 2," *Faslnameh tarikh-e mu'aser-e iran* [The Contemporary History of Iran Quarterly] 1, 2 (summer 1997): 131–32. See also Jalil Bozorgmehr, *Taqrirat-e Mosaddeq dar zendan* [Mosaddeq's Statements in Prison], ed. Iraj Afshar (Tehran: Entsharat-e farhang, 1359 [1980]), 126–31. According to Mosaddeq, Ala and Heshmat-Dauleh met together with Mosaddeq at the latter's house, 126.

39. Ala, "Daily Reports," 132.

40. Bozorgmehr, *Taqrirat,* 127.

41. Ala, "Daily Reports," 133–34.

42. *Gahnameh,* 2: 610–12; Bozorgmehr, *Taqrirat,* 128; *Ruzshomar,* 1: 483–84.

43. *Gahnameh,* 2: 610–11.

44. Ala, "Daily Reports," 132–34. Curiously, this same sentiment is expressed by a CIA operative working then at the Greece-Turkey-Iran branch of the Office of Current

Intelligence (OCI): "You get a strong figure like Razmara or Mossadeq or sometimes Qavam, they seem to develop the point of challenging the Shah, rather than using the Shah to achieve national goals. Do you understand what I'm suggesting? Whatever the goal was of Razmara or Modsadeq, or maybe Qavam, or may be even much later of [General] Bakhtiar, whatever their original goals may have been, it seems like ultimately it boiled down to a challenge to the Shah. I think that Iranian politicians missed a number of good opportunities to advance the interests of Iran and of reform and so on, by aiming at the Shah (to supplant or supersede him or shove him into a purely ceremonial position) instead of coopting him." FISOHA interview with Ernest R. Oney, by Seyyed Vali Reza Nasr, Bethesda, Md., 22 and 29 May 1991, 7–8.

45. *The Times,* Monday, 9 March 1953.

46. Henderson to State Department, Report of Interview with Dr. Mosaddeq, 9 March 1953, PRO FO 371/104614.

47. *Kayhan,* 29 Esfand 1331 (20 March 1953); PRO FO 371/104614, EP 1531/224.

48. Commonwealth Relations Office to U.K. High Commissioners, 21 March 1953, PRO FO 371/104614, EP 1531/197.

49. Mosaddeq interview with Homer Bigart, *New York Herald Tribune,* 30 April 1953.

50. Henderson to State Department, 10 May 1953, PRO FO 371/104581, EP 10345/10.

51. Peter G. Boyle, *The Churchill-Eisenhower Correspondence, 1953–1955* (Chapel Hill: University of North Carolina Press, 1990), 53.

52. Message from Dr. Mosaddeq to President Eisenhower, 28 May 1953, PRO FO 371/104581.

53. Homer Bigart, "Extra Aid for Iran Ruled Out," *New York Herald Tribune,* 8 July 1953.

54. *Gahnameh,* 2: 620–22.

55. Gold was owed Iran as part of payment for the damages Iran had sustained during the Allied occupation. The agreement had been signed between Iran and the Allies on 18 March 1943. Since the Soviet ruble was inconvertible, the Soviets agreed to make part of the payment (approximately $12.5 million) in gold. After a decade of negotiations, on 1 June 1955 they delivered to Iran 11.8 tons of gold and additional monetary credits to satisfy approximately $20 million of debt.

56. Ibid., 622.

57. Ibid.

8. TPAJAX

1. *Gahnameh,* 2: 618–22; *Ruzshomar,* 1: 484–87.

2. *Gahnameh,* 2: 622–25; *Ruzshomar,* 1: 488–99.

3. *Gahnameh,* 2: 626.

4. Esmail Rain, *Asnad-e khaneh-e Seddon* [Documents from Seddon's House], (Tehran: Tarjomeh va nashre ketab, n.d. [orig. pub. 1351 (1972)]).

5. Richard Helms, *A Look over My Shoulder: A Life in the Central Intelligence Agency* (New York: Random House, 2003), 82–83, 113–14, 116.

6. Ibid., 117.

7. Helms is quite loquacious on later CIA operations—Cuba (MONGOOSE) and Chile (the Allende affair), for example. See ibid., esp. 201–26 for Cuba and 393–408 for Chile.

8. FISOHA interview with Richard Helms, by William Burr, Washington, D.C., 10 and 24 July 1985, 4.

9. Arthur M. Schlesinger, Jr., *Robert Kennedy and His Times* (New York: Ballantine Books, 1978), 489.

10. Ibid., 490.

11. On 16 June 2000, *The New York Times* published on its Web site PDF files of a secret CIA report: "CLANDESTINE SERVICE HISTORY, OVERTHROW OF PREMIER MOSSADEQ OF IRAN, November 1952–August 1953," an operation planned and executed by the CIA and British SIS: http://www.nytimes.com/library/world/mideast/041600 iran-cia-index.html. References to this report (hereafter referred to in the text as the Secret Report), are based on Donald Wilber's account and the original plan as extracted directly and indirectly from the *Times* publication. According to the Secret Report, Donald N. Wilber, who wrote a draft of the plan and subsequent operations in March 1954, was in 1953 a covert consultant to the CIA Near East and Africa Division (NEA), which at the time was being administered by Kermit Roosevelt. On 13 May 1953 Wilber was dispatched to Nicosia to work out a plan with the SIS, represented by Norman Mathew Darbyshire, the officer in charge of SIS's Iran Branch. "Discussions were concluded on 30 May 1953 and the completed draft of a recommended operational plan was cabled by Wilber to Headquarters on 1 June." See also Kermit Roosevelt, *Countercoup: The Struggle for Control of Iran* (New York: McGraw-Hill, 1979).

12. Eisenhower's Diary, 8 October 1953, quoted in Stephen E. Ambrose, *Eisenhower, vol. 2, The President* (New York: Simon and Schuster, 1984), 129.

13. C. M. Woodhouse, *Something Ventured: The Autobiography of C. M. Woodhouse* (London: Granada Publishing, 1982), chaps. 8 and 9. (I am currently unable to locate the English edition; page citations are to the Persian translation by Nezameddin Darbandi, *Asrar-e kudetay-e 28 mordad* [Tehran: Offset, 1364 (1985)].)

14. Anthony Cavendish, *Inside Intelligence: The Revelations of an MI6 Officer* (London: HarperCollins, 1997), 139.

15. Anthony Verrier, *Through the Looking Glass: British Foreign Policy in an Age of Illusions* (London: Norton, 1983); cited in Cavendish, *Inside Intelligence,* 139.

16. Woodhouse, *Something Ventured,* chap. 8.

17. Stephen Kinzer, *All the Shah's Men: An American Coup and the Roots of the Middle East Terror* (Hoboken, N.J.: Wiley, 2003), 6, 7, 2.

18. Woodhouse, *Something Ventured,* 75.

19. Ashraf Pahlavi, *Faces in a Mirror: Memoirs from Exile* (Englewood Cliffs, N.J.: Prentice-Hall, 1980), 134–40. On Khojasteh Hedayat see FISOHA interview with Princess Ashraf, by Ahmad Ghoreishi, New York, 5 June 1982, 35.

20. Kinzer, *All the Shah's Men,* 11. Roosevelt's account of his meetings with the shah is in Roosevelt, *Countercoup,* 156–67.

21. Kinzer, *All the Shah's Men,* 10.

22. Ibid., 11; and see Roosevelt, *Countercoup,* 161.

23. Kinzer, *All the Shah's Men,* 11.

24. Ibid.; and see Roosevelt, *Countercoup,* 168.

25. Kinzer, *All the Shah's Men,* 12.

26. FISOHA interview with Ardeshir Zahedi, by Gholam Reza Afkhami, Montreux, Switzerland, 5 July 2001, tape 2, side 1.

27. William Warne, *Mission for Peace: Point 4 in Iran* (Bethesda, Md.: IBEX, 1999; orig. pub. 1956), 116–17, 41.

28. Zahedi interview, tape 2, sides 1 and 2.

29. Ibid.

30. Ibid.

31. Ezzatollah Homayounfar, *Az sepahigari ta siasatmadari* [From the Military to Politics] (Geneva: Abnus, 1997), 243.

32. Homa Katouzian, *Musaddiq and the Struggle for Power in Iran* (London and New York: I. B. Tauris, 1999; orig. pub. 1990), 187.

33. Noor Mohammad Asgari, *Shah, Mosaddeq, Sepahbod Zahedi* (Stockholm: Arash, 2000), 107, quoting an interview with Bashir Farahmand in 1979.

34. Zahedi interview, tape 2, sides 1 and 2.

35. FISOHA interview with Majid A'lam, by Ahmad Ghoreishi, Walnut Creek, Calif., 22 May 1991, 9–11. FISOHA interview with Yahya Adl, by Gholam Reza Afkhami, Paris, 20 August 2000, tape 3, side 1.

36. Ardeshir Zahedi, "Panj ruz-e bohrani" [The Five Critical Days], *Ettela'at-e Mahaneh,* Shahrivar 1336 [1957].

37. Kinzer, *All the Shah's Men,* 183 (based on Roosevelt, *Countercoup,* 193–94).

38. Kinzer, *All the Shah's Men,* 183–87.

39. Gholamhossein Sadiqi, "28 va 29 Mordad 1332" [19 and 20 August 1953], *Ayandeh* 14, 3–5 (Khordad–Mordad 1367 [May–August 1988]): 120–40.

40. Ibid. Sadiqi may be confused here. According to the Iranian press, Mosaddeq had already dismissed Colonel Ashrafi, whom he had appointed military governor of Tehran on 21 July 1953, on 18 August (the day before), replacing him with Brigadier Daftary. On the other hand, Ashrafi might have remained in the headquarters to complete the handing over of the command to Daftary. See *Ruzshomar,* 1: 489, 491.

41. Sadiqi, "28 va 29 Mordad 1332."

42. Reported by General Khosrodad, who had several conversations with the author between 1975 and 1978.

43. Kinzer, *All the Shah's Men,* 180.

44. See Homa Sarshar, ed., *Sha'ban Ja'fari* (Beverly Hills, Calif.: Naab Publishers, 2002), 159–207.

45. FISOHA interview with General Reza Azimi, by Farrokh Ghaffari, Paris, June 1990, 4.

46. FISOHA interview with Abolfath Atabai, by Ahmad Ghoreishi, New York, 6 June 1982, 34.

47. British Ambassador in Baghdad to the Marquess of Salisbury, 19 August 1953, PRO FO 371/104570, EP 1015/218.

48. Ibid.

49. *Ruzshomar,* 1: 490.

50. British Ambassador to the Marquess of Salisbury, 19 August 1953.

51. Ibid.
52. Atabai interview, 35.
53. British Ambassador to the Marquess of Salisbury, 19 August 1953.
54. Atabai interview.
55. Ibid.
56. Princess Ashraf interview, 38.
57. Alexander Solzhenitsyn, *Lenin in Zurich,* trans. H. T. Willetts (New York: Farrar, Straus and Giroux, 1976).
58. Atabai interview, 38.
59. Ibid., 39
60. *Gahnameh,* 2: 629–30.
61. Atabai interview, 40.
62. *Gahnameh,* 2: 631–32; *Ruzshomar,* 2: 11–12.

9. A NEW VISTA

1. FISOHA interview with Ardeshir Zahedi, by Gholam Reza Afkhami, Montreux, Switzerland, 5 July 2001, tape 3, side 1.
2. Ibid.
3. Loy Henderson to Washington, No. 466, 23 August 1953; in Department of State, *Foreign Relations of the United States 1952–1954,* vol. 10, *Iran, 1952–1954* (Washington, D.C.: Government Printing Office, 1989). All further communiqués cited from Henderson are in this volume.
4. Ibid.
5. Text of Zahedi's and Eisenhower's statements printed in *Kayhan,* 12 Shahrivar 1332 (2 September 1953).
6. William E. Warne, *Mission for Peace: Point 4 in Iran* (Bethesda, Md.: IBEX, 1999; orig. pub. 1956), 259–60.
7. Farhad Kazemi, ed., *Khaterat-e natamam-e doctor Parviz-e Kazemi* [Memoirs of Dr. Parviz Kazemi] (New York: BAF, 1995), 157.
8. Henderson to State Department, No. 357, 27 August 1953.
9. Henderson to State Department, No. 360, 1 September 1953.
10. Henderson to State Department, No. 368, 18 September 1953.
11. Zahedi interview, tape 3, side 1.
12. *Ruzshomar,* 1: 491.
13. Zahedi interview, tape 3, side 1.
14. Warne, *Mission for Peace,* 261.
15. *Ruzshomar,* 2: 12.
16. Text of Mosaddeq's trial in *Ruzshomar,* 2: 430–59.
17. *Gahnameh,* 2: 660.
18. Zahedi interview, tape 3, side 2.
19. Anthony Cavendish, *Inside Intelligence: The Revelations of an MI6 Officer* (London: HarperCollins, 1997), 139; Cavendish cites Anthony Verrier, *Through the Looking Glass: British Foreign Policy in an Age of Illusions* (London: Norton, 1983).
20. Secret memo, 21 August 1953, PRO FO 371/104577, EP 1024/1.

21. Foreign Office to Washington, No. 3342, 28 August 1953, PRO FO 371/104577, EP 1024/5.

22. U.S. ambassador in London to Marquess of Salisbury, 9 September 1953, PRO FO 371/104577, EP 1024/10G.

23. Foreign Ministers Conference, 17 October 1953, PRO FO 371/104577, EP 1024/12.

24. Quoted in W. M. Jablonski, *Journal of Commerce,* 6 October 1953.

25. Ibid.

26. Henderson to State Department, No. 388, 19 November 1953.

27. Ibid.

28. *Gahnameh,* 2: 647; *Ruzshomar,* 2: 26.

29. *Ruzshomar,* 2: 26.

30. *Gahnameh,* 2: 653.

31. Ronald Ferrier, "The Iranian Oil Industry," in *The Cambridge History of Iran* (Cambridge: Cambridge University Press, 1991), 639–701, at 664–65. See also Gholam Reza Afkhami, ed., *Tahavvol-e san'at-e naft-e iran: Negahi az darun* [The Evolution of Iran's Oil Industry: An Insider's Assessment], An Interview with Parviz Mina (Bethesda, Md.: FIS, 1998); hereafter cited as Mina. Fuad Rowhani, *Tarikh-e melli shodan-e san'at-e naft-e iran* [A History of the Nationalization of the Iranian Oil Industry] (Tehran: Jibi, 1973).

32. Mina, 31–32.

33. Ebrahim Safai, *Eshtebah-e bozorg, melli shodan-e naft?* [A Grand Mistake? Nationalization of Oil] (Tehran: Ketab Sara, 1371 [1992]), 289.

34. *Gahnameh,* 2: 684.

35. *Ruzshomar,* 2: 40.

36. Seyyed Jalal-ud-Din Madani, *Tarikh-e siyasi-e mu'aser-e iran* [Contemporary Political History of Iran], 2 vols. (Tehran: Daftar-e Entesharat-e Eslami, 1376 [1997]), 1: 313–14.

37. *Official Gazette,* Proceeding of the Eighteenth Majlis, 5 Mehr 1333 (27 September 1954).

38. Mina, 12–13.

39. Fuad Rowhani, *San'at-e naft-e iran: Bist sal pas az melli shodan* [The Iranian Oil Industry: Twenty Years after Nationalization] (Tehran: Jibi, 2536 [1977]), 1.

40. U.S. State Department, *Bulletin* 28, 729 (15 July 1953): 833.

41. Dwight D. Eisenhower, *Waging Peace, 1956–1961* (Garden City, N.Y.: Doubleday, 1965), 505.

42. *Gahnameh,* 2: 721.

43. Ibid., 724–27.

44. Ibid., 722.

45. Zahedi interview, 5 July 2001, tape 3, side 1. President Eisenhower, press conference, 15 December 1954; reported in *New York Times,* 16 December 1954.

46. Interview with Ardeshir Zahedi, by Barry Zevan, 1 October 1998, reproduced in Pari Abasalti and Hushang Mirhashem, eds., *Ardeshir Zahedi: Untold Secrets* (Los Angeles: Rah-e Zendegi, 2002). Zahedi interview, 5 July 2001, tape 3, side 1.

47. Zahedi interview, 5 July 2001, tape 3, side 1. The Sa'dabad Pact was a treaty signed by Iran, Afghanistan, Iraq, and Turkey at the Sa'dabad Palace in Tehran on 9 July 1937,

by which the signatories agreed to refrain from interference in each other's internal affairs, to respect their mutual frontiers, to refrain from aggression against each other, and to consult together in the event an international conflict should threaten their common interest.

48. This was one of five agreements signed between Iran and the Soviet Union in 1927, covering fishing rights in the Caspian, return to Iran of the installations at the Caspian port of Pahlavi, commercial relations, customs tariffs, and guarantees of mutual neutrality and security, the latter usually referred to as the 1927 Agreement.

49. *Gahnameh,* 2: 678.

50. Ibid., 738–39.

51. Mohammad Reza Pahlavi, *Ma'muriat baray-e vatanam* [Mission for My Country] (Tehran: Nashr-e Ketab, 1353 [1974]; orig. pub. 1961), 206.

52. See Majid Tafreshi, ed., *Chehel sal dar sahneh: Khaterat-e doctor Jalal Abdoh* [Forty Years on the Stage: Memoirs of Dr. Jalal Abdoh], 2 vols. (Tehran: Rasa, 1989), 1: 562–68.

53. Abolhassan Ebtehaj, *Khaterat-e Abolhassan Ebtehaj* [The Memoirs of Abolhassan Ebtehaj], ed. Alireza Aruzi, 2 vols. (London: Paka Print, 1370 [1991]), 1: 297–307, 323–27; hereafter cited as Ebtehaj. See also Bank Melli, "History of Iran's Seven-Year Plan: Organization, Development, and Construction," Bureau of Statistics and Economic and Financial Studies, no. 98 (Tehran: Bahman-Esfand, 1327 [1949]).

54. Ebtehaj, 323–27.

55. Ibid., 328, 333.

56. Sir Roger Stevens to The Rt. Hon. John Selwyn Lloyd, Foreign Office, 1 January 1956, PRO FO 371/120710, EP 1011/1.

57. Stevens to Foreign Office, 27 and 31 May 1954, PRO FO 248/1542, PE 1018/1/54G and 1018/5/56G.

58. Stevens to Foreign Office, 21 March 1955, PRO FO 248/1554, EP 1014/28/5S.

59. *Ruzshomar,* 2: 49–51.

60. *Gahnameh,* 2: 744–46.

61. See Ezzatollah Homayounfar, *Az sepahigari ta siasatmadari* [From the Military to Politics] (Geneva: Abnus, 1997), 394–99.

62. FISOHA interviews with Naser Zolfaqari, by Farrokh Ghaffari, Paris, 11 May, 9 and 23 September, 5 and 28 October 1989, 89.

63. Zahedi interview, 5 July 2001, tape 2, side 2.

64. Soraya Esfandiaryi Bakhtiari, *Le Palais des Solitudes,* 1st ed. (Paris: Michel Lafon, 1991), 130.

65. Zahedi interview, 5 July 2001, tape 2, side 2; Zolfaqari interview, 89.

10. THE WHITE REVOLUTION

1. Abolhassan Ebtehaj, *Khaterat-e Abolhassan Ebtehaj* [The Memoirs of Abolhassan Ebtehaj], ed. Alireza Aruzi, 2 vols. (London: Paka Print, 1370 [1991]), 1: 375; hereafter cited as Ebtehaj.

2. Ibid., 239.

3. Ibid., 374, 384–85.

4. Gholam Reza Afkhami, ed., *Omran-e khuzestan* [Khuzistan's Development], Interviews with Abdol-Reza Ansari, Hassan Shahmirzadi, and Ahmad Ali Ahmadi (Bethesda, Md.: FIS, 1994), 24.

5. David E. Lilienthal, *The Journals of David E. Lilienthal,* 7 vols. (New York: Harper and Row, 1964–83), 4 (1969): 179–81.

6. Mohammad Reza Pahlavi, interview in exile on *Answer to History,* by Christine Godek and Tom Weir, Cairo, 27 May 1980, tape 3.

7. Ebtehaj, 1: 430.

8. Farmanfarmaian in Gholam Reza Afkhami, ed., *Barnamerizi-ye omrani va tasmimgiri-ye siyasi* [Ideology, Process, and Politics in Iran's Development Planning], Interviews with Manuchehr Gudarzi, Khodadad Farmanfarmaian, and Abdol-Majid Majidi (Bethesda, Md.: FIS, 1999), 144. Hereafter cited as Gudarzi, Farmanfarmaian, or Majidi.

9. *Ruzshomar,* 2: 95.

10. Farmanfarmaian, 143.

11. Ebtehaj, 1: 446.

12. The author was the host of the meeting as the president of the association.

13. *Gahnameh,* 3: 1109–10; *Ruzshomar,* 2: 111.

14. *The Washington Post,* 20 February 1961.

15. *Ruzshomar,* 2: 123–24.

16. Ibid., 84–85. See also FISOHA interview with Nasser Zolfaqari, by Farrokh Ghaffari, Paris, 11 May, 9 and 23 September, 5 and 28 October 1989, 117–18.

17. Zolfaqari interview, 117–18.

18. *Ruzshomar,* 2: 84–85. See also Zolfaqari interview, 126–27; Amir Hushang Asgari, "Chand khatereh az doctor Amini" [Remembering Dr. Amini], *Rah-e Zendegi* [Way of Life], no. 455, 12 Aban 1368 [October 1989]): 34–35.

19. Majidi, 252–54; see also interview with Gudarzi, a leading member of the group.

20. FISOHA interview with Dean Rusk, by William Burr, Athens, Ga., 23 May 1986, 12.

21. Pahlavi interview, tape 3.

22. Rusk interview, 10.

23. Ibid., 11, 12.

24. FISOHA interview with Philips Talbot, by William Burr, New York, 21 November 1985, 8, 13.

25. FISOHA interview with Armin Meyer, by William Burr, Washington, D.C., 29 March 1985, 1.

26. Ibid., 2.

27. *Gahnameh,* 3: 1148, 1150; *Ruzshomar,* 2: 119.

28. FISOHA interview with Robert W. Komer, by William Burr, Washington, D.C., 27 April and 11 August 1987, 2–7, quote at 7.

29. Ibid., 9, 11.

30. Farmanfarmaian, 118.

31. Ibid., 135.

32. Majidi, 258–59.

33. See Farmanfarmaian, esp. 115–24, and Majidi, 255–66.

34. Farmanfarmaian, 152.

35. Ibid.

36. Majidi, 262, 263.

37. *Gahnameh,* 3: 1249.

38. Majidi, 264–65.

39. Stuart Rockwell for the Ambassador, U.S. Embassy, Tehran, no. 358, 3 February 1962, in "Iran dar band," *Asnad* 6 (winter 1969): 1–9.

40. *Ruzshomar,* 2: 141.

41. Record of conversation between the foreign secretary (Sir Alec Douglas-Home) and the shah of Iran in Tehran on Friday, 3 March 1961, PRO FO 371/157621.

42. Mohammad Reza Pahlavi, *Ma'muriat baray-e vatanam* [Mission for My Country] (Tehran: Nashr-e Ketab, 1353 [1974]; orig. pub. 1961), Introduction.

43. Ibid., 327–33.

44. Ibid., 336–38.

45. Ibid., 340, 341, 346, 348.

46. Ibid., 349–50.

47. Ibid., 350–52.

48. Ibid., 353–55.

49. Ibid., 361.

50. Ibid., 363–64.

51. Ibid., 364.

52. Ibid., 385–86.

53. FISOHA interview with Gholam Hosein Jahanshahi, by Mahnaz Afkhami, Juan Les Pins, France, 31 August 1989, 15–16.

54. For a comprehensive account of the land tenure system in Iran before the passage of land reform laws, see Anne K. S. Lambton, *Landlord and Peasant in Persia: A Study of Land Tenure and Land Revenue* (Oxford: Oxford University Press, 1953).

55. *Ruzshomar,* 2: 145–47.

56. *Gahnameh,* 3: 1261–62.

57. Ibid., 1266, 1268, 1269, 1272.

58. Ibid., 1279, 1290, 1293.

59. Jahanshahi interview, 7.

60. Ibid., 8.

61. Ibid.

62. See D. R. Denman's account in George Lenczowski, ed., *Iran under the Pahlavis* (Stanford, Calif.: Hoover Institution Press, 1978), 253–301, 263. Amouzegar came under attack by opponents of land reform who wrongly and underhandedly accused him of implementing some American design. See an example of the accusations and Amouzegar's response in *Rahavard,* winter 1992, 264–66.

63. *Gahnameh,* 3: 1297, 1298.

64. *Ruzshomar,* 2: 150.

65. Gholam Reza Afkhami, ed., *Jame'eh, dowlat va jonbesh-e zanan-e iran: 1320–1357* [Women, State, and Society in Iran: vol. 1, 1941–1978], Interview with Mehrangiz Dowlatshahi (Bethesda, Md.: FIS, 2002), 124–26, 128; hereafter cited as Dowlatshahi.

66. *Ruzshomar,* 2: 148–49.

67. *Gahnameh,* 3: 1303–4; *Ruzshomar,* 2: 150. Contrary to expectations, women activists had encountered no opposition when they voted for the first time in the referendum. "It should be remembered that women went out to vote with their families and the men everywhere supported them. Men, therefore, also voted for the women's right to vote," Mehrangiz Dowlatshahi reasoned; Dowlatshahi, 133–34.

68. *Gahnameh,* 3: 1310; and see Dowlatshahi, 135–36.

69. *Gahnameh,* 3: 1314.

70. *Ruzshomar,* 2: 153.

71. Gholam Reza Afkhami, ed., *Siyasat va siasatgozari-e eqtesadi dar iran, 1340–1350* [Ideology, Politics, and Process in Iran's Economic Development, 1960–1970], Interview with Alinaghi Alikhani (Bethesda, Md.: FIS, 2001), 39; hereafter cited as Alikhani.

72. *Gahnameh,* 3: 1316, 1324, 1328.

73. See Report of the Political Officer, U.S. Embassy, Tehran, no. 260, 3 December 1964, in *Asnad,* 6: 10–18.

74. *Gahnameh,* 3: 1324, 1328.

75. FISOHA interview with General Mansur Qadar, by Gholam Reza Afkhami, Washington, D.C., 30 April and 4 May 1986, 20–21.

76. *Ruzshomar,* 2: 463, 464.

77. Alikhani, 40, 41.

78. Jahanshahi interview, 14.

79. Ibid., 15.

80. Interview with Kambiz Atabai, by Gholam Reza Afkhami, New York, 5 February 2001.

81. FISOHA interviews with General Mohsen Hashemi-Nejad, by Marvin Zonis, March 1982, and Seyyed Vali Reza Nasr, April 1989, Washington, D.C., 48.

11. WOMEN AND RIGHTS

1. For a panoramic discussion of women in Iran before the nineteenth century, see Guitty Nashat and Lois Beck, eds., *Women in Iran from the Rise of Islam to 1800* (Urbana and Chicago: University of Illinois Press, 2003).

2. For a sympathetic discourse on Tahereh Qurrat-ul 'Ain, see Farzaneh Milani, "Pardeh ra bedarim, begozarim keh ehsas hava-i bekhorad" [Let Us Tear Off the Veil and Let Feeling Have Some Air], *Nimeh Digar* 15/16 (fall and winter 1991): 56–61; also Ali Akbar Mahdi, "The Iranian Women's Movement: A Century-Long Struggle," *The Muslim World* 94, 4 (October 2000): 427–48.

3. Mansureh Nezam-Mafi and Cyrus Saadvandian, eds., *Khaterat-e Taj-us-Saltaneh* [Memoirs of Taj-us-Saltaneh] (Tehran: Nashr-e tarikh-e iran, 1362 [1983]), 14.

4. See Fereydun Adamiayat, *Ideolozhi-ye nehzat-e mashrutiat-e iran* [The Ideology of Iran's Constitutional Revolution] (Tehran: Entesharat-e payam, 2535 [1976]); Ahmad Kasravi, *Tarikh-e mashruteh-e iran* [A History of Iran's Constitutional Movement] (Tehran: Amir-Kabir, 1340 [1961]); Nikki Keddie and Mehrdad Amanat, "Iran under the Later Qâjârs, 1848–1922," *The Cambridge History of Iran,* 7 vols. (Cambridge: Cambridge University Press, 1991), 7: 174–212; and *Iran Nameh* 11, 3 (summer 1993), issue devoted to the Constitutional Revolution. See also Janet Afary, *The Iranian Constitu-*

tional Revolution 1906–1911: Grassroots Democracy and the Origins of Feminism (New York: Columbia University Press, 1996).

5. Seyyed Ali Kamali, *Qur'an va maqam-e zan* [The Koran and Woman's Status] (Qom: Sadra, 1363 [1984]).

6. See, among others, Mahnaz Afkhami, ed., *Faith and Freedom: Women's Human Rights in the Muslim World* (London and New York: I. B. Tauris, 1995); Ann Elizabeth Mayer, *Islam and Human Rights: Tradition and Politics,* 4th ed. (Boulder, Colo.: Westview Press, 2006), especially chapter 6, "Restrictions on the Rights and Freedoms of Women"; Fatima Mernissi, *The Veil and the Male Elite: A Feminist Interpretation of Women's Rights in Islam* (Reading, Mass.: Addison Wesley, 1991); Ziba Mir-Hosseini, *Islam and Gender: The Religious Debate in Contemporary Iran* (Princeton: Princeton University Press, 1999). For a modern Islamist interpretation of the position of women in Islam, see the works of Morteza Motahhari, especially *Nezam-e hoquq-e zan dar eslam* [The System of Women's Rights in Islam], 8th ed. (Qom: Sadra, 1974).

7. Gholam Reza Afkhami, ed., *Jame'eh, dowlat va jonbesh-e zanan-e iran: 1320–1357* [Women, State, and Society in Iran: vol. 1, 1941–1978]), Interview with Dowlatshahi (Bethesda, Md.: FIS, 2002), 25–27.

8. FISOHA interview with Nayyereh Ebtehaj-Samii, by Shirin Samii, Dover, Mass., 6 April 1984, 6. It should be noted, however, that years before the official unveiling in 1936, certain upper-class and intellectual families lived practically unveiled, though not in public. The tension between the traditionalist majority and modernist minority was in many ways focused on women. See Mohammad Tavakoli Targhi, "Women of the West Imagined: The Farangi Other and the Emergence of the Woman Question in Iran," in *Identity Politics and Women: Cultural Reassertions and Feminisms in International Perspective,* ed. Valentine M. Moghadam (Boulder, Colo.: Westview Press, 1994), 98–120.

9. See Haideh Moghissi, *Populism and Feminism in Iran* (New York: St. Martin's, 1996), notably chapter 5 and part 3; Parvin Paidar, *Women and the Political Process in Twentieth-Century Iran* (Cambridge: Cambridge University Press, 1995); Nahid Yeganeh and Azar Tabari, eds., *In the Shadow of Islam: The Women's Movement in Iran* (London: Zed Books, 1983).

10. Dowlatshahi, 82, 86–87. Compare with the opinions stated by several left-leaning writers on this subject, for example, Paidar, *Women and the Political Process;* Eliz Sanasarian, *The Women's Rights Movement in Iran: Mutiny, Appeasement, and Repression from 1900 to Khomeini* (New York: Praeger, 1982); Yeganeh and Tabari, *In the Shadow of Islam.*

11. Dowlatshahi, 66–80.

12. The nine were Mehrangiz Dowlatshahi, Saideh Zanjani, Mehri Sadeqinejad, Parvin Khanlari, Forugh Shahab, Shokuh Riazi, Qamar Ariya, Mehri Ahy, and Parichehr Hekmat. See ibid.

13. Ibid., 57.

14. Ibid., 119.

15. *Gahnameh,* 2: 1027.

16. *The Times,* 2 January 1960.

17. *Gahnameh,* 3: 1346–49.

18. The new crop of women in legislative bodies was in the tradition of Badr-ul-Moluk Bamdad, one of the first women to attend university, a woman leader, and author of a seminal book on the women's movement in Iran. See B. Bamdad, *From Darkness to Light: Women's Emancipation in Iran,* ed. and trans. F. R. C. Bagley (Hicksville, N.Y.: Exposition Press, 1977).

19. Noushin Ahmadi Khorasani and Parvin Ardalan, *Senator: Fa'aliatha-ye Mehrangiz Manuchehrian bar bastar-e mobarezat-e hoququi-e zanan dar iran* [The Senator: Mehrangiz Manuchehrian's Efforts in the Context of Women's Activities Concerning Equal Rights in Contemporary Iran] (Tehran: Tose'eh, 1382 [2003]), 238–39.

20. Mehrangiz Manuchehrian, *Enteqad-e qavanin-e asasi va madani va keyfari az nazar-e hoquq-e zan* [A Critique of Iran's Constitutional, Civil, and Criminal Law from the Standpoint of Women's Rights] (Tehran: Sazeman-e davtalaban-e hemayat-e Khanevadeh, 1342 [1963]), Muqaddameh (prologue).

21. *Official Gazette,* Senate Debates, 7 Esfand 1342 (26 February 1964).

22. Khorasani and Ardalan, *Senator,* 252–57.

23. *Eradeh-e Azarbaijan Weekly* 693, 15 Bahman 1345, cited in ibid., 259.

24. Dowlatshahi, 151. On *mut'a* see Shahla Haeri, "The Institution of Mut'a Marriage in Iran: A Formal and Historical Perspective," in *Women and Revolution in Iran,* ed. Guitty Nashat (Boulder, Colo.: Westview Press, 1983), 231–52; and Haeri, *Law of Desire: Temporary Marriage in Iran* (London: I. B. Tauris, 1989). See also Motahhari, *Nezam;* and Muhammad Husayn Tabatabai, *Ezdevaj-e movaqqat dar eslam* [Temporary Marriage in Islam] (Qom: Sadra, 1985).

25. *Sahifeh Imam* [A Collection of Imam Khomeini's Works] (Tehran: Nashr-e asar-e emam, 1378 [1999]), 1: 314, cited in Khorasani and Ardalan, 281.

26. *Gahnameh,* 1: 561.

27. *Gahnameh,* 4: 1666.

28. *Gahnameh,* 4: 1677–78

29. Around the World with Bernice Q Johnson, in http://www.geocities.com/ Heartland/Village/8168/24iran.html.

30. *Ruzshomar,* 2: 210.

31. Text in English in Farah Pahlavi, *An Enduring Love: My Life with the Shah* (New York: Miramax, 2004), 157.

32. *Gahnameh,* 4: 1679.

33. Dowlatshahi, 105.

34. Gholam Reza Afkhami, ed., *Jam'eh, dowlat va jonbesh-e zanan-e iran: 1342–1357* (Women, State, and Society in Iran: vol. 2, 1963–1978), An Interview with Mahnaz Afkhami (Bethesda, Md.: FIS, 2003), 49–50; hereafter cited as M. Afkhami.

35. Ibid., 69–70.

36. *Ettela'at,* 8 Aban 1346 (29 October 1967).

37. *Ettela'at,* 18 Aban 1346 (8 November 1967).

38. *Zan-e Ruz* [Contemporary Woman], 23 Dey 1346 (13 January 1968).

39. Senate Debate, Session 33, 8 Khordad 1351, cited in Khorasani and Ardalan, *Senator,* 325–30.

40. M. Afkhami, 103.

41. Some scholars have argued that Manuchehrian failed because what she proposed

had not been initiated by the shah or his family. This is at best a dubious proposition. See Paidar, *Women and the Political Process;* and Homa Hoodfar, "The Women's Movement in Iran: Women at the Crossroads of Secularization and Islamization," *Iran Chamber Society,* winter 1999. The latter may be accessed at http://www.iranchamber.com/podium/history/020312_women_secularization_islamization1.php.

42. M. Afkhami, 105–6.

43. Mohammad Reza Pahlavi, *Ma'muriat baray-e vatanam* [Mission for My Country] (Tehran: Nashr-e Ketab, 1353 [1974]; orig. pub. 1961), 479–80.

44. M. Afkhami, 95–96.

45. Charter of the Women's Organization of Iran, adopted 31 April 1973, in Khorasani and Ardalan, *Senator,* 560–65.

46. From the shah's speech, printed in *Kongereh-ye bozorgdasht-e chehelomin salruz-e azadi-ye ejtema'i-ye zanan va aghaz-e sal-e jahani-ye zan* [The Congress to Celebrate the Fortieth Anniversary of Women's Social Freedom and the Beginning of the International Year of the Woman] (Tehran: Women's Organization of Iran, 1353 [1975]), 7–12.

47. Ibid.

48. "Declaration Presented by Her Imperial Highness Princess Ashraf Pahlavi to the Secretary General of the United Nations on December 10, 1974" (Tehran: Women's Organization of Iran, n.d.), 12, 15.

49. United Nations, http://www.choike.org/nuevo_eng/informes/1453.html.

50. ECOSOC, E./Conf.66/CC/L.1, 3 March 1975.

51. UN World Plan of Action, reproduced in "A National Plan of Action for the Improvement of Women's Status in Iran" (Tehran: Women's Organization of Iran, September 1978).

52. Mahnaz Afkhami became the second woman to be appointed to the cabinet in Iran and also the second woman in the world to be appointed as minister of women's affairs. The first, Françoise Giroux, had been appointed minister of women's affairs in France some months before, a fact presumably not unrelated to the decision made in Iran.

53. UN World Plan of Action, in "A National Plan of Action," 6.

54. "A National Plan of Action," 12.

55. M. Afkhami, 146.

56. *Kongereh-ye bozorg-e zanan-e iran* [The Grand Congress of Iranian Women] (Tehran: Women's Organization of Iran, 2536 [1978]), 3–5.

57. M. Afkhami, 138.

58. Ibid., 188–89.

59. Ibid., 214.

12. MASTERING OIL

1. The eight companies so designated were Exxon Corporation (then Standard Oil of New Jersey), Texaco Incorporated, Mobil Oil Corporation, Gulf Oil Corporation, Standard Oil Company of California, British Petroleum (Anglo-Iranian Oil Company), Royal Dutch Shell, and Compagnie Française des Pétroles.

2. Muhammad A. Mughrabi, *Permanent Sovereignty over Oil Resources* (Beirut: Middle East Research and Publication Center, 1966), 56.

3. Fuad Rowhani, *San'at-e naft-e iran: Bist sal pas az melli shodan* [The Iranian Oil Industry: Twenty Years after Nationalization] (Tehran: Jibi, 2536 [1977]), chap. 4.

4. Gholam Reza Afkhami, ed., *Tahavvol-e san'at-e naft-e iran: Negahi az darun* [The Evolution of Iran's Oil Industry: An Insider's Assessment], An Interview with Parviz Mina (Bethesda, Md.: FIS, 1998) 23; hereafter cited as Mina.

5. Rowhani, *San'at,* 65–66.

6. *Gahnameh,* 2: 901.

7. Mohammad Reza Pahlavi, *Answer to History* (New York: Stein and Day, 1980), 96–97.

8. Mina, 26–28.

9. Speech on the occasion of the seventh anniversary of 28 Mordad (19 August, the day Mosaddeq fell), quoted in Rowhani, *San'at,* 166.

10. Ibid., 167.

11. Franklin Tugwell, *The Politics of Oil in Venezuela* (Stanford, Calif.: Stanford University Press, 1975), chap. 3.

12. The Organization of Petroleum Exporting Countries (OPEC) is a permanent, intergovernmental organization, created at the Baghdad Conference on 10–14 September 1960 by Iran, Iraq, Kuwait, Saudi Arabia, and Venezuela. The five founding members were later joined by eight other members: Qatar (1961); Indonesia (1962); Socialist People's Libyan Arab Jamahiriya (1962); United Arab Emirates (1967); Algeria (1969); Nigeria (1971); Ecuador (1973; withdrew 1992); and Gabon (1975; withdrew 1994). OPEC had its headquarters in Geneva for the first five years of its existence, then moved to Vienna on 1 September 1965. See the OPEC Web site at www.opec.org.

13. In Farrokh Najmabadi's opinion, at least two of the top Iranian delegates to the first conference—Fatollah Naficy and Fuad Rowhani—were technological and legal giants, respectively, compared to the delegates from other participating nations. Interview with Farrokh Najmabadi, Bethesda, Md., 14 September 2005. The only other comparable member in terms of technological and political prowess was Venezuela, which, in any case, could hardly assume formal leadership in an organization whose other members were all drawn from the Persian Gulf region.

14. Rowhani, *San'at,* 201.

15. Mina, 78.

16. Rowhani, *San'at,* 193. The Iranians remembered their lot during the nationalization crisis of the early 1950s, when Iranian oil was replaced by extra oil pumped out of Saudi Arabia, Iraq, and other countries, quickly and without fanfare. See chapter 6.

17. *Kayhan,* 21 Mehr 1341 (13 October 1962).

18. Maurice Bridgeman to Abdollah Entezam, 25 October 1962, cited in Persian in Rowhani, *San'at,* 182.

19. *Kayhan,* 24 Mehr 1342 (16 October 1963).

20. In line with the Consortium Agreement, which recognized two entities representing Iran—the government, represented by the minister of finance, and the NIOC.

21. In the oil industry, especially where the owner of the land and the government are not the same, royalty—that is, the right of ownership—and taxation are two different and distinct concepts. The owner of the land is always assumed to have a right to the commodity extracted from the land. In Anglo-Saxon countries the owner has all

the rights. In most other countries, especially those that adopted continental European law, especially French law, the state has the ownership right of the underground resources. In Iran, the underground resources belonged to the state, which, based on certain rules and regulations, conferred certain rights on individuals. The law of foreign trade gave the government a monopoly on foreign trade. The government then would pass on the right to the private sector under certain conditions. The Consortium Agreement recognized these principles — the separation of owner's royalty and the taxes, both of which in Iran's case belonged to the government. The owner's share in the Consortium Agreement was 12.5 percent of the posted price. According to the agreement the government could take the money or the oil. As things stood, it did not make any difference which, since the 50–50 principle included the sum of royalties plus taxes. But if 50 percent taxes were paid, then clearly 6.25 percent in each barrel would be added to Iran's income. This was called the expensing of the royalty, that is, the putting of the royalty to the account of the expenditure. Again, according to the agreement, the royalty of 12.5 percent was paid to the NIOC, which, according to the law, had control of the underground oil. The rest, bringing the total payments to 50 percent of the posted price, was paid to the government.

22. Amir Asadollah Alam, *The Shah and I: The Confidential Diary of Iran's Royal Court, 1969–1977,* ed. Alinaghi Alikhani, trans. Alinaghi Alikhani and Nicholas Vincent (London and New York: I. B. Tauris, 1991), 39.

23. Ibid., 37.

24. *Ruzshomar,* 2: 26.

25. Alam, *The Shah and I,* 33–40.

26. Alinaghi Alikhani, ed., *Yaddashtha-ye Alam* [Alam's Diaries], 5 vols. (Bethesda, Md.: IBEX, n.d.), 1: 191; hereafter cited as Alam, *Yaddashtha.*

27. Ibid., 1: 194, 164–66.

28. Ibid., 175.

29. Ibid., 192.

30. Ibid., 193–94.

31. Ibid., 200–201.

32. Ibid., 231.

33. At the conference in 1975, again in Vienna, Amouzegar and other OPEC ministers were taken hostage by Ilich Ramirez Sanchez, alias Carlos "the Jackal," a young Venezuelan turned Palestinian guerrilla who was at the time attached to the Popular Front for the Liberation of Palestine (PFLP). Taken on flights to Algiers, Tripoli, and then back to Algiers, Amouzegar and the Saudi oil minister, Zaki Yamani, were told they had been sentenced to die, according to Yamani because of their countries' alliance with the United States. However, they were ransomed with money paid by their respective governments and by a promise of safe passage, which allowed Carlos to go to Damascus, where he was expelled from PFLP for failing to carry out the sentence on the two ministers. Carlos ended up in Sudan and subsequently was handed over to France, where he was sentenced to life imprisonment. See Planet Ark, http://www.planetark.org/dailynewsstory.cfm?newsid=8054.

34. Mina, 32–33.

35. Ibid., 33–34; see also Gholam Reza Afkhami, ed., *San'at-e gaz-e iran: Az aghaz ta*

astane-ye enqelab [The Evolution of Iran's Gas Industry: Organization, Policy, Assessment], An Interview with Mohsen Shirazi (Bethesda, Md.: FIS, 1999), 19–23.

36. Mina, 34–35.

37. Speech at the Tenth Anniversary of the Shah-People Revolution, 3 Bahman 1351 [23 January 1973], reproduced in Rowhani, *San'at,* 374–76.

38. Mina, 37–39.

39. Jamshid Amouzegar, "Khatereh-i az salhay-e gozashteh" [A Remembrance of the Years Past], *Rahavard* 61 (winter 2002): 351–52.

40. Ibid.

41. The shah knew of Alam's connections to Britain and used this to his advantage while remaining confident of Alam's loyal allegiance to him. In fact, had he not been so certain of his loyalty, he would not have allowed himself the adventurous freedoms he did in Alam's company.

42. Mina, 83–84.

43. The government take of $7 per barrel was based on taxes computed at 55 percent and interest computed at 12.5 percent of the posted price. See Rowhani, *San'at,* 304–5.

44. *Oil and Gas Journal* 7 (September 1970).

45. Alam, *Yaddashtha,* 4: 231–33.

46. *Gahnameh,* 5: 2291.

47. For a full account of the North-South Conference, see Jahangir Amuzegar, "A Requiem for the North-South Conference," *Foreign Affairs* 56, 1 (October 1977): 136–59.

48. Ibid., 146.

49. Ibid., 147.

50. A. Pezeshki, ed., *Siasat-e khareji-ye iran bar mabna-ye farmayeshat va neveshteh-haye a'lahazrat homayun shahanshah aryamehr* [Foreign Policy of Iran Based on the Writings and Speeches of His Imperial Majesty Mohammad Reza Shah Pahlavi Aryamhr Shahanshah of Iran] (London: n.p., 1985), 31–32.

51. King Khalid to the shah, 7 August 1975, in Alam, *Yaddashtha,* 5: 198–200.

52. Shah to King Khalid, 21 Mordad 1354 [12 August 1975], in ibid., 201–2.

53. Shah to King Khalid, 15 Shahrivar 1354 [6 September 1975], in ibid., 221.

54. President Gerald Ford to the shah, 9 September, 1975; in ibid., 227–28.

55. Shah to President Gerald Ford, 10 September 1975, in ibid., 229–31.

13. COMMANDER-IN-CHIEF

1. General Hassan Arfa', *Under Five Shahs* (London: Murray, 1964).

2. General Abbas Qarabaghi, *Haqayeq dar bare-ye enqelab-e iran* [Facts about the Iranian Revolution] (Paris: Suhail Publications, 1984), 103–4. Qarabaghi was the last chairman of the Supreme Commander's Staff under the shah.

3. Conversation with Lt. General Ahmad Ali Mohaqqeqi, Richmond, Va., August 1984; also FISOHA interview with Mohaqqeqi, by Vali Reza Nasr, 26 June 1989, Washington, D.C., 11 (appendix).

4. Gholam R. Afkhami, *The Iranian Revolution: Thanatos on a National Scale* (Washington, D.C.: Middle East Institute, 1985), 120.

5. According to one observer, "in 1942 the State Department launched its advisory

program for Iran in which advisers were to become the instruments of an American-sponsored 'New Deal.' The program encompassed five key missions, one each to the army, the Ministry of Finance, the gendarmerie, the urban police, and the Ministry of Food and Supply." Mark Hamilton Lytle, *The Origins of Iranian-American Alliance, 1941–1953* (New York: Holmes and Meier, 1987), 103.

6. Arthur Millspaugh, *Americans in Persia* (Cambridge, Mass.: Da Capo, 1976), 214–15.

7. Students Following the Line of the Imam, 70, *The U.S. Military Advisory Mission in Iran* (1) (Tehran: CPUSEDD, 1990), 119.

8. Agreement signed in Tehran, 6 October 1947, by George Allen and Mahmud Jam, Iran's minister of war; text in ibid., 37.

9. Ibid., 47.

10. Ruhollah Ramazani, *Iran's Foreign Policy 1941–1973: A Study of Foreign Policy in Modernizing Nations* (Charlottesville: University Press of Virginia, 1975), 291–92.

11. See Ray Takeyh, *The Origins of the Eisenhower Doctrine: The U.S., Britain and Nasser's Egypt, 1953–57* (New York: Macmillan, 2000), chap. 3.

12. Ibid., 219–22.

13. *Pravda* and *Izvestia,* 25 June 1956 and after; *New York Herald Tribune,* 26 June 1956; *New York Times,* 14 July 1956; *Christian Science Monitor* and *Manchester Guardian,* 18 July 1956.

14. Majid Tafreshi, ed., *Chehel sal dar sahneh: Khaterat-e Jala Abdoh* [Forty Years on the Scene: Memoirs of Jalal Abdoh], 2 vols. (Tehran: Rasa, 1368 [1989]), 1, 375.

15. *Gahnameh,* 2: 829–34, 831.

16. *Gahnameh,* 2: 858–59; *Ruzshomar,* 2: 72.

17. For a documentary survey of the Suez Crisis, see James Eayrs, *The Commonwealth and Suez* (London: Oxford University Press, 1964); also Alexander L. George, *Avoiding War: Problems of Crisis Management* (Boulder, Colo.: Westview Press, 1991), chap. 9; Gustav Krecsks, "The Suez Crisis and the 1956 Hungarian Revolution," *East European Quarterly* 35 (2001). For the shah, see *Gahnameh,* 2: 855–61.

18. Document signed and delivered to Congress 5 January 1957 (H. Doc. 46, 85th Cong., 1st session), *Congressional Record,* 103: 181.

19. *Pravda,* 26 November 1957.

20. See Tahmouress Adamiyatt, *Gashti bar gozashteh: Khaterat-e safir kabir-e iran dar shoravi* [A Promenade in the Past: Memoirs of an Iranian Ambassador to the USSR (1945–1965)] (Tehran: Ketab Sara Co., 1989), 160–75.

21. Interview with Ardeshir Zahedi, Montreux, Switzerland, 5, 6, and 7 July 2001, tape 3, side 2.

22. K. Afshar, Harvard Iranian Oral History Project; www.fas.harvard.edu/~iohp/afshar1.pdf, 19–21.

23. K. Afshar, Harvard Iranian Oral History Project; www.fas.harvard.edu/~iohp/afshar2.pdf, 3–7.

24. Mohammad Reza Pahlavi, *Ma'muriat baray-e vatanam* [Mission for My Country] (Tehran: Nashr-e Ketab, 1353 [1974]; orig. pub. 1961), 225–26.

25. Pravda called the Iranian note "immaterial and nonsense." *Pravda,* 5 March 1959.

26. *Gahnameh,* 2: 993.

27. "In the Neighborhood of the Bear," An Interview with Ahmad Mirfendereski, by Ahmad Ahrar, *Kayhan* (London), [April 1995], English translation by Nayer Mostofi Glenn. Unpublished, in FIS.

28. FISOHA interview with Dean Rusk, by William Burr, Athens, Ga., 23 May 1986, 17.

29. Mohammad Reza Shah Pahlavi, "A Future to Outshine Ancient Glories," *Life,* 31 May 1963, 52–74, 73.

30. Rusk interview, 14–15.

31. Ibid., 31.

32. Ibid., 15–16.

33. FISOHA interview with General Hamilton Twitchell, by William Burr, Washington, D.C., 1 April and 3 June 1988, 14.

34. FISOHA interview with Armin Meyer, by William Burr, Washington, D.C., 29 March 1985, 30.

35. Department of State to the Embassy in Iran, 23 May 1966, FRUS, DEF 19–8 US-IRAN. Files on U.S.-Iran relations for 1964–68 (Johnson administration) are available at www.state-gov/www/about_state/history/vol_xxii/index.html.

36. Armin Meyer to Washington, 31 August 1965, FRUS, 1610Z POL 15–1 IRAN.

37. Ibid.

38. Ibid. Secret, limited distribution. See also Meyer's 9 September 1965 telegram, FRUS Central Files, AID 6 Iran.

39. Meyer to Washington, 31 August 1965.

40. "Reassessment of Non-Soviet Threat to Iran," FRUS, Washington National Records Center, RG 330, OSD Files: FRC 70 A 4443, Iran 381, 28 January 1966, Secret.

41. *Kayhan,* 9 Esfand 1344 (28 February 1966).

42. Meyer to Washington, 2 March 1966, 1250Z, FRUS, POL 15–1 IRAN.

43. Students Following the Line of the Imam, 8, *U.S. Interventions in Iran* (1) (Tehran: CPUSEDD, 1985), 1, 2.

44. Telegram 1572 from Tehran, 23 May 1966, FRUS, POL 1 U.S.

45. Memorandum from the Assistant Secretary of State for Near Eastern and South Asian Affairs (Talbot) to the Under Secretary of State for Political Affairs (Harriman), Washington, 6 June 1964, FRUS, NEA/IRN Files: Lot 69 D 30, Staff Studies. Confidential; and Department of State to the Embassy in Iran, Washington, 8 June 1964, FRUS, POL 7 IRAN, Confidential.

46. Memorandum from Robert W. Komer of the National Security Council Staff to the President's Special Assistant for National Security Affairs (Bundy), Washington, 27 June 1964; Johnson Library, Austin, Tex., National Security File, Country File, Iran, vol. I, Memos & Miscellaneous, 1/64–12/65, Secret. And see From the Department of State to the Embassy in Iran, Washington, 2 July 1964, FRUS, DEF 19 US-IRAN, Confidential.

47. Embassy in Iran to the Department of State, Tehran, 24 September 1965, 1110Z, FRUS, DEF 19–8 US-IRAN, Confidential. And From the Embassy in Iran to the Department of State, Tehran, 12 November 1965, 0950Z, FRUS, DEF 19–8 US-IRAN, Confidential.

48. From the President's Special Assistant (Rostow) to President Johnson, Washing-

ton, 27 May 1966; Johnson Library, National Security File, Memos to the President, Walt W. Rostow, vol. 5, 27 May–10 June 1966, Top Secret.

49. From the Assistant Secretary of Defense for International Security Affairs (Warnke) to the Deputy Secretary of Defense (Nitze), Washington, 23 August 1967; Johnson Library, National Security File, NSC Files of Harold Saunders, Visit, Shah of Iran, 22–24 August 1967, Confidential. For relevant information see also the following. Harold H. Saunders of the National Security Council Staff to President Johnson, Washington, 23 August 1967; Johnson Library, National Security File, Country File, Iran, Visit of Shah (con't.), 22–24 August 1967, Secret. From Vice President Humphrey to President Johnson, Washington, August 24, 1967; Johnson Library, National Security File, NSC Files of Harold Saunders, Visit, Shah of Iran, 22–24 August 1967. From Harold H. Saunders of the National Security Council Staff to President Johnson, Washington, 25 August 1967; Johnson Library, National Security File, Country File, Iran, Visit of Shah of Iran, 8/22–24/67, Secret; no distribution.

50. See the following, in FRUS. From the Department of State to the Embassy in Iran, Washington, 22 March 1968, 0125Z, DEF 19–8 US-IRAN, Secret. From Harold H. Saunders of the National Security Council Staff to the Assistant Secretary of State for Near Eastern and South Asian Affairs (Battle), Washington, 22 March 1968, DEF 12–5 IRAN, Secret. From the Embassy in Iran to the Department of State, Tehran, 23 March 1968, 0850Z, DEF 19–8 US-IRAN, Secret. From the Department of State to the Embassy in Iran, Washington, 9 April 1968, 2226Z, DEF 19–8 US-IRAN, Secret. And from Secretary of State Rusk to President Johnson, Washington, 19 April 1968; Johnson Library, National Security File, Country File, Iran, Secret. From the President's Special Assistant (Rostow) to President Johnson, Washington, 29 April 1968; Johnson Library, National Security File, Country File, Iran, Secret.

51. Memorandum of conversation, Washington, 5 December 1968; Johnson Library, National Security File, Country File, Iran, Secret.

52. Fereydun Jam, "Dar safar-e mahabad che gozasht" [What Happened on the Journey to Mahabad], *Rahavard* 11: 44 (spring and summer 1997): 236–40, at 240.

53. FISOHA interview with Major General Ellis Williamson, by William Burr, Arlington, Va., 10 February, 11 March, and 13 April 1988, 127.

54. Twitchell interview, 40, 45, 102.

55. Ibid., 90.

56. Williamson interview, 129.

57. Ibid., 89.

58. British dislike of the Pahlavis is well documented in the official correspondence between London and British envoys in Tehran from the 1940s to the 1970s. See the observations of Sir Reader Bullard (World War II), Sir Roger Stevens (1950s), and Sir Peter Ramsbotham (1970s), in the following communiqués, for example. Bullard to Foreign Office, 24 October 1941, PRO FO 371/27248, E 6943, No. 1037; Sir Roger Stevens to Mr. Selwyn Lloyd, last dispatch from Tehran, 26 August 1958, PRO PREM 11/3397, EP 1015/38; Sir Peter Ramsbotham to Sir Alec Douglas Home, 11 October 1971, PRO FCO 17/1517. Ramsbotham quotes Harold Nicholson, the British chargé in 1926, in support of his opinion of Iranians: before Reza Shah, Iranians had a "childish and

gentle charm"; nationalism made them "conceited and disagreeable." See the next note for Sir Denis Wright (1960s).

59. Sir Denis Wright to Roger Stewart, 1 March 1965, PRO PREM 13/409, 19.

60. On economic and political reasons, see Jeffrey Pickering, *Britain's Withdrawal from East of Suez: The Politics of Retrenchment* (London: Polgrave Macmillan, 1998); and for strategic reasons, Saki Dockrill, *Britain's Retreat from East of Suez: The Choice between Europe and the World* (London: Polgrave Macmillan, 2002).

61. Interview with Ardeshir Zahedi, Montreux, Switzerland, 7 July 2001, tape 4, side 2.

62. Meyer interview, 21–22.

63. Address by Richard M. Nixon to the Bohemian Club, San Francisco, 29 July 1967; The Richard Nixon Library, Yorba Linda, Calif., Nixon Papers.

64. Richard M. Nixon, "Asia after Vietnam," *Foreign Affairs* 46, 1 (October 1967): 113–25. See also Henry Kissinger, *American Foreign Policy: Three Essays by Henry Kissinger* (New York: W. W. Norton, 1969), 51–97; and Richard Nixon, "U.S. Foreign Policy for the 1970s — The Emerging Structure of Peace," a report to the Congress on 9 February 1972, reprinted in *Department of State Bulletin* 66, 1707 (13 March 1972): 314.

65. Zahedi interview, tape 4, side 2.

66. FISOHA interview with Richard Helms, by William Burr, Washington, D.C., 10 and 24 July, 1985, 2–60.

67. William Isaacson, *Kissinger* (New York: Simon and Schuster, 1992), 656.

68. Gary Sick, "Iran: a View from the White House," *World Affairs* 149, 4 (1987): 210.

69. Williamson interview, 149.

70. Ibid., 53–54.

71. Ibid., 2–3.

72. Ibid., 12, 61.

73. Ibid., 12, 5.

74. Ibid., 11–12.

75. For example, joint press conference with President Echeverria of Mexico at Mehrabad Airport, 21 July 1975; *Gahnameh,* 5: 2362.

76. Author conversation with Reza Qotbi, September 2004.

77. FISOHA interview with Lieutenant General Mohsen Hashemi-Nejad, by Seyyed Vali Reza Nasr, Washington, D.C., 12 April 1989.

78. Williamson interview, 143.

79. FISOHA interview with General Reza Azimi, by Farrokh Ghaffari, Paris, June 1990, 7.

80. Interview with Queen Farah, Paris, 1 July 2001, tape 2, side 2.

81. FISOHA interview with General Karim Varahram, by Seyyed Vali Reza Nasr, Washington, D.C., 9 April 1989, 19.

82. FISOHA interview with Amin Alimard, by Gholam Reza Afkhami, 3 December 1994, Bethesda, Md., 25.

83. For Tufanian's appointment, see *Daily Ettela'at,* 25 Bahman 1344 (14 February 1966).

84. FISOHA interview with General Hassan Tufanian, by Seyyed Vali Reza Nasr, 18 March and 7 April 1989, Chevy Chase, Md., 1: 26.

85. See, for example, Students Following the Line of the Imam, 60, *U.S. Interventions in Iran* (9) (Tehran: CPUSEDD, 1986), 154.

86. Tufanian interview, 26–30.

87. Williamson interview, 168–69.

88. Twitchell interview, 69–70.

89. Williamson interview, 169.

90. *U.S. News & World Report,* 22 March 1976, 57.

91. Meyer interview, 41.

92. Eric Pace, "Iranian Prime Minister Assails Unethical Foreign Corporations," *New York Times,* 4 March 1976, 53.

93. Tufanian interview, 25.

94. Barry Rubin, *Paved with Good Intentions: The American Experience and Iran* (New York: Penguin, 1981), 163.

95. Williamson interview, 168–69.

96. Ibid., 102–3.

97. FISOHA interview with James Schlesinger, by William Burr, Washington D.C., 15 May and 7 June 1986, 40–43.

98. Rubin, *Good Intentions,* 164–65.

99. Mohammad Reza Pahlavi, *Answer to History* (New York: Stein and Day, 1980), 197.

100. Tufanian interview, 31.

101. Rubin, *Good Intentions,* 163–65.

102. Tufanian interview, 29–30; Gholam Reza Afkhami, ed., *Barneh-ye enerzhi-e atomi: Talashha va taneshha* [Iran's Atomic Energy Program: Mission, Structure, Politics], An Interview with Akbar Etemad, the First President of the Atomic Energy Organization of Iran (Bethesda, Md.: FIS, 1997), 142–51.

14. DEVELOPMENT AND DREAMS

1. See Khodadad Farmanfarmaian in Gholam Reza Afkhami, ed., *Barnamehrizi-ye omrani va tasmimgiri-ye siyasi* [Ideology, Process, and Politics in Iran's Development Planning], Interviews with Manuchehr Gudarzi, Khodadad Farmanfarmaian, and Abdolmajid Majidi (Bethesda, Md.: FIS, 1999), 158–59.

2. Gholam Reza Afkhami, ed., *Siyasat va siasatgozari-e eqtesadi dar iran, 1340–1350* [Ideology, Politics, and Process in Iran's Economic Development, 1960–1970], Interview with Alinaghi Alikhani (Bethesda, Md.: FIS, 2001), 8; hereafter cited as Alikhani.

3. *Gahnameh,* 3: 1308; *Ruzshomar,* 2: 151.

4. Alikhani, 34.

5. Gholam Reza Afkhami, ed., *Jame'eh, dolat, va jonbesh-e zanan-e iran, 1320–1357* [Women, State, and Society in Iran, vol. 1, 1941–1978], Interview with Mehrangiz Dowlatshahi (Bethesda, Md.: FIS, 2002), 134–35; Alikhani, 38–39.

6. Alikhani, 48–49.

7. Ibid., 61–62.

8. Shah to the Second National Conference of Labor, 27 April 1970. See *Kayhan,* 28 April 1970 (8 Ordibehesht 1349).

9. Majidi in Afkhami, *Barnamehrizi,* 211–13.

10. Conversation with former Central Bank president Hassanali Mehran, FIS, Bethesda, Md., 29 November 2004.

11. Ibid.

12. Pourhomayoun was the opposite of Ebtehaj, according to Hassanali Mehran. He quoted Mehdi Samii, who reportedly said: "Ebtehaj's pencil was famous for its strong color and indelible effect on paper. Pourhomayoun's was famous for never leaving a trace"; ibid.

13. Alikhani, 81, 84–85.

14. Ibid., 81–83.

15. Charles Issawi, "The Iranian Economy, 1925–1975: Fifty Years of Economic Development," in *Iran under the Pahlavis,* ed. George Lenczowski (Stanford, Calif.: Hoover Institution Press, 1958), 129–66, at 135–37.

16. Alikhani, 107–8.

17. Conversation with Mahmud Khayami, Cannes, France, 23 July 2003.

18. Alikhani, 103–7.

19. Khayami conversation.

20. Alikhani, 101.

21. Ibid.

22. Farmanfarmaian, in Afkhami, *Barnamehrizi,* 202–6.

23. Majidi, in ibid., 321.

24. Robert S. Stobaugh, "The Evolution of Iranian Oil Policy, 1925–1975," in Lenczowski, ed., *Iran under the Pahlavis,* 201–52, at 248.

25. *Barnameh-ye panjom-e omrani-ye keshvar (tajdid nazar shodeh 1352–1356)* [The Fifth Development Plan, 1973–1977 (revised)] (Tehran: Sazeman-e barnameh va budjeh, 1353 [1974]), 2.

26. Ibid., 13–14.

27. Jahangir Amuzegar, *Iran: An Economic Profile* (Washington, D.C.: The Middle East Institute, 1977), ix, 248. For a comparison with Iran's economic and social conditions at the beginning of the twentieth century, see Julian Bharier, *Economic Development in Iran 1900–1970* (London and New York: Oxford University Press, 1977), chap. 1

28. Issawi, "The Iranian Economy," 163.

29. "M. Hoveyda au Monde," *Le Monde,* 11 February 1975.

30. *Durnama-ye eqtesadi va ejtema'i-ye iran, 2531–2551* [A Social and Economic Perspective of Iran, 1972–1992] (Tehran: Plan and Budget Organization, 2535 [1976]), 2–3.

31. Ibid., 57–62, 78.

32. Ibid., 82–84.

33. For a general account of the development policy of France, see http://fr.wikipedia.org/wiki/Am%C3%A9nagement_du_territoire; also http://www.diplomatie.gouv.fr/fr/france_829/decouvrir-france_4177/france-a-z_2259/territoire_2559/amenagement-du-territoire_4741.html.

34. Conversation with Rahmat Jazani, Iran's director of the project, Bethesda, Md., August 2004.

35. *National Spatial Strategy Plan: First Stage Final Report* (Tehran: Center for National Spatial Planning, Plan and Budget Organization, May 1976), 17.

36. Ibid., 17–18.

37. Ibid., 21.

38. Majidi, in Afkhami, *Barnamehrizi*, 354.

39. "Proposed Strategies," in *Barnameh-ye omrani-ye sheshom, 2537–2541* [The Sixth Development Plan, 1978–1982] (Tehran: Plan and Budget Organization, 2535 [1976]), 1–7.

40. Ibid., 17.

41. Mohammad Reza Pahlavi, *Toward the Great Civilization* (London: Satrap Publishing, 1994; orig. pub. in Persian as *Besu-ye tamaddon-e bozorg,* 1978), 124–25.

42. Ibid., 140.

43. Ibid., 145–56.

44. Ibid., 157–61, 126–30.

15. GAS, PETROCHEMICALS, AND NUCLEAR ENERGY

1. Soviet translation to Persian of Khrushchev's press conference, 12 July 1960, from *Pravda,* 13 July 1960; cited in Tahmouress Adamiyatt, *Gashti bar gozashteh: Khaterat-e safir kabir-e iran dar shoravi* [A Promenade in the Past: Memoirs of an Iranian Ambassador to the USSR (1945–1965)] (Tehran: Ketab Sara, 1368 [1989]), 164.

2. Ibid., 167–76, quote at 171.

3. Michael P. Gehlen, *The Politics of Coexistence* (Bloomington: Indiana University Press, 1967), 72–75.

4. *Gahnameh,* 3: 1266; Habib Ladjevardi, ed., *Khaterat-e Mahmoud Foroughi* [Memoirs of Mahmoud Foroughi], Harvard University Iranian Oral History Project (Bethesda, Md.: IBEX, 2003), 113–21.

5. Ladjevardi, *Foroughi,* 113–21; Sir G. W. Harrison to Foreign Office, 14 November 1962, PRO FO 371/164188, EP 1023/2, No. 73.

6. Harrison to Foreign Office.

7. Interview with Queen Farah, Potomac, Md., 3 June 2001, tape 1, side 2.

8. *Gahnameh,* 3: 1369; this was the Treaty Banning Nuclear Weapon Tests in the Atmosphere, in Outer Space, and under Water, signed in Moscow by Sir Alec Douglas Home, Dean Rusk, and Andrei Gromyko.

9. *Gahnameh,* 3: 1376; *Ruzshomar,* 2: 167.

10. By 1978, production capacity had reached 2 million tons, and plans were under way to expand the Isfahan plant in three stages to 8 million tons by the end of 1980s. Conversation with Farrokh Najmabadi, former minister of industries and mines, Bethesda, Md., 30 March 2005. See also "Zowb-e ahan-e ariyamehr" [The Aryamehr Steel Complex], by Abdolhamid Sheibani, the manager of the Isfahan complex, p. 50; deposited at FIS.

11. Gholam Reza Afkhami, ed., *Siyasat va siasatgozari-e eqtesadi dar iran, 1340–1350* [Ideology, Politics, and Process in Iran's Economic Development, 1960–1970], An Inter-

view with Alinaghi Alikhani, (Bethesda, Md.: FIS, 2001), 175; hereafter cited as Alikhani.

12. Ibid., 176.

13. FISOHA interview with Taqi Mosaddeqi, by Gholam Reza Afkhami, Washington, D.C., 30 November 1987, 20.

14. *Gahnameh,* 4: 1959.

15. See Gholam Reza Afkhami, ed., *San'at-e gaz-e iran az aghaz ta astane-ye enqelab* [The Evolution of Iran's Gas Industry: Organization, Policy, Assessment], An Interview with Mohsen Shirazi (Bethesda, Md.: FIS, 1999), prologue by Farrokh Najmabadi and Shirazi, 31–34 (hereafter cited as Shirazi); Alikhani, 174–83; Gholam Reza Afkhami, ed., *Tahavvol-e san'at-e naft: Negahi az darun* [The Evolution of Iran's Oil Industry: An Insider's Assessment], An Interview with Parviz Mina (Bethesda, Md.: FIS, 1998); Mosaddeqi interview, 14–20.

16. Shirazi, 71–72.

17. Mosaddeqi interview; Shirazi, 104–7; Alikhani, 182–84.

18. Alikhani, 114.

19. Shirazi, 103.

20. *Gahnameh,* 5: 2392; *Ruzshomar,* 2: 302.

21. Mosaddeqi interview; Shirazi, 107–16.

22. Shirazi, Prologue, 22.

23. Ibid., 126–36.

24. Mosaddeqi interview.

25. Mohammad Reza Shah Pahlavi, "A Future to Outshine Ancient Glories," *Life,* 31 May 1963, 66D.

26. Gholam Reza Afkhami, ed., *San'at-e petroshimi-e iran: Az aghaz ta astaneh-ye enqelab* [The Evolution of Iran's Petrochemical Industry], An Interview with Baqer Mostowfi, FISOHA (Bethesda, Md.: FIS, 2001), 49–50; hereafter cited as Mostowfi.

27. Ibid., 63–64.

28. Alikhani, 158.

29. Robert B. Staubach, "The Evolution of Iranian Oil Policy, 1925–1975," in *Iran under the Pahlavis,* ed. George Lenczowski (Stanford, Calif.: Hoover Institution Press, 1978), 224.

30. Mostowfi, 76–77.

31. Ibid., 85.

32. Ibid., 86–88.

33. Ibid., 98–99.

34. FISOHA interview with Reza Qotbi, by Gholam Reza Afkhami, Bethesda, Md., 4 June 2002, tape 1, side 1.

35. *Gahnameh,* 5: 2247.

36. Qotbi interview, 4 June 2002, tape 2, side 1.

37. Gholam Reza Afkhami, ed., *Barnameh-ye enerzhi-e atomi-e iran: Talashha va taneshha* [Iran's Atomic Energy Program: Mission, Structure, Politics], An Interview with Akbar Etemad (Bethesda, Md.: 1997), 11; hereafter cited as Etemad.

38. Ibid., 17.

39. Mosaddeqi interview, 24.

40. Etemad, 18, 29.

41. Address by Mr. Dwight D. Eisenhower, President of the United States of America, to the 470th Plenary Meeting of the United Nations General Assembly, Tuesday, 8 December 1953. http://www.iaea.org/About/history_speech.html.

42. Etemad, 36.

43. Ibid.

44. Alikhani, 72.

45. Etemad, 36.

46. Ibid., 102.

47. Ibid., 102–3.

48. Interview with Queen Farah, 3 June 2001, tape 1, side 2.

49. Etemad, 160.

50. *Gahnameh,* 5: 2266–67, 2443–44.

51. Etemad, 159–67.

52. Alireza Aruzi, ed., *Khaterat-e Abolhassan Ebtehaj* [Memoirs of Abol-Hassan Ebtehaj] (London: Paka Print, 1991), 384–85.

53. Nixon wrote, "I want to say to you quite directly that there was no excuse for Mr. Simon's rhetoric, and you have our apology. As I indicated in my press conference, I dissociate myself and my government from his remarks." Text of the letter in Alinaghi Alikhani, ed., *Yaddashtha-ye Alam* [Alam's Diaries]), 5 vols. (Bethesda, Md.: IBEX, n.d.), 4: unpaged insert between 24 and 25.

54. A. David Rossin, "US Policy on Spent Fuel: The Issues," *Frontline.* http://www.pbs.org/wgbh/pages/frontline/shows/reaction/readings/rossin1.html.

55. See President Gerald Ford's State of the Union address, 15 January 1975, C-Span .org; also at www.ford.utexas.edu/library/speeches/listpres.htm.

56. Secret letter from Henry Kissinger, dated 4 January 1975, in Alikhani, *Alam,* 4: unpaged insert between 312 and 313.

57. Etemad, 31; Dafna Linzer, "Past Arguments Don't Square with Current Iran Policy," *Washington Post,* 27 March 2005, A15. http://www.washingtonpost.com/wp-dyn/articles/A3983–2005Mar26.html.

58. Linzer, "Past Arguments."

59. Henry Sokolski, "The *Washington Post* Bombs Nuclear History," *The Daily Standard,* 28 March 2005.

60. Rossin, "US Policy on Spent Fuel."

61. Etemad, 171–72.

62. Text of the letter in Alikhani, *Alam,* 5: 491–92; Etemad, 172–73. The letter was prepared at the court based on the copy Etemad had drafted. Much to Alam's embarrassment, the shah had found a typographical error neither Alam's deputy, who had grammatically edited and finalized the letter, nor Alam, who had "read it carefully twice," had noticed. Alam was moved to write in his diary: "Wow. What intelligence and precision is this that diminishes never"; Alikhani, *Alam,* 5: 489.

63. Etemad, 173.

64. Ibid., 43.

65. Alikhani, *Alam,* 5: 262. Nothing much seems to have followed from the royal order.

66. Etemad, 45–46.

67. Ibid., 43–51. A second company, Coredif, was also established, which enriched uranium and in which Iran held a 20–30 percent share, but it did not last beyond the end of the 1970s, when the demand for nuclear energy had substantially decreased.

68. Uranium Information Center, Ltd., Melbourne, Australia. http://www.uic.com .au/index.htm.

69. Etemad, 113.

70. *Durnema-ye eqtesadi va ejtema'i-ye iran: 2531–2551* [A Social and Economic Perspective of Iran, 1972–1992] (Plan and Budget Organization, 2535 [1976]), 85–94.

71. Etemad, 95.

72. Ibid., 182–88.

73. Ibid., 197–98.

74. Ibid., 60–61.

75. Ibid., 61–62.

76. Ibid., 62–66.

77. Charles S. Costello III, "Nuclear Nonproliferation: A Hidden but Contentious Issue in US-Japan Relations during the Carter Administration (1977–1781)," *Asia-Pacific,* May 2003. http://www.pacificrim.usfca.edu/research/perspectives.

78. Texts of letters and speeches by Carter, the shah, and Etemad in Etemad, 240–47.

79. Ibid., 247.

16. POLITICS AND TERROR

1. "The Dangerous Mosque," *Time Magazine,* 28 November 1955.

2. See the Navvab Safavi Web site, http://www.navabsafavi.com.

3. See Amir H. Ferdows, "Khomaini and Fadaiyan's Society and Politics," *International Journal of Middle East Studies* 15, 2 (May 1983): 241–57.

4. See the Web site of Mohammad Mehdi Abd-e Khodai, member of Fadaiyan Islam and son of Ayatollah Sheikh Gholam Hossein Tabrizi, http://www.kayhannews .com/810326/other3.htm#other307.

5. Mohammad Tavakoli-Tarqhi, "Baha'i-setizi va eslam-gera'i" [Anti-Bahaism and Islamism in Iran, 1941–55], *Iran Nameh* 19, 1 and 2 (winter and spring 2001); available at www.fis-iran.org/index.php/_121/Item4224d92880cf7.

6. In shari'a criminal law, *hudud* (plural of *hadd*) are "limits" set by God, the contravention of which leads to a prescribed and mandatory penalty; *ta'zirat* (plural of *t'zir*) are crimes not included among the *hudud* because their punishment is discretionary; and *qisas,* or retribution, is concerned with crimes against the person, such as homicide and battery. Though punishment of such crimes is set by law, the victim may wave such retribution by accepting blood money or financial compensation *(dieh),* or by foregoing the right altogether. See *The Oxford Encyclopedia of the Modern Islamic World,* 4 vols. (Oxford: Oxford University Press, 1995), 1: 329.

7. Ruhollah Khomeini, *Kashf al-asrar* [Revealing Secrets] (Qom: n.p., 1323 [1944]), 184–292; Mojataba Navvab Safavi, *Ketab-e rahnemay-e haqayeq* [Guide to the Truth] (Tehran: n.p., 1329 (1950]), 25–55.

8. Khomeini, *Kashf al-asrar,* 104–5.

9. Hamid Ahmadi, "The Cold War and Political Islamic Fundamentalism," *Iran-shenasi* 13, 3 (2001): 570–72.

10. Mohammad Reza Pahlavi, interview in exile on *Answer to History,* by Christine Godek and Tom Weir, Cairo, 29 May 1980, tape 2.

11. Navvab Safavi Web site, http://www.navabsafavi.com/Shahid-Navvab-fadaeean/default.htm. See also Abd-e Khodai Web site, cited above.

12. Babak Amir-Khosravi and Fereydoun Azarnour, eds., *Khatirat-e Iraj Eskandari* [Memoirs of Iraj Eskandari] (Berlin: Hezb-e democratic-e mardom-e iran, 1366 [1987]), Part One, 156–57; also cited in Ahmadi, "Cold War," 589.

13. *Ruzshomar,* 1: 415–16.

14. Ibid., 427.

15. From Khalil Tahmasebi's second interrogation session, 8 March 1951, reproduced in Mohammad Torkoman, *Asrar-e qatl-e razmara* [Secrets of Razmara's Assassination] (Tehran: Rasa, 1370 [1991]), 137–39.

16. Ibid., 149, 286.

17. Ibid., 286–89.

18. Abd-e Khodai Web site. This is a sophisticated analysis; it may be that Khodai attributes this idea he has learned during the revolution posthumously to his leader, Navvab Safavi.

19. Ibid.

20. Students Following the Line of the Imam, Note 423, Embassy of the United States to Imperial Ministry of Foreign Affairs, *The U.S. Military Advisory Mission in Iran* (2) (Tehran: CPUSEDD, 1980), 3; hereafter cited as *U.S. Military Advisory Mission.*

21. Interview with Stuart Rockwell, by Habib Ladjevardi, Cambridge, Mass., 20 May 1987, Iranian Oral History Collection, Harvard University. http://www.fas.harvard.edu/~iohp/baheri.html.

22. Note 8800, Ministry of Foreign Affairs to Embassy of the United States, 11 March 1963, *U.S. Military Advisory Mission* (2), 5.

23. Ahmad Mirfendereski (in conversation with Ahmad Ahrar), *Dar hamsayegi-e khers: Diplomasi va siasat-e khareji-e iran az sevvom-e shahrivar 1320 ta 22 bahman 1357* [In the Neighborhood of the Bear: Diplomacy and Foreign Policy of Iran from 25 August 1941 to 11 February 1979] (London: Book Centre Limited, 1998), 50–64, 57 (for immunity), 59 (for Rambod).

24. *Official Gazette,* Majlis Discussions, 21 Mehr 1343 [13 October 1963], Session 104.

25. Ibid.

26. No. 448, Rockwell to Washington, 27 October 1964, *U.S. Military Advisory Mission* (2), 86–87.

27. No. 398, To Secretary of State, embassy telegram, 14 October 1964, ibid., 78.

28. *Official Gazette,* Majlis Discussions, 21 Mehr 1343 [13 October 1963], Session 104.

29. Memorandum for the Files, 29 October 1964, *U.S. Military Advisory Mission* (2), 92.

30. No. 398, To Secretary of State, embassy telegram, 14 October 1964, ibid., 78.

31. Rockwell, Confidential Memorandum for Files, 2 November 1964, ibid., 116–18.

32. *Ruzshomar,* 2: 465–68.

33. Ibid., 180.

34. Memorandum for the File, Meeting of the Ambassador [Armin Meyer] with the shah, 17 September 1964, *U.S. Military Advisory Mission* (2), 20.

35. Abd-e Khodai Web site.

36. Ibid.

37. Ibid.

38. Rockwell interview.

39. FISOHA interview with Lieutenant General Mohsen Hashemi-Nejad, by Marvin Zonis and Seyyed Vali Reza Nasr, Washington, D.C., March 1982 and 12 April 1989, 41.

40. Author conversation with Manuchehr Gudarzi, Bethesda, Md., 22 September 2004.

41. Hashemi-Nejad interview, 42.

17. SAVAK

1. FISOHA interview with General Mansur Qadar, by Gholam Reza Afkhami, Washington, D.C., 30 April and 4 May 1986, 5–7.

2. FISOHA interview with Nasser Zolfaqari, by Farrokh Ghaffari, Paris, 11 May, 9 and 23 September, 5 and 28 October 1989, 107–8.

3. FISOHA interview with Colonel Gratian Yatsevitch, by William Burr, Camden, Me., 5 November 1988, and Washington, D.C., 12 January 1989, 1: 72; FISOHA interview with Earnest R. Oney, by Seyyed Vali Reza Nasr, Bethesda, Md., 22 and 29 May 1991, 49–62.

4. Qadar interview, 6–11.

5. Zolfaqari interview, 43–44.

6. Mark Bowden, "The Dark Art of Interrogation," *The Atlantic Monthly,* October 2003, 51–78, at 57–58. The manual was unearthed in 1997 under the Freedom of Information Act by the *Baltimore Sun* reporters Garry Kohn, Ginger Thompson, and Mark Mathews.

7. Interview with Mohammad Reza Pahlavi, by David Frost, Panama, January 1980; televised on *20/20* (ABC), 17 January 1980.

8. Interview with Queen Farah, Potomac, Md., 3 June 2001, tape 2, side 1.

9. Hamid Shokat, ed., *Negahi az darun be jonbesh-e chap-e iran: Goftegu ba Mehdi Khanbaba Tehrani* [Iran's Left, a Look from Within: Conversation with Mehdi Khanbaba Tehrani] (Paris: Vajeh Desktop Publishing, 1990), 132–33; and Shokat, ed., *Negahi az darun: Goftegu ba Kurosh Lashai* [An Insider's View: A Conversation with Kurosh Lashai] (Tehran: Nashr-e Akhtaran, 1381 [2002]), 34–35; hereafter cited as Lashai.

10. FISOHA interview with Lieutenant General Mohsen Hashemi-Nejad, by Marvin Zonis and Seyyed Vali Reza Nasr, Washington, D.C., March 1982 and 12 April 1989, 2–41.

11. Amir Taheri, *The Unknown Life of the Shah* (London: Hutchinson, 1991), 185–86.

12. FISOHA interview with Reza Qotbi, by Gholam Reza Afkhami, Bethesda, Md., 20 June 2002, tape 1, side 1.

13. FISOHA interview with Mohammad Baheri, by Shirin Samii, Paris and Cannes, December 1983, March 1984, tape 59, side 1.

14. Lashai, 295.

15. Ibid.

16. Ibid., 120, 123.

17. Ibid., 139–40.

18. *Gahnameh,* 3: 1395; *Ruzshomar,* 2: 175.

19. Lashai, 185–86.

20. Author's conversation with a SAVAK agent, Washington, D.C., 5 August 1984.

21. Lashai, 190–93.

22. Ibid., 194–99.

23. *Gahnameh,* 2: 1742.

24. Baheri interview, tape 53, side 2, and tape 54, side 1.

25. See Andrei S. Markovits, "The European and American Left since 1945," *Dissent,* winter 2005; available at www.dissentmagazine.org/article/?article=264.

26. Showkat, *Negahi,* 338–40.

27. See *The New Left in Contemporary Iran,* Series on Contemporary Iran, No. 5 (Washington, D.C.: The Foundation for Constitutional Government in Iran, September 1985), 8–11.

28. See *Islamic Marxism: The Case of the Iranian Mojahedin,* Series on Contemporary Iran, No. 2 (Washington, D.C.: The Foundation for Constitutional Government in Iran, January 1985).

29. Alinaghi Alikhani, ed., *Yaddashtha-ye Alam* [Alam's Diaries], 5 vols. (Bethesda, Md.: IBEX, n.d.) 5: 69, 52.

30. Conversations with Professor Yahya Adl, an aside to FISOHA interview with Yahya Adl, by Gholam Reza Afkhami, Paris, 20 August 2000.

31. Alikhani, *Alam,* 5: 147.

32. Lashai, 287–88.

33. Qotbi interview, tape 2, side 2.

34. FISOHA interview with Kambiz Mahmoudi, deputy general manager, NIRT, by Behruz Nikzat, Washington, D.C., 10 September 1982, 56–62.

35. Qotbi interview. Jafarian was executed by the Islamic Republic together with Parviz Nikkhah.

36. Ibid.

18. A CELEBRATION AND A FESTIVAL

1. FISOHA interview with Mehrdad Pahlbod, by Mahnaz Afkhami, Los Angeles, 25 and 30 May 1984, 73.

2. "Asnad-e mahramaneh-ye jashnha-ye dohezar-o pansad saleh-ye shahanshahi" [Classified Documents of the Anniversary of the Twenty-Five Hundred Years of Iranian Monarchy], *Tarikh-e Mo'aser-e iran* [Contemporary Iranian History] 2, 5: 103–88, at 122–32.

3. It may be that at the beginning Alam did not favor the Celebrations, if one was to

go on a statement made to Kambiz Atabai by Mrs. Alam after the revolution. Interview with Kambiz Atabai, by Gholam Reza Afkhami, 5 February 2003, tape 1, side 1.

4. Text of the letter (Shafa to Alam) dated 8 Khordad 1349 (29 May 1970), in *Tarikh-e Mo'aser-e iran* 2, 5: 156–59.

5. Text of letter (Mottaqi to Alam) dated 18 Tir 1349 (9 July 1970), in ibid., 164–68.

6. FISOHA interview with Abdorreza Ansari, by Gholam Reza Afkhami, 27 February and 1, 2, 4, and 6 March 1991, Bethesda, Md., tape 10, side 1.

7. Ibid. The council members were Asadollah Alam, Culture Minister Mehrdad Pahlbod, Imperial Court Protocol Chief Hormoz Qarib, Deputy Court Minister for Culture Shoja'eddin Shafa, Deputy Court Minister for Administration Amir Mottaqi, NIRT Managing Director Reza Qotbi, SAVAK Chief General Nematollah Nasiri, Mehdi Bushehri, and Abdorreza Ansari.

8. Ibid. Alam's point was not off the mark, though the reference to the nomadic tradition deflects the real intention. There are several descriptions of the tents erected for the Achemenid kings, especially Xerxes in the Greek campaign, by Greek historians. There is also an account of Alexander's awe at the splendor of the tent of Darius III when he entered it after his victory at the battle of Issus in 333 B.C.E. "Its treasures included a golden throne and bath, carpets, jewels, gold and silver drinking cups and more. Alexander, being brought up in more spartan conditions, commented: 'This, it seems, is royalty.'" From Plutarch's *Life of Alexander the Great,* cited in http://members.ozemail.com.au/~ancientpersia/index.html.

9. Ansari interview.

10. According to Ministry of Education figures, the total number of such schools run by the education corps was eventually raised to 10,566 and the total number of students to 412,800. *Gahnameh,* 5: 2017.

11. Text of letter (Ramsbotham to Qarib) dated 28 August 1971, reprinted in *Tarikh-e Mo'aser-e iran,* 2, 5: 141.

12. Ansari interview.

13. Ibid.

14. Interview with Queen Farah, Potomac, Md., 3 June 2001, tape 1, side 2.

15. *Sahifeh Nur: Majmu'eh rahnemud hay-e emam* [Book of Light: Collection of the Imam's Directives] (Tehran: Ministry of Culture and Islamic Guidance, 1980), 1: 158.

16. Hamid Shokat, ed., *Negahi az darun be jonbesh-e chap-e iran: Goftegu ba Mehdi Khanbaba Tehrani* [Iran's Left, a Look from Within: Conversation with Mehdi Khanbaba Tehrani] (Paris: Vajeh Desktop Publishing, 1990), 332.

17. William Shawcross, *The Shah's Last Ride* (New York: Touchstone, 1988), 43–44, the cost figure, 47. This is still less than the "up to $500 million" cited by the BBC.

18. Marvin Zonis, *Majestic Failure: The Fall of the Shah* (Chicago: University of Chicago Press, 1991), chap. 3, and 67, 66, 61. Italics are mine.

19. *Ruzshomar,* 2: 256.

20. Cyrus Kadivar, "We Are Awake: 2,500-Year Celebrations Revisited," 25 January 2002. http://www.iranian.com/CyrusKadivar/2002/January/2500/index.html. The difference between Alam's figure and Ansari's may have resulted from Alam's confusing rials and dollars—both using amounts containing the digits 16.

21. Interview with Queen Farah, 3 June 2001, tape 1, side 2.

22. Shojaʿeddin Shafa, speech, University of Sorbonne, Paris, 10 April 2004. http://1400years.org/ROCShafa.asp.

23. Farah Pahlavi, *An Enduring Love: My Life with the Shah* (New York: Miramax, 2004), 227–38, quote at 228.

24. Pahlbod interview, 74.

25. FISOHA interview with Farrokh Ghaffari, by Akbar Etemad, Paris, November 1983 and July 1984, 35–36.

26. Ibid., 50.

27. Quoted in http://www.robertwilson.com/bio/bioMaster.htm.

28. In the years when *taʿzieh* was also included, the number rose to 140,000, though this did not affect revenues because the *taʿzieh* sessions were free. Farrokh Ghaffari, "We have been slow to defend ourselves and our work," *Kayhan* (London), 15 June 1988, 7, 9.

29. Ibid.

30. Don Shirley, "New Theatre Festival," *Washington Post*, 13 June 1977, B9.

31. Farrokh Ghaffari, "We have been slow to defend ourselves and our work," part 2, *Kayhan* (London), 22 June 1988.

32. Ibid.

33. Conversation with Reza Qotbi, Bethesda, Md., 9 September 2005.

34. Mel Gussow, "Stages: Squat Abuses West 23rd Street," *New York Times,* 17 November 1977.

35. Qotbi conversation.

36. Ghaffari, "We have been slow," part 2 (22 June 1988), 7.

37. Maurice Fleuret, "Revue de Polytope de Persépolis," *Nouvelle Observateur,* 6 September 1971.

38. http://www.asphodel.com/cat/asp_2005.html.

39. Qotbi conversation.

40. "L'Etoile Iannis Xenakis a rejoint sa galaxie," *Le Monde,* 6 February 2001.

41. Qotbi conversation.

19. THE RASTAKHIZ PARTY

1. Gholam Reza Afkhami. ed., *Siyasat va siyasatgozari-e eqtesadi dar iran 1340–1350* [Ideology, Politics, and Process in Iran's Economic Development, 1960–1970], An Interview with Alinaghi Alikhani (Bethesda, Md.: FIS, 2001), 225–29. The shah left for the Winter Olympic Games at Innsbruck on 22 January 1964 and returned to Tehran on 1 March. According to Alikhani, the meetings, in which he participated, took place before and after the shah's trip. For the dates of the shah's trip, see *Gahnameh,* 3: 1381–87.

2. Gholam Reza Afkhami, ed., *Barnamerizi-ye omrani va tasmimgiri-ye siyasi* [Ideology, Process, and Politics in Iran's Development Planning], Interviews with Manuchehr Gudarzi, Khodadad Farmanfarmaian, and Abdolmajid Majidi (Bethesda, Md.: FIS, 1999), 282–84.

3. *Gahnameh,* 3: 1389.

4. Interview with Queen Farah, Paris, 1 July 2000, tape 2, side 2.

5. Afkhami, *Siyasat,* 239–40.

6. Interview with Queen Farah, 1 July 2000, tape 2, side 2.

7. Interview with Reza Golsorkhi, New York, 14 May 2001, tape 1, side 2.

8. Interview with Queen Farah, 1 July 2000, tape 2, side 2.

9. See Gholam R. Afkhami, *The Iranian Revolution: Thanatos on a National Scale* (Washington, D.C.: Middle East Institute, 1985), 50–53.

10. Ibid., 55.

11. Asadollah Alam and Yahya Adl were both associated with the Mardom Party, and both soon came to believe that the two-party system was essentially a sham. Adl believed the shah would get reports that the parties had so many members, which "the shah believed or pretended to believe." FISOHA interview with Yahya Adl, by Gholam Reza Afkhami, Paris, 20 August 2000, tape 3, side 1.

12. Conversation with Cyrus Ghani, New York, 28 July 2005. Ghani was present when the shah asked aloud, as the guests had stood in two rows at either side of the hall, which row was heavier. Bushehri, Princess Ashraf's husband, said the right row because Ghani, then somewhat overweight, was in that row. Another person said Hushang Ansary, small and underweight, lowered the weight on the left. The shah, looking at Ansary, said, to everyone's surprise, Ansary's weight was all in his brain.

13. The author was one of the deputy ministers presented. Amin Alimard and I were the dean and associate dean of the School of Economics and Political Science at the National University of Iran, respectively. I was drafted for and had agreed to the appointment because I had spoken for some time on the need for greater decentralization and participation, a position Amouzegar agreed with. In a reformulation of tasks, I was designated to be in charge of the upcoming election. Nothing I had learned or taught in school taught me as much about the Iranians' political culture as did the experience of the months I was engaged in that election. Much of what follows on this election and the transformation of the party system to Rastakhiz, the Resurrection Party of the Iranian Nation, is based on personal experience. See also Afkhami, *The Iranian Revolution,* chap. 2.

14. Each poll station was supervised not only by a supervisory board, as stipulated by law, but also by a representative of both candidates. Though absolute care was taken to have a clean election, it is possible that one of the poll stations in a faraway village in the wooded mountains might have been tampered with. Still, it does not change the general point being made here.

15. *Gahnameh,* 5: 2285; *Ruzshomar,* 2: 289.

16. Alinaghi Alikhani, ed., *Yaddashtha-ye Alam* [Alam's Diaries], 5 vols. (Bethesda, Md.: IBEX, n.d.), 4: 334.

17. Ibid., 4: 318–19.

18. Text of the letter (Kissinger to shah) dated 4 January 1975, in ibid., 4: unpaged insert between 312 and 313.

19. Ibid., 4: 325.

20. Habib Ladjevardi, ed., Interview with Abdolmajid Majidi, Harvard Oral History Project, 61–66. http://www.iranian.com/History/Aug98/Madjidi/p5b.html.

21. Adl interview.

22. Interview with Queen Farah, Potomac, Md., 3 June 2001, tape 2, side 1.

23. *Kayhan,* 3 March 1975.

24. Adl interview.

25. The author was a member of the group. I drafted the project, titled "Tarh-e tajhiz-e mellat-e iran," a rather pompous title meaning "Project to empower the people of Iran." (The word *empower* has come into vogue relatively recently. At the time, *tajhiz* was used in its Persian dictionary meaning as "to supply someone with the wherewithal to enable him/her to accomplish a task," which, more or less, means "to empower.") The analysis was based on my work on political development, especially my Ph.D. dissertation, titled "A Conceptual Scheme for the Analysis of Relationships between Political Development and Public Bureaucracies in Transitional Systems." The terminology, in vogue in the American universities in the mid-1960s, was difficult to impart to the uninitiated in Persian. Thus, independently of the virtue or lack thereof of what was said or written, some of the ideas might very well have been misinterpreted. What follows is my recollection of the text, copied out in the far superior penmanship of my late colleague and dear friend Amin Alimard, which was handed over to and discussed with the queen.

26. See Afkhami, *The Iranian Revolution,* 68–69.

27. I was totally surprised when I heard the shah on television on the evening of 2 March 1975, calling what he proposed the Rastakhiz.

28. Azmun subsequently played an important role in the Sharif-Emami cabinet. He was summarily tried and shot by the Khomeini regime. See Afkhami, *The Iranian Revolution,* 71, 80, note 22.

29. Ibid., 71–72. The experience with reformed communists in Iran supports Theodore Adorno's suggestion that it is always easier for the political extremist to jump from the extreme left of the political spectrum to the extreme right than to accept the uncertain give-and-take situation of the middle. See Theodore W. Adorno et al., *The Authoritarian Personality* (New York: Harper, 1950).

30. *Asasnameh-ye movaqqat-e hezb-e rastakhiz- mellat-e iran* [The Provisional Constitution of the Resurgence Party of the Iranian Nation] (Tehran: Kayhan Publishing House, 1976).

31. In the first days after the establishment of the Rastakhiz, the shah's position seemed to veer to conceiving the new party as possibly becoming a movement. He told Court Minister Alam that "within the Rastakhiz factions might develop and come together to form powerful majorities that supported a particular government." Subsequently, on 20 March 1975, correcting Ambassador Richard Helms, who said it was difficult to justify a one-party system to the world, Alam objected that "this is not a party, this is a Rastakhiz, a Resurrection." Alikhani, *Alam,* 4: 347, 358.

32. Ibid., 4: 346.

33. *Barresi-ye natayej-e entekhabat-e rastakhiz* [Analysis of the Rastakhiz Elections], unpublished report for the Ministry of the Interior, 1975. The study was done by the NIRT Communications Research Institute in conjunction with the Industrial Management Organization.

34. Being in charge of the election, I knew many of the candidates and most of the ones elected to the Majlis. The decisions made by the party leadership appeared inexplicable to most of them, a feeling many of them, especially those affiliated with the Progressive Wing, unabashedly expressed.

35. Reza Qotbi, then head of NIRT, objected to the broadcasts on the grounds that the policy was ill-conceived and that it also took too much television time. A day later, he received the shah's reaction: "Has NIRT become Marxist-Leninist that it sabotages a major policy of the state?" "His Majesty of course did not really think I am a Marxist-Leninist. He had told me many times, as he had told others, he believed I was a nationalist; maybe a bit on the liberal side, but nationalist and devoted to him. But the thing is that I probably thought it was no use to try. Not that [the shah] would not listen, but I simply did not have the energy or the power to fight all those who wanted to do this." FISOHA interview with Reza Qotbi, by Gholam Reza Afkhami, Bethesda, Md., 20 June 2002, tape 1, side 2. This was probably representative of other high government officials as well, including Prime Minister Hoveyda after his twelve years in office.

36. Majidi in Afkhami, *Barnamerizi,* 331–32.

37. See Gholam Reza Afkhami, "Iran: The Nature of the Pahlavi Monarchy," in *Ideology and Power in the Middle East: Studies in Honor of George Lenczowski,* ed. Peter J. Chelkowski and Robert J. Pranger (Durham and London: Duke University Press, 1988), 31–55, at 49.

38. I was called upon by Prime Minister Hoveyda to present to the cabinet a project on decentralization and political participation I had prepared at the behest of both Amouzegar and Majidi. The positions described here were stated in the ensuing discussion. The best I can recall is that Hoveyda himself took what was being said as another idea that the shah seemed to insist on but that in practice, given his proclivities, carried little meaning.

39. Bank-e Markazi-e Iran [Central Bank of Iran], *Annual Reports,* 1974–75, 1975–76, 1976–77.

20. THE GATHERING STORM

1. Many years later in exile in reference to the shah's dismissing Hoveyda in 1977, the queen's friend Fereydun Javadi heard her observe to the shah as they reminisced: "You tried for six months to tell Hoveyda the time had come for him to go. At the end, when you convinced yourself that it had to be done, it was as hard for you as giving birth to a baby." Interview with Fereydun Javadi, Bethesda, Md., 9 November 2003, tape 1, side 2.

2. *Karnameh-ye yeksaleh-ye dowlat* [Annual Balance Sheet of the Government], Tehran, August 1978.

3. Throughout the 1970s wages had tended to increase — dramatically in January–March, with a rollback in April–June, then again rising in July–September and continuing to rise, albeit at a lower rate, in October–December. Under Amouzegar in early 1978 wages rose 41.1 percent in one quarter, the highest rate ever recorded. See Charles Kurzman, *The Unthinkable Revolution in Iran* (Cambridge, Mass.: Harvard University Press, 2004), 96–104, at 98.

4. See *Mesl-e barf ab khahim shod: Mozakerat-e shoray-e farmandehan-e artesh Dey-Bahman, 1357* [We Will Melt Like Snow: Minutes of the Debates of the Council of the Commanders of the Armed Forces (January–February 1979)] (Tehran: Nashr-e Ney, 1365 [1986]).

5. Amouzegar tells of one exception: two brothers, whom he names, were issued

monopoly permits to import bananas and citrus fruits during the new-year period, and they paid part of the profits to the Ayatollah Shariʻatmadari. Amouzegar repealed the monopoly permit, which made the brothers stop paying Shariʻatmadari. Amouzegar makes other allegations, some of which are difficult to substantiate. See "Nameh-ye doctor Jamshid Amouzegar" [A Letter from Doctor Jamshid Amouzegar], *Rahavard* no. 65 (winter 1382 [2003]): 256–57.

6. See Dariush Ashuri, "Ostureh-ye falsafeh dar miyan-e ma: Bazdid-i as Ahmad Fardid va nazariyeh-e gharbzadegi" [The Myth of Philosophy among Us: A Review of Ahmad Fardid and the Theory of Westoxication], http://ashouri.malakut.org/archives/Fardid.pdf. Fardid's name in Iran is associated with Heidegger. According to the philosopher Daryush Shayegan: "Heidegger, interprété par la grille messianique de Ahmad Fardid (1912–1994), fondateur en Iran du groupe des heideggeriens islamisants et par les disciples de ce dernier qui voient dans leur gourou un personnage prophétique incarne un mal qui paralyse tout esprit critique et rejette dans les ténèbres la tradition des Lumières dont nous avons tant besoin aujourd'hui." Daryush Shayegan, "Heidegger en Iran," *Le Portique* no. 18 (October–November 2006).

7. See Mehrzad Boroujerdi, *Iranian Intellectuals and the West: The Tormented Triumph of Nativism* (Syracuse: Syracuse University Press, 1996).

8. See especially Frantz Fanon, *Black Skin, White Mask* (New York: Grove Press, 1967; first published in French in 1952), and *The Wretched of the Earth* (New York: Grove Press, 1965; first published in French in 1961).

9. Jalal Matini, "Doctor Ali Shariati dar daneshgahe Mashhad [Dr. Ali Shariati at Mashhad University], *Iranshenasi* 5, 4 (winter 1994): 835–99, at 849, 853–55.

10. For an expansive biography of Ali Shariati, see Ali Rahnema, "Political Biography of Ali Shariati: Teacher, Preacher, Rebel," in *Pioneers of Islamic Revival,* ed. Ali Rahnema (London: Zed Books, 1994), 208–50.

11. See Farhad Khosrokhavar, "The New Intellectuals in Iran," *Social Compass* 51 (February 2004): 191–202.

12. Ali Shariati, *Majmuʻeh Athar,* no. 1, 13, cited in Matini, "Doctor Ali Shariati," 878.

13. Said Amir Arjomand, *The Turban for the Crown: The Islamic Revolution in Iran* (New York: Oxford University Press, 1988), 93.

14. Abdolkarim Soroush, "Farbeh-tar az ideolozhi" [Fatter than Ideology], *Kiyan* no. 14 (Shahrivar 1372 [September 1993]): 3–4.

15. Matini, "Doctor Ali Shariati," 879–80.

16. Ali Rahnema, *An Islamic Utopian: A Political Biography of Ali Shariʻati* (London: I. B. Tauris, 1988), 274–75.

17. Abdolkarim Soroush, "Shariʻati va jameʻehshenasi-ye din" [Shariʻati and the Sociology of Religion], *Kiyan* no. 13 (tir va mordad 1372 [summer 1993]): 10.

18. See http://www.drsoroush.com/English/Interviews/E-INT-19970311-Intellectual_Autobiography_An_Interview_of_Abdolkarim_Soroush.html.

19. *Kayhan,* 18 and 21 Ordibehesht 1356 (1977); *New York Times,* 10 February 1978; *Ruzshomar,* 2: 318.

20. *Ruzshomar,* 2: 322.

21. *Kayhan,* 20 Mordad 1356 (11 August 1977).

22. *Kayhan,* 14 Mordad 1356 (5 August 1977).

23. Principles 18 and 19; *Ruzshomar,* 2: 325.

24. *Kayhan,* 22 Shahrivar 1356 (13 September 1977); *Ruzshomar,* 2: 327; Amir Taheri, *The Spirit of Allah: Khomeini and the Islamic Revolution* (London: Hutchinson, 1985), 208.

25. FISOHA interview with James Schlesinger, by William Burr, Washington, D.C., 15 May and 27 June 1986, 65, 92.

26. William H. Sullivan, *Mission to Iran* (New York: W. W. Norton, 1981), 122–24, quote at 124.

27. Ibid., 126–27.

28. Interview with Queen Farah, Potomac, Md., 3 June 2001, tape 1, side 2.

29. Sullivan, *Mission to Iran,* 127.

30. Interview with Queen Farah, 3 June 2001, tape 1, side 2.

31. Jimmy Carter, *Keeping Faith: Memoirs of a President* (New York: Bantam Books, 1982), 434.

32. Ibid., 434, 436.

33. Hamilton Jordan, *Crisis: The Last Year of the Carter Presidency* (New York: Berkley Books, 1983), 77–78.

34. Carter, *Keeping Faith,* 436.

35. Ibid., 436–37.

36. Gary Sick, *All Fall Down: America's Tragic Encounter with Iran* (New York: Random House, 1985), 29.

37. Reprinted in Farah Pahlavi, *An Enduring Love: My Life with the Shah* (New York: Miramax, 2004), 272–73.

38. Schlesinger interview, 92.

39. Sick, *All Fall Down,* 31.

40. Khomeini's statements included in *Sahifeh-ye nur: Majmu'eh-ye rahnemudha-ye emam Khomeini* [Book of Light: Collection of the Imam's Directives] (Tehran: Ministry of Culture and Islamic Guidance, 1361 [1982]), 249–50, 255–56.

41. Part of the problem is that many people believe this article was the beginning of the end for the regime. Writing it, therefore, smacked of ill will if not outright criminality. Naturally, no one would like to own it. It is now more or less established, however, that the author was Farhad Nikukhah, Hoveyda's deputy at the imperial court. Some people have attributed the initiating of the idea to Hoveyda, suggesting that he wished to hit at Amouzegar, who not only had usurped Hoveyda's office of prime minister but also was about to add insult to injury by taking over the party as well. This is not only unlikely; it is also mean-spirited. Hoveyda was unhappy at the turn of events and, as we shall see, instrumental in the writing and printing of the article but not as a means of disparaging Amouzegar. Rather, he was among those who thought Khomeini was trouble and that the regime ought to take arms and come out strongly against him. In January 1978 no one imagined that the regime would fall in a year.

42. See Safa'ud-din Tabarraiyan, "Enfejar-e yek maqaleh va pas-larzehha-ye an" [The Explosion of an Article and Its Aftershocks], *Tarikh-e mo'aser-e iran* [Contemporary History of Iran] 6, 24 (1381 [2002]): 7–48.

43. For both agreements, see *Ruzshomar,* 2: 336.

44. Ibid., 337.

45. FISOHA interview with Reza Qotbi, by Gholam Reza Afkhami, Bethesda, Md., 20 June 2002, tape 1, side 2.

46. *Ruzshomar,* 2: 339–40.

47. Qotbi interview, 20 June 2002, tape 2, side 1.

48. See Kurzman, *Unthinkable Revolution,* 44–49, and for references, 200–203.

49. *Ruzshomar,* 2: 348.

50. Ibid.

51. FISOHA interview with Reza Qotbi, Bethesda, Md., 24 May 2001, tape 2, side 2. Qotbi was present at the meeting. ⸱

52. *Ruzshomar,* 2: 352.

53. Ibid., 353.

54. Ibid., 354.

55. "I volunteered to go to Abadan as I had gone in the past to any part of the country where some calamity had befallen the people. But Mr. Amouzegar did not want me to go. I thought if we ourselves have lost faith in our standing in the country, then we must surely be in a bad way." Interview with Queen Farah, 3 June 2001, tape 2, side 1.

56. Reuters, 24 August 1978.

57. "I never should have allowed this wise and unbiased counselor to withdraw," said the shah in 1980. See Mohammad Reza Pahlavi, *Answer to History* (New York: Stein and Day), 1980, 160.

58. Ibid.

59. Houchang Nahavandi, *Carnets secrets: Chute et mort du chah* [Secret Reports: The Fall and Death of the Shah] (Paris: Éditions Osmondes, 2003), 118.

60. Ibid., 118–19.

61. Ibid., 124–25.

62. *Ruzshomar,* 2: 356.

63. Ibid.

64. See Kurzman, *Unthinkable Revolution,* 62–63.

65. Claire Brière and Pierre Blanchet, *L'Iran: La revolution au nom de Dieu* [Iran: Revolution in the Name of God] (Paris: Seuil, 1979), 45–46; cited in Kurzman, *Unthinkable Revolution,* 63. This tactic became the scourge of the military.

66. Qotbi interview, 20 June 2002, tape 2, side 2.

67. I have derived these thoughts in part from the shah's interview in exile with Tom Weir and Christine Godek in Cairo in 1980 on the final and official rendition of his book *Answer to History.* I have also drawn from my own conversations with officials and others close to the shah, for example, the following account from Reza Qotbi and Akbar Etemad, head of the Atomic Energy Organization: After the Tabriz demonstrations of February 1978, Qotbi began to prepare reports for the shah on the events that were unfolding in Iranian cities. In one report, he argued rhetorically that unless serious measures were taken, Iran might be moving toward a revolution. The shah did not like the report, as he showed by treating Qotbi coldly. "We were in a meeting discussing recent events. His Majesty asked everyone's opinion except mine. Well, I knew I was in the doghouse. A few days later, during the Noruz vacations in Kish, I tried to explain what I thought was happening, but he did not give me encouragement. I had to find other ways."

Qotbi explained his problem to Akbar Etemad, who as head of the Atomic Energy Organization had regular meetings with the shah. When in a good mood, the shah usually invited his interlocutor to expound on whatever he wished by asking generally about the news. He asked the same of Etemad after he had finished with his report. Etemad talked about the riots and the turmoil. The shah said the Americans and the British wanted to rid themselves of him. "They think if they take me out, things will go their way. They are mistaken. If they succeed in doing so, there will be chaos and they lose." Etemad went straight to Qotbi's office. Both of them were surprised at the shah's response to the events—not what he believed, but how he expressed his belief. He did not say he would fight them, and they would lose. He said they would depose him and they would be sorry. Qotbi interview, 24 May 2001, tape 2, side 3.

68. *Ruzshomar*, 2: 358.

69. Kurzman, *Unthinkable Revolution, 64*.

70. John D. Stempel, *Inside the Iranian Revolution* (Bloomington: University of Indiana Press, 1981), 114–15.

71. Kurzman, *Unthinkable Revolution,* 65 (including reference to taxicabs); *Ruzshomar*, 2: 359.

72. Nahavandi, *Carnets secrets,* 132–33.

73. FISOHA interview with Ardeshir Zahedi, by Gholam Reza Afkhami, Montreux, Switzerland, 25 July 2003, tape 2, side 1.

74. *Asnad va tasaviri az mobarezat-e khalq-e mosalman-e iran* [Documents and Pictures from the Struggles of the Muslim People of Iran] (Tehran: Abuzar, 1978), vol. 1, part 1, 87–89; cited in Kurzman, *Unthinkable Revolution, 64*.

75. Ali Davani, *Nehzat-e ruhaniyun-e iran* [The Movement of the Iranian Clerics], 10 vols. (Tehran: Bonyad-e Farhang-e Emam Reza [The Cultural Foundation of Imam Reza], 1998), 7: 231–32. In his book on the fall and death of the shah, Houchang Nahavandi reports a story about the 8 September events at Zhaleh Square that if correct is, as he puts it, truly bizarre. In France in July 1980 he met a former employee of the Ministry of Development, a pro-Khomeini activist during the revolution, who, realizing he had made a mistake, had turned against Khomeini and the new regime and left for Europe. He told Nahavandi that "his apartment windows opened on the path of the demonstration. He was contacted by a group of Islamic Marxists who sent him two armed Palestinians. Posted at the windows, they opened fire not only on the soldiers but also on the demonstrators, indiscriminately, their purpose to make blood flow, to create the irreparable. Other shooters, he told me, placed here and there at the windows opening on the square, did the same." Nahavandi, *Carnets secrets,* 139.

76. According to *Ruzshomar*, 2: 361, Shapur Bakhtiar of the National Front had a precise number: 2,450; Abolhassan Bani-Sadr in Paris claimed 3,000. For the cabinet estimate, see Nahavandi, *Carnets secrets,* 138.

77. See Cyrus Kadivar, *Ruzegar Now,* 8 August 2003 in http://www.emadbaghi .com/en/archives/000592.php#more.

78. Sohbatollah Amra'i, "Barresi-ye moqe'iyat-e ejtema'i-ye shohada-ye enqelab-e eslami az shahrivar-e 1357 ta akharin-e bahman-e 1357" [Analysis of the Social Background of the Martyrs of the Islamic Revolution from August 1978 to February 1979],

master's thesis, Department of Sociology, University of Tehran, Iran, 1982; cited in Kurzman, *Unthinkable Revolution,* 71.

21. "I HEARD THE MESSAGE OF YOUR REVOLUTION"

1. Jimmy Carter, *Keeping Faith: Memoirs of a President* (New York: Bantam Books, 1982), 438.

2. Zbigniew Brzezinski, *Power and Principle: Memoirs of the National Security Advisor, 1977–1981* (New York: Farrar, Straus and Giroux, 1983), 361.

3. Cyrus Vance, *Hard Choices: Critical Years in America's Foreign Policy* (New York: Simon and Schuster, 1983), 326.

4. Mohammad Reza Pahlavi, *Answer to History* (New York: Stein and Day, 1980), 161.

5. Brzezinski, *Power and Principle,* 361.

6. Vance, *Hard Choices,* 326–27.

7. Brzezinski, *Power and Principle,* 362.

8. Vance, *Hard Choices,* 328.

9. Brzezinski, *Power and Principle,* 362.

10. Ibid.

11. Vance, *Hard Choices,* 328.

12. Parviz C. Radji, *In the Service of the Peacock Throne: The Diaries of the Shah's Last Ambassador to London* (London: Hamish Hamilton, 1983), 255–56.

13. Brzezinski, *Power and Principle,* 362. Carter relied heavily on his longtime friend the Georgia lawyer Charles Kirbo and often referred to Kirbo's advice. According to James Schlesinger, Kirbo was largely uninformed about international relations and "had less of a geopolitical sense than any man" Schlesinger had encountered. FISOHA interview with James Schlesinger, by William Burr, Washington, D.C., 15 May and 27 June 1986, 2–70. See also Hamilton Jordan, *Crisis: The Last Year of the Carter Presidency* (New York: Berkley Books, 1983), 371.

14. Brzezinski, *Power and Principle,* 364.

15. Ibid., 365.

16. *Ruzshomar,* 2: 373.

17. Ibid.

18. FISOHA interview with Amir Aslan Afshar, by Mahnaz Afkhami, Nice, France, 10 and 12 September 1988, 24–25.

19. Ibid.

20. Interview with Queen Farah, Potomac, Md., 3 June 2001, tape 2, side 2.

21. William H. Sullivan, *Mission to Iran* (New York: W. W. Norton, 1981), 178.

22. Ibid., 179.

23. Ibid.

24. Interview with Queen Farah, 3 June 2001, tape 2, side 2.

25. This statement was made to the author in an audience in September 1978.

26. The following account is from the author's conversation with Reza Qotbi, Bethesda, Md., 3 May 2001.

27. Conversation with Seyyed Hossein Nasr, Washington, D.C., 11 December 2003.

28. Afshar interview, 26.

29. Interview with Kambiz Atabai, by Gholam Reza Afkhami, New York, 3 February 2003, tape 1, side 1.

30. Afshar interview, 27.

31. Interview with Queen Farah, 3 June 2001, tape 2, side 2.

32. Nasr conversation.

33. Fereydun Jam, "Moruri bar khaterat-e arteshbod-e sabeq Fardust" [A Review of the Memoirs of Former General Fardust], in *Pazhuhesh: Naqdi bar ketab-e khaterat-e arteshbod-e sabeq Hossein Fardust* [A Critique of the Memoirs of the Former General Hossein Fardust], ed. Mohsen Mobasser (London: Peka Print, 1996), 106–7.

34. Atabai interview, tape 1, side 1.

35. Qotbi conversation.

36. Atabai interview, tape 2, side 1.

37. Mohammad Reza Pahlavi, interview in exile on *Answer to History,* by Christine Godek and Tom Weir, Cairo, 27 May 1980, tape 7.

38. Radji, *Peacock Throne,* 242.

39. See Chapour Bakhtiar, *Ma fidélité* (Paris: Albin Michel, 1982), 170, 171.

40. The author was a witness to university professors looking at the moon to detect Khomeini's image on it.

41. See "Liberal Misperceptions," chapter 6 in Gholam R. Afkhami, *The Iranian Revolution: Thanatos on a National Scale* (Washington, D.C.: The Middle East Institute, 1985), 173–93.

42. Bakhtiar, *Ma fidélité,* 119.

43. Ebrahim Yazdi, *Akharin talash-ha darakharin ruz-ha* [The Last Efforts in the Last Days] (Tehran: Rushdieh, 1363 [1984]), 33.

44. *Al Mustaqbal* [Beirut], 6 November 1978.

45. Khomeini interview with Swiss Radio-Television, 16 November 1978, cited in Yazdi, *Akharin,* 35–36.

46. *Ruzshomar,* 2: 374–75.

47. Houchang Nahavandi, *Carnets secrets: Chute et mort du chah* [Secret Reports: The Fall and Death of the Shah] (Paris: Éditions Osmondes, 2003), 175–76.

48. Conversation with Reza Qotbi, 3 May 2001.

49. The number is usually given at two million. The main marching column started out at the Fawzieh Circle at the east end of Shah Reza Street and ended at the Shahyad Circle at the west end of Shah Reza Street, a distance of exactly six kilometers. According to the live reports at the time, when the first group of marchers reached Shahyad, the last group left Fawzieh. This means that all of the marchers starting from Fawzieh were at some point on Shah Reza Street. The marchers, of course, walked freely, many with their children walking and running about. But if we assume the most economic and efficient pattern of the march, that of military marches, the following figures emerge. The most efficient distance between rows of marchers allowing for a maximum of participants is one meter. This would allow for six thousand rows of marchers in the main column. Given the width of the street, and assuming shoulder-to-shoulder march, each row would optimally contain forty marchers. The total comes to 240,000 (40 × 6,000). Even if we assume another 240,000 joining the procession at Shahyad and 100,000 to 200,000 watching the event on the sidewalks coming and going, there would be no more

than 600,000 participants. This is the figure also mentioned by General Moqaddam, the chief of SAVAK, at the Council of Commanders, described below.

50. These events are narrated in a letter dated 29 March 2003, addressed to Kambiz Atabai from Lieutenant Colonel Morteza Eshqipur of the Immortals, who was present at the time of the shooting. I am indebted to Kambiz Atabai for providing me the letter.

51. Carter, *Keeping Faith,* 441.

52. Brzezinski, *Power and Principle,* 370–72.

53. Ibid., 373.

54. Carter, *Keeping Faith,* 441–42.

55. Sullivan, *Mission,* 210–12.

56. Brzezinski, *Power and Principle,* 368.

57. Conversation with Princess Ashraf Pahlavi, Sa'dabad, September 1978; audience with Mohammad Reza Shah, Niavaran, Jahan Nama Palace, September 1978.

58. Ardeshir Zahedi, a distant relative of Amini's, told him that if he really wished to be prime minister and thought he was the man to do the job, he (Zahedi) would do his best to get a *farman* for him from the shah. If not, there was no sense in debilitating Sharif-Emami. Amini, according to Zahedi, wanted to help but was not sure how. He was against Zahedi's choices, Aliqoli Ardalan or Abdollah Entezam, for minister of court. And he would not say that he was interested himself. Abdollah Entezam and his brother Nasrollah said they were not able to handle the responsibility, given the prevailing conditions. Abdollah Entezam agreed to serve as the chairman of the board and managing director of the NIOC. Aliqoli Ardalan, a former minister of foreign affairs and a venerable octogenarian, agreed to serve as the shah's last minister of court. Pari Abasalti and Hushang Mirhashem, eds., *Ardeshir Zahedi: Untold Secrets* (Los Angeles: Rah-e zendegi Publishers, 2002), 54–55.

59. Conversation with Ali Amini, Tehran, 2 November 1978.

60. According to Houchang Nahavandi and Amir Taheri, the shah ultimately rejected Sadiqi because he did not wish to stay in Iran, as Sadiqi had requested, since the United States and Great Britain had asked him to leave. This, as I suggest in the text, is unlikely. See Nahavandi, *Carnets secrets,* 214; Amir Taheri, *The Unknown Life of the Shah* (London: Hutchinson, 1991), 283–84. According to Shapur Bakhtiar, Sadiqi withdrew because Karim Sanjabi made it impossible for him to accept. "Je savais qu'il avait empêché Sadighi de parvenir à un accord avec le roi et qu'il ne voulait à aucun prixvoir quelqu'un d'autre réussir dans cette tentative de formation d'un gouvernement" [I know he had prevented Sadiqi from reaching agreement with the king and that he would pay any price to prevent any other person from succeeding in the attempt to form a new government]. Bakhtiar, *Ma fidélité,* 132.

61. Atabai interview, 3 February 2003, tape 1, side 1.

62. Ibid., tape 1, side 2.

63. Ibid. Houchang Nahavandi presents Baqai as a more serious candidate, supported by Ardeshir Zahedi and also a number of military officers, including air force commander General Rabii. Baqai was intent on executing a plan named Khash, after a town in Baluchestan, where a large number of the opposition would be taken. A recent book on Zahedi repeats Nahavandi's version almost verbatim, although Zahedi did not mention this as an important matter in the interviews I had with him for this book. Nor is

the matter mentioned in the collection of interviews in Persian and English, Abasalti and Mirhashem, *Ardeshir Zahedi*. See Nahavandi, *Carnets secrets,* 214–16; Mansoureh Pirnia and Daryoush Pirnia, *Ardeshir Zahedi: Farzand-e toufan* [Ardeshir Zahedi: Son of Storm] (Rockville, Md.: Mehr-e Iran, 2005), 312.

64. Bakhtiar, *Ma fidélité,* 17–30.

65. Ibid., 47–62.

66. I have established the date on the basis of Jamshid Amouzegar's account in *Rahavard* (he says five or six weeks after his resignation on a Thursday) and Ahmad Ghoreishi's statement that his conversation with Bakhtiar and Razmara and subsequently Amouzegar was close to the shah's birthday. For Amouzegar, see Jamshid Amouzegar, "Majeray-e vapasin ruzha-ye farmanrava' i-ye shah" [An Event of the Last Days of the Shah's Rule], *Rahavard* 11, 39 (summer 1995): 146–48. For Qoreishi, several conversations with the author, the last a telephone conversation on 30 March 2006.

67. Amouzegar, "Majeray," 146–48.

68. Bakhtiar, *Ma fidélité,* 119–22.

69. 27 October 1978, *Ruzshomar,* 2: 371.

70. Farah Pahlavi, *An Enduring Love: My Life with the Shah* (New York: Miramax, 2004), 292. Sanjabi had been arrested on 11 November 1978 in Tehran, shortly after he returned from Paris. He was released on 5 December 1978; *Ruzshomar,* 2: 375, 379.

71. Interview with Queen Farah, 3 June 2001, tape 2, side 2.

72. Ibid.

73. Interview with Reza Qotbi, Bethesda, Md., 20 June 2002, tape 2, side 2.

74. Ibid. Bakhtiar's account of the meeting in his book is somewhat different; Qotbi later objected to Bakhtiar about this. The queen states that Bakhtiar asked the shah to leave, which accords with what Bakhtiar states. The shah, on the other hand, does not mention his departure as one of Bakhtiar's demands. However, some ten days separate Bakhtiar's first and second meetings with the shah, during which time both the shah and Bakhtiar, each for his own reasons, had concluded that the shah should leave. Bakhtiar states that the shah's departure was not his position at first but events had made it necessary by the time he formed a government. The time frames, however, differ somewhat. See Bakhtiar, *Ma fidélité,* 130; Farah Pahlavi, *An Enduring Love,* 292–93.

75. Qotbi interview, 20 June 2002, tape 2, side 2.

22. "MELTING LIKE SNOW"

1. Cyrus Vance, *Hard Choices: Critical Years in America's Foreign Policy* (New York: Simon and Schuster, 1983), 329.

2. Zbigniew Brzezinski, *Power and Principle: Memoirs of the National Security Adviser, 1977–1981* (New York: Farrar, Straus and Giroux, 1983), 367–68.

3. Shaul Bakhash, *The Reign of the Ayatollahs: Iran and the Islamic Revolution* (New York: Basic Books, 1984), 52–53.

4. William H. Sullivan, *Mission to Iran* (New York: W. W. Norton, 1981), 199–202.

5. Vance, *Hard Choices,* 329–30.

6. Brzezinski complained about the "woeful state of our political intelligence in

Iran" and got the president also to complain about it to the director of the CIA, Stansfield Turner, and Secretary Vance, apparently to little avail. Brzezinski, *Power and Principle,* 367.

7. Ibid.

8. Mohammad Reza Pahlavi, *Answer to History* (New York: Stein and Day, 1980), 165.

9. General Robert E. Huyser, *Mission to Tehran* (New York: Harper & Row, 1986), 6–10.

10. Ibid., Haig's Introduction and 15–17.

11. Ibid., 43–44.

12. Jimmy Carter, *Keeping Faith: Memoirs of a President* (New York: Bantam Books, 1982), 445.

13. Valéry Giscard d'Estaing, *Le pouvoir et la vie* [Power and Life], vol. 1 (of 3) (Paris: Compagnie 12, 1988), 88–117, esp. 108–11.

14. Ibid.

15. Carter, *Keeping Faith,* 446.

16. Ibid.

17. Huyser, *Mission to Tehran,* 73–74.

18. The shah also told Huyser in their meeting of 11 January that "their only plans were for an external threat. They hadn't given an internal threat a second thought, and their war reserves were quite inadequate for an internal operation." Ibid., 77.

19. General Abbas Qarabaghi, *Haqayeq dar bare-ye enqelab-e iran* [Facts about the Iranian Revolution] (Paris: Suhail Publications, 1984), 178, 180.

20. Ibid., 168–69.

21. Ibid., 197.

22. Chapour Bakhtiar, *Ma fidélité* (Paris: Albin Michel, 1982), 146.

23. See Shapur Bakhtiar, *Si-yo haft ruz pas az si-yo haft sal* [Thirty-Seven Days after Thirty-Seven Years] (Tehran: Radio Iran Publications, 1361 [1982]), 51; and Qarabaghi, *Haqayeq,* 204.

24. Qarabaghi, *Haqayeq,* 154–55.

25. Ibid., 157–58.

26. Ibid., 207, 208.

27. *Ettela'at,* 21 Dey 1357 (11 January 1979).

28. The following were the members of the Regency Council: Prime Minister Shapur Bakhtiar, Senate President Mohammad Sajjadi, Majlis President Javad Sa'id, Court Minister Aliqoli Ardalan, Chief of SCS Abbas Qarabaghi, Seyyed Jalaleddin Tehrani, and Abdolhossein Aliabadi, Abdollah Entezam, and Mohammad Ali Varasteh.

29. *Ettela'at,* 26 Dey 1357 (16 January 1979).

30. *Mesl-e barf ab khahim shod: Mozakerat-e shoray-e farmandehan-e artesh Dey-Bahman, 1357* [We Will Melt Like Snow: Minutes of the Debates of the Council of the Commanders of the Armed Forces, January–February 1979] (Tehran: Nashr-e Ney, 1365 [1986]), 39–40; hereafter cited as *Mozakerat.*

31. Ibid., 48–49.

32. Ibid., 52–53.

33. Ibid., 56–57.

34. Ibid., 62–63, 66–67.

35. Ibid., 70–71.
36. Ibid., 72.
37. Ibid., 74–75.
38. Ibid., 81–85.
39. Ibid., 85–87.
40. Ibid., 87–89.
41. Ibid., 127–41.
42. Ibid., 148–50.
43. Ibid., 162.
44. Ibid., 167–69.
45. Ibid., 169–72. Moqaddam's account of Oveisi agrees with Queen Farah's, who thought Oveisi less decisive than his reputation suggested. Interview with Queen Farah, Potomac, Md., 3 June 2001, tape 2, side 2.
46. *Mozakerat,* 179.
47. Ibid., 187–93.
48. Kathleen Teltsch, "Ramsey Clark Meets Khomeini and Relays Plea to Washington," *New York Times,* 23 January 1979, A5.
49. *Ettelaʿat,* 4 Bahman 1357 (24 January 1979).
50. *Ettelaʿat,* 8 Bahman 1357 (28 January 1979).
51. Ibid.
52. *Mozakerat,* 205–7.
53. Ibid., 213–14.
54. Ibid., 216–17.
55. Ibid., 218–19.
56. Ibid., 219–20.
57. Ibid., 220–21.
58. Ibid., 225–26.
59. Ibid., 227–30.
60. Ibid., 231–32.
61. Ibid., 234–35.
62. Ibid., 241–43.
63. Ibid., 244.
64. Ibid., 245–47.

23. TREK TO NOWHERE

1. Interview with Kambiz Atabai, New York, 3 February 2003, tape 1, side 2.
2. Interview with Queen Farah, Potomac, Md., 3 June 2001, tape 2, side 2.
3. Atabai interview, 3 February 2003, tape 1, side 2.
4. Pari Abasalti and Hushang Mirhashem, eds., *Ardeshir Zahedi: Untold Secrets* (Los Angeles: Rah-e zendegi, 2002), 9.
5. Atabai interview, 3 February 2003, tape 1, side 1.
6. FISOHA interview with Amir Aslan Afshar, by Mahnaz Afkhami, Nice, 10 and 12 September 1988, 36.
7. Ibid., 31.

8. Zbigniew Brzezinski, *Power and Principle: Memoirs of the National Security Advisor, 1977–1981* (New York: Farrar, Straus and Giroux, 1983), 375–77.

9. Afshar interview, 30.

10. The shah was one of the pillars of the 1969 Islamic conference on the al-Aqsa Mosque. The conference was convened in Rabat rather than Tehran because Iran and Egypt did not then maintain diplomatic relations, although relations between the two countries had improved as a result of the shah's material and moral support in the 1967 war. See Ardeshir Zahedi, "Cheguneh conferans-e eslami payehgozari shod" [How the Islamic Conference Was Established], *Rahavard* 12, 45 (fall 1997): 228–35, at 228.

11. Jehan Sadat, *A Woman of Egypt* (New York: Pocket Books, 1987), 340–41.

12. Interview with Queen Farah, Potomac, Md., 6 June 2001, tape 1, side 1.

13. Ibid.

14. Afshar interview, 42.

15. Jimmy Carter, *Keeping Faith: Memoirs of a President* (New York: Bantam, 1982), 447–48.

16. Interview with Queen Farah, 6 June 2001, tape 1, side 1.

17. Pierre Salinger, *America Held Hostage: The Secret Negotiations* (Garden City, N.Y.: Doubleday, 1981), 16.

18. William H. Sullivan, *Mission to Iran* (New York: W. W. Norton, 1981), 235–36; Cyrus Vance, *Hard Choices: Critical Years in America's Foreign Policy* (New York: Simon and Schuster, 1983), 338.

19. Brzezinski, *Power and Principle,* 385.

20. Huyser estimated the number of daily desertions at one hundred to two hundred as opposed to the two thousand to three thousand the international press suggested. General Robert E. Huyser, *Mission to Tehran* (New York: Harper & Row, 1986), 160.

21. Sullivan, *Mission to Iran,* 237.

22. Brzezinski, *Power and Principle,* 388. Brzezinski, on Brown's report based on a Huyser communication, was under the impression that Bakhtiar had said he would turn Khomeini's plane to a southern island if he attempted to return. However, according to Huyser, the idea had come from General Rabii of the air force at an NSC meeting and had been discussed at some length, but no decision had been made on it. Huyser, *Mission to Tehran*, 175.

23. General Abbas Qarabaghi, *Haqayeq dar bare-ye enqelab-e iran* [Facts about the Iranian Revolution] (Paris: Suhail Publications, 1984), 175.

24. Interview with Fereydun Javadi, Bethesda, Md., 9 November 2003, tape 2, side 1.

25. Interview with Queen Farah, 6 June 2001, tape 1, side 2.

26. Carter, *Keeping Faith,* 446–47.

27. Chapour Bakhtiar, *Ma fidélité* (Paris: Albin Michel, 1982), 167–70.

28. Farah Pahlavi, *An Enduring Love: My Life with the Shah* (New York, Miramax, 2004), 306.

29. Atabai interview, 3 February 2003, tape 2, side 2.

30. Complete text of the speech in *Ruzshomar,* 2: 469–71.

31. Ibid., 406.

32. Carter, *Keeping Faith,* 449–50.

33. Huyser, *Mission to Tehran,* 274.

34. *Ruzshomar,* 2: 409.

35. Bakhtiar, *Ma fidélité,* 181.

36. Qarabaghi, *Haqayeq,* 445–76.

37. See *Mesl-e barf ab khahim shod: Mozakerat-e shoray-e farmandehan-e artesh, Dey-Bahman 1357* [We Will Melt Like Snow: Minutes of the Debates of the Council of the Commanders of the Armed Forces, January–February 1979] (Tehran: Nashr-e Ney, 1365 [1986]), 230.

38. For Afshar, Afshar interview; for Sepahbodi, http://users.sedona.net/~sepa/moezzi.html. The receipt of the bill the shah paid for is shown on the Web site.

39. Farah Pahlavi, *An Enduring Love,* 310.

40. Interview with Queen Farah, 6 June 2001, tape 1, side 1.

41. The author witnessed Hoveyda's statements on television. See all Iranian press for 23 and 24 Bahman 1357 (12 and 13 February 1979). See also Shahram Javidpur, *Shuresh-e 57 dar a'ineh-ye matbu'at* [The Revolt of 57 in the Mirror of the Press], vol. 1, *Fehrest-e ruzberuz-e vaqaye'-e iran az 26 Deymah 1357 ta 26 Deymah 1358* [Day-by-Day Account of the Iranian Events from 26 Dey 1357 to 26 Dey 1358 (16 January 1979 to 16 January 1980)] (n.p.: n.p., 1992), 53.

42. Afshar interview, 29–30.

43. Javidpur, *Shuresh-e 57,* 53–54.

44. Interview with Queen Farah, 6 June 2001, tape 1, side 1.

45. Farah Pahlavi, *An Enduring Love,* 307.

46. Interview with Princess Ashraf, New York, 5 February 2001, tape 1, side 1.

47. Interview with Reza Golsorkhi, Princess Ashraf's chief of staff, New York, 14 May 2001, tape 1, side 2.

48. Princess Ashraf interview, tape 1, side 1.

49. Mohammad Reza Pahlavi, *Answer to History* (New York: Stein and Day, 1980), 13–14.

50. Carter, *Keeping Faith,* 452; Vance, *Hard Choices,* 344.

51. Vance, *Hard Choices,* 344.

52. Farah Pahlavi, *An Enduring Love,* 311.

24. THE AYATOLLAH'S SHADOW

1. Farah Pahlavi, *An Enduring Love: My Life with the Shah* (New York: Miramax, 2004), 311.

2. Interview with Kambiz Atabai, New York, 3 February 2003, tape 2, side 2.

3. Interview with Queen Farah, Potomac, Md., 6 June 2001, tape 1, side 2.

4. "Shah's Strategy," *New York Post,* 12 March 1979.

5. Interview with Queen Farah, Potomac, Md., 25 November 2002, tape 2, side 1.

6. FISOHA interview with Amir Aslan Afshar, by Mahnaz Afkhami, Nice, 10 and 12 September 1989, 50.

7. Interview with Queen Farah, 25 November 25, tape 2, side 1.

8. The information on the shah's illness in this and the next paragraphs is taken from letters in the form of a report written by Professor George Flandrin to Professor Jean Bernard. The text of the letters is reproduced in Farah Pahlavi, *An Enduring Love,*

243–48, 252–57, 263–65, 267–68, 302–4, 316–18, 323–28, 333, 352–60, 370–72, 375–79, 382–84.

9. FISOHA interview with Yahya Adl, by Gholam Reza Afkhami, Paris, 20 August 2000, tape 4, side 2.

10. Interview with Queen Farah, 6 June 2001, tape 1, side 2.

11. According to the election headquarters at the Ministry of the Interior, 20,288,021 participated; 20,147,055 voted yes; 140,966 voted no. Shahram Javidpur, *Shuresh-e 57 dar a'ineh-ye matbu'at* [The Revolt of 57 in the Mirror of the Press], vol. 1, *Fehrest-e ruz-beruz-e vaqaye'-e iran az 26 Deymah 1357 ta 26 Deymah 1358* [Day by Day Account of the Iranian Events from 26 Dey 1357 to 26 Dey 1358 (16 January 1979 to 16 January 1980)] (n.p.: n.p., 1992), 95–96.

12. See interview with Sadeq Khalkhali in *Kayhan*, 14 Tir 1382 (5 July 2003), 12. The interview, according to the interviewer, is a reconstruction of conversations with Khalkhali when the judge was severely ill with cancer and almost incapable of carrying out a structured conversation. One of the aims of the interviewer is to exonerate Khomeini from the charge of ordering the killings.

13. Jean d'Ormesson, "Justice pour le vaincu" [Justice for the Defeated], *Le Figaro*, 17–18 March 1979, 1, 3.

14. Interview with Queen Farah, 6 June 2001, tape 1, side 2.

15. Atabai interview, tape 2, side 2.

16. Interview with Queen Farah, 6 June 2001, tape 1, side 2.

17. Fereydoun Hoveyda, *The Fall of the Shah* (New York: Windham Books, 1980), 212.

18. Jimmy Carter, *Keeping Faith: Memoirs of a President* (New York: Bantam Books, 1982), 452.

19. Zbigniew Brzezinski, *Power and Principle: Memoirs of the National Security Advisor, 1977–1981* (New York: Farrar, Straus and Giroux, 1983), 473.

20. Carter, *Keeping Faith*, 452.

21. Ibid.

22. Letter and memorandum from John McCloy to Honorable Warren Christopher, 16 April 1979; McCloy Papers, Amherst College Library, Archives and Special Collections, Box SH 1, Folder 12.

23. Christopher to McCloy, 18 April 1979; McCloy Papers, Folder 12.

24. McCloy to Christopher, 20 April 1979; McCloy Papers, Folder 12.

25. McCloy to Brzezinski, 27 April 1979; McCloy Papers, Folder 10.

26. Brzezinski, *Power and Principle*, 473.

27. Memorandum of telephone conversation with the former shah of Iran at 12:30 P.M., 3 May 1979, with Mr. Joseph V. Reed, Jr., present and listening in on the telephone conversation; McCloy Papers, Folder 20.

28. Atabai interview, tape 2, side 2.

29. Memorandum from McCloy to Christopher, 31 May 1979; McCloy Papers, Folder 12.

30. Flandrin to Bernard, in Farah Pahlavi, *An Enduring Love*, 317.

31. Ibid., 317–18.

32. Mohammad Reza Pahlavi, *Answer to History* (New York: Stein and Day, 1980), 15.

33. Carter, *Keeping Faith,* 453–54.

34. Ibid., 453.

35. See Robert Armao's statement according to Hamilton Jordan, in Jordan, *Crisis: The Last Year of the Carter Presidency* (New York: Berkley Books, 1983), 194.

36. Pari Abasalti and Hushang Mirhashem, eds., *Ardeshir Zahedi: Untold Secrets* (Los Angeles: Rah-e Zendegi, 2002), 67.

37. Farah Pahlavi, *An Enduring Love,* 319.

38. Interview with Queen Farah, 6 June 2001, tape 1, side 2.

39. Pahlavi, *Answer to History,* 17.

40. Farah Pahlavi, *An Enduring Love,* 322.

41. Interview with Queen Farah, 6 June 2001, tape 1, side 2.

42. Flandrin to Bernard, in Farah Pahlavi, *An Enduring Love,* 323–28.

43. Draft of the letter from Princess Ashraf to President Carter, dated 8 August 1979; McCloy Papers, Folder 4.

44. Brzezinski, *Power and Principle,* 474, which also gives mid-August for the sending of the letter.

45. Joseph Verner Reed (JVR), Memorandum for the record, 9 September 1979; McCloy Papers, Folder 23.

46. Cyrus Vance, *Hard Choices: Critical Years in America's Foreign Policy* (New York: Simon and Schuster, 1983), 370–72.

47. Brzezinski, *Power and Principle,* 475.

48. Interview with Queen Farah, 6 June 2001, tape 1, side 2.

49. Pahlavi, *Answer to History,* 19.

50. Flandrin to Bernard, in Farah Pahlavi, *An Enduring Love,* 333.

51. Interview with Queen Farah, 6 June 2001, tape 2, side 1.

52. Memorandum of conversation, John J. McCloy, 12 November 1979; McCloy Papers, Folder 20.

53. Jordan, *Crisis,* 16–30; Pierre Salinger, *America Held Hostage: The Secret Negotiations* (Garden City, N.Y.: Doubleday and Co., 1981), 44–47.

54. Pahlavi, *Answer to History,* 21.

55. Memorandum of telephone conversation, David Rockefeller and the President of the United States, Thursday, 15 November 1979; McCloy Papers, Folder 28.

56. Jordan, *Crisis,* 46.

57. Ibid., 54.

58. Ibid., 58–59.

59. Mexico was a candidate for membership in the United Nations' Security Council, and the rumor was that Castro had promised to withdraw Cuba's bid for the seat and give Mexico its vote if Mexico refused to readmit the shah.

60. Pahlavi, *Answer to History,* 24.

61. Salinger, *America Held Hostage,* 64–65; William Shawcross, *The Shah's Last Ride* (New York: Touchstone, 1988), 290.

62. Jordan, *Crisis,* 62–63.

25. ALMOST BARTERED

1. Interview with Queen Farah, Potomac, Md., 6 June 2001, tape 2, side 1.

2. Interview with Kambiz Atabai, New York, February 2003, tape 3, side 1.

3. "Report on Pahlevi Children, Background"; McCloy Papers, Amherst College Library, Archives and Special Collections, Box SH 1, Series 28.

4. WABC TV and ABC Television Network, *The Iran Crisis: America Held Hostage,* 2 December 1979.

5. Interview with Queen Farah, 6 June 2001, tape 2, side 1.

6. ABC, *Iran Crisis.*

7. Interview with Queen Farah, 6 June 2001, tape 2, side 1.

8. John M. Crewdson, "Shah Moves to Suite on Air Base and Is Said to Be in Good Spirits," *New York Times,* 4 December 1979, A18.

9. Ibid.

10. Hamilton Jordan, *Crisis: The Last Year of the Carter Presidency* (New York: Berkley Books, 1983), 83.

11. Ibid., 62.

12. Zbigniew Brzezinski, *Power and Principle: Memoirs of the National Security Adviser, 1977–1981* (New York: Farrar, Straus and Giroux, 1983), 482.

13. Jordan, *Crisis,* 70.

14. Ibid., 69, 72.

15. Ibid., 73.

16. Ibid., 77.

17. Ibid., 77–78.

18. Ibid., 79.

19. David Rockefeller, Memorandum for the Record, 7 December 1979; McCloy Papers, Folder 29.

20. Jordan, *Crisis,* 79.

21. Pierre Salinger, *America Held Hostage: The Secret Negotiations* (Garden City, N.Y.: Doubleday and Co., 1981), 89.

22. Jordan, *Crisis,* 80.

23. Ibid., 92, 84.

24. Brzezinski, *Power and Principle,* 482.

25. Jordan, *Crisis,* 84–85.

26. William Shawcross, *The Shah's Last Ride* (New York: Touchstone, 1988), 307.

27. Mohammad Reza Pahlavi, interview in exile on *Answer to History,* by Christine Godek and Tom Weir, Cairo, 28 May 1980, tape 8.

28. Interview with Queen Farah, 6 June 2001, tape 2, side 1; Robert Armao and Mark Morse, in Lisa Myers, "Rockefeller's Aides Blast Carter Administration's Handling of Ill Shah," *Washington Star,* 25 January 1981, A7; Shawcross, *Shah's Last Ride,* 320.

29. Interview with Queen Farah, 6 June 2001, tape 2, side 1.

30. Ibid.

31. Myers, "Rockefeller's Aides."

32. Mohammad Reza Pahlavi, *Answer to History* (New York: Stein and Day, 1980), 30.

33. Interview with Queen Farah, 6 June 2001, tape 2, side 1.

34. Myers, "Rockefeller's Aides."

35. "Iran Notifies Panama That It Intends to Ask for the Shah's Return," *New York Times,* 29 December 1979, 6. See also Shawcross, *Shah's Last Ride,* 327–28.

36. This account is from Pierre Salinger, *America Held Hostage,* 142–45. Shawcross quotes Salamin as stating that he and Torrijos assumed that the extradition request was a fiction, that in reality the Iranians wanted to end the crisis. Thus they proposed a fiction: "That they should ask for extradition and Panama should ask for the release of the hostages." Shawcross, *Shah's Last Ride,* 329.

37. Jordan, *Crisis,* 102–6.

38. Ibid., 111–33.

39. Cyrus Vance, *Hard Choices: Critical Years in America's Foreign Policy* (New York: Simon and Schuster, 1983), 399.

40. *Kayhan,* 3, 4, and 5 January 1979; Jordan, *Crisis,* 118–26; Salinger, *America Held Hostage,* 146; Shawcross, *Shah's Last Ride,* 329–30.

41. Salinger, *America Held Hostage,* 162–67.

42. Ibid., 170.

43. Ibid., 181.

44. Mohammed Heikal, *Iran: The Untold Story* (New York: Pantheon, 1982), 21–24, 25, 187–89.

45. Salinger, *America Held Hostage,* 181.

46. "'In fact you are being duped right now,' Bourguet responded [to the commission]. 'You know about the little boy with no arms. You believed he was a victim of the Savak. In fact he lost his arm in an automobile accident, and his mother has been using him to make money.'" Ibid., 179.

47. Ibid., 185.

48. Jordan, *Crisis,* 178.

49. According to William Shawcross, the shah is said once, in late February, to have accepted General Noriega's offer to go on a *gardesh,* the kind of outing arranged for him in the past by royal pimps or directly by friends like Alam. This is unlikely since by that time the shah's health had significantly deteriorated. See Shawcross, *Shah's Last Ride,* 335–42.

50. Interview with Mohammad Reza Pahlavi, by David Frost, Panama, January 1980; televised on *20/20* (ABC), 17 January 1980.

51. Shawcross, *Shah's Last Ride,* 344–45.

52. Interview with Queen Farah, Potomac, Md., 25 November 2002, tape 1, side 1.

53. Ibid.

54. Ibid.

55. George Flandrin to Jean Bernard, in Farah Pahlavi, *An Enduring Love: My Life with the Shah* (New York: Miramax, 2004), 352–60; Jordan, *Crisis,* 181–84.

56. Confidential letter, McCloy to Honorable Cyrus R. Vance, 11 March 1980; McCloy Papers, Folder 14.

57. Interview with Queen Farah, 25 November 2002, tape 1, side 1.

58. Jehan Sadat, *A Woman of Egypt* (New York: Pocket Books, 1987), 422–24.

59. Jordan, *Crisis,* 197–206.

60. Interview with Queen Farah, 25 November 2002, tape 1, side 2.

61. Jordan, *Crisis,* 206.

62. Interview with Queen Farah, 25 November 2002, tape 1, side 2.

63. Jordan, *Crisis,* 207.

26. CLOSING IN A DREAM

1. Interview with Queen Farah, Potomac, Md., 25 November 2002, tape 1, side 2.

2. Hamilton Jordan, *Crisis: The Last Year of the Carter Presidency* (New York: Berkley Books, 1983), 211.

3. Ibid.

4. Jehan Sadat, *A Woman of Egypt* (New York: Pocket Books, 1987), 424.

5. Mohammad Reza Pahlavi, *Answer to History* (New York: Stein and Day, 1980), 33.

6. Sadat, *Woman of Egypt,* 424.

7. George Flandrin to Jean Bernard, in Farah Pahlavi, *An Enduring Love: My Life with the Shah* (New York: Miramax Books, 2004), 370–72.

8. Interview with Fereydun Javadi, Bethesda, Md., 9 November 2003, tape 1, side 1.

9. Farah Pahlavi, *An Enduring Love,* 374.

10. FISOHA interview with Amir Aslan Afshar, by Mahnaz Afkhami, Nice, 10 and 12 September 1988, 44. None of the individuals mentioned worked closely with the son after the father died.

11. Mohammad Reza Pahlavi, interview in exile on *Answer to History,* by Christine Godek and Tom Weir, Cairo, 27, 28, 29, 30 May and 1 June 1980. The first draft of *Answer to History* had been finished in September 1979 in Mexico, in Persian and French. A French version was published in the same year by Albin-Michel and an English translation was produced in 1980 by Michael Joseph, Ltd. Based on it, the Panama and specifically the Cairo conversations were intended, as the shah declared, to produce "the final definitive text."

12. Flandrin to Bernard, in Farah Pahlavi, *An Enduring Love,* 375–80.

13. Javadi interview, 9 November 2003, tape 1, side 1.

14. Flandrin to Bernard, in Farah Pahlavi, *An Enduring Love,* 384.

15. Ibid., 384–85; FISOHA interview with Amir Pourshoja, by Mahnaz Afkhami, Washington, D.C., 12 December 1990, 51–53.

16. Sadat, *Woman of Egypt,* 432.

SELECTED GLOSSARY
OF TERMS AND EVENTS

AIOC	Anglo-Iranian Oil Company
APOC	Anglo-Persian Oil Company
ARAMCO	Arabian-American Oil Company
arbaʿin	forty; fortieth day after *ʿashura,* which gives it religious import
ARMISH	United States Military Mission with the Imperial Iranian Army
Aryamehr	The Light (Sun) of the Aryans
ʿashura	tenth day of the Muslim month of Muharram; the day of martyrdom of Hussein, the Prophet's grandson and Third Imam of the Shiʿa
ayatollah	"sign of God"; an honorific title with hierarchical value in Twelver Imamite Shiism
CENTO	Central Treaty Organization
Comintern	Communist International (established in March 1919)
Consortium	the group of oil companies that signed an agreement with Iran in 1954, after Iran's nationalization of oil; also the agreement itself
Constitution	Basic Law of 1906 and its Supplement of 1907
Constitutional Revolution	events of 1905–11 launching and finalizing the constitutional struggles
fadaiyan	devotees; committed fighters
faqih (pl. *fuqaha*)	one learned in *fiqh*
farang	West, Europe, France
farman	decree, edict
fiqh	the science of Islamic jurisprudence
GENMISH	United States Military Mission with the Imperial Iranian Gendarmerie

gharbzadegi	Westoxication
gharbzadeh	Westoxicated (one too much influenced by the West)
haj; haji	one who has successfully performed the pilgrimage to Mecca
hajj	pilgrimage to Mecca required of Muslims under certain conditions
hezb	political party
HIM	His Imperial Majesty
hujjat-ul-Islam	"proof of Islam"; a *mujtahid,* one learned in Islamic law
IBRD	International Bank for Reconstruction and Development (World Bank)
id al-fitr	celebration ending fast at the end of the Islamic month of Ramadan
jang-e mosallahaneh	armed struggle (warfare)
jihad	struggle (for or against)
khalq	the people (in politics, used mostly by leftists, especially Chinese communist-oriented leaders and organizations)
khan	courtesy title, "mister"; tribal leader; big landlord (term of Mongol-Turkic origin)
MAAG	Military Assistance Advisory Group
marja (pl. *maraji*) *taqlid*	"source of emulation"; a *mujtahid* whom a group of believers choose to go to for religious guidance
mashruteh	constitutional
mashrutiat	constitutionalism
melli	national
mojahed	struggler, fighter
mujtahid	one learned in Islamic law
NIOC	National Iranian Oil Company
Noruz	Iranian New Year (spring equinox in northern hemisphere)
NPT	Nonproliferation Treaty
NSA	National Security Agency (U.S.)
NSC	National Security Council (both U.S. and Iran)
Point IV	U.S. aid program launched under President Truman
Qanun-e asasi	Basic Law ratified in 1906 and, together with its Supplement of 1907, establishing the Constitution of Iran before the advent of the Islamic revolution in 1979
Rastakhiz	resurrection; resurgence (Resurrection Party)
RCD	Regional Cooperation for Development
Sa'dabad	royal residential palace compound north of Tehran

Sardar Sepah	Commander of the Armed Forces; title conferred on Reza Khan by Ahmad Shah Qajar in 1921
SEATO	Southeast Asia Treaty Organization
Sepah-e behdasht	Health Corps
Sepah-e danesh	Education Corps
Sepah-e tarvij	Development Corps
seyyed	title for descendant of the Prophet through his daughter, Fatemeh
shahadat	martyrdom
shahanshah	king of kings (originally from the Achemenid period)
shahbanu	queen (pre-Islamic title conferred on Queen Farah on 20 March 1961)
Shahnameh	*The Book of Kings* (major Iranian epic by Ferdowsi)
shari'a	framework of Islamic law based on the Koran and the *sunna*
sunna	actions and sayings of Mohammad and, in shi'a, also of the imans
talabeh (pl. *tullab*)	student of religion studying in religious school
taqiyeh	dissimulation (usually of a political nature)
ta'zieh	ritual drama based mainly on traditions of Iranianized Islam
toman	currency unit equal to 10 rials
tudeh	masses
ulama	body of religious learned men
uliya'	religious tutelaries
USIA	United States Information Agency

INDEX

Abadan: cinema fires, 458–59, 465, 468, 664n55; Makki, 127; oil, 64–65, 124, 126, 139, 145, 151, 263, 272, 343; Shatt al-Arab near, 202, 271–72, 301

ABC: and extradition attempts on shah, 579; Frost interview, 385–88, 400, 547, 585–86, 596; Morocco photo-op, 532

Abdorreza (shah's half-brother), 77, 84–85

Abd-ul-Ilah, Crown Prince of Iraq, 179, 183, 203

Acheson, Dean, 107, 129, 140, 143, 145

Acker, William P., 570, 571

'adalatkhaneh (house of justice), 5

Adamiyatt, Tahmouress, 335

Adl, Catherine, 399

Adl, Yahya, 50–51, 53, 433, 615n34; daughter killing gendarme colonel, 399; Mardom Party, 431–32, 659n11; Perron surgery, 113; royal parties, 43; and shah's illness, 550; and two-party system, 428

AEOI (Atomic Energy Organization of Iran), 315, 347–50, 354–56, 360–62

Afkhami, Mahnaz, 251–52, 256, 258, 261–62, 640n52

Afshar, Amir Aslan: protocol chief, 472–73, 479, 527–28, 531–32, 540–41; shah recommending to son, 596; shah's funeral, 598; and shah's plane, 538

Afshar, Amir Khosro, 292–93, 469, 482

Afshartus, Mahmud, 155, 158

Aftandelian, George, 47

Agah, Manuchehr, 322

Aghevli, Fazlollah, 11, 102

Al-Ahmad, Jalal, 443–44

Ahmad Shah, 8, 10, 12, 17, 22, 23

Ahmadzadeh, Masud, 397

al-Ahram, 584

Ahy, Majid, 75, 81, 92

Ahy, Mehri, 242, 250

AIOC (Anglo-Iranian Oil Company), 63–66, 88, 106, 115–36; Abadan, 64, 65, 126, 139, 145; British Petroleum, 268, 277, 640n1; compensation, 124, 127–28, 136, 143–47, 151–53, 198; Consortium Agreement and, 127, 197–99, 263; and Iranian nationalization of oil, 115–36, 143–47, 151–53, 195; Khuzistan economic development and, 209; in Majors, 640n1; and Tudeh party, 88, 158

Akhavi, Hassan, 162

Ala, Hossein: ambassador to U.S., 98, 118–19; and Ashraf joining women's associations, 241; assassination attempt on, 210, 365, 370, 371, 372; court minister, 142, 144, 149, 191, 210, 405; death, 405; demonstrations for shah (1952), 150–51; discussion meetings, 55, 616n48; and Mosaddeq, 132, 144, 149, 151, 155, 168; prime minister, 124, 125, 207, 210, 614n17; shah's father's body, 85; UN ambassador, 97, 98; Zahedis and, 157–58, 168

A'lam, Amir (shah's doctor), 25, 27, 50

Alam, Amir Asadollah, 112–13, 206, 425; and Algerian president, 431; Anniversary Celebration, 405–12, 414; Celebrations Council, 657n7; court minister, 53–54, 113, 270–72, 277, 355, 390–94, 399, 405–12, 548, 660n31; illness and death, 441, 548; and intellectuals, 55–57; interior minister, 207; and Iraq, 271–72; Khomeini arrest (1963), 234–36, 271; loyalty to shah, 235–36, 277, 399, 425, 431, 441, 643n41, 652n62; Mardom Party, 211, 430, 659n11; oil issues, 270, 271, 277; prime minister, 113, 226–37, 317–18, 321,

Designer:	Sandy Drooker
Text:	10.5/13.5 Adobe Garamond
Display:	Akzidenz Grotesk Super
Compositor:	BookMatters, Berkeley
Indexer:	Barbara Roos
Printer and binder:	Sheridan Books, Inc.